813.54   Kerouac, Jack, 1922-
Ker   1969.

         Jack Kerouac and
         Allen Ginsberg.

JACK KEROUAC AND ALLEN GINSBERG: THE LETTERS

HOTEL LUIS MOYA, CUARTO #16, ~~LUIS MOYA 94~~ MEXICO CITY, MEXICO

Dear Allen — (1418½ CLOUSER ST. ORLANDO, FLA.)

This is by way of being a letter to Bill also, to tell him
that Bill Garver is dead, buried somewhere in Mexico City
with Joan, died last month or so — That was the first
catastrophe, then I went to Esperanza's hotel, she's disappear'd
then that night the earthquake which made me tremble
and hide under the bed in this hotel room with a 20-ft.
ceiling (woke up from deep sleep to what I wordlessly
thought was the natural end of the world, then I said
"It's a giant earthquake!" and waited as the bed
heaved up & down, the ceiling creaked deeply, the loose
dresser doors moansqueaked back & forth, the deep
rumble and SILENCE of it in my Eternity Room) —
One horror after another as usual in Doom Mexico —
Now, a few days later, I walk & see the building that
used to say "Burroughs" on it is divided in two, all
the windows broken and only "Burrou" left of the
name in front — Anyway I wrote the article they
want, EXPLAINING THE BEAT GENERATION, all about
our visions, yours, mine, Bill's, Philip Lamantia's, Gregory's
visions of "devils and celestial Heralds," Joan's,
Henkey's, Gary's, Phil's — even Alene's and the Times
Square Kid of the Second Coming — I hope they publish the article, in it I show that "beat" is the
Second Religiousness of Western Civilization as prophesied
by Spengler — I also mention Neal's religiousness and
Lucien's attempt to gain asylum in a church, which
is really the most Gothic mad event of all — Also,
I'm writing new scenes for DOCTOR SAX but I've decided
to showdown with Cowley by inserting a clause in
the contract against removal of (Gothic) phantasie
and in fact against extensive editorial fucking-up
— I have $17 left, however, and am waiting to
be saved — Will start back Sept. 15 and so to
New York in October — Joyce wanted join me here —
I keep thinking of Bill Garver ... and of November
when we were all together here — I have no typewriter
and thinking of looking up old painter Alfonso for
one, or Donald Demarest of the Mexico City News
who mentioned you & Denise Leverton last Sunday
in a review about a painter's autobiography (the
painter, Lester Epstim, is an "aficionado" of yours
& Henry Miller, it says) — I asked Viking to send
you copy of ON THE ROAD — O what a lonely room
I have, 20 foot ceiling, whorehouse mirrors, no windows,
right downtown — Except for writing-work, I haven't
got a single reason in the world to be here, especially
since Catastrophe No. 3 was my visit to Panama Street,
the whores have been driven off the streets completely,
apparently by spreading Cancer of Americanism — And
I'm without my holy weed too! WRITE TO ME IN
FLORIDA, AM LEAVING Jack

(left margin, bottom to top) LATEST LATEST NEWS — I GOT ASIATIC FLU & GOING HOME

(right margin, bottom to top) Even Club Bombay closed, Hell Peter — Love to Alan Ansen — LATEST NEWS: Alphonse Michel also dead!

ALSO BY JACK KEROUAC

THE DULUOZ LEGEND

Visions of Gerard

Doctor Sax

Maggie Cassidy

The Sea is My Brother:
    The Lost Novel

Vanity of Duluoz

On the Road

Visions of Cody

The Subterraneans

Tristessa

Lonesome Traveler

Desolation Angels

The Dharma Bums

Book of Dreams

Big Sur

Satori in Paris

POETRY

Mexico City Blues

Scattered Poems

Pomes All Sizes

Heaven and Other Poems

Book of Blues

Book of Haikus

Book of Sketches

OTHER WORK

The Town and the City

The Scripture of the Golden Eternity

Some of the Dharma

Old Angel Midnight

Good Blonde & Others

Pull My Daisy

Trip Trap (with Albert Saijo and
    Lew Welch)

Pic

The Portable Jack Kerouac

Selected Letters: 1940–1956

Selected Letters: 1957–1969

*Atop an Underwood: Early Stories
    and Other Writings*

Door Wide Open (with Joyce
    Johnson)

Orpheus Emerged

Departed Angels: The Lost Paintings

*Windblown World: Journals
    1947–1954*

Beat Generation: A Play

On the Road: The Original Scroll

Wake Up: A Life of the Buddha

*You're a Genius All the Time: Belief
    and Technique for Modern Prose*

*And the Hippos Were Boiled in Their
    Tanks* (with William S. Burroughs)

TELEPHONE CENTER

U. S. MARITIME SERVICE TRAINING STATION
Sheepshead Bay, Brooklyn, New York

august 12.

Chèr Jean —

"L'Automne déjà" ... Il y a une année, jadis,
si je me souviens bien, que le monde a venu à son fin.
Today is Sunday; this evening, or on the 14th, we violent and
pensive children will be reenacting our crimes and
judging ourselves. The year somehow has passed
quickly, almost has eclipsed itself. At moments
when les remords sont crystalisées by some proud
proustian feature, I think of the season of hell with a
willing sentimental yearning. Today while
I was trying to sleep I heard a negro singing softly, "you
always hurt the one you love," and I began singing it
myself in hommage. You must change your life!

The abrupt fluctuation of your personal fortunes
vis à vis stable employment have ceased to surprise me,
though they still are "kind of amusing."
I can't criticise again leaving the camp, but what
I miscalled "Emotional smugness" — a sense of
something missing in your head besides bourgeois
idealism — was responsible for your getting
yourself into such bitness.

ALSO BY ALLEN GINSBERG

POETRY

Collected Poems 1947–1997

Airplane Dreams

Cosmopolitan Greetings: Poems
  1986–1992

Death & Fame: Last Poems 1993–1997

Empty Mirror

The Fall of America: Poems of These
  States 1965–1971

First Blues

The Gates of Wrath

Howl and Other Poems

Howl Annotated

Illuminated Poems

Iron Horse

Kaddish and Other Poems 1958–1960

Luminous Dreams

Mind Breath: Poems 1972–1977

Planet News 1961–1967

Plutonian Ode: Poems, 1977–1980

Poems All Over the Place

Reality Sandwiches: 1953–1960

Selected Poems 1947–1995

White Shroud: Poems 1980–1985

PROSE AND PHOTOGRAPHY

Allen Ginsberg Photographs

Allen Verbatim

As Ever (with Neal Cassady)

The Book of Martyrdom & Artifice:
  First Journals and Poems 1937–1952

Composed on the Tongue

Deliberate Prose: Selected Essays
  1952–1995

Family Business: Selected Letters
  Between a Father & Son
  (with Louis Ginsberg)

Indian Journals

Journals: Early Fifties, Early Sixties

Journals: Mid-Fifties: 1954–1958

The Letters of Allen Ginsberg

The Selected Letters of Allen Ginsberg
  and Gary Snyder

Snapshot Poetics

Spontaneous Mind: Selected
  Interviews, 1958–1996

Straight Hearts' Delight
  (with Peter Orlovsky)

The Yage Letters
  (with William S. Burroughs)

JACK KEROUAC AND ALLEN GINSBERG: THE LETTERS

EDITED BY

Bill Morgan and David Stanford

VIKING

VIKING
Published by the Penguin Group
Penguin Group (USA) Inc., 375 Hudson Street, New York, New York 10014, U.S.A. • Penguin Group (Canada),
90 Eglinton Avenue East, Suite 700, Toronto, Ontario, Canada M4P 2Y3 (a division of Pearson Penguin Canada
Inc.) • Penguin Books Ltd, 80 Strand, London WC2R 0RL, England • Penguin Ireland, 25 St. Stephen's Green,
Dublin 2, Ireland (a division of Penguin Books Ltd) • Penguin Books Australia Ltd, 250 Camberwell Road,
Camberwell, Victoria 3124, Australia (a division of Pearson Australia Group Pty Ltd) • Penguin Books India
Pvt Ltd, 11 Community Centre, Panchsheel Park, New Delhi – 110 017, India • Penguin Group (NZ), 67 Apollo
Drive, Rosedale, North Shore 0632, New Zealand (a division of Pearson New Zealand Ltd) • Penguin Books (South
Africa) (Pty) Ltd, 24 Sturdee Avenue, Rosebank, Johannesburg 2196, South Africa

Penguin Books Ltd, Registered Offices: 80 Strand, London WC2R 0RL, England

First published in 2010 by Viking Penguin, a member of Penguin Group (USA) Inc.

10 9 8 7 6 5 4 3 2 1

Frontispiece of letter from Jack Kerouac to Allen Ginsberg: Allen Ginsberg Papers, Rare Books and Manuscript
Library, Columbia University. Frontispiece of letter from Allen Ginsberg to Jack Kerouac: Harry Ransom Humanities
Research Center, The University of Texas at Austin.

LIBRARY OF CONGRESS CATALOGING IN PUBLICATION DATA
Kerouac, Jack, 1922–1969.
  [Correspondence. Selections]
  Jack Kerouac and Allen Ginsberg : the letters / edited by Bill Morgan and David Stanford.
      p. cm.
  Includes index.
  ISBN 978-0-670-02194-9
  1. Kerouac, Jack, 1922–1969—Correspondence.   2. Ginsberg, Allen, 1926–1997—Correspondence.   3. Authors,
American—20th century—Correspondence.   4. Beat generation.   I. Morgan, Bill, 1949–   II. Stanford, David,
1951–   III. Ginsberg, Allen, 1926–1997. Correspondence. Selections.   IV. Title.
  PS3521.E735Z48 2010
  813'.54—dc22
  [B]   2010003213

Printed in the United States of America
Designed by Carla Bolte • Set in Warnock

I've all these two days spent filing old letters, taking them out of old enve-lopes, clipping the pages together, putting them away . . . hundreds of old letters from Allen, Burroughs, Cassady, enuf to make you cry the enthusiasms of younger men . . . how bleak we become. And fame kills all. Someday "The Letters of Allen Ginsberg to Jack Kerouac" will make America cry.

— Jack Kerouac, in a letter to Lawrence Ferlinghetti, May 25, 1961

CONTENTS

Editors' Introduction   xxi
Acknowledgements   xxvii

1944

ca. mid-August 1944: Allen Ginsberg to Jack Kerouac   3
ca. September 1944: Jack Kerouac to Allen Ginsberg   4

1945

ca. late July 1945: Allen Ginsberg to Jack Kerouac   9
August 10, 1945: Jack Kerouac to Allen Ginsberg   11
August 12, 1945: Allen Ginsberg to Jack Kerouac   12
August 17, 1945: Jack Kerouac to Allen Ginsberg   14
August 22, 1945: Allen Ginsberg to Jack Kerouac   16
August 23, 1945: Jack Kerouac to Allen Ginsberg   17
September 4, 1945: Allen Ginsberg to Jack Kerouac   19
September 6, 1945: Jack Kerouac to Allen Ginsberg   20
after September 6, 1945: Allen Ginsberg to Jack Kerouac   25

1948

ca. April 1948: Jack Kerouac to Allen Ginsberg   31
May 18, 1948: Jack Kerouac to Allen Ginsberg   34
after May 18, 1948: Allen Ginsberg to Jack Kerouac   35
July 3, 1948: Allen Ginsberg to Jack Kerouac   37
summer 1948: Allen Ginsberg to Jack Kerouac   38

September 9, 1948: Jack Kerouac to Allen Ginsberg   40

ca. late summer 1948: Allen Ginsberg to Jack Kerouac   41

September 18, 1948: Jack Kerouac to Allen Ginsberg   42

after October 19, 1948: Allen Ginsberg to Jack Kerouac   46

ca. December 1948: Allen Ginsberg to Jack Kerouac   50

ca. December 1948: Allen Ginsberg to Jack Kerouac   51

ca. December 16, 1948: Jack Kerouac to Allen Ginsberg   52

ca. December 1948: Allen Ginsberg to Jack Kerouac   58

ca. December 1948: Jack Kerouac to Allen Ginsberg   62

1949

ca. April 23, 1949: Allen Ginsberg to Jack Kerouac   67

ca. early May 1949: Allen Ginsberg to Jack Kerouac   68

before May 15, 1949: Allen Ginsberg to Jack Kerouac   70

May 23, 1949: Jack Kerouac to Allen Ginsberg   73

after May 23, 1949: Allen Ginsberg to Jack Kerouac   75

June 10, 1949: Jack Kerouac to Allen Ginsberg   80

June 13, 1949: Allen Ginsberg to Jack Kerouac   83

June 15, 1949: Allen Ginsberg to Jack Kerouac   86

ca. June 29, 1949: Allen Ginsberg to Jack Kerouac   92

July 5–11, 1949: Jack Kerouac to Allen Ginsberg   93

July 13–14, 1949: Allen Ginsberg to Jack Kerouac   98

July 26, 1949: Jack Kerouac to Allen Ginsberg   106

1950

January 13, 1950: Jack Kerouac to Allen Ginsberg   113

January 21, 1950: Allen Ginsberg to Jack Kerouac   114

ca. February 1950: Allen Ginsberg to Jack Kerouac   117

February 24, 1950: Allen Ginsberg to Jack Kerouac   120

ca. March 1950: Allen Ginsberg to Jack Kerouac   122

July 8, 1950: Allen Ginsberg to Jack Kerouac   125

1952

ca. February 1952: Allen Ginsberg to Jack Kerouac
and Neal Cassady   131

ca. February 1952: Jack Kerouac to Allen Ginsberg   135

February 15, 1952: Allen Ginsberg to Neal Cassady
and Jack Kerouac   137

February 25, 1952: Jack Kerouac to Allen Ginsberg   143

ca. March 8, 1952: Allen Ginsberg to Jack Kerouac
and Neal Cassady   144

March 15, 1952: Jack Kerouac to Allen Ginsberg   145

March 20, 1952: Allen Ginsberg to Neal Cassady
and Jack Kerouac   149

ca. late March 1952: Allen Ginsberg to Jack Kerouac   150

late March 1952: Jack Kerouac to Allen Ginsberg   156

late March–early April 1952: Allen Ginsberg to Jack Kerouac   159

May 10, 1952: Jack Kerouac to Allen Ginsberg   162

May 15, 1952: Allen Ginsberg to Jack Kerouac   169

May 18, 1952: Jack Kerouac to Allen Ginsberg   173

June 12, 1952: Allen Ginsberg to Jack Kerouac   176

October 8, 1952: Jack Kerouac to Allen Ginsberg   178

ca. November 1–7, 1952, but before November 8, 1952:
Allen Ginsberg to Jack Kerouac   180

November 8, 1952: Jack Kerouac to Allen Ginsberg   185

1953

February 19, 1953: Allen Ginsberg to Jack Kerouac   189

February 21, 1953: Jack Kerouac to Allen Ginsberg   190

February 24, 1953: Allen Ginsberg to Jack Kerouac   191

May 7, 1953: Jack Kerouac to Allen Ginsberg   192

May 13, 1953: Allen Ginsberg to Jack Kerouac   193

July 2, 1953: Allen Ginsberg to Jack Kerouac   194

July 13, 1953: Allen Ginsberg to Jack Kerouac   195

November 21, 1953: Jack Kerouac to Allen Ginsberg and
William S. Burroughs   196

1954

before January 12, 1954: Allen Ginsberg to Jack Kerouac,
Neal Cassady, and Carolyn Cassady   201

January 18–25, 1954: Allen Ginsberg to Neal Cassady, Jack Kerouac,
and Carolyn Cassady   205

February 18–19, 1954: Allen Ginsberg to Neal Cassady,
Carolyn Cassady, and Jack Kerouac   208

ca. March 1954: Jack Kerouac to Allen Ginsberg   211

April 4, 1954: Allen Ginsberg to Neal Cassady,
Carolyn Cassady, and Jack Kerouac   213

ca. late May 1954: Jack Kerouac to Allen Ginsberg   218

June 18, 1954: Allen Ginsberg to Jack Kerouac   220

after June 18, 1954: Jack Kerouac to Allen Ginsberg   222

ca. July 10, 1954: Allen Ginsberg to Jack Kerouac   228

July 30, 1954: Jack Kerouac to Allen Ginsberg   230

ca. early August 1954: Allen Ginsberg to Jack Kerouac   232

August 23, 1954: Jack Kerouac to Allen Ginsberg   235

September 5, 1954: Allen Ginsberg to Jack Kerouac   238

before October 26, 1954: Allen Ginsberg to Jack Kerouac   244

October 26, 1954: Jack Kerouac to Allen Ginsberg   246

November 9, 1954: Allen Ginsberg to Jack Kerouac   248

November 26, 1954: Allen Ginsberg to Jack Kerouac   250

December 22, 1954: Jack Kerouac to Allen Ginsberg   253

December 29, 1954: Allen Ginsberg to Jack Kerouac   254

1955

January 12, 1955: Allen Ginsberg to Jack Kerouac   261

January 14, 1955: Allen Ginsberg to Jack Kerouac   262

January 18–20, 1955: Jack Kerouac to Allen Ginsberg   266

February 10, 1955: Jack Kerouac to Allen Ginsberg   272

February 14, 1955: Allen Ginsberg to Jack Kerouac   276

March 4, 1955: Jack Kerouac to Allen Ginsberg   280

March 13, 1955: Allen Ginsberg to Jack Kerouac   281

April 20, 1955: Jack Kerouac to Allen Ginsberg   282

April 22, 1955 : Allen Ginsberg to Jack Kerouac   282

May 3, 1955: Jack Kerouac to Allen Ginsberg   285

ca. May 10, 1955: Allen Ginsberg to Jack Kerouac   286

May 11, 1955: Jack Kerouac to Allen Ginsberg   287

May 20, 1955: Jack Kerouac to Allen Ginsberg   289

May 27, 1955: Jack Kerouac to Allen Ginsberg   291

May 27, 1955: Allen Ginsberg to Jack Kerouac   292

June 1, 1955: Jack Kerouac to Allen Ginsberg   294

June 5–6, 1955: Allen Ginsberg to Jack Kerouac   296

ca. June 10, 1955: Jack Kerouac to Allen Ginsberg   300

June 27–28, 1955: Jack Kerouac to Allen Ginsberg   300

June 29, 1955: Jack Kerouac to Allen Ginsberg   302

July 5, 1955: Allen Ginsberg to Jack Kerouac   303

July 14, 1955: Jack Kerouac to Allen Ginsberg   304

after July 14, 1955: Allen Ginsberg to Jack Kerouac   311

August 7, 1955: Jack Kerouac to Allen Ginsberg   314

before August 15, 1955: Allen Ginsberg to Jack Kerouac   315

August 19, 1955: Jack Kerouac to Allen Ginsberg   317

August 25, 1955: Allen Ginsberg to Jack Kerouac   319

August 30, 1955: Allen Ginsberg to Jack Kerouac   320

September 1–6, 1955: Jack Kerouac to Allen Ginsberg   321

1956

March 10, 1956: Allen Ginsberg to Jack Kerouac   325

ca. late May 1956: Allen Ginsberg to Jack Kerouac   326

August 12–18, 1956: Allen Ginsberg to Jack Kerouac   327

September 26, 1956: Jack Kerouac to Allen Ginsberg   330

October 1, 1956: Allen Ginsberg to Jack Kerouac   331

October 10, 1956: Allen Ginsberg to Jack Kerouac   332

October 10, 1956: Jack Kerouac to Allen Ginsberg   335

December 26, 1956: Jack Kerouac to Allen Ginsberg   336

1957

ca. late April–early May 1957: Jack Kerouac to Allen Ginsberg
and William S. Burroughs   341

May 17, 1957: Jack Kerouac to Allen Ginsberg   344

May 31, 1957: Allen Ginsberg to Jack Kerouac   345

June 7, 1957: Jack Kerouac to Allen Ginsberg, Peter Orlovsky,
William S. Burroughs, and Alan Ansen   348

July 21, 1957: Jack Kerouac to Allen Ginsberg,
Peter Orlovsky, and Alan Ansen   351

August 9, 1957: Jack Kerouac to Allen Ginsberg   353

August 13–September 5, 1957: Allen Ginsberg to Jack Kerouac   354

September 28, 1957: Allen Ginsberg to Jack Kerouac   355

October 1, 1957: Jack Kerouac to Allen Ginsberg   356

October 9, 1957: Allen Ginsberg to Jack Kerouac   360

October 16, 1957: Allen Ginsberg to Jack Kerouac   363

October 18, 1957: Jack Kerouac to Allen Ginsberg   365

November 13–15, 1957: Allen Ginsberg to Jack Kerouac   367

November 30, 1957: Jack Kerouac to Allen Ginsberg   372

December 5, 1957: Allen Ginsberg to Jack Kerouac   374

December 10, 1957: Jack Kerouac to Allen Ginsberg,
Peter Orlovsky, and Gregory Corso   376

December 28, 1957: Jack Kerouac to Allen Ginsberg   379

1958

January 4, 1958: Allen Ginsberg to Jack Kerouac   383

January 8, 1958: Jack Kerouac to Allen Ginsberg   384

January 11, 1958: Allen Ginsberg to Jack Kerouac   387

January 16, 1958: Jack Kerouac to Allen Ginsberg   389

January 21, 1958: Jack Kerouac to Allen Ginsberg   390

ca. February 26, 1958: Allen Ginsberg to Jack Kerouac   392

April 8, 1958: Jack Kerouac to Allen Ginsberg   394

June 26, 1958: Allen Ginsberg to Jack Kerouac   396

July 2, 1958: Jack Kerouac to Allen Ginsberg   399

August 11, 1958: Jack Kerouac to Allen Ginsberg   401

August 20, 1958: Allen Ginsberg to Jack Kerouac   403

August 28, 1958: Jack Kerouac to Allen Ginsberg   405

ca. August 31, 1958: Allen Ginsberg to Jack Kerouac   407

September 8, 1958: Jack Kerouac to Allen Ginsberg   408

ca. September 16–17, 1958: Allen Ginsberg to Jack Kerouac   409

October 5, 1958: Jack Kerouac to Allen Ginsberg   412

October 28, 1958: Jack Kerouac to Allen Ginsberg   412

October 29, 1958: Allen Ginsberg to Jack Kerouac   416

November 17, 1958: Allen Ginsberg to Jack Kerouac   417

November 19, 1958: Jack Kerouac to Allen Ginsberg   420

December 16, 1958: Jack Kerouac to Allen Ginsberg   421

1959

March 24, 1959: Jack Kerouac to Allen Ginsberg,
Gregory Corso, and Peter Orlovsky   427

May 12, 1959: Allen Ginsberg to Jack Kerouac   428

May 19, 1959: Jack Kerouac to Allen Ginsberg   430

June 18, 1959: Jack Kerouac to Allen Ginsberg   432

July 1, 1959: Allen Ginsberg to Jack Kerouac   434

October 6, 1959: Jack Kerouac to Allen Ginsberg   435

October 16, 1959: Allen Ginsberg to Jack Kerouac   437

November 2, 1959: Jack Kerouac to Allen Ginsberg   439

November 5, 1959: Allen Ginsberg to Jack Kerouac   440

December 24, 1959: Jack Kerouac to Allen Ginsberg   441

December 29, 1959: Allen Ginsberg to Jack Kerouac   443

1960

January 4, 1960: Jack Kerouac to Allen Ginsberg   449

June 20, 1960: Jack Kerouac to Allen Ginsberg   450

September 19, 1960: Allen Ginsberg to Jack Kerouac   454

September 22, 1960: Jack Kerouac to Allen Ginsberg   457

ca. October 13, 1960: Allen Ginsberg to Jack Kerouac   459

October 18, 1960: Jack Kerouac to Allen Ginsberg   461

1961

April 14, 1961: Jack Kerouac to Allen Ginsberg   465

1963

June 29, 1963: Jack Kerouac to Allen Ginsberg   469

October 6, 1963: Allen Ginsberg to Jack Kerouac   473

Index   477

EDITORS' INTRODUCTION

"Let you not to the marriage of true minds admit impediments—love is not love which alters when it altercation finds—O no! 'tis an ever fix'd lark."

—The twenty-two-year-old Jack Kerouac paraphrasing William Shakespeare
in his first letter to the seventeen-year-old Allen Ginsberg

It is now common to lament the gradual demise of the handwritten or hand-typed letter over the past decades. Significant blame is often placed, and rightly so, on the radical lowering of phone rates. Up through the mid-1960s, for many people calling long-distance across country was a rare and costly luxury, only to be indulged in for an emergency or to share news of a birth or death. But as technology improved, people could increasingly afford to pick up the telephone and talk through the details of their lives with friends and loved ones, instead of taking the time to sit down and write. More recently, the advent of e-mail has further diminished the flow of snail mail correspondence.

The question now becomes whether writers who prove to be of lasting interest, and who correspond extensively about their lives and their craft via e-mail, will take the trouble to maintain accessible records for use by future scholars and readers. But whatever lies ahead in this regard, it is unlikely we will often see a body of correspondence between two important writers that yields more insight into their work and their lives than does the collection of letters and postcards between Jack Kerouac and Allen Ginsberg. Their prodigious output is remarkable enough merely for its sheer volume and for the longevity of the literary friendship enacted and developed through it. But it is truly extraordinary in its range, quality, and intimacy. An extended correspondence of such richness is a rare thing.

Kerouac and Ginsberg have proved to be two of the most influential writers of the second half of the twentieth century. Kerouac's *On the Road* and Ginsberg's *Howl* are seminal works that have inspired innumerable readers, including many artists working well outside the field of literature, who cite these books as liberating and life changing. Kerouac's novels had a great impact on the way American writers write and helped shape the worldview of several generations. Ginsberg's poetry, his compelling public performances, and his role as an activist and teacher made him a cultural force for decades. The legacy of their writing and their lives continues to unfold, to such an extent that their place in history cannot yet be definitively assessed.

This selection makes a significant contribution to both their bodies of work, and to the understanding of that work. Two-thirds of these letters have not been published before. The Ginsberg-Kerouac friendship was the pivotal axis for the literary movement and cultural construct that became known as the Beat Generation and was essential to both men throughout their adult, professional-writing lives. Their unique quarter-century of correspondence offers passionate self-portraits, a vivid record of the cultural scene they helped create, key insights into the literary explorations at the core of the Beat movement, a unique chronicle of their mutually encouraged spiritual explorations, and a moving record of a deep, personal friendship.

That friendship began when Ginsberg was an undergraduate at Columbia University in 1944 and their correspondence commenced the same year. The letters record a long, intense conversation, one that continued, with varying periods of frequency and intensity, until shortly before Kerouac's death in 1969.

Both men were committed, from early on, to a life in literature; and their letters were an important workshop in which their ever-evolving ideas were shared and endlessly debated. Whether they were in agreement or following divergent strands of thought, they wrote with great open spirit to one another in trust. In their letters, Ginsberg and Kerouac emerge first and foremost as writers of artistic passion, innovation, and genius. Both their careers involved endless struggle, hard work, and sacrifice to enact their literary visions; and each man provided a steadfast reference point for the other in times good and bad. Their correspondence illuminates both their convergences and their conflicts as writers. They shared an uncanny and remarkable versatility as word "sketchers," both devoted to fully exploring writing as disciplined "spontaneous thought." Ginsberg's relentless support and encouragement helped Kerouac profoundly. Ginsberg's social skills and irrepressible efforts to connect people to one another were important in promoting the very idea of a Beat Generation. Kerouac's innovations as a writer were central to Ginsberg's work. As Ginsberg once noted, "My own poetry's always been modeled on Kerouac's practice of tracing his mind's thoughts and sounds directly on the page."

"Friendship is love without his wings," Lord Byron wrote. Surely he was wrong, as this book is evidence of a lifelong friendship that was love with wings. These two friends soared to the heights in their correspondence as the letters flew back and forth. Sometimes they wrote so eagerly to each other that their missives crossed in midflight. The letters were an essential part of their work, and often the vehicle through which that work evolved. Phrases were shared and pondered, books recommended, writers and friends analyzed, poems exchanged, and ideas tried out, their responses to each other helping to determine the next step forward. There is madness here and mad joy, play and suffering and erudition, as well as daily life strategy, money struggle, and detailed logistical planning to coordinate meetings and events. They kept track of friends and forwarded each other letters by those friends, precious in those prephotocopy days when the original was often the only copy.

Some of their letters are stunningly extensive single-spaced epics, longer than published stories or articles. There are aerogrammes from afar, words jammed to the edges, filling every inch, and handwritten letters on lined pages, tiny notebook sheets, old letterhead. Add-ons are scrawled on envelopes, and sometimes-lengthy postscripts tucked in. There is an ongoing attention to publishing strategies, the painful year-after-year efforts to get their work—and the work of their friends as well—into print. There are agents and editors and publishers to discuss, anger and frustration to share, new directions, renewed resolve, despair. There are arguments, and moving past those and underlying all across the years, an oft-voiced mutual appreciation and affection. "Cher Breton," Allen would write. "Jackiboo," "Mon cherami Jean," "Kind King Mind," and "Ghost." "Cher Alain," Jack would begin, "Cher jeune singe," "Alleyboo," "Irwin," "Old Bean."

When Kerouac's attention turned to Buddhist thought, he diligently sought to engage Ginsberg's interest as well, taking copious notes on his extensive reading and enthusiastically sharing them, instructing and urging. Eventually Kerouac turned back away from his practice, but Ginsberg embraced Tibetan Buddhism and practiced seriously for decades. His memorial service was held in a Manhattan temple. The origins of both men's explorations of Buddhism are in these letters.

The attention success brought Kerouac was not his friend. He recoiled from much of the sixties counterculture and, in his final years, pulled back into himself. Ginsberg fully embraced the era, assuming a unique role by bringing art and politics together. The correspondence between them continued during the Sixties, but only sporadically. The occasional phone call became the main emotional link sustaining their bond. By the time Kerouac died, in 1969, Ginsberg was just hitting his stride, and followed through in every aspect of his work for the next thirty years.

A few years after Jack Kerouac died, Allen Ginsberg and poet Anne Waldman cofounded the Jack Kerouac School of Disembodied Poetics at the Naropa Institute in Boulder, Colorado. While teaching there one summer, Ginsberg asked Jason Shinder, his student assistant at the time, to help him collect copies of all the correspondence between himself and Kerouac. Fortunately, both Ginsberg and Kerouac were mindful of posterity and had organized and saved nearly everything. By that time, most of their letters were already in the collections of two great research libraries: Kerouac's at the Columbia University Library, Ginsberg's at the University of Texas. It was Ginsberg's hope that someday a book of their letters might be published, but once the mountain of material had been gathered, it was clear that the job of transcribing everything was overwhelming. Nothing much was done for the next thirty years.

In editing this book, we began with nearly three hundred letters. Every one has qualities in its favor, and it would have been satisfying to simply include them all, but this was impractical. In the end we included two-thirds—the best. Our goal was to publish as many strong letters as possible, and toward that end we let the last few years of sporadic correspondence go. Those letters were mere supplements to person-to-person conversation. The book ends on a high note, with a spirited exchange between the old friends several years before Kerouac's voice fell silent.

For the most part we included entire letters, but on a few occasions judiciously cut portions, indicating these by ellipses within square brackets [. . .]. Both Ginsberg and Kerouac occasionally used ellipses in the letters themselves as a form of spacing, and these have usually been preserved, but square brackets indicate deletions to the text. Sometimes postscripts were eliminated if they had nothing to do with the flow of the letter and were inessential; often these were inquiries about friends, or directions, or greetings to pass along to other people. Both writers sometimes included poems and texts with their letters, and some of these have been left out.

Assigning precise dates to some of the letters has been problematic. Where the exact dates were not known, the editors have made educated guesses, and those approximate dates are noted by brackets, as are corrections to the authors' own dating, as in the case where a previous year is mistakenly used out of habit for several months into the new year. In general, simple spelling mistakes were corrected unless it was obvious or likely that incorrect spelling was deliberately creative—"eyedea" for instance, and "mustav." Some errors were made by the authors consistently, as in Ginsberg's use of "Caroline" for "Carolyn," and "Elyse" for "Elise," and those are noted the first time in each letter and corrected thereafter. Other errors are more variable. Kerouac might use *On the Road* in one sentence and *On The Road* in the next. The city in Morocco might appear as Tanger, Tangier, Tangiers, or even Tangers, with little concern for consistency.

Ginsberg's handwriting can be particularly difficult to decipher, and some of Kerouac's both-sided letters have extreme show-through, making it hard to read every word, even with the aid of a magnifying glass. Therefore, in instances where the editors were making a well-calculated guess regarding a particular word, the word is included in brackets, [thus]. Similarly, where a word or passage is completely illegible it is indicated by [?].

Footnotes have been added in order to help identify people and events that might not be widely familiar, but the editors have tried to keep footnotes to a minimum, and we refer readers to their own reference sources. The life stories of Kerouac and Ginsberg have been well told in biographies. In this volume, the Editors' Notes, which appear throughout the text, are meant as stepping stones to bridge the reader across gaps in chronology, or to fill in missing context for a letter. The storytelling is in the letters, and we leave it to the reader to discover it.

ACKNOWLEDGEMENTS

The editors, Bill Morgan for the Ginsberg Estate and David Stanford for the Kerouac Estate, wish to thank the following:

The Allen Ginsberg Trust; trustees Bob Rosenthal and Andrew Wylie, and a special note of thanks to Peter Hale, who really is the workhorse of the Ginsberg world. Steven Taylor kindly made suggestions to the final manuscript. Judy Matz as always was the unsung hero of the editing process.

The Wylie Agency: in particular Allen Ginsberg's agent, Jeff Posternak.

The Estate of Jack Kerouac; John Sampas, executor, with a special note of appreciation for John's many years steadfastly guiding the continued unfolding of Kerouac's work, and ensuring the preservation of his writing for future generations.

Sterling Lord Literistic; in particular Kerouac's longtime agent Sterling Lord, with whom it is always an elegant pleasure to work—and of whom Kerouac said, "The Lord is my agent, I shall not want."

Penguin USA, specifically Viking-Penguin, and even more specifically our editor Paul Slovak, with deep gratitude for his longtime furthering of Kerouac's canon at the house formerly known as The Viking Press, where he and David Stanford burned the midnight oil together for many years in happy hardworking camaraderie. Also big thanks to veteran wordherder Beena Kamlani, whose painstaking labors on other books by Kerouac and Ginsberg made her the ideal colleague for this project.

The following libraries: Harry Ransom Humanities Research Center, The University of Texas at Austin; Butler Library, Department of Special Collections, Columbia University; and Green Library, Department of Special Collections, Stanford University.

We would like to honor the memory of editor, writer, and poet Jason Shinder, who worked on this project in its earliest stages. When interest in bringing it to fruition was revived, he signed on to coedit on behalf of the Ginsberg Estate. His untimely death deprived him of that opportunity. In drawing on notes from the cowritten book proposal, we have undoubtedly incorporated some of his thoughts into the editors' introduction. We acknowledge his contribution, and, as fellow editors, we salute him.

David Stanford offers ever-thanks to the divine Therese Devine Stanford, his beloved delightful wife, ally, sweetheart, and friend.

1944

Editors' Note: *The earliest letter between Ginsberg and Kerouac was written six or seven months after the two met. During those months, they had become close friends and saw each other almost daily on or near the Columbia College campus on Manhattan's Upper West Side. Then on August 14, 1944, they were involved in a tragic murder, when their mutual friend Lucien Carr killed David Kammerer, an older man who had been infatuated with him for years. Kerouac helped Carr dispose of evidence, and when Carr turned himself in to the police a day or so later, Kerouac was arrested and held as a material witness. Not able to post bail, he was remanded to the Bronx County jail.*

Allen Ginsberg [New York, New York] to Jack Kerouac [Bronx County Jail, New York]

ca. mid-August 1944

Cher Jacques: on the subway:

I've been escorting *la belle dame sans mercip* [Edie Parker[1]] around all morning—first to Louise's,[2] now to jail. I haven't a permit, so I won't visit you.

I saw her carry *Dead Souls* to you yesterday—I didn't know you were reading it (she said you'd started it). We (Celine [Young[3]] *et moi*), took it out of the college library for Lucien [Carr], too. Anyway, and to get to the point: Good! That book is my family Bible (aside from the *Arabian Nights*)—it has all the melancholy grandeur of modder Rovshia [Mother Russia], all the borscht and caviar that bubbles in the veins of the Slav, all the ethereal emptiness of that priceless possession, the Russian soul. I have a good critical book on it home—I'll send it to you (or, I hope, give it to you) when you're finished with the book. The devil in Gogol is the Daemon Mediocrity, I'm sure you'll therefore appreciate it. Anyway, I'll finish some other time.

Edie and I looked into D. Klavier [David Kammerer]'s old room—all the penciled inscriptions on the wall had been painted over by some philistine housepainter. The little graphite mark above the pillow is no more—it once bore emblem (where plaster had fallen off the wall) "Lu—Dave!" The snows of yesteryear seem to have been covered by equally white paint.

To get off this morbid *recherché tempest fortunatement perdu*, I'm reading

[1] Edie Parker was Kerouac's girlfriend at the time.
[2] Ginsberg frequently used pseudonyms to disguise the true identity of the people he was writing about. Here it seems probable that Louise was either Joan Vollmer Adams, with whom Edie and Jack were sharing an apartment, or Lucien Carr, who was in jail. Adams later became the common-law wife of William Burroughs.
[3] Celine Young was Lucien Carr's girlfriend at the time.

3

Jane Austen and finishing Dickens's *Great Expectations*. I also started Brontë's *Wuthering Heights* for the second time for an English course; and of course I am also plowing thru about 4 history books at a time (when Edie isn't chewing my ear) mostly about revolution in Europe in the 19th century. When I am finished I will start one here.

Give my fondest love to Grumet [Jacob Grumet, the assistant district attorney]—*A pet de eu fease.*

Allen

Editors' Note: On August 25, 1944, Jack Kerouac and Edie Parker were married while Jack was still in police custody. Edie was then able to borrow money from her trust fund to post Jack's bail. This letter appears to have been written just as the newlyweds were about to leave New York to live with Edie's mother in Grosse Pointe, Michigan.

Jack Kerouac [New York, New York] to Allen Ginsberg [New York, New York]

ca. September 1944

Dear Allen:

Let you not to the marriage of true minds admit impediments—love is not love which alters when it altercation finds—O no! 'tis an ever fix'd lark . . .

Our wedding anniversary fell on the day of the liberation of Paris. I suppose this news Lucien now views morosely—he who wanted to be in Paris among the first. That event will have to wait now . . . but surely it will come about.[4] I'd like to go to Paris after the war with Edie, Lucien, and Celine—and a little money for a decent flat somewhere in Montparnasse. Perhaps if I work hard now, and establish my fortune swiftly, I can realize that transcendent ambition. You yourself might lay down your legal labours[5] for awhile and join us there. The new vision[6] would blossom . . .

But this is all speculation, mediation, nay, emasculation . . . Thanks for the letter. It moved me at times. I find in you a kindred absorption with identity, dramatic meaning, classic unity, and immortality: you pace a stage, yet sit in

[4] Lucien Carr spent the next two years in prison.
[5] Allen Ginsberg had gone to college originally to become a labor lawyer.
[6] The "new vision" was a term that Kerouac and Ginsberg's small group of friends in Morningside Heights used to describe their own philosophy, which they hoped to express through their art. They picked up many of their ideas from Baudelaire's notion of "poet as alchemist," the Symbolists' attitude of spiritual defiance, and Apollinaire's *l'esprit nouveau*, which pitted "experimental" arts against growing social conformity.

the boxes and watch. You seek identity in the midst of indistinguishable chaos, in sprawling nameless reality. Like myself, you deserve the Adlerian verdict, but we don't care about that: Adler[7] can name our egocentricities, but only because he himself is an egocentric . . . (the dirty bastard.)

This mania stems from the great Germans, Goethe and Beethoven. He who seeks all knowledge, and then all life and all power—and he who identifies himself with thunder. He is egocentric. But how paltry is the definition.

Lucien is different, or at least, his egocentricity is different, he hates himself intensely, whereas we do not. Hating himself as he does, hating his "human-kindness," he seeks new vision, a post-human post-intelligence. He wishes more than Nietzsche proscribed. He wants more than the next mutation—he wants a post-soul. Lord only knows what he wants!

I prefer the new vision in terms of art—I believe, I smugly cling to the belief that art is the potential ultimate out of the humankind materials of art, I tell myself, the new vision springs. Look at *Finnegans Wake* and *Ulysses* and *The Magic Mountain*. Lord only knows the truth! Lord only can tell!

Well, goodbye . . . and write: tell me more about the shadow and the circle.

    Ton ami,

      Jean

---

[7] Alfred Adler was a Viennese psychologist who split away from Freud's methods during the early part of the twentieth century.

1945

Editors' Note: After spending only a month in Michigan, Kerouac returned to New York City and renewed his friendships with Ginsberg and William Burroughs. Once again they were in daily contact, so there was little need to write, and when they did correspond it was only to arrange meetings here and there around the city. During the summer of 1945, Kerouac went off to find work and Ginsberg signed up for training at the Maritime Service Training Station in Sheepshead Bay, Brooklyn.

Allen Ginsberg [n.p., Paterson, New Jersey?] to Jack Kerouac [Ozone Park, New York]

ca. late July 1945

Cher Breton:

I am sorry that we could not rescue a final meeting from our departure. The good Dr. Luria [a doctor with the Merchant Marine] told me you'd called, and I sent another postcard in haste. I'm writing a last time in the hope of reaching you before your voyage. *A moi*—Tomorrow morning, all the preliminaries having been dispensed with, I shall sign into the Merchant Marine. *Incipit vita nuova!* Monday I shall leave for Sheepshead Bay, where I hope to tutor myself anew in all these strange realities I have learned from the purgatorial season.

Your letter came to me after I returned from a fruitless journey into New York to recapture the grandeur of another time, and it came, almost, as a letter from the past, and conjured up in me all the emotions I had been seeking the days before.

But, Jack, rest assured that I shall return to Columbia. Bill [Burroughs] never advised me to stray from the fount of higher learning! I should return, however, to finish college, even if it were only a pilgrimage of acceptance of former time.

I hear from Celine [Young] from time to time; I saw her two weeks ago. I'll probably see her before I leave. Hal [Chase] has returned to Denver for the summer (a week ago.) Nothing from Joan [Adams] or John [Kingsland]. I still see [Lionel] Trilling[1] from time to time, he's invited me to his house (yes, I received the invitation, I acknowledge, with my usual pleasure at such things.) I hope I hear from you from Paris; at any rate, please write when you get back to the U.S., before you leave for California.

I understand, and I was moved that you were openly conscious that we were not the same *comme amis*. I have known it, and respected this change, in a way.

---

[1] Lionel Trilling, an author and literary critic, was one of Ginsberg's professors at Columbia.

But perhaps I should explain, for I have felt myself mostly responsible for it. We are of different kinds, as you have said, and I acknowledge it more fully now than before, because at one time I was fearful of this difference, perhaps ashamed of it. Jean, you are an American more completely than I, more fully a child of nature and all that is of the grace of the earth. You know, (I will digress) that is what I most admired in him, our savage animal Lucien. He was the inheritor of nature; he was gifted by the earth with all the goodness of her form, physical and spiritual. His soul and body were consonant with each other, and mirrored each other. In much the same way, you are his brother. To categorize according to your own terms, though intermixed, you are romantic visionaries. Introspective yes, and eclectic, yes. I am neither romantic nor a visionary, and that is my weakness and perhaps my power; at any rate it is one difference. In less romantic and visionary terms, I am a Jew, (with powers of introspection and eclecticism attendant, perhaps.) But I am alien to your natural grace, to the spirit which you would know as a participator in America. Lucien and yourself are much like Tadyis [the young, handsome boy in *Death in Venice*]; I am not so romantic or inaccurate as to call myself Aschenbach [the old professor who is infatuated with Tadyis], though isolate; I am not a cosmic exile such as [Thomas] Wolfe (or yourself) for I am an exile from myself as well. I respond to my home, my society as you do, with ennui and enervation. You cry "oh to be in some far city and feel the smothering pain of the unrecognized ego!" (Do you remember? We were self ultimate once.) But I do not wish to escape to myself, I wish to escape from myself. I wish to obliterate my consciousness and my knowledge of independent existence, my guilts, my secretiveness, what you would (perhaps unkindly) call my "hypocrisy." I am no child of nature, I am ugly and imperfect to myself, and I cannot through poetry or romantic visions exalt myself to symbolic glory. Lest you misunderstand me, I do not, or do not yet, own this difference to be an inferiority. I have sensed that you doubted my—artistic strength—shall we call it? Jean I have sincerely long ceased to doubt my power as a creator or initiator in art. Of this I am sure. But even if I would, I cannot as you look on it as ultimate radiance, or saving glory, redeeming genius. Art has been for me, when I did not deceive myself, a meager compensation for what I desire. I am bored with these frantic cravings, tired of them and therefore myself, and contemptuous, though tolerant, of all my vast powers of self-pity and self-expressive misery. What am I? What do I seek? Self-aggrandizement, as you describe it, is a superficial description of what my motives are, and my purposes. If I overreach myself for love, it is because I crave it so much, and have known so little of it. Love as perhaps an opiate; but I know it to be creative as well. More as a self-aggrandizement that transcends the self-effacement that I unconsciously strive for, and negates the power of self-aggrandizement. I don't know if you can understand this. I renounce the pain of the "frustrated ego," I renounce poetic passive hysteria; I have known them too long, and am worn and enervated from seeking them too successfully. I am sick of this damned life!

Well, these last years have been the nearest to fulfillment of my desires, and truthful feeling I thank you for the gift. You were right, I suppose, in keeping your distance. I was too intent on self-fulfillment, and rather crude about it, with all my harlequinade and conscious manipulation of your pity. I overtaxed my own patience and strength even more than I did yours, possibly. You behaved like a gentlemen; though I think that you did take me too seriously, assign too much symbolic value to my motion and friction. There is much that was not merely ironic, but also purposeless and foolish in myself and my activity. I can't forget Burroughs' tolerant smiles as I mockingly and seriously explained to him all the devious ways of my intelligence. Still, Jack, I was conscious of all that I did, and inwardly sincere at all times, and this I have always been. I wonder if you comprehend the meanings which I can't explain. Well, though in poetry I shall lie whitely and elevate these frustrations to "wounds," I shall have flashes of insight and know better. At any rate, if you are able to understand me, I ask your tolerance; if not, I plead for your forgiveness. When we meet again I promise you that seven months will have elapsed profitably, that we will meet again as brothers in comedy, a tragedy, what you will, but brothers.

What is ahead I do not know; a valediction is our heritage; the season dies for a time, and until it is resurrected we must die as well. To all who perish, all who lose, farewell; to the stranger, to the traveler, to the exile, I bid farewell; to the penitents and judges of the trial, farewell; to the pensive and thunderous youth, farewell; to the gentle children and the sons of wrath, to those with flowers in their eyes, of sorrow or of sickness, a tender adieu.

   Allen

Jack Kerouac [Ozone Park, New York] to Allen Ginsberg [Maritime Service Training Station, Sheepshead Bay, Brooklyn, New York]

August 10, 1945

Hello Allen:

It didn't develop so well at camp,[2] work and pay not being what I was led to believe, so I'm home again now. You make first with the letters.

---

[2] That summer Kerouac had been hired to work at a summer camp, before finding a job closer to home as a soda jerk.

I'm going to soda-jerk occasionally, enough to pay the fare to L.A. Also am writing a batch of potable magazine love stories, hope I can sell one of them.

(They wanted me to clean latrines at $30 a week at camp. Pfui.)

Let me know how you like or dislike Sheepshead.

Comme toujours
Jean

Allen Ginsberg [Sheepshead Bay, New York] to Jack Kerouac [n.p., Ozone Park, New York?]

August 12, 1945

August 12.

Cher Jean:

"L'Automne deja."... Il ya une annee jadis, si je me souviens bin, que le monde a venu a'sou fin. Today is Sunday; this evening, or on the 14th, we violent and pensive children will be reenacting our crimes and judging ourselves.[3] The year somehow has passed quickly, almost has eclipsed itself. At moments when *les remords sont crystalisees* by some Proustian gesture, I think of the season of hell with a willing sentimental yearning. Today while I was trying to sleep I heard a negro singing softly, "you always hurt the one you love," and I began singing it myself in homage. You must change your life!

The abrupt fluctuation of your personal fortunes *vis-à-vis* stable employment have ceased to surprise me, though they still are "kind of amusing." I can't criticize your leaving the camp, but what I miscalled "Emotional Smugness"—a sense of something missing in your head besides bourgeois idealism, was responsible for your getting yourself into such [bettises?]. Don't you even know what you're signing up for? You have what my grandmother calls a *Goyeshe Kopfe*—a *Goy's* head—as differentiated from a *Yiddishe Kopfe*—a shrewd Yiddish foresight somewhat *a la* Burroughs. I haven't heard from him.

A *moi-l'histoire d'un de mas folies*—I've been encamped here for twelve days now. The boys here are all overgrown or warped adolescents—all screaming neurotics. Me, with all my highly advertised guilts and frustrations, *moi*, I was able to absorb the change to service with an equanimity and dispassionate benevolence unknown to the maritime. The second day here we were shown a botched version of Freud in a movie short, explaining to the demons of the streets that their backaches, leg pains, headaches, fainting spells, and melancholies were all

---

[3] A reference to the Carr-Kammerer murder, which had taken place one year earlier, on the night of August 13–14, 1944.

functional—that their troubles were purely psychic. Some naive professional tough guy on my left leaned over and whispered in a sort of scared voice that jeez maybe he ought to see the psychiatrist like they say? I was surprised to find such an overwhelming preponderance of nervous wrecks who cracked under the initial "strain." There is a great deal of stupidity in the management of this place. The petty officers etc. are all fat buttocked Marine sergeants with loud voices. They talk a lot about order and discipline but the administrative and ordering sections are the most confused, contradictory, undisciplined and disorderly crowd I've ever met with and the atmosphere breathes lack of definition and fosters anxiety. The first thing I did was follow a maxim of Burroughs' and find out the layout; I cased the joint; got all the regulations down pat, and defined myself. So I had no surprise and tension in my *Yiddishe Kopfe* when all went through with smoothness. I know the techniques of "fluffing off" (escaping duties and punishments and details). The routine here is routine; the telos is periphery, the preoccupation is "detail work," which surprised me somewhat. I hadn't thought about what any army trains for. It merely maintains itself here with no exterior purpose. So I wash clothes, and practice neatness at all times, stow my gear properly in a clean locker, make my bunk, giggling to myself unobtrusively. There is also buffing detail. Buffing the floors (pushing buffing rags with the feet) is the standard routine for keeping the trainees busy. Since even cleaning reaches a point of declining output, when no more can be cleaned, we are put to doing it all over. This keeps us busy, teaches us discipline and attendance to duty. Since my presence here is voluntary and experimental, I don't take it all so hard and don't find myself itching to knock out anybody's teeth or go A.W.O.L. The Thomas Wolfish reaction to all this, of romantic disapproved and fiery rejection, doesn't particularly interest me. I question the consciousness and validity of gestures. Anyway, I'm enjoying myself, since I don't take it personally, and the change is, ah, refreshing. There is a beach here where I swim and laze in the sun on weekends. I miss music most of all. There are radios here but you know the story.

I've begun to use Burroughs' critiques and begun criticizing them. For one thing, he tends to type all individuals that he doesn't know personally, and thus perhaps he would have difficulty in evaluating a mob of individuals. And these are all individuals—they are reminiscent of one type or other, some character types (the regressive fairy, the mother loving crybaby, the dead end kid, the sadist, etc.) and others more neatly anthropological. But though each has a reminiscent theme, they are people on their own to whom I am drawn with a certain sympathy. Incidentally, I failed to maintain a mask of the "regular guy" in that I couldn't prevent myself from airing my ego from time to time. Fortunately, I was also able to talk the language; then, I had welding experience, which I exploited—it made me a mechanic, a normal human being. And so I am afraid that I am perhaps a "brain" (I was caught reading Hart Crane and the mailman delivered your post-card saying it was in French—he saw the last line, which was in French I think.) But it hasn't tended to prejudice my relations with the good guys, and I am accepted ("Heaven be praised for that") as one of the guys by all. I find them coming to me for sympathy (which I give) and advice, since I am one of the oldest in my section. Also, they keep telling me about their women. This sex talk is a real pistol. So I tell them about this cunt Joan Adams I used to live with, and how she laid for me in the afternoon. My language is usually restrained; when I want to be "regular" I use a slight southern accent and talk about Denver, and Saint Louis and curse the niggers. So all goes well and I am not victimized, nor do I have any anxiety on that score.

I like a few of the boys (friendly-like, you know, no more). One is a redhead, a spindly virgin named Gaffney who is a little scared by it all. Another calls himself a "man of steel" and sends his mother one of those hideous green and purple silk pillow covers with a sentiment (rhymed) embroidered in it.

I haven't written anything but occasional poems. This bothers me some-what. I got a letter from Joan who will be in N.Y. in September's first week. John [Kingsland] writes to her, using Celine's name on the back of the letter to deceive Joan's parents. Now they think she is so friendly with Celine that maybe they ought to invite her up to Albany. Celine wrote: she is up in Lake Champlain. Lancaster is working as a waiter in a country club.

I don't feel much like writing now, I'm tired.

Allen

Jack Kerouac [Ozone Park, New York] to Allen Ginsberg [Sheepshead Bay, New York]

Aug. 17, '45
1 Ozone Parc

Mon garcon,

Yes, my friend, I long to be the proud possessor of a *yiddishe kopfe's* head. There is a head which senses the only true values: Returning from the summer camp last week, I had occasion to sit next to a gentleman of *Yiddishe kopfe* material. He was about fifty. I was reading *The Counterfeiters* [by André Gide]— (it was a gesture, I must confess!)—when my companion reached over and took the book out of my hands. Needless to say I was pleased by his informality. "Ah very good book!" he said, prodding me with his finger. "Ah very valuable book!"

"Yes? You like it?"

Nodding, he thereupon opened the book (whilst I relaxed in anticipation of a treatise on the choicer scenes) and removed the jacket. The jacket he examined very carefully, smoothing it lovingly with his sensual fingers. Then he bent the book back until the binding groaned, and examined that for a while. Finally, he turned the book upside down and peered like a watchmaker at the cover, at the gold paint, and then at the very pages themselves! These he felt between his fingers, and sighed. I said, "Do you want to read it? If you like you can, I've some other books here in my bag."

"Oh," he said, "you sell books."

"No—but I have some with me." I reached down and produced Plato's *Republic*. He immediately took it from my hand and presto!, with quick unerring judgment, with *yiddishe kopfe* foresight, with a sad yet somehow shrewd smile—he handed it back to me. He tapped the book as it lay in my hand, and shook his head. "Not so good, not so good."

So I went on with Plato while he, perhaps improperly, but certainly without conscious reprehensibility, continued to sigh over, and fondle, our good friend Andre Gide.

Bill [Burroughs] in town. "Surrender night" found us reunited. We went out with Jack and Eileen. Bill and I didn't talk much. There was much drinking and charming madness, though I'm sure it didn't charm Bill. In the end he and I were alone trying to pick up women. He was wearing a Panama hat and something about his appearance must surely have had something to do with our failure to find women . . . As he stood on Times Square, one had the feeling that he surveyed not a sea of heads but a vast field of poppies "as far as the eye can see." Or maybe he looked like Lucifer's emissary, *charge d'affaire de l'Enfer* himself, and passer-by women caught a flash of red lining inside his coat. This is all nonsense of course. It was a night for servicemen, not for a Marijuana Tycoon, sober, and a hoodlum, drunk. After Bill went home, I went to Eileen's and laid her while Jack slumbered beside us.

Bill is going to join you at Sheepshead! You may now abandon your strenuous efforts to adjust yourself, for Bill is going to approach you and cry, "SNOOPY! When did you get out? DID YOU BEAT THAT INDECENT EXPOSURE RAP IN CHI??"

I suggested he approach you and say, "SNICKERS! How CHARMING! WHERE have you been, YOU ELUSIVE THING!"—But Bill decided it wouldn't be in the best interests of either one of you.

I'll see Bill tomorrow and hope to talk things over with him.

When you write letters to me, try not to be sophomoric and moribund about your criticism of Jean *et son weltanschauung*. A little more finesse, please, or if

possible, a dash of humour. Some of the cracks you make are *PM*-ish[4] if anything; and you know, not at all in keeping with one's laborious tendings towards
perfect Lucienism. *He* would be satirical, *mon ami*, but never ponderous and
paranoiac. You "question the consciousness and validity of gestures." Never
would you subscribe to "Thomas Wolfish fiery rejection and romantic disapproval." It pains me, my friend, it pains me. Perhaps you judge me too harshly,
especially with reference to my latest *goyesha kopfe* "fiery rejection" at the
summer camp, for you see, I was a busboy, and busboys live on tips, and tips
must be substantial in order to provide for the livelihood of *goyesha kopfe* busboys who read Thomas Wolfe, only, you see *mon vieux*, in this melancholy instance, the guests at the camp were 100% middleclass *yiddishe kopfe*, and after
all, one has to make a living you know, so, with romantic disapproval, I sallied
forth from there, and came away with Byronic dignity—a gesture, I fear, that
meets with your unromantic disapproval, but which was, after all, grounded in
the strictest urgency of reality, unless it be that I flatter myself, in which case I
certainly deserve all the mild censure, the pity, and the sympathy which you
have always held in reserve for me at crucial moments.

    Happy *cauchemars*!

      Your affectionate monster,

        Jean

Allen Ginsberg [Sheepshead Bay, New York] to Jack Kerouac [n.p., Ozone Park, New York?]

Aug 22, 1945
In Service of My Country.

Cher ape:

    I was overjoyed (is this too strong?) to hear that Bill [Burroughs] was in
town. What is his address? I'm curious to know what flophouse he's picked for
a front this time. Is it adjoining a Turkish bath? But that he is to join me at
Sheepshead is something too good to be true! Tell him to send me or send me
yourself details of his swearing in and departure-time, day, etc. (and I'll see that
there's a welcoming committee at the gates to meet him.)

    As for this jack-off sophomorism, screw you Jean. And if these "Laborious
efforts at Lucienism" are supposed to be mine, make it up yours. I'm not in the
mood myself. *Je sais aujourdhu comment orluer la beaute avec l'yiddishe koffe.*
I meant by the way that the peckerhead romanticism came in where you fun-

---

[4] *PM* was a socialist newspaper published in New York.

gled up the choice of jobs until you are so screwed up that the only practical thing is to be Wolfish. O.K. So it wasn't your fault that you were pushed into the wrong job. But it could only happen to you. My letter was ponderous but please god not paranoiac.

Allen

P.S. I have liberty this weekend I think and I want to see Bill's face again and yours if possible. *Pro tem*, I'll be at the Admiral Restaurant at 5:30 on Saturday. Now write me a letter or postcard post haste *s'il vous plait* and give me details as to when you can meet me and Bill, and what his phone and address is. Change the time and place if you wish; I can be in N.Y. by 3:00 o'clock.

I got a pistol of a letter from Trilling. I'll bring it.

Your clinging vine,

A.

Editors' Note: In this letter a new Bill appears, Bill Gilmore. Gilmore and other people with the common name Bill will make appearances, but they will always be identified clearly by their family name given in square brackets. If there is no such identification, the reader should assume that the reference is to William Burroughs.

Jack Kerouac [Ozone Park, New York] to Allen Ginsberg [Sheepshead Bay, New York]

August 23, '45

Cher jeune singe:

I shall answer all your stupid questions, as there is nothing else to do. Bill [Burroughs]'s now at Sheepshead, has been there since Monday the 20th. Of course he won't look you up right away—that's his system, he wants us not to think that he is too eager. He'll look you up in good time, unless you happen to run into him. Don't be too surprised!—Now, he was in New York five days before he called me up, or that is dropped me a line, telling me he was around. I immediately went to see him, not being wary of my own eagerness. He was not living in a flophouse this time—he lived in a Park Avenue hotel at $4.50 per day. It did not adjoin a Turkish bath (I'm still answering your questions) but the place itself was a well known Turkish bath, as the saying goes.

I've scoured your letter for any further questions, and there are no more. Strange!—I had had the notion that it was full of whys and whats. All well and good . . . there is no Why. The mystery is this: that there should ever have entered our heads the notion of Why! That's the mystery, among others. Death is a mystery almost as enigmatic as life. But enough of that.

You were right about my "peckerhead romanticism." Of course. I perfectly agree with you. Now it is all settled. We can begin worrying our little heads about something else now.

The other night, the last night I saw Bill, that strange thing happened to me . . . I got very drunk and lost my psychic balance. It doesn't always happen, remember, but sometimes it does, like that night. [Bill] Gilmore had some fellow come to our table . . . we drank . . . all went to his apartment, where we drank much more. Even Bill was a little silly. We were all silly. I hated the guy. You know of him, he was with that large party at the Cafe Brittany that night we were there with Gilmore and Uncle Edouard, that large noisy American party, shot through with ensigns and society girls. I shall have to tell you about that night I lost my psychic balance. Only one thing did I carry away with me from the welter of silliness . . . a book! I stole a book. *Voyage Au Bout De La Nuit* by Celine. In a remarkable English translation. And also, I carried away with me much drunkenness. It was the second time I saw Bill, and still we did not talk. For awhile we were alone, in a restaurant, and it occurred to me we had nothing more to talk about. That's the way it has developed; that's what it's come to. We have nothing further to talk about. We've exhausted the possibilities of each other. We are tired. Another few years, an accumulation of new possibilities, and we will have something to talk about. As for you, my little friend, there is always something to talk about because you are so unutterably vain and stupid, and that always leaves a splendid electrically charged gap for argument. *Merde a toi!*—that's what I say.

In view of all that, I suppose we can meet at the Admiral, providing you are serious about meeting me there. As to eating there, I don't know. The place has deteriorated, service and food and all. It's a disgusting biological change, like cancer. Bring along the Trilling letter. I may as well begin to find out now what kind of a fool he really is . . . whether he is a bigger one or lesser one than you or I or anybody else.

It may surprise you to know that I have been writing in prodigious amounts. I am writing three novels at this very minute, and keeping a large diary to boot. And reading! . . . I have been reading like a madman. There's nothing else to do. It's one of those things you can do at the moment when all else isn't any more interesting, I mean, when everything else can't exactly prove to be much more worthwhile. I intend to do this sort of thing all my life. As for artistry, that is now a personal problem, something that concerns only me, so that probably I won't bother you about that ever again. All well and good. A line from my diary: "We are all sealed in our own little melancholy atmospheres, like planets, and revolving around the sun, our common but distant desire." Not so good, perhaps, but if you steal that line of mine, I'll actually kill you, for a change.

5:30 *a l'Admiral, Samedi* . . .

        Bye bye petit,

            Jean

Editors' Note: *Ginsberg became sick and had to spend a few weeks in the base hospital. He missed the brief visit of William Burroughs to the base and the dinner with Kerouac at the restaurant in New York, as mentioned in this letter.*

Allen Ginsberg [Sheepshead Bay, New York] to Jack Kerouac [n.p., Ozone Park, New York?]

Monday afternoon
Sept. 4, '45 [*sic*: Monday was September 3, 1945]

Dear Jean:

I was well enough to leave my bed today and so I slipped out to my barracks and got my mail which has been waiting. I got your letter, and was so excited by the prospect of seeing Bill [Burroughs] immediately that I ran over to B-1 which is the reception building to look him up. He arrived you said on the 20th. After begging the authorities to tell me how to locate him, I got one petty officer to open the books. I was told he's disenrolled from Sheepshead on the 22'd, two days after he'd arrived. I am just returned to sick bay much bewildered and disenheartened. What has happened? Where is he now—have you heard from him since? Back on Park Ave. I suppose. I very strongly want to see him, but I am restricted here for the next few weeks. But now I feel anticlimactical, hopelessly confused.

I wait with some impatience to hear your description of *La Nuit De Folie.* I hope you'll have regained your psychic balance by the time I hear it; I enjoy hearing your labyrinthine expositions of rescued masculinity—This was unnecessary. But mostly I'd like to hear you describe the degenerate looking limbo character whom I remember quite well. As to the police, [serucisient?], don't let your guilt or repentance upset you, as I fear from your tone that it already has.

Your letter sounds somewhat tired, of a fatigued spirit, whether speaking of your conversations with Bill, or your ennui (the particular cause of your heavy reading), or your unexplained attacks on my "stupidity and vanity," which distressed me rather than amused or wounded, whatever you were aiming at. What is the matter? At any rate, don't shepherd your artistic problems back into the cave; I'd like to hear of them since I suppose they are almost the most important season of your supernal journey, to borrow your metaphor.

Alas! I am sorry about the Admiral the other Saturday. My absence was unavoidable as I explained in the postcard I sent last night. I am feeling much better now, although for a day I was so sick that I found myself worrying about the future of man's soul, my own in particular. Did you show up? What did you do, what did you think, how did you curse in my absence?

I have been reading while in bed, since it was the only thing for me to do. I finished *The Way of All Flesh*, at last, Thornton Wilder's *Bridge of San Luis Rey*, neither of which I was particularly moved by. Now I have begun, at last, *War and Peace* and am finished with 825 pages of it. I do not think that I like Tolstoi as much as Dostoevsky (whatever the confession means), but I am enjoying myself with *W&P* more than any novel I've read since *The Idiot*. I enclose Trilling's letter. [. . .]
> Allen.

Jack Kerouac [n.p., Ozone Park, New York?] to Allen Ginsberg [Sheepshead Bay, New York]

September 6, 1945

Thursday night Sept. 6

Dear Allen,

Your little letter moved me, I must say . . . particularly the line, "I was so sick that I found myself worrying about the future of man's soul, my own in particular." There you elicited the true picture of things terrestrial . . . namely, disease and loss and death. I like the way Rilke faces these facts in his un-bourgeois way, and I must say I don't particularly approve of forgetting the facts of life and death in an orgy of intellectual pseudo-synthesis . . . Shelley's "dome of white radiance" has become a sort of rose-coloured dome now, shedding technicolor pinkness on us all. However, I don't think there's much point in telling *you* all this because I know you don't represent the average intellectual softy. Or punk.

Some of my most neurotically fierce bitterness is the result of realizing how untrue people have become . . . and you must admit that I am in closer touch with public vulgarity than any of us. Although Bill reads the *Daily News* also, I go him one better, alas, and take the trouble to listen to the radio . . . *and* suffer myself onto *P.M.* as well. Archetypal morality in its modern high-pressure Orson Welles O.W.I. [Office of War Information] and Hearst regalia—you see, there are no right and left distinctions, and never were, in spite of what I think the Lancasters and Fritz Sterns[5] would say—have become for me a kind of windmill to my Quixote . . . I think of what Joan Adams and Kingsland would say about all this; this makes of me a most ludicrous figure. I'm wrestling with the passé . . . that's what you're probably thinking. Well, let's have no more of this for now . . .

News of Burroughs is what you want . . . I haven't seen him and I don't know where he is. However, I've mailed a card to the University Club in the hopes that it will be forwarded to him, and he may let me know where he is. Gilmore's roommate, Francis Thompson (!) is under the impression that Bill is still in New York . . . Gilmore himself is staying at a cottage on Cape Cod writing a novel. The reason why Bill disenrolled from Sheepshead is because he wanted to go in the MM [merchant marine] as a purser, and very likely they wouldn't see it his way . . . Francis believes that Bill is going to try again. That about sums up all I know about Burroughs for the present, but the moment I'm in receipt of his new address, it shall be sent on to you. There remains but one additional item re Burroughs . . . Joyce Field says he is "leprous." That I must tell Bill . . .

I was moved by your letter, I repeat. Partly because you'd been and still are sick . . . Partly because of Trilling's letter, which represents something I'd like to happen to me someday, namely, to be liked and admired by someone like him. Although there's something a little wearying about his emphasis on "effect" in poetry, that letter he wrote you is certainly a marvelous example of how an entrenched man of letters can inspire confidence in a young poet. There's something French about it . . . I mean, it smacks of Mallarmé encouraging the young author of Le Cahier d'Andre Walter [André Gide]; or of [Paul] Verlaine praising the tempestuous provincial lad in a letter addressed to Charleville; or of Gide bestowing his warm appreciation and admiration on the young and unknown Julian Green. I say all this gauchely in my haste, but honestly I envy you. I think we none of us realize the importance, nay the sweetness, of admiration; it is one of the dying virtues of character. Look for instance at the way Lucien [Carr] is neurotically resented all around Columbia by a lot of bloodless fish who couldn't out-argue him or something, or who couldn't get away with wearing red shirts and striking white masks on the streets, as he did. A recent visit at Columbia, where Carr is still very much in evidence, reveals, I suppose, and to coin a pat and disgusting phrase, the neurotic nature of our times . . . Here are all these jerks snarling out of the corners of their mouths at everything—and particularly at Lucien. There is none of the loving perception of "Look! Look!" . . . no one grabs your arm eagerly to seduce you sweetly with a point . . . there is no Germanic enthusiasm, no thick guttural cries . . . just so

[5] Both were fellow Columbia College students.

much monotonous epigram-making, and as far as that goes, there are no Oscar Wildes at Columbia. Save Wallace Thurston, of course . . .

I was there and I saw Celine Young, Joyce Field, Grover Smith, Joan [Adams] and John [Kingsland], Auerbach the sophomoric bore, Wallace Thurston, [Arthur] Lazarus (who asked about you), and others I can't remember. Celine got drunk and showed me a letter from [Hal] Chase. She says they've broken up, but I don't think they have . . . It would have amused you to see the wonderful understanding Celine and I reached that night: just like brother and sister, it was, all except the wrestling. But vraiment, I think Celine is a remarkable girl . . . She's lost fifteen pounds, she looks like something out of Mann's sanatorium—ineffable, beautiful, self-corroding doomed, a bit mad. She told me, with a melancholy air, that Lucien did not love her and that he would in the future seek his love elsewhere . . . she added to that, that no girl could satisfy Lucien. I was so kind to Celine that night . . . Do you know, Allen, that Celine and I can never again be lovers? It's as though she wanted me more as a brother . . . And I'm inclined to like it, since she's lost all sex-appeal to me in a sort of mystic immolation of desire. But the maddening thing! . . . she's resigned herself to all kinds of fates, including an affair, mind you, with Don Kahn! The situation is straight out of Dostoevsky, my little friend! Look at it this way: she likes Edie [Parker Kerouac] a great deal and reserves the right thereby to ask for my friendship. Secondly, she has always desired my confidence. Everything but romance, as it were. Finally, in view of all that, she decides to have affairs with anyone who wants her . . . Now she says she doesn't want Chase any more; she speaks of that Kahn fellow. I can't get over the irony of all this. I feel more and more like Myshkin[6] as time goes on . . . I am in love with a lot of people at this moment, and Celine no less than the others. Being the sensual Breton, it is hard for me to resist sex in relations with women. But here I find myself gladly playing the father-confessor, the sympathetic Raskolnikov to her Sonia,[7] while her charms are reserved, as by tacit agreement, for a bunch of nobodies. *O merde à Dieu!* The novelty is there, of course, and I am young enough to wade into new ponds. And anyway I'm going to California in October . . .

I asked Edie to meet me at Columbia this weekend. There's going to be a sort of get-together, which will include Edie, Joan, John, Grover, Celine, Kahn, myself, and I hope, Burroughs—if I can locate him. We will drink a toast to you, I'll see to that. Though Kingsland may giggle and Burroughs smirk and Edie turn up the corner of her mouth and Joan make a crack and Celine smile sweetly and Grover make a pun, I'll suggest a toast to our bed-ridden little *copain*.

---

[6] Prince Myshkin is the central character in *The Idiot*, by Fyodor Dostoevsky.
[7] Raskolnikov and Sonia are characters in *Crime and Punishment*, by Fyodor Dostoevsky.

Your curiosity regarding *la soiree d'idiocie* is understandable. True, I did feel remorse . . . So much so as to cancel an appointment with Burroughs for the next day, which probably bored him altogether. He has no patience for my kind of neurosis, I know . . . But since then I've been facing my nature full in the face and the result is a purge. You understand, I'm sure. Remember that the earlier part of my life has always been spent in an atmosphere vigorously and directly opposed to this sort of atmosphere. It automatically repels me, thereby causing a great deal of remorse, and disgust. There is a kind of dreary monotony about these characters, an American sameness about them that never varies and is always dull . . . Like a professional group, almost. The way they fore-gather at bars and try to achieve some sort of vague synthesis between respectability and illicitness . . . That is annoying, but not half so much as their silly gossiping and snickering. If they were but Greeks, things would take on a different tone alto-gether. I am repelled, then, largely by these social aspects, an overdose of which I got that night. As to the physical aspects, which as you know, disgust me consciously, I cannot be too sure . . . whatever's in my subconscious is there. I am not going to play the fool about that. My whole waking nature tells me that this sort of thing is not in my line. It keeps on telling me. It drums in my nature, telling me, until I begin to suspect its motive. But I shan't worry my pretty little head about it anymore. I think that in the end it will just be a matter of "Drive on!"—you have heard that story about Phil the junky, haven't you? I shall let my neurosis dissolve in the white fire of action, as it were. Strangely, the thing that annoys me the most is the illusion everyone has that I'm torn in two by all this . . . when actually, all I want is clear air in which to breathe, and there is none because everybody's full of hot air. The remorse you detected in my last letter is not all for the reasons you imagined . . . Once I was in bed with a girl, down in Baltimore; I had picked her up in a bar and she promised me she would come across. When we got to bed, she fell asleep and couldn't be awakened . . . I spent the whole night wrestling around with her limp rag of a body, as she snored. It is a horrible experience, that . . . You feel remorse the next day, ashamed of your desire; perhaps you feel like a necrophiliac, maybe there's a fear of necrophilia in all of us, and this business of wrestling around with an unconscious woman is the closest thing there is to necrophilia . . . Well, that's the kind of remorse I felt, for exactly the same reasons. But I knew there would be no clear air vouchsafed me the next day . . . There was no one I could tell the story to who wouldn't in return blow a lot of hot air my way . . . It's almost as though my neurosis were not ingrown, but that it was the result of the air, the atmosphere around me. For there are a lot of horrible things I've done in my life, in the dark away from everything, and not only to me. I am not a Puritan, I don't answer to myself; rather, I'm a son of Jehovah—I advance with trepidation towards the scowling elders, who seem to know about every one of my transgressions, and are going to punish me one way or the other. As a little boy, you know, I started a very serious forest fire in Massachusetts . . . and it's never worried me in the least, because I've had only my own blithe self to answer to for that crime . . . If on the other hand, I'd been caught, I would have suffered terribly. This then, is the kind of remorse I felt . . . But that too is now purged . . . I trust.

You shouldn't have been "distressed" by the tone of my last letter. It was only a mood . . . and a not malevolent one either, not at all. It was all done as an older brother. Sometimes you give me such a feeling of superiority, say, moral superiority, that I can't restrain myself . . . Other times, I feel inferior to you—as I doubtlessly do this moment. I'm afraid that you'll never understand me fully, and because of that, sometimes you'll be frightened, disgusted, annoyed, or pleased . . . The thing that makes me different from all of you is the vast inner life I have, an inner life concerned with, of all things, externals . . . But that would be discussing my art, and so intimate is it become that I don't want to babble about it. You may deplore the fact that I'm "shepherding artistic problems back to the cave," but it's certain that that's where they indeed belong. The bigger and deeper this inner life grows, the less anyone of you will understand me . . . Putting it that way may sound silly, it may particularly amuse Burroughs, but that's the way it is. Until I find a way to unleash the inner life in an art-method, nothing about me will be clear. And of course, this places me in an enviable position . . . it reminds me of a remark Lucien once made to me: he said: "You never seem to give yourself away completely, but of course dark-haired people are so mysterious." That's what he said, by God . . . Then you yourself referred to a "strange madness long growing" in me, in a poem written last winter . . . remember? I just thrive in this, by God. From now on, I think I'll begin to deliberately mystify everyone; that will be a novelty.

After all my art is more important to me than anything . . . None of that emotional egocentricity that you all wallow in, with your perpetual analysis of your sex-lives and such. That's a pretty pastime, that is! I've long ago dedicated myself to myself . . . Julian Green, among others has one theme in all his work: the impossibility of dedicating oneself to a fellow being. So Julian practices what he preaches . . . There is just one flaw: one yearns so acutely to dedicate oneself to another, even though it's so hopeless . . . There's no choice in the matter.

I was telling Mimi West last summer how I was searching for a new method in order to release what I had in me, and Lucien said from across the room, "What about the new vision?" The fact was, I had the vision . . . I think everyone has . . . what we lack is the method. All Lucien himself needed was a method.

I understand Trilling's impatience with the High Priest of Art . . . There *is* something phony about that. It's the gesture adopted when the method doesn't prove to be self-sufficient . . . after awhile the gesture, the Priestliness, begins to mean more than the art itself. What could be more absurd?

But let's not let the whole matter deteriorate, as I feel it will in mentalities such as Trilling's—that to adopt art with fervor and single-minded devotion is to make the High Priest gesture. No, there's a distinction to be made, without a doubt.

So goodnight for now . . . About the Admiral [Restaurant], I'd received your card in time and so was forewarned. I'm keeping Trilling's letter for awhile in order to show it to a few people: this must make you realize that the quality of my friendship for you is far purer than yours could ever be for me, you with your clay-pigeon complex. There's nothing that I hate more than the condescension you begin to show whenever I allow my affectionate instincts full play with regard to you; that's why I always react angrily against you. It gives me the feeling that I'm wasting a perfectly good store of friendship on a little self-aggrandizing weasel. I honestly wish that you had more essential character, of the kind I respect. But then, perhaps you have that and are afraid to show it. At least, try to make me feel that my zeal is not being mismanaged . . . as to your zeal, to hell with that . . . you've got more of it to spare than I. And now, if you will excuse me for the outburst, allow me to bid you goodnight.

[. . .]

Jean

Allen Ginsberg [n.p., Sheepshead Bay, New York?] to Jack Kerouac [n.p., Ozone Park, New York?]

after September 6, 1945

Dear Jack:

I got your letter yesterday. I said to Joan [Adams] when I saw her in the W.E. [West End Bar] "Celine [Young] reminds me of Natasha or whatever her name was in the *Magic Mountain.*" Your remark to the same end in your letter—is this telepathy? Thus surprised me Joan didn't agree though. I think she's thinking of the healthy Celine, paramour of the up and coming lawyers (though that somewhat fits in with Mann, even.) As you have been father confessor of late, I have been brother (or sister?) confidante for some years now and I know the feeling; I suspect that there's some transferred libido in the role.

As there is also, I suppose, in my and Bill's sharp curiosity *vis à vis* your various *affaires de folie.* The assumption on my part (now half habitual) of

25

your double nature and the conflicts there from—"the illusion that every-one has that I am torn in two by all this," was formerly a sort of half prurient wish-fulfillment. You have got me there. Still you can not arrive at a verdict yourself—that in a sense you are being persecuted by an atmosphere—so easily as you do by "as it were" dissolving it in the white ice of action. I am repelled by the atmosphere of Larry's and Main Street, and by [Bill] Gilmore's patterns of innuendo, at the same time I find myself revolving about in that particular universe (to use a phrase of yours). It is much the same with you; after all, the atmosphere is one that you have chosen from other than aesthetic impulses, you are also drawn by a prurient curiosity which you are conscious of I sup-pose. You could even accept them (these posy people) as Greeks, though you have contempt and some fear for them as they are. And the "remorse" that you feel is avowedly exteriorized, you are afraid of Burroughs's inquisitive sardoni-cism, of external consciousness of your fatal flaws. Burroughs or Gilmore are perhaps trying to drive you to this level, you on the other hand provoke them by manifestations of fear, by trying to maintain yourself on another level from them and ignoring or rationalizing all evidences to the contrary. You are more Greek than Gilmore, and more American than Greek, and so you need not be so tense about it.

I don't enjoy sitting at your feet being thrown into consternation by fits of divine madness—alternately "frightened, annoyed, disgusted or pleased." You are not a toy you know, nor am I a well meaning simpleton ineffectually trying to fathom you. At the same time your conservation of speculative energy and growing aloofness in a promiscuous exhibition of your wares hit me as another corridor in the gamut of emotions, on surprisingly Burroughsian and (I bow) mature in the line of development. Your art is as you say more important to you than anything, mine is an emotional egocentricity. I accept this because I would relegate art to a purely expressive and assertive tool—here I am more Rimbaud, I think. And for me its equal purpose is as a tool for discovery. But the assertion—myself—and the discovery—external—are my aims; I am dedi-cated to myself. It is you who do not recognize the impossibility of dedicating yourself to your fellow-beings, you are dedicated to your art. My art is dedi-cated to me.

Anyway, if we traced the currents of poetry, I think that in the end the whole art making machine (in yourself as in myself) would be egocentric, whether we wish to deceive ourselves with other ideas. And in the end, and with Julian [Lucien Carr]. He does not wish to dedicate himself to another, except as far as for him it will dedicate another to him. Love is only a recognition of our own guilt and imperfection, and a supplication for forgiveness to the perfect be-loved. This is why we love those who are more beautiful than ourselves, why we fear them, and why we must be unhappy lovers. When we make ourselves high priests of art we deceive ourselves again, art is like a genie. It is more powerful than ourselves, but only by virtue of ourselves does it exist and create. Like a genie it has no will of its own, and is, even somewhat stupid; but by our will it moves to build our gleaming palaces and provide a mistress for the palace, which is most important. The high priest is a cultist, who worships the genie that someone else has invoked.

You say you are keeping Trilling's letter, my true friend, and that I shall realize the quality of your friendship by advertising it for me. My self-souled aggrandizing lust seems to have convinced you of the validity of my clay pigeon complex. Well, you *are* the ungrateful one—and I had the temerity to tell Trilling (half year ago) that you were a genius. This is the thanks I get! (Incidentally, I think that half the reason I told him that was to get him to think that my friends were geniuses and by implication, etc. Still, I risked my reputation on you.)

Aside from all of this frivolity I was surprised by your belief that whenever you show your affectionate nature to me I become condescending—I think that it has been oppositely so. Do you really find it like that?

Incidentally—I was ashamed to tell you before Burroughs—I wrote Trilling an 8 page letter explaining (my version) the Rimbaud *Weltschaung*. It was mostly an exegesis of Bill's Spenglerian and anthropological ideas. I feel sort of foolish now—over bumptious.

I think I'll be in N.Y.—at Bill's—Saturday night, maybe Sunday. I expect to have Monday off. I have no money, so I'll have to seek introspective entertainment—C.

Is Gilmore really writing a novel?

Here are two sonnets on the poet which contain half of my versions of art.[8]

     Allen

P.S. Don't write unless there is something special. I don't want to take your time and I will see you soon enough. Somehow I'd like to save your letters for tragic occasions, long farewells, or for voyages.

---

[8] Ginsberg included two poems here that can be found reprinted as "The Poet: I" and "The Poet: II" in his *The Book of Martyrdom and Artifice* (DaCapo, 2006).

1948

Editors' Note: Between September 1945 and April 1948 the letters were few and far between. During these years Jack and Allen spent a good deal of their time together, which made writing unnecessary. When their correspondence picks up again here, in 1948, they have both spent time at sea, met Neal Cassady, and made their first cross-country trips to the West to visit him, and their friendship has had its ups and downs.

Jack Kerouac [n.p., Ozone Park, New York?] to Allen Ginsberg [n.p.]

ca. April 1948

Saturday night

Dear Allen

Distractions, excitement, and evil influences prevented me from absorbing what you were saying about Van Doren and the proposed publication of your doldrums.[1] Thus, sit down and write me a letter about it. I'd go to see you about it only I'm so near to the end of my book that I tremble at the thought of leaving it for one moment. Exaggeration—but I can see you next weekend. Meanwhile I'd like to hear about it, more about it, circles of it briefly.

Meditating on the *yiddishe kopfe* heads I wonder if you were right about my taking *Town and City* to Van Doren instead of a publisher. Tell me what you think about that in your considered well-groomed Hungarian Brierly-in-the-bathrobe[2] opinion. It seems to me perhaps that if I took my novel to publishers they would glance at it with jaundiced eyes knowing that I am unpublished and unknown, while if Van Doren approved of it, everything would be quite different. I imagine that's what you think, too. We creative geniuses must bite fingernails together, or at least, we should, or perhaps, something or other.

Have you heard from Neal [Cassady]? Reason I ask, if I go to Denver on June 1st to work on farms out there I'd like to see him. It's strange that he doesn't right (write)—and as I say, he must be doing ninety days for something, only I hope it's not ninety months, that's what I've been really worrying about.

Hal [Chase] has been reading my novel and he said it was better than he thought it would be, which everybody says. As a matter of fact I don't know much about it myself since I never read it consecutively, if at all. Hal is still

---

[1] Mark Van Doren was a Columbia professor of English at the time to whom Ginsberg had shown his poem cycles *The Denver Doldrums* and *Dakar Doldrums*.

[2] Justin Brierly was a Columbia alumnus from Denver who had recommended that both Hal Chase and Neal Cassady attend Columbia.

amazingly Hal—you know, Hal at his best and most *mysteriously intense* self. What a strange guy. With a million unsuspected naiveté's jumping over the monotone of his profundity. And it is a real profundity.

It's funny that whenever I write to you nothing seems to sound right due to the fact that I keep imagining you saying, "But why? why is he saying *that*? what is the meaning of all this? what is it for?" Do you know, that sounds like Martin Spencer Lyons, big philosopher. Says, "What are you doing?" and you say: "Writing a novel" and [he] says: "WHY?"—with the voice of Gabriel, supposed to lay you flat under the why-and-wherefore of the universe. I tell you, man, a guy like Martin Spencer Lyons has been into the house of doubt-and-why and had to sneak out the *back way*, whereas you take *me*—I've been in that house and I wandered around all the rooms and I came out the way I came in. Ask me about the whys and wherefores of doing anything, or about the insanity of unconsciously contrived action, and I will say to you in my cardiest Mark Twain tone, "Shit, I even know the wall-termites in the house of why-and-wherefore by their first names." Good, hey? All of which is supposed to mean that one shouldn't ask *why* all the time, and therefore don't ask *why* I'm writing you this letter. Actually it's because I have a sudden urge to talk to you about it and also, subliminally, to complete a little circle we began last Saturday night when I borrowed a buck from you and we both smiled graciously like two old Jews in the garment business who know each other *so* well that they can smile falsely. Also, the buck is not forthcoming perhaps until I might see you this weekend.

So when you see Van Doren—tell him I plan to take my novel (380,000 words) to him, tell him I *will* take it to him in the middle or end of May, completed novel: tell him it's the same one I told him about 2½ years ago and go and tell him that I have laboured through poverty, disease and bereavement and madness, and this novel hangs together no less. If that isn't the pertinacity or the tenacity or something of genius I don't know what is. Go tell him that I have been consumed by mysterious sorrowful time yet I have straddled times, that I have been saddest and most imperially time-haunted yet I have worked. And tell Martin Spencer Lyons, poor rueful ramshackle oddity that he is, that he has succeeded in annoying a man of action. So long man. Tell me of Hunkey [Huncke].

Man of enigma-knowledge and despair of aggression,

J.

P.S. The thing I like about Van Doren is this: he was the only professor I personally knew at Columbia who had the semblance of humility without pretensions—the semblance, but to me, deeply, the reality of humility too. A kind of sufferingly earnest humility like you imagine old Dickens or old Dostoevsky having later in their lives. Also he's a poet, a "dreamer" and a moral man. The moral man part of it is my favorite part. This is the kind of man whose approach to life has the element in it of a moral proposition. Either the proposition was made to him or he made it himself, to life. See? My kind of favorite man. I have never been able to show these things to anyone from a fear of seeming hypocritical rather than sympathetic, or simpatico. Thus, if he should happen to like my novel, I would get the same feeling that Wolfe must have gotten from old [Maxwell] Perkins at Scribner's—a filial feeling. It's terrible never to find a father in a world chock-full of fathers of all sorts. Finally you find *yourself* as father, but then you never find a son to father. It must be awfully true, old man, that human beings make it hard for themselves, etc.

P.S. Dig this line from my novel, in a Greenwich Village sequence: "In all these scenes (Greenwich Village parties) the grave Francis was like some veritable young officer of the church who had been defrocked early in his career after a scandal of tremendous theological proportions."

P.S. And dig this description of New York: "They saw Manhattan itself towering across the river in the great red light of the world's afternoon. It was too much to believe, near, almost near enough to touch (like the stars), and so huge, intricate, unfathomable and beautiful in its distance, smoking, window-flashing, canyon-shadowed realness there, with the weave of things touching and trembling at its watery apron below, and the pink light glowing on its highest towers as bottomless shadows hung draped in mighty abysms, and little things moving in millions as the eye strained to see, and the myriads of smoke rising and puffing everywhere, everywhere from down the shining raveled watersides right up the great flanks of city to the uppermost places, etc. etc." Then it gets darker—"And it was so: the sun was setting, leaving a huge swollen light in the world that was like dark wine and rubies, and long sash-clouds the hues of velvet purple and bright rose above, all of it somber, dark, immense, and unspeakably beauteous all over: everything was changing, the river changing in a teeming of low colors to darkness (dig that?), the abysses of the streets to darkness, etc., fabulous thousand-starred glitter, etc., etc., and finally,—" as you look across the river to Brooklyn—"the swoop of the bridges across the river—the river like pennies—to Brooklyn, to the teeming, ship-complicated, weaving-soft incomprehensibly ruffled water's-end and very ledge of Brooklyn."

P.S. More, much more, but I'm tired

So long

Jack Kerouac [n.p., Ozone Park, New York?] to Allen Ginsberg [n.p., New York, New York?]

Theme: All the young angels rolling to the music of celestial honkytonks. (in a roller skating rink)
Tuesday night May 18 '48

Dear Allen:

Thanks for writing. I'll be seeing you perhaps this Friday night, but now I don't want to discuss your letter[3] in detail due to the fact that it's a lot of ancient material with me. In answer to all your questions: yes. I have the same problems, of "personal-ness" in expression striving at the same time to be communicative (sweetly if you like.) . . . and all that, and yes, I have worked it out in my own way. In *Town and City* not as much as later, also. We can talk about it. Assured that I have "matured up to it" all-right; how could I miss?—I haven't done anything but write for years and years, and you know I'm not stupid and unintelligent. Perhaps I can help you by pointing out pitfalls. As to the novel, I already handed it in to Scribner's two weeks ago, and they're reading it now; no word yet.

But here is news that will interest you a lot, I heard from Neal [Cassady]. Oh these are the sweet dark things that make writing what it is . . . Anyway I heard from Neal, and I had to fill out an application blank for his employer attesting to his character. Assured that I piled it on in the best Bill Burroughs letter-manner. I think I said that he would be of "great initial value to your organization and purposes," etc. The job is as a brakeman on the Southern Pacific railroad. From which I assume—and I guessed right—that Neal got in trouble, got three months, and they're getting him a job out of a jail agency of some sort. No peep out of Neal himself, however. The Southern Pacific is the most wonderful railroad in the world incidentally . . . on a Sunday morning, riding down through the sunny San Joaquin Valley of grapes and women-with-bodies-like-grapes, I reclined on a flatcar reading the Sunday funnies with the other boys, and the brakemen smiled at us and waved cheerful. It is the hobo's favorite road. Anybody with any sense in California can ride between Frisco and LA endlessly on that road, once a week if they want to, and nobody will ever bother them. When the train stops at a siding, you can jump off and help yourself to fruit if you're near a field. So wonderful Neal is working for a wonderful railroad, in the Saroyan country . . . (if there's any beastly murderousness it's not my fault or Neal's or Saroyan's.) The Santa Fe brakemen will kill you if they catch you and if they have enough clubs. But not the SP.

---

[3] Kerouac is referring to a Ginsberg letter of mid-April 1948, which is not included in this volume.

I had a season, Allen, I had a season. It lasted exactly four days. She was eighteen years old, I saw her on the street, was riven, and followed her into a roller skating rink. I tried to roller skate with her and fell all over the place. Young and beautiful of course.—Tony Monacchio, Lucien's friend (and mine) was conversant with my beautiful season . . . He thought that the girl, Beverly, was too dumb for me, not vocal enough. I hated the thought of it . . . you can't imagine how madly in love I was, just like with Celine [Young], only worse, because she was greater. But finally she rejected me because "she didn't know me, she didn't know anything about me." I tried to get her over to my house to meet my mother for God's sake but she was afraid I was trying to trick her, apparently. Sweet love softly denied. She thought I was some sort of gangster . . . she kept hinting. She also thought I was "strange" because I didn't have a job. She herself has two jobs and works herself to a bone, and can't understand what "writing" is. Tony Monacchio and I found Lucien dead drunk in Tony's room after a party—on the night that Lucien was supposed to fly to Providence for his 2-weeks vacation. We helped him to the Air Lines bus. He was bleary-eyed, blind, wearing brown-and-white saddle shoes like a Scott Fitzgerald character of the 20s. I suddenly realized that Lucien is drinking too much after all and that Barbara [Hale][4] is not doing anything about it. I mean he was really sick. Tony said to him, "Jack's girl is sweet and beautiful but dumb." And Lucien, out of this dizzy sickness of his, said—"Everybody in the world is sweet and beautiful but dumb." Allen, these are the things, these are the things, don't worry about the *theory* of writing, not at all. Then Lucien thanked us for escorting him to the "airplane" as he called the bus, and there was a farewell. That afternoon my little girl rejected me. So now, how are you? How's everybody in the sweet beautiful dumb world?

        Jack

Allen Ginsberg [n.p., New York, New York?] to Jack Kerouac [n.p., New York, New York?]

        after May 18, 1948

Monday Night : 1:30

Dear Jack:

I got your letter Sat. evening—I had been in Paterson for a few days. I will be in this weekend (in N.Y.).

You seemed overly proud that it was "ancient material." What I was saying

---

[4] Barbara Hale was Lucien Carr's girlfriend at the time.

in part (lesser part) was that it was not recognizable (to me in your prose) but but but. This is not the same old maturity that I (as [Bill] Gilmore) have been talking about before. This is something I wouldn't have the slightest idea if Gilmore would understand and don't care much. But you are right, perhaps it's under my nose in you. This is a kick I don't want to continue.

School is over and I have been reading Dante, which I have found very inspiring. I finished the *Divine Comedy* during the term, and am reading books including *The Vita Nuova* (New Life) [by Dante Alighieri]. I dreamed up an enormous tentative plan tonight, which I will tell you about. My interest in reading is the profit by other men's experience. I sometimes find (only lately) authors talking directly to me, from the bottom of their minds. I think I am going to write a sonnet sequence. I want to read Petrarch and Shakespeare, Spencer and Sidney, etc. and learn about sonnets from beginning to end, and write a series on love, perfectly, newly conceived. I conceived the whole idea all at once seeing the first word in a title embedded in a page of the *Vita Nuova*: my poems have always been prophesied by their titles. That is, a poem often has a single "transcendent, personal, and serious idea" behind it, as a novel—a single image. I want to celebrate my "lovers" in all various manners, intellectually, wittily, passionately, raptly, nostalgically, pensively, beautifully, realistically, "soberly," enthusiastically, etc., every possible perception fitted out in inwrought, clear, complex stanzas—including the one as yet undefined or unstated mood, or better, knowledge, that I have and that at times you are aware that I have, no matter how silly I get. The title of this is: "The Fantasy of the Fair." Just repeat it aloud, it carries the whole idea in it. One of the major ideas is the dynamic sense of "Lucien's Face" which you once propounded to me and which I half understood at the time. I want to formulate it poetically, if possible as the end of the poem, but without any private or subjective, or N.Y. idea of L.I. [Long Island] use the name to bridge at the moment. I am talking about humanity, and beginning to try to write in eternity.

I have been enduring a series of troublesome dreams lately about Neal [Cassady]. Your notice comes at about the crisis of them, though it is not a passional crisis and is accompanied by no tempests of intellect. I wonder what he is doing in his eternity. I feel so far away from people, without loneliness, that I am rather happy now. [. . .]

I'm not worried about the theory of writing, I am only just vering the practice. The Doldrums are antiquated. For that reason I am sending poetry out for the first time. I got my first rejection slip from *Kenyon*; a note from J.C. Ransom, editor and poet: "I like very much this slow, iterative, organized and reflective poem. At times it's like a sestina. Thank you for sending it. But still I think it's not for us exactly. I guess we need a more compacted thing."

36

I had sent them "Denver D. [Doldrums]" but, as luck would have it, I have some compacted things around that he will get next week.

Your season sounds beautiful. I particularly wish I had seen Lucien so drunk. Make what you want out of that.

No, it sounded like you. (Some one is singing a ditty "So please pass a little piece of pizza") and it makes me wish I were alive, that's why I can't say any more.

Everybody's fine, but it's sweet, beautiful, but not so dumb, this world. Lucien means dumb because we don't know what we know. I mean, won't admit how much we know.

White[5] said that Scribner's rejected you, too, just like the goil. Can I see the novel [*The Town and the City*]? But don't worry, it really don't mean a thing. That's my opinion.

Grebsnig

Allen Ginsberg [East Harlem, New York] to Jack Kerouac [Ozone Park, New York]

July 3, 1948

Dear Jack:

[. . .]

Yes, daddio I am in Harlem, reading *Huckleberry Finn*. I have a radio and I listen to everything when I like it, Durgin[6] comes in and out all hours of the night drunk giggling over silly absurdities, we have short and long mad, even gleeful conversations, and I sit and write, and he sits and writes on T. Aquinas and Martin Buber and Shakespeare, and coughs. I am working up a great brotherly feeling for him, he is pretty great, and really sad. He knows all the bars all over the city: he knows the city, and he doesn't care, he is too thoughtful over the Soul in a theological way. He is going away to have his lung deflated up in Saranac[7] in a few days. I sit and tell him improvised stories about walks I take into Harlem, about seeing Lester Young at the Apollo, who Lester is, how he looks when he blows, about the landlady who is an old Jewess named Mrs. Bitter, etc.

What happened to [Allan] Temko[8] in Frisco? Couldn't take it? What does he

---

[5] Ed White was a fellow Columbia student from Denver and an acquaintance of Neal Cassady.

[6] Russell Durgin was the student in whose apartment Ginsberg was living at the time.

[7] Saranac Lake, New York, in the Adirondack mountains, was the home of a famous tuberculosis sanatorium.

[8] Allan Temko was a Columbia classmate of Ginsberg and Kerouac. One of their Denver friends, he later became an architectural critic in San Francisco, and won a Pulitzer prize.

know about Horror? What does he care, why doesn't he get a job and stay there like an honest man? Why doesn't he go to Paris and stay there and roll in the gutter? I can see him making a niggling fortune in the black market and sitting in Rumpelmeyers taking his perspectives. Tell him to take a pilgrimage to Aix (Cézanne) or Charleville.

I am learning by the week, but my poesy is still not my own. New rhyme new me me me in words. I am not all this carven rhetoric.

If you want to see swirl come to Harlem.

I am off this weekend to Paterson to dig poppa Louiay [Louis Ginsberg]. Come in anytime after that, say, Monday night or any night thereafter. I can be caught by phone on weekday mornings at the Academy of Political Science[9] if you call Columbia regular Universal number, and ask for Academy, and ask for me, anytime before 10:30 in the morn.

I am struck by your ending. It might be great. It is the most promising if you just don't fuck it up with Wolfe brooders.

"Anything you do is great."

I wrote Neal a long letter, so long I had to send it in a package, and I copied out everything I've written beginning with "Dakar Doldrums."

Mop, Ow.

Editors' Note: During the summer of 1948, while living in Russell Durgin's apartment at 321 East 121st Street in East Harlem, Ginsberg experienced a series of cosmic visions and hallucinations. The first was of the voice of William Blake reciting poetry. That was followed by a period of heightened awareness that lasted on and off for a few weeks. These visions influenced Allen dramatically and were to occupy his thoughts for the next decade. In the following letter Ginsberg writes to Kerouac, trying to express what he has been going through spiritually.

Allen Ginsberg [East Harlem, New York] to Jack Kerouac [n.p., Ozone Park, New York?]

Summer 1948

Dear Jack

I hope you remember still with me the conversation we had last week on 14 St. There was an element that entered into it of something that, has not been

[9] Ginsberg was working for the journal of the Academy of Political Science.

so clearly realized in our previous conversation—namely that X which I have (and you, and everyone for that matter) continually harped on for the last few months. It is important that we clearly understand (if anything is important to understand intellectually) the complete other-ness of the other world. It does not at any time come into our conscious worlds—except perhaps at rare moments—but I believe it is the only valuable thing, the only possession, the only thought, the only labor of worth or truth, and to that I have dedicated my self or to make it less of a self-hood, to that somehow I have been dedicated— much as the Kafka hero who wakes up one morning to find that something mysterious has found substantial form and is persecuting or prosecuting him, giving no rest—a time life and death struggle. The unreal has become for me the most real, now. That is perhaps why my conscious thought-life is so far removed from yours. What you shuddered at as madness—what you glimpsed as the fantastic—the most fantastic possible—possibility is I have seen for several months the only thing, the inevitable—the one. There is no evasion of it for me—I can't forget what I have seen, and seen by myself for a few disparate moments more clearly than we guessed together last week. I once saw clearly beyond my life, and saw I had to go there. You may be annoyed at my repetitive use of words like "literal" and "actually" or "actuality" etc. but for lack of a vocabulary—and for lack of the immediate presence of what I was talking about I have been trying to express myself about a miracle.

I have been at it now for months trying intellectually to define, to describe, to show the existence of that something else that we know—something that we can know if we are able to shoulder the responsibility of destroying our present lives, but it is by its nature so far beneath or above existence as I normally know it that it is of no use except to invoke (as in a few conversations) the vague sensation of something dreamlike and white, arden-esque, ghostly about us—and that sense of fairy tale is the nearest in our conscious minds that we can approach. Once I give up this attempt I will be nearer to the ultimate realization that I strive for, for this is vain and defensive against the awful sensation of knowledge. If I did not have faith in the mechanical procedure of psychoanalysis as a way of making me face myself and god I would no longer wait here in the city for a vision, but I would have despaired of life here and left—on an actual pilgrimage, as of old— across the land, would throw myself on the mercy of the elements and die out of this life of vanity and fear, give up completely, and wander, without home, until a home were everywhere. It may seem anachronistic for me to combine such ambitions spiritually with psychoanalysis that will change everything—towards that goal. But that is my own life and choice, and I can't presume to prescribe any medicine but suffering to anybody else—suffering to exhaustion, and exhaustion of suffering. Nothing that I know matters. Do you remember Spengler's description of the magician idea of god?—on p. 235[10]—"as body and soul he belongs to himself alone, but something else, something alien and higher, dwells in him, making him with all his glimpses and convictions just a member of a consensus which, as the emanation of God, excludes error, but excludes also all possibility of the self asserting ego . . . the impossibility of a thinking, believing, and knowing ego . . . the idea of individual wills is simply meaningless, for 'will' and 'thought' in man are not prime, but already the effects of deity upon him." I have more self asserting ego after all than anyone—a more vicious ego than you—a more "slopping" ego? and who but I would realize the ultimate of fantasy-nature of my ego? of all ego, all individual mind, personality? With all my demonic individualism, it is you who defend the ego and refuse to give your self up when it comes to that last battle for the inner heart. But that is the crucial battle—there is no inner heart but one with god, which is the same substance as everything else; no power of inwardness and secrecy has any meaning or force but as it is an expression of pride and fear of the one nation, the one spirit, the one emotion—the one unthinkable. Is it not so? But what I am talking about is veritable apocalypse (not merely mysticism) and so there is no use in my beating my meat so. Dies Irae! Someday when I enter another world I will find all this talk to have been an attempt to deceive others as to the true nature of the apocalypse. But let there be terror in your heart for that day, as well. We will all be judged.

I may be in NY Wednesday. If so I will stop by the New School. Here, meanwhile, is a key to my apt.

Your fellow creature,
Allen

Jack Kerouac [Ozone Park, New York] to Allen Ginsberg [n.p., New York, New York?]

September 9, 1948

Allen ami:

Yes, want to see you, but why don't you simply come to my house at Ozone Monday—if not afternoon, evening or late night. I'm very busy staving off the horror of form-letter rejections from publishers and plotting new attempts. Must revise even more, too. Barbara Hale thought novel was "great but awkward"— but the Talking Class which runs publishing is looking for slickness of course. I'm going to North Carolina in few weeks to run brother-in-law's parking lot

---

[10] A reference to Oswald Spengler's *Decline of the West*.

and woo a nurse and have a rest from this awful shallow literary world I have to do business with. What's this about Claude de Maubri [Lucien Carr]? . . . actually true? I turned down job at U.P. [United Press] because it is beneath my dignity, with a novel like that written and rejected like silent sorrowful Sam Johnson. Pfui! Saw *The Idiot*, loved Rogozhin most. Come over! (*Lundi*)

J.

Editors' Note: Once again Ginsberg wrote to Kerouac about his visions, this time denying that they had happened. Jack wrote in the margin of the letter, "when he was flipping," which was accurate. Ginsberg was never closer to madness than he was during this period.

Allen Ginsberg [n.p., East Harlem, New York?] to Jack Kerouac [n.p., Ozone Park, New York?]

ca. late summer 1948

Dear Jack:

I am insane does that surprise you? Ha! I think my mind is crumbling, just like crackers. If I had written five minutes earlier I would have wept, if I had written ten minutes earlier I would have told you to leave me alone, if I wait any longer I won't write at all. I'm afraid I can't answer you sincerely at the moment. Your letter was so obviously natural. What am I supposed to say? I can see you reading this and telling me coldly to stop posing, because I am posing, posing as if I were posing from the Underground. But I have a great faith in the supreme physician.

Be that as it may I thought that I impressed you so much with my latest vision that you wouldn't dare speak to me again without falling on your knees. Well no I don't think so any more, not because I am more sensible or more just to you, but because I have found a better way of tormenting you, since you're so open. The whole vision, it's just rubbish, just a big fantasy. I'm not making this up now, I really knew it while I was telling you, though I only realized it fully later. In fact I don't even care about it. If you think that that's my major virtue, a vision, oh no, I have more important things to think about. However, just to ease your mind, the "Vision" had elements of nature in it but it was just a cover up for something more deep and horrible. No not just sex either.

If you want to know my true nature, I am at the moment one of those people who goes around showing his cock to juvenile delinquents.

I can't really answer your letter, though I want to with a good deal of wishing and perception of what level you are on and I would be on.

You speak of me as obnoxious and I am.

Let me get out of this rut. Come and see me. No. I will come and see you. I have something to tell you.

Jack Kerouac [Ozone Park, New York] to Allen Ginsberg [Paterson, New Jersey]

Sat. night Sept. 18, '48
Wizard's Shelf

Dear Allen:

I've been having some very mad thoughts since I saw you . . . visions that tell me there is no such thing as "life's bitter mystery," (Wolfe and others), but— never more clearly could I see that it is a beautiful mystery. And it *is* a mystery, you know. None of us understand really what we're doing, whether it's intentional or not, or whether we consider it this or that—it's something else we're doing, all the time, and very beautiful. Even the sharply inpiercing Carrs cannot always know what they're really doing. After you left that day, I received a call from Tom Livornese[11] and went to his house. We drank and stayed up all night, and went to N.Y. to transact some business of his. I waited for him in a Third Avenue bar, filled with visions. Your Cezanne paper swirled in my head, that is, the understanding of sight. I saw—and especially as New York was bright like a bonnet that day due to low humidity—I saw everything in its true contour and light. But this is not my point (the spiritual esthetic.) Not now. When he came back—it was now eleven in the morning—I called Lucien. Tom and I wanted to go on drinking, and I knew it was Lou's day off. Lucien told us to come down and wake him up. We had Tristano[12] records with us. We played them, and Lucien lay in bed trying to wake up, listening intently, after awhile, to Tristano; after which he got up. He had had a big hangover. I kept wondering how I should act to impress Lucien. But suddenly I just took sick, nauseous from no sleep and no eat, and just lay on the couch with my eyes closed. Lucien came over and yanked at my leg and grinned. He talked to Tom. Finally he gave me milk and I felt better. "I have a splendid idea," he says, "we'll go sit in Washington Square." Barbara [Hale] was out of town, by the way, or of course? . . . We started down Sixth Avenue in that Cezanne light of the day. I pointed it out to Lucien, and he agreed. We went into a Parisian bar (the Rochambeau) and had three pernods. The bartender carefully iced the glasses, took the ice out,

[11] Tom Livornese was a student friend of Kerouac who knew Vicki Russell and Little Jack Melody. He was also a part-time jazz pianist.
[12] Lennie Tristano was a jazz pianist and composer.

poured pernod, and water, and handed us the smoky green drink. Like the light of the day, and the light of Lucien's intelligence, the pernod brought in another light. It warmed us, all three, in the pit of our stomachs. We sat radiantly together at the bar and drank slowly. Then again we wandered down the beautiful streets of the day. We went to visit some St. Louis friends of Lucien and had a hiball there and talked with them. They were very condescending young socialites, but Lucien was delighted to point out afterwards that their condescension nowhere approached that of Tom Livornese, who is after all richer than they. At this time Tom delighted Lucien forever by going into a certain nightclub . . . We were out of money and wanted to drink all day and night . . . by going into the nightclub and saying, "Does the name Livornese mean anything to you?" and they said certainly, and they cashed a $20 check for him, or that is, they gave him $20 on trust . . . I don't know exactly, I was waiting outside the club looking at people go by, with new eyes. Lucien rushed out and told me that people were always going to get money by some ruse, some daring ruse like Tom's, but never succeeded, but he had. We stood on the corner eating hotdogs then, and Lucien mentioned this to me with delight, as Tom was talking to him, and Tom turned to me and said: "Tell me later what he said." Can you just see the rapport of all this? Then Tom left us $5 and went to dinner with his girl, saying he would meet us at another bar. Lucien and I drank and talked. He told me about you and him, just as you told me. And then he regretted that I had to be a "disreputable writer" and could not get into the economic system as he had done. But I knew he was saying that because he had once believed in "artistic communicative this-and-that" art that you and he used to talk about at Columbia, remember? I mean, for the first time, I am able to hear what people are saying from the other world. We don't know what we're saying: it appears that only God must know. We communicate to each other depthlessly, without the words we use. And it is the same in "bad" writing. And we continually worry about how we feel towards each other, whereas if we were God we would know that we always feel love for each other, without deviation, only with variations of complicated obtrusion and inversion of intent . . . well, confusion among other things. But more, more . . . Lucien and I then walked out of the bar because we wanted to see the light of the day before it sank in the West. It was now reddening in the streets, and we wandered to Washington Square together. There, among all the children, we walked. We saw a little girl fall down on her skates and scrape her knee, and get up and stamp up and down with pain and grief and resentment because she was hurt. Lucien said, "It's so wonderful the way children express their pain." He went over and patted the little girl on the head and said she would be all right. She pouted and blushed, and turned away. Her little companions giggled . . . and somehow they misunderstood what he said, and

43

Lucien turned and said, "Oh now I didn't say that . . . I said she would be all right." But further misunderstandings, very small, ensued, and Lucien walked back to me a little defeated, embarrassed, but pleased, and the children were pleased. These swift obtrusions of real meaningful intent gave me an insight into what our communicative troubles are about: it's just a kind of fear of being understood, or misunderstood, with love as the basic energy—for to be understood completely implies a kind of vacuum. Realize, Allen, that if all the world were green, there would be no such thing as the color green. Similarly, men cannot know what it is to be *together* without otherwise knowing what it is to be apart. If *all* the world were love, then, how could love exist? This is why we turn away from each other in moments of great happiness and closeness. How can we know happiness and closeness without contrasting them, like lights? In the truth of light and color, is the same truth, moral and psychological, and spiritual. Then, we walked along the park, and Lucien, tripping along on the edge of a pool, said, "And you know, Jack, it gets more and more joyous all the time." He had been talking about his days at Elmira[13] and all the hopes he had nurtured there. It occurred to me, you see, that Lucien was a man who was saved because he had once lost everything—in the same sense that Jesus advises us to lose all, to gain all. And that Lucien was not only saved, but gone—because of that loss once. This is what Bill aims at too, that is why he is a harlequin now. They have gained the kingdom by throwing all their earthly possessions and prides away, in a deeper sense. "It gets more and more joyous all the time . . . "—spoken in the reddening sun of Washington Square.

People were staring at Lucien because, I imagine, he was so beautiful. I asked him why people were always staring at him. He said, "They've always done that." There was no way to explain it—actually, people do always stare at Lucien. And I was full of loving insights that day: I knew all about him that day.

We walked to another bar in the Bowery and there we ran out of money. But, trying to be like Tom, I wangled a free drink for him from the bartender somehow, and he was delighted. We talked more, and he told me that the difference between me on one side, and he and you on the other, was that I was involved with everyone to the point of always being worried what they thought of me, and you and he were involved in a way which I could never understand. He said you and he have a being that stands apart, examining, that says, "Can this be *me*?" "Pah!"—Whereas I always said, "Oh this is me and what will the others think!" You see, it was compliment, and as a matter of fact, though, I want no

---

[13] Lucien Carr had spent two years in an Elmira prison in upstate New York after pleading guilty to manslaughter in the death of David Kammerer.

theories made out of this, because it separates us, and as all theories do, separates the world which is not after all dissimilar. Since then I have said "Pah!" too, so Lucien was lovingly wrong.

Well, finally, we got hold of Tom again, and joined at another bar on Sixth Avenue. On the way Lucien and I picked up Jinny Baker.[14] My heart was pounding at the sight of her again, but immediately I saw her I knew something was wrong. I cannot understand Jinny. I deliberately walked in back of her and Lucien, and sure enough she kept saying, "Walk with me, you make me sad back there." But the moment I walked with her she looked at me with contempt, and once when she used the word "Hysterical," I grabbed her by the sleeve and said "Who's hysterical? Eh? Who's hysterical!" and she covered me with a look of loathing. Why does she hate me? Why did she like me the first time she saw me, why did she make me fall in love with her, and why does she do this now? Where shall I walk—behind her, or in front (in front did not interest her), or at her side, despised? Meanwhile Lucien laughed at her and said very dirty things to her. We went in the bar and waited for Tom. Then we went to the apartment on 12th Street and there, no longer able to understand Jinny, I started to go home, knowing full well that Lucien couldn't be caught alone with Jinny in Barbara's place, with Barbara coming home any minute. Lucien said, "But you know I can't stay here with her."—and I said, "Well then throw her out," in a loud voice. But Lucien made me stay. I deliberately borrowed a dime from Jinny to go home on, as a sign of my own loathing for her. Suddenly, as Lucien began to scare her by grapping her lecherously, "she began to like me again," and like a fool I began believing it again, and danced with her and devoured her with my eyes. Then Tom came in, laughed at her, and he and Lucien went out to drink and to leave us alone to make love. Tom even put on Mel Torme's "Gone With the Wind" on the phonograph. But the moment they were out of the room Jinny began loathing me again. I cannot understand this. She said, "And please don't ever call me up again." I bit her finger real hard, and suddenly she seemed interested in that. You see, I guess she wants to be maltreated, and she wants to maltreat others all the time so that they can maltreat her with logic and conviction. I am not involved in that kind of inversion. Perhaps I understand? "All right, you may as well go home. You can walk home alone, can't you?" "Oh yes," she said. At the street corner she said again, "And please don't call me up again." I shook her hand and looked at her and said, "I don't understand you, and you don't want me." (But all the time Lucien was whispering in my ear, back at the place, that everything she was doing was

---

[14] Jinny Baker was a young girlfriend of Kerouac's who appears as Jinny Jones in *On the Road.*

45

for my benefit. Can this be true? How about the street corner? Was Lucien fooling me?) She walked home, logically sad . . . perhaps she always wants to be logically sad, to be sent home alone, so she can brood and gain some satisfaction being sadder than her sisters and Victor Tejeira.[15] It's something like that, but as I said at the beginning, no one knows what they're doing, but there's a divineness behind it all, even in Jinny. And I cannot think of any way of saying that to her *when I'm with her*. You see, there's life right there, all of it, all of it. That's it.

So, alone, I went back to the bar, where Lucien and Tom were having a great time talking. You'd be amazed to know how much they like each other. As I came in Lucien was asking Tom why it was that every time Tom said something, Lucien understood immediately what he meant. He said they had the same minds, with different words. Tom was a little turned away by this perfection of understanding, you see what I mean? We drank and drank, and at one time Lucien was saying something to Tom about me, which I didn't hear, but which was flattering, that is, good. I don't mean to say flattering all the time, I realize how petty that is, that is, I don't *realize* it, what difference does it make to you whether I *realize* it or not. You see? So long as it existed and I sort of noticed it from the other world. So we went back to 12th Street, and Barbara was there in bed, and says to me, "What's the big idea of getting Lucien drunk the moment my back is turned." I said to her, later, "Be serious, Barbara." Lucien ended the night dancing with a frying pan, hitting himself with it softly, bing-bong, bing-bong, bing-bong, sadly at dawn, as I sat watching. We knew, we knew. Not so?

Jack

Allen Ginsberg [n.p., New York, New York?] to Jack Kerouac [n.p., New York, New York?]

after October 19, 1948

Wed

Dear Jack:

Letters or speech as we speak is vague, but only because we are vague. There is no such thing as life's bitter mystery, and yet you say also that it is a beautiful mystery. It is a mystery to us, that's all. "None of us understand what we're doing" but we do beautiful things anyway. The something else that we are doing

---

[15] Victor Tejeira is described as Victor Villanueva in *On the Road*.

is always recognized by us one way or other. I want to know what I am doing/I want to recognize this. This can be recognized. That is what psychoanalysis, religion, poetry, all teaches us, that it can by its nature be recognized, sin is not recognizing. Cézanne is a beginning of recognition for me but it is not the real thing, just still an intellectual-sense substitute. All the fascination and beauty of people meeting and echoing comes from our innate instinct which is not yet emerged to consciousness, that we are here, that something specific is there that we are arguing our love about. It is one thing to accept it as such and wander around like in a dreamland struck with uncomprehending wonder of the mystery of the beauty. But if anyone throws back a direct shock of communication—not mysterious, but direct, some people are capable of that—it would be frightening to me and you because it would disrupt the whole dream of ambiguously intended beauty. What if I said stop trying to kid me, stop play acting as if I didn't know what you were talking about? You don't say what you mean, particularly in your explanation of what if anything Lou meant by saying that he was sorry that you weren't a socially acceptable writer.

"We don't know what we are saying." "It appears that only god must know." What if we really did and were just hiding it. That is what we are doing. What did you really mean when you told me to stop peering into your soul? I was just understanding too much. Understanding sensations and feelings of gibbering idiocy that you had that you didn't want spoken of, much less enacted. Everything that you say in your letter is true, but still partial because it really tries to deceive with a gentleman's agreement. I am more afraid of a gentleman's agreement not to hit below the belt than any other. Everyone knows about the gentleman's agreement not to get to the real point, and that doubt in the back of the head is the very area of knowledge. Any attempt even to agree on the existence of this doubt and then act as if it didn't matter when it is the whole point will not bring happiness or art. "If we were god we would always feel love, only with complications." Yes that is so, and we are already in this state. The thing to do is get rid of such complications, not ignore them or explain them away as part of a meaningless business that had better be left vague, or you know what will happen. "It is just a kind of fear of being understood." True, absolutely. With love as the basic and only, exhaustive, all meaning and absolute thing that is being understood. That is why I reach out to touch people, physically. I enact the form perhaps? without content. That is because I believe in action. If you were understood, you say, completely, there would be no more meaning to the understanding, therefore the necessity of sin. "Realize Allen, that if all the world were green, there would be no such thing as the color green. Similarly, men cannot know what it is to be together without otherwise knowing what it is to

47

be apart. If all the world were love, then how could love exist!" This is the root of your dishonesty and in a similar way mine. You try to keep it back. The point is that all thought is inexistence and unreality, the only reality is green, love. Don't you see that it is just the whole point of life not to be self conscious? That it must be all green? All love? Would the world then seem incomprehensible? That is an error. The world would seem incomprehensible to the rational faculty which keeps trying to keep us from the living in green, which fragments and makes every thing seem ambiguous and mysterious and many colors. The world and we are green. We are inexistent until we make an absolute decision to close the circle of individual thought entirely and begin to exist in god with absolute unqualified and unconscious understanding of green, love and nothing but love, until a car, money, people, work, things are love, motion is love, thought is love, sex is love. Everything is love. That is what the phrase "God is Love" means. There is one law and most men try to live as if their law were different, as if they had an understanding of their own. You don't realize that your only personality not merely your true personality, which other people see, and even you see, as you, as your only personality, is not that which you set up for yourself and others to see, your individual self enclosed rebellious, egoistic mental system, your childishness. Your personality has nothing to do with you, what you want it to be like in your deception. It is what you are which you don't admit that I actually see you as. It would be an awful shock for you to realize that. It is also some thing you kept saying to me once. The unbelievable in the back of the head, that is the one thing that people see clearly in each other, not their reasons for not believing it which they have the gentleman's agreement not to "misunderstand" each other. What the fuck do you actually care whether or not you know you are love in the false way that you seem to think you "know" things now? Why are you afraid to submit to the annihilation of such stupid meaningless unreal knowledge. This is the abyss. Everything is green, love, without the logical fantastic equivocations that we invent so that we won't actually have to face each other. That is the death truly that Jesus advises, which everyman faces and dies in in different forms but never completely to the point of complete submission. They pass though the phase of possibility of such a death, face it, fear it, put it off, construe it to a meaningless verbal complex, avoid it, are changed and entrenched by the experience. Do you really believe that Lucien totally died, or that he and Bill re-entrenched themselves, but stayed the same? Nobody that we know is dead.

Can this be me? Every time I see myself as I am I am staring into a cosmic mirror in which I see myself with my thoughts broken into nothing, and my unequivocal physical self weaving and gyrating in the universe in an incomprehensible monkeylike babbling idiocy, a sordid frightening picture. Actually would at that stage be a saint, or an ordinary natural man, but so different are my mental conceptions from reality, that I think I am a monster when I see what could be. I have only faced this mirror for a few moments at a time, actually a few frightened split seconds, at maybe three different times in my life. That is what my equilibrium with L. [Lucien] is. I attempt, or flirt, with that image, a sexual one also as it is one and the same, and because I trust and acknowledge his just mind, and his love, I have only myself to blame if I do not turn before him into the monster. So instead I tell him what I saw in the mirror, and he believes me, at the same time we both realize that we are deceiving each other when we don't change into what we are. I was frightened as a kid by the transfiguration scene in Jekyll and Hyde. That is because it recalled my true self to me. So miraculous and unbelievable is this true self, is life, that it seems like an image of horror, once we accept that horror we see that it was all a fit, that horror was the birth pains, the pangs of recognition of self deception, and we are in love (in green). Blake and Emily Dickinson and lots describe this specifically.

"To find the western path,
Right through the gates of wrath
I urge my way:
Sweet morning leads me on.
With soft repentant moan,
I see the break of day."

This is the moment of death. This is the nectar whereof each one tells. This is why Lucien sadly hits himself on the head with a frying pan at dawn, he has never done it. I have not yet. Yes, for fuck all this, I am crazy. All this is raving babbling. I am I talk and read and write and the circle of destiny narrows and closes around me: die, go mad, what you think now is mad is really love and sane. Die, go "mad." This is schizoid. I am now monomaniacal in my preoccupation with this moment of will.

I think what I say is true in one way or another, though you can't understand it, I think, because I have not made myself clear. Perhaps I could have said all this by saying, of your letter, I understand what you are saying, more or less. I understand because not that I am smart, but that you have actually understood what you were writing. I heard what you were saying. I did not understand fully because you were not clear enough, because you were beginning to understand, but it was not complete you yet. When it becomes more complete, I will understand more. Don't say that it never becomes complete because what I am saying is that that is just the whole point, even of you, that it can be complete. All green. Abandon everything else.

Allen

Allen Ginsberg [New York, New York] to Jack Kerouac [n.p., New York, New York?]

ca. December 1948

Dear Jack:

I have moved to 1401 York Ave.—3 flights up to the back, left side. (That is at 74th St. east of 1st Ave.) My last weeks in Harlem were very bad but also baffling (everything is bad and baffling now.) Huncke moved in, yakked at me irritably for a week and a half, ate my food, took my last nickel, and walked off with my last suits, a jacket, Russell [Durgin]'s winter clothes (suits, coats, etc.) and twenty or thirty expensive books—(hundreds of dollars worth of books) full of theological notes. Nor have I [a] typewriter any longer as you knew. I will have to pay Russell for all of this, don't you see. Huncke sent a letter to him a few days later to notify Russell that he was aware of his sins and would someday (perhaps in the month) "try to make it up as soon as he regains his fortunes"— much like the old retired army captain lush in *The Idiot*.

I was repaid by God however because a man left me his apartment, $13 a month cold water, 3 rooms fastidiously furnished (one of them is).

Don't stay away because you think I don't want to see you. Don't think ill of me.

Lucien and I had a long conversation the other night. I explained my new Faith (you can call it) first in terms of *Cezanne* (which he bought) but as I went deeper and deeper and approached my own central point he listened responsively. He told me that he thought I was mad. My father thinks I should see a psychiatrist. You think I am getting ugly (same thing?) (Bill understood everything I said but he did not have the experience to be with me, and he wished me luck.) Leaving Bill out, perhaps—assuming I am mad (Ha!) god, how I must have suffered, to go mad. And all the time I was calling to people to save me and no one put out his hand and held it. This is like suicide, only I am alive and looking out of this living death I can *see* the people weep and feel sorry. Alas, nobody even weeps. It's all a dream.

Love,

Allen

Allen Ginsberg [Paterson, New Jersey] to
Jack Kerouac [n.p., New York, New York?]

ca. December 1948

Dear Jack:

Have we been in touch with each other? I heard from W. [Walter] Adams through someone else that you asked for my address. It is, as I wrote you (did you receive my letter?) 1401 York Ave., third floor back.

My circle or at least one more cycle is complete. I have returned to Paterson to live—for the while. I look at this as semi eternal, that is, it really marks the closure of some kind of gyre, five years in the running. What really made it complete (that is about all that it did) was that I finally went to bed with Lucien. I will speak to you of it when I see you. The earth did not turn over in its grave, but another sphere did open. We always wonder at these levels and levels, cycle after cycle. You see them as *life*, and complete and beautiful in themselves. I think sometimes that that is enough, since I understand that beauty, although not with the ripeness and humility that you do. For me however, there is something else, a supreme cycle of which all these are a part—a single real (actual) (literal) (practical) vision of which all new visions are the shadow. The shadows get lighter and lighter with me, my understanding comes nearer and nearer to final knowledge. Veil after veil is removed—by our action in removing it, too. My consciousness interposes itself between my soul and the world, and makes a part of me unreal and perhaps that is the ugliness you spoke of. Someday, I will have destroyed this consciousness, and will be myself. I am most myself lately I think, too. But I always have kept saying this. Once I was convinced that I was wrong. But I have been right—as far as I am concerned. I know that now too well to question. But even such stories as this that I am telling I will cease to tell, as until you will have nothing more to object to, and everything to love. I mean my consciousness won't get in the way.

My school has as usual been giving me trouble. I flunked a course in Victorian literature [summer 1948] because I wrote an exam on the dead authors based on a living idea of eternity. Teacher said it was "Pretentious generalization." I guess it really was, too, but what is one to do on that score?

And you? I haven't been talking to you all this time, I know. I wish I already had your humble courtesy. You are a pot of gold, don't think I don't realize it. Lawrence[16] rejected your novel because of reasons of security. Well, don't de-

---

[16] Earlier that year Seymour Lawrence, editor of the Harvard literary magazine *Wake,* had turned down "The Death of George Martin," a section of *The Town and the City.*

spair, we are on the right track. It's too bad our problems are not solved more easily. But that is an old stupid complaint. Still the others are stupid. It is as if to save ourselves we had to save them too. That is why genius must suffer—it has to bear the burdens of the whole world. Our happiness and reality depends on the happiness and reality of others. Remember Rimbaud's remark when he said that some day he would have to leave Verlaine and help others? Dear soul, that's not a very tasty proposition. My humor is getting senile—that is because my wit is tired and irrelevant, not because it is vague in itself. Well, as I was saying, maybe if you have to be refused by them you will have to break down even more, break down another defense, break down the falseness of your rhetoric. Dear soul, it's not a very tasty proposition. The soul must speak, you must speak out directly, not through literary symbols like "Brooding." *You must assume every responsibility in the novel that evades you.* Total, total, no super-fluity. But you sense the superfluity so completely that the situation is sad. I think you are right to put off the decision to the next novel. This one is good enough. The only trouble practical is with the world. Well, this is where the trouble starts for you, I guess, the real trouble, with your art. The only thing is to look that directly in the face. The world will force you to, and that is good, unless you weaken and take to rage and illusion. I am really talking to myself, not to you. These are my decisions that I'm speaking of I guess and projecting them to you. How true they are for you I don't know. But you are certainly advanced beyond my comprehension, when I try to comprehend or "help" in a sacerdotal way, etc. etc.

I want to see you. I feel more and more at home with you now actually than ever before, I feel you more, actually more clarity, more confidence, more trust. I will be in Paterson for several weeks. Will you come in, at last?

Jack Kerouac [n.p., North Carolina?] to Allen Ginsberg [Paterson, New Jersey]

ca. December 16, 1948

Allen:

I am aware that Reginald Marsh, and his cool change from tense faults and naturalism, to God's-eye view of man in the God-real world, is great. (SPOKEN IN A DEEP VOICE.)

Not screaming over the telephone—you and Barbara [Hale] are queers.

You ought to go to the Rehn Gallery and dig "New Gardens."

Do you know what I think?—People in this century have been looking at

52

people with a naturalistic eye, and this is the cause of all the trouble. I think women are beautiful goddesses and I always want to lay them—Joan [Adams], Barbara, all—and I think men are beautiful Gods including me, and I always want to put my arm around them as we walk somewhere.

Last night I wrote an apocalyptic letter to [Allan] Temko and I made a copy of it to show to you and maybe [John Clellon] Holmes. It is full of "frightening" and inescapable predictions, scatalogically smeared with an evil leer sometimes, much as "old me, old spontaneous me" is that way. All truthful words are that way . . . "Snake Hill was so-called for a very real, snaky reason." "If that's the case, then I am glad that shadow changes into bone."

I said to Temko—"When we get out of the narrow 'white light' of our surface rationality—when we get out of the room—we will see that mystic makes no mud."

However, I hate you. Because years ago you and Burrows [Burroughs] used to laugh at me because I saw people as godlike, and even, as a husky football man, walked around godlike like, and Hal [Chase] did that too, and still does. We long ago realized our flesh happily, while you and Bill used to sit under white lamps talking and leering at each other. I think you are full of shit, Allen, and at last I am going to tell you. You are like David Diamond[17]—you confused your claw with the hand of a godly man; you confused affection. I am sick of you, I want you to change: why don't you die, give up, go mad, for once.

I have decided that I am dead, given up, gone mad. Thus I speak to you freely. I don't care any more. I may get married soon, too— to Pauline maybe. We'll run away. I am on the verge now of loving my geekish guilty-flesh self—thus reverting to the original sanity of the Hal-days. The reason why I always dream of torturing and murdering Bill (as last night) is because he made me geekish in the name of something else. However, I wrote a big letter to Bill and am sending him Tea Party. I am lost. The only thing to do is to give up—I am giving up.

Thinking of getting a job in a gas station, I shudder as before. I'm lost. If my book doesn't sell, what can I do? As I write this to you I am on the verge of falling dead from my chair. Just now I felt myself swooning. It is too much, too close to death, life. I must learn to accept the tightrope.

Do you know what Hal does? Like Julien Sorel,[18] the moment he enters a seminary, he says to himself, "There are 383 seminarists in here, or rather, 383 e-ne-mies . . ." The only seminarist who befriends him is, therefore, "of the 383 enemies the one and greatest enemy." I think Hal is full of shit.

[17] David Diamond was a New York composer who appeared in Kerouac's *The Subterraneans* as Sylvester Strauss.
[18] Julien Sorel is the protagonist in Stendhal's novel *The Red and the Black*.

I am full of shit too. Don't you see? we're ALL full of shit, and therefore we can be saved.

In the picture on the beach there is a man embracing a woman front-wise, naked, and this is all I want to do—nothing else. So please don't bother me with your verbiage. Write me a big verbal letter. I don't believe anything I say.

However, I believe in love. I love Ray Smith. I also love Pauline, my mother, Lucien (in a way), Bill and you (in a way), little children, and finally I love everything about little children. Goombye. Chinaman.

There is a false note throughout this letter that hides from you the real me, which is simply the madman-child I am . . . and forgive me for saying you are full of shit, in fact. I don't know what to think or say, Allen, and so it begins . . . that is, why think? why say? let me just be. You were right sending me the picture. Let us be gods saying nothing much, just standing like the two men on the beach looking at the ocean. There is too much talk nowadays, isn't there? Yet you and Neal hate me for not-talking and for "dignity" as you called it. ah, well, ah, well, ah, well, ah, well, ah, well, ah ah ah

I don't have to tell you what I believe, because you don't believe in belief, and neither do I, but I do believe . . . (I really do).

I believe in shelter from the cold, and good food, and drinks, and many women all around, the interplay of the sexes, and much happy meaningless talk, and tales, and books, and Dickensy joy. I even believe in your existence. I believe that soon we will all die, go mad, give up, drop off. I believe in children and everything (see how false that sentence?) I believe that when I talk to you I feel I have to be false. Thus the hysteria of the subway. I used to be more truthful to you when I used to glare at you and call you names. Now I pretend to believe like you and to be like you. I don't.

I believe that I have to continually remind you of my love for women and children only because I feel (perhaps inaccurately) that you hate women and children. I believe (perhaps wrongly) that you are a cosmic queer and hate everything but men, and hate men, therefore, the most, and hate me the most (as you hate Neal, how you must hate Neal.) I believe in shelter from the cold. I have rages, too, and hang up from the phone and will continue to do so. Barbara and I are lions, we meet at the watering-place of the lions and don't notice the fawns, the giraffes ([Alan] Harrington) or the weasels ([John Clellon] Holmes) or the panda bears (Marian [Holmes])—or the cardinal birds ([Alan] Wood-Thomas) or the cats. bla bla bla bla bla. This is all hysteria and I wonder why I have to be hysterical with you, when I used to be old-brotherish. You see how honest-dishonest I am? You see how good-bad the world? You see how we must shelter ourselves from the cold-warmth?

you see how we must shelter ourselves?
you see how we must?
you see how?
you see?
you?
me?
who?
what?
I don't un-stan'
I am speaking to you as I would like to speak to everyman
No one else would take this shit but you
Thank you

Finally, when we're all honest, we will cut down our sentences as above and end up saying nothing. With our new deep voices we will simply say—"mooo." or "shmooo." or "beeee"—or "faaaa." and we'll all know. And our belief will have become us. Then everybody will walk around gravely like gods—like in the picture, you see. The two gods looking at the sea will say, "Beeee." The other will say, "Roooo." And the man facing the woman will say, "Geeee." and she'll say— "Chaaaaa." And food will taste more delicious than now, orgasms will last longer, warmth will be sweeter, children won't cry, fruit will grow quicker. Finally, out of his mind, God himself will appear and have to admit that we did it alright alright.

Excuse me again for trying to be mad . . . Roooo . . . like you; I am your crazy pal.

Now that I have more or less settled that, and expressed my appreciation of our new life and regard for each other, let me go on to the next "great" thing: (you see, I used "beautiful" and "great" only in quotes now to show you I am conscious of our former hypocrisy)—

It is this, "dear" Allen . . . (you see? but you don't have to see any more, we have dead eyes now, we'll be quiet)—

Neal is coming to New York.
Neal is coming to New York.
Neal is coming to New York for New Year's Eve.
Neal is coming to New York for New Year's Eve.
Neal is coming to New York for New Year's Eve in a '49 Hudson.
etc. . . . in a '49 Hudson.

I have almost real reason to perhaps almost believe that he stole the car, but I don't know.

The facts: last Wednesday, Dec. 15, he long-distanced me from San Fran, and I heard his mad Western excited voice over the phone. "Yes, yes, it's Neal, you see . . . I'm calling you, see. I've got a '49 Hudson."

Etc . . . I said: "And what are you going to do?"

He says "That's what I was going to say now. To save you the hitch-hiking trip out to the Coast, see, I will break in my new car, drive to New York, test it, see, and we will run back to Frisco as soon as possible, see, and then run back to Arizona to work on the railroads. I have jobs for us, see. Do you hear me, man?"

"I hear you, I hear you, see."

"See. Al Hinkle is with me in the phone booth. Al is coming with me, he wants to go to New York. I will need him, see, to help me jack up the car in case I get a flat or in case I get stuck, see, a real helper and pal, see."

"Perfect," I said.

"You remember Al?"

"The cop's son? Sure."

"Who? What's that Jack?"

"The cop's son. The officer's son."

"Oh yes, Oh yes . . . I see, I see,—the copson. Oh yes. That's Al, that's right, you're perfectly right, that Al, the copson from Denver, that's right man, see."

Confusion.

Then—"I need money. I owe $200 but if I can hold off the people I owe it to, see, by telling them or perhaps by giving them $10 or so to hold them off. And then I need money for Carolyn to live on while I'm gone, see . . ."

"I can send you fifty bucks," I said.

"Fifteen?"

"No fifty dollars."

"Allright allright fine. See." And so on. "I can use it for Carolyn, and to hold off these people I'm in debt . . . and my landlord. Also I have another week's work left on the railroad so I'll make it. It's perfect see. Reason why I call is because my typewriter broke down, and it's being traced (sic! I'm only exaggerating here)—and I can't write letters, so I called."

Anyway, how crazy it was. So I agreed to all our new plans, of course; I had been writing him asking him to go to sea, but this is better we both agreed, more pay, too. $350 a month. And Arizona, see. He says he traded in his Ford and all his savings for the '49 Hudson. That car is the greatest in the country, in case you don't know. We talked about it more than anything else.

But come Saturday, and I'm in New York with Pauline my love, and Neal calls up again and beseeches my mother to warn me not to send the money to him in name but in another name he would mail me, and another address. I

56

had, however, already sent the money to him airmail registered . . . but only $10, I couldn't make my mad happy miscalculation of the phone. My mother's report included a certain remark he seemed to have made without connection, viz., "I ain't there." (?)

Unless he means 160 Alpine Terrace, or something.[19]

Secondly, when I sent him the $10 I asked him to pick me and my Maw up in North Carolina on his way East, so we could use the money saved to our advantage and to return to Frisco and Arizona. He agreed to this with my mother over the phone, altho he mentioned going to Chicago too, which is pretty far North off the Carolina course. But he apparently will do that . . . both.

I know nothing. If he stole the car, or what's with Carolyn, or his landlord, or something, or debtors (creditors?), and what's with the cops, or that phony address he wanted to send me. All I know is that he is tremendously excited about the car, and that "He's off," of course.

So I expect to see him in North Carolina around the 29th of December, and we will be back in New York for New Year's Eve, and of course you're going to begin right now arranging a big BIG party in your York Ave. place for New Year's Eve inviting everybody . . . especially [Ed] Stringham and Holmes, etc. We will rotate the party to the Holmeses and your place and Ed's and Lucien's and then Harlem after-hours or anything, in our big car. Invite a select group— Ed Stringham, the Holmeses (I will have Pauline), and of course Lou and Babala [Barbara Hale]; and Herb Benjamin for tea and for kicks. I will try to get Adele [Morales][20] for Neal.

However, if you wish, don't arrange anything, inasmuch as *it is no longer necessary* to arrange things anymore; we have changed. Use your judgment. Meet me at Kazin's Wednesday night and we'll talk. On the other hand no, meet me at Tartak's at 4 Monday afternoon (today if you get the letter Mon.)

If . . . well, to hell with it. That's it,

Jack

P.S. You may not believe this but as I write, a little child is looking over my shoulder . . . a real little child who is visiting us with his aunt, and who is amazed because I type so fast. Now what that little child is thinking is it, see.

[19] Carolyn Cassady had rented a house in San Francisco at 160 Alpine Terrace the previous summer while she was pregnant.
[20] Adele Morales was a girlfriend of Kerouac, and later married Norman Mailer.

Allen Ginsberg [Paterson, New Jersey] to
Jack Kerouac [n.p., New York, New York?]

ca. December 1948

Dear Mistah Krerouch:

When you scream over the telephone I first begin to recognize your voice. Isn't it you? You never heard me scream over the phone. That is why I sit here in Paterson and rock back and forth on my heels masturbating and crying to god.

> Why do ageless angels cry
> against their own eternity?
> All their fallen faces feign
> Thoughts of uncertain certainty
> That what was sure will be as sure again.

> I think I would be content to live
> All of a thousand years, and give
> A thousand thoughts to melancholy;
> I'd trickle endless till I'd sieve
> My thoughts all down to one, and that one holy.

> A thousand years alas! are given
> If I wish, till I am shriven;
> It is a miracle to believe.
> What thousands have I not forgotten?
> And why do all the other angels grieve?

[...]

Years ago when you saw people as godlike—if you truly did—I had no idea that such a thing was possible. I have only to believe you and you dare not lie. Did [Hal] Chase and you actually have *the* vision (not mine) but *the*? If so "I bow to my offended heart / Until it pardon me." (W. B. Yeats). I will say in my defense that I do confuse the claw with the godly hand. You want me to change; I also want to change. That is why I speak of the gate of wrath—my own coming shame.

I shall feel shame for all that you accuse me of truly. My heart leaps up for wrathful joy when you say that you are sick of me—my ego. I wish you were and were not afraid to show it. This gives you complete freedom henceforth.

Don't you know why I wanted you to beat me up in the subway? O Jack . . . Shame!

For Bill and his white leer you must be gentle, as he is not yet ready . . . I am not either, perhaps, that is why you contradict your hatred. I hate you for the same things in you where my suspicious mind fancies they exist.

I am nowhere near going mad. I must sooner or later; at that time there may be a temporary rupture between us. You realize that it works both ways?

When we were talking before [John Clellon] Holmes, didn't it sound to him as if we didn't know each other at all? Didn't we sound naive? Were we? Yes and no.

I and Bill made you geekish in the name of something else. True. Also, you couldn't have been made so if you were not already a fallen angel. Blake accuses us (me particularly) of the "wish to lead others when we should be led."

The tightrope you speak of is what I live on. Anyone can give me a push either way. You and Bill help steady me, Lucien once and a while gives me a push off, so does the rest of the world. People like Van Doren and Weitzner[21] and W. Shakespeare tell me to realize I'm really on one and get over to the other side . . . or something. They don't insist on pushing me though. They just make it so obvious to me where I am. Chase also. He must be wise.

"IF my book doesn't sell, what can I do" that paragraph about the tightrope was true . . . you were speaking and seeing the truth. Even if you sold your book would that change anything now? The abyss is more real than present flesh or future fancy. What should you do?

"To find the western path . . ." or, apropos, not really so clear, though a poem: mine. I wrote 3 poems over the weekend.

> You cannot tell the time it's taken
> To live into another life.
> First the thought, beyond belief
> Jams the mind; then the heart breaks;
> Everything breaks down to soul.
> Lives are changing, even Time
> Time is nothing, all is all.

Can you believe me when I say my heart has been broken? My very heart, center of my existence. (What's to come is still unsure.)

No, I don't hate Neal; perhaps I really love him—basically we are all angels.

[21] Richard Weitzner was a friend and fellow Columbia student.

59

I would rather be hated, than hate. I am afraid to hate. Maybe my shame is that I really hate him—you—Chase—Carr etc.

I once had a talk with Joe May[22] about the Broken Heart. Told me I was too young—when I was 18–19 all you want to do is fuck. Then go fuck. You're free. Stop worrying I tell you.

I didn't mean to send you a picture as a lesson—though I hoped that all signs from god should be exchanged for their instructive value. I didn't send it out of contempt.

I don't really hate you. Love takes many forms. I mean, I, too believe in shelter from the cold, painless dentistry.

Believe me, if you compromise yourself on my account you are making a mistake. I realize how difficult it is for you to act sincerely to me because that involves so many conflicting rages. At the same time perhaps I was more surprised than you when I realized (in our conversation at Barbara [Hale]'s) that you were imitating me. For I have always felt that the other way around. I thought I was being "gleeful" like you. So you see it is a comedy of errors as usual. Pardon the silly tone of the above, but you must see, and I must see, that we are both being hypocritical. By an old mathematical law that makes us the same at bottom. We should amend our ways. Would you like to have it out with me violently? I should welcome that in the next few weeks. This is something you (at Harlem) spoke to me of, and I evaded; another time perhaps I spoke to you. Why don't we take time out next time we meet and be honest, if possible, without compromising. I used to fear your glare of disgust. I still do, but then it was a fear of the unknown, the inconceivable. Now it is conceivable and welcome. However I won't take it lying down. I may scream and shout.

I am a cosmic queer, that's true; if you only knew what an isolated existence that exiles me to in comparison with your moderately healthy outlook in the universe.

Don't you see we both suffer? Yes, of course you do. That really is the basis of our "friendship." The secret knowledge of reciprocal depths—of hatred perhaps, but suffering and loneliness. That is why we are so tenderly hypocritical. That's what I liked about Neal. He knew. That's why also breaches of the unknown are good, are a good.

Come what may we will get our just deserts, from each other and the world. Nothing can be lost, nothing can be saved. So we must or I must not fear the unknown.

Let us be brothers from now on. You be my big brother. I am your little brother just out of college.

[22] Joe May was a gay friend of Ginsberg's.

The abyss: you wonder, what if all your novel came to naught.

My poetry has in my deepest and surest knowledge come to naught—has come. I have been aware of that for ½ year. I cannot turn to it now for consolation except the merest vain and transitory security which disappears in an hour, and I also have begun to accept that. My rock, if I have one, is elsewhere now. It is just as well.

> "Men come, men go.
> All things remain in god"

> (W. B. Yeats. Song of a Whore)

> "I don't understand"
> "you ask what makes me sigh, old friend
> What makes me shudder so?
> I shudder and I sigh I think
> That even Cicero
> and many minded Homer were
> Mad as the mist and snow"

Have you read W. B. Yeats' poesy? I will give you the book for a temporary present this Xmas. I have studied him and he knows all the problems. You might enjoy reading him. Say no if it bores you. He has a voice like an echo chamber.

And others, others are there. Mr. Jethro Robinson, whom you will remember as a friend of Lucien and R. Weitzner in Colorado Springs now, has been writing a novel. He recently published a small pamphlet self printed—sonnets and other poems—he sells them himself at a dollar each. They are so wise they make me shudder jealously. Some of them are as good as Shakespeare—the secret of the open sea he knows. I sent for his pamphlet. I enclose the letter I sent him. See the undertone of despair and irony that old man Allen has in the version II I sent. I wrote it out on the paper you see, and copied it on a clean sheet to send him. Funny.

My next poem is entitled (curtsey)

Classic Unity.
It goes:

> See the twisting puppets twirled
> In and out that changeless light.

As if they act beyond their world
They turn around the stage in fright.

All these puppets are the Lord,
Their tangled loins, his only rod.
Their mouths are bloodied with the Word.
Every eye is blind with God.

"Dead eyes see" or "Blind Vision" is what R. Weitzner points out in certain of my earlier poems as the true phrases. The rest, he says, have no content. He said that after I asked him, too, didn't volunteer the information.

If I am temporizing after the crisis of your letter, it is because you didn't come right out with it.

Important Announcement. I am leaving Paterson tonight for NY in 10 minutes. I think I am almost sure, hold your breath! I'm excited. I have a job! Hee hee hee! with Associated Press as a copyboy. O Rockefeller Center! O Life.

I have really been moved to your prescription of work, write, live. Once I get to NY I will live.

Jack Kerouac [Ozone Park, New York] to Allen Ginsberg [Paterson, New Jersey]

ca. December 1948

Sunday afternoon
Home

Dear Allen:

Altho I read your letter only once, last night late arriving from town, I remember and am particularly pleased by your sincere reaction to my tired attack. However, none of this can be settled "violently"—as I often do with Lou [Lucien]—because there is no violent feeling, only a rarefied communication. It isn't necessary for you to send me smutty pictures (the cock) because they don't "scare" me, they only scare whoever reads my mail—"society," I guess, for whom you apparently have respect ("A.P. you see is in Rockefeller Center.") I am very glad that I got sore at you and that you wrote back so "stoutly." And now we are on a good level and we might stay there, I don't know. I see all your theories now for what they are; and mine too. The fact that 3-years of work on *T & C* turned out to be the delusions of a cracked madman doesn't bother me any more, I had already gauged my chances there. As Pauline says, I have "two hands" and therefore I can earn my bread. The realization that art is cracked anyway (mostly) only makes me become a Factualist now. I will begin again with a Factualist art, perhaps a la Dreiser-Burroughs-"On the Road." Like you, I consolidate my lines and move on. On our deathbeds we will realize one thing is as good as another anyway; as you yourself say, "nothing can be lost, nothing can be saved." Relax.

And in any case half of life is death. This is my latest greatest thought. Psychoanalytically, it has made me realize that I associate home and mother and farms and *Town and City* etc. with a kind of childish *immortality* (the "genius," etc., who will be redeemed.)—and that I associate the "outside world" (you and Neal and Bill and wars and work and hitch-hiking and cops and jails and taking my chances making women win-or-lose without childish remorse and petulance) I associate this outside world with "half-of-life-is-death." There is a tight-rope only when you wish to be "immortal" (childish.) After that, it is solid but still as yet dangerous ground, but only the dangerous real ground of the forest which also has tigers and lions as well as lovers. To see all things as they are is of course the simplest truth—you can't tell me that the tiger and the lion are lambs (I wouldn't even care if they were.) They are lambs only in God. But in the world they are carnivorous. That is why you have to "look beyond" to God to find your stare through rock and stone, because you can't do it in the carnivorous world that poured past us uncaring on Union Square. I like you again now that I see you as you are—and particularly, most "beautifully", because you thought you were being "gleeful" with me and therefore I am given to see (naive of me I admit) that we were trying to please each other, I by hysteria, you by glee. The energy behind that is, even if deluded, fantasized, etc., is real. Because we were trying to live half of which is dying. Please, by the way, read these observations on "my level," and not on your God-level . . . merely for the sake of digging at the moment. Your God-level is a beyond, and I buy it, but these explanations are of this world right now. By Factualism, also, I don't mean Naturalism . . . but simply the acceptance of the fact that I will die, that half of life is death, that I am no better (no more privileged) than any one else, that I have to earn my bread, that I have to limit my love (in marriage), that I must make my way through "this world" as well as through the "beyond." In fact, my whole theory now is that I have no theory. I am writing a paper for Slochower[23] on the "Myth," in which I will tell that pedant that Myth is nothing but concept built on a particular which is never repeated, sad tho to relate. I will go my way

[23] Harry Slochower was a professor at Brooklyn College and wrote many books, including *No Voice Is Wholly Lost.*

without concept, without "prevision" (Neal's word), but only with a sense of my own and your own depth and depthlessness . . . like Lucien after all. And I begin to see that "it gets more and more joyous," to repeat.

The only change I want from you is to see with your dead eyes. (he-he!) We will now be sad and perceptive and active, like Lucien after all. You must change also in the way you wrote to Jethro [Robinson] the former jerk—become a quiet old child. (he-he!) We will recall he-he! as our ignorant attempt to please each other, and it is just as real as Bill's drawling act for Phil White et al. For the first time in a long time I feel a philosophical excitement running between you and me—because we decided we were hypocrites and move on knowing.

1949

Editors' Note: After this flurry of letters, Kerouac rode with Cassady back across the country to San Francisco, but before long he returned by bus to his mother's house in Ozone Park. In the meantime, Ginsberg had gotten himself into another terrible situation. He had allowed Herbert Huncke, Little Jack Melody, and Vicki Russell to store stolen merchandise in his apartment, and after a car crash the police discovered the stolen property and everyone, including Ginsberg, was arrested. The following letter was written from jail as Allen awaited the disposition of his case.

Allen Ginsberg [Long Island City, New York] to Jack Kerouac [n.p., New York, New York?]

ca. April 23, 1949

1 Court Square
Long Island City
New York
Sat. Morn

Dear Jack:

I have a restless anxiety about my journal and correspondence which was taken [by the police], otherwise am well in spite [of] a severe car crash and the uncertainty of the immediate future. My case is not too bad. Call up Eugene[1] for details if you are interested in details—his office (he is acting as lawyer).

Herbert [Huncke] is across the cage; I can't see him well as I lost my glasses in the crash. The few hours before the arrest were confused by the shock and horror—self-horror mostly as I saw patterns of activity so clearly. Everything happens in a suggestion of what will happen (to men I mean). I keep letting things happen to me, want them to.

You might notify Denison and his sister [Burroughs and Joan] what has happened. They (the police) also have your letters. I hope they are returned—5 years of literary correspondence that is a priceless treasure for the future.

Read the first few pages of "Rogue Male" (25¢ book) by Geoffrey Household. I kept thinking of that, after I got out of the overturned car.

I feel pretty well; wrote a poem:

> Sometimes I lay down my wrath
> As I have lain my body down

---

[1] Ginsberg's brother, Eugene Brooks.

Between the ache of breath and breath
and have to peaceful slumber gone.

All I tried to be so kind
All I meant to be so fair
Vanish, as the death of mind
Might leave a ghost alive in air

To gaze upon a spectral face
And know not what was fair or lost,
Remember not what flesh laid waste
or made him kind as ghost to ghost.

Allen

Editors' Note: With the help of his family and a good lawyer, Ginsberg was re-leased from jail. It was agreed that in lieu of prison he would go to a mental hospital for treatment. While arrangements were being made, Allen stayed at his father's house in Paterson.

Allen Ginsberg [Paterson, New Jersey] to Jack Kerouac [n.p., New York, New York?]

ca. early May 1949

Wednesday Eve.

Dear Jack:

I am back, as you put it, in the bosom of my family. It's quiet around here but I can get work done if I want to. I filled a 150 page notebook in the last four days with a detailed recreation of the events of the last month. This was for my lawyer who wants to get to understand me and find out why I associated with such people and did the things I did. He asked me to write him a journal. I didn't work it out carefully, but in the writing (and before) I think I came to a clear understanding at last of [Herbert] Huncke and his total relationship with people; something I have been seeking for a long time, and the lack of which left me powerless to act towards him before in a positive way. I (perhaps we) had dehumanized him before. The nearest and clearest of him he himself obscured to us all; he needs a mate first like anybody else. The same with me, and Neal, too. I spoke of this to Vicki [Russell] and I found that she, too, had never realized just what Huncke secretly wanted from us, or we from him. I guess Bill knows Huncke.

My family problems have become more complicated and strange since my mother first was released from the hospital. She is living for the moment in the Bronx with my aunt. I saw her Monday. She is a little flighty, but natural, and my aunt doesn't understand that; but she is a sister and there are other sisterly understandings. I don't know what she will do, or be done, next. Gene and I will not live with her; I'm afraid to, and besides the doctors (at the hospital) forbid it; so that problem isn't mine. But Naomi will have to be financed by my brother and father and aunt, and so that puts an added financial strain on them. Everything seems to have happened all at once.

I don't know what is happening on my case; it is mostly out of my hands in the lawyers'. My family and lawyers are taking the attitude that I am in bad company, so that will make a lot of long range social problems for the future, since I'm so far in as far as having to (gratefully) accept their financial and legal aid. Also they would want me to betray and squeal on everybody to get myself out. It is past the point where I, like Huncke, can try to explain my position with any certitude on my part or assurance of understating, and so I am uneasy. Fortunately I know so little that I have little to squeal about. But presumably Vicki, Herbert, and Jack [Little Jack Melody] will try to arrange the guilt among themselves according to their own lights, and I fear to be maneuvered into some statement which will disrupt their own stories. The situation is delicate. Of course it won't exist as anything meaningful in another (or 10) years. But at the moment I am prayerfully walking a tightrope. I would hate to have to pick up the toilsome balloon and try to maneuver my own lawyer to advance my case according to my own wishes; but that seems to be my present responsibility. At any rate, he thinks I will have to plead guilty, have charges dropped, be placed in the hands of a psychiatrist; or take a suspended sentence with psychiatrist. I saw [Lionel] Trilling, who thinks I am crazy; and [Mark] Van Doren, who thinks I am sane but doesn't sympathize beyond a limit (he kept winking at me as we talked). He wrote Morris Ernst, a big criminal lawyer. But it is too late for Ernst for my family already have arranged for lawyers. I also saw Meyer Schapiro[2] (Trilling sent me to him.) He told me to come over, and sat talking with me about the Universe for 2½ hours; also told me about how he was in jail in Europe for being a stateless bum. He asked about you, apologized again for not being able to get you into his class. My problem, *vis a vis* the above with my lawyer, would be less complicated were it not for Bill's letters, which make

[2] Meyer Schapiro was an art historian who taught at Columbia University and the New School.

69

it imperative for me to settle on other terms than my own nearest and clearest and easiest, and get them out of harm's way before lightning strikes Bill again. It's possible; I am afraid to take chances. I have no idea how deep the Divine Wrath has been planned and will continue.

I am at present thinking a lot about Thomas Hardy's poem "A Wasted Illness," p. 139 of his *Collected Poems*, if you run across a copy. I wonder what Lucien thinks of it, or if he takes it (that particular poem) seriously? The poem is all clear, and as far as I am concerned especially the last stanza. It comes a page after the poem you drew my attention to at [Elbert] Lenrow's house, "The Darkling Thrush." I have also been reading Shakespeare—*Macbeth*. The irony of neglected and forgotten misunderstandings and complacencies returning like ghosts to wreak vengeance.

I would like you to come to Paterson.

Write me about Lucien. Has he told you his stories? Has he begun writing them? Also, please write Bill again, telling him, if you haven't, the total situation. Tell him to clear his household of crime entirely, wherever he is. I said so. He doesn't need it. Has Neal written?

> Mustapha

Allen Ginsberg [n.p., Paterson, New Jersey?] to Jack Kerouac [Ozone Park, New York]

before May 15, 1949

A Rainy Day in May.

Dear Jack:

Thank you for writing, your letter[3] came via my father (also opens my mail now) like a Halcyon to my troubled waters.

I was in N.Y. all weekend, and called up [John Clellon] Holmes for news of you. When you're in town, I can be reached in the late morning or early afternoon, usually, at my lawyer's; at evenings perhaps at my aunt's house; at night at Charles Peters. Eugene [Brooks], also, is most likely to know my whereabouts.

No news yet as to what will happen. I feel more and more deeply involved. Van Doren gave me a straightforward lecture telling me that people around Columbia were sick and tired of my mock-guilt and my "Satanism," which I am supposed to have fostered. They are bored with all my "mush." Well, I guess he is right. There are two sides to every question [but?] I have begun to feel more and more lost and unsure of myself. Which is a good feeling, I guess, as usual.

---

[3] A reference to a letter that is now missing.

Never mind, I'll try to explain all the above when I see you. Anyway my bullshit is coming back to haunt me. Things get more real.

I called up [Elbert] Lenrow and told him O.K. for Friday, so I will see you then at 4:00 at his house. It will be a state occasion.

When you write, if you have any news of anybody out of the way, give them novel-names: Pomeroy [Cassady], Claude [Carr], Denison [Burroughs], Virginia (Vicki). Junky [Huncke] call Clem (nice name?) If I am in the future to put efforts out in correspondence I might as well think to prepare safeguards from the beginning.

Maybe I should invent a secret code.

Allen

I asked my father what he thought of the poetry you enclosed; he "didn't care for it" as the figures of speech were "clouded" and foggy. I have wondered what you might do with poetry. I don't know enough about its real inner secrets or technical measures, so I can't say what I will with "authority!" (I mean I'm not sure I'm right). It seems to me that you have pure feeling for the trust veins— the prophetic-biblical ("I am he who watches the lamb") and the prophetic— joyful ("Pull my daisy, Tip my cup.") The *saving* of the latter is what is most desired. As it happened you were already equipped with meaningful or sig- nificant symbols, taken from life around—Yeats, in a book called [*King of*] *the Great Clock Tower*—1935 says, describing how he went to Ezra Pound and an- other mystic called A.E. for literary advice: "Then I took my verse to a friend of my own school, and this friend did go on like that. Plays like the *Great Clock Tower* always seem unfinished but that is no matter. Begin plays without know- ing how to end them *for the sake of the lyrics*. I once wrote a play and after I had filled it with lyrics abolished the play," etc. That is one way to get the purity of inspiration and language in a meaningful background. You ought to write a beautiful book someday which like Rabelais and Quixote and Boccacio is filled with tales, poems, riddles, lyrics, and secret phrases. What I meant to do in the doldrums is to write so many poems that, though, on their own, none would seem significant, by the time the book were read, their whole purpose and *real- ity* of purpose would be evident. At this point, for instance, writing about ghosts, angels, specters, etc.; the way has been already prepared for the use of these symbols by what has gone before—and will be modified by what has to come after. This is all *a propos* of what you said about the poem I read in your notebook that I thought was such pure poetry.

The symbols in this poem (and the one in notebook) seem to me more clear and with real reference than you admitted yourself (as far as the notebook) what seems to be emerging in you is the first mouthings of the real Lamb, which is an awesome thing to behold, and to some (including yourself?) a cloudy sight. Unless I am wrong you will see in the poetry (or you see in the prose) more and more real significance (I mean all in what you *have* written and why you might write) (Everything is *possible*, in fact, probable, as far as "prophetic" power, or what I call here prophetic power.) What remains, when the meaning of the poems (aside from their passionate, frenzy-poetic being) comes clear to you is to organize them and direct them consciously. The same, or similar elevation of style, I mean, is possible with a purely practical, pragmatic purpose, provided naturally such a level of mind is attained. In other words what you may feel to be false ("I have written some truly amazing poetry, if you can call it that . . . ") about the manner or content of the poetry you write, is really false, and that element of falseness must be dealt with, not necessarily by changing to a meaner, more limited style and ambition and liking, or inclination, or penchant; but by following out the inclination to its end and seeing ultimate truth. So you can call it "poetry"—what you're writing seems to be potentially great poetry. You are doing no different (as you know) than what any true poet does; only doing it with more shining and profound manner than any poets I know of our generation. You should not necessarily investigate poetic measure (rhyme and metrical tradition). Your poetry has abrupt stops transitions due to its *improvised* nature. That can only be solved in the fulfillment of ripeness of purpose, not by constricting the rhythm artificially to conform. I have done that and I made a mistake. I have to learn how to talk *naturally* in verse again; find out how to say great things or beautiful things naturally. You do that already.

I have been improvising, what I mean really, is that when you say of yourself "I am he who watches the Lamb," I believe it. My father doesn't, and maybe doesn't believe in the Lamb, even, so he thinks its all foggy.

I have been at our poem again:

> This token may I tup
> Runneth over broken.
> Pull my Daisy,
> Tip my Cup,
> All my doors are open.

also:

> Who is the hooded mummer of the night
> green haired and mouldy in the eye
> that reddens in the window pane's dim light
> and startles old men, and makes children cry?

Who is that shroudy stranger in the street
to shadowed children, stinking of the dead,
and dance unfixed, though bound in phantom feet,
Behind the child who weeps with limbs of lead?

Who is the secret and familiar shade
That walks through bedrooms, where the sleeper curled
With open eye lies still? No sign is made.
World must beckon vainly unto world.

The above is a first version, a little diffuse with not enough concentrated imagery. I have to dye it green all over.

> *Bon ami,*
>> Allen

Editors' Note: On May 15, 1949, Kerouac arrived in Denver and set up a house for his mother and sister. He had finally received an advance for The Town and the City *and felt that his success was now just a matter of time. In June his family and furniture arrived, but as it turned out both would return to the East Coast early in July.*

Jack Kerouac [Westwood, Colorado] to Allen Ginsberg [Paterson, New Jersey]

May 23, 1949

6100 W. Center Ave.
Westwood, Colo.

Dear Allen:

Just a note till I get my typewriter. Am living alone in this new house in the foothills west of Denver waiting for family . . . and any signs. Leased $75-a-month house for one year. Dancingmaster D.[4] negotiated inside info for me. He is just like us, incidentally. Said he knew all the Denver birds worth knowing—I told him he was saving me a lot of trouble. He smiled. He's okay. Met another Denver bird—big social science genius.

My house is near the mountains. This is the wrath of sources—the Divide where rain and rivers are decided. Here, too, soft meadows in the rumorous

---

[4] The Dancingmaster was a nickname they gave to Justin Brierly, a reference to his ability to manipulate people.

afternoons. I am Rubens and this is my Netherlands beneath the church-steps. (Remember that Rubens I showed you?) This place is full of God, and yellow butterflies.

Pomeroy [Neal Cassady] is in Frisco. A girl told me (Al H. [Hinkle]'s sister) that she dropped him off two weeks ago somewhere at Russian Hill. Therefore Pommy has no car. Russian Hill is white tenements with crooked roofs.

Dancingmaster said you were a great poet.

I hitch-hike into Denver and sit in Larimer poolhalls and go to 20¢ movies to see the myth of the gray West. Mostly I'm writing . . . and hiking, "leaping over brooks."

Will copy all latest stuff when I get typewriter. All about the Mississippi River at Port Allen Ol Port Allen—for rain is alive and rivers cry too, cry too— Port Allen like Allen poor Allen, ah me.

The Bridge of Bridges there over the water of life. "It is where rain tends, and rain softly connects us all, as we together tend as rain to the all-river of togetherness to the sea."

"And the sea is the gulf of mortality in blue eternities."

"So the stars shine warm in the Gulf of Mexico at night."

"Then from soft and thunderous Carib—(Clem's)—comes tidings, rumblings, electricities, furies and wraths of life-giving rainy God—and from the Continental Divide come swirls of atmosphere and snow-fire and winds of the eagle rainbow and shrieking midwife harpies—Then there are labourings over the waves—and little raindrop that in Missouri fell and in Louisiana is gathered earth and mortal mud; selfsame little raindrop indestructible—rise! be resurrected in the Gulfs of night, and Fly! Fly! Fly on back over the down-alongs whence previous you came—and live again! live again!—go gather muddy roses again, and bloom in the waving mells of the waterbed, and sleep, sleep, sleep . . ."

(In other words, am beginning to find out *why* rain sleeps. You encouraged me greatly, therefore I continue in this kind investigation previously disallowed me.)

Also—

Poem Decided Upon in Ohio
It's a helluvan—Ohio
In the hullabaloo of the bees
When you're out in the hay
On a mulberry day
a helluva hullabaloo.

It's a helluvan—Ohio
In the lullaby-loo of the hay
In the hullabaloo and the lullaby-loo
Of the bees and the hay and the bees-hay.

Please write. Try my new address. Next year I'm getting a mountain ranch. Worry about the green face, not laws. (I was once in nut-house, y'know.)
J

P.S. I'm anxious to know how everything turns out. I hope you will keep a large correspondence with me. Write as soon as you can and as often—and I'll do the same.

Allen Ginsberg [Paterson, New Jersey] to Jack Kerouac [Denver, Colorado]

after May 23, 1949

324 Hamilton Ave.
Paterson 1, N.J.

Dear Jean-Louis:

Whichaways is Westwood? I remember little foothills north (?) leading to Central City mountains; and the long plateau and red deserts south toward Colo. Springs; but West? When are your family going to go out? After long negotiations, I wrote your brother-in-law [Paul Blake] to get the bed; he did, with my brother helping him. I didn't see them meet and it was all an accident that they ever did under the skies of N.Y., but they did. I always thought the Dancingmaster was O.K. but so much like me that I felt like a reincarnation of him, after several new lives and purifications. Strange how well I feel I know him—or does everybody really recognize Mr. Death? and feel akin? I owe Death $10; tell him I'm sorry but am not as usual in a position to pay up my debts to him; but that I will before the great accounting; and since I know that, tell him I know that, and that his $10 will ultimately reach him. (Unless it is miraculously forgiven—but don't tell him that.) Yes, I remember the dancing feast of rubes—is everything so alive and free for you really? All God and butterflies? I envy you. I am caught still in the grey moils of selfhood and thought, that I fear I shall never feel past the divide in life, and never feel the rain running down my face, and never swim in the dark river. Pomeroy [Neal Cassady]? What is he all alone for?

You must be alone yourself in Denver, living in a big house. Speaking of rubes there is a scene in one of the Faust legends where the master leaves his study, having just renounced alchemy and metaphysic lore, and steps outside into just such a celebration as the one in the picture. I don't remember what else he says or does except he sings a song or writes a poem in praise of the dance and then goes back into his house and calls up the Devil—who appears. I saw Thomas Mann lecture on "Goethe and Democracy"—perhaps the same lecture that Pomeroy saw last year. Mann is wiry and energetic and very young; he sends electric thought into everybody but usually they don't know it and he is weary of people; but praises "Life."

I don't know what the rain is about and hope you find out why it sleeps but like I said I don't know what the rain is about. Oh I am weary of thinking that I encouraged you. It's hard for me to maintain. The rhetoric is fine, the music's lovely, but as Clem [Huncke] used to say "Shit, another, I can't dance." Did you ever hear him say that? He'd be wandering around the house abstractedly, and he'd drop a napkin, or sink into a chair wearily, saying that. How like a little girl at dancing school he is, all hung up on his mother. I have his extant collected works (about 30 pages) with me.

Things have taken a turn, I guess, here. I myself am sick and tired of hearing all these people around me judging and judging without (it seems) any idea of what they are saying. But I am too confused now to fight back. Anyway, I am being taken to a hospital, a mental hospital, soon, I believe. My lawyer took me to a psychiatrist (highly recommended by Trilling, and a nice man) who suggests that for the immediate picture I am "too sick" to do anything but go to the hatch—sicker than I or anybody knows (He-He!) except him. I breathe a great sigh of relief; at last I have maneuvered myself to the position I have always fancied the most proper and true for me. As you say you were in a nut house but I ought to repeat what I've said over and over, I really believe or want to believe really that I am nuts, otherwise I'll never be sane. Or to put it more simply; yes, I take this development seriously and wish to cooperate with the authorities who want to help me they say. Unfortunately I (like evil Burroughs who is damned) don't trust them (you, Kerouac, are crazier than me) but *moi*, I can be saved because sometimes I'll break up in hysterics and beg their pardon for having ever doubted them. Unfortunately they continually contradict themselves, too—but I must forget that and curb the unreasonable intellectual pride or vanity which makes me inhuman and makes me think that I (like Denison [Burroughs]) am smarter than them. Anyway I'm caught as you can see in the toils of my mind again; this time I hope it is decisive. Of course I am sick and tired of all the attendant introspective bullshit, and tired of the

76

inactivity and self-laceration of madness, and tired of fighting with people—lawyers, parents, Clem [Huncke], school, etc. tired of my continual absorption in enervating introspection which has gone past control into at this point a wild-land and wonderland of horror and joy in external *action*—now to be sent free to a psychoanalytic clinic (on 168th St.) as an inpatient (I think that is what will happen) is O.K. I don't want to wind up in decadence and gooey abstraction, I'd rather go West to the sun. But at the moment I don't really know how and am caught like a rat in a trap. I thought all along I was getting clearer in the head and saner and wiser and truer, but the truth is that Chase was always right, and I feel now as if I've gotten so hung up on myself now it isn't funny any more. I stop in the middle of conversations, laughing shrilly—stare at people with perfect sobriety and remorse—and then go on cackling away.

I called Claude [Lucien Carr] up once, the Friday nite that you left. He said nobody had asked him any questions. He was O.K. Said "I'm in your corner, kid; keep your chin up." How strangely true I felt his seriousness was.

I had, before the madhouse, intended to settle down in Paterson for good, as you suggested—I discovered myself that I had to do it. But no. How ironic, that I should not finally return home, but should have another fate open (perhaps a good one?) yet. All my doors are open, I feel that more and more. I let people take enormous liberties. How madly they rush past me, rocking to and fro in the business of the world! My lawyer tells me I am crazy, that I have subjectivized my sexual *ideas*, even; so I believe him. He talks on until I realize that he is so innocent he does not know that women also blow men, and that that happens in America naturally—I tell him about the Kinsey Report; he tells me I am exaggerating my own delusions. Ah me. But no! I *will* believe everybody! Just like Van Doren told me to choose between criminals (Huncke) and society (my lawyer). I asked for a middle choice, but he said that this was The Choice. How frightened I was; and I chose Society. He (Van Doren) told me that I had exaggerated and romanticized Clem out of his class, while he was just a common hoodlum; and my lawyer describes him as a "filthy stinking mess—one look at him and you can tell he's no good." But I believe them, too! The thing is, Jack, that I have been intimidated into believing everybody because I don't know what I myself believe, and now I am so confused I can't even write poems, hardly. But (*Ah!*) *they will all be judged*, thank god. My judgment (I feel) is now, during this life. They may never get judged till their deaths; but they will burn for every thoughtless word, every [unclean?] wound, every dead-eyed evil done, every insult and indignity! They'll burn! He! He! He! I am burning already, I can afford to laugh. I have put it to rhyme

(Ah! *Si je me venjece! Les damnes!*)
Write me about Denver and Birds.

The Complaint of the Skeleton to Time

1.

Take my love, it is not true,
So let it tempt no body new;
Take my Lady, she will sigh
For my bed where'er I lie;
Take them said the skeleton,
    But leave my bones alone.

2.

Take my raiment, now grown cold
To sell to some poor poet old;
Give the dirt that hoods this truth,
If his age would wear my youth;
Take them said the skeleton,
    But leave my bones alone.

3.

Take the thoughts that like the wind
Blew my body out of mind;
Take the ghost that comes at night
To steal away my heart's delight;
Take them said the skeleton,
    But leave my bones alone.

4.

Take this spirit, it's not mine,
I stole it somewhere down the line,
Take this flesh to go with that
And pass it on from rat to rat;
Take them said the skeleton,
    But leave my bones alone.

5.

Take this voice, which I bemoan,
And take this penance to atone,
Grind me down, tho' I may groan
To the starkest stick and stone;
Take them said the skeleton,
    But leave my bones alone.

This is a complaint of praise to all destroying time. I am not sure whether the bones represent the core of self which is the last to be given up; or whether I'm telling everybody they can do what they want as long as they leave the god-bone alone.

I am reading a lot and writing as usual, on and off. I will write you next time more coherently; the truth is, I would have, today, but I had to *deal* with all of that rainy weather in *your* letter, so I put up my umbrella and walked out into the storm.

I am beginning to think, aesthetically, in terms of images of dreams (like the green face) and to weave (I hope to) these images into poems now, instead of using abstractions and wit-rimes. I am writing a ballad around the ditty I dreamed up a few months ago (remember)?

> I met a boy on the city street,
> Fair was his hair, and fair his eyes,
> Walking in his winding sheet,
> So fair as was my own disguise;
> He will not go out again
> Bathed in the rain, bathed in the rain.

It is essentially an *image*, a beautiful white-visaged youth, walking around at night dead. From now on, also, I shall stop trying so hard to gather metaphysical implications into the image as I used to try to do (as sun through a magnifying glass?)—for to try to force all levels to meet intellectually is impossible; but it is just possible for them to come together on their own in a self-born image. (That is the secret of Dr. Sax?) So I have a *method*.

I would like to go to Haldon [Chase] to see him but am afraid to. I wish he would etc. . . . I think (or thought last month) about him a lot. Oh, well, maybe someday will get together. I am in no condition to now.

Next time I write I will send you facts and sobriety.

Do you think I am right or wrong. sane/crazy?

         Allen

I mean, the above, what do *you* think? You know. I'm really quite perplexed by a very confused situation, right now. I sometimes wonder if I could really get out of it (West to the sun) even if I wanted to, at this point. [. . .]

Jack Kerouac [Denver, Colorado] to
Allen Ginsberg [Paterson, New Jersey]

June 10, 1949

Dear Gillette:

Your big letter occupied my mind for a whole day here in what was then my hermitage. In answer to your question about what I think about you, I'd say you were always trying to justify your ma's madness as against the logical, sober but hateful sanity. This is really harmless and even loyal. I can't say much about it, after all what do I know? I only want you to be happy and to do your best toward that end. As Bill says, the human race will become extinct if it doesn't stop doing what it don't want to do. As for me, I think you are a great young poet and already a great man (even tho you get sick of my evasive goldenness.) (For which there are dross-ish reasons, you know; and you know.)

I'm no better off than you are with respect to doing what I want. I have to work on a construction job now and can't stay up all night dreaming up the mouthings of the Lamb. (But there is something else in this business of Forest-of-Ardening around people, all day, at work.)

If you ask me, Clem [Herbert Huncke] really dances when he says "Mother I can't dance."

The Rubens I meant was not the White Arms Over the Void Horizontal Dance, but the other one of fowls beneath the church-steps and a great Netherlander field . . . but what does it matter now? No, my life is not that dance either.

Reading over your Holier Than Thou poem last night (or "Lines Writ in Rockefeller Center" ["Stanzas: Written at Night in Radio City"]), I saw something weird, in comparison to my own lines. For instance, let's start with my recent "crazy" poem, then yours.

> "The God with the Golden Nose, Ling,
> gull-like down the Mountainside did soar,
> till, with Eager Flappings, above the Lamb
> so Meek did Hang, a Giggling Ling.
>
> And the Chinamen of the Night
> from Old Green Jails did Creep,
> bearing the Rose that's Really White
> to the Lamb that's really Gold,
> and offered Themselves thereby, and
> the Lamb did them Receive, and Ling.

Then did Golden Nose the Giggling Ling go down
and He the Mystery did Procure—
all wrapp'd in Shrouds that greenly swirl'd,
which barely He, nor Chinamen, could hold,
so Green, so Strange, so Watery it was:
but the Lamb did then the Mystery Unveil.

Saith the Lamb: "In this Shroud the Face
is Water. Worry therefore not for Green,
and Dark, which Deceptive Signs are,
of Golden Milk.
    Beelzebub is but the Lamb.
Thus did the Lamb his Mouthings end."

I find that your lines evoke yourself, and mine, myself . . . which is proper. "Not a poppy is the rose" has a strange lecherous sound; not only that, but "up-in-the-attic-with-the-bats" and the line about the superfine poppy. Not that I want to go into that . . . but, poetically, the combination of sensual hint, wink-of-the-eye lechery, dirty ditty goes with your work. This is comparable to Herrick:

"A winning wave, deserving note, / in the tempestuous petticoat: /
A careless shoe-string, in whose tie / I see a wild civility"

Picture Herrick's picture of the petticoat, etc.

Enuf of this. I live west of Denver, on the road to Central City.

When I can, I now read French poetry: De Malherbe, and Racine the French Shakespeare. But I have little time. Brierly gave me Capote to read. He winked at me today during a big luncheon at high school among teachers and labor leaders and tycoons.

As I run miserably around Denver I wonder what Pomery [Neal Cassady] would do.

I'll write a longer letter next time. It's always "next time" now with us . . . why? Because there's too much to say.

The family is here, the furniture is here, and cats, dogs, horses, rabbits, cows, chickens, and bats abound in the neighborhood. Last night I saw bats flapping about the Golden Dome of the State Capitol. If I were a bat I'd go and get gold. Up-at-the-dome with the goldy bats. There are so many beautiful girls around. I ache. A little girl has fallen in love with me . . . a pity. A crush for an older man, me. I gave her classical records and books, and am become a dancingmaster. Dancingmaster Wink.

I rode in a rodeo, bareback, this afternoon and almost fell off.

I decided someday to become a Thoreau of the Mountains. To live like Jesus and Thoreau, except for women. Like Nature Boy with his Nature Girl. I'll buy a saddlehorse mix for $30, an old saddle on Larimer St., a sleeping bag at Army surplus, frying pan, old tin can, bacon, coffee beans, sourdough, matches, etc.; and a rifle. And go away in the mountains forever. To Montana in the summers and Texas-Mexico in the winters. Drink my java from an old tin can while the moon is riding high. Also, I forgot to mention my chromatic harmonica . . . so I can have music. Thus—without shaving—I'll wander the wild, wild mountains and wait for Judgment Day. I believe there will be a Judgment Day, but not for men . . . for *society*. Society is a mistake. Tell Van Doren I don't believe at all in this society. It is evil. It will fall. Men have to do what they want. It has all got out of hand—began when fools left the covered wagons in 1848 and rode madly to California for gold, leaving their families behind. And of course, there ain't enough gold for all, even if gold were the thing. Jesus was right; Burroughs was right. Why did Pomeroy turn down Dancingmaster's help to go to high school? I saw their graduation exercises last night and the 18 year old valedictorian, using a false deep voice, spoke of the fight for freedom. I am going to the mountains, up in the eagle rainbow country, and wait for judgment day.

Crime is not what men want either. I have often thought of robbing stores and didn't want to do it finally. I didn't want to hurt nobody.

I want to be left alone. I want to sit in the grass. I want to ride my horse. I want to lay a woman naked in the grass on the mountainside. I want to think. I want to pray. I want to sleep. I want to look at the stars. I want what I want. I want to get and prepare my own food, with my own hands, and live that way. I want to roll my own. I want to smoke some deer meat and pack it in my saddlebag, and go away over the bluff. I want to read books. I want to write books. I'll write books in the woods. Thoreau was right; Jesus was right. It's all wrong and I denounce it and it can all go to hell. I don't believe in this society; but I believe in man, like Mann. So roll your own bones, I say.

I don't even believe in education any more . . . even high school. "Culture" (anthropologically) is the rigmarole surrounding what poor men have to do to eat, anywhere. History is people doing what their leaders tell them; and not doing what their prophets tell them. Life is that which gives you desires, but no rights for the fulfillment of desires. It is all pretty mean—but you still can do what you want, and what you want is right, when you want honestly. Wanting money is wanting the dishonesty of wanting a servant. Money hates us, like a servant; because it is false. Henry Miller was right; Burroughs was right. Roll your own, I say.

It will take me a long time to remember that I can roll my own, like our ancestors did. We'll see. This is what I think.

So leave my bones alone. I think that is a wonderful poem. Write me another. Write me that coherent long letter. All is well.

Go, go; go roll your own bones. Bone-bone. Roll-bone your own go-bone. etc.

Quelle sorciere va se dresser sur le couchant blanc?
Quelle bone va se boner sur le bone-bone blanc?
Go, go; go roll your own bones.

Jack

Editors' Note: Ginsberg must have written the following before receiving Kerouac's June 10th letter.

Allen Ginsberg [Paterson, New Jersey] to Jack Kerouac [Denver, Colorado]

June 13, 1949

June 13

Dear Jack:

No letter from you, and I forgot about you last 2 weeks, after writing. I am waiting to go to the clinic, and in the days I have been putting together my book, working from noon far into the hours after I put out the light and lie in bed dreaming up poems. Last night I dreamed more stanzas of our poem—

> I asked the lady what's a rose,
> She kicked me out of bed,
> I asked the man, and so it goes,
> He told me to drop dead.
>   Nobody knows,
>   Nobody knows,
> At least, nobody's said.

Then more purely in our own metrical and abstract image scheme. (read the first lines fast and see how it sounds)

> I'm a pot and God's a potter
> and my head's a piece of putty
>   Break my bread
>   And spread my butter,
> I'm so lucky to be nutty.

But the nicest stanza almost as good as "Pull my daisy, tip my cup," goes:

> In the East they live in huts,
> But they love where I am lolling.
>   Cut my thoughts
>   For coconuts,
> All my figs are falling.

"Cut my thoughts for coconuts" will someday be part of the speech of the world. Another contribution to city imagery—did you ever hear of the Alley-Mummy? I revised the poem "Who is the shroudy stranger of the night?" and the second stanza begins, "Who is the Walker, laughing in the street," "The Alley mummy, stinking of the one . . . ?" Can't you just see him coming out of the garbage strewn, beery dank of Paterson and Larimer Street in the dead waste and middle of the night? He is lying there among all the broken bottles and rain soaked newspapers and bags, in the garbage can, wound in the soiled bandages some old man had wrapped around his legs, bound in old Kleenex and women's rags. Everybody knows how frightening alleys are—the dark alley, the dark corridor—think of all the street phantoms and gutter elves and roof gremlins there must be in the Kasbah. Also, did I ever tell you about the face in the television set, the poor ghost that calls to children in the living-room, "Please open the window and let me in"? I thought of him about half a year ago. I also revised the Psalms that I showed you at your house, they are almost an even poem now, and a lot of small lyrics and longer poems—all the nightingales—I retyped and cleaned up everything and in a few days I hope to have my book ready and I left a lot out, too, that was formless and passionate. Only complete poems—but even then, there are weak spots, long rhetorical diatribes about eternity and Light and Death that have no corporeal home, and no true form—but I left them in, some of them, because I hope nobody will notice that they are not truth. They are so pretty when I have finished I will really turn to something new—longer real poems about people, with plots—then poetic drama—a tragedy of light-doom-ridden Pomeroy [Neal Cassady]—Clem [Herbert Huncke] in the prison. In the hospital. But I am sorry that I did not try harder in the past to publish what I wrote, because I have small heart to send individual poems out to magazines in a full dress attack; and without previous magazine publication it is hard to get a collection of poems published. If I cannot get a publisher, and I still feel that I want to be read, I would print them up like Jethro [Robinson] did, myself—but I haven't any money in the hospital. Well, I'll see. Perhaps you will do me the honor of writing a preface, since near the time I am ready you will be a famous author. As I started to say, I finished the heaviest work this evening

84

and was relaxing trying to be peaceful and serene, and I turned on the radio and picked up your last letter. The long paragraph ending with the Waving Mells of the Watched, I was surprised and moved by more than the first time I read it. The first time it seemed less like a profound call to the raindrops; and reading it tonight I felt just like a little raindrop indestructible being told by the sea to rise! Rise! and fly back over the Down-Alongs. Paterson is making some changes in me. I'm getting more thought about the Down-Alongs of the old houses I lived in, my schools, and childhood, my father. Also I've taken a slight historic interest in the town. You must locate the myth of the rainy night here, near New York, for do you know there is a snake hill with an actual real castle, a castle, overlooking the city? And a river in the middle of the town? The castle was built by old Mr. Lambert in 1890 or so, and has a history much like yours, but now it belongs to the park system of the County and is a vast and crazy museum of art objects imported by Lambert (great Titians and Rembrandt visions and Reynolds ladies, Italian statuettes, medieval Bacchuses) mixed with hundreds of items of local importance having to do with Passaic County—it is a treasure house with a long history—(Paterson was settled before the revolutionary war). A poet named William Carlos Williams, incidentally, is using a lot of this. There are old bronze dogs that used to hang over a shoemakers shop in 1840, maps of the great wild Passaic falls, bustles from the 1870s, lampposts from the 18th century. The castle is an immense turreted place (half of it was torn down a few decades ago) on the slope of a mountain 5 minutes from town and far away— and on the top, away from the castle, is a huge stone tower, like a dungeon tower from Annabel Lee, overlooking all the valley to the dim spires of New York beyond the Palisades. You can see it from the downtown area—but nobody ever goes there, much. And on the top floor lives the museum caretaker and his wife. And also, Mr. Hammond, a silly old lady who is the principal of School 16 and Chairman of the park system, has an office there, and is a great specialist in Passaic County marginalia. (I know all these people, incidentally—it might surprise you how well known my father is here as Paterson's principal poet—and I have met all the mayors and newspapermen and schoolteachers and bank officials and rabbis at one time or another. Someday I will be free to wander here and give an account of the growth of the demon-child in the Silk City (that's what Paterson's called—we used to make silk products before the depression).

I am as I say, still waiting to go to N.Y. [the mental hospital] and it ought to be soon—there was a little hitch last week. I don't know what has become of the other defendants—I am sheltered and isolated, and don't need to go out of shelter. I called Claude [Lucien Carr] up last week—he's O.K., congratulated me on the efficiency and cleanliness with which I'd seen my case through to a successful end—a surprise, pleasant—for him to congratulate me as if I were the sensible brains behind what is happening. I guess he's congratulating me (without knowing it) for leaving my hands off and accepting whatever my lawyer does on his own in the upper spheres of legalistic huckstering. It was a nice feeling, being told by Claude that I'd done well in an affair of the world, so I accepted the compliment. Otherwise I know little of him. He did write his short story, said "Christ, you waste more time fiddling around, looking for cigarettes, than you actually put in writing. Being an artist," he said, "is easy if you just mind your business and get it over with." Those aren't his words, but near—he meant, or said, it wouldn't be so bad if you could get down to it. I will call him again soon. He says he is going out with a girl, but not completely coed or something; I didn't get him to talk about that over the phone.

Adieu. Write to Denison [Burroughs]—if necessary (have you his address?) care of Kells,[5] at Pharr, Texas. I want to know what's with him. Give him news from me. Tell him conditions are not propitious for a letter from me, but that I think of him. Also say I am liable to be silent for a considerable length of time, until I know in what sphere I am alive. Find out how he is. Please do this now, Jack.

Write me here. Has your family arrived? Are you all settled? It seems to me if you could as a veteran, you might get a loan for a house, and pay that out, instead of paying $75 a month for rent—but you have a lease, I see.

I enclose the ticket to the museum.[6] Do you know that Lenrow is an ignu? He gave me the ticket to keep, instead of throwing it away; he not only realized that in my romantic way I would seize on the unused ticket as an object of nostalgia—but he offered it to me, with a pleasant comment about the possibility of my wanting it.

But, incidentally, the word Ignu is only for the Dennisons and Pomeroys of the world.

Also find a clipping from a magazine article on folk singing.

Oh lordy, dem bones, dem bones, dem dry bones . . .

Allen Ginsberg [Paterson, New Jersey] to Jack Kerouac [Denver, Colorado]

June 15, 49

Dear Jack:

I got your letter today, so add this as a postscript to one which I wrote yesterday, and [the one] which you received a week ago. Great news: Pomeroy

---

[5] Kells Elvins was one of Burroughs's oldest and closest friends.
[6] Elbert Lenrow had been planning to take Kerouac and Ginsberg to the Museum of Modern Art to see a screening of Carl Dreyer's film *The Passion of Joan of Arc* before Allen's arrest.

[Cassady]'s address in Frisco is 29 Russell St. I got a letter from Goodyear Service requesting information, so I sent them a recommendation of his vigor and imaginativeness, congratulating them on their association with him, assuring them he'll give them satisfaction. Reminds me of the time he told [Hal] Chase's woman to leave a note in her box. Poor Pomeroy, imagine him depending on beat out refugees like me to be his solid stable reference. Oh, what we dancing masters don't have to endure. Well, write him; I will not (as with Denison [Burroughs] or anyone else) for a time; maybe just a couple of months. Give regards, explain events. Also, my lawyer tells me that I have been cleared by grand jury; no indictment, though Melody, Vicki, and Herb were indicted. I was not at hearing, did not even know it had taken place till later; fine lawyer is keeping me away from all the melee; all the war goes on in upper airs. Apparently an analyst, Van Doren, Mr. and Mrs. Trilling, and Dean Carman[7] had to be present and speak; I don't know any details. But I must say that's mighty cricket of them all. I was really worried last month; and I had reason to be, except for work of others who assumed all the burden. I feel grateful. Shouldn't I? That's what Van Doren means by society I suppose; people getting together to keep each other out of trouble (or away from tragedy) till they got an inkling of what they're getting into. Do you know, incidentally, that 22 years ago Van Doren wrote a little book on Light and E.A. Robinson, "It is not good, one can imagine Mr. Robinson saying, to know too much of anything; but it is necessary for great people thus to err—even while it is death for them to do so. Tragedy is necessary." He ends beginning half of book so. In and out are comments like, "Bartholow, in other words, has seen too much; he is blinded by his light." And "I have spoken more than once of the image of light as being the image in which he saw life reflected. The six poems are all concerned with men who have seen a light and who are both punished and rewarded for doing so." I believe that Van Doren is talking about that specific miracle of vision which I have attempted to point to and specify the last year; his poems are about it; and in conversation with him it seems so; but since 22 years ago he has gone on beyond that light and seen its relationship to the world of time or "sober but hateful sanity"; I say gone on beyond not to mean that he has abandoned it or it him, but that it has assumed a new significance beyond its original occasional appearance as the actual existence of some transcendent fact; perhaps he has learned to see eternity in human laws, to put it bluntly, and god's ways in organized society; perhaps he even believes now without a further thought any, even to us weak willed, complaint against lawbreakers and holds the lawbreakers responsible for some outrage against other men which they really

[7] Harry Carman was a dean at Columbia University.

were aware of; and if they (like me) were not aware of it it's just as well that folks give them "a good slap in the face, so that they can hear the ring of iron." The quote is from his lecture to me. Maybe he sees me and the hipsters hassling against society while cream and honey pour down unnoticed. Maybe he thinks its all a big secret joke, and that the trouble with me is that I am taking it (and myself) too seriously. In fact, these are his opinions. However he had an exaggerated idea of my self hood based on what recently he had been told by Hollander[8] and others about my fancying myself as Rimbaud. Oh those pinheads. Yes, he thinks I am taking myself too seriously. Is there anything more hateful to hear from a wise man? Jack, your book is a big balloon, you take yourself too seriously. And its true. O Lord what temptations thous placest in the way. Deliver me from my own thoughts and the thoughts of others, too, I think Van Doren probably thinks almost the same as you, that it's all a matter for the giggling lings, so what's all this intense investigation of evil.

Remember the discussion about prayer we had? I had this week a trembling on the edges of revelation again, and came up with a fish, half flesh, half abstract; no real revelation so no true fish (incidentally I do not believe that I will have any more guideposts of Light given free for a while now). I have been praying previously for God's love; and to be made to suffer; and to be taken (I wish he'd pull my daisy); it says here in my (new) notebook, for June 14 "Say not, Love me, Lord," but "I love you, Lord!" Only lately has this aspect of the way been clear to me in its meaning. You have said this in one form or another to me a number of times; and Claude [Lucien Carr] has told me the same. I was wrong.

Of your poetry. Yeats warns to beware of Hodos Chameliontos. You know what that is? (I was reading his autobiography, borrowed from Lenrow). That is a big dragon, all Chinese, except that it is a chameleon; and one minute you have one Chinese image, the next minute you are bumping along on a Mayan spider; and before you know it it turns into a North African porpentine, and an Indian geek, and a western cat.

"Worry therefore not for green, / And dark, which deceptive signs are, / Of golden milk./Beelzebub is just a lamb." Or "Twas a husk of doves."

Hodos Chameliontos is also worrisomely mechanical, and very abstract. Do you know that my lecherous wink is by now become so repetitious and stale and mechanical that I am caught with my pants down? This is because I am not dealing with real things; but abstract relations between values; on the basis of a true inspiration; but the inspiration is departed, the lesson remains and is repeated by rote with many changes of symbol but not of formula. But that

---

[8] John Hollander was a Columbia classmate of Ginsberg, and became a poet and conservative literary critic.

is the way my mind works, in its illusory Beulah. Beulaah. Beulaaah. That is the trouble I suspicion in the Myth of the Rainy Night, as far as symbols are concerned; that also was what was wrong with my Denver birds and nightingales and dawns; I got so hung up on a series of words that I went around abstractly composing odes, one after another, until even now I can't tell them apart and what they mean, and had, for instance, to throw all of the birthday ode of Willi Denison[9] out the winder, when I was making up my book. That is what is the trouble with the "Divide where the rains and river are decided." Well, you have worked out a myth for the symbol (rain being Time, events, things; the river and sea all the holy raindrops connected) (No?) and these are good and stable currency to work with; will you have trouble amplifying and extending? Eliot complains that Blake was, alas, a great minor poet, not a major one, since he made up a lot of crazy symbols of his own which nobody understands. Even I can't read the weird beautiful prophetic books because they are full of Hodos. (I'm reading a commentary on them now by Mona Wilson) whereas I get not only understanding but the actual illumination of wisdom from the short "Ah, sunflower." That is why you are so lucky and wise to be a novelist with an epic of storied events to work on; and why you are inclined (is this not so?) to leave the Myth of the Rainy Night a great big detailed fable-story, and not (as I was trying to suggest,) an allegory with a big worked out symbolism. The Giggling Ling itself is not an aspect of Hodos, for instance, because in addition to its chinoiserie, it also winks out a stale real sound effect which gives it away; it is an actual emotion of reality reconstructed. So the thousands of details of Myth of Rain, will reveal themselves; not through an artificial system of thought. I hearken back to your letter to say, that the dirty ditty in my work comes from the feeling that I have that all I and other people secretly want is . . . also it's happened to me several times that while walking up a rainbow, when I get to the other side I find not a pot of gold but a bedpan, full. But I am not disappointed, because shit is gold. What else would gold be, but that, and rain? or water? So that the key, has been to remind them (people) that the shroudy stranger has a hard on; and that the key to eternal life is through the keyhole; and so I make great big sensual hints; and not dirty jokes, mind you, but serious hidden invocations. And when someone will read it, and see, under the surface of my poem, as under the surface of his mind, a golden pole, and a holey goals, and a silver shower; I hope to accomplish someday an outright sensual communion; and as my love grows purer and less lecherous, when someone peeks under the surface of what I say, they will really be made love to. And not only

[9] "Birthday Ode," written for the birth of Bill Burroughs's son, was later retitled "Surrealist Ode" and published in Ginsberg's *The Book of Martyrdom and Artifice* (DaCapo, 2006).

that, I'll have this long serious conversation with them, just as if the two of us were in the same head. And furthermore, it will only be under the surface for those who are themselves under the surface; but anybody truly akin will recognize it outright, because that's what I'll be talking about all the time right on top down front. And I will be writing about boys and girls in love in dreamland, like Blake, about the pale youths and white virgins rising from their graves in aspiration for "where my sunflower wishes to go;" and, "if her parents weep, / How can Lyca sleep?" and "abstinence sows sand all over / the ruddy limbs and flaming hair." And if I find out any more about death, as other poets actually have, so they say, then I will have a way of communicating that too. Unfortunately, my present hang up is sexual and so I have recourse to that for key symbolism; but that in time will evaporate into a healthier and less frustrated truthfulness. Also, I learned from a mutual acquaintance, learned "In bodily lowliness, and in the heart's pride / A woman can be proud and stiff (i.e. love is physical) / When on love intent, / but love has pitched his mansion / In the place of excrement." That's my favorite poem of all, because it is so literal, it has really only one meaning, and that's what Yeats means. I am not just dirty to be cute; it's partly that (when in a poem I say blows, not smokes the flower super-fine); but because I am calling the attention of the poem and reader to a state of fact, which is hidden, either from consciousness, or real attention, if conscious. Yes, I too see [Robert] Herrick in his cups writing soft lyrics about his lady's petticoats. Remember walking down the street, reading the Bible, shouting from Jeremiah, "The filth is in her Petticoats?"

Ah, yes, I remember well the road leading to Central City, and the small hills there. I was hoping you lived there. Pommy [Neal Cassady] and I once rode around there all over the side roads leaving firecrackers under people's porches in the middle of the night. When you write, tell me how your mother is feeling about Denver, and what she says. Also, is there any difficulty about writing? I mean, about your receiving letters from me? If there is, we should do something practical to straighten out that. I could write care of general delivery.

Yes, however, I believe that Dennison is right, too.

When I next write—incidentally I will for sure be in the crazy house when I next write, so don't worry—I will probably have finished a poem about the lines I wrote a while ago

"I met a boy on the city street,
Fair was his hair, and fair his eyes,
Walking in his winding sheet,
As fair as was my own disguise."

I have some of it written: it will tell Pommy; I am writing a prophetic poem for Pommy; it will see all, hear all, know all; I am the witness for Pommy, though he doesn't know; it endeth:

"And so I pass, and leave these lines
Which few will read, or understand;
If some poor wandering child of Time
Sees them, let him take my hand.

And I will take him to the Stone,
And I will lead him through the grave,
But let him fear no light of bone,
And fear no more the dark of Wave . . .

Followed by several more as yet unwritten stanzas describing the mansions of the Lord. Maybe I will also throw in, for good measure, that my name is angel and my eyes are fire, and that All Who Follow Shall Be Rewarded With My Favor.

May I have the title for "Tip My Cup," to use bookishly? Also, think up more, and send them to me; better we will write our own mutual poem, and I will publish it in my book under your name, and you in yours in mine, and he and she in It's. We'll call it the Natural Top. Who shall it be dedicated to? Poe? Walter Adams?[10] Ignu VII of Egypt? Oscar Bop? The survivors of Thermopylae? Bobby Pimples? Hysterical Larry?

Speaking of epileptics (and I promise you that this is the last time I mention Pommy's name) do you know that Fyodor was, as you say, just like Pommy? I read a book written by Mrs. D. [Dostoevsky] describing the days when he was gambling in Baden, and how she used to weep and cry alone at home, expecting a baby, while Fyodor was gambling his last ruble, his last kopeck, even, and finally coming home, throwing himself weeping at her feet, offering to commit suicide to demonstrate his love for her, and making her give him her shawl off her shoulders so that he could pawn it to play some more. She poor wretch, didn't know what to do, prided herself on being understanding, and then felt justified when one day he came home with a fortune he'd won; they celebrate, and then he goes out and loses it all the next day; and all starts up again, and happens every week and goes on for weeks and weeks and months, and a whole half year, with hysterical scenes and pacifications and entreaties every other

---

[10] Walter Adams was a classmate of Ginsberg's, and the son of poet Kathrin Traverin Adams.

night, like a hotel room in Denver, until at last he's so beat that he can't go on—he hasn't any more money, blames himself, cries that he is a failure. Finally he falls at her feet sobbing like an injured child, helpless and in an epileptic; so she bundles him up in her coats and takes him down the R.R. station and they go to Russia. What a great, mad book, by Mrs. D. Probably in Denver Library. Years later he writes about it (in a few letters) and what he says about her, sounds like a wise and aged Pommy recollecting his own lifetime. But a wise and aged Pommy, naturally still vigorous, much more insight, on account of years. If you are curious what Pommy might be really truthfully (to self) thinking in years.

See, I have without planning, spent hours writing you. I hereby present them to you as a gift, free. No strings.

Allen

Editors' Note: After waiting for nearly two months Ginsberg was finally admitted to the New York State Psychiatric Institute at Columbia Presbyterian Hospital on West 168th Street in Upper Manhattan.

Allen Ginsberg [New York, New York] to Jack Kerouac [Denver, Colorado]

ca. June 29, 1949

From the Wizard of Paterson
To the Wizard of Denver

Mon Cher Jean Louis:

Enfin J'ai arrivais au maison du Koko; ici les animaux sont tres interresant, il y est un homme in de vinget et n annees, une surrealiste qui me fait riri avec son inspire imagination fauve, et aussi son weltanschaunung est comme cela de M. Denison [Burroughs], *mais ce jeune homme ci (tres laid) est une jinf de Brom/ et anssi une Hipster. Mais il est fou. Ech, ce francois ci m'enneri.*

The atmosphere is weird. I have an idea (how true it is I will I suppose find out soon enough) that the attendants have not too clear an idea as to the nature of madness; to them it is characterized by absurdity or eccentricity mostly. I rather had hoped to come to a judgment of my soul under the clear light of sane eyes. Tomorrow night we see a performance of Rumpelstiltskin, however.

Ecrivez moi, ecrivez moi, j'attend, faisey-vous l'effort de etre du moins au moins un pen balance et grave, pas trop fou (perhaps it will improve your literary style?) *mais ecrivez avec une style libre* anyway. The mail is read before it gets to me. Say what you want, but don't write me tracts suggesting that I dynamite the establishment for instance. I mean, they may take offense.

> Love,
> Allen

Give me news of whoever is newsworthy.

OK. I got a mad long letter from [John Clellon] Holmes—asking me about my soul. I replied at great length. He kept disclaiming personal interest and insisted that he was interested in the Visionary in relation to the Lyric Poem, and the processes of literary creation. It would be a big joke on me if he was really interested in cold facts. He is at Cape Cod. No news from or to Claude [Lucien Carr]. I am now a bleak prophet. (Bleak eternity) (Bleak heavens) (Bleak smile) I have come to love the word bleak, it suggests just the quality of timeless joy possible that I feel in a key.

Jack Kerouac [Denver, Colarado] to Allen Ginsberg [New York, New York]

July 5–11, 1949

July 5, 1949
6100 W. Center Ave.
Denver 14, Colo.

Dear Allen:

I admire you for delivering yourself to an actual bughouse. It shows your interest in things and people. Be careful while convincing the docs you're nuts not to convince yourself (you see, I know you well.) Isn't it interesting that Holmes' letter demanding information about your soul should reach you there? Relax on the roof and get fresh air anyway.

In connection with this sort of thing, let me quote from an article I read last night in the *Pharr Gazette*, by a certain M. Denison [Burroughs] (a local editor with a fiery temper): He says, about another farmer in the region, called Gillette [Allen Ginsberg], who was taken to a sanatorium in Houston after he killed his wife:—"What's with Al Gillette talking about the Wrath of God? Has he flipped his lid? We have the W. of G. down here in the shape of Border Patrol agents, deporting our field hands, and D. of Agriculture Beaurocrats telling us what, where and when to plant. Only us farmers have other names for it. And if any obscenity bunch of beaurocrats think we're going to sit on our (ass) and let the W. of G. take over, they will learn that we are not Liberals." (!) (Notice the spelling—beaurocrat, a kind of southern plantation spelling, a Missouri aristocrat spelling.)

The editor goes on (in Immortal Complaints in the Chaunce [*sic*] of Time):— "If your editor were in Gillette's place he would say 'Go ahead and place your charges, if any.'" (The editor considers Gillette innocent in the case, which took place in Clem, Texas.) "His present position is insufferable. Imagine being herded around by a lot of old women like Louis Gillette [Louis Ginsberg] and Mark V. Ling [Van Doren]. Besides I don't see why V. Ling puts in his 2 cents worth. Sniveling old Liberal fruit . . . All Liberals are weaklings, and all weaklings are vindictive, mean and petty. Your editor sees nothing to gain from this Houston deal. A lot of New Deal Freudians. Your editor wouldn't let them croakers up there treat his corn let alone his psyche."

After reading this amazing editorial I called up Denison, and among other things he said to me: "I have just done reading Wilhelm Reich's latest book *The Cancer Biopathy*. I tell you Jack, he is the only man in the analysis line who is *on that beam*. After reading the book I built an orgone accumulator and the gimmick really works. The man is not crazy he's a F—— genius." He added, concerning the editorial: "The overpaid beaurocrats are a cancer on the political body of this country which no longer belongs to its citizens."

Incidentally I am going down there to visit, in August.

Sad things happened in Denver. My mother was lonely and beat, and went back to New York yesterday and got her shoe-factory job back. She is *right*, as usual. I'll explain later. So I am moving back to New York and will live there forever now. My mother is a great trooper—wants to earn own living.

Also, Edie [Parker Kerouac] and I are practically back together again, by mail. Now that I sold my book she is most interested in me. She said "When you're a Hollywood writer and live in a big mansion, I have first dibs for parasiting off of you." I am going to try to make her go to school in New York this fall (she studies Floralculture.) Her mother married the Berry of the Berry Paint, and they all live in a mansion on Lake Shore, Detroit, now; Edie has a room in the tower (!) And in the Spring I will bring her to Paris with me, and write *Doctor Sax*. If I have enough money by then I am definitely financing your own Voyage there. I envision a season in New York and then an Immense Season in Paris in 1950 (including Claude [Lucien Carr], and even Vern [Neal Cassady] if I am rich enough.) If I become rich we'll all be saved by overcoming the bigness of the night, the red, red night.

Well I began writing "The Rose of the Rainy Night" this week, to amuse myself while doing *On the Road* and to prepare for the "Myth [*Doctor Sax*]." "The Rose" is a big Spenserian work of many cantos. It opens:

"So doth the rain blow down
Like melted lutes, their airs condenst,
And water harps and waterfalls
And all manner of concertina
Th'arcanums of the night alluring."

As you see, it isn't so good, but I'll fix it. I merely put down what comes into my head, though not recklessly. This way, I'll pile up a big Rose and have something to pluck out, petals: —

"Unfolding petal—*A me peloria*!—
The rose of the rain falls open,
And drooping lights the sky
With firkins of softest dew."
[. . .]

However, now I understand poetry and am just going along. My prose has improved because of these studies. I'll just copy one sentence, it would be too much, you'll read it all later:

"And by and by all the lights but one dim hall-light were out, and the men were shrouded in May-night sheets, preparing their minds to sleep." This is in a jail. The hero, Red, is listening . . . "To his right Eddy Parry seemed to moan, alone; to roll his own bones on the hard, hot pad; unless he moaned to someone in the next cell further."

This demonstrates the utter gravity and importance of our poetic experimentations, for they reach the rational atmospheres of the prose-sentence as in Melville's prose make it more than that, much, much more.

Here again, the influence of pure preoccupations with language appearing in, and strengthening, the scaffolded exigencies of the reasonable and light-of-day prose sentence—

"And when the silence increased, then it was possible for Red and anyone else who was awake and listening, to hear the great sea-roar of New York outside: the rumorous Saturday night stretching its tide far over the wash of the vast eventful plain—with its towering Knight-island, and basins, and outreaching apian dark flats to Rockaway, and to Yonkers cliff, to blue-shawled New Jersey, and the Jamaican reaches that guttered like altar waxes on the hooded horizon—the Saturday night of ten million secret and furiously living souls to which Red, now considering it half-heartedly and half drowsy, would soon return, himself a secret and furious and excited motion in that ocean of life antique. For what reason? Why had he no wild interest in the mere day? the mere night? in here? anywhere?"

But later that night Red has a vision (all minutely and swirlingly described) and is Resurrected out of Glooms: —

Among his visions are:

"Now, inexplicably, he was sitting in the movie looking avidly at the crazy-serious gray screen and what it was showing; and looking at the curtains beside the screen, and even at some hunchbacked old man with a top hat who scowled there beside a stepladder. He then saw a kind of vision of a candy bar, an immense Mr. Goodbar—a candy he always ate as a kid in movie,—and began eating it slowly from the corner inwards, peanut by peanut, all hunched over it with hugging delight. Also, it was raining outside, but warm and dark in the movie where he jubilantly lay hidden with his feet on the forward seat. It was the Marx Brothers on the screen, with everything going mad and almost exploding, Harpo hanging from a rope from the attic window, Groucho gliding in the marble hall with a lion, something collapsing, a woman screaming in the closet. And then it was a western movie, Buck Jones in arid plains rolling along in clouds of dust on a big white horse—a rainy gray myth on the screen, the myth of the gray West, with crooks in vests pursuing behind on ordinary horses, and another posse roaring in from the creaky rickety town. A big face appeared on the screen turning slowly in profile, a man's face with fluttering eyelashes. Who was this? Vern?"

Red has all these visions, it's his last night in jail, and finally he says a prayer on his knees. Then begins the Pilgrimage hitch-hiking with benign imbecilic Smitty to California to look for his father, whom he only finds the following winter gambling in Montana saloons, after many dusty travails and crazy rides around the country with Vern, and many things including my own version of the Dark Angel and the Madman (remember Dostoevsky at the Apollo?) (In San Francisco this.) Finally everybody leaves and Red's alone, and that's where the story ends. This is I. (Also, there's a Mystic Tenorman who hitch-hikes around the country and Red keeps running into him, a wild colored cat, until Red's scared; he even sees him in the middle of the night walking in the Mansion of the Snake, the Bayou of New Orleans, with his Tenor Horn, and steps on the gas.) This is like the shrouded stranger. *On the Road* is the name of this opus; I want to write about the crazy generation and put them on the map and give them importance and make everything begin to change once more, as it always does every twenty years. When I die I'll be a shroud swimming in the Parade on the River, with skinny white arms and Lotus-Eyes, and that will be that, at night.

Thank you for telling me about Hodos Chamelientos. I'm reading Eliot and

Crane and Dickinson and Robinson and even Keinvarvawc (a Celtic poet) and
The Faerie Queene. More later. See you in September.

Old friend

Jack

1. Brierly invited me to a big party for Lucius Beebe here. He claims to be the
"last of the Bourbons" and is a big fake . . . that is, he says the world interests
him only insofar as it offers "the last remaining best things." He's always plastered, and not happy drunk, either. I met Thomas Hornsby Ferrill and all the
big society of Denver. I behaved like a fool. I yelled and told dirty stories and
got drunk. Then I came back to my shack in the hills here, and rested and
mused. I am surrounded day in day out by hordes of children and dogs, who
come in the house. Today there were a thirteen-year old girl, a six-year old girl,
a four-year old boy, an infant, a bird-dog, a mud-hound, two Chihuahua dogs
and a cat. The thirteen-year old girl wrote a story on my typewriter about the
Giant in the garden and the little children who were afraid to go in because
they thought the garden door was locked, but it wasn't at all and the door
opened, and they went in, and the Giant cried with joy. This proves to me that
children really know more than adults. Children are preoccupied with the same
things Shakespeare knew . . . gardens and fairies and enchanted islands and
Giants and wizards and the whole stock of what might be called Metaphorical
Cerebration in the Metaphysical Phantasy.

Is this not so?

Am I the Giant?—the one in the garden? Of course I am.

I love these little children and I love the Rubens countryside here and I am
sorry that the whole world is not one small garden so everybody could be together all the time before they die and rot in the grave. And I will love Edie
again before she goes.

Do you know what I think of the *mind*?—that it is made of various ordered
myths, each with a direction of its own, and a hope (foolish or not); and that
when you analyze and dissect these ordered myths (associative constellations)
you shatter them and in their place erect One White Myth of Reason, which
then arbitrarily directs and commands you; all that has happened is a loss of
riches. The mind may become more coherent, but an organic tangle of vines is
gone. Just as a jungle can be torn down for a cement factory. All the vines and
the flowers and the cockatoos and the tigers go, and they make cement in noisy
dusts. I see no reason to laud this. It is just another foolish mistake of man's.
Centuries from now he will laugh and play.

The Denver Birds? I know a kid here who believes that everybody should be
happy at his little job, making cement, etc., and be *predictable* so the Social

Scientists can keep their papers in order. I feel like that fellow Denison. It's all a big mistake, everything but the flesh, and the mind is the flower petal of the flesh. It is the same juice as the flesh. Albert Schweitzer[11] is at present saying this at the Aspen Goethe Festival here. I would love to hear his lecture in French tomorrow.

My editor [Robert] Giroux is flying out next week and Brierly and I are taking him to the Central City opera. It is very possible I will fly back with him, so I'll see you soon perhaps, if they allow it. I wish you would place your weary bones in lesser inaccessible demesnes . . . like the Dixie hotel or something, or Pokerino, or the Mills Hotel, or the Waldorf-Astoria. What fun is there in the Medical Center? Hey? What is it that finds you there?

(wink)

P.S. Hal [Chase] is dead.

Allen Ginsberg [New York, New York] to Jack Kerouac [Denver, Colorado]

July 13–14, 1949

July 13, 1949
Wed. Eve.

Dear Jack:

Comprenez, I did not deliver myself to an actual bughouse to see what it was like in the sense that you meant, things and people. Write a letter to the editor—tell him that *I take my madhouses seriously*. That's how it is. As to selling my soul to the New Deal, that does not interest me now, the fear of doing that—I have been fighting and seeking punishment from an abstraction (society) and I have found the punishment in myself. (Weary am I of my sad majesty) The reactionaries have been prideful and arrogant too long, perhaps, but that is their affair. Perhaps Hal [Chase] is not dead—he knew me, and made me shudder. Sanctity is love and humility, and there is truth and self—A Great White Myth—vaster than the jungle of the unreal. I will be a lamb to "society," I was never a jackal like Denison [Burroughs] or a lynx like Joan [Adams], though I have tried to be like everyone but *moi*. No?

Je Changerau. There are no intellectuals in a madhouse. The rest of the people here see more visions in one day than I do in a year—tho profound gulfs appearing everywhere. Do you know what amnesia is? If you cannot speak a

[11] Albert Schweitzer was a missionary, doctor, and theologian who later won the Nobel Peace Prize.

name which is on the tip of your tongue, which you don't remember—a line of poetry, or a person, etc. But what if that condition extends through greater areas than a single instance? What if you can't pronounce what's just beyond your mind—what if all memory is gone? The whole world new, and you familiar but unknown, even your name gone? People like this everyday here—and we speak of visions—others are lost. Nightmares are daily occurrences.

I have discovered that I have no feelings, just thoughts, borrowed thoughts taken from someone I admire because he seems to have feeling. I am tired of thoughts against the New Deal. If the New Deal can teach me to *feel* love for it, I will love it.

Words mean only what they say, what they state on the surface; infinity, nothingness, are literally inexistent. The only thing real is on the surface.

The bureaucrats are right—the proof is that I have spent my life fighting them. Why shouldn't they be right, except that if we thought so it would upset our established spiritual order? Very well, upset our old order. A revolution? Why not? Do you know what it would mean to the reactionary editor if he found out all of a sudden that he had wasted his life in a quixotic meaningless war against a true reality represented by the "bureaucrats." The lice of eternity, the pits of reality—"O bitter reward of many a tragic tomb. The murderous innocence of the sea." O Bleak Bill. He is afraid that I will find out that he is crazy, that his analysis of me was a tragic farce—not an absurd farce, but a tragic real one—that he has led me astray. Very well—write a letter to the editor declaring that one reluctant subscriber now finds that he has, despite his parent's warnings, been led astray—by wastrels and perverts. The scion of a noble family. Put that in yer pipe and smoke it, and make of it what you will, I am not Jesus Christ. I am Jerry Rauch.[12] *Mon pere avait raison. Ma mere elait fou.*

> Behold! the swinging Swan
> Where the geese have gamboled.
>   Say my oops,
>   Beat my bone
> All my eggs are scrambled.

Reality, as Claude De Maubri [Lucien Carr] well knows, is that familial and social community which we, as madmen, have discontinued. Oedipus Rex—he, he alone, caused the plague in the play.

If we were to love as intensely as we now hate, without hate's contradictions— and love the very things we hate?

---

[12] Jerry Rauch was one of their Columbia friends.

And what else would be the answer, except that it is *we*, not they, who are crazy? That is a foreign policy alien and vast to the local isolationist publicists. I contemplate incredible logical revolutions different from any in the past decade.

What is this seasonal madness and pride in spirit that we have cultivated but a premeditated insult to other people? A defense against their love? The attendants in the madhouse love me, they want to help me. Why should I resent them and make jokes at their expense? I laugh alone. Roll my bones, roll my bones, don't leave my bones alone. We are all really crazy. You are crazy, too.

In sum I consider myself a sick man. Denison [Burroughs] was in a madhouse once but instead of learning something new he suspected that everybody there was trying to torture him. You too. Think of Kafka. That is the very Gate of Wrath.

You do not give me credit for sufficient abandon of spirit. I am happy, also, that Wilhelm Reich is right. He is probably more right than the rest of the analytic schools. I am also happy, also, that you and I will be together in New York in years to come. I might have gone to Denver if you stayed. Now we will call each other from our penthouses to our country houses by telephone each night in 1954.

Walter Adams is back. I have not seen him yet, but I will this Saturday. He wrote me 3 lines here—saying he would like to see me. Where is your mother going to live?

And Edie [Parker Kerouac] too!

Claude I called last weekend—short phone talk. All O.K. He is going out with someone, but won't say who over the phone. We are not going to meet again till fall.

Do you really want to finance this poor broken spirit on a trip to Paris? I will accept when the time comes if I am still crazy. Did you hear from Pomeroy [Neal Cassady]?

(Ha! How I intend to frighten Pommy someday!) I think of your stanzas the same thing that you do. Six water angels is the best, also waterharps and waterfalls, (I think all it needs is one running coherent *plot* to make it coherent—otherwise Arodos) (But you have that?) (water is your medium). Watery shrouds, 6 water angels sing enthroned—you are saying that it's all bullshit, all the symbolism. Bleak Blook the same.

Your prose has many more *bleak echoes* than before, is all you say it is also: "The utter gravity of our investigations." That is what I felt in Cézanne originally, and your novel which converted me, amazing how our early frivolity changes alchemically. All balloons go up. Shadow changes into bone.

We will all be together again soon, don't worry. I personally will go get Pommy and Denison . . . when I go sane. I believe in the Great White Myth, I don't believe in the jungle anymore, really. Down with the associative constellations! Down with the constellations! I want to be directed and commanded by "Arbitrary Reason." Which is as much to say 1.) God, reality is not arbitrary, but necessary, because true and in existence. The jungle is a big camp, a big fake. It doesn't exist, it's an illusion. What exists is real, what doesn't exist doesn't exist, it's nothing. *De nihil de nihil*. The great white myth is not cement and noisy dust, it is actually love in disguise. So far I'm the first (except Claude and perhaps Haldon [Chase]) to see this. 2.) To tell the truth I am a little doe who has just been devoured by a tiger and I don't believe in jungles anymore; and I seek the inmost shade.

But all our thoughts (even Denison's though he doesn't know it) meet in heaven. But I really don't agree with the editor anymore.

Now enough of this—and I will tell you tales of the madhouse—facts, anecdotes, stories, descriptions. I have tried to answer your real question of your whole letter, the last sentence—"Hey? What is it that finds you there?" Something that I am learning—becoming—something that I think is true, that the tone of your letter gently derides, anyway.

Thursday Afternoon [July 14, 1949]

Ignore everything I said except by reading between the exaggerations to what I can't express easily. I take my madhouses seriously; it seems I have been threatening and winking for years on the same kick. "What they undertook to do They brought to pass:

> All things hang like a drop of dew
> Upon a blade of grass"
> In Gratitude to the Unknown Instructors—Yeats.

There is a pale Bartleby here, a Jewish boy named Fromm, (there are so many crazy Jews here) who sits in his chair. The first time I came in, I sit on a chair in the hall, waiting to be called to the preliminary routines of being shown my bed. He sat opposite me slumped over; he notices everything but won't say nothing. A big fat German refugee who helps run occupational therapy, a woman, came up to him and said "Don't you want to go up to O.T. today? Everybody else is there now. You don't want to sit here alone?" He raised his pale, weak head and looked at her inquiringly, but didn't say anything. Very gently she asked him again, hoping that he'd suddenly get up, perhaps, and follow her, repenting his loneliness. He looked at her a long time, pursed his lips, and slowly shook his head. Didn't even say "I prefer not to," just shook his head meditatively, after a long time in which he seemed to have been considering the

101

question seriously; but shook his head, no, rationally. I immediately assumed that I could penetrate his mysterious secret refinement—but no—he was a poor lost wandering child of time. But the doctors (a whole hospital full of liberal minded social experimenters) have been treating him here since time immemorial trying to make him say yes. He has gone through insulin and/or electric shock therapy, psychotherapy, narcosynthesis, hypnoanalysis, everything but a lobotomy, and he still won't say yes! He rarely talks—only once have I heard him raise his voice in the wilderness. I was told that it was a great disappointment to hear him at last, because he has a nasty whining complaining voice, that's why he won't talk. When I heard him, just two days ago, he was complaining about some bureaucratic mix up. It seems he had started to shave, finished half his face, and then was called to breakfast. He came back and found the razors locked up. He stood in the hall arguing with the nurse. She was saying "Mr. Fromm, but you must realize that there are certain set hours for shaving." And he "But—But—But—I still have the soap dry on my face, I still have half my face shaved only," etc. Once in awhile they take it in their heads to drag him by force up to occupational therapy, or to the roof. He doesn't say a word, just resists; they have to bend his arm back, painfully, and take him to the elevator. But he stands near the elevator door and mournfully taps on it indicating that he wants to leave, go back to his chair. He [never] makes any trouble otherwise.

Well, last night, I heard an awful hysterical shriek down the hall and rushed to investigate. I met Fromm rushing away from the scene. He looked up at me (his eyes, walking fast, on the ground) with a half-embarrassed, half-pleased smile. I hardly smiled back, thinking he was rushing away in fear from some awful scene of psychic carnage (patients often blow their tops, alone, or attack others) and I refused to acknowledge that I was afraid, so I didn't half smile back, but half I did, because the *scenes* here are awesome. (The shriek, incidentally, was laughter.) What had happened? Fromm was sitting in the same chair, drooping, listless, quiet—and two other patients (one I will describe) were talking together, exchanging perhaps sarcastic jokes about the fact that they were in the bughouse—when suddenly, Fromm's face lit up, he raised himself in his chair, and without a word, he began imitating everybody in the madhouse, making bleak mimicries of even patients that just entered, doctors, nurses, me, the people he was talking to, savage, hopeless gestures that caught and caricatured everybody. I would like to show him what I have just written, but I really don't know what's under his skin. He would probably hand it back to me with no sign at all—(after reading it carefully.)

(The danger of such stories as this is that they are wishful exaggerations of possibility. *O, Les maupions de l'eternite!* But this is true nonetheless.)

There is a boy here named Carl Solomon[13] who is the most interesting of all. I spend many hours conversing with him. The first day (in the chairs) I gave way to the temptation of telling him about my mystical experiences. It is very embarrassing, in a mad house, to do this. He accepted me as if I were another nutty ignu, saying at the same time with a tone of conspiratorial guile, "O well, you're new here." He is also responsible for the line: "There are no intellectuals in madhouses." He is a big queer from Greenwich Village, formerly from Brooklyn—a "swish" (he used to be he says) who is the real Levinsky—but big and fat, and interested in surrealistic literature. He went to CCNY and NYU, but never graduated, knew all the Village hipsters, and a whole gang of Trotskyite intellectuals (this generation's Meyer Schapiros), and he is familiar with a great range of avant garde styles—also a true Rimbaud type, from his teens. Not creative, he doesn't write, and doesn't know much about literature really, except what he reads in little magazines (he had *Tyger's Eye, Partisan* and *Kenyon*) but he knows everything about that. Jumped ship and spent months wandering through Paris—finally at the age of consent he decided to commit suicide (on his 21st birthday) and committed himself to this place (entering a madhouse is the same thing as suicide he says—madhouse humor)—presented himself practically at the front door demanding a lobotomy. He apparently was full of great mad gestures when he first came in (with a copy of *Nightwood*[14]) threatening to smear the walls with excrement if he didn't get a seclusion (private) room so that he could finish his book in peace. Also threatened the nurses, "If I ever hear anyone saying to me 'Mr. Solomon you're raving,' I'll turn over the ping pong table," that happened almost immediately. There is a perfect opportunity here for existentialist absurdity—he is quiet now—speaks in a sinister tone to me of how the doctors are driving him sane by shock therapy "Making me say 'momma!'" I tell him I want to be made to say momma and he says "of course (we do)." You can see what a weird sinister atmosphere here it is, Kafkian, because the doctors are in control and have the means to persuade over the most recalcitrant. Ha! I'd like to see Dennison exposed to these awful abysses and dangers. Here the abysses are real; people explode daily and the doctors! the doctors! my god, the doctors! They are fiends, I tell you, absolute Ghouls of Mediocrity. Horrible! They have the truth! They are right! They are all thin, pale lipped, four eyed, gawky, ungainly psychology majors from the colleges! All the seersucker liberals, dressed in the same suits, always with a vapid, half embarrassed, polite smile on their faces. "What? Mr. Solomon doesn't eat today? Send him down to shock!" All the stoops from the past years, the blood-

[13] This is the first mention of Carl Solomon, to whom Ginsberg would address *Howl*.
[14] *Nightwood*, by Djuna Barnes, was published in 1936.

less apoetic bourgeoisie, the social scientists and rat experimenters, the blue eyes who went to the proms, who debated about socialism—went west on bus through the rolling wheatfields to study social psychology and medicine, the squares and ignoramuses, the Jews from Bronx. They all look the same, I tell you, I can't tell one from another, except for some obviously crazy East Indian midget who also is a psychiatrist. What is he doing here in America psychologizing drug store cowboys with nervous breakdowns? These are the men who are going to fudge my immortal soul! Heavens! Where is Denison? Where is Pomeroy? Where is Huncke? Why don't they come to my rescue? It is just like Russia! The machine men from the N.K.U.D. are making me recant my rootless cosmopolitanism.

Speaking of this, because of Solomon, I am reading in all the little magazines about the latest Frenchmen. One is named Jean Genet, he is about the greatest— greater than Céline, perhaps, but similar. Huge apocalyptic novels by homosexual hipster who grew up like Pomeroy in jail—an article in April 1949 *Partisan Review* talks about him—a book called *Miracle de La Rose*, a massive autobiography, a long prose poem on prison life! The hero is the Assassin Hercamone— "Whose shadowy presence in the death cell radiates throughout the prison a mystical intensity that is taken as the standard of Beauty and Achievement and to whom the author attaches the symbol of the rose. (His life lasted from his death sentence to his death . . .)" I speak the very language used by the mystics of all religions to speak of their gods and their mysteries. I read a 3 page excerpt on the mysteries of shoplifting ending (as I remember) "and so it is that at the judgment of the apocalypse God will call me to the dolmen realms with my own tender voice, crying, 'Jean, Hean'." (Dolmen realms is my own phrase).

Also a man named Henri Michaux—interesting prose poems about the weird *Aivinsikis* (Heaven-seekers?) in *Kenyon* and *Hudson Reviews*.

Most of all, a madman lately died named Antonin Artaud—spent 9 years in Rodez, a French madhouse ("*M. Artaud ne mange pas au juurd'hue. Apportez lui au choc.*") Solomon was wandering around Paris and suddenly he heard barbaric, electrifying cries on the street. Terrified, penetrated, totally come down, frozen—he saw this madman dancing down the street repeating be-bop phrases—in such a voice—the body rigid, like a bolt of lightening "radiating" energy—a madman who had opened all doors and went yelling down Paris. He wrote a big poem—article about Van Gogh (translated in *A Tiger's Eye*)—saying the same things about U.S. that I said about Cézanne. Solomon said it was the most profound single instant he ever had (till he came here where the doctors have insulin—and "the drugs fight it out.")

Several days ago a tongue tied boy of twenty named Bloom came in (he had been here several years before, too) talking about "concentrations of time" and eternity—he escaped, also, ran away, with attendants chasing him down the block, escaped into the subway. You see I am not unique in my formulations. I think Richard Weitzner would do well here. Before I came in I told him "If I'm mad, you're madder—and I'm mad." He looked at me, interested, and said "Really?"

What does old J.B. [Justin Brierly] the dancing master, say about my presence here? Did he predict it before? He took me for the sane and bureaucratic type (between the two of us) when we were in Denver. Do you know? He said he wasn't sure about you (you were kind of Bohemian, while I was the well-groomed Hungarian) but took you for O.K. since Ed White vouched for you (as I remember the conversation).

Van Doren asked to see my book, (after I offered to show it to him).

I haven't done any writing here at all—no pen, no place to write, no calm yet. Wrote a poem ending:

> Never ask me what I mean
> all I say is what I seen
> though it seems to be a shame,
> anyone can say the same
>   anyway it happened.

It begins:

> It happened when the rain was grey,
> a gloomy, doomy, cloudy day.
> I don't remember what it was
> But then it seemed as clear as glass,
>   And anyway, it happened.

This illustrates my desire to write a poem or a ballad with a real story line—but I wound up writing a poem about an unmentioned mystical "It"—a joke.

I am beginning to hate my mother.

Adieu—

When you get to N.Y. call up my brother [Eugene Brooks], and he will tell you how to get to me. I can go out weekends—running around too loose is discouraged, though. Someone has to sign me out and take responsibility for me, and sign me back in—relative, sometimes a friend. When you get back, we'll go away on a weekend maybe—to Cape Cod—where [John Clellon] Holmes, [Alan] Ansen, [Bill] Cannastra, [Ed] Stringham and many others are. I'll only be able to see you on weekends for the time, but if I get better, I may have more privileges.

105

I dreamed of Claude for two nites after I called him up.

Send me news of Joan? I may write a letter to the *Pharr Gazette* [William Burroughs] in a few months.

> *Adieu ancien ami;*
>> Allen

P.S. Incoming letters are *not* censored. My mistake.

I am going to a dance—the men and women patients—Local 802 musicians—on the roof—in a half hour—I wear white trousers, Fitzgerald shoes, yellow T-shirt.

I am painting, too (for occupational therapy) a series of *Revelations of Golgotha*—Christ on the cross, great flaming white wings, and the great yellow Rose of Paradise for a halo, surrounded by thieves, one an idiot, one with a death's head. (I always write you from institutions—Sheepshead, Paterson, Columbia, etc.)

Jack Kerouac [Denver, Colorado] to Allen Ginsberg [New York, New York]

July 26, 1949

July—49

Dear Allen:

This must be brief. This is all the paper I have in the empty house a-moving—I think now I know what you mean. If only you could be straight like Yeats and come right out with it—and if I too did so. I sit here at the table. Your letter at my side.

> "What they undertook to do
> They brought to pass:
> All things are like letters
> Stamped and addressed—
> To me? Dear God to me?
> I flinch, now I flinch.
> All things are like this,
> They reach me finally.
> They sit there waiting for me.
> All things are like the
> Loaf of bread on the shelf,
> Brought to pass, deliver'd,

To me, Happy Home Bread.
All things are like the pencils
On the shelf, and my cat
Who sits alive, and the Sugar Bowl
On the table, and the raindrops making.
All things were intended to be
What they have become in silence.
Yes, the editor does not know,
Or knowing, doesn't care,
Or you knowing, never mind,
It's all undertaken and done,
And silence is your living middle prayer.   All this means
'Tis bleak to know what knowing is.   that everything
'Tis not seeing as seeing is known,   ←——that exists, exists
But inside-eyes and bones that wait.   anyway, because
All things are actually done and doing?   of reality.
Are you glad life lives? O Bleak!—
O Bleak substantial bone all shadow."—

Of course, I did not yet come out with it. But dear Allen I will yet. O folder-blash.

Now listen:—I have told Robert Giroux all about you and he is of course interested. This is the man who went to see Ezra Pound at the nuthouse, with Robert Lowell. (Tell you all about details.) When he was leaving, Pound shouted from the window: "Where are you going? Aren't you eligible?" Since then Lowell went mad. Giroux is a little scared. He went to see Thomas Merton at the monastery. He knows [T. S.] Eliot. He is a big intellectual Catholic N.Y. Ignu—You'll see. Bring him your volume of works to Harcourt Brace at 383 Madison—tell him your name. He knows you. He agreed that dead eyes see. But remember that he is also a big businessman like [Alan] Harrington[15] would like to be—a stockholder in the company, editor in chief and member of the Opera Club (with Rockefellers.) Be smart, now, and don't shit in your pants. The world is only waiting for you to pitch sad silent love in the place of excrement. Okay? By sad silent love I guess I mean some kind of compromise. But a *bleak one*, see? In daylight be bleak. All set. You may be published now.

Your stories of the madhouse are so actual that I feel again as I did in the Navy nuthouse[16]—scared and seeing through heads. I used to sit with the worst

---

[15] Alan Harrington was a friend of Kerouac and Holmes who later wrote *The Immortalist*.
[16] Kerouac had spent time in a Navy mental hospital in Bethesda during the spring of 1943.

ones to learn. Be kind and allow that I sought to see. Oh for Krissakes, I know everything . . . don't you know that? We all do. We even all know that we're all crazy. All of us are sick of our sad majesties. Don't be so pedantic. *Mush!*

Hal [Chase] is really dead. By that I mean that over the phone his voice yearned to see me, but he did not mention that it was Ginger told him not to see me in Denver. I know, thru his father who was my inadvertent spy. It is perhaps Ginger who can make us shudder all. She's stark gone.

Dancingmaster I love. I told him. I never knew Dancingmaster was so great. He took Giroux and I to the mountains at 85 miles per, to the opera. He had a woman with him, an old Edie, whom I screwed just a few hours ago, who gave me money.

I wandered around Denver the other night looking for Pommy [Cassady] somehow. A black gal said "Hello Eddy." I know I was really Eddy—was getting closer to Pommy. It was a mystic night in the Mexican-Nigger Denver. There was a softball game. I thought it was Pommy pitching. I thought any moment LuAnne[17] would sneak up behind me and grab my cock. The stars, the night, the lilac-hedge, the cars, the street, the rickety porches. *Down in Denver, down in Denver, all I did was die.*

How many times have you died?

Then I saw your Denver Doldrums in my desk—Ah. Do you know what Giroux did? He revised the child saying from a dark corner—"I see you . . . peek-a-boo!" to just: "I see you . . ." I asked him if he knew what he had done and he said "Of course." He likes me, by the way: we're friends now; I like him; we're going to go to shows and operas together in N.Y. A new great friend of my life. He hitch-hiked with me so as to understand *On the Road.* He is Eliot's editor, remember, and Van Doren's pal. He knows everybody—[Stephen] Spender et al, Jay Laughlin (New Directions) etc. He hitch hiked with me in my wilderness.

I am hitch-hiking to Detroit tomorrow. No more letters to 6100 W. Center. See you in N.Y. in two weeks. I don't know anything about those crazy Jewish cats in your nuthouse. Maybe I will in time. They remind me of Norman.[18] Talk to Walter Adams who is bleak. [Allan] Temko wrote me a big letter from Prague. I am getting some money Xmas—want to go to a school in Italy with Edie, and meet Giroux in Rome in spring and go to Paris. Won't be rich till October 1950. So live cheaply first.

Please do what you say—go get Denison [Burroughs] and Pommy. I've written twice to Pommy, no answer. What's the matter? I'll write to Denison and

---

[17] LuAnne Henderson was Neal Cassady's first wife.
[18] Norman Schnall was an early friend of Ginsberg and Kerouac, and is mentioned in the scroll version of *On the Road.*

tell him to move to N.Y. Why are we all camping in California, Texas and Colorado? I would love Denison to go to Europe with me. Also his trust fund would be a fortune out there, where one lives well on $30 a month. Ask Adams if this is not so. Know what, Edie wrote to me?—"Maybe you and I are just a dream." Also:—"I guess we'll always be night birds." Finally—"I love to drink coffee with people in the morning." She now sounds like a sad, straight woman. I yearn for her cunt. Every now and then I feel like Pommy about that—more and more. I want us all together before it is too late, before the Season dies from neglect (as they always do in time.) Why? Do you mind my questions?

C'est tranquil sa—Excuse my soul.

As ever,

Jack

Thanks for your huge and amazing letter—read it to Giroux, too.

1950

Editors' Note: Kerouac left Denver, originally planning to stop in Detroit to see his former wife, Edie, but instead he headed for San Francisco where Neal Cassady promised him free room and board for as long as he wanted to stay. That arrangement didn't last long, and, by August, Neal and Jack were both in New York City. Throughout the fall, Ginsberg remained in the mental hospital (although he received his mail at his father's house in Paterson, where he went every weekend). He continued to hope that something positive would come out of his therapy, but as time went by, he began to think that the doctors didn't know much more about mental illness than he did. His dream of a sudden cure to his problems faded.

Jack Kerouac [New York, New York] to Allen Ginsberg [Paterson, New Jersey]

January 13, 1950

Dear Allen:

Tonight while walking on the waterfront in the angelic streets I suddenly wanted to tell you how wonderful I think you are. Please don't dislike me. What is the mystery of the world? Nobody knows they're angels. God's angels are ravishing and fooling me. I saw a whore and an old man in a lunchcart, and God—their faces! I wondered what God was up to. In the subway I almost jumped up to yell, "What was *that* for? What's going on up there? What do you mean by that?" Jesus, Allen, life ain't worth the candle, we all know it, and almost *everything* is wrong, but there's nothing we can do about it, and living is heaven.

Well, here we are in heaven. This is what heaven is like. Also in the subway I suddenly shuddered, for a crack had opened, like cracks open in the ground when there's an earthquake, only this crack opened in the air, and I saw pits. I was suddenly no longer an angel, but a shuddering devil.

Mainly, I wanted to tell you how dearly I regard your soul, and value your existence, and wish for your recognition of my heart's desire, in short, I admire and love you and consider you a great man always. Let me boast a moment in order to give value to this, for what good is regard from a dunce, a spook, an elephant or a chocolate drop: My English editor, (ain't met him yet) sent G. [Giroux] a postcard showing picture of the antique Counting House in their firm, and said, "Place looks exactly like it did when we published Goldsmith & Johnson. Please tell Kerouac [he] is in good company, and what is more, is worthy of it."

A beat American kid from a milltown, me, is now side by side with Goldsmith & Johnson. Isn't it strange historically? if not actually? Let us get on with the mystery of the world.

For instance, why do I write you this note in spite of the fact that I'll see you tomorrow night?—and live in the same city with you. Why is everybody like Sebastian [Sampas][1] in the record, stammering, stumbling at the end, fainter and fainter with all the scratching, saying, "So long, Jack old boy . . . take it easy, please . . . goodbye . . . old friend . . . see you soon, I guess . . . goodbye . . . take care of yourself, now . . . farewell . . . I guess . . . 'bye . . . so long . . . goodbye old man." Most people spend their lives saying that to their best friends; they're always putting on their coats and leaving, and saying goodnight, and going down the street, and turning to wave a last time . . . Where they go?

Let me tell you what the Archangel is going to do. At a big Walter Adams party, or a [Bill] Cannastra party, the Archangel is suddenly going to appear in a blinding flash of white light, among actual waterfalls of honey-light also, and everybody will keep still while the Archangel, with its voice, speaks. We will see, hear, and shudder. Behind the archangel we will see that Einstein is all wrong about enclosed space . . . there will be endless space, infinities of Celestial Vine, and all the gores of the mires below, and the joyful singing of angels mingling with the shudders of devils. We'll see that everything exists. For the first time we'll realize that it's all alive, like baby turtles, and *moves* in the middle of the night at a party . . . and the archangel is going to tell us off. Then clouds of cherubs will fall, mingled with satyrs and whatnots and spooks. If we were not haunted by the mystery of the world, we wouldn't realize nothing.

> Jack

Allen Ginsberg [Paterson, New Jersey] to Jack Kerouac [n.p., New York, New York?]

Paterson Midnight, Jan. 21, 50

Dear Jack:

The Letter of the Archangel was received here but unfortunately my father misplaced it and it can't be found. He did not do it purposely. We spent a long time looking. I told him not to worry.

I was sick and vomited last time we were at Neal's,[2] and when I rose in the morning you grabbed the bed. I was weak on my knees and still sick and that

---

[1] Sebastian Sampas was a childhood friend of Kerouac's who died in combat during World War II.
[2] Neal Cassady was staying with Diana Hansen, and they were splitting their time between her New York apartment and her mother's in Poughkeepsie. They married later that year.

was why I was so avaricious to get back into bed. I felt so lousy I was willing to exasperate you. I remember you got stuck on the chair but what could I do? I hope you are not still angry.

I went to a party last night—a sweet sixteen party for my sister Sheila—and was a wallflower half the night except for a few moments when I danced with some teen age girls, and the end of the night when I got drunk with my step brother (who thought everybody at the party was "phony") and told him tales about Dakar witch doctors and New Orleans whorehouses. I was surprised by the boys there—most of them sharply dressed poker playing frat brothers, all full of experience and sensuality more mature than my own. I began to feel so miserable that I almost left, feeling no reason for my own existence—like a cockroach—till Harold (my step brother) wandered in late with a frown of anger and looked at the crowd of necking couples and cursed them all up and down for a bunch of phony slobs. Ah, me! I began sheepishly asking him what was wrong, were they really nowhere or was I and he nowhere. He insisted it was them and we got drunk after that. After a while he began insulting all the young girls who came through the kitchen where we were drinking, calling them whores, and spilling water on their dresses (down their bosoms). I had a feeling all the people noticed me and asked who was that jerk. O Paterson, what crucifixions do I not suffer for love of thee? I hope someday to become familiar with them all and accepted when I have earned the honor. The reason I want to return home is to suffer fully the abyss between myself and my generation and home and understand the years that have separated us and go back and learn to live unselfconsciously with my people. So far I am Francis in the attic. I am amazed how much I think of him and how true he is; but I am Francis after his own death returned to life with another chance to be humiliated and not reject the humiliation. (Your novel was a world that is dead, and the characters are still alive walking through the same labyrinth on the other side of death, which is the last page of the written book.)

When I slept last night I dreamed a dream. I had just left Henry Street and was looking for Bill [Burroughs]. We had no appointment [to] meet with each other, because we thought that the world was dead, and didn't know what we would have to tell each other. But we knew that we would meet each other somewhere in New York. It would be a casual meeting, and very short: he would have business, and I would go on to a movie, though we hadn't seen each other in a long time. While I walked down the street toward Eighth Ave. I looked at the sky, and there I saw an eastern auroral halo, as from the moon. And I turned and I looked to the west, and I beheld a halo in the sky on the opposite half of the sphere. Each of the two haloes was a dim circular light exactly similar, far up in the heavens, and yet large enough to cover a piece of the night equal to the size of ten moons. After I saw this, I wished that Bill was there and hoped that he saw it wherever in the city he was. I couldn't find him on the Avenue, nor could I find the bars between 42–43 St., then I discovered I was on Seventh Avenue not Eighth Avenue. I went to Eighth Avenue, and tried to find him, but it was too late, he had gone, and not waited for me.

This dream is like one that I once had and dimly remember when I was lost on an unknown vast subway system, and was looking for a home-pad in Brooklyn.

There is a political fight in Paterson between the corrupt powerful old Republican Party, which has lost the last two elections, and a young powerful Democratic Party which has become corrupt since its victories. My father is vociferously in favor of the Democrats. I tried to get a job on the *Morning Call* paper, Democratic, but they are small and run by old men and have no jobs. I went to friends who worked on the *Evening News* (Republican) but they badgered me for hours with questions of loyalty to the paper's policies and reproaches about my father's public opinions and speech makings. It turns out that the owner would be stupid to do a favor for Louis Ginsberg's son when Louis has been openly making violent attacks on the paper and its candidate in the last years, though he is a friend of the editor. I was told that Paterson is run on a strictly cutthroat dollar and power basis and that because my father had stuck his neck out for no reason other than dreamy political idealistic opinions, and had been taken advantage of for his good name to get the votes of the Jews by the mayor, I was considered an unlikely and absurd person to give a job to (not to mention my ill fame, which didn't hit the papers here last spring, but was brought to the attention of the editors, etc.) I next will try the *Passaic Herald News* (three miles away). A fast and growing conservative newspaper which owns a television station too. I am beginning to get a touch of just how strange and actually sordid the atmosphere here is among those who run the city officially. But perhaps that is just out of the hassle of trying to hustle a job that involves "responsibility." Most people here who seem to be at all sensitive or powerful or rich seem to live lives and think thoughts dominated by the smallest sounding (to an outsider) fears for social security and business position. Friendship is actually political. I would not generalize so but these are just the impressions of the weekend surface scratching done with no axe to grind (not even aesthetic that is while I was in action I did not think how mean it was of the paper to refuse a minor job to their frustrated genius) and the real actual degradation of personality and love and work, the cruelty of the system—the system as an actual horrible machine to be felt and suffered in the middle, watching people lie and cheat each other staggering their own imaginations and mine for its reality—makes me wonder if it turns out to be true, what will happen to me here. Perhaps I shall actually be crucified after all. If what I am beginning to suspect is true it will be just like rolling off a log. If it is true Lucien can't see because he is on top, not in the grass roots. Everybody is sick at heart at home and full of blatant terrorist machinery. In some south sea islands they have cruel puberty rites, because the old men are so evil, and, not that they want to hurt the young, but they want to teach them a lesson in one complete formal explosion without individual humiliation.

I am beginning to wonder how evil the world is again. I thought that by accepting chaos it would make everything all right.

I took Varda (the Assyrian looking girl at Simpson's) out on a date last weekend and she introduced me to her best girlfriend and made supper at her house (the girlfriend, who gave me a painting she made). I guess I will see her mostly for a while, of the run of females I know. I wish I could meet a really gone sweet girl who could love me. But I guess a really gone sweet girl is too much to expect.

Why is everything so hard?

The last lines of Orwell's *1984* are stubborn self-willed exile from the loving breast! "But it was all right, everything was all right, the struggle was finished. He had won the victory over himself. He loved Big Brother."

Leave word with [Carl] Solomon or someone accessible where you will be this weekend. I will try to be around.

I turned to write you in respite from the ugliness of the last days, archangel.

Love,

Allen

Allen Ginsberg [New York, New York] to Jack Kerouac [New York, New York]

ca. February 1950

Sunday Night

Dear Jack:

I went home, and after settling all practical matters and putting others off, I sat down and read your book [*The Town and the City*] through on Saturday—from about 10–1:30 and then 3–2 at night.

First things first (or easiest things to speak of first) I was overly pessimistic before about Giroux's effect. The book is definitely helped in some very important ways—two principally:

1. There was hardly any point at which I felt that your prose was exaggerated or overstrained beyond sympathy.

2. I saw (as I did not see the first time—perhaps this is the effect of rereading) the structure more clearly and was continually pleasurably surprised by

the inevitability of section after section of development of the history of each character, each thing in its turn. It seemed at moments clearly consummately in control. Your manly (Goethean) intelligence emerges and created its effects in a way of ease and "virtuoso" of craft that I feared to hope for and only half realized was possible anyway—you continually surprised me and led me along.

On the other hand (to speak negatively for a moment) I think it is unfortunate that many beautiful and sometimes necessary solo flights were eliminated. I mean:

1. Rain sleeps
2. New York and Dennison [Burroughs]
3. The Figure of Waldo
4. The "Vultures of the Andes" on press boxes
5. Francis Martin's experience with the Three Witches at the funeral.

I can't remember of course what has been taken out and number 1 and 4 are only slight changes of rhetoric (sentences or paragraphs) but the elimination of 5 is unfortunate to my eyes. I will speak of that presently. The New York scene is excellently compact now but it lacks focus on the immediate moment of tragic crises—you don't see the death of Waldo, and loses some of the impact—it seems less important than I think it is (unless you want to eliminate the whole wood sub-plot and make it an incidental scene). I wish the shuddering blind man and Palmyra Towers were still there. The way it is now you don't really feel that Kenny is inwardly as tied up with Waldo (spiritually) as he really is.

I also seem to remember a beautiful panoramic description of a truck drive thru the west which I was looking for and is gone—Joe.

As I always said (before) I felt that you gave Francis too little nobility at times. In the beginning and through most of the scenes (especially the figure in the dark perch) he has great dignity. I wish he (and maybe Wilfred Engles) were greater men at parties, or do you really mean he is all dried up? But the light of comprehension was shining most strongly in his late arrival at the funeral and the rippling waves of the 3 ladies. So that he is left a little unfinished at the end—and he is one of the most beautiful characters too.

But to conclude this speech about surface—I think Giroux is definitely O.K. and I'm sorry that I mistrusted him. Further if you want my (prophetic) opinion— it's a truly great book deserving of a great response and I am pretty sure that it will make a big stir and get singing reviews. I think that it will swing in every way, swinging I mean. Furthermore if anybody gets nasty call me in and I'll challenge him to a duel—you have nothing to be humiliated about in any way, it would be crass perversity to dislike your work (and you).

Now I will answer your letter, which I avoided doing. Angel, you amaze me.

(I must tell you I am inconsiderate and impercipient.) The first time I read your book I cried because your sense of the world was so beautiful—but not merely that—really rock bottom true, and ultra bony there, real and with the quality of gentleness, tenderness, care, selflessness and experience and the wisdom of life which there can be—which makes me cry whenever someone shows me it. But I always fall back to careful slothful levels and underestimate you even at the moments when I seek you most—and to find in you such sweet expressiveness again shakes tears out of my Hebrew face. I am made of the same gentle stuff as thee—I know you and I know again that you know me.

Perhaps it is true that knowledge is not known day to day but only in lifetimes or art eternities but I am grateful for your forbearance if such it is until our eyes meet again in your laborious work.

I know your power full well in your work and I am amazed that it is so clear and ripe "concluded" (your art is conclusive)—amazed past envy (at moments) into tears or (not so much awe) but revelatory wonder. You teach me over about the Lamb. I only wish I knew how to meet you in the present light of our soul daily and show back openly some part of the peace I bare thee sometime when I read thee right.

I know you are honest but I never realized how sincere you are. Your book continues and concludes with final sincere self-statements (not horrible revelations but peaceful) that exhaust possibility—the real thing, if I may use a Huncke and turn a maudlin phrase.

I wish we could show our true face more often. I don't want to say any more because you know how I feel. I don't want to be rhetorical (though through images I may summon up a Flash of the Shepherd). I hate to short change you by losing sight of you in an abstract ecstasy of our funeral or whatever life is. [Sentence washed out by water.] Just the same I hate to lose the opportunity to pitch a little woo.

As a result of your book I was able to see Neal more closely today and we were more than gravely polite to each other tonight and I brought Varda up to Diana's for an hour for him to meet.

Isn't everything really complete, though?

Well, Zagg,[3] I guess I'll close now because I have to go to bed.

I am going if possible to see Schapiro sometime Thursday afternoon; and then to Neal's lot that night to show him the paintings. Get in touch with me somehow this week so I can call you up and tell you what exact arrangements have been made for Meyer Schapiro—through Holmes? C. Solomon is going away for a week.

---

[3] Zagg was one of Kerouac's nicknames from childhood.

Also I expect to see Lenrow (to return a book and perhaps have supper) Friday afternoon, if you would enjoy seeing him then call him.

I would like to write prose and may soon. Still afraid of work, but might also write a longer "Shroudy Stranger" poem with embalmess and ecstasy of unreals and corruption, visions of the Booder [Buddha], ghost tidings, window's aglory, pigs asses, dungeons of the lamb, dark shaggy things of the sea, the monstrous lights of the Sahara, and tears out of my Hebrew face and gas.

O Tears out of my Hebrew face.

Allen

P.S. Also your poem is comprehensible now.
I was jealous of Neal's blood-brotherhood.

Allen Ginsberg [Paterson, New Jersey] to Jack Kerouac [n.p., New York, New York?]

Paterson February 24, '49 [*sic*: 1950]

Mon Cher ami Jean:

Because I left the hospital today and carried my belongings directly to Paterson, I will not see you this week, and so am writing.

I received a letter from Giroux sent Feb. 17. He tried unsuccessfully to peddle my poems, and said that he went out of his way to do it because he liked them. He does not think the book is publishable yet, and in addition thinks that my private idiom needs a channel to the public through magazines first; and suggests prose, which he will look at, to make a name first. Half page letter, concluding with presentation of Saroyan's *Assyrian*,[4] signed Bob. I went to the office and picked up my material, and also stole a copy of *Cocktail Party* [by T. S. Eliot] (the world owes me at least that $3 worth of heart balm). He also suggested I try *Poetry* magazine (now edited by one Karl Schapiro). I saw Van Doren briefly, told him the results, said I would try *Poetry* (once again, as they rejected poems this year already), and asked him to intercede with *Partisan*. It seems so far that I have not been able to make any magazine, which is not right. I will be surprised if I can't place anything at all that way in the next year at least. I do not know if this situation has anything to do with the lack of drive I have to work. But no more complaints, I don't find that publishing has the same glory that it once had when I wanted to be supreme.

---

[4] *The Assyrian and Other Stories,* by William Saroyan.

I am in Paterson and I move into the house tomorrow. As soon as I am settled and the weather looks to be warm, come out. I will be in N.Y. Monday, Tuesday, and Thursday morning for the next months to see my doctor. I can see you around 1:30 Thursday anywhere. Send postcard to my new address which is 416 East 34 Street, Paterson.

A turning point has been reached in that I am not going to have anymore homosexual affairs anymore: my will is free enough now to put this in writing as a final statement.

Verne [Neal Cassady] seems a little pathetic and dizzy from time to time as I visit him at Diana's. I had to get back home one night this week, and he refused to say goodbye or understand that I wanted to go but kept on reading me passages and pages of Hindus-Céline[5] past my pumpkin hour; and then when I forced the issue by interrupting him to apologize and say goodbye he accused me (jokingly) of wasting time. (Time, he meant by that, I should be out the door instead of explaining that I was sorry that I had to interrupt) Ah. But the mono-maniacal, almost purposeful (on purpose) way in which, though he knew I had to go by the minute, he just kept reading to me, irritated me. Sheer perversion. He was trying to formulate some tender communion other than this attritive imposition; that is his trouble. He doesn't know what he is doing. I am annoyed by his insistence that he does: he thinks so because he has built a wall of mental plans. You can hardly get a word or a look in edgewise, the way he juggles Time to keep it from settling. I know this because I know from feeling-sight, as well as from the fact that when he is cool or not on edge, on some good days, he is altogether different. But there is so much invisible burden of the past on his mind that he seldom can escape. Verne is very young in spirit.

I will not speak of my creative plans (which are beginning to bud again). I am going to write non-metrical poetry for a while, I think. I have learned enough about surface. Is *The Gates Of Wrath* a good short novel title? Or is it like Steinbeck?

Do you find me distant or frigid of sentiment lately? I'm not, I assure you, Jean. Not toward Verne, either.

The American myth of Wolfe and power and pathos is changing in this decade. What is happening I realized this week, reading Wolfe's credo, is that we are nearer to the edge of inevitable social transformation that are going to affect us in thought and sense: for one thing, do you realize how much nearer the alignment of east against west has become, especially since English sway in elections? If we could carry this off, it were different; but I feel in my bones that

[5] *The Crippled Giant: A Literary Relationship with Louis-Ferdinand Céline,* by Milton Hindus.

we are not really the world-spirit-power, but that Russia is actually stronger, militarily already, potentially more overwhelming, perhaps even in her myths now, and I think that Wolfe's "lost" America may be reduced to the pathetic status of self-deception. We are used to thinking of ourselves in sophisticated life and fortune power thoughts, but it may actually be that we are swollen with pitiful pride and history will bypass us (even me and you) in the next half century. We will become a sort of greater Spain, or Portugal. Dig? And not merely *Life* magazine myth, that is just the false formal consciousness of America—but pioneer America will not have the significance that it once had. Did you see the subway ads for *Texas, Li'l Darling*?[6] It looks like a decadent capitalist satire in crude form out of Russian propaganda magazine, satirizing chauvinistic Americans machine enthusiasms. Nobody here is (Paterson) aware that anything might happen—depression, war—to shake up the U.S. again from top to bottom. Nobody knows seriousness outside of self.

These are random thoughts of the moment. Don't know if they mean anything. Might however be prophecy about real time.

400,000 unemployed in N.Y. on relief.

Stepmother thinks your book (half read) is much better than most novels.

> *Ton ami.*
> Allen of Paterson

Allen Ginsberg [Paterson, New Jersey] to Jack Kerouac [n.p., New York, New York?]

ca. March 1950

Dear Jack:

Missed you last Thursday. How was Lowell? Well, it is now arranged that you make your literary debut (in the little mag. that is) in *Neurotica* in the same issue as me. I went down on my knees (practically: took me days to recover from the fury) to Landesman[7] to get him to publish "Pull My Daisy." He finally agreed but I had to chop the poem down to half its size so he could squeeze it in; it still looks good. I did that on the basis of my service to him by recommending [Carl] Solomon to his attention. I ran back and forth and Carl turned out a great hip-cool essay on insulin and madness and hospital and sanity.[8]

---

[6] *Texas, Li'l Darling* is a musical by Johnny Mercer and Robert Emmett Dolan.
[7] Jay Landesman, the editor of *Neurotica*, published their collaborative poem under Ginsberg's name with the title "Song: Fie My Fum" in the spring 1950 issue.
[8] Carl Solomon's piece also appeared in the spring 1950 issue of *Neurotica* under the pseudonym Carl Goy.

Landesman and [John Clellon] Holmes read it and agree its probably the best article they ever printed. It too will be with our issue. Make sure, incidentally, that you do give them your work, so that everything will not be anticlimactic in my eyes. I was so pleased by Carl's success (Landesman, college Joe himself, thinks that Carl is a great new discovery) that I ran to Neal and started him off on an article on car stealing, hoping that some small achievement of his might give everybody a shot in the arm; also for sentiment. Well, he was pleased like little boy (his better nature) at so much responsibility. I make it a point to cut in at 75 St.[9] early Monday and Thursday morning (8:30) for two hours before going uptown to my Doc.

Also last Thursday I had lunch with poetry editor of *New Yorker* [Howard Moss]. I sent him poems which he passed on to chiefs but they rejected them on three different occasions. He will look at my book and see if he can find anything they can use. Probably will be able to find something. He also invited me to a party at his house next Thursday (this Thursday) at 11 at nite: young poets who are speaking at a YMHA poetry series, in their honor. He will also introduce me to Dylan Thomas in two weeks. I think if I get around and meet people I may be able to get poems published. Lucien will come to party with Barbara [Hale]; you come too, if you can.

I saw Lu [Lucien Carr] last night. We agreed that your book [*The Town and the City*] had no advertisement and this was a serious situation. Suggest you talk to somebody at Harcourt and if this fails wire Giroux explaining situation and asking what's up. It doesn't seem natural for there to be so little advertising, at such a crucial time, and it may make a tremendous difference. *T&C* could sink into obscurity if they don't make a lot of noise. This may sound like old wives gossip but my original optimistic prognosis, reinforced in my mind by reviews, is being rapidly undermined in my own mind by fears about some commercial slipup unforeseen brought on by Harcourt. Do something. Man the lifeboats. Get Rome on the phone. You have a duty to protect your investments. Don't hesitate. Time is crucial. I am serious. Why is that stinking company advertising nothing in the Sunday papers but Merton? This can ruin everything.

You will he happy to hear that Lucien (himself) said that L.M. Jones's review in the magazine was a lot of "obvious" literary bullshit. Remember, Lucien is a realist. I write this down because I was taken aback by it myself, as I guess you were.

Don't have a mind of my own. Do you?

I see you as a slob, too, in the same way that I see myself as a self-conscious

[9] Diana Hansen's apartment, where Neal Cassady was staying, was on 75th Street in Manhattan.

wreck (at the Paterson party), and, as I understand Claude [Lucien Carr], himself, actually sees himself. Trouble with Neal is that he won't admit that he is just a slob to himself. The slob is the truth (not the whole, but a major aspect of the true truth) and it is on this humility that we are true to life. As you spoke of yourself in the Damnation of Pokipsie [Poughkeepsie], 27 years old and alone, fat bellied, that is how I see you. You should look around seriously as you propose to find someone who'll love you for yourself alone, and not your golden hair, and who'll you'll seriously respect in family humility. I am slowly finding that the only future. I look to Carl, in my imagination, as a kind of teacher in this respect. Carl says "The world is a wonderful place," on the phone this morning: he woke me up to read me a poem called "Thank you, Sir" and quoted me a line of Melville's "The yearning voids recoil, for terrible is earth." Terrible here meaning awesome; the void-gone-yearning is afraid of the family density of life.

I told Neal to go to the hospital.

I feel the approach of a permanent spring fever. The best spring fever is that which seeks love and warmth, and is without ideas or fever or nerves, and spends sunny Sunday walking in the park and realizing how peaceful life is.

I am glad that Fitzgerald[10] likes me, in any phase, and that he digs me as Levinsky. I will write him a note (fifty pages) the first spring day.

Carl said that I should lay down the law to Neal when he tries to get me into a witch dance. He said: "Neal has to come down. Neal has to come down. Neal has to come down."

Your suggestions about my writing usually set me off inanimately for hours. (mass-observation note) [. . .]

Henceforth let's enjoy life. No more suffering, no more woe. I hope this letter finds you in a merry mood.

Your buddy,
Allen of Paterson

Editors' Note: Ginsberg's stay in the mental hospital led him to believe that he could cure his own homosexuality if he wanted to. For this reason he tried to find women sexually attractive and finally he lost his virginity with a woman that summer in Provincetown, Massachusetts, as he described in this letter to Kerouac, who was visiting Burroughs in Mexico.

[10] Jack Fitzgerald was a classmate of Ginsberg's at Columbia and a jazz aficionado.

Allen Ginsberg [Paterson, New Jersey] to Jack Kerouac [Mexico City, Mexico]

Saturday Night, July 8, 1950

Dearest Jack:

If you are in any ennui or doldrums, lift up your heart, there IS something new under the sun. I have started into a new season, choosing women as my theme. I love Helen Parker, and she loves me, as far as the feeble efforts to understanding of three days spent with her in Provincetown can discover. Many of my fears and imaginations and dun rags fell from me after the first night I slept with her, when we understood that we wanted each other and began a love affair, with all the trimmings of Eros and memory and nearly impossible transportation problems.

She is very great, every way—at last, a beautiful, intelligent woman who has been around and bears the scars of every type of knowledge and yet struggles with the serpent knowing full well the loneliness of being left with the apple of knowledge and the snake only. We talk and talk, I entertain her in grand manner with my best groomed Hungarian manner, and I play Levinsky-on-the-trollycar, or mad hipster with cosmic vibrations, and then, O wonder, I am like myself, and we talk on seriously and intimately without irony about all sorts of subjects, from the most obscure metaphysical through a gamut to the natural self; then we screw, and I am all man and full of love, and then we smoke and talk some more, and sleep, and get up and eat, etc.

The first days after I lost my cherry—does everybody feel like that? I wandered around in the most benign and courteous stupor of delight at the perfection of nature; I felt the ease and relief of knowledge that all the maddening walls of Heaven were finally down, that all my olden aking corridors were traveled out of, that all my queerness was a camp, unnecessary, morbid, so lacking in completion and sharing of love as to be almost as bad as impotence and celibacy, which it practically was, anyway. And the fantasies I began having about all sorts of girls, for the first time freely and with the knowledge that they were satisfiable.

Ah, Jack, I always said that I would be a great lover some day. I am, I am at last. My lady is so fine that none compare. And how can she resist me? I'm old, I'm full of love, when I'm aroused I'm like a veritable bull of tenderness; I have no pride of heart, I know all about all worlds, I'm poetic, I'm antipoetic, I'm a labor leader, I'm a madman, I'm a man, I'm a man, I've got a cock. And I have no illusions, and like a virgin I have all of them, I'm wise, I'm simple. And she,

she's a great old woman with a beautiful face and a perfect fair body that everybody in the neighborhood calls a whore. She's so sharp, and she never makes me shudder. She don't want war, she wants love.

Apparently I have quite respectable precedents—she was engaged to Dos Passos for over a year, he took her and kids to Cuba then, she lunched with Hemingway, knows all kinds of literary people. She was also engaged awhile and helped midwife Thomas Heggen with *Mister Roberts*; he later suicided. (he-he!) But none, she says, compare to me. That's what a woman is for, to make you feel good, and vice-versa.

Then, her children, they are the most knocked out pair of flaming red haired, angelic, wise young boys (age 5 and 10) I ever saw. They need a father, which alas (this is the crux of practical problems) I am sure I cannot be, for financial and other unhappy reasons, such as not wanting to get stuck permanently with the situation. So we talk about this too.

I am in Paterson—I still work, so can't see her much, though I pine. She offered to set me up with her in Cape Cod, she working, I staying home writing and caring for kids, but I can't see it as I still see doctor and want to get in a position of being financially stable somehow (though at the moment I am so beat for money I am a dog). Then to Key West for winter, if I want. Ug, so much joy!

Hal Chase sure picked himself a screwy cold chick.

Tell Joan [Burroughs] that my fair damsel originally reminded me of her, and much of their personal inborn style is alike. You must also tell me what weary, skeptical comments Bill comes on with.

I only wish you were here to talk to. Lucien is so much himself—he patted me on the back mockingly, kept buying me drinks at 4 AM the night I got back in town, asking me sardonic lascivious and practical questions, declaring that he didn't believe a word I said.

By god, I've been canorked with a feather!

Neal rearrived here 2 weeks ago, his car broke down in Texas so he planed back. He and Diana [Hansen] are having trouble between them, partly over practical plans—at this point he's acting slightly gruff and mean, and she weeps; he's also kind of shuddery and nervous. I would be if I were him. He never should have let her have a baby—they were doing ok till she began to try capturing him with authority and ritual, and the baby was or became a kind of trick, which he let pass ambiguously; now its marriage, they were in Newark the other day (with [John Clellon] Holmes and [Alan] Harrington) to get a license. Now he is restive, lost his job, had a call from the Frisco railroad, and is going back west in a few days. He promises to write, he will save money, he will be back when he's laid off; but she, that foolish girl, is beginning to see that she is stuck with the fruit of her too-greedy lust for him; and in the long run I believe she's fucked herself up, and him too, somewhat, by disturbing the balance they had before. She knew what she was getting into, but it was not only serious love, it was a kind of soupy insistence born of jealousy and vanity, that made her assume she would succeed in "fixing" him up.

I never saw him so detailed and rich as in his high description of Mexico, the quartz crystals, and the mambo in that side town.

Helen, I meant to tell you, knows everyone of all sorts—Cannastras, Landesmans, even the Trotskyite and hip types like bearded viper Stanley Gould at San Remo. (Know him?) I saw him the other day in Minetta [Tavern], he was shrunk and thin with junk; and such a messed up youngster too, who doesn't know what he is missing, and is full of hip despair and terrible pride. I was so heart-shaken—not having seen him for half a year, and having met him on the first steps of the road downward, if I may call it such, since he's degenerating with dissipation into a mere substitute for the right, intelligent active cat that he is, that I said to him, haltingly, "You ought to eat more. Guard your health, its the only thing you have." And he smiled on me, half hinkty, and said, "Sure man, are you carrying anything?" in the most intimately viperish tone I heard since Huncke went away to become a cowboy.

How is your novel coming along? I am going to give Helen my copy of *T&C* [*The Town and the City*] to read. I am poor, I write nothing. I keep fearing for the permanence of this sad nothingness of creation.

I got your letter and read it as an opera on Wotabulshit most terrible of all. Write me, make a plan for me.

> Love,
> Allen

Tell Bill that my fright as he described it is quite accurate, and it took me a long time to get over it; but it also was a fear of having put my money on the wrong horse spiritually and sexually; and I was frightened when I discovered that I had, though the race was not yet over; and my bet had consequences to others besides myself—such a responsibility! yet!

1952

Editors' Note: Later in 1950, Jack Kerouac married Joan Haverty, whom he had known only for a few weeks. While they were living together, Jack composed a long scroll version of the novel he had been working on for several years, which eventually became On the Road. *When Joan became pregnant the couple split up. Jan Kerouac was born in February 1952. During this period, Ginsberg continued to live in Paterson and work at temporary jobs while writing poetry. He and Jack communicated in person more often than via the mails. Their correspondence picked up again in 1952, at which point Kerouac was in San Francisco visiting Neal Cassady and William Burroughs was awaiting trial in Mexico, having accidentally shot his common-law wife, Joan, in a tragic incident the previous September.*

Allen Ginsberg [Paterson, New Jersey] to
Jack Kerouac and Neal Cassady [San Francisco, California]

ca. February 1952

Dear Jack: and Neal:

O I'm so full of delirium today! Your letter arrived, and last night I opened a strange letter from the Hotel Weston in New York, I couldn't figger out who it was from. But I wrote W.C. Williams a crazy jazz letter (mentioning you) last week and sending him weird poems. And his letter (I repeat it entire for the sweetness of it) sed:

"Dear Allen:

Wonderful! really you shall be the *center* of my new poem—of which I shall tell you: the extension of *Paterson*. (I shall be proud to bring you the *Paterson IV*.)

For it I shall use your "Metaphysics" as the head (as some shit uses a quotation from some helpless Greek in Greek—to precede his poem)

How many of such poems as these do you own? You *must* have a book. I shall see that you get it. Don't throw anything away. These are *it*.

I am in N.Y.C. for a winter vacation. Home Sunday. The next week-end we'll do something. I'll get in touch with your father.

yours,

devotedly,

Bill"

I opened it and said aloud "God!" The poems he is referring to (he is also referring to an earlier request to me to take him down to River Street Paterson for an addition to his poem, after my father wrote him inviting him here, and he replied yes and sent me a message that he wanted to dig my Shrouded Street area) a bunch of short crappy scraps I picked out of my journals and fixed up like poems, the like of which I could write ten a day to order: like:

Metaphysics
This is the one and only
firmament; therefore
it is the absolute world;
there is no other world.
I am living in Eternity:
The ways of this world
are the ways of Heaven.

and

Long Live The Spiderweb
Seven years' words wasted
waiting on the spiderweb,
    seven years'
thoughts hearkening the host,
    seven years' lost
sentience naming images,
narrowing down the name
to nothing,
    seven years'
fears in a web of ancient measure,
the words dead
flies, a crop
of ghosts.
The spider is dead.

and [seven other poems . . .]

Now you realizes you old bonepoles, the two of you, whuzzat means? I can get a book out if I want! New Directions (I guess). Whaw? An you realize further, [William Carlos] Williams is also nutty as a fruitcake. It also means we can *all* get books out (just you and me and Neal) (don't tell Lamantia,[1] he's too polite) all we got to do: I have a new method of Poetry. All you got to do is look

---

[1] Philip Lamantia was one of the poets who read at the famous Six Gallery reading in 1955.

over your notebooks (that's where I got those poems) or lay down on a couch, and think of anything that comes into your head, especially the miseries, the mis'ries, or night thoughts when you can't sleep an hour before sleeping, only get up and write it down. Then arrange it lines of 2, 3 or 4 words each, don't bother about sentences, in sections of 2, 3 or 4 lines each. We'll have a huge collected anthology of American Kicks and Mental Musseries. The American Spiritual Museum. A gorgeous gallery of Hip American Devises. Like:

> Today I am 32.
> What! So soon?
> Wha' hoppen to my wife?
> I kilt her.
> Wha hoppen to my hop?
> I smokt it.
> Wha hoppen to my kids?
> I et em for dinner
> lass week.
> Wha hoppen to my car?
> Smasht it agin a telephant pole.
> Wha hoppen to mine career?
> Down the drain, down the drain.

So much for that.

I canna make tail of your letter? Who signed what? Who calleth me sweetheart? Don't you guys got names no more?

Stamp money I, impoverished, will send you. What happened when my poetry was read aloud? Anybody cry? Send me Peotl [peyote]. Tell Lamantia I need Peotl for my methaphysical moo. Good! you wrote Bill [Burroughs]. I will give Ginger one big abstraction. I still never seen John H [Clellon Holmes]. But he will appear.

BUSINESS!!!!!

See? Carl [Solomon] sent contract. Lousy contract (what no million?) but its O.K.[2] Look it over. Also, finish book soon, so you don't have to wait alla way to 1954 to collect more moolah. Gene [Eugene Brooks] sent you legal letter. See boy? Alan Ansen[3] they will publish, but don't really want to give him advance. Carl also asking French major friend of mine to translate Genet's *Journal du Voleur*. Also Carl pushing Bill [Burroughs]'s book for a Wyn paperbound. That's

[2] Solomon, working at Ace Books for his uncle, A. A. Wyn, gave Kerouac a contract for *On the Road*, offering him a $1,000 advance, but Kerouac never signed it.

[3] Alan Ansen was a friend and poet, at one time working as W. H. Auden's secretary.

OK it means money, and posterity will have it, same as if it was New Directions. But I will work on New Directions.

Yes Jack *On the Road* will be the First American Novel. By gum we going places. Prose in letter was great. California and Neal are great for you. But what amante shall we find for Neal to make him keep writing? If I came out there would he do it? No, I'm afraid I'd only annoy the pants offa you, boy. But rillly, I'm feeling so fine—and there's a huge Eastern snowfall on my doorstep in Paterson.

Yes yess, add, add addup. Finish the novel soon. We'll all be on kicks. Speaking winkwise, I believe you its the first modern novel.

Oh Lucien he's just newly married, that's all that's wrong with him aside from a slight case of being a congenital sourpuss. Love Lucien, anyway.

But what can be done with Hal [Chase]? Nobody even knows his address? How can I reach him? Tell me in detail—or have [Al] Hinkle write me details etc. I will compose a huge insane letter and send him it; he won't know what to think, so maybe he'll answer. He's not sick, he's just showing off. First thing Kind King Mind must do is dye his golden hair green.

Really this letter is silly.

Pretty poems on Melville and Whitman. I sent Van Doren our mutually typed Melville notes. Haven't talked to him since.

Young friend named Gregory Corso[4] left for coast, didn't see him before he left, but you may run into him. Two years ago he used to watch Dusty [Moreland] undress through window from furnished room across the street. I introduced him. He was in love with her. He too's a poet. But Dusty won't marry me, I asked her? What can I do? But I'll present your petition too. Maybe she'll marry all three of us? Think of the great wedding night ball.

You must meet [William Carlos] Williams, he digs us, I'm giving him your books and will show him your letters. He's old, and not hip in our way, but he's innocence itself and picks up himself just like that.

Your abstraction is shore superior. Save the pastels. I incidentally knew it was yours minute I laid eyes in it. Like a signature.

I have been sleeping with all the girls around Columbia, from Barnard, I mean. I'm entering a huge transformation to passivity now. I don't know when it happened, I don't make love no more, I just lay back and let people blow me. (It don't work on Dusty though—never lay her no more). Send on your whale of a bitch and I'll see that it gets in print, or send it to Carl and he'll do the leg work, I'm getting too hincty to do that free anymore (except for total recalcitrants like Neal who don't know what they're missing by not farting in public.)

---

[4] Gregory Corso became one of the leading poets of the Beat Generation.

The only man alive who really writes like us at all is Faulkner. *Soldier's Pay*. 25¢ pocket book.

I didn't read about Moby Dick, send clipping. I have huge candid photos from Lucien's wedding [January 1952]. No, I'm shipping NMU [National Maritime Union] soon as I see Williams, as dishwasher on passenger ship, then after month being yeoman. Then come back and get ANALYZED. Yahh! Make Neal write me via wire recorder, you transcribe.

Whazzis 12 Adler?[5] Whooz Ed. Roberts?

     gone,

         Allen

Jack Kerouac [San Francisco, California] to Allen Ginsberg [n.p., Paterson, New Jersey?]

ca. February 1952

Dear Allen:

Williams is right: the original impulse of the mind is in the "prose seed" or first wild draft of the poem, the "formal ode" is a dull suit covering the great exciting nude body of reality etc. I think these your great poems here but I think (also) your rooming house poems about the cockroach on the door and the growing old in the floor is just as great but mainly this is the—I'm trying to talk seriously about your work in a hurry . . . but no hurry. Death's head Dusty is great lil poem: "Sunset is greater this way, because steel is naked like naked thoughts unplanned but ored up from dark mind." In fact the "blood" (remember) you later inserted, probably for carnal,—is not something that's "missing" from this poem but is the seed of another about sundown steels. I believe this and know my own mind on subject. Remember Van Doren talking about tightrope Shakespeare over the abyss, or that he was a balloon floating over it? I like "imagined purposes" in eternity. (Say, why haven't you commented on my great ink angel with the poem?) Your Metaphysics is worthy of Williams' quote and by God he must be a great man not only to "do this for you," but to be so smart as to use pure lines like that at the head of his great next-extending epic *Paterson* of late-life flow towards eternity . . . Dostoevsky was the wildest writer in the world at 57; we're young punks. Is "Long Live the Spiderweb" spontaneous as presented or reworked?

Listen, I love you, you knew that didn't you?—still you—fuck Lucien, he's my—he doesn't respond, he stepped on me but I don't know why and especially

[5] Adler Place was a popular neighborhood bar in North Beach, San Francisco.

the times with all meaningless sadisms. But why do I say this? in a letter of critical mentions. "Negroes climbing around" is a supreme example of your funny
vision of the world—also looking for that toilet—as if you were saying hm as you
traversed spiderweb halls in long black pants, stroking your chin, among iron
rings, covered with dust of big tears in the black rent curtain of the sky somewhere beyond . . oh hell, negroes climbing around is just like the place where
those kids swim back O' the mills. Also it's like yr old vision of the negroes digging NY from a Harlem eminence in a park. Say, I have a gone line—a poem too:
but never mind. ("Paranoia about a crash." (say it out loud). The Trembling of the
Veil is perfection itself; it reminds me of a poem *Richmond Hill* I wrote:

> A cluster of yellow November leaves
> in an otherwise bare
> and sheepish castrated tree
> send up a little meek PLICK
> as they rub together
> preparing to die—
> When I see a leaf fall
> I always say goodbye.*

[five lines crossed out here and beside them written "Phooey"]

> *
> . . . The area breathes to want
> to tell something
> intelligible to me.

Don't show this note to Williams, he'll know I wrote it just so he could see
it. The arms of the trees bending at once when the wind pushes them, is like
Whitman for awe and suspense and like dewdrop flowerstems sunflowers and
all your favorite Alice in Wonderland miracles of poesy. See, the value of your
mind is in its spontaneity, it has no other. Considered thought is for existential
generals who love battles anyway and for Spenglerian high late men who are all
embroiled in squadrons of bureaucracy and expensive [?] and cuckoldry
in midtown funny cocktail blahs. Please dig my closing lines of *On the Road*
John has—every time I compliment you on a line I have to think of one of my
own to draw a compliment in return from you, but be that as it may, don't go
around thinking that I ain't the old boy still with these shit slingings in the page,
who was it first fardeled you and threw crinnicks in your hair, when the—dig
this: " . . . at night now drove back, north, right out Insurgentes the way we
come in, Ferrocarril Mexicano hunting his left hubcaps, in the dark, across the

136

holy biblical plains by the first starlight the wise men made. Far across the dewy cacti the coyote crowed his oats with a long dog grin a burley sack hung from a nail, an icon flickered in the tree, the wines of repentance flowed in the stream. Bent over his wheel like a madman (Neal this is, driving back to NY), shirtless, hatless, the moon leering on his shoulder, the apex of the night sweeping back in a fast shroud, he unrolled his old word-joint by cracking the door over the bumps and [?] of night. Did he see any lights?" (late chapter of *On the Road*, in which dig Neal (Crafeen) as a traditional Irish hero.) Also, I further, commenting on his handsome snapshots, how his children will look at them. Our, his children will look at (those pictures) and say "My daddy was a strapping young man in 1950, he strutted down the street as cute as can be and for all a few troubles he has that Irish fortitude and strength—ah coffin eatest thou old strength for they meal, and throw worms?" (or "pass worms" which is best?)* How can the tragic children tell what it is their fathers killed, enjoyed and what joyed in and killed them to make them crop open like vegetable windfalls in a bin . . . poor manure, man," But that's enuf quotes, you won't appreciate them in these rough little letters, better on a big manuscript page. Ask Williams if you can what he thinks of that prose.

Please write often; join the MCS! [Marine Cooks and Stewards Union]—
Jack

* shit worms?

P.S. I haven't written Bill [Burroughs] yet—don't want Kells' [Elvins] wife to know my address.

Allen Ginsberg [New York, New York] to Neal Cassady and Jack Kerouac [n.p., San Francisco, California?]

New York
10:PM: Thursday Feb 15, 52

Dear Neal and Jack:

I am living in the same house as you saw on 15th St., Jack, but now upstairs in the garret. Last night I had my eyes closed sleeping (half asleep) and thinking about Neal's birthday, which led me to think of my own in 6 months—I will be 26 like Neal. It has been occurring to me often that years now seem shorter, more fast to fly. At 26 we are almost 30 actually, and I woke with a powerful knock of awareness at my heart, my eyes flew open, I saw time flying like an enormous bird. We are getting to our age of most power, our peak. I feel older and clearer than I ever did—though at the same time more irretrievable isolated in the huge dream of the world. I don't really see much future, since by now I should be more *connected* to outside things, like $ and society. Whatever I want, I still am not what I wanted to be, none of the many kinds of things I wanted to be—and perhaps will not. The opening of eyes goes on.

I will tell you about New York. Claude [Lucien Carr] was married at a huge party—enough of social details. Now he and C. [Cessa] live around the block from [Jerry] Newman's store—they drink and throw things at each other, just like always, only a little different since Claude thinks now that he always has to make up one way or the other. I see him every week. He says, "Why did Jack leave before the wedding without saying goodbye." I say "He thought you were rejecting him." He says, "Well, he sure thought right." But he has asked me several times why you weren't there, and what did you think? He is just the same. He likes his father in law, old Von Harz was standing on his balcony a few doors down from Dusty's old apt. on a snowy day, surveying the street. Claude came down the street and threw a snowball at him, "right in the puss." Old Van Harz said "Well you're feeling in high spirits but you could have broken the French window." Claude then explains that Von Harz broke it himself a week before in rage, while tugging and pushing at it impatiently when it was stuck.

Burroughs has been writing. He is very lonely—write him, care of Kells, Turf Club, Mexico DF. His boy [Lewis] Marker left him temporarily on a visit to Florida, is to rejoin him in Ecuador any week. I've been calling Laughlin[6] but no word yet. Still considering (seriously apparently) Bill says: "Meanwhile things seem kind of dreary around here. Several other people I like left about the same time. I want to get the case settled and clear out." His kids have been claimed by respective grandparents. No word of Hal [Chase].

I saw [Bill] Garver[7] (did I see you since then, Jack?) who says Phil White killed himself in Tombs[8] because he was up on three raps, tried to get out of it by stool pigeoning on an old *schmecker* who didn't sell to whores and kids only to respectable criminals. Thereby he got out on two raps. Last rap (non-narcotics) still hung him, was going to bring him to Rikers. But old *schmecker* and the boys were waiting for him at Rikers Island. So hung self in Tombs. Like tragic movie. Said Garver "I never thought he had much character. But what else could he do, he was washed up as a junkie in N.Y." Said Burroughs (letter January 19) "He was so uncompromising and puritanical about stool pigeons. He used to say 'I don't

---

[6] James Laughlin was the owner and publisher of New Directions Books.
[7] Bill Garver was a small-time thief and drug dealer befriended by Burroughs.
[8] The Manhattan House of Detention in lower Manhattan was commonly referred to as "The Tombs."

understand how a pigeon can live with himself." I guess Phil couldn't after what he did. Even so I still haven't changed my opinion of Phil."

Dusty has returned and has new greater apartment with shy frightened mother at 19 Barrow Street—same place as Henri Cru[9] used to live, right around corner from Louis' Bar. I dream of marrying her but don't have the force or money, and we don't love each other. We are great tired friends now—we talk a lot, sleep once in a while, but never screw. I am, myself, getting tired of sex. Which reminds me of a limerick I used to know:

> There once was a young man from Datchet
> Who chopped off his cock with a hatchet,
> And said "Well, that's over,
> But my little dog Rover
> Is hungry. Here Rover! Now catch it."

The great line is the third. This reminds me of a joke I once told you. Carl S. [Solomon] and I were sitting around with a Subterranean in his old pad on 17th Street. The third guy was a young villager I had met briefly several years earlier—tall, thin, rather big boned, white faced and pale, with (as I remember) dark? hair. He was reputed to be one of the most intelligent people, an apocalyptic, and poet. He said very little, was not surly, though, just very silent and too gone hipwise to talk. So Carl and I embarked on a conversational conspiracy—we told silly jokes, limericks, dirty jokes—very neighborly like and relaxed and dull (including the above limerick.) Suddenly John Hoffman[10] (the subterranean, whose name and fortune you know) started to tell a joke, in a very straight and low voice—he had a lugubrious solemn voice, very deep and weary.

"There was a cat who killed his mother—to collect on the insurance. They lived in an old house in Frisco and he didn't get along with her anyway. He wanted to collect the insurance on her so he could take things cool for a change. But he knocked her off with a hatchet and suddenly he dug that if he tried to collect on her, he'd wind up taking a murder rap instead. So he decided not to blow his top and he finished off the job by chopping up her anatomy carefully; and every night he'd pick up a leg, or a shoulder, put it in a paper bag, and carry it out to the city dump. So he got rid of his old lady piece by piece until on the last night, he was beginning to breathe easier again. He was walking down the street toward the dump and he had in his paper bag her heart, the last of her corpse. Just when he went to cross the street he slipped off the curb unex-

[9] Henri Cru was a classmate and friend of Kerouac's at Horace Mann who appeared as Remi Boncoeur in *On the Road*.
[10] John Hoffman was a poet who died in Mexico in 1952 at the age of 24.

pectedly and went down, falling right on top of the bag, squashing it. He almost blew his top and picked himself up, cursing, when all of a sudden he heard a sad, frightened voice: 'Did I hurt you, son?'"

I remember how his story shocked me, it fell like a maniacal bombshell, told in that solemn and world empty voice. That's the deepest I remember of Hoffman.

I see you are digging Lamantia, who is a very interesting chap. Neal, I remember, met him (and possibly H. [John Hoffman]) years ago at Solomon's. Give him my regards, I am glad you know each other. Of course he's cool—but did I ever tell you how, in the long space of dreary time when Jack was away, and Claude up the river, and I had not met Neal, I used to haunt the art library at Columbia, in a post Rimbaud love, and read Surrealist magazines. Well, I was astounded one day, when in *VVV*[11] (3 V's) a N.Y. transplantation of the style, a magazine like *View*, I ran into the poems of thirteen year old Lamantia (1945–4)—and I even remember envying and admiring him. I even remember two lines from a meaningless poem

> at the bottom of the Lake
> at the bottom of the Lake

a refrain of some sort. I followed his career vaguely, and ran into him in N.Y. also 2 years ago with great joy at the widening circle. Now you have him around.

Send *me* some peyote. Who else you know? How about digging Henry Miller?

Carl is serious about Neal's manuscript. Neal, get to it, honey lamb. He'll give you money and you are a great man.

How I miss both of you, and wish I were there with you so that we could share hearts again. I know I am hard to get along with and proud. I insulted Jack before he left and felt many twinges of sadness, that's what I meant in the telegram. I only hope that you two are not laughing at me or mocking me when I am here away from your warmth. Write me, I think about you all the time, and have no one to talk to as only we can talk.

So I have been reading a lot of things—Balzac (*Goriot* and *Distinguished Provincial*) Herman Hesse, Kafka's great diaries, Faulkner's *Requiem* and *Soldier's Pay*, cumming's *Enormous Room*, W. C. Williams' Autobiography, R. Lowell's poetry, Goethe's *Werther*, Lawrence's *Plumed Serpent*, Hardy's *Jude the Obscure*; Gogol's unknown novels; Stendhal's *Charterhouse*, Ansen's essays on Auden; Holmes' book, Genet's *Miracle of the Rose*, etc. Genet is the

---

[11] *VVV* was a magazine of Surrealist writing, published from 1942 to 1944.

most beautiful. He is also a great poet, I am translating a poem called "*Le Con-damne a Mort*" ("Man in Death Cell")—Maurice Pilorge, his lover says—a long poem—65 huge Dakar Doldrums—pornographic stanzas of love—great as "*Bateau Ivre*." In the Cell, he says—

1. *"Ne chante pas ce soir les 'Costeauds de La Lune'"*
(Tonite don't sing me the "Hoods of the Moon.")
2. *Gamin d'or sois piutot princesse d'un tour*
(Golden boy, go be a Princess in a tower)
3. *Revant melancholique a notre pauvre amour*
(With a melancholy dream of our poor love)
4. *ou sois le mousse blonde qui veille a la grand' hune.*
(or be the blond cabinboy up on the mast)
(like Melville's dream)

The stanza before goes

Dis moi quel malheur fou fait eclater ton oeil
D'un desespir si haut . . .

Tell me, what crazy unhappiness lit up your eye with a despair so high . . . etc.

Well there's a lot of great golden-obscene poetry—I can't have time to write it, like

"Enfant d'honneur si beau / corrone / de lilas!
[. . .]

John Holmes' novel [*Go*] is no good, I believe. I was shocked when I got his eyedea of me. But maybe I'm so prejudiced. John Hall Wheelock, his editor, says that Holmes' conception is of a real poet, and that the poems (imitations of mine) are profound mystic poetry. Whore! Whore! Whore! as old Bull uster say; or how wondrous doth the Wheel of the World turn! But I say Wheelock is a fool, and Holmes because he talks nice and treats self badly in book, as badly as me or you, is not so much of a fool.

However Marian and John [Holmes] have actually separated. He lives some-where else now. I went by to see him, he wasn't home, I haven't heard of him since. I wait developments.

I've been spending weekends out at Alan Ansen's house (you and Neal drop him a hello Valentine)—and am acting as his agent. He's also writing a strange literary but very sad novel about a spectre of a party at Cannastra's. Perhaps I will be able to get Auden essays in book by him through Mardeau's [Alene Lee] publisher (Goreham Munson, an old-time midtown ninny.) Ansen sends regards to Al Hinkle. So do I, thank them for the pretty Christmas card they sent me.

I love a great new group of Subterraneans—I pointed out one Bill Keck, the N.Y. peyotl connection, to Jack. See if Lamantia knows him (and Anton [Rosenberg], Norrie, and Stanley Gould of course) and I see Peter Van Meter, and may move in with him while I'm waiting for a ship.

I registered Jan. 7 with NMU [National Maritime Union], have a tripcard as a yeoman, but have been going to the Hall, and no tripcard yeoman's job has come up. That's all besides reading, writing and socializing that I've been doing. I go there every day from 10 AM 11-/ to 3 PM. My registration is running out, I don't know *what* I'll do, except hang on and really make a ship, as I do want to. I don't know how you would do if, Jack, you came east. Norfolk, of course, perhaps but who knows what's going on in Norfolk? There are very few tripcard yeomen in N.Y. but still no free jobs.

As for Wyn, Jack, the whole thing will be easily resolved if you: 1. Write A.A. Wyn (Jollson) a note of two paragraphs, saying you are working on the novel and feel sure that a first version of it will be complete on (_____) you fill in date, but not too near, give yourself at least one year to integrate your notes and ideas.

Tell him in as few words as possible and in as *least* alarming manner as possible that you have changed your plan or method of approach somewhat, but like what you have as a result.

And say that of course you know he will have the final say-so on publication, you have that in mind and feel sure that you and he will see eye to eye on completed manuscript, and you are of course willing to make revisions as he suggests, compatible with your own idea of integrity of structure.

On this basis (knowing that you may have to do some re-integrative revision, or that is, have to sweat out a little extra work,) tell him that contract as proposed by Carl is O.K., and that Carl knows how you want money apportioned. (Carl hasn't showed him your other letter yet)—(and also Carl will consult with Eugene [Brooks] on legal details—that's all there is to it.) Let's see you rejoice with the Ball of God. Send the letter, if O.K. by you, immediately, and you'll have contract signed and O.K. in jiffy and be free to do what you want and finish book.

It sounds O.K. to me as described in Carl's letter, broken up sections and all—just like last Faulkner book. All I wonder is if you're trying to escape (as I always do) the sweat of patient integration and structuring which you slaved over on *T. and C.* This my aside, is what Carl is worried about. Aside from that book sounds O.K. as it is if it is as you describe it.

Please also write Laughlin (New Directions) 333 6th Ave. N.Y.C.—a short note telling him how much you like Bill's book recommending it for prose and great archive value, and telling him you're out of town and I'm Denison [Burroughs]'s connection here for moment. I wrote him six page letter (to Laughlin) telling him why it's great book. I have revised version Bill sent up two weeks ago,—smoother, now, not so weird Reichian. Great book. If Laughlin no want, we'll peddle it to cheap paper cover 25¢ Gold Medal or Signet books, like *I, Mobster.*

How or when will I ever hear your records? I sit here and my soul lacks you Neal and you Jack. I hope my ship goes your way to Frisco. I don't want ever to fade from your minds.

> Love,
> Allen

I read this over and it sounds so weak and matter of fact and hung up on details so as to bore you, while I see your bloody-red clouds of the western flood and Pacific riding by me here to the Atlantic. Send me a smoke signal from the cloud factory.

Jack Kerouac [San Francisco, California] to Allen Ginsberg [Paterson, New Jersey]

February 25, 1952

Dear Allen:

Your latest poem, about the poor young cowboy in his Texas shroud automobile ["A Crazy Spiritual"] is almost the best and maybe the best you've ever done and Neal himself specifically thought so tonight and leave it just as it is, except, leave "wooden leg" instead of "pegleg" it's better rhythm and purer and originaller, so that's a great, great poem.

I think you should call your collected poems *Don't Knowbody Laff Behind My America Hunchback* and use a picture on the cover of you sitting in that shroudy stranger sewage pipe Wilburg Pippin Central Park, remember?

Also, when you find time, tell Carl [Solomon] the picture for the cover of *On the Road* is in Pippin's[12] possession. [. . .]

Go down there and get your own picture of shroudy sewer too and I want my *On the Road* picture the one with the cigarette; Sara Yokley[13] has only other

[12] Gene Pippin was a Columbia classmate.
[13] Sara Yokley was a girlfriend of Kerouac's.

copy (and while you're at it pick up picture of Neal at mantelpiece with dollar over his cock, remember?)

Bill [Burroughs] just wrote and's waiting for me to join him at 210 Orizaba [Mexico City] . . . his case still pending. I'm ready to fly soon. [Lewis] Marker being gone, he resumed habit "for health."

Incidentally do NOT tell Bill I'm writing a book about him because he may get self-conscious and uninteresting and I really want to sketch him unawares, you dig.

What'll I call this latest new book after *Road*?

How about *DOWN*?

Yes, your latest poem is the finest suprafine, nothing wrong with anything you do lately, and so write to me again, I like to hear everything, etc.

I sent Carl excerpt of *Road* to reassure him and proposed papercover separate shorter edition of *Road* (sexy party) and also publication in papercover of Lucien novel (the one Bill and I wrote together 1945 [*And The Hippos Were Boiled In Their Tanks*]) but you must beware of telling Lucien who will object and have us thrown in the madhouse the whole literary movement and slam the door after us in the name of politics of the United Press and the United States of Amerkee.

Don't nobody fuck with the spiderweb.

What's wrong with the spiderweb ["Long Live the Spiderweb"] is that you *didn't* spend seven years wasting on it, you did a lot of other too, ha hee hee.

(It's okay, don't worry).

and your Harlem vision I don't understand the difference between abstract description of something and mystical description . . . if you feel my Richmond Hill tree poem is, as you say, "exactly the same kick" then how can you make big tsimmis about one vision when, as proved by Richmond Hill to me, you can get high and "mystical" or "abstract" anytime anywhere; goes for you too of course, you so high alla time whatsa matter you dumb dope you hey stumboutsa mougavala, yr current poetry is, to me, best.

Allen Ginsberg [n.p., New York, New York?] to Jack Kerouac and Neal Cassady [San Francisco, California]

ca. March 8, 1952

Mon Cher Jack, Mon Cher Neal:

Things is going great. Since I last wrote you I have been working steadily at typewriter piecing together mad poems—I have already 100 of them, I'm jumping. Listen to this: I'm putting together fragments of "Shroudy Stranger," with a small descriptive poem—too busy on fragments to get to the EPIC which will be next. [the draft of "Fragments of the Monument" was included here]

Now, what I want to know from you: my fantasies and phrases have gotten so lovingly mixed up in yours, Jack, I hardly know whose is which and who's used what: like rainfall's hood and moon is half yours. I am enclosing copies of poems that seem to stem from you, like rhetoric at end of "Long Poem"—is "very summa and dove" yours? I'm not haggling I just want to know if it's OK to use anything I want that creeps in?

Spoke to [William Carlos] Williams on phone, go down to River Street tomorrow. He said he already (he hasn't seen the whole hundred, just about five poems) spoken with Random House (I thought it was going to be New Directions) and book may be there. Isn't this crazy? I've been off my nut with work and giggling. Speaking of which one poem enclosed beginning "Now Mind is Clear" sounds like synopsis of Giggling Ling. Is that OK? Also I enclose, "After Gogol." Do or did you use the idea? If I use it will it screw up you? Fuck, lets both use it. [John] Hollander thinks I have burst forth like Rilke and cries whenever he looks at me, for amazement. But I tell you really, though I'll be depressed and incompetent and in a bughouse in three weeks, I swear I really have got the whole metrical problem at last by the balls, and that been holding me up—meter, breaking out of it, and talking like we really talk, about madtown. I was all wrong.

Listen to these "poems": (a book if any will be called *Scratches in the Ledger*; and will be dedicated to Jack Kerouac, Lucien Carr and Neal Cassady: "VAST GENIUSES OF AMERICA WHO HAVE GIVEN ME METHOD AND FACT")

Jack Kerouac [San Francisco, California] to Allen Ginsberg [Paterson, New Jersey]

March 15, 1952

Dear Allen:

Blow, baby, blow!

I never knew you'd realize you're great poet without my help (in telling you, that is, not in genius, "assistance") (is completely your own). Summa and dove.

In fact your letter was read by big great Neal and, without even knowing of its existence, Carolyn found it under the garbage sink where the baby girls threw it; otherwise I might never have seen it. (Neal loves you—he just works sixteen hours, twenty hours a day at hard crazy labour, for no reason except alleviation of his anxieties about the world and also saving up for a big Carolyn-homecoming trip to Tennessee in their station wagon all five of 'em—Jamie, Cathy, Jack Allen, Neal, Carolyn—I may ride with them far as Nogales to go get me a store of T. [marijuana] for my next litry effort—but Neal's awright, disregard he can't write, he has no thumb.)[14]

The only phrase which I have used in *On the Road* is "strange angel"—disregard ANY worries about "stealing from each other"—I steal from you all the time, it's okay—anything that creeps in is the only truth . . . we're creeping in the shroud. Please however, make these two improvements in your poems

1. it was to be a mass of images moving on a page . . .

(NOT "moving on *the* page"—see?)

moving on a page is like "paranoia about a crash."

Correction No. 2—also,—

Cuban cousin meets Cuban cousin

in a dim-lit listing focasle.

not "in a dim-lit foc'sle" because that spelling is too labored, obvious and stupid, as we all know . . . by deliberately misspelling focasle (instead of forecastle) you are using a poet's prerogative which was once a seaman's—I know everything about language, I'm like Ezra Pound in a past.

I must type up *On the Road* at once but dammit Neal and the railroad keep pestering me with work, and I keep losing the money I painfully earn in stupid accidents and connections that don't come back with my loot, I'd rather lay up in the attic with my innumerable moans, broke.

What will
I care if I faced my responsibilities
instead of my mysteries?

is I guess the greatest statement you ever made. Didn't I show this kind of enthusiasm before Random House? When you "open your mouth to sing," however, you are the end . . . and the beginning . . . the greatest living poet in America and I guess the world, "no hyacinthic imagination can express this cloaked man"

Now we shall go to Paris and Venice together, within a year.

CARROUASSADY is the name of the 3 vast geniuses, but don't fuck up your dedication with *that* anagram.

---

[14] Cassady had struck LuAnne Henderson on the head and injured his thumb. It became infected, and a portion was amputated.

One possible furtherbility

make "jumping with jazz *into* the Pacific" like you mused . . . maybe, only maybe . . . LATER, in a bum beanery on 3rd St.

I must be headed for a big breakdown, I've never been so exhilarated and exuberant—like you, I'm blowing my top with words words—They come to me muting in a mad dream, I have it all solved, etc.—Good bad, so what, okay, Allen, Neal C. I'm going to see him in fifteen minutes at his tire-recap garage, drink wine from my pocket while he works, we'll talk about you, go home for supper together, pick up a can after in the evening, we're inseparable, immitigable, unsolvable, won. The "French onion soup" in this bum joint tastes like a shroudy stranger tincan special. I threw horseradish in.

I think it would be a good idea for you to use those side-remarks like you have in your letter to me—"I think of this week's humiliations" capped with "opening statement" on the side, you know what I'm talkin about . . . and "the shame of my poor beat down brother" is capped "example," and then "the whole crooked ass unlazarus like lot of em" capped curse, and then "not a come in a carload" is "expansion of curse," a pure method. Incidentally, too, don't say "crooked assed" but just let "crooked ass" adverb its way by itself.

Love for sale, daddy, love for sale

Let me know about [William Carlos] Williams on River Street if you did it together.

I haven't written to Bill [Burroughs] but will tonight because I think I'll go to Mexico for two months now.

When do you think we should go to Paris? I'll be passing thru NY before year's out, as seaman, so we can plan and write; a colored buddy of mine is going to make it with me there, either meet me, or go with me, his intention being, to eat lovely white girl's cunts and mine to fuck and eat them . . . but with you it would be big Genet underground explorations at the same time and the glamour of our two books about to come out and [Bob] Burford, [Allan] Temko, all of em,[15] and wine, the gamut. I am have become completely sexmad and completely incidentally straight, that is no virile Ow without aMOw . . . When you realize that the "shrouded stranger" itself was my original phrase, and as you say, "lovingly mixed up with my phrases" etc. there's nothing we can do about it—I think I could find some of my prose which uses some of your feelings, lemme see, but anyway, don't worry about that at all because I'm

[15] In 1949, Kerouac had hoped to join a group of his Denver friends—Ed White, Bob Burford, Allan Temko, and others—who were all living in Paris

overflowing and don't need anything or to worry about anything, so long as I've got my wine and shit and cunt I guess. Haven't been laid for three months except—shit, tell Dusty. No on the other hand, hell, fuck it—Just now dammit two men walking down the street with wine bottles and a swaddled baby, pause a while in a waterfront door to slug, the baby's too young to know—I realized they just don't know how completely sad life or themselves or the whole void is, damn I'm high and gone and a crazy one—drunk now, on wine, writing this to you, let me know, (O for Fhri cirhe eu) P

Please tell Carl Solomon to mail me, at once, the first 23 pages of *On the Road* so I can see what I'm working on, I have no copy of that myself. Okay? please do, it's important.

Eugene [Brooks] sent me splendid efficient legal papers that will save the day for me; I appreciate him hugely; he doesn't ask for fees; but when I see him, or in the future, soon, I can give him, if he needs, what ever it is, or whatall, you know, embarrassing; but in any case he's great and thank him personally for me in your own words, as I've thanked him in a letter recently.

I'm going to start typing my novel this week.

I'm just rambling, don't know what I'm saying, got to go buy bread now and Neal pays no attention to anything some days like today, he just says "Yeah, yeah," to everybody and anything, isn't listening, in fact is slightly deaf, and just doesn't care,—and this, finally is the reason why I can't establish a permanent formal relationship with him . . . I don't care if he *is* relaxed, I'm interested and excited and that's all, and will go to my founts without him. He's the most un-reassuring guy in the world. Incidentally, write a note to Carolyn next out, she really is a gone gal and the one likely successor to Joan (not Dusty, who isn't intelligent like C).

Well so long buddy I gotta go—morderoga. bye Allen Mountain

Give my best to everybody—say hello to Alan Ansen if you see him and how I'm still sorry I missed our appointment at his pad in Elmhurst when I came out here instead.

"Across from that rocky village with its cactus foundations is an earth of the young Jesus; they're bringing the goats home, long stepping Pantrio comes fumilgating along the maguey rows, his son gave him up a month ago to walk barefoot to Mexico City with home made mambo drum, his wife gathers blossoms and flax for his embroideries and kingdoms the young inquisitive carpenters of the village quaff pulque from urns in the goateries and shelli-meeli-mahim of Mohammedan Worldwide Fellaheen dusk and nightfall, Ali Babe be blessed."
Road

But please don't use any of my new words (such as fellaheen on a big scale like I'm doing for instance) till later altho I dig "inquisitive" as a you-word.

Jack

148

Allen Ginsberg [n.p., New York, New York?] to
Neal Cassady and Jack Kerouac [San Francisco, California]

March 20, 1952

March 20?

Dear Folks:

Well Neal I read your novel and it's coming along fine. Even the early tight-assed section on parents reads easily now (on 3rd or 4th reading. I read it a few times two years ago) and it improves with each reading—all that effort despairing as it was was not wasted but should be kept as is. It also gets better from rereading I notice more and more humor in it—the sections you invented are very great—as I was once struck with the collapsed porch and old man Harper. You seem right to me in thinking you are picking up pace and ease in jumping along in detail blowing Proustwise. As described in your letter to Carl [Solomon]—whether or not you had faith in yourself to go on in that way—you are right. The more frantic and personal you blow the better, it sounds more and more beautiful by the page.

I gather from Carl he is sending you letters telling you to go to writing classes (though he does accept and like your novel—more, even than he admits in public) but I think he—in fact I know he—is very hung up with his own personal metaphysics of publishing—and it is a metaphysical structure of no mean—and in fact it is a great structure—proportions who's labyrinths he is haunting these days (the last year)—so really disregard—I say, from my vantage point on top of the ass-teasing skyscraper pinnacle of the East—everything he says and continue to follow your and Jack's hearts. Carl is worried about form—and literally has confused whatever "form" is with the temporary, in fact weekly shiftings of necessity and opinion in his publishing office.

You see (both of you) he has now on hand a million strains and squabbles at Wyn's. He's really the only one there with any knowledge and everything hip he does is so fucked up and made problem of by his office he is having a nervous breakdown almost. He went off, in fact, this week, for a week's rest. Alone in the woods upstate N.Y. in a rest camp for "physically—mentally tired businessmen." Among his problems have been:

1. Worrying how Jack's novel will turn out—he got frightened by Jack's description.

2. The de Angulo[16] book which Wyn handed posthumously to an editor

---

[16] Jaime de Angulo was an author and expert in anthropology and Native American culture.

whose revisions have now precipitated a major literary squabble between de ngulo's widow and office on one side, and Ezra Pound himself on the other.

3. The fact that Wyn has invested in several dear books like Jack's and are afraid to put out more money for [Alan] Ansen's novel (which is great Ansen) even though they actually want to publish it when its done and Ansen won't write any more unless they like gentlemen give him a token advance of $150–250 (with Carl caught in the middle).

4. Several great ideas of Carl's which they will sooner or later accept but due to office reorganization haven't noticed, etc.

5. My own crazy poetry and Holmes's book which his office rejected and which have found success elsewhere.

6. Wanting and not being able to get Alan Harrington's book yet.

All in all Carl—with my pushing him and yakking at him and trying to influence him all the time to counteract evil effects of office (we're even planning a Huncke revival)—has actually begun to officialize the new movement in literature which, Jack, as you said, years ago, is only us after all. All things considered I have really come to believe that between us three already we have the nucleus of a totally new historically important etc. etc. American creation. Nobody knows how ripe we are now already, yet.

I have therefore put all aside, including my shipping, to type up my poems and yak at Carl. Also he's taken *Junk* back by Bill and is trying to get them to read it and they're too dreamy to see yet but will inside of three weeks I think.

So this was to say for Neal that it is important to the future of America that he work fast—Denver is lonesome for her heroes, she waits with tears in her dreams like Billie Holiday and work as he wants not as Carl says—because the final thing is what interests Neal, You, which is great or anything.

It is us that is important—(not so much our juvenile egos but) our hearts our true hearts of our own—that is the end—whatever way we see it. Tee hee.

    Love

      Pope Ginsberg

Allen Ginsberg [New York, New York] to Jack Kerouac [San Francisco, California]

ca. late March 1952

Dear Jack:

I got your letters, got first note through John. You're the only one who's really understood the poetry—[William Carlos] Williams knows a lot but hasn't got the whole naked junkyard in the moonlight of his intelligence like you. I don't think—so far he's been acting like W.C. Fields—country doctor a little; keeps talking about "invenshun" of pure speech and knows whereat it lies—but certain things of our generation or mutual understanding escape him—however he's been perfect so far, no bitches, no egos, just amazing cooperation—said in fact he'd write an introduction, said to leave thoughts unfinished if I wanted—"like Cézanne left his canvasses unfinished" if he didn't figger what to do with a corner of the canvas.

We went out in Paterson, but got a little drunk in expensive downtown restaurant, talking about friend of his I met in Mexico, about Genet (who he likes), about Pound and Moore—I pointed him out antlers heads and silly signs in restaurant. Then we went to look at old swimming hole in middle of coteries, rode around in car on street, stopped and picked up a handful of trash at riverbank and made a poem then and there about its contents under the light of a riverside advertising signboard (piece of old concrete, sliver of tin, pin from a loom, 200 yr. old dogturd.) I wanted to take him to bars but he was old and wanted to go home, we went into one and vaguely dug the people, broken down white orchestra with accordion, then rode me home; sat in car. He said, "What's it all for?" I said, "Why?" He said, "I'm getting old—two years more and I'll be seventy." I said, "Are you afraid of death?" He and I looked into the asphalt suburban street road and he said, "Yes, I think that's it." So we talked for a minute about the asphalt pavement (what is there in it?) as if it were the walls of the universe. Saw him later at his house, went upstairs to his writing room, looked over book I left with him, discussed arrangement of poems and how hard it will be to publish. Read me a letter from Robert Lowell in Amsterdam ("it's like a grey Midwestern city"). Lowell is called Cal—or Caligula for short, on account of some old school class apocalypse years ago when they were talking about Rome—and Lowell leaned out of the hotel window in Chicago a few years ago and screamed "I AM JESUS CHRIST" before Alan Tate, eminent critic, pulled him back in and called doctors. Just like Cannastra and R. Gene Pippin combined. But nowhere I think. Will show Williams your letter.

But your specific understanding of certain things is my salvation: Lucien, for instance, liked poems, but said that the best ones were the "amusing ones." Hollander around Columbia liked them but worried about arrangement and Greek titles for them so they'd look like poems; Kingsland liked recherché ones about Marlene Dietrich. Dusty liked (eek!) the metaphysical ones best. But thoughts "ored up unplanned from dark mind" is the only true level. Thank you for specific comments, they matched my own ideas completely—despite all you did "talk seriously" about work; more incisively than anyone else knew. I guess that's the test now. So much for generalizations.

"Long Live the Spiderweb" is experimental poem; some seed of it was spontaneous, but it was only one consciously worked and re-worked for half rhymes, rhythms, arrangement of lines on the page, and structure of image (spider, web, flies, etc. etc.) I tried then to write a poem that looked "moderne" like in *Poetry* magazine. Lucien and Dusty like it, so Hollander. But I thought it was too arty and formal, sort of, though perhaps (what Lu thought, it contained horror-seed). Do you think this type is worth doing, or is as good or fresh as rest? I noticed you noticed it and asked if it was like others or "re-worked") (what sensitivity of you!)—what did you think—it was pretentious—I thought so a little, but am not sure. Would like your opinion—need only half sentence or two words answer on this—just as I'm not sure what to do—method—in future. Cockroach-rooming house poem Williams likes as part of whole too, that gets kept in.

Williams incidentally said he never was actually in Paterson except as younger man, he used to wander around—the whole poem itself, of his is just a head imagination—wanted to look at River St. for an epilogue about actuality, after all play is over (like an epilogue in hell or outside of world).

Neal I think must have "Ode to Sunset" (formal) around in an old letter (if he keeps them around) look it up maybe, and compare. I guess informal might be better—but in hospital I worked for six months line by line composing formal ode—practically wrote only that one poem all that time. Understand one is naked thought. But so much mental work, time, patience, craft gone into other. Wish I could publish them side by side.

You can write Bill [Burroughs] at 210 Orizaba and warn him not to let Kell's wife know your address. He's still at 210 Orizaba. Got enclosed letter from Laughlin rejecting *Junk*. Still working on Wyn paperbound, may work out.

I know you love me but I am not traveling around and am tied down yet by ideal of doctors, and not on kicks with you in Frisco and Neal, and don't hold it against me. I felt like an outsider when I wrote you first (on yellow ruled lined paper) and tried to get back in club. Don't nobody laff at me or insult me behind my American hunchback. Great picture you sent, would have liked to be in it. Enclose wedding party photo of me and Lucien, folded up. I have quadruplicate of same photo so am messing it up to send. Neal looks older, Jewish, very serious and on powerful integrity drive. I have information from above that he has passed intact through his Hell of being damned and is now ascending purgatory, perhaps is out of it, and is in no longer any danger for his soul, in fact has recently been accorded grave, the worst is over for him and he has entered a new universe. I think that's why he has been so silent, and withdrawn, to all appearances, the last two years.

"Trembling of Veil": written in journal two years after East Harlem, or a year.

At time when trying consciously to regain mystical eyesight; that's what title was. Veil not totally rent, just trembled. The aspect of appearance of tree verging on total mystical presence that flooded sight of universe during East Harlem visions. Tried to describe instead of abstractly, a specific thing how it looks mystically. Entry in journal that day (in Paterson) substantially the same as poem; followed two sentences later by parallel notation and explanation of method of eyesight in words about imagined purposes in eternity. Both really same poem, same note in journal, perhaps will combine. That was what I was talking about alla time about visions. Except eyesight was clear and total for few moments on everything in universe at once for a few seconds—sixty perhaps—in bookstore and out of Durgin's window. I keep explaining this because I was trying to check up my own thought and find out if anyone did does same (off tea)—do these poems say same to you as I've already over explained, or have you understood it already? Have I made too much of a tsimmis over this one point? I mean did those poems present anything new to my explanation? Your own "Richmond Hill" seems to me on exactly the same kick—certainly should keep five lines in middle about ants in orchestras, its the same thing as rest, and makes things even clearer, its very clear. ("That has a sound (PKICK) which is lost unless there is a country stillness etc.") Why'd you say phooey? Same reason I didn't realize value of own naked thoughts? It's very deceiving—I don't really know when I'm communicating myself, and when not—gives me a good feeling about realness of my own thoughts, that others understand them. Such a surprise, too—but few really understand. Those that do actually do though. The part about area breathes is important too. Can you write me a prefatory poem (you and Neal together or one each?) about similar subject—not about angels and shrouds so much as mysterious actual communications of very strange true thoughts that we have in common? Or anything you want anyway.

Actually didn't think till you write about strangeness of phrase arms of the trees. Thought green hairy protuberances was the neediest. That's why its confusing to me—I never noticed—can anyone—what's going on, in poem.

Didn't realize how seriously you were working in dreamy sentences and compound phrases in streams. Gets very good. Have just started reading Joyce's *Finnegan's Wake*, with skeleton key. Joyce is too hard—too much fooling around with verbal ideas and historical abstractions, so it's hard to understand him when he's referring to esoteric literary matters. But an American Joycean mode (bop inventions in lines, "shirtless, hatless, the moon leering over his shoulder" is great—think that's fine for you—gets the whole point of your personal myriad sense of enormousness of Neal-Bill-Huncke-me-tree across) would work and be read. Faulkner does it a little too, and understood. (I guess not too many shrouds and lots of particular moons, best.) Also coyote with dog grin, I noticed, in fact things of that paragraph I noticed were: Coyote, icon in tree didn't like wines of repentance on account of its like title of some middleclass novel (my Martha Gellhorn[17] Drapenport-Chicken-every-Golgotha); liked sentence bent over wheel, moon; liked fast shroud, but wondered about whole apex-shroud clause; liked old ford joint etc etc. Got to talk.

Whole sentence about "my daddy strutted" is on, including through vegetable bin.

Now second letter received on back of RR forms. Neal is working too hard on money problems, too bad he can't get some kind of peace for his own work. Don't he know he's forgiven and don't have to make up by crucifying self on practical exhaustion? anymore? Will have to think in a year when possible about getting him a subsidy.

You bastard I outright deny you made up phrase Shroudy Stranger, you'll hear from Brooks the lawyer tomorrow. I natcherly steal from you. But didn't you and I make it up together that day on York Avenue? Don't you go stealing my glory. Hole.

John [Clellon Holmes] wants to call his book "*GO.*" (so suggested his editor Burroughs Mitchell. Yes? How about *GO, MAN*. But maybe go. Better "*GO!*"

The two improvements you suggested are accepted, esp. focasle. Too bad I can't see you before book out, but probably will anyway. "River Street Blues" is other consciously worked poem, not finished yet—will be a long poem with real blues songs in it and more details about Paterson.

Mysteries—responsibilities was something I thought you said right out to me a long time ago.

The rhetoric of Song and our Hart Crane I don't know how or where to use so it will mean anything yet.

Paris? Would like to go but how should I know when? Williams says he will get me $1,000 Arts and Sciences grant after book out. Maybe on that?

What other side remarks did I have on crooked ass—poem? I forgot. You mention all up to expansion of curse (except the first) put them down and send them, I'll put it in.

If you hit NY you can live in my attic—I'm not there all the time, costs me only $4.50 per week to maintain.

I haven't been really laid for months either. Dusty ain't interested, have not been seeking anything out. Too tired, too unsuccessful. But got to get back to

---

[17] Martha Gellhorn was a novelist and war correspondent, and was married to Ernest Hemingway.

it, am losing touch with world without. But we can't be anywhere really while we're so hungup sexless and without relation with any females. Ask Caroline [Carolyn] for advice. Actually we're crazy, and that's no joke, that's why I don't want to go so much to Europe and play the Whitman character in front of well meaning admirers, who I'll vanity like take foolish. Why carry on in Europe, for me? Maybe I'll find love there, that's a reason, but everybody has empty Hemingway affairs in Europe or had. I don't want to go to Paris so I can write.

> How strange I am in Paris.
> I'm sitting up on top of
> the Eiffel Tower looking at
> an angel on the sacred heart
> church, wishing it were
> alive and looking me in the eyes.
> Gee Paris is Paterson. etc.

You know what I mean? It's such egotism to be a lonely writer in Europe, and I don't too much want to go there for that. However there will be maybe mad adventures. Kingsland met Genet in Paris, by the way. Kingsland had a great party (I wasn't there—he thought I was away) at which were Hohnsbean, Auden and his boys, [Chester] Kallman, etc.; famous harpsichordists and counts and patrons, and Marianne Moore, etc. Very amazing of Kingsland. He's living with an old queen, nice guy, on 57 St. Right around the corner from Marian Holmes, who is always drunk and John is not there (J. Holmes I mean) anymore.

Don't write me, don't send me eggsurps, I'll see them from Carl, don't waste time, but do write often short letters maybe with short facts about what's going on—don't take up your time. I have time to write, so I do and will.

I enclosed note to Neal, read his work and believe in it as much as I believe in mine for me and yours for you, and don't believe in Bill's *Junk* or John's *Go*. He [Neal] always reminded me of grim Julius Caesar on the trolley in Denver and iron bones of purity are emerging in his *First Third*. The end should be the most serious expression of serious soul ever seen, in these days in America if he goes on natcherally as he has done. He can afford to relax and let the perminess take over. The true gyzm (jizem, gyzem) of Cassady will roar o'er the pages like Niagara.

> Love,
> Allen

Jack Kerouac [San Francisco, California] to
Allen Ginsberg [Paterson, New Jersey]

late March, 1952

Dear Allen:

[. . .]

Appreciated your thing about you and Williams—I saw him, it's a classic night, he's 68, what's he got left . . . good thing he was at least a doctor, I feel shame all the time from all this poetry, I don't know how the hell I manage to live with myself being so open and cuntlike and silly like *ROAD* will be and you with your tragic "sandwich of pure meat" made me shudder and wish I could help you on Judgment Day . . . not in the face of God but your own when you realize . . . That pix of you and Lucien, he says your poetry is amusing in it . . . he looks like a successful snob, you look like a hipster from San Remo but I love you, don't doubt that part of it.

I'm just being Lucien like now. News of Bill's book astounding—I *knew* it, who else writes a full confession, hamstring your cunty old Merton's in a hog-farm, blah, Bill is still great; I wrote TWO weeks ago and asked him to take me to Ecuador with him and [Lewis] Marker, am waiting for his reply: here's a quote from the letter he wrote me:

"Dear Jack, I do not know how much longer I will be here. I am charged as a 'pernicious foreigner' and the immigration dept. will request my departure as soon as the case is settled . . ." (later) (talks about his new novel about queer, I'm suggesting he call it *Queer*, it's sequel to *Junk*, he says it's better, I bet it is too . . .) "And let me tell you, young man," (he writes) "that I *did not* 'leave my sexuality back somewhere on the opium road', that phrase has rankled with me all these years. I must ask of you, if I am to appear in your current opus, that I appear properly equipped." (and then adds, beyond period) "with male facilities. Jesus, man, you sure can pick your women. You needn't have cautioned me not to reveal your address to Kell's wife, she and me don't hardly say hello, I gather she don't like me" (this sounds like old Runyon 8th avenue bill don't it?) the PS is as follows: "Another thing, I am not entirely happy about appearing under the name of Old Bull Balloon, I cannot but feel that the epithet Bull contains an uncomplimentary reference, and I am by no means old . . . you'll be equipping" (equip again, the word twice) "me with white hair next book". Isn't that interesting from Bill? . . . in new book he is Bill Hubbard, incidentally. He says Dennison has been discovered by his mother, in *Town and City*, so he will have to use Sebert Lee as name in *Junk*, but to hide from Maw, but . . .

"I thought of Sebert Lee, but Sebert is like Seward and Lee is my mother's name. I guess it will do though." (end of letter). (crazy?)

If he sends for me, my third novel will be underway immediately . . . it will be about Bill sinking into South America, no title as yet, as vast as *On the Road*, tell Carl, also tell Carl I'm sending in *Road* completed and neatly typed and all considered and pruned no later than April. So I can start on novel No. 3, I want to hit onwards, one of these years I will knock off THREE masterpieces in one year like Shakespeare in his Hamlet-Lear-Julius Caesar year,—I didn't ask you to go to Paris with me because I need you, I was only being kind to a fellow writer and being traditional, fuck you too.

     Ti-Jean

       xxx

Hey, how lucky you are to have a home address like that Paterson home of your Paw's even tho as I know there, you, a ghost, etc. feel like an outsider and crazy but worse than that unliked or strange and from mars, but me, I have a terrible guilt and no-home and will never feel the same again on account of that cruel cruel little bitch [Joan Haverty] who really I think wants to have me killed—but that's alright, but they can't I'm too fast and strong, but Allen, you're awfully lucky to have your father still alive, and your brother at your side, even tho your poor mother is sick, you're a lucky good little kid, I wish I had a home in Paterson, I'm getting awfully tired of roaming and now (keep it to yourself for Christ sake, my mother writes that cops are haunting the house and priests are calling on her wanting to know my address, tell Eugene [Brooks] it's that Goddamn Brooklyn Uniform Support of Dependents and Abandonment Bureau of the DA there, the bastards want to change the country to "meet a problem," there're one million men in this country trying never to see their wives pusses again and these socialistic think-they're-well-meaning-pricks are trying to "solve" that, you and your bureaucracy, Tit, don't tell nobody but I have to leave even Frisco in due time course shit man I wish I was innocent again) to Ecuador, . . . which means equator, jungles, disease, Burroughs and his rotten martinis rotting . . . good enough for pricks like me.

    Well Allen, adieu

P.S. Tell John Holmes "Go, Go, Go" was the title of a story I wrote about me 'n Neal in a jazz joint, it was Giroux made up the title; he called his novel *Go* is a good idea for him, I got nothing to do with it, he wrote and asked me if it was one of my old rejected titles, Jesus Christ what am I supposed to be Jesus Christ? Also, yes, shrouded stranger you make up yourself talking to me that spring morn, Lucien woke up and talked to Huncke an hour later (I started by talking of pursuing figure in desert and you called him shrouded stranger and pulled a chair up to touch my knees and said "Well now lets talk about the s.s. [shrouded stranger]."

Are you really being published by Random House?

Might as well finish paper. Wish you were here. Having wonderful time. How's Harrington?

J'ever see Jose Garcia Villa anywheres? or whozit? Tell Cessa von Hartz Carr to hang on to that copy of *Town and City*, I'll pick it up in the next century the way things are going.

The pix of party made me wish I was back in my New York, which I originated.

Tell Lucien I wish I had been there to repay him in kind for what he done for me MY wedding party, being there, lending me money then giving me a fin, and being there that's all; he looks great with that carnation, he's a lovely fellow, tell him I look forward to drinking him under the table any time, I've changed and can now drink him under the table my gullet is so hugened.

I'm a wino in Frisco temporarily.

John Holmes is a latecomer, or that is, a pryer-intoer of our genuine literary movement made up of you, me, Neal, Bill, Hunkey (as yet unpublishable) and mebbe Lucien someday . . . just like other literary movements, and therefore John Holmes is really riding our wagon without knowing where actually it's headed (but you know and I know). (Boy)

Remember Joe May laughing in the streets of 14th bookshops? hey?

I don't understand your spiderweb. Get me an Arts and Science Grant, I'm starving in the wilderness, I have nothing but my seabag and no ship I have nothing, my mother gets all that Wyn money (most).

I've been getting laid lately, plenty, it makes no difference in what you write, it just makes your cock come alive again.

Could I live in your attic? the law would catch me, I'm a criminal, I'm going to *hurle dans les rues de Paris* soon, or someday, shoot somebody in Brussels, get elephantiasis in Port Stettenham mid Malaya,—I only want to go to Italy so a couple Lombard blondes sit on my head. dig? Listen, in late June a great cat is coming your way, Al Sublette off the *President Monroe*, treat him well, I'll hip you later, a great Negro simple hero, no intellectual or nothin, a friend of jazz musicians in St. Louis, I can' describe his greatness—later. Neal is great, his book is great, I'm disappointed in Carl's [Solomon] intelligence telling him to study Mickey Spillane, what does he think our boy is an idiot? Would I write a book about a dope?

Allen Ginsberg [n.p., New York, New York?] to
Jack Kerouac [n.p., San Francisco, California?]

late March–early April 1952

Dear Jack:

No news of my book's fate yet, is with [William Carlos] Williams and Random House, also another copy at *Commentary* magazine to see if they want anything. Showed Van Doren who liked and took me to Faculty Club twice in same week for lunch; made me feel accepted again almost. As we walked in the second time, I headed for bathroom before going to lunch, holding copy of poems under arm, he suddenly said, "Here you better let me hold that. You might pee on it." Said it right out of the blue. I can't understand that man. Also (after all these years finally) opined as I had obviously had a "Revelation" at some time or other to speak so plainly now. Said goodbye, and don't know when I'll see him ever again, out in the world on my own.

What will I realize on Judgment Day, seriously, about your comment on sandwich of pure meat? (Incidentally, I had to edit that poem, I originally had lines:

I ate a sandwich of pure meat, an
enormous sandwich of human flesh;
I noticed it also included a dirty
asshole while I was chewing on it.

I don't remember if I included that in version I sent you. Lucien shuddered and said to take it out it was disgusting, so I did, also for publisher, but that's why it says in heaven.)

Bill's book is going thru usual publishers crap which I am handling; they want to change things, etc. etc.; it's too short as is, they want *Queer* (a title Carl and I figured out simultaneous with you; such loving intermixture of thought) in first person (Bill's writing in 3rd) to fill out, want more outside detail on Bill's myth and life. Difficult mediations, and I see why Carl's going crazy there; it's so hard to be practical and sympathetic at once. And those people also are dumb, which makes matters worse, harder to deal with them.

I read last chapter you sent Carl, and liked it; missing the lines you sent in John Holmes's letter which were beautiful and I thought were to conclude book, too. No? Carl upset, doesn't understand references made, thought it was surrealist free association. Haven't got chapter here with me or would say more. Interested to know how book is organized now: how many sections of what kind in

159

what order? Hope will not have trouble at Wyn, but that's possible. I made Carl promise to let me see it and explain its virtues to him first before bringing it to office, as he is easily overwhelmed by violent prophecies of total catastrophe at the least sign of difficulty; that is due to his position at the nerve center of practical concerns. I have liked all the prose you sent me so far. I sent your letter to Williams. Hope he will become our ally. Possibly we will need such. Wish I had more experience and self-confidence in regard to dealings with Bill's book.

Sorry I was so stupid about Paris, I was talking straight and viewed possibility of Paris sans poetry as actual possibility and was weighing it in mind. I am submitting a short story I just wrote to *New Story* Contest (address: New Story Young Writer's Contest, 6 Boulevard Poissoniers, Paris 9 France). First Prize is trip to Paris and back plus month freeloading and living at *New Story*'s expense. Mine is called "The Monster of Dakar," about sea trip, futile search for hop and boy in Dakar, ending with assignation under streetlight made by pimp for me with local Mongolian idiot, only one he could find to sleep with me. Word limit is 7,000 and Saroyan among judges. Suggest you also enter if can make up or find story type story that length, must be done and postmarked May 1. Also money second prizes. One of us should wind up with something. Maybe we could actually wind up in Paris.

I am lucky to be taken care of, but it's only temporary unless I want to wind up the village idiot of Paterson, grubbing off family and eating their bread and having to obey my father and live under someone else's sway. Must get out of that and become independent, like you must; only can't figure way, but must, more important to me than writing, though writing may be my way of getting independence.

Carl upset you still starving and that your mother keeps your money. Why don't you use it yourself? You are in a worse hole than your mother. I spoke to Gene [Brooks] about wife and he said either change your address to keep safe or send Joan [Haverty] money (from another postal town) according to agreement. If want to stay in country safe and without anxiety, that's only way. You better do that with Wyn money. OK to visit Bill, but no use doing that because you're in such a hole you have to to be safe. You're letting yourself get too unnecessarily tangled up in sad fate. Must work out some free-er and happier way. Write me, what exactly is your financial situation, your mother's, and that in respect to Joan. Let's figure a way to clean things up before it gets further, makes writing paranoid, and life lousy. After all it's only question of enuf money to live and alimony. Don't go down the other side for nothing like that. Was upset by sadness of your last letters. That's strictly situation, external, not absolute and fixed fate for you unless you leave it be fixed fate. Am not being analytic-moral. None of us are fast and strong enuf to battle society forever really, it's too sad, and grey. Just felt you were feeling too crazy lately, and am putting out friend-hand. Tell me real situation as you see it and we can figure out something; maybe get more gold from Wyn. Can't never maybe be innocent again; have maybe to make own home. (This last lyrical abstract). But must not let situation drift to intolerability. We got too much else to do besides suffer.

Incidentally if you can get a copy of *American Mercury* for April 1952, there's a snotty story in it by Herb Gold about me (called the "Widening Flaw," like the widening gyre) which is more unpleasant than Holmes's book. Such notoriety. Really about me too. I didn't review that bastard's book for *Commentary* half year ago because I didn't like it and didn't want to bother saying anything unsympathetic or negative as matter of principle. Shows the difference in breed. He wrote me an apology (I sent him a card saying story stank and he was putting needles in my wax doll) saying he wrote it for money and also it wasn't really about me, the stupid liar. Such a Dostoevskyan position it put me in. If I write him back I have to be proving that an insulting story was really written about me.

[Alan] Harrington's wife (do you know?) has T.B. and she's away at a hospital, I haven't seen him. Never see Jose. Lucien said to tell you he was sorry you weren't there, too, and that he can drink you under the table anytime even if your guts was so hugened "they filled up your whole insides." We went to the circus, double date with me and Cessa's old roommate, and he said, when, over public address system, someone was paged, "Oh god mothers done it again, she's out on the Grand Concourse nude again."

[...]

Agree about Holmes. And he's so secretive, though. Lives alone now, is supposed to have a girl, but never says nothing, nobody knows what he's up to. The most mysterious of anybody. But a poor writer.

[...]

Carl is a friend, but is working for publisher; he's ok himself but has duties to do which may for temporary time be against the grain of our interests: i.e. changes in Bill's book, necessitated, they think, possibly rightly, by economic needs of publishing. Therefore deal with him as someone you have to deal with, though friend. He ain't you, you ain't him. That's as it gotta be. Only among lovers can we consider ourselves each other. Publishers are not lovers. They can't be and stay in business. However, they are not infallible in their own business. It's just all got to be worked out patiently. And, sad tho true you know often their business interests are actually not compatible with what is artistically and honestly true, or long-range beautiful. Not always incompatible, just sometimes: like can't publish Genet unexpurgated as would be put in jail. Or even can't publish my book as being for moment completely unprofitable. I decide that's O.K. They really can't. Like you can't stay away from work or lose job. They don't want to lose business, I don't necessarily want them to; just when I don't like them at all. This something conservative Alan Ansen taught me. Alan is a reactionary like Lucien, i.e. realist.

Jean Genet is in jail now in France on a murder charge, Carl found from publishers here. Catholic existentialists (Francois Mauriac) want to cut his head off. Big literary battle. Sartre trying to save him. Very wild death days for him. I think he wants to die like Cannastra. Don't know anymore facts. Write [Bob] Burford? Hear from Seymour [Wyse]? I did, he's ok said he wrote you. I saw Ed White. Not much to say. Will see him again for drunk talk.

Love,
Allen

Will pick up manuscript from your mother soon. Must tell Lucien, win him over. Swear he's the type he'd sue anyway. Will look over book, consider situation before digging him on it.

O.K. Hunchback, will ask Williams. Sounds crazy to me, too crazy, but who knows.

Richmond Hill: I can't do it anytime, only in moments of extreme wareness. Maybe that's the whole secret of my being nuts. Moments before were such, swept over me, knocked me down, opened my eye. Now I look at something; just a dead tree, or the idea of a live tree, but not the living presence, unless I make my mind do tricks; and mind tricks never so visionary as those that sweep over unawares and authentic.

DON'T ANSWER MY LETTERS just drop me a little line, answering specific questions. When you off to Mexico?

Jack Kerouac [Mexico City, Mexico] to Allen Ginsberg [Paterson, New Jersey]

May 10, 1952

May 10
c/o Williams (Burroughs)
Orizaba 210, Apt. 5
Mexico City, Mexico

Dear Allen:

It took Bill and I ten days to find this splendid typewriter and ribbon and only recently we resumed work on our respective books.

I have no idea how it could have been possible for Hilda, Joan [Haverty]'s siren friend from Albany (you know, the brunette) to write, a month ago, a letter to Kells' wife telling her I was coming to Mexico unless somebody in New York who knows my movements is hipping her and possibly Joan, not that it matters but why? Try to figure this leak for me, it ain't right.[18]

Neal left me at Sonora, Arizona, on the Mexican border. He had his car with the seats all out (station wagon) and had pillows and babies and Carolyn all gypsied and happy in the back. I left the happy domestic couple and started on my new adventure, at dawn. Crossed the wirefence into Sonora (it was Nogales Arizona, excuse me into Nogales Sonora I went). To save money I bought 2nd class bus tickets south . . . it became a tremendous Odyssey of bouncing over dirt roads through jungles and changing buses to cross rivers on makeshift rafts with sometimes the bus itself fording the river up the wheeltops, great. I hooked up soon enough, around Guyamas, with a Mexican hipcat named Enrique by asking him, as we stood in front of some nepal cactus if he ever tried peotl; yes he had; he showed me you could also eat the fruit of the nepal for the palate; mescal is the peotl cactus. He started teaching me Spanish. With him he had a handmade radio repair ohms and amperes gadget for appearances, also it was one of his crafts (he's 25) but actually we ended up using it for, *pour cacher la merde*, if you dig, which we picked up in an Oriental village or town called Culiacan, the opium center of the New World . . . I ate tortillas and carne in African stick huts in the jungle with pigs rubbing against my legs; I drank pure pulque from a pail, fresh from the field, from the plant, unfermented, pure milk of pulque makes you get the giggles, is the greatest drink in world. I ate strange new fruit, erenos, mangos, all kinds. In the back of the bus, drinking mescal, I sang bop for the Mexican singers who were curious to hear what it sounded like; I sang "Scrapple from the Apple" and Miles Davis' "Israel" (excuse, it was written by Johnny Carisi whom I once met in Remo) (wearing checked topcoat with fur collar). They sang me all the songs, did "Ah ya ya ya yay yoy yoy" that Mexican laugh-cry; in Culiacan we got off bus, me, Enrique, and his 17 year old footman tall six foot Indian Girardo, like a safari and started off down hot dobe streets of midnight, straight for the stick hut Indian outskirts of town; near the sea, in the tropic of cancer, hot night, but pleasant, and soft, no more Friscos, no more fogs. We came to a gigantic space between the dobe town and some huts and crossed in the moonlight; one dim light ahead, in a stick hut; E. knocked; door was opened by white garbed Indian in big sombrero but with downturned hunkey like Indian face and scornful eyes. Some talk, we went in. On the bed sat a big gal, Indian's wife; and then his buddy, an Indian goateed (not by style but didn't shave) hipster-junkey, in fact opium eater, barefoot and tattered and dreaming on the bed-edge, and Hunkey like;

---

[18] Kerouac was trying to avoid Joan Haverty, his second wife, during this period.

and on the floor a drunken snorting soldier who'd just eaten some O [opium] after lush. I sat on bed, Enrique, he squatted on floor, Big Girardo stood in corner like a statue; the host, scornful, made several angry remarks; I translated one of them, "Is this Americano following me from America?" He had once gone to America, to L.A., for maybe twelve hours, and someone rushed . . . well he the hero of the gone heroes tribe of Mexican Fellaheen Afternoons and Mexico (I saw the Lord Star from a bus) gave me a medallion to look at which was either torn from his neck or from another torn, see, but I think it was torn from him but he recovered it and he gestured showing how this American (maybe cop) tore it from his neck in L.A., that's what he did, was crucified in Los Angeles and returned to his Night Huts. Thus anger . . . understand, Allen that everything is going on in Indian dialect Spanish and that I am digging everything, all of it, almost perfectly, with my French Canadian mind in the middle of the Dakar village.

I thought I was beyond Darwin's chain,
A phosphorescent Jesus Christ in space, not a champion of the
    Fellaheen night
With my French Canadian mind.

Then Scornful, who was very husky and good-looking and dark, handed me a pellet and instructed my boy Enrique (who was squatting on the floor pleading for friendship and coolness but had to go through certain tests, just like two tribes meeting) so I looked at the pellet, and said opium, and Scornful laughed and was glad; pull'd out the weed, rolled several cigars, sprinkled O in them, and passed around. I got high on the second drag; I was sitting right next to the Indian Opium Saint who, whenever he succeeded in breaking into the conversation, made apparently vacuous or maybe mystic remarks that they in their practicality and hopness avoided—everybody, young Girardo, blasting. I got high and began to understand everything they said, and told them so, and chatted in Spanish with them, Scornful brought out a statue he'd made in Gesso . . . you turn it over and it's an enormous cock; they all put it on their flies seriously to show me, laffing only a little, and on the other side a, I think, woman of some kind, or human figure. They told me (it took a half hour, with writing in my notebook) that in Spanish the other word for Gesso was Yis, or Gis. I showed them things like Zotzilaha, the Bat God, Yohualticitl, Lady of the Lights, Lanahuatl, Lord of Lepers, Citalpol, the Great Star; and they nodded (from my notebook). Then they apparently talked about politics, and at one point, by candlelight, he the host said "The earth was ours," "*La terra esta la notre*" or however . . . I heard it clear as a bell and looked at him and we understood (about Indians I mean) (and after all my greatgreatgrandmother in Gaspe, 1700, you know, was an Indian, married my ancestry French baron) (but so they say in the family)—then it was time to retire, the three travelers went into Hunkey's hut and there they gave me the choice of the bed or the ground, the bed was a straw pallet on crisscross sticks with a piece of cardboard for insulation under which the Saint Junkey kept his fixings and shit. He was offering his bed to all three of us, it was too small, so we stretched out on the ground with my seabag as a common pillow, I tossed with Girardo for the outside position, I lay down, Hunkey went out to get some shit, and we blew out the candle. But first Enrique promised to tell me all the mysteries of that night in the morning, which he later forgot. I wanted to know if there was a secret underground Indian hipster organization of revolutionary thinkers (all of them scornful of American hipsters like John Hoffman and Lamantia who come down among them not for shit or kicks but with big pretenses of scholarship and superiority, this is what Scornful indicated) and not with pure Allen Ginsberg-like friendship on the corner on Times Square is what these Indians of course want, see, no bullshit and hinct, they need Hunkies) (in Frisco, the last week I visited Lamantia with Neal, he is living in the former stone small castle of Hymie Bongoola (you know the name [Jaime de Angulo]) overlooking Berkeley Calif. He was reading *The Book of the Dead*, was reclined in sumptuous couch with book and Hymie's old cancerous fourteen year old angora cat, and fireplace and rich furnishings and turned us on, three friends from Calif. U dropped in, a psychology major who is apparently his Burroughs, a tall handsome owner of the house (who is somewhat the Jack K.) (lounging on floor and sleeping eventually altho maybe his queer lover) and a young eager intelligent kid who was like you; this was his circle, and of course he was being Lucien, they talked about psychology in terms of "I saw that damned black background to the pink again in yesterday's peotl," "O well (Burroughs) it won't hurt you for awhile." (both snickering) Then: "Try this new drug, it may kill you, the greatest kick of all, man." (snicker, turning away, real serpentine and hateful he is, Lamantia, very unfriendly, very queer, I touched his hand briefly while exchanging joint and they were cold and snakelike). He showed me his poems about the Indian tribes on the San Luis Potosi plateau, I forget tribe name, they deal with his visions of Peotl, and they, the lines are,

    arranged
     like
       this, for effect, but more complicated.

But I was disappointed in Neal that night for not at least digging the [?] instead holding the floor all night talking about [?] shit, "Chug chug, there's the

165

engineer easy as you [?] as I told him later, we were like two Italian mountain peasants allowed by local nobles of the castle to chat with them for a night and had failed on account of Guidro talking about his cart and horse all the time. This made Neal mad, and the next night, for the first time in our lives, we had a fight—he refused to drive me to Lamantia, outright. He made up for it the next day (at Carolyn's urging because she loved us both) by buying a Chinese dinner, my favorite. But when I left Neal at Nogales I felt an undercurrent of sad hostility and also that he had hustled me there awful fast instead of the picnic we were going to have by the side of the road in Arizona or Imperial Valley even. So it goes, I dunno. But Neal was great and generous and good and my only complaint is cheap, i.e., he never talked with me any more, just "Yeah, yeah," almost sullen, but he was busy, but he is dead, but he is our brother, so okay, forget it. He needs another explosion, I can tell you that much; for now he is all hungup on complete all-the-way-down-the-line materialistic money and stealing-groceries anxieties and nothing else, positively. Carolyn has to stay in the house for months at a time while he works every day, seven days on railroad and other jobs, to pay for things they never use, like cars not a drop to drink in house usually, no shiazit any more, nothing and Neal always gone. This was my observation; Carolyn is a great woman. I think it will work out when they move to San Jose, in the country, and then C. can at least grow a garden and get her kicks in sun, there being no sun where they live now, or nothing, although I never was so happy in my life than in that splendid attic with 11th edition *Encyclopedia Britannica* . . . but my complaints are the least of it, and I want to tell you in person later, and you understand, I don't want to appear to be the ungrateful brother in law guest yakking in behind their backs which I ain't, I was happy and secure for the first time in years and the first thing Neal said was "Do anything you like, man." But to Culiacan: the candle out, I lay awake for an hour listening to the night sounds in the African village; footsteps crunched close to our door, all three of us stiffened; then they moved on; and sounds, rhythms, beasts, insects. Hunkey came back and slept, or dreamed. In the morning we all leapt up simultaneously and rubbed our eyes. I took a crap in a 1000-year old Indian stone crapper in the outdoors. Enrique went off and got me about two ounces of shit for equiv. $3, which is expensive down there but I had dough they knew. Then I got high again and sat listening, squatted, to noon sounds of village, which is a cooing, crooning, African, world Fellaheen sound, of women, children, men (in the yard was Scornful with a spear splitting twigs on the ground with great strokes of perfect aim, chatting and laughing with another spear wielder, mad); Hunkey just sat on bed with eyes open, moveless, a dead mad mystic Francis I tell you, down. Enrique rolled enormous Indian joints, laughed at my American sticks I rolled. In fact they roll em just the size of

Lucky Strikes so they can smoke on street unnoticed, round, firm. Then I got shakes (from no eat and bouncing for days) and they wondered at me; I sweated. Scornful went out and brought me hot food; I ate happy; they gave me hot peppers to revive my system; I drank a pop with it; they kept rushing out for soup, etc. I heard them high on tea discussing whose food it was . . . "Maria" . . . they gossiped after her; I saw enormous complexities of Indian noon-time gossip and love affairs, etc. Hunkey's wife came in for a brief giggling look at me; I bowed. Then I was surrounded by cops and soldiers. Guess what, all they wanted (tho my heart sank) was some tea; I gave a lot of it away. "I'm going to be arrested in Mexico finally," was my thought but nothing happened, and we left, safari, waving, and cut; in the heat of the day Enrique made us stop in the old church for a minute to rest and pray; then we moved on, left Girardo in Culiacan with tea and twenty pesos, got bus for Mazatlan, were entertained by young intellectual busline employee (two mission oranges) (at sidewalk crazy cafe) who said he read Flammarian . . . I told him I read existentialists, he nodded, smiled. Enroute to Mazatlan Enrique got a woman who offered us her house and food for ten pesos in Mazatlan that night, Enrique accepted cause he wanted to lay her, but I didn't feel like being a watcher of Spanish lovers, but I agreed; in Mazatlan we took our gear to her two aunts' house in the Dakar slums (you know Mazatlan is just like an African city, hot and flat right on the surf, no tourists whatever, the wonder spot of the Mexicos really but nobody hardly knows, a dusty crazy wild city on beautiful Acapulco surfs) and then Enrique and I went swimming, blasted bombers on sand, turned and [?]

"Look at the muchachas make the center of the world"—three little Biblical gals in robes and (I don't know why I'm writing this I've got to do my typing) Let me finish, instead of staying the night with the gal I insisted we move on to Guadalajara, anxious now, as I got close, to see Bill the Champ. So he kissed her bobye and she got mad and yelled at me but we cut, and in the morning Guadalajara, where we wandered in the great market eating fruit. The beach at Mazatlan when we look'd at the girls five miles away and the red, brown, and black horses in the distance, and the bulls and cows, the enormous verdures, flat, the great sun setting in the Pacific over the Three Islands, was one of the great mystic rippling moments of my life—I saw right then that Enrique was great and that the Indian, the Mexican is great, straight, simple and perfect. Towards late afternoon, bussing now from Guadalajara (incidentally went through Ajijic little stone village of Helen but rolling) I slept; there is no more beautiful a land and state than that of Jalisco, Sinaloa is also lovely. We arrived in Mexico City near dawn. Not wake up Bill we instead walked in slums and slept in a criminal's hovel for five pesos, all made of stone and piss, and blasted, and slept on miserable pad . . . he said to look out for the gunman. I avoided his

167

learning Bill's address, for obvious reasons, told him I'd meet him that night in front of post office, went to Bill's, with seabag, the dust of great Mexico on my shoes. It was Saturday in Mexico City, the women were making tortillas, the radio was playing Perez Prado, I ate a five centavo powder candy that I first dug two years ago with Bill's little Willy; odors of hot tortilla, the voices of the children, the Indian youths watching, the well dressed city children of Spanish schools, great clouds of the plateau over piney thin trees of morning and future.

Bill was like a mad genius in littered rooms when I walked in. He was writing. He looked wild, but his eyes innocent and blue and beautiful. We are the greatest of friends at last. At first I felt like a beat fool brought to a far flop in a land of centipedes, worms and rats, mad with Burroughs in a pad, but not so. And he persuaded me to stick to him instead of Enrique, somehow got me not to meet the kid that night, and I ain't seen my saint Enrique since. That is, a guy who could teach me where, what to buy, where to live, on nothing-a-month; but instead I turned my mind again to the great St. Louis of American Aristocracy and has been so ever since. Wasn't that right decision? The kid, I mean, I feel sorry for standing him up—but Bill can't afford any contacts save Dave[19] you know, his position is delicate. His *Queer* is greater than *Junk*—I think now it was a good idea to put them together, with *Queer* we can expect big Wescotts, Girouxs and Vidals to read it avidly, not only Junkie-interested types, see. Title? "Junk or Queer" or something . . . hey? JUNK OR QUEER OR JUNK, OR QUEER JUNK AND QUEER But title must have indications of both. Bill is great. Greater than he ever was. Misses Joan terribly. Joan made him great, lives on in him like mad, vibrating. We went to the Ballet Mexicano together, Bill danced out to catch bus we went on a weekend to Tenecingo in the mountains, did some shooting (it was an accident, you know, no doubt about it anywheres) . . . In the mountain canyon there was depth. Bill was up on the hill striding along tragically; we had separated at the river in order to go separate ways—always take the *right road* Bill had said night before about cobblestone road and asphalt regular road to Tenencingo—so but now, he was taking left road, climb along ridge to mouth of cut, and back along, to road, avoiding river—I wanted to in the inexpressible softness of Biblical Day and Fellaheen Afternoon wash my feet at the place where the maidens left their cloth parts, and sat on a rock (shook spiders from it first but they were only the little spiders that watch the river of honies, creek of God, God and honey, in the flow of the gold, the rocks are soft, the grass just reaches to the lip, I washed and laved my poor feet, waded across my Genesee, and headed for the road (holes in my

---

[19] Dave Tercerero was Burroughs's friend and drug connection in Mexico City.

shoes now, I'm at my last ten bucks in this foreign land) interrupted just once by canyon where depth and tragedy made me circle further, met Bill in a Tenencingo soda fountain waiting. We came back that night, after Turkish baths, etc. Bill's Marker [Lewis Marker] has left him; I have had two women so far, one American with huge tits, and a splendid mex whore in house. Met several great Americans . . . but they all got arrested yesterday for weed, tell you their names later (Kells [Elvins] among them, as if Kells was a teahead) (or pusher) Bill and I clean, cool; we have Dave [Tercerero]. Bill and I want huge letter from you about Wyn situation, for both of us (my manuscript coming soon, 550 pages); more news about [Jean] Genet, first-degree murder? news about everything, and again I want to know where are the first 23 pages of *On the Road* goddamit! (Will insert into manuscript for me?)

    Write

       J.

Allen Ginsberg [Paterson, New Jersey] to Jack Kerouac [n.p., Mexico City, Mexico?]

416 East 34 Street
May 15, 1952
12:00 Noon
Paterson, N.J.

Most Dear Jack:

Just received your letter which am answering immediately. Guessed you were in Mexico; this was a monumental trip, followed it on map. Lucien and I went to Mazatlan last summer also, via Ajijic and Guadalajara (Ajijic you know rendezvous for Subterraneans). But hardly nobody goes to Culican, through Sonora, ever, it's all unknown.

I must be the leak somehow. Unless impossible through presence of Kells' wife, I will cover your tracks totally by announcing to world (Seymour [Wyse] in London, [Bob] Burford in Paris, everyone in N.Y.) that you have shipped out.

Your sight of Mexico is the greatest I have ever read.

"I thought I was beyond Darwin's chain" also eerie expression, any more stanzas of that?

I know that rock in Neal, that is him in his fate which makes love impossible to go beyond; but that is OK because there is where another unknown Neal begins (and writes), and who knows what self that hood hides, what personal disgust at world, or rocky glare.

I can't come to Mexico because I am terrified of going off into the night again, toward death maybe, or oblivion beyond the pale tenderness of New York daily life. I don't want to feel alone in the dark at the mercy of you and Bill—for I have no money of my own—traveling deeper and farther away from world I know and love a little. Your letter was monumental and frightening to me, I wanted immediately to come on down, just like you said, happily and gaily, but instead of kicks under control I am afraid of bum kicks of police, penniless, ragged days. I don't write much, just a few hours a day—depression, beatness, unknown; also I could not call on parents for help then, and am afraid could have to, all these things, childish and timidly pale. I remember trip with Lucien as great kicks and torment of continual threat of death. I would not be able to stand my despair if I thought of no road open but that going deeper into night. I will come down as soon as I have enough money to be able to relax. I am still traumatized and impotent with York Avenue apocalypses and jails and lawyers, [Bill] Cannastra, Joan [Burroughs]. I don't know what I think, but your letter inspires great fear in me, for you, though I know the grandeur of the scene, and for myself, though I know if I strode into the house it would be the greatest meeting we have ever had. Ah, let me tarry awhile till my fate is more firmly fixed before I go down the other side.

> My heart sank beating
> and honey filled my limbs
> when we lay down together
> in each others arms;
>
> there was so much gladness
> bound into our embrace,
> it weighed on naked thigh
> as on soul's nakedness.
>
> Ah Davalos,[20] thy look!
> thy sigh, it is too late;
> The heaviness is gone,
> Gone into the night.

Third line from last no good, can't find another for the moment. Ran into Dick Davalos in Remo the other night, and we stared at each other and in low voices exchanged compliments, and met in rainy night two days later on Lex-

[20] Dick Davalos was a friend and actor with whom Ginsberg had a brief affair.

ington Avenue and went home and had a ball again. Almost in love again, but spontaneous sweetness of first meeting does not last, the clouds come down, can't make joy again, once satisfaction is in sight, as if the accident, and later the imagination, released more feeling than later with designed meet. I'll see him tomorrow night and read him your letter. He asks after you, kept going to Lex Bar to find us months after, never received invite to Thanksgiving party. Explain to Bill.

[. . .]

When I see you will tell you about our Mazatlan, yes remember Three Islands, the greatest vision of the earth I ever had (except Harlem natch) was the great rolling plain of Spain between Tepic and Guadalajara, just a few miles outside of Tepic—we rolled down the vast slope in sunset, the biggest grassy plain I ever saw, coming down from the mountains, long masses of clouds hanging midway between earth and sky, you could see over the clouds we were on slope, and saw little lost city Tepic huddled in the distance. And do you remember, in that area, the uphill down dale road among miniature mountains, a whole little kingdom of huts off road among small jungled hill?

You are so alone your washing of feet in creek near Tenincingo in eternal afternoon, must have arrived at ripeness of alone in universe there.

Kells [Elvins] arrested sounds horrible, write me what happens to him, what he said. Give him my regards.

No news yet about Genet, however plans going to publish him in pocketbook in drugstores all over America, Carl's idea.

Now, as I wrote to Frisco two or three weeks ago (I guess after you left). I found your first 23 pages of *On the Road*, Carl sent it off to Frisco, (against my advice) but it is in safe hands and I'll write and have it returned here. If you want it write me and I'll send it to you.

Everything at Wyn waiting on receipt of manuscript. Send on books soon as can. Nothing new there since I wrote Bill last. Also, Jack, advise you send me your book first, before Carl so I can read it immediately and prepare situation if there's going to be trouble. I know how good it is and want to get with it soon as possible, as Carl may give trouble, being as I say caught in commercial tangle (you have no idea how tangled the commerce is), so if you please, send it on to me in Paterson, and I'll deliver to Carl. No agent charge, etc. just want to make sure as I can that everything is going all right with publisher. Carl already worried and talks about revisions, at contract rate of 100 per month.

Nothing however is happening up here but hot air. My book not accepted yet either. Saw Louis Simpson, wanted your book, same actually with Scribner's, so don't worry, but I wished I had seen your contract.

I am in touch with Burford, or I wrote him, asking that I get editorship of one issue of *New Story*: will publish Carl, Self, You, Bill, Huncke (maybe Harrington and Holmes and Ansen) all together in one blockbusting issue.

I am increasingly interested and hung up on your idea of sketches. Please tell me contents and whereabouts of your works. My own poems are mostly just like your sketches in parts, in theory.

I enclose copy of picture you sent me, I have great beautiful enlargement and extra copies plus negative, so will never get lost. Enlargement, monumental figures in repose, on my desk in Paterson at this moment.

Your plans sound great; I promise to join you in perhaps a year when ripe time for me comes. I feel I'm missing a lot. But how can I join you when I haven't any money at all, just meager unemployment checks and no prospects except after my own book. Can Bill and you take care of me? Will have to wait to see what your finances will be.

Tell Bill I said you shouldn't schmeck, absolutely not, Jack, Ti-Jean, do not schmeck around.

Yes do not tolerate changes in book except possibly in clearing up some references or sentences: for instance, I have a little difficulty understanding your letters (mostly possibly because of Aesopian language talking about T. [marijuana] and O. [opium])

Did you get my last letter? to Frisco? Will Neal forward that?

All right, will show Carl your letter, and will report developments as they develop. Tell Bill nothing new, waiting for *Queer*. Also I sent out his short story to *American Mercury*, if not taken will use it for *New Story* or *Hudson* or something like that.

Stick with it everybody and for god's sake don't get into any trouble, it would break my heart.

     Love,

        Allen

You see I am hung up on commerce with publishers: if I don't do it I know nothing would ever happen here. As soon as I establish everybody's position and reputation, will get on better kick. But all would die in NY if I weren't around to clean up messes. They're all in another world.

P.S. Davalos is secret kick in NY. No mention in return letters except by code—dargelos perhaps. (La Coq du Classe). I do want to go to the Amazon, (will make it somehow). I saw Ed White, got letter from Seymour—who never says anything except "How are you old boy?" He's going to Paris to meet Burford and Jerry Newman, who left for Paris a month ago.

Jack Kerouac [Mexico City, Mexico] to
Allen Ginsberg [Paterson, New Jersey]

May 18, 1952

Dear Allen,

Bill says he will write you a letter contesting your "fear in the dark" reasons for not coming down—while at the same time he doesn't want you to leave until *Junk* or *Queer* is settled, natch. We want you to become big hep New York agent and later editor now, if we make money you can open yourself an office, handle the manuscript of everybody . . . Holmes, Harrington, Ansen, Neal, yourself, Carl, Hunk. By the way where *is* Hunkey?

I myself am leery of going into dark jungles with Bill . . . he scares me with stories of snakes . . . "they have a boa there that's really tree-bound till the age of so and so then it takes to the water" (in a bored yawning voice). And the malarial mosquito takes a dip with its ass when biting you, it's different from regulars; and the danger of sleeping on the ground is a certain kind of viper with so much venom that there's no cure, you just die. And the Auca, man-killing tribe; and lawless provinces and lawless towns like Manta on the coast; and the staple diet in jungle is monkeys, etc. But I will go if I have the dough, of course. At some point, keep this to yourself, possibly en route from Ecuador to Paris, I will zoom thru New York for a week of reunions and kicks on the sly, mebbe a month hey?

I know you will love *On the Road* [21]—please read it all, no one has read it all yet . . . Neal had no time, nor Bill. *On the Road* is inspired in its entirety . . . I can tell now as I look back on the flood of language. It is like *Ulysses* and should be treated with the same gravity. If Wyn or Carl insist on cutting it up to make the "story" more intelligible I'll refuse and offer them another book which I'll commence writing at once, because now I know where I'm headed. I have *Doctor Sax* ready to go now . . . or *The Shadow of Doctor Sax*, I'll simply blow on the vision of the Shadow in my 13th and 14th years on Sarah Ave. Lowell, culminated by the myth itself as I dreamt it in Fall 1948 . . . angles of my hoop-rolling boyhood as seen from the shroud. Also, of course, now that *On the Road* is in, I'm going to start sketching here in Mexico . . . for the general basis of my Fellaheen south of the border book about Indians, Fellaheen problems, and Bill the last of the American Giants among them . . . actually a book about Bill. That's

---

[21] At the time Kerouac was calling this manuscript *On the Road*, but it was later published as part of *Visions of Cody*.

two things. And at any leisured moment near libraries (say, if I lived on the Columbia campus, or in Paterson, or a cheap room near 42nd and 5th Avenue) I'm going to execute my Civil War novel which I want to parallel Tolstoy's 1812 hang-ups in 1850s, in other words a historical novel, a big personal gone with the wind about Lucien-like cavalry heroes and Melville-like Bartlebies of draft riots and Whitman-like nurses and especially dumb soldiers from the clay hills staring into the gray mist and void of Chickamauga at dawn. Learning facts of Civil War as I go along. But I'm not sure which (of the first two) ideas will be completed first . . . should be *Doctor Sax*.

Now here is what sketching is. In the first place, you remember last September when Carl first ordered the Neal book and wanted it . . . Sketching came to me in full force on October 25th, the day of the evening Dusty [Moreland] and I went to Poughkeepsie with [Jack] Fitzgerald—so strongly it didn't matter about Carl's offer and I began sketching everything in sight, so that *On the Road* took its turn from conventional narrative survey of road trips etc. into a big multi-dimensional conscious and subconscious character invocation of Neal in his whirlwinds. Sketching (Ed White casually mentioned it in 124th [Street] Chinese restaurant near Columbia, "Why don't you just sketch in the streets like a painter but with words?") which I did . . . everything activates in front of you in myriad profusion, you just have to purify your mind and let it pour the words (which effortless angels of the vision fly when you stand in front of reality) and write with 100% personal honesty both psychic and social etc. and slap it all down shameless, willy-nilly, rapidly until sometimes I got so inspired I lost consciousness I was writing. Traditional source: Yeats' trance writing, of course. It's the *only way to write*. I haven't sketched in a long time now and have to start again because you get better with practice. Sometimes it is embarrassing to write in the street or anywhere outside but it's absolute . . . it never fails, it's the thing itself natch.

Do you understand sketching?—same as poetry you write—also never overdo it, you should normally get pooped in fifteen minutes' straight scribbling—by that time I have a chapter and I feel a little crazy for having written it . . . I read it and it seems like the confessions of an insane person . . . then next day it reads like great prose, oh well. And just like you say the best things we write are always the most suspected . . . I think the greatest line in *On the Road* (tho you'll disagree) is (apart of course from description of the Mississippi River "Lester is just like the river, the river starts in near Butte Montana in frozen snow caps (Three Forks) and meanders on down across states and entire territorial areas of dun bleak land with hawthorn crackling in the sleet, picks up rivers at Bismarck, Omaha and St. Louis just north, another at Kay-ro, another in Arkansas, Tennessee, comes deluging on New Orleans with muddy news from the land and a roar of subterranean excitement that is like the vibration of the entire land sucked on its gut in mad midnight, fevered, hot, the big mudhole rank clawpole old frogular pawed-soul titanic Mississippi from the North full of wires, cold wood and horn.")

How do you think I arrived at last four five words if not in trance?

I explained all this method to Neal.

But here's that (best) line "The charging restless mute unvoiced road keening in a seizure of tarpaulin power . . ." This is obviously something I *had* to say in spite of myself . . . tarpaulin, too, don't be frightened, is obviously the key . . . man that's a road. It will take fifty years for people to realize that that's a road. In fact I distinctly remember hovering over the word "tarpaulin" (even thought of writing tarpolon or anything) but something told me that "tarpaulin" was what I'd thought, "Tarpaulin" was what it is . . . Do you understand Blake? Dickinson? and Shakespeare when he wants to mouth the general sound of doom, "peaked, like John a Dreams" . . . simply does what he hears . . . "greasy Joan doth keel the pot; (and birds sit brooding in the snow . . .")). However I got very tired of blowing all that poetry and am now resting and getting hi and going to movies etc. and trying to read Gore Vidal [*The*] *Judgment of Paris* which is so ugly transparent in its method, the protagonist-hero who is unqueer but all camp (with his bloody tattoo on a thigh) and craptalk, the only thing good, as Bill says, are the satirical queer scenes, especially Lord Ayres or whatever his name . . . and they expect us to be like Vidal, great god.) (Regressing to sophomore imitations of Henry James.) If Carl publishes Genet in drugstores all over America he will have done a service to his century.

Listen, last December, on a whim, I sent Eric Protter a little short story about J. [Jean]—title was "What the Young French Writers should be Writing" and it was that dream of Neal (remember the dialog where he says "I don't understand that spectral canal of yours, Brooklyn scares me, the el's are too mad, I want to go back to the white hills of Frisco" (facsimile) "that pump of yours, those potatoes, those wild orgies with sailors and the bourgeois running across the burning bridge with dogs under their arms, help me" (and all that) I sent to *New Story*, changing all the names to French names (Neal was Jean) and the cities to French cities (New Orleans—Bordeaux) but the little pissyass shit sent it back saying he wanted something more conventional. You know the type. So beware.

You want me to send you (my dear agent you are now boy) some sketches etc. well it's all in *Road* . . . be sure and extract what you like for individual publications, I am egal on the whole thing, it's all good, all publishable . . . (except obvious cases). You can make short pieces out of any part . . . send jazz parts to *Metronome*, to Ulanov[22] the vain cock, he thinks the sun rises and sets on his dictionary.

As for peotl—it's grooking in the desert to eat our hearts alive.

What you might do, if Lucien comes to Mex again this summer with Cessa, come with him, if we're still here.

Good for dargolos [Davalos] . . . he sure put old Dusty down that night. What Ed White say? Where's Holmes? Calling for Rock and Rise is in *Road* somewhere . . . around page 490. I won't comment on your splendid letter . . . let us now begin negotiations; write often because (if you have time) I and Bill are lonely. My contract is 10% for first 10,000, then more, 15% . . . we can show *Road* to Scribner's or Simpson or Farrar Straus (Stanley Young) if necessary, change title to *Visions of Neal* or something, and I write new *Road* for Wyn.

But methinks none of such crap necessary. Isn't *Queer* great?

Jack

Allen Ginsberg [New York, New York] to Jack Kerouac [Mexico City, Mexico]

June 12, 1952

Dear Jack:

All right, the manuscript arrived a few days ago, *On the Road*. Carl read it, I read it once, and [John Clellon] Holmes has it.

I don't see how it will ever be published, it's so personal, it's so full of sex language, so full of our local mythological references, I don't know if it would make sense to any publisher—by make sense I mean, if you could follow what happened to what characters where.

The language is great, the blowing is mostly great, the inventions have full-blown ecstatic style. Also the tone of speech is at times nearer to un-innocent heart speech ("why did I write this?" and "I'm a criminal"). Where you are writing steadily and well, the sketches, the exposition, it's the best that is written in America, I do believe. I'm not stopping now to write you praise-letter, tho maybe I should etc. etc. but on my mind I am worried by the whole book. It's crazy (not merely inspired crazy) but unrelated crazy.

Well you know your book. Wyn I'm positive won't take it now, I don't know who will. I think could be published by *New Story* people in Europe, but will you be revising it at all? What you trying to put down, man? You know what you done.

---

[22] Barry Ulanov was a jazz critic and an early supporter of bebop.

176

This is no big letter, can't see Bill's for reason. I will, all by myself, read book second time, next week, and write you twenty page letter taking book section by section figuring my reactions.

For an on the spot minute guess:

1. You still didn't cover Neal's history.

2. You covered your own reactions.

3. You mixed them up chronologically, so that it's hard to tell what happened when.

4. The totally surrealistic sections (blowing on sounds and refusing to make sense) (in section following tape-records) is just a hang-up, hang-up.

5. Tape records are partly hang-up, should be shortened and put in place after final trip to Frisco.

6. Sounds like you were just blowing and tacking things together, personally unrelating them, just for madness sake, or despair.

I think book is great but crazy in a bad way, and *got* aesthetically and publishing-wise, to be pulled back together, re constructed. I can't see anyone, New Directions, Europe, putting it out as it is. They won't, they won't.

HODOS CHAMELIONTOS in Yeats is series of unrelated images, chameleon of the imagination diddling about in the void or hang-up, meaning nothing to each other.

Should keep *Sax* into framework of a myth, a FRAMEWORK, and not violate framework by interrupting *Sax* to talk about Lucien's formerly golden hair or Neal's big cock or my evil mind, or your lost bone. The book is the lost bone, itself.

On the Road just drags itself exhausted over the goal line of meaning to someone else (or to me who knows the story); it's salvageable. I mean it needs to be salvaged. You're handing up the whole goddam junkyard including the I agh up erp esc baglooie ain't you read what I'm shayinoo im tryinting tink try I mea mama thatsshokay but you gotta make sense you gotta muk sense, jub, jack, fik, anyone can bup it, you bubblerel, Zag, Nealg, Loog, Boolb, Joon, Hawk, Nella Grebsnig. And if you doan wanna make sense, shit, then put the nonsense on one page boiled down to one intense nervous collapse out of intelligibility (like [William Carlos] Williams did in a section of *Paterson*, scrambling up the type, and followed it real cool by a list of the geological formations of shale etc. under the fuckin falls, and then went on to say "This is a poem, a POEM.") and then go on talkin like nothing ever happened cause nothin did. Nothing jess *interrupted* something. But nothing juss keeps breaking in out all over the joint, you'll be talking along, and say "he come out of the room like a criminal—then you'll add—like a shrouder (whoever heard of ?) then you'll add—like black winged rubens—then you'll go poetic and say—like pink winged

Stoobens, the hopscotch Whiz of grammar school, hopscotch, the game of Archangels, it's hevvin, it's clouds, meanwhile he was alla time juss commin out of that room, but you got us not only up inna clouds, via Steubenville and urk ep blook, but via also I am JK interrupting myself.

Well maybe it's all three dimensional and awright aesthetically or humanly, so I will re re re read your whole buke, puke anall, (and jeez, Joyce did it, but you're juss crappin around thoughtlessly with that trickstyle *often*, and it's not so good.) reread your whole book I will,

and give you a blow by blow account of *how it comes off.*

And incidentally don't be too flabbergasted flip at my foregoing because I Allen Ginsberg one and only, have just finished cutting down my book from 89 poems to a mere perfect 42, just to cut out the comedy and crap and personalia jackoffs, for leanness, and humanness, it is ACTION WHICH IS DEMANDED AT THIS TIME. That's what he sez, though god know what kind of action he talkin about.

Editors' Note: Kerouac was staying with William Burroughs in Mexico when he received Ginsberg's letter. He was working on the manuscript of Doctor Sax *and was penniless as usual. After borrowing some money from Burroughs he returned to his sister's house in North Carolina for a brief visit and then headed to San Jose to live with Neal Cassady, who offered to help him get a railroad job.*

Jack Kerouac [San Jose, California] to Allen Ginsberg [Paterson, New Jersey]

October 8, 1952

Allen Ginsberg

This is to notify you and the rest of the whole lot what I think of you. Can you tell me even for instance . . . with all this talk about pocket book styles and the new trend in writing about drugs and sex why my *On the Road* written in 1951 wasn't ever published?—why they publish Holmes's book [*Go*] which stinks and don't publish mine because it's not as good as some of the other things I've done? Is this the fate of an idiot who can't handle his own business or [is] it the general fartsmell of New York in general . . . And you who I thought was my friend—you sit there and look me in the eye and tell me the *On the Road* I wrote at Neal's is "imperfect" as though anything you ever did or anybody was perfect? . . . and don't lift a finger or say a word for it . . . Do you think I don't realize how jealous you are and how you and Holmes and Solomon all would give your right arm to be able to write like the writing in *On the Road.* And leaving me no alternative but to write stupid letters like this when if instead you were men I could at least get the satisfaction of belting you all in the kisser—too many glasses to take off. Why you goddamn cheap little shits are all the same and always were and why did I ever listen and fawn and fart with you—fifteen years of my life wasted among the cruds of New York, from the millionaire jews of Horace Mann who'd kissed my ass for football and now would hesitate to introduce their wives to me, to the likes of you . . . poets indeed . . . distant small-sized variants of same . . . baroque neat-packaged acceptable (small print in the middle of neat page of poetry book) page . . . Not only have you grieved me now by your statement that there is nothing in *On the Road* you didn't know about (which is a lie because at just one glance I can see that you never knew the slightest beginning detail of even something so simple as Neal's work life and what he does)—and [Carl] Solomon pretending to be an interesting saint, claims he doesn't understand contracts, why in ten years I'll be lucky to have the right to look into his window on Xmas eve . . . he'll be so rich and fat and so endowed with the skinny horrors of other men into one great puff-ball of satisfied suckup . . . Parasites every one of you, just like Edie said. And now even John Holmes, who as everybody knows lives in complete illusion about everything, writes about things he doesn't know about, and with hostility at that, (it comes out in hairy skinny legs of Stofsky and "awkward" Pasternak, the sonofabitch jealous of his own flirtatious wife, I didn't ask for Marian's attentions . . . awkwardness indeed, I imagine anybody who walks on ordinary legs would look awkward around effeminate flip-hips and swish like him)— And the smell of his work is the smell of death. . . . Everybody knows he has no talent . . . and so what right has he, who knows nothing, to pass any kind of judgment on my book—He doesn't even have the right to surl in silence about it—His book stinks, and your book is only mediocre, and you all know it, and my book is great and will never be published. Beware of meeting me on the street in New York. Beware also of giving any leads as to my whereabouts. I'll come up to New York and trace down the lead. You're all a bunch of insignificant literary egos . . . you can't even leave New York you're so stultified . . . Even [Gregory] Corso with his Tannhauser chariots running down everyone else has already begun to pick up . . . Tell him to go away . . . tell him to find himself in his own grave . . . My heart bleeds every time I look at *On the Road* . . . I see it now, why it is great and why you hate it and what the world is . . . specifically what you are . . . and what you, Allen Ginsberg, are . . . a disbeliever, a hater, your giggles don't fool me, I see the snarl under it . . . Go ahead and do what you like, I want peace with myself . . . I shall certainly never find peace till I wash my hands completely of the dirty brush and stain of New York and everything that you and the city stand for . . . And everybody knows it . . . And Chase knew it long ago . . . that is because he was an old man from the start . . . And now I am an old man too . . . I realize that I am no longer attractive to you queers . . . Go blow your Corsos . . . I hope he sinks a knife in you . . . Go on and hate each other and sneer and get jealous and . . . My whole record in NY is one long almost humorous chronicle of a real dumb lil abner getting taken in by fat pigjaws . . . I realize the humour of it . . . and laugh just as much as you . . . But here on in I'm not laughing . . . Paranoia me no paranoias either . . . Because of people like you and Giroux . . . even with G. you fucked me up from making money because he hated you . . . and came in with Neal that night and Neal right away wanted to steal a book from the office, sure, what would you say if I went to your N O R C [National Opinion Research Center] and stole things and made fun of it . . . and Lucien with his shitty little ego trying to make me cry over Sarah and then telling me at the lowest ebb of my life that I would be awful easy to forget . . . He must know by now unless be-sotted and stupid with drink that it is so about everybody . . . how easily one may disappear . . . and be forgotten completely . . . and make dark corruption spot in dirt . . . well alright. And all of you, even Sarah I don't even care to know any more or who will ever hear of this insane letter . . . all of you fucked me up . . . with the exception of Tony Monacchio and a few other angels . . . and so I say to you, never speak to me again or try to write or have anything to do with me . . . besides you will never probably see me again . . . and that is good . . . the time has come for all you frivolous fools to realize what the subject of poetry is . . . death . . . so die . . . and die like men . . . and shut up . . . and above all . . . leave me alone . . . and don't ever darken me again.

Jack Kerouac

Allen Ginsberg [New York, New York] to Jack Kerouac [San Francisco, California]

ca. November 1–7, 1952, but before November 8, 1952

Dear Jack:

I just finished *Doctor Sax*, it's hard to write you because of all previous crap with *On the Road* and your letter—hard to accept or deny reality of your letter—but that aside.

I think *Dr. Sax* is better than *On the Road* (I'm expounding here on just harmony and appearance—*On the Road* has great original method to be sure) and I think also it can be published—unlike what I thought of *On Road*. *Sax* is a big success for my money, as a completed project.

Though I think you can still do more with it and it ought to be rewritten it's still muddy and creaky here and there. But on the whole its construction is mainly perfect—particularly the final revelations of the last pages, and the general sanity of whole approach makes it possible to appreciate the delights of moment to moment verbal creation.

I believe with *On the Road* and *Sax*, which makes that tendency crystal clear, you really have hit a whole lode of originality of method of writing prose—method incidentally though like Joyce is your own origin and make and style, similarities only superficial your neologisms are not foggy philological precisions but aural (hear-able) inventions that carry meanings.

And the aural cadence of your prose which Joyce also specializes in—is done without much damage to natural sequences of sentence construction. He had to melt and fuckup sentences, and fuggup words and fog them to get them to join in melodious series. I notice your melodies are often in an Irish-Joyce mélange of the sentence, but in a natural Nealish speak cadence.

Your imagery—which is simple like Lucien's, is also new-old humble poetry (illustration later on)

The philosophic line is satisfactory and has moments of sublimity. By satisfactory I mean harmonious and symmetrical. Not just a Chinese puzzle.

The structure of reality and myth—shuttling back and forth, is a stroke of genius: casting the myth within the frame of childish fantasy, so giving it reality [?] in terms of its frame.

The trouble with the reality side of your book, I think it isn't too interesting all the time, I get bored by it, because it's partly a series of incidents unrelated except by process of general association—i.e. it has not much compel[ing] inner structure to make you want to read on and find out what is going on or what is happening in the real life of [?] that is being symbolized by this grand fantasy life. Also it waters down interest in real life recollections not to have them tied down to anything personally central—except the hint of discovery of Sex. The flood, too helps maintain interest as it builds up, in real life. Perhaps if you felt inclined to improve this book you might put in what was actually there—some great reality crisis as what you've had in last years, or some earlier reality crisis like sex, I don't know, whatever in real terms the imaginary myth might correspond to in real life human development preadolescent trials and traumas. I'm not being clinical, tho I'm not writing poetry here, just observations. The real life side of the books was held together for me by the intrinsic interest of the experiences described, anecdotes, and incidents etc. and secondly held my interest to it by the continual brilliance of the language—so that at times I even felt that nothing was happening at all except verbally, but that was enough—though as in parts of *On the Road*, that can be too much meaningless bop to keep the attention fixed upon, even if you try to follow.

I have described the flaw I thought about the naturalistic side; that is to say I respect the total structure of the book but wish to estimate it clearly for you as I see it, in its particulars, also, still, despite possible horrors of criticism.

I would have to read book over again to figure out what I think is wrong with the mythological structure as it is interwoven. Mainly at the moment it seems to me almost just right. I felt it was too sketchy at first till I reached the long explanations of Dovish politics, Blook, etc. page 191—explanations so breathless and coming just at a point when I was getting so irritated with the confusion (I was cursing you—that stupid Kerouac hasn't even bothered to shove in a plot to all the supernatural gossip—just left an undigested mass of images and references and rumors) but there you came in with a whole explanation—which by this time I couldn't think possible to give, anyway, but now so clear it seemed like a miracle (like cleanup of detective story with clues). Thank god.

Blook isn't as interesting as he might be—as he was in conversation, not an important creation, you fell down on old Blook—the scene where he meets child while burying an onion is not here—and rushes screaming away in fright, you could have said "up walks Ti Jean just at that moment behind the bush where bleak Blook stood timidly soliloquizing the onion grave" or some such nonsense utilizing the phrase bleak Blook. Perhaps with Sax on trip to the castle.

The conceptions are all very original and must have been hard to set down to do, though, though great delight to conceive, as they were to read. Great idea of trip to castle, great moment observing the town with Sax and boy, great Dovish and Evilist controversy—in fact I think more attention and time spent to details of the myth would be just great—it is the real caviar of the whole book—so intelligent, so apt as metaphysical and *social* commentary, so *hip* and yet so public in reference. I don't see why you can't do more of that and wave book greater.

Would love to talk to you—on plot.

[. . .]

Section of reality about the poems is confusing. Where are all the old poems you had in Diana's apartment years ago? I think I have some. I don't too much dig the poems, nor the seeming sloppy and foggy way you worked them into the text. Seems to me like jerry built intrusion. Should be poems (more meaningful ones, in specific context of dovish or evilist significance, or final giant-bird significance, or Sax preparation significances. But on first reading your poems seemed to be just fucking mells and mells and I said "O shit" when I saw them, I thought they were going to be really funny, but it was just a bunch of interesting lines (hodos chameliantos—chameleon imagery) with a few illuminating ones scattered here and there—the poems weren't part of the whole conspiracy enough, just tacked in by your enthusiasm it seemed.

Have you as a child ever visited someone older (like old negro or teacher) and sat daily in their parlor among brocades listening to their transaction of life, fed cookies watching their world go on without understood significance before your innocent eyes?

So perhaps there should be an earlier meeting and rapport with Sax, with more detailed plot of the preparation shown the reader, more action and familiarity with the Dutchess, Blook, Sax. The wizard (all those great creations, you realize, have scarcely a page or two apiece—and they are the great figures of the book—devoted to their characters and daily life and humor-actions and gossips etc and anecdotes—so that I hardly know anything about Condu and the Wizard—they seem like the same persona practically, and not different identities—and Adolphus Ghoulens (does he mean to appear as the author of the document?) (just for the joke of the name?) and Amadeus Baroque—all these figures good for real fine Mozartean comedy (like the wonderful career of Boaz Jr. until it gets too confused with frozen children imagery—a little out of anachronism with focus of reality) are neglected and not given full life—you treat them as if they were just around to be mentioned and dismissed as part of the general joke, but they need further development—otherwise their full significance (which you know now only in your own head) is lost on the average reader, and that includes me too.

The apparition should be more detailed—not complexified—the plot's complex enough, just simplified and oriented solidly. Words works, I don't know exactly what I mean. But like, the Dutchess you see thrice, you don't know really just what relationship all the evilists have to each other—you don't ever see an actual dovist, just hear rumors (maybe that's ok) of them. The gnomes and all the more complicated machinery is a little too science fiction farfetched. If you want I will send you a detailed appraisal of how much of the myth detail succeeds and how much seems to be anachronism—this is a very important point. Mainly the whole myth succeeds, it's built like a brick shithouse as a grand symbol, some of the details (old shmecker conversations about B between the batman and the contessa) are brilliant, and on the whole most of it was polish, sophistication, intellectual suavity—all of which (intentionally) you failed to achieve in *Town and City* in Francis intellectual decadent sections—but here that awkwardness never everything's real high comedy as you would like to imagine it.

At this point, to recapitulate letter, I have covered what I thought wrong (and OK) about the two wings of your bat book, the reality narrative and the myth narrative and structure.

[...]

In *On the Road* you failed to produce that eerie human vision of Neal mostly.

This book is an *actual* vision, first one in American lit since who knows?

Practically speaking—that evilists should go down with the ship, be destroyed with the snake, is a great pure pun on happenstance—it happens, like Joan A. [Adams]

Incidentally, in your great long letter you mistake me for an evilist because I am no longer a professed dovist. I am like Ti Jean, a practical boy who feels at certain moments that Dr. Sax is mad and had better be escaped from. A Fieldsian attitude too.

I have been hoping to hear from you. My father said I have a letter at home in Paterson, from Cassady, possibly reply to my postcard, but he sent it on to me but I have not received it, hoping it will not be an evil thing, hoping it will be a pipperone or at least a level crawyak.

I have not written the Shrouded Stranger. Your book poses quite a challenge. We will see about my mediocrity when and if I finish that. Till then I can only admit that since genius is 9/10 perspiration etc. I am worse than mediocre, I am a total failure. And yesterday I received a letter from Carl, counseling me to burn *Empty Mirror* as it was not entertaining, just a "suffering of this self-pity type is worthless."

I am working at the same place I was when I last saw you. I saw Herb [Huncke] briefly for five minutes several days later. I don't want to see him yet. I have a sweet little pad in Lower East side with heat and hot water, very neat and clean, your own mother wouldn't be ashamed to live there if you know what I mean. Three small rooms, bedroom, kitchen, parlor all $33.80 a month furnished even. Anyone who wants to come visit or stay over is invited, plenty privacy.

My address is 206 East 7th Street Apt. 16 NYC (between Avenue B&C). Dusty [Moreland]'s clothes etc. are here but she is not, we've about broken up by now, I don't know where she sleeps. Being sparse on details as I want to finish this letter with the necessary information.

Give me lowdown if wish on what you intend to do financially. I think I know how *Sax* could be published, with or without revisions (though Jack I still say listen to me when I say what I think about your writing). I will consult with Carl and Holmes (who I don't know how they'll be for actual agenting.)

Suggest you get MCA to handle if they accept it—doubt they will.

[Bob] Burford I believe would publish as is. [New] Directions might publish revised. So also Bobbs-Merrill Louis Simpson if revised, maybe as is.

Incidentally nothing in the book strikes me as sexually verbally offensive or censurable, could all be left as is.

Watch out on progress selling *T.&C.* [*The Town and the City*] to paperback.

184

M.C.A. should be asked to. Will write practical details on all of above if asked. You sure shat on me last time I tried to help—

As ever love to
Allen

All in all Jack the book is a real triumph for you, a Beethovenian-Melvillian triumph just as you imagine (or don't) imagine.

Do you want me to show it to Van Doren? He would be delighted.

I have been exploring the Lower East Side for the first time really exploring its depth and vastness that I never realized—some streets like Mexican Thieves Market.

Jack Kerouac [San Francisco, California] to Allen Ginsberg [Paterson, New Jersey]

Nov. 8 1952

Dear Allen,

I read your letter many times. It's very nice, you are very nice to understand my writings. I felt honored. *Doctor Sax* is a mystery. I'm going to leave him the way he is, but not for the same reasons as *On the Road* (enraged, etc.) but because I really like it the way it is, a few things you suggest I will do, like bleak Blook and the child. *Doctor Sax* is only the top of the pot about Lowell . . . the truth buried insane in me, in my head that becomes so inflamed sometimes. I'm trying to speak to you brother to brother, like we were French Canadian brothers. Literature as you see it, using words like "verbal" and "images" etc. and things like, well all the "paraphernalia" of criticism etc. is no longer my concern, because the thing makes me say "shitty little beach in the reeds" is pre-literary, it happened to me to think that way before I learned the words the litterateurs use to describe what they're doing. At this moment I'm writing directly from the French in my head, *Doctor Sax* was written high on tea without pausing to think, sometimes Bill [Burroughs] would come in the room and so the chapter ended there, one time he yelled after me with his long gray face because he could smell the smoke in the yard. You know I was mad at you, but you know it doesn't take me long to stop, and many times I wanted to write you and say "Well, you understand, sometimes I get mad," etc. I always thought you my little brother, my little petushka, even tho you're Jewish, because you're like a little Russian brother. Lucien has always said to me not to get mad at you—if I get mad, to get mad at those who try to hurt me, like himself? Neal got mad at me, he wasn't talking to anybody, he hung the phone on me, I got me a fine little room in Skid Row at $4 a week and I was arranging myself so well (and writing a big new novel like *Town and City*) that I was happy for the first time in years, and was saying to myself, "Well, Neal has always been crazy, since the day he put his head in my door at Ozone Park and was making me believe he wanted to learn to write," quel bull shit eh what? But I was sleeping one night on the railroad, on an old ratty couch, hard asleep after three days and three nights of work and no sleep, Neal was bent over me, hung over me, laughing, "*There* you are buddy! Come on, now, come on, now, no words, come on, now," so, me, I am here to try to be nice, I go along with him and move back to his house, and then CAROLYN gets mad at me, etc. Bitchy people, I hate people, I can't stand people any more. The phone just called me gotta go to work again, I'm sick and tired of it—This is why it took me so long to answer you, the railroad.

Let's let John Holmes handle *Doctor Sax*, another thing about your letter, and you, always afraid it isn't "right," etc. like Arthur Schlesinger Jr. and Adlai Stevenson and the Harvard Law School and United Nations and Dean Acheson ready to fly at any instant with a detailed appraisal of something . . . for what? for what? for what? for what?

See?

GO is alright when you see it between book covers, it's sincere, each page . . . Truman Capote, Jean Stafford are full of bull on every page . . . so Holmes is better than they I say.

Ah I'd love to see you, maybe I will this Xmas according to my plans of travel. Good Morning to the whole gang.

> Your friend
>
> Jack

P.S. When you said to yourself "Oh that stupid Kerouac hasn't bothered to put in a plot, just left an undigested mass of images and references etc." you weren't remembering were you that once it was LOVE animated our poesies, not no anxious techniques. Yes the digging by you of Balzacian jewelpoint (and ah I can't) it means you REALLY did comprehend the book like I thought nobody could, our clairvoyance is together—my good boy.

1953

Editors' Note: Kerouac spent much of the winter working on the railroad in California, while Ginsberg in New York worked to find publishers for the books of his friends. In order to publicize Burroughs's first book, Junkie, *which Carl Solomon was helping to publish through his uncle's company, Ace Books, Allen asked that Jack allow his name to be used in the publicity. On the top of the following letter, Kerouac later wrote "Cause of Tiff."*

Allen Ginsberg [New York, New York] to Jack Kerouac [San Francisco, California]

February 19, 1953

Thursday Night 10:30

"JOHN KEROUAC AND Clellon Holmes, both experts on the Beat Generation, Holmes though his recent *Times Magazine* section controversy, say that they "dig" the pseudonymous William Lee as one of the key figures of the Beat Generation.

"Lee first appeared lurking in the shadows of both of their books, respectively *The Town and the City* and *Go*, portrayed as an underground character. Lee's professional debut in the open on his own as an author is announced by Ace Double Books with the publication of *Junkey: The Confessions of an Unredeemed Junk Addict*, which comes up from underground April 15.

"Author-Junky Lee has not stayed around to gather whatever plaudits are due and was last heard from on an expedition into the Amazon basin in search of a rare narcotic."

Dear Jack:

On the reverse is rough draft [text in quote marks above] of news gossip item for the *Times* that Carl [Solomon] and I and Wyn publicity figured up. I read it to Holmes and it's OK by him. Will be given to *Times* gossip litterateur, David Dempsey.

Please give your permission for your name to be used, and also please send me, for now or later use, with this item, a two sentence plug for Bill [Burroughs] as intense and hi-class as you can make it. Twenty-five words or so. Holmes will contribute also—emphasizing literary value, whatever it is, personality, or perhaps balloonish foolishness of whole project of JUNK.

I am expecting to go out of town this weekend to Paterson on Saturday tho I may be here Friday nite.

John never made it last week to Birdland in time anyway, he came in from Queens, or wherever, half hour late and thought perhaps it was his own fault.

189

I will call Lu [Lucien Carr] tonight and move into his apt. in a few days perhaps Monday or Tuesday. He'll go away for a month so perhaps we could see
him again once before.

Adios. Write that please and send me this week. For dear Will [Burroughs]'s
sake.

> Yours
> Allen

*Editors' Note: Kerouac responded immediately using his mother's New York
City address, his "official" residence, since he saw this as an important business
matter.*

Jack Kerouac [Richmond Hill, New York] to
Allen Ginsberg [New York, New York]

Feb. 21, 1953

Dear Allen and Sirs:

I do not give my permission for my name to be used in the notes prepared
by you and A.A. Wyn and Carl Solomon for David Dempsey's *New York Times*
literary notes column. I do not want my real name used in conjunction with
habit forming drugs while a pseudonym conceals the real name of the author
thus protecting him from prosecution but not myself and moreover whose
work at the expense of my name is being bruited for book trade reasons.

In this "rough draft publicity" I do not want *The Town and the City* mentioned in juxtaposition to *Go*, by association hinting at some professional and
artistic semblance, and I deny permission to place my name next to Clellon
Holmes as a co-expert on the *Beat Generation*.

Especially I do not want to be misquoted as saying that I "dig the pseudonymous William Lee as one of the key figures of the Beat Generation." My remarks on the subject of either the pseudonymous author William Lee or the
generation are at your disposal through the proper channels, from my pen and
through my agent.

> Yours most respectfully and strictly business,
> John Kerouac

Editors' Note: Ginsberg responded with a large dose of sarcasm.

190

Allen Ginsberg [New York, New York] to
Jack Kerouac [San Francisco, California]

February 24, 1953

Mr. Jack Kerouac
94-21 134 Street
Richmond Hill, New York

Dear Sir:

Thank you for your two prompt replies of the 21st to my letter of the 20th.[1] I am sincerely aggrieved that my original appeal appeared to violate certain proprieties of your situation which you explained in your letters, and I hasten to set this matter right on all counts.

Before I proceed let me congratulate you on the charm and incisiveness of the quotation which you authorize; which quotation I will naturally submit to your agent for his (her) approval before making use (there)of.

There are two delicate matters which I wish to mention: While I approve your wish to dissociate your own literary position with that of the author of *Go* (who incidentally gave his general permission, etc. without consulting MCA) and while I will do everything in my power to aid you in doing so, especially in this instance, it behooves me to remind you as a friend that, adopting your suggestion of separate statements, no further reference will be made by me to anyone that it was at your request. In other words, let us do this as quietly as possible, so as not to risk offending Mr. Holmes. If you wish to make a public matter of this, of course, that is your privilege, and I will follow suit.

Secondly, you know of course that great secrecy is desirable *vis-a-vis* your new relationship with MCA, particularly as there is still a delicate situation to be dealt with at A.A. Wyn. Solomon knows nothing of your recent activities. I have, by your express instructions, said nothing to him of any import on anything remotely concerning your present publishing position. So, if you do see him, and speak of this matter, or any other, I beg you for your own sake to breathe not a word about MCA. And certainly, if you wish to see him, avoid MCA as intermediary, until they say so.

I applaud your discrimination in choosing the method of praise which you have consented to accord to Mr. Lee's writings. I am sure that he, as well as myself as his agent, would be gratified by this instance of your esteem, were he apprised of the facts. He is, as you know, traveling in South America now and cannot be reached for consultation on matters of publicity. I have been pro-

---

[1] Only one letter is included in this volume: the letter dated February 19, 1953, on page 189.

ceeding carefully as possible on my own in his behalf, though mistakes are to be made and unmade I am sure.

A further question, perhaps to be decided by your agent: do you really feel the possibility of threat of persecution for drug reasons as a result of your contribution to the publicity? The pseudonym conceals the author's name as he confesses, as you know, to a number of statutory crimes. This does not involve a threat, except perhaps of social disapproval, to anyone who chooses to praise his writing.

A further word as to my own position: though your name is being cried on the streets for book trade reasons, I would not dream of participating in this particular request to you except for reasons of high literary seriousness. I have faith in the quality of the book I am dealing with. I would not, as well, make use of your name for any other purpose publicly. The motives of the publisher, A.A. Wyn, are, as far as I am concerned, for the most part beneath my interest; and I do not find it necessary for my purposes to concern myself with their motives except infrequently for tactical reasons. As evidence of the latter I adduce my paragraph consulting you to keep silent about your arrangements with MCA until MCA makes it public.

I cannot close this letter without thanking you once again for your paragraph which seems to combine all the proper elements and catch the spirit of admiration which I hope one day will be universally accorded to the work we are dealing with.

> Yours most respectfully and in the spirit of strictest commerce,
> Allen Ginsberg

P.S. Once again let me apologize for bothering you on this matter. I will of course follow your suggestion and clear such matters with MCA first, on this situation and on any others to come.

Editors' Note: Typically, their disagreement was short-lived, and before long Kerouac was again asking Ginsberg to represent him with publishers in New York City.

Jack Kerouac [San Luis Obispo, California] to Allen Ginsberg [New York, New York]

May 7, 1953

Dear Allen:

Are you willing to take a chance with *Sax* and *Maggie Cassidy* primarily *Sax*. They're in the upper right hand drawer of my rolltop desk at 94–21 134th—If you agree to agent *Doctor Sax* (We disagreed over *ROAD*, not *SAX*, right?) I'll write and notify my Ma to give them to you when you call. Further, if Phyllis Jackson drops *T&C,* that would devolve to you too. I just don't see the sense of letting *Doctor Sax* rot in my desk. Send it anywhere—but just don't let every Tom Dick and Harry read it *(Sax)*—the first thing you know that style will begin to appear in *New Writing* and elsewhere—fuck Martha Foley's son[2] and his excerpt shit—get *SAX* published nobly as the architectural creation and symphony it is, please—if you don't want to handle *Sax* (and also *Maggie*) let me know soon—I'm still miserable—in fact worse—my mind has begun to narrow in its spin, like the lip the throat of a whirlpool—I'm going going—But also I'm peaceful and work and sleep. How about you?

Note

Neal [Cassady] got badly injured here—fell off, was knocked off a boxcar, fell on an iron end bumper, slashed his chest, cracked his foot back to touch his ankle—is now home on crutches—write to him—I saw him at the hospital—I haven't seen Carolyn yet but may go live with them—I am now in the mountains—braking—this summer I plan to go up into the wilderness and learn to survive by myself fishing and making Indian acorn mush and hunting etc. in preparation for when I won't be able to make it in culture and civilization any more.

What's with A.A. Wyn and *Maggie Cassidy?*

Well,—I hope you are well—Please give me Bill's latest address and ask him to—well I'll ask *him,* for Kells Elvins' address, he is in Frisco someplace, yachting—

I am so bored, aren't you?

Jack

Allen Ginsberg [New York, New York] to Jack Kerouac [n.p., San Luis Obispo, California?]

May 13, 1953

Dear Jack:

I got your letter yesterday. I'll write to Neal immediately. I wrote to Bill today giving him your address. His is now: W.S. Burroughs c/o U.S. Consulate, Lima Peru. He'll be there another two weeks maybe. He's writing YAGE book.

I have a lot to tell you—got a job with a literary agency, got fired, am unemployed (though have money from work for brother) and full of ideas and writing. In next letter will explain all. I will write all summer, have book to put together (another) and a great new work founded on the imagination and new philosophy.

[2] Martha Foley was the editor of *Story* magazine.

Dr. Sax and *Maggie* are publishable and I will take steps immediately to publish them.

You must leave everything to me, or trust me, or something. Do the following things. Inform your mother that I will be out to see her (not bringing the monster) and will pick up both books. Send me a letter enclosing a note to Phyllis Jackson at M.C.A. saying:

"Please take whatever steps are necessary to publish *Dr. Sax* and *Springtime Maggie* (*Maggie Cassidy* or whatever) at your convenience as soon as possible. Allen Ginsberg will be able to speak for me and handle my affairs in connection with these two books during my absence from NYC."

That's all the note should say. I have been on the telephone arranging things today. Wyn has rejected *Maggie Cassidy*.

Any further communications should be through me, Jack, please. I am sure that I know how to handle this situation completely.

I will operate through the facilities of M.C.A. who are willing to cooperate in the manner that I have arranged with them. If they cannot place it—though they are interested and will try—I will peddle it further myself, with their OK and goodwill.

Send me the above note to transmit to them, and don't get in touch with anybody till I tell you (anybody in publishing).

(Cowley[3] doesn't know, incidentally, that you have any other ideas about *On the Road*, such as you expressed to me in N.Y. He is still friendly disposed professionally.)

I will write further tomorrow. Answer by return mail sending the note above.

All my love,
Allen

Allen Ginsberg [New York, New York] to Jack Kerouac [n.p., New York, New York?]

July 2, 1953

Thursday Noon

Dear Jack:

"Just" a note on general plans:

1. Could you bring in other copies—carbons—of *Sax* and *Maggie*. This way I think it is good, we will also publish sections in *New Writing*, and several

---

[3] Malcolm Cowley, American writer, editor, and critic. An editorial consultant to the Viking Press, his support of *On the Road* was instrumental to its publication.

other large anthologies I have in mind (*Perspectives*). Circulate at same time and save time.

2. Do you have any short pieces at all around of any kind that you would like published in such (above places). Bring them too.

3. Will you make (yourself) a list of selections or excerptable sections from *Maggie*, and *Sax*, for above purposes? (As M. Lowry did)

4. Are there any parts of *On the Road*, Version I or II which you think will be in the final version or which you would like to see printed now? Bring those in.

5. Can you give me copies of *On the Road* I and II for my own use to study (for my own poetry) and for my projected essay:

INTRODUCTION TO THE PROSE OF JACK KEROUAC

which I have been thinking of for half a year and which I am ready to begin.

I am off all weekend from Fri. at 4:00 to Monday morning on account of the holiday. Walter Adams is supposed to come early evening Friday; and Alan Ansen invited me out to Woodmere Saturday night tentatively. I would like really to go away to shore or mountain for the days (I never get two days off as a rule—this is July 4) but I don't know where to go. If I could think of somewhere I would cancel all others and scram.

As ever, as Bill says,
Allen

In fact I may cancel others anyway on general principles.

Allen Ginsberg [New York, New York] to
Jack Kerouac [n.p., New York, New York?]

July 13, 1953

Dear Jack:

Business:

I finally picked up *Maggie* from Wyn & a letter of rejection, and delivered them to MCA. Hard as pulling teeth, they kept putting me off and evading, God knows why.

The following documents are necessary for me to have:

1. A copy of your contract with Wyn. Do you still have that at all or did I understand that you mailed it back to them? If you have it, need it. If not I will get one from them.

2. All correspondence from Wyn that has anything of business in it. Par-

ticularly letters (if any) rejecting *On the Road* (*Visions of Neal* version) and *Dr. Sax*. Did they ever send you those letters, or was all dealings mouthly? If not, I will also get them from Wyn. Also letters asking for revisions, etc.

This makes three definite documents I need, and all supplementary ones you have around. This is very important. Mail them to me or bring them this week. If you haven't any one of the three let me know.

Carl [Solomon] shouldn't know any more (than he does) about present publishing plans. So if you see him or anyone likely to converse with him about you, don't say anything. As far as I said today was that I was trying to place *Maggie* and *Sax*, didn't talk about anything else. He knows about [Malcolm] Cowley etc. from last season but should not know an inch more, and further conversation on that score should be wrapped in confusion and obscurity. Unless you have alternative plans, of which please let me know. This too is very important. Delicate. Subtle.

MCA thinks the short piece in Cowley's hands is publishable *here* (or foreign), and will find out what he has done with it. He's away for last three weeks, be back in seven days.

I have a note from P.O. saying three registered letters are in (from Burroughs) at post office for me to pick up tomorrow. The continuation of *Yage*.

I am off Wednesday (so is Lucien that rat) so am free Tuesday evening, and Wednesday.

Finished *Confidence Man*. It's about the void between friends, the break in continuity of innocent faith, between man. Exploration of that skull "reality" which suicided *Pierre*.

Began your essay.

  Love,

    Allen

Jack Kerouac [Richmond Hill, New York] to Allen Ginsberg and William S. Burroughs [New York, New York]

Nov 21 53

Dear Allen and Bill:

 Feel the need to write a letter to the two of you, sittin in front of my typewriter with goofball in, wine glass out—just wrote to [Malcolm] Cowley on business about *New World Writing* but threw in the following: "I see from the latest *New World Writing* where Libra or Gore Vidal is trying to tear you down to lift himself up to position of big new dean critic which is such a laff he's just such a pretentious little fag. They told me in 1950 that the homosexuals were very powerful in American Literature but since then what's troubled me is not that, so much as the certain dull individuals who happen to be homosexual who have grabbed off the limelight and therefore the temporary influence second rate anecdote repeaters like Bowles, pretentious silly females with flairs for titles like Carson McCullers, clever dramaturgists, grave self-revelers too naive to see the shame of their position like Vidal, really it's too much—think I'll come out soon and make a statement—every single original musical genius in America, for instance, "has been to jail or prison; I assure you the same holds true for literature"—How's that? and next line in letter reads: "This is the time"—(the musical geniuses like Bud Powell, Bird, Bill Holiday, Lester Young, Jerry Mulligan, Thelonious Monk)—So that's tellin em! hey? I'll fix that Vidal; I'll libra him; I'll ad astra that ass hole a?

Purpose of this letter is not to yak like this, tho, but serious necessity, to say, I had the Dolophine Visions now and after 48 hours of hi American chemical synthetic I am actually now junksick I guess and so lushing and barbitrating—but in the midst of that feeling such great tenderness and love for you two fellows, together or alone, wish there was some heavenly accolade I could lay on you or something you'd value—and soon we are going in three directions—but eventually and about a year probably we all probably be in Mexico City anyhow—but now I want to make a speech, an after dinner speech, a big successful fat cigar big steakdown after dinner speech, don't know really what to say, ain't no George Jessel, know you understand, etc. and just writing and mailing this letter and goofballs got me now, you boys okay, you boys gonna go heaven ya, you boys, coupla fine fellows, that what, tha wha, you bonna be do all right, okay, in heaven dog, love you.

   As ever

    Jack

1954

Editors' Note: By the end of 1953, Ginsberg had saved enough money for a trip to visit Neal Cassady in San Jose. He decided that he'd make it a leisurely visit and stay for an extended period of time, and perhaps get a job in San Francisco and find his own apartment. He left New York in December and traveled by way of Florida, Cuba, and Mexico, writing long descriptive letters on the way. Since he was on the move in a remote part of Mexico, Kerouac did not have any way of writing to him, so the correspondence from this period is one-sided.

Allen Ginsberg [Merida, Mexico] to Jack Kerouac, Neal Cassady, and Carolyn Cassady [San Jose, California]

before January 12, 1954

Dear Jack and Neal and Carolyn:

I am sitting here on the balcony of my Merida "Casa de Huespedes" looking down the block to the Square at twilite—have a big $5 peso room for the nite, just returned from eight days inland. Came by plane from horrid Havana and more horrid Miami Beach. All these tropical stars—just filled my gut with big meal and codeinettas and am sitting down to enjoy the nite—first rest I've had in longtime.

Saw Bill [Burroughs]'s Marker [Lewis Marker] in Jacksonville—a sweet fellow who donated $12 to my trip on his own hook, very simpatico—but, and, I *must* say Bill's taste in boys is macabre—(to say the least etc.) he is so starved looking and rickety and pitifully purseymouthed and "laid"—French for ugly and with a disgusting birthmark below left ear—and skin the texture of a badly shaved hemophiliac. The first sight of him was a shock—poor poor Bill! To be in love with that sickly myopic pebblemouthed scarecrow! Had great long talk about mystical ignus personality and drank rum and stayed in big moldy apartment in slums house that he owns.

In Palm Beach I called up the Burroughs family and was given big welcome— Xmas dinner and put me up at fancy hotel and drove me around town sightseeing and asked me about Bill, who I told them was "a very good and perhaps become a very great writer" which I think they liked to hear said, and was glad to say it in most conservative Bob Merims[1] considering manner. Old Burroughs very nice, some of Bill's innate wisdom-tooth. Miami Beach I stopped overnite for $1.50 and saw all the mad hotels—miles of them—too much for the eye, the lushest unreal spectacle I ever saw. Also ran into Alan Eager[2] at a Birdland they

---

[1] Bob Merims was an engineer and friend of Lucien Carr.
[2] Alan Eager was a jazz musician whom Ginsberg and Kerouac knew from New York.

have there. Key West pretty like Provincetown, nothing happened there, rode on Keys on truck at nite. Havana I won't talk of—kind of dreary rotting antiquity, rotting stone, *heaviness* all about and don't dig Cubans much even in Cuba. Got lost penniless twenty miles out of town in small village and had to be sent home on train with man who bought me drinks. So sad, so hospitable, but I wanted to get away, can't dig his fate. Marvelous first airplane air vistas of the earth, Carib Isles, great green maplike Yucatan Coast maplike below with sinkholes in earth of limestone crust and narrow road and trails like antpath down below and little cities like mushrooms in pockets and hollows of afternoon hills, and windmills.

Stayed in Merida three days at this place, ran into two Quintana Roo Indians and drove in horse carriage round city, met mayor's brother so got invited to big City Hall ceremonies New Years day—free beer and sandwiches overlooking plaza on balcony City Hall; that nite, New Years, formal dress— New York-Paris-London society type "Country Cloob" (Club) champagne free and French and English and German speaking industrialists and young Yucatan Spanish girls fresh from New Orleans finishing school—all dressed in tux and party evening dress at tables under stars—nothing happened I just wandered around and talked to people, then after went downtown and heard poor mambo in dancehalls and drank little and slept at 5 AM. Next day to Chichen Itza where I got free house next to pyramid and spent days eating in native hut for 7 pesos a day, wandering around great ruins—at nite take hammock up on top of big pyramid temple (whole dead city to myself as living in archeologists' camp) and look at stars and void and deathheads engraved up on stone pillars and write and doze on codeinetta. Free guide from where I eat, and drink every nite before supper at Richman's Mayaland Hotel talk to rich Americans, meet thirty-five year old Ginger B. all hung up on Yucatan songs and costumes, dumb, drag, talking bitch sad. Stars over pyramids—tropic nite, forest of chirruping insects, birds and maybe owls—once I heard one hooting—great stone portals, bas relief of unknown perceptions, half a thousand years old—and earlier in day saw stone cocks a thousand years old grown over with moss and batshit in dripping vaulted room of stone stuck in the wall. A high air silent above niteforest— tho a clap of hands brings great echoes from various pillars and arenas. So then left for Valladolid—money already running out—in central Yucatan and nite there with amigo speaking English who showed me the tower and I ate at his middleclass family house where his wife bowed respectful and a movie about ghosts—and next day awful miserable ten hour train to town name of Tizinia [*sic*: Tizimin] for the oldest fiesta of Mexico; most venerable Indians from Campeche and Tabasco on train with great sacks full of food and babies and hammocks; started on train at 4 A.M. morning rode till afternoon cramped no place to stand, train ran off rails, hold-ups, arrive at really crowded small town middle of nowhere—with silly bullring and 400 year old cathedral, mobbed by old Indians, candles, three wooden kings old as the conquest they came to see (three Mages)—the air of cathedral so smoky and so full of candles the wax on the floor was inches deep and slippery—thought I was the only American in town but later found a Buffalo optometrist on train back who said famous documentary film maker named Rotha[3] was there with movie cameras—(I saw Rotha pix in Museum of Modern Art once)—trip back horrible—the *boxcars* with benches on sides and down center, wood, Mex-made and all crude, 110 people to car, people hanging on platform and even *steps* for hours—me too—so uncomfortable to sit it was insane, for 10 hours—and had left my codeine behind! (*No* have habit by the way only used two times) old women and babies falling asleep on my shoulder and lap, everybody suffering meaningless hour-long stops in the nite to change tracks or engines.

Had met priest at Tizimin Cathedral who took me backstairs and smoked and cursed native pagan rite of the feast, and so went with him to his village "Colonia Yucatan" a lumber town *a la* Levittown or Vet housing project—and he drove me by jeep next day to forests of Quintana Roo and back—then to train and horrid ride. Then another day at great silent Chichen Itza—recalling a dream I once had about a future world of great plateaus covered with grass and levels and plains of plateau leading to horizon with grassy roofs on many levels of dripping stone chambers and wild sculptured ornament all round the sides—stood up and looked from top at jungle spread all around circle to horizon, dream actualized. Who came up but the optometrist, with his nice camera.

Came back to Merida today. Met bunch of Mexico City painters on junket to study provinces and talked French and will go to a big *gran baille* (dance) tonite (Sat. nite)—and tomorrow look up Professor Stromswich for info on Mayapan ruins—also must pick up letter from Bill from Rome at Consulate and telegram perhaps with money from home—down to $25 dollars, enuf to get to Mexico City but not much more and want to see more Mexico south so sent for some more $ from Gene [Eugene Brooks]. My Spanish is got to point where I can find out what I want easily but I keep making mistakes that have cost me money from time to time—enough to wish I knew—like I bought the wrong kind of hammock and so lost out nine pesos the other day.

Also in Merida a "homeopathic druggist" i.e. I don't know, different from

[3] Paul Rotha was a British documentary filmmaker and critic.

pharmaceutical druggists—name of George Ubo been everywhere in U.S. and Yucatan and told me how to get everywhere on big ten foot map he has. So far everywhere I have run across someone or other who showed me the town in English or French or English-Spanish mixture but have not met anyone great— except one nite in the rich hotel in Merida last week, wandered into bar for one peso rich-man's tequila and ran into a drunk brilliant elderly Spaniard who talked to me in French in great world weary monologue full of filth and Paris and N.Y. and Mexico City and who was later led off by his bodyguard to be sick in the urinal—later found out he was the richest man in the area Yucatan Peninsula— famous character who married a whore twenty years ago and owns everything everywhere and gets drunk every nite with venerable looking Jaime de Angulo white bearded spic internationalists at the hotel—who were there that night winking and calming him down—sort of an old evil Claude [Lucien Carr] he was, full of misery and rich and drunken disregard of life.

Mosquitoes down here awful—all beds come with M-nets and I have bought one for my hammock.

Jack, incidentally—they won't let you past customs in Merida without health card and all the Indians have vaccination marks they wear "proudly"—it's really a 50-50 necessity. Have had dysentery and took pills and it went away, so no suffer. No such thing as a natural man untouched by medicine around here— it's not for touristas, tho it's a tourista routine—it is for everyone.

If I had more money, I found a way to get thru Quintana Roo involving busses and narrow gauge mule driven R.R. and an afternoon walk thirteen kilometers on rocky mule path thru jungle—or else a forty peso boat around peninsula—but cannot go cause too costly for my purse. But will be fine trip for someone someday. Many people all over ready to help the traveler—it's like a frontier—with engineers building a road thru that never gets done.

Received a letter from [Bill] Garver saying he's still in D.F. [Mexico City] and will see me there.

The man here, head of archeology, name given me by Museum Natural History in N.Y.—turned out valuable—gave me pass to stay on archeologist's camps, free, everywhere there's a ruin I go. Great way to travel and see ruins. Write me note to Mexico City Embassy.

Love,

Allen

P.S. Had a great dream—must go to Europe to make movie about Bill riding on trains from Italy.

Allen Ginsberg [Palenque, Mexico] to Neal Cassady, Jack Kerouac, and Carolyn Cassady [San Jose, California]

January 18–25, 1954

Palenque, Chiapas, Mex.
Jan 18 '54

Dear Neal and Jack and Caroline [Carolyn]:

Since I last wrote I have been from Merida to Uxmal to Campeche (a port on the peninsula on the way) to Palenque where I am now.

I am beginning to really hate Mexico and almost wish I were out of it, as traveling with so little money I am continually obsessed with saving it, and consequently making mistakes in spending what I have and building up great reserves of anger at whoever gets in my way—usually a Mexican—when I spend it. As it is I have about thirty-four bucks left to get to D.F. on where (I presume) I have more waiting from the telegram and it better be there—though with dear old Bill Garver around I suppose I won't become a public charge. However I ain't going to hit a lot of cities on the way that I wanted to—partly no money to get there (San Cristobaldo Las Casas way down South Chiapas) or time and $ to find out how to get there—travel around here mainly by R.R. but I am sure there are roads. By R.R. it would take days and days to San Cristobal from here, which is only 100 or so miles away as bird flies.

Uxmal where I was last week is the 2nd most important Yucatan Roon [ruin] but is the best to live at I think—more glory though less grandeur than Chichen Itza. Have much to say about ruins but am more concerned with a typical paranoid incident occurring ten miles out of Merida the day before I left—having nothing to do I got on a local bus to a small town twenty miles away where there was a small party (a Kermesse they called it—sounds French) advertised. On the way two young fellers picked up on me—at a time when I didn't really want to try to talk this rotten language anymore—it's too exhausting just to work out the necessities like food drink and transportation to carry on further trying to make self understood—(in a very bad mood tonite having trekked in mud for hours in a real jungle too hung up picking my way thru slime and thorn trees to get to see any jungle though it was there—and thirsty, little water around—and slightly dysenteric, and with a lousy cold been with me ten days) so as I say not wanting to try to talk no more Spanish that day, just ride and see and eat tortillas, I got hung up.

The lights there went out (Jan 25 is today) and I have not had a chance to continue this letter till now (a week later) and am not at Palenque and the story is half forgotten—be that as it may I got on the bus and got involved in dull conversation with two youths and got off bus half way to get drunk with them and went on to fair and returned at dark and was given over in the small half-way town to what intuition and all told me was the local queer who began singing songs of Corazon on this road at nite and I really didn't dig the situation as he was a 35 yr old . . . child effeminate this Mexican, an archetype of a kind—I'm sure I've seen him somewhere—and I got a bus and returned home. Point is not understanding Spanish I couldn't make anything of the drunken paranoia—much like Jack's Mexico.

Well anyway to get off this bum kick of incomprehensible story.

I was walking around Palenque and ran into a woman who grew up around here—the edge of the most inaccessible jungle area of South Mexico—who had returned six years ago after various careers in the States, a professional archeologist whose family had owned the Palenque site so that she knew it inside out. As result I am spending a week on her cocoa finca (or plantation)—have been here seven days—don't yet know when I'll leave—located in middle of jungle a day's horseback ride out of Palenque. Last week we set out on march, took jeep to path, then she, I, another girl (wandered thru forest on foot to Palenque from city on Pacific, a student, ugly), an old Indian retainer and a boy being taken to live at the Senora's finca—four horses and a mule set out for seven hour ride thru beautiful dark jungle—soldier ants, anthills, lianas, orchids, vast trees covered with parasite cactus and fern, big leaved plantain trees, parrots screeching and wild deep roar of howler monkeys in trees sounding like Tarzan Jungle. First time I ever rode a horse—on mucky path, full of little up and downhill wind, trees fallen over path full of hunky-like fungus growths, small streams—and always every few miles a small hill covered with stones which was a part of the City of Palenque (forty square miles)—the woman knowing from childhood all parts everywhere, and more, being a sort of mystic and *medium* type personality, as well as *learned* in the subject— perhaps the person in the world most emotionally and knowledgably tied to these ruins and this area—so that I found after a few days talking, she had been on foot and plane all thru jungles down to Guatemala and in lost cities all places, some even she discovered, had written books (her editor is Giroux) and learned papers and worked for Mexican government reconstructing Palenque and others, owned a few cities in her great tract of land here (hundreds of sq. mi) *and*, most important, was the only person in the world who knew of a lost tribe of Mayans living in Guatemala on a river who still possibly could interpret codices and were specially on a mission to keep alive Mayan flame—and she told me all sorts of secrets, beginning with outline of Mayan metaphysics and mystical lore and history and symbolism, that would have delighted Bill, who doesn't know—that it is all still extant. This lost tribe apparently had brought her up as child, being in area where her father owned $3,000,000 dollar ranch here and having selected her for confidence. Well all this is sort of corny and amusing but the curious thing is that much of it is true in its most classically corny aspects. It is a great kick to enjoy her hospitality in the jungle—she being starved for ignu conversation tho she is not an ignu herself—and go out everyday with machete and rifle in jungle trails, on 3–4 mile walks, hunting, swimming in great clear little rock pools surrounded by giant ferns, in crystal water, returning at nite in darkness when jungle begins stirring, talking Mayan metaphysics. We live in an open sided room with continual fire for coffee and food at one end tended by an Indian, hammocks strung up across the room, a great unexplored mountain right ahead looking very near—a few hundred feet thru the brush behind the house are six native huts with families—who work on the plantation, a sort of feudal system of which she is queen and we are royal guests. Party includes a young Mexican Point 4 apprentice who is supervising the cultivation of the cocoa (which is chocolate). I will leave here sooner or later by horseback for two hours and then by Kayuko (a big tree hollowed out for a boat) up a river to a R.R. town. Then by plane for 80 pesos to San Cristobal, where I have decided to go after all. Plane is cheapest way—there being no way to get across Isthmus except by five day roundabout rail or five day by horse, just as expensive, more so, can't afford—tho horses are only 6 pesos a day here. At San Cristobal I meet Franz Blum who is a famous archeologist— Hal Chase in disgrace with universities in States, an old lush now gone tropical, who everybody says is the most brilliant man in Mexico and lived with Sherwood Anderson and Faulkner in New Orleans years ago before he came down here and discovered Palenque, etc.—he being now the foremost authority on Indians and Mayans and a friend of my hostess, etc.

I am sending this by Kayuko ahead of me, will leave in a few days more. If you get this letter send me a note care of U.S. Embassy Mexico D.F.

Allen

Have no place on which to write and can't write comfortable so excuse this sloppy letter effort—can't concentrate and compose.

What is the situation in Frisco—I am dawdling here and will dawdle in Mexico as long as my money lasts—another two or three weeks perhaps? Then will go to your cheerful household—I have many photographs too with me I will develop in Frisco—about 200 photos, maybe 25 interesting ones.

I had a dream: Everyone I knew killed (by knife) frightening series of murders as in a movie—Gene, Jack, Bill. Police called me in for questioning.

Allen Ginsberg [Tacalapan, Mexico] to Neal Cassady, Carolyn Cassady, and Jack Kerouac [San Jose, California]

February 18–19, 1954

Tacalapan, Palenque
Chiapas, Mexico
February 18, 1954

Dear Neal, Caroline [Carolyn], Jack:

Well I am still here in the state of Chiapas and don't know for sure when I will leave, maybe next week maybe next month. Doesn't depend on anything for sure, just when I come out of a sort of retreat or limbo and push on for bright lights alcohol and sex joys. Here, I am on the brush field surrounded by big forest trees looking over typewriter past leaning thin palm to a great long green mount, a tropical Greylock nobody's ever been on, supposedly Mayan and enchanted with gold and an old guardian and ruins near a white rocky bluff, triangle shaped, which can be seen on some days; and the contour of the mount changes daily, sometimes can be seen as being far far away, sometimes seems close up and detailed, especially in eerie cloud light of dusk; sometimes seen as a series of ridges with huge valleys unknown between, which it actually is, tho looks daily most like one solid long green mount, name of Don Juan.

In daily walks thru jungle (or nightly) saw a huge rust reddish colored spotted blossom which when smelt appalls the mind with a fetid charnel house odor, stink of flesh manufactured by blind blossom on vine to catch flies.

Feb 19, '54

Have a beard, a goatee, black and mustachio, long hair, heavy shoes, ride horses, go fishing at nite in streams with natives giggling with focos (flashlites) and long stick with prongs to catch great crawfishes size of lobsters. Or go walking midday naked up a mile of rocky clear stream, bluey sky, with lianas and elephant ear trees and angel hair trees of plantain leaves and giant saibol (mahogany) trees filled with monkeys, on bank or dank islands midstream, ankle or waist or neck deep walk. A few mosquitoes.

And every hour or so get up from hammock and sit and idle with my drums, especially at dawn, at dusk, and during dark hours by fire before mosquito net is opened over hammock. Drums: smallest is three and a half feet, longest is seventeen feet and stands on a vine and stick support for vibrations to hang free. I went out and tapped rubber trees for black hard balls to tip heavy foot long sticks with for proper bong. I play several hours daily, mostly very soft

208

listening, and when a file of Indians rides in thru the trails from Agua Azul, Eden like little town in hills an hour ride away, I break out in African reverberations which can be heard for miles around. Am known as Senor Jalisco.

I read the *Cloud of Unknowing*, anonymous 14th century handbook of abstraction and in this limbo have developed a feeling again for possibilities of sitting and with stark blankness conceiving a familiar uncanny sensation which never comes to me whole, presumably too divine. Time spent here has been mainly contemplative of this fixed idea, and I had one day of excited agitation thinking I should go be a monk, but no need to do that, can develop anywhere and such agitations are passing. What hung me up on *Cloud of Un.* was the lovely and obviously true idea that a contemplative doesn't have to do anything but what he feels like, sit and think or walk and think, don't worry about work, life, money, no hang-ups, his job is to have no job but the unknown abstraction and its sensations, and his love of it. I have a tentative offer if I want to stay here till August alone when owner of ranch goes off to make money in states and manage it passively, no duties, just be here and see nobody sets fire to house or steals cocoa. Probably a very small pay like 100 pesos month, but perfect refuge and learn a lot. However want to get back to states and am lonely for someone to share pleasures with, wish someone were here to understand beauty of the drums, they're so big they would make Newman[4] for instance cream if he were not beyond the creaming state in his bald sunburned pate age.

Plans: Every several nights I have a melancholy dream that I am embarking for the ancient parapets of Europe: passageways, captains, gangplanks, staterooms, bunks, huge decks cluttered with people in furs *a la* '20s or deckchairs, nite lunches, foc'sls, arrangements with family, breaking up of apartments, foghorns in N.Y. harbor mist near docksides, Front Street or Telegram Street; and one night as summary I had a picture of N.Y. in color, in oval frame, enclosing Hohnsbean, Kingsland, Dusty, Keck, Anton [Rosenberg], D. Gaynor or others, Durgin, Merims, was Cannastra?, a compressed proustian moment in oval frame of all characters in activity at a psychic party Technicolor, all NY in one picture as you, Jack (are you there?) must have had many times over from road to road.

So, after waking up from four of these in two weeks I realized (especially after dream of Burroughs on Italian 2nd class train going to Spain) that as soon as possible must go to live awhile in Europe—think of the marvelous facades and palaces of dank Venice alone for instance, which will be digged in spacious St. Mark's Square dusk by us among pigeons of Europe and Eyetalian

---

[4] Jerry Newman owned Esoteric Records and taped Kerouac reading his work. He appeared as Danny Richman in *Visions of Cody*.

beggars as in some slow silent stage presentation of melancholy cloaked Byronic traveler passing thru in sad ballet. To say nothing of hollow old Catholic Rome. Prague! the very name conjures a mirage of centuries, the Golem, ghettoes, stone kings and fountains of dark lions and grey cherubs, students drinking beer and dueling thru the night. And perhaps sweet Moscow. Then there is Paris. Paris! City of Light! *ici mouru* Racine! Here Proust sipped his delicate tea, here Jean Gabin stared out over the roofs with his mistress crying in bed, glum. Memories, ancient waltzes, *tristesse de la lune*, all the tenderness of antiquity and the angel gentility of civilization, with the Eiffel tower and strange city mystics *a la* Cocteau and Rimbaud and most the tearful reality of the old world places. Even wish to see Londres, London of great bells and banking houses old as time, where liveth still in silence Seymour [Wyse] waiting for a winking eye from us undoubtedly.

As I sit here under the mountain at the moment of noon, sun white in that green high palm tree leaves, butterflies in the meadow, contemplating a voyage to the old world, having seen a ruin in the new, head full of abstraction and memory, there are sitting beside me four Gauguin maids conversing in Spanish (I half understand and can follow) barefoot in bright store clothes, with big safety pins in bosom of dresses for ornament, complaining about their ailments to the senora who has medicines: codeine, barbiturates, W.C. Fields Wampole drink for the weary and worried, vitamins that would mystify and delight Burroughs. And last week a murderer, having avenged the death of his father (sister of one of these girls), young boy with bullet holes in hand and arm, came at dawn for refuge from law and help, and we operated, cutting open upper arm to take out bullet (I felt faint, watching her cut with a Gillette double edged blade) and put him up for two days till rumors of a posse (just like frontier) reached us one night and we sent him to the woods to hide. Two weeks ago we had a meteor so grand, big as star of Bethlehem, illuminated blue and red the whole half horizon. Same day my first trembler; which earthquake, I later found, had half destroyed the back-interior town of Yajalon (Yah-ha-lone), the church in ruins, lava coming up, a new volcano like Paracutin—though this is rumor, another man passing thru said the mountain top went to the bottom and the bottom went to the top—meaning a landslide? *Quien sabe*? however adding that the priest who was supposed to have perished screaming in the tottering cathedral four centuries old really was still alive though seriously wounded, as he had been konked by a single brick shook loose. As well as a perfect lunar eclipse I saw the nite I left Palenque.

I live among the thatch roof huts, eat tortillas and frijoles at every meal with mucho pleasure, amazing how a real strong taste for them can be developed, like for potatoes with eggs, meat, vegs. etc. I pass banana groves and work in them for an hour or so weekly, cutting, pruning, gathering the bunches, eat them fried and raw, daily also. And work a few hours or a day in the cocoa grove, cutting, washing, fermenting and drying cocoa (makes chocolate)— washing particularly, very pleasant, with group of injuns barefoot each with a woven basket swushing the gooey nuts around to rid them of guk, squatting in sunlite under hot greenery by rocky stream. Well not always a group of in-juns, but often. And at nite I sit in huts by fires watching violin and drum, sometimes.

La Senora, in case I forgot to say last time, is a Giroux-Harcourt authoress, once wrote a best seller about jungle (*Three in the Jungle*). Ugh. Writing another about mystical Mayans, interesting facts for Bill but she's a strange case, some good and some nutty and some tiresome about her; her best feature aside from real (tho perhaps indefinite mystic hang-up) being pioneer type-operating-on-the-indians-grew-up-around-here-carries-a-machete-and-runs-plantation aloneness, real archeological pro.

Yesterday I laughed to myself with delight at the thought of finally leaving here sometime and really making it to Frisco; and tho I will, and arrival in Frisco is sure shooting barring unforeseen changes in soul atmosphere here or there or seismic phenomena unwonted or civil states and wars unheard of here as yet (no seen newspaper in two months) (me), I don't know when. It's like a dream of Europe. I ordered my mail sent down here from D.F. and other places so if you've written me, I'll get it this coming week. Can be reached here: HOTEL ARTURO HUY, c/o Karena Shields, Allen Ginsberg, Salto De Agua, Chiapas, Mexico. When I leave mail if any will be forwarded and I'll write then anyway.

Shutting up shop—man bit by bushmaster in next village and must find horses in field rush with razors and antiviperina. But eat first, we sent medicine ahead. Stupid corrupted blood Indians who play poor drums don't even know enuf to cut open and bleed snakebite. Older time real Indians know savvy more lore.

Croak.

A. Groan.

Jack Kerouac [San Jose, California] to Allen Ginsberg [n.p., Mexico City, Mexico?]

ca. March 1954

Dear Allen:

This large enclosed interesting letter from Burroughs in Tangier indicates that he needs a "completely new approach" and shows how all of us in only the past four or five months have suddenly changed and taken up new positions around what we like to think is the sun, or the moon, or the everything and zenith. Neal, for instance, has suddenly become religious and is espousing Reincarnation and Karma.[5] Carolyn is firm on the subject of Karen Horney ("Inner Conflicts" or the later one.)[6] . . . saying it's all the same thing, in different approach. In fact a general Bahiaism all over and even on the radio you hear a preacher say that it is "false individualism" that makes a man refrain from "labor."—and so everybody getting wise to the terms "false" and "true," "essence" and "form" and etc. I, on receiving your Chiapas letter, was high with Al Sublette and Neal, listening to Gerry Mulligan and Chet Baker, and read about your proper bong drums how the Indians come single file to the store and you jump up and drum popeyed to impress them and they call you Jalisco and you have an act with medicine. Did not ye find those secret eroticism you went there for? Is it worth visiting?

Shall I come down there and sit, or shall I go back to New York, or shall I live under a tree by the railroad track in California, or shall I move into an abandoned dobe hut in the Valley of Mexico and see [Bill] Garver every Saturday afternoon? Alone or with Al Sublette? Or go down to Chiapas with or without Al Sublette? Al says he wants to sit and let it all go but admits his weakness for drugs, lush, cunt and all the countless anxious intoxications of the jazz age and the machine. He's not an intellectual. I prefer going off alone on all counts for everything now but can't tear myself away from bondage and bondhood to friendhood ship and have long since realized that not only am I the Messiah deceived but you too, and Neal too, and Bill, and Zilen, and Zunkey, and Mush, and Crush. From the ten quarters of the universe it is said they come and lay radiant hands in a wheel on your brow. This is in appearance, like the moths of light, and that Atlantis radar machine we saw in the sky over the New School when you said it had been there since the beginning in eternity anyway, and now Neal claims they had atomic power in Atlantis and Gurdjieff and Ouspensky and Bill Keck and all the social details so drearsome come flooding in to repeat what we know has already happened and will happen again. A girl will come to me again; and I will be an accomplice after the fact to a crime again; and I will find rest again and sleep deep within the golden light in the womb of the mind again. But all of it has to be, we must have a conference, or nothing, east meets west or nothing; that's why, I want to arrange a meeting between us or none at all, naming place, time, laying bare plans for livelihood, ideas; I have the teaching to impart to you. The teaching, the Dharma, is lost to Neal. He has

[5] The Cassadys had discovered the teachings of the American mystic Edgar Cayce.
[6] Karen Horney was a psychologist and the author of *Our Inner Conflicts*.

already and as I say at the same time espoused a teaching (of Edgar Cayce a supernaturalist recently dead who cured people by self hypnotic diagnosis) and is like a Billy Graham in a suit, and talks rapidly explaining that here at last is "scientific proof" of the truth of reincarnation and Neal's interest in the subject curiously Melvillean, "the world would be flooded with evil if there wasn't an inner good" and a wheel of justice turning us dog murderers from bad to worse till we repent and become dogs and are killed by dog murderers and are reborn contemplatives and perfect to finish. But let him tell you himself. That's the big main thing, that he tell you himself, so you'll judge for yourself (the nature of his what amounts to materialistic heresy here). But the difference amounts only to choice of celestial contacts, different connections, I suppose the pusher is the same. Neal begins there is no beginning and end to the world, the karmic etheric akasha essence substance vibrating continuously in all the billion universes and our atman-entities rushing around . . . and I believe that there was emptiness and silence, and will be, after this hassle ends, by our own volition undone thread by thread and our egos and entities vanish but so we took benny tonight and I'll write this big letter and empty my notebooks to you so you can judge and Neal will dictate later.

Allen Ginsberg [Yajalon, Mexico] to Neal Cassady, Carolyn Cassady, and Jack Kerouac [San Jose, California]

Yaljalon
March [sic: April] 4, 1954

Neal:

Carolyn:

Jack:

Forgive me for not answering your letter about spiritualism earlier. I received it in a kayuko in the Rio Michol traveling toward Salto de Agua when we met a messenger with months old mail, so I read it and a flippant letter from Claude [Lucien Carr] and Burroughs' messages under the trees leaning back on my knapsack while the Indians rowed in green crocodile water. That Neal is religious is a great piece of news: I always wondered what he would be like with some overpowering Awful thought humbling his soul to saintliness. But wait! I have been doing some magnificent deeds in the last week, and now am sitting in awful dumps all gone wrong and will tell you about it first.

I got to Salto with your letter two weeks ago. To make a long story short, I hitchhiked a plane ride into deeper Chiapas, Yajalon where all the earthquakes have been. I heard about Mt. Acavalna—Tzeltal for Night House? What does that mean—Refuge from Darkness, or Place to Suffer Darkness—casa obscura. A mystery. Acavalna (roll that name, its Blakean, on your lips)—in the mountains beyond Yajalon—haven't got time to tell you all the Mayan sierra and mystery forest ruins details, nor the meaning of names—Tumbala, Bachahon, Lancandon etc. But Acavalna is in that direction. According to geologists source of the quakes—still going on here every day after two months.

So in Yajalon with 100 pesos and no toothbrush and dirty clothes on my back, nothin but a fountain pen stepped off plane empty handed—small Mexican south town, 400 year church at end of ten blocks long, four blocks wide, walled in by high mountains on either side, fantastic scenery—approachable by plane that crashes every ten days or three days of mule inland from railroad town Salto.

I went to Presidente and said I was a periodista on vacation and wanted to visit Acavalna—no newsman ever been there, just one geologist climbed it ten days before and reported nothing but a big crack in its front, said maybe no volcano. But two days later Instituto Geologica his office said maybe there was volcano, in papers. Much confusion, Yajalon frightened. President promised mule free and guide. Next day no mule, just guide, I started over La Ventana—mountain wall between Yajalon and Acavalna—till halfway up a kind of Mexican saw my beard and in midpassage gave me his mule to ride up (he continuing his trip down on foot—true courtesy of local road). I arrived in afternoon at finca or plantation named Hunacmec—was treated as honored important guest—we sent mule and guide back. Hunacmec is at foot of Acavalna. That late afternoon, was loaned hammock and blanket for cold air mountain, given guide and horse to go spend the night at Zapata—a central Indian village lost in side of Acavalna where men wear white and women wear black and pigs gobble your crap by the river, pushing you aside to get it before you're finished. Meanwhile joined by two Laurel and Hardy Yajalontecans who ran up and down mountain after me to go along. Night—drums, primitive church, bamboo pipe, (greatest hollow primitive drums I ever saw by the way they make brilliant drums here) guitars, men on cedar logs around wall, women in black pool at center in front of altar lighting long sinister pagan candles in front of glasscase altar covered with bunting and 1890 German religious paintings containing dolls of Jesu Christi and bearded black Indian saints, another drum hanging from thatch roof—entertainment for me—suddenly boom, stupendous under ground roar like the subway of the End [West End Bar] under years of concrete pavement, and the whole mountain begins to shake, the thatch roof adobe church creaking, tortilla sized adobe chunks falling by my shoulders, women screaming and rushing out the door into the black shaking night, me trembling for my stupid pride in coming to dread Acavalna. Horror of the awful power under the mountain making so much noise and moving so much, and building up the noisy shuddering—then stopped, everything quiet except for dogs barking and cocks crowing and women screaming. It was the worst shake they had since Feb. 5, the first earthquake, and me on top of the fucking mountain right there. Nobody killed or nothing.

Well to make a long story short again, next day at dawn we got together an expedition of 54 men Indians all beautiful and numberless boys and dogs more, from Zapata, from Tzahala, dirty town south, and Chiviltic, over the next mountain—everybody scared, and we started a great high dreadful climb under hanging stone thru milpas, to the unknown forest at the top of the mountain to see if there was a volcanic fissure, or ruins, as was rumored, or a secret lake, also rumored. High cedar forest, we caught a monkey—they eat monkeys. Can't tell you how I enjoyed the situation—curious my psychology but it was a perfect set up—I was the leader, I organized and supplied the general power and intelligence—and I was deferred to, boys carried my morale (little bag) and my food, special Indian coffee and eggs for me—the rest drank ground maize for lunch, they asked me questions, dozens of Indians ready to run up and down mountains to get me horses or carry messages or perform any mysterious white man with beard wish. At same time I was weaker on horse or mountain or locality know how, and my weakness deferred to with the greatest love and chivalry. This was the sensation I had anyhow. Well anyhow we got to the top—two or three small noisy tremblers on the way (there were twenty a day)— not exactly unknown, I should say as the geologist had got there with a few Indians last time. They were all afraid to go when he was here, but this time all the men of all three villages who weren't sick or busy went with me—the point being to calm the injuns all over the area who think a volcano is smoking on top. So we got to the top and saw all the mountains around and found nothing and set afire for joke smoke a great cedar tree to scare Chiapas, came down and I sat in middle of a circle and took names and we made a declaration to send to the Indians and towns saying exactly what's going on in the mountain—for there is immense rumor inaccurate of every kind all over around here—and stamped it with official seal of the three villages.

Went back to Hunacmec thinking I'd had a great trip into rarely seen parts more obscure than where I've been all along, though I know well of parts more obscure toward the Usumacintly—and we must sometime with mule go traveling through these parts. I know Spanish now and a little bit of Mayan, pocitito, and I love Indians and get along with them great, really, I think I could go anywhere practically—but anyway, the next morning when I woke up I found forty Indians sitting on my doorstep of the tile roof finca house at the

215

foot of Acavalna. They were from La Ventana, across the way, had got up and walked five miles before dawn to talk to me, they wanted to know what we saw on the mountain—and wanted me to come with them to the other side. There was a legendary cave, they said they didn't know it, but two men from the village had been there years before, and the geologist didn't believe them, and they wanted to see if the earthquakes had closed the mouth. They said [I] should come and spend the night at their village and they would give me horses and guides to get back to Yajalon next day. So I went along on foot, and we stopped at another village on the way and they put me up on a horse in the middle of them—a long line of forty white robed Indians filing up and down the hills—till we came to the end of the mulepath—and I got off horse and twenty men went ahead to clear a path, so we climbed up the east side of the mountain through the brush, till we reached great boulders of ancient volcanic rock, like the great waste plain at Paracutin—climbing over these—mountains ready to shake or explode or god knows what: then shouting ahead, they found it. When I came out in the clearing I saw a hole in the side of the mountain as big as St. Patrick's cathedral, entrance to the great legendary cave—first stranger other than Indians ever there—solving riddle of name of mountain—House of Night—dark cave. Indians have great poetic imagination for names—a mountain anciently named house of night and forgotten why except for one or two who nobody believes centuries later. Well this cave was there, and I climbed over the brush and went in first—I had to do something brave to justify the honor—and we all started staring and wandering in the mouth—suddenly another boom from the mountain, I sat down hard and waited but nothing happened, and there was another innocent trembler fifteen minutes later when we were all deeper in, and could hear stalactites crashing down interior—the mouth of the cave had caved in and enlarged in earlier quakes, so it was very scary. Beautiful cathedral like stalactite formations—it's an enormous cave, one of the big world caves. I never visited caves before like Crystal Cave, but this one is as big I'm sure or bigger, it's just stupendous, and right now thinking of it, it's like some awful dream vision, that big you know—and full of pulpit formations, and naves and arches, like a Piranesi drawing don't you know, pilasters and arks and giant dark religious figurations.

Well we drew up a declaration of La Ventana later and I returned to Yajalon and read the mayor my declarations. I became a local hero—the cave was legendary, I was the first to verify it officially, as I had the forty La Ventana witnesses and the seal, etc. So they asked me to stay and write up my story for newspaper and inform the Geological Institute at Mexico and have them come down and see if the tremblers have anything to do with the cave (I don't know)—and gave me a room in the president's house and told the local restaurant to send the bill to city hall and everybody in town wants to talk with me and invites me for coffee and merchants sell me cigarette packages cheap and don't charge me for pineapples and suchlike.

Chapter 2: Treachery in New York

Meanwhile first thing I do is spend thirty pesos wiring Claude [Lucien Carr], giving him a scoop for his Mexican U.P.—for Mexican newspapers are full of Acavalna tho no mex newsman as I say has ever seen the place, just typical Mexican rumors via the geologist about secret lakes that don't exist (the cave has a river)—and mail him the documents to make sure and write up 3000 words describing trip, Indians, night of quakes on mountain, discovery of cave. Asking him to have mex U.P. inform the geologist, etc. so he can have the story first and me maybe a little money like 50 bucks say for expenses.

In this telegram I said went to the top unvolcanic and next day discovered legendary cave secret of name.

In the middle of this sentence my typewriter began shaking—and the room trembling back and forth, dust falling from walls, I'm in the president's house in Yajalon, another earthquake, a kind of shuddering sound, but not like in the subway up in the mountain. No damage, though they say a house fell down at the end of the street near the airfield, I'll go and see when I'm done writing.

And said to Claude in this telegram that geologist don't know, etc. and described cave. I wait three days and I get back: UNVOLCANIC CONDITIONS KNOWN STATESIDE APPLAUD MAGNIFICENT DISCOVERIES GONE BRAZIL WRITE

Which means, the ironic stupid bastard, that he misunderstood my telegram and thought that I thought I was telling him something new about the top of the volcano (whereas I was giving him my itinerary shorthand) and that the cave didn't register, or mean anything to him—and that he was going to Brazil (his vacation is April 2 or something to visit De Onis) and wouldn't receive my explanation about the cave nor the interesting description in detail about what it's like in a primitive Indian church in the middle of the night when an earthquake shakes the mountain. In short I am left hung up on Yajalon with no money to telegraph anybody about anything, all my sweat writing three days no carbon in air to no hands in N.Y. and all my adventure slipping from my hands into the anonymity which it so richly deserves. So I'm leaving this dump, I've got 10 pesos left and soon my welcome here will be worn thin. I wrote Von Harz to read Claude's mail from me and use what he can—but it will be a week before anybody in N.Y. gets the idea and meanwhile I can't delay informing the Mexicano Institute, which will give the story to the Mexican press and maybe I'll get my name in the papers here but no chance of collecting any small $$$ if there ever was one—though to be sure I haven't seen a paper for months and have no idea how absurd all this sounds in U.S. ears unless anybody has enough imagination to see the importance and news value, however minor, of the cave. Well, I have some money—20 dollars in Salto, will return to the finca for rest and to still my troubled irritated nerves and explore legendary mountain Don Juan there and wait for another 20 bucks in checks the stupid embassy in D.F. returned to sender with the rest of my mail. *World Telegram* back wages they were. If I get that I'll have enuf money I guess to get out, and come to Frisco right off the bat. Meanwhile if you get a sudden wire from me asking for 25 dollars please get it to me if you have to pawn the family jewels because it will mean I am desperate and broke. Incidentally anyplace I wire from, Salto if anywhere, will receive money wired back. I add this glumly since the last time my family sent me money the U.S. bureaucracy tried to say there was no such place on the wireless maps. Write me if you haven't since last.

  Love,
    Allen

And if that damned cave hasn't been reported by the time you get this letter do something—write Giroux or my mother in Pilgrim State.

P.S. Jack: Re a meeting—I won't be in Mexico much longer—don't have plans yet, waiting for money to get out—write and wait.

Jack Kerouac [New York, New York] to Allen Ginsberg [n.p., San Jose, California?]

ca. late May 1954

May

Dear Allen,

Please be reassured, angel, I think dearly of you whenever I do think of you, which is often, as I'm sure you do think of me often and dearly, naturally, and I'm not trying to be mysterious, or quiet, or anything, but just have reached the essence center of things where nothingness resides and does quite absolutely nothing, and this is my Chinese position.

I won't quote you the Tao, or make demands or impositions, or go into detail about what I been doing, except to mention, as you'll hear from Edgar Cayce Cassady and Carolyn, my discovery and espousal of sweet Buddha, which has been I guess in a wordly maybe even you sense my undoing, because, tho I always did suspect that life was a dream, now I am assured by the most brilliant man who ever lived, that it is indeed so, consequently I don't want to do anything any more, no writing, no sex, no nothing, I have abandoned and that is, hope to abandon, all evil outflowings of "life" for all good non-outflowings of mind essence recognition . . . no more Subterraneans to harass you with, or Alenes to kick myself in the ass with and no more anything but a kind of like 1948 realization of the nothingness and the who-cares-anyhow of Lucien drunks . . . tho once in a while I go out, because people call and write, and drink and fuck a little, but always come back, to my room, to do nothing, to take the privilege of doing nothing and claim it for my own, and so that, if my mother should want me to leave, I will and would go to El Paso Texas at first, to wash dishes and live across the river in $4 a month dobe cottage where with my Buddha Bibles and bean stews I would live life of mendicant thinker in this humble earth dream.

As for all your latest Mayan discoveries and poems, I want to hear every word of it if you want to transmit it, or tell it when we meet, but don't expect me to get excited by anything any more.

I love you, you are a great man, a great little kid in my mind, full of bullshit but innocent of why you fully of bullshit, like a Lucien Carr hero properly, to give something for the Lucien Satan to rave and rant about I guess at dawn in front of his believing cribs and arrant wives, Allen boy, okay, make it Maya, Maya, Maya, which in Sanskrit, means, dreamlike, the earth, all living things in the Universe must be regarded as Maya, the reflection of the moon on the lake, ask Carolyn to let you read the big letter of about May 20 that I sent her, for a résumé of my philosophical expository thinking; and have good time with wonderful Neal who will certainly show you around as no one else could, the crazy inevitable American California, the likes of which, etc., and I'm so tired of all such discriminations which come and go with little radiant lifetimes one after another; if possible we meet again sometime and I'll tell you about the gypsy shrouds, pull out the crystal meaning balls, and show you the secrets of the magic saints and the radiant perfumed hands of the Tathagatas that may one day be laid in a wheel shimmering upon your awakened brow, if I have anything to do with it before I lost myself in the recognition that I have no self, no ego, and therefore can no longer act as "I" and because of that don't find you or see you; until which time I hope to see you, to help you angel, in the final great radiant final filial heavenly discovery that believe me your you-sad-sublime boy has accidentally and only accidentally recently and completely found—so after big Californias and washlines and rail roads and speeches and go dig my cactus grove in the backyard, and Jamie and Cathy and Johnny [Neal and Carolyn's children], and Maw Cassady's Pizzas, and the wine in the store across the street, and Neal's tennis-chess-and kicks, write, if you want, for full explanation of the Blessed One, and I send, if, as I say, I'm still alive, or still recognize that you are Allen Ginsberg old friend of Jack Kerouac, which I guess even in and after eternity I won't forget, but don't you forget our liquid giants ogling behind buildings, and the eternity radar machine in the sky, and dead eyes see, because, boy, I've now found out that it was all instinct pure and true, and I must say, we weren't so dumb, as I will prove, as I say, if I ever see you again, which, after all, may not be, for I am weary of the world and wish to weary from this globe, to other blobs where bloblessness grows more apparent with each passing kalpa—O So have a drink of wine, and dig the liquid sad ungraspable, fault-sour suffering Samsara sea of mournfulness for me, O Allen saint, *Arhat*, goodbye . . . I'll see you in the Tathagata Worlds anon.

Jean

Allen Ginsberg [San Jose, California] to Jack Kerouac [n.p., New York, New York?]

June 18, 1954

Dear Jack:

I am in San Jose, have your letters, have heard Neal's Cayce; nothing has happened among us here yet. I sent you card from North Mexico; have answered Burroughs etc. all that's out of the way, except to say that I wasn't being mysterious in Mexico. I kept writing letters to one and all every week or so, some never got there, also I was in an isolated locality where mail was difficult; I didn't intentionally create a mystery though was pleased afterward by all the fuss. In *T and C* [*The Town and the City*] you mention Stofsky's ability to disappear as one of his virtues (disappear on trip or whatever and suddenly reappear) and that's what I thought of when I got word that I was missed.

Well, let me get on to this letter.

If you left here the end of March you didn't see the letters I wrote to you and Neal here; I don't know if you've seen Lucien who also got account of what happened. But I will give you the story assuming you haven't been informed. [Ginsberg retells the story of his Mexican earthquake visit, as already described in his April 4 letter.]

[. . .]

I wound up spending last night in Mexico overlooking the poor barrio Kasbah outside of my room on the garbage cliff of Mexicali, tin shacks down the cliff, white roofs and dirty little gardens with superhighway and other cliff leading to uptown border hipsters streets, so anyway I stood on a garbage cliff in the darkness to see I was at the end of my Mexico trip.

The first night I got here (after spending week with relatives around L.A.) Neal got me hi and talked continually building the whole fragmentary Cayce structure like an unfinished reverie. The great thing, despite all obvious absurdities, is that he has conceived of possibility of a final idea, got religion, whether Voices of Rock or Buddha balloon or Cayce transmigrations, new level of conceptions opened for him as actual possiblies and necessaries. These are the roads to heaven, I do not forget liquid giants ogling, and forests of absolute Arden on 8th Ave., the sensations of the sublime we ken, great steps and hints of the stairway:

On codeine on the bus up to Veracruz: an image, as in a Giotto painting, likeness of a heavenly file of female saints ascending a starry gold stairway winding up into the sky, daintily regularly stepping up the miniature gold steps, the thousands of little saintesses in blue hoods with round sweet smiling faces looking out directly at me the beholder, their hands beckoning up, palms out, as they climb. Salvation! it's true, as simple as in the picture.

The above is just a random conception.

And now with all this conflict of theologies, I made out my credo:

CREDO

1. The weight of the world is love.

2. The mind images all visions.

3. Man is as far divine as his imagination.

4. We go create a world of divine love as much as we can image. (That is, we must go on interpreting recreating the given blank world (lack of imagination is death by physical starvation) according to the most extreme absolute of divine love divinity that we can conceive.)

I haven't said much about Neal but will in next letter whenever it is. At the moment my greatest pleasure has been in looking at him as in a great dream, the unreality of it, that we are in the same space-time room again. As if resurrection from dead past, fresh and full of life, though with the drag of old knowledge, but we have not yet begun to talk. I don't know what it is I want to tell him. Or he me yet.

As to you Kerouac, it is clear that your heavenly duty, your Buddha balloon, is to write, and that your unhappiness is undeserved in a way that only acceptance can make clear.

What I mean to say is there stands the structure of your works and sublimity towering in my imagination untarnished. My tea leaves still read $$$ and FAME for you whether or not in the next ten years probably in this lifetime.

[...]

Your isolation like mine is sad and frightful mainly the blind alleys of money and love but life is not over, and much to be written and much to be respected in all of us not just for being humanity but for having tried and actually achieved a thing, namely literature and also possibly a certain spiritual eye at this point.

And Neal who has money and love is desperate at the gate of heaven for he is unhappy with his existence. God knows what starvation's behind the blankness, was behind, now he is seeking in his soul. As for Bill he thinks he is lost. Lucien knows his way but may have a period of having to expand his spiritual horizon in order to accommodate the depth and height of possibility and this may be preceded by the appearance of a prison in his soul, not his existence.

> Love,
> Allen

PS: I am not finished with my poem so will send this as is and send the fine poem soon.

Neal will read *Visions of Neal* if you will send it registered and insured here. We talked about him not reading those things.

What are you writing now since I last saw you?

Have you seen Lucien?

Have you seen Holmes, Kingsland, Solomon, and the others, Alene [Lee], and Dusty [Moreland]? Please give me news of them.

Write me when and if you want, don't worry.

> As ever
> Allen

Please return the pages about Acavalna. There is no other copy.

I will be reading *Bagavad Gita* and some Buddhism soon, if you have directions or advice.

Jack Kerouac [New York, New York] to Allen Ginsberg [n.p., San Jose, California?]

after June 18, 1954

Dear Allen,

Starting last Friday afternoon drunk on wine, and ending this morning sober, with bat in between in town seeing Kingsland, Ansen, Holmes, Cru and Helen Parker, here's a big semi-silly letter; reason I won't throw away silly parts is because they may amuse you and you would be amused instead of not amused. They were written drunk, are gossipy, but maybe funny; first four pages . . .

I'm enclosing a Bill letter from Bill in Algiers containing material I'm not sure you've seen, and that I want you to be as sure of sending back, as I am right now of returning your Acavalna paper. Be sure now!

Your letter was happily received, as I thought something had gone wrong and you wouldn't write me big letters any more. I felt a warm glow of pride and happiness reading it, that you should write it to me.

And I wanted to tell you many gentle and brotherly things. [. . .]

I recently had an affair with a junky girl call'd Mary Ackerman that you may know of, friend of Iris Brody's, saw me and Kells [Elvins] in his yellow jeepster in Cuernevacas in 1952; knows everybody, but is so hot and so Camille [Carolyn Cassady] like suicidal and crazy I can't follow her around; she [Mary] just went to hospital for an overdose, for instance. And it's too late anyway for me to love, to love love, that is, or love women, I mean, I mean sex and involvement and common-law marriage like, or I'm talking thru my hat. I saw your big letter to Kingsland.

I see Chester Kallman[7] all the time now, and his Pete [Butorac]. I've been getting sillydrunk again lately in Remo and disgusting myself *a la* Subterraneans. I want to live a quiet life but I am so weak for booxe booze. I am very unhappy and have nightmares; when drinking; after a week of abstinence, I am happier than ever before in life, but slowly become bored and wondering what to do now; am writing two big books only because have nothing else to do and it would be a shame to waste all that experience in "talent"—as Carolyn says— and generally speaking, I have crossed the ocean of suffering and found the path at last. And am quite surprised that you, innocent, novice-like did enter the first inner chamber of Buddha's temple in a dream; you're going to be saved—There would be rejoicing and hosannas in heaven if anything once in heaven WERE a thing, or could rejoice, where rejoicing is is a naught—heaven is nothing—[. . .]

WALTER ADAMS I ain't seen.

DIANA HANSEN CASSADY I seen, on the street, she showed me pictures of Curt [Diana and Neal's son] and she said she got big letters about Edgar Cayce, is this giving something away? but she can't find the books he alludes to and anyway she doesn't care and she stood on the sidewalk goofing but I was late and she was the same.

JOSE GARCIA VILLA was on the village sidewalk and as Lucien and I strolled along he came up, sad, Phillipino, and we talked, and he said, "How are you Lucien"? and then he gave us address of his new magazine . . . but I didn't send him any poems.

    Little anger Japan
    Strides holding bombs

---

[7] Chester Kallman was a companion of W. H. Auden.

To blow the West
To Fuyukama's
Shrouded Mountain Top
So the Lotus Bubble
Blossoms in Buddha's
Temple Dharma Eye
May unfold from
    Pacific Center
Inward Out and Over
The Essence Center World.

This is from my new book of poems *San Francisco Blues* that I wrote when I left Neal's in March and went to live in the Cameo Hotel on Third Street Frisco Skidrow—wrote it in a rockingchair at the window, looking down on winos and bebop winos and whores and cop cars—and I quote it to draw your attention to the fact, we have consistently been clairvoyant of each other's minds for years now, this poem has "bubble" in it which you used with Buddha in your letter (tho you deleted it for "balloon")—and it hints of the temple, the inner chamber, of the Mongolia wall, of which, incidentally, I too have a dream, in *Book of Dreams* (which I'm now finishing the typing of)—[. . .]

A thousand other examples of our clairvoyance oneness later.

LUCIEN I saw, as I say, went to his house one Sunday afternoon, bringing a pint of whiskey cause I owed him three bucks from another night, and tho Cessa was like displeased, I insisted we mix it all up with ice in a bottle to take to the park with us, where she wanted to sun child, so on the park Lou and I are belting from this magnificent huge cocktail and here comes HELEN PARKER and BRUCE and TOMMY [Parker's two boys] and sits with us, and then I got to go for a leak in Washington Park toilet so I walk with Tommy across, and we pass STANLEY GOULD who says, "Who is that, Tommy Parker?" and here comes GREGORY CORSO with black skin tan of Scandinavian ships and cut his hair off in crew cut and looks like great beachcomber poet and he takes my Buddha book and reads one line coldly, but then says, "I know it's great, you can't lend it to me can you?"—"No, I gotta have it by my side all the time."—"I know," he says, and we talk about you, and he says, "When Allen gets back I won't pay no attention to him, fuck him"—I say, "Why do you talk like that about Allen, whatsamatter with you and Allen"—"Fuck him" he says, like agonized over something . . . I warn Mary Ackerman not to hate Gregory, like she wants to do, I tell her, "He's no different than you, all is the same essence," and over comes hepcat to talk to us.

I was at HELEN PARKER'S and had a ball and then ALAN ANSEN came with WILLIAM GADDIS and I didn't like Gaddis cause it seemed to me he was making Ansen unhappy . . . I put my hand on A's head and rubbed his head and he went off with Gaddis and came back again to me and Helen and we got drunk in the night and danced the mambo . . . sweet Helen in the morning put on her Easter bonnet and went to work down the streets of Village—good brave gal—Finally got rid of JACK ELIOT the singin cowboy who apparently was costing her a lot of money but poor Jack, he can't work, he's like the robin, he sings . . .

So I walk down the streets of the village with JACK ELIOT and we just been banging two colored sisters all night, and he's playin the Memphis Special, and other songs, and we run into BILLY FAIR a great five string banjo genius from N'Awrleans, and bang ? BILL FOX drives by and I stop him by yelling at his car, and he comes out, and I say, "Bill, give these boys an audition for Esoteric" and we have a songfest and a hundred and two school children gather around to listen and up comes an old Frisco wino with his bottle and broken pulpy nose and he likes Jack Eliot's singing so much he says, reach in in his shirt, by god, boy, I'm gonna give you my lass sandwich."—"I'm from Oklahoma meself"— and the sun goes down—and I have a pimple on my nose.

ALENE LEE calls me on the phone, it seems she's now a hardworking wait-ress at Rikers restaurant on Columbia campus at 115 and Broadway, so I go to her house, bringing manuscript of *Subterraneans*, as promised, and I tell her I still love her and we hold hands going down the street, cause you know, boy, I love all women . . . but instead of being big swain I get drunk with JORGE D AVILA Ed White's boy and his great buddy from Porto Rico HERNANDO, who is the very first peron I have met in this world who has completely and instantly understood the words of Buddha . . . a great cat, you meet later, architect, so far . . . You see Allen all there is to Buddha, is this,—All life is a dream—but later, I'll explain later . . . it isn't AS IF it was a dream, it IS a dream . . . see? So I get drunk with the boys in the West End [Bar] and JOHNNY THE BAR-TENDER is still asking for his copy of *The Town and the City*, and at midnight I take a peek in Rikers, and there's Alene rushing around on little twinkling legs with her arms sawing along her thighs, real intent on being "sane" and just madder than ever if you asks me . . . all this tainting and defiling these lesbian psychologists are putting down on these poor innocent avant guarde negresses, really my dear, the things I could tell that little cunt and won't.

JOHN HOLMES, I rush up to his place at 123 Lexington and ring the door-bell and he's laboring up the stairs with a bagful of gin, and we go in, there's Shirley [Holmes], we get drunk, I rush out and fetch Mary, she jolts, we go back, we play old Billies, old Lesters, it goes on, we pass out, next day when Shirley goes to work me and Mary and John go to a 3rd Avenue bar and drink and talk all that day and I say to John brothers forever, and mean it.—Shirley comes home at night, sees three drunk lushes bums in her room, sighs, leans against door just like Marian [Holmes], and all it's the same thing again as Marian, and John "writes" during the day, and they haven't published *Go* in pocketbooks, for some reason, and he's "broke"—he says, "In 1952 I had a lot a money" "but now" . . . and he is sad, and for money I guess, but we talked, and made up okay, and of course he asked about you with concern and intelligence. But he is suspicious of the reason for my visits—so I'll leave him alone.

JETHRO ROBINSON I haven't seen.

HENRY CRU is back, has a pad on West 13th Street and Mary stayed there awhile and regularly on Saturday afternoons he goes out looking for stray furniture in the streets and lays $50 bills on bookies in front of Remo (keeps losing on Correlation) and on Saturday nights has barrels of beer and Mucho Coukamongas, Kerouac, don't you DARE bring any males to my party, you know I'm not fruit don't you, I want you to bring every last couchkamongo you can find to my beer party but God help you if like the last time you bring these fruits (I had brought Pete Butorac and Chester Kallman, at four)—Kerouac, I'm going to have to REPRIMAND you, do you hear me, I'm going to have to" etc. and Mary was taking nude baths in front of him, and he does an imitation of it, and he keeps drinking beer in giant glasses a foot tall and has cases of it around and is constantly eating and fat and when he has his blessed couckamongos at night he never touches them and when presented with the opportunity as Mary and I done, when we turned on two Mexican sixteen year old sisters in the dark room, he blushes and makes jokes, poor old lost Henri.

SEYMOUR [Wyse] I done heard about, from SAM KAINER, I was over to Mark Van Doren's house to pick up *Doctor Sax* where I'd left it, with his son CHARLES, Mark wasn't there and had already written me a note saying that *Sax* was "monotonous and probably without meaning in the end," saying, at first, "quite a work but I don't know where to place it," whereby I realized he is really nowhere, face it, but Charles was friendly, he is having a novel published by Giroux soon (my dear) and he had his sweetheart with him VARDA KARNEY who is all gushing and fascinated in my talk about Buddha and wants to know how to practice *dhyana* and *samadhi* and *samapatti* and in comes a gang of young kids, and Sam Kainer, I say "Sam Kainer, where'd I hear that name?" and of course!! it's the cat who lived in Seymour's pad in St. John's Wood all this time, blasting with him, conducting bop session, he wears a goatee and is very cool and Philip Lamantia like and hep—and says Seymour for awhile was Ted Heath's band manager, Ted Heath big band like Woody Herman in England.

JERRY NEWMAN I went to Sayville with him and we cultivated his vast crop o couckamonga green and corn, and I went with him to antique shops where he got lamps for his huge new CBS style by-his father-billfooted studio which is the most beautiful, vast thing you've ever seen with soundproof walls so we could have screaming agonized orgies in there and nobody'd ever know (right around the corner from Holmes) and where he is makin big records and big money now—and says he will have big sessions with Brue Moore and Alan Eager and Al Haig.

BRUE MOORE I finally met, with Gould my Buddy, and Brue says he's from Indianola, Mississippi, not far from Greenville, on River, and says "Let's you and me drink wine, you think I drink whiskey, you ought to see me drink wine, we'll go down to the Bowery and light a fire in the alley and drink wine, and I'll play my horn"—with Gould, we'll do this, in October. Be sure to be with us, Melville. I'm in Love With You Always.

NOW LISTEN ALLEN, do NOT FAIL to look up, if possible, Al Sublette, at the Bell Hotel at 39 Columbus St. Frisco, with, or without Neal, so Al can take you around the Great Frisco and show you, remember and don't fail . . . he's a great boy, and sell me to him, please, he mad at ma, at me—big mad good by and maybe the first hep Negro writer in America maybe, if he digs—Not that he's avant guarde, he's, understand a straight simple hepcat with a GIANT FLAIR FOR WORDS, a wordslingin fool, don't know it, a real POET in the sense in which it was known in Elisabeth's time, and, not surprisingly, a wino, and jolts too. I just could write epics about his vision of America, 's, what I mean, Al.

PHILIP LAMANTIA, Ed Roberts, Leonard Hall, Chris McClaine, Rexroth,[8] look them up while you're in Frisco. Its your big chance to dig the Berkeley axis,—Is Saint there? . . . Jaimie d'Angulo's house . . . big peotl heroes like Wig Walters obtain from there; dig Wig if you can, the "Cash" of Bill's *JUNKIE* novel.

[. . .]

Jack

P.S. Sal Paradise *On the Road*, which I re-titled *Beat Generation* so I could sell it was just turned down by Seymour Lawrence at *Atlantic Monthly*—Little Brown with the same little tune about "craftsmanship" he sang in 1948 about "The Death of George Martin" I'd sent to *Wake*—remember? Book is now at E.P. Dutton's—Arabelle *New World Writing* is sitting on four of my pieces—All the others are in my agent's drawers unread and dusting—what the hell's the use?

---

[8] Kenneth Rexroth was an influential poet and writer who lived in San Francisco.

Allen Ginsberg [San Jose, California] to
Jack Kerouac [n.p., New York, New York?]

ca. July 10, 1954

Dear Jack:

Thank you for your letter. I always delight when we get on kick of immense letters.

Now I am trying to finish and conclude and type the poems I mentioned to you, a fragment of which I put in Kingsland's letter which you saw. So don't want to take a day to write you now, except for general gossip, which will do so at length.

I will study Buddhism with you. I can't get the fucking books here. I haven't been to main San Jose Library yet but will in day or so and find what I can. The Warren[9] is probably there. Eliot mentions it in *Wasteland* notes. Send me your document, let me begin with that.

"Let me see you imagine nothing, and I give you heaven." I understand perfectly. Am not joking, but the fixed principles of destroying my imaginations of paradises and god and systems has been the one block or wall which since my 1949 visions of whatever they were—perhaps your *samhadi*?—has prevented me from entering any deeper unknowing. I hope you are not offended by my recurring to my 1949 [*sic*: 1948] flashes. They were the strongest experiences that have occurred to me. I would appreciate your thinking on them and commenting. We have never had an understanding on that. If you feel they are in the way of your blackboard or present awareness I will put them aside. (They were however the consummation of sensations of Forest of Arden and Billboard monsters) I willingly put them aside however.

Neal does not understand unknowing, he thinks cornily that it is a negative approach to life, which obviously it could be in the wrong mind. I mean a negative blah blah, just words.

Your vision of two pages. Is the clarity of it new? You have shadows of this in end of *Sax* (walk thru backyards) but do I understand correctly that this sensation came to a crystallization more overwhelming than before?

Van Doren is wrong. What else did he say? I will write him sooner or later and try and explain he had mistaken judgment.

I enclose Bill's letter. The new approach seems to have hit him with all these credos in his first page about the forces of death destroying, I wrote him to come out here if he wished, a kind letter, though really I shudder at the prob-

---

[9] *Buddhism in Translations*, by Henry Clarke Warren.

lems, but I said I would be happy to see him, which I naturally will, though I am aweary and he may be wearying. He seems better. He wrote yesterday and said he was sick, some bone trouble, arthritis perhaps.

I will correspond in details soon, I beg you excuse me to prepare my poems for you.

I spent three days and two nites laid up in Hotel Bell with Al Sublette, who received me with great delicacy of feeling and we drank two gallons of tokay and talked, slept, walked to Coit Tower. He asked about you fondly, bears absolutely no ill will, no selling job was necessary. Yes I dug Sublette, now, it's complete, that circle. Will write more later.

Carolyn and I dig and understand each other. I am Myshkin with Neal to the best of my ability though often the pain of losing love and naked body lusts drives me wild, yet am trying to give soul, heart, feeling irrespective of returns, a universal problem. This formula Carolyn is picking up on and seems that Neal responds and opens up a little.

I applied for a brakeman's job and there are none at the moment, but I will wait a few weeks and reapply. I think I can make it if I get a job. Should I who have entered the Cave of Night be afeared of an engine? Send more NY gossip. Love to Lucien.

　　　Allen

PS: My regards to Holmes, Ansen and Helen [Parker] and everybody. Show Holmes or Ansen whatever of my letters they'd be interested. Tell Alan specifically please I would like him to let me know what he saw of Bill in Europe. He added a note to an early letter that was very funny. If he has time to write. I have piles of miscellaneous correspondence left over from Mexico and want to stop all this, except to Bill and yourself, however.

Don't show anyone neurotic sex stuff.

What does Lucien say?

When I am thru collectivating my book I will think about publishers again. Meanwhile I advise by all means keep trying to peddle your works thru regular and irregular channels as they rise. You never can tell what accident. Probably something by law of averages will happen. When this method has been completely exhausted we will invent our own. But maybe you will have some luck. Have you also done this, maybe it's a good idea: who in NY of any power might dig it? Who, who? Not Hershey. Faulkner is far far away. Try to get hold of Faulkner, maybe. The really great will dig. Let's cut out piddling with intermediaries like Cowley. Go to the horses mouth. Can you think of any? Off hand I can't. By the way did we finish trying New Directions? Ah, I know you're sick of it but for moment let's try do something.

I can't write a *Visions of Bill*, I haven't your imagination and heart for detail, you are after all the greater driver. It is all I can do to sit down and scribble fragments of thoughts for poems. When I write prose I get so deliberate it turns out bare and hopeless really nowhere like the Acavalna paper. I wrote it for facts for Lucien. Bill and Ansen tell me to try prose but I don't understand what they're talking about, it's impossible, it would kill me to keep sitting at a desk going off into abstract tangents writing and writing and writing. I'm too sick at heart for such an effort. I do what I can without putting myself thru torment. It doesn't seem to torture you to write prose but it is really nerve-wracking for me. It seems such shit, prose I've written. I'm not being humble like Neal who can, either. I admire your prose but feel too hopeless to ever catch up with all the massive detail and freedom and blowing.

    Love, Baby.

        Allen

Jack Kerouac [New York, New York] to Allen Ginsberg [n.p., San Jose, California?]

July 30, 1954

July 30,

Dear Allen,

    I've been very depressed all day and now I'm having a well needed rum and coke; I wondered if you've been depressed all this day too, Friday July 30th, judging from our past telepathies . . . I've been so generally down all week I have not yet mailed the [*Some of the*] *Dharma* to you, which I do Monday when I buy a big envelope . . . I hope you like it; I hope it instructs you . . . Myself, having really just reach'd the nadir of Nirvana-understanding, am probably depressed as an aftermath . . . I tell you I had a vision of emptiness to put an end to all of em . . . More later in the letter.

    Lucien came to my house one night, sneaking in the door like my old Paw's buddies used to do, squeaking followed by Jim Hudson and Jim Crayon and quarts of Irish Whisky. We drank in my lil room and Lucien took your big letter, your 2nd smaller letter and all the pictures he could find and stuffed them in his pocket . . . [Here, four lines of the letter are completely blacked out, with a marginal notation "He read Neal's letter and didn't like it."] I saw Lucien again several days later, after, that first night, we drove wildly around Long Island looking for newspapermen, squeaking wheels, Lou making wild U-turns right on the turfed dividers of superhighways, fast, leaping over curbs and just missing park benches, reminding me of your Mexico hayride and I wasn't scared . . .

several days later Kells Elvins called Lou to get me, and we all met in Sellman's, then Lucien kindly offered to drive Kells to a girl's house in New Jersey, tho he had to be at Cessa's at 10 . . . at 10 we were sneaking and whispering down his street in the Village and getting into his car, Kells, him, me, three girls, and Hudson—went out to New Jersey and had a good time. Generally Lucien seems fine and the same as ever, which means, he is Lucien and indefatigably manly.

I passed the Swiss Oaks bar and peeked in and Dusty [Moreland] saw me and came out and wanted me to take your pictures to her and tell her what you're doing and show her your letters. I confess I ain't done this. Please write to her, she's anxious to hear. She looked good.

Alene [Lee] turned out to be a real little tit, called me and asked me to bring *The Subterraneans* and then we were sposed to discuss it and instead she had Sherman Hikox in her sack when I knocked on the door, he made cracks, such as, "She's gone to publish *The Subterraneans*," so I started to break the door down and got my *Subs* back. However every tom dick and harry read it while she had possession of it, including Gregory [Corso], who is contemptuous of it, and Gould,[10] who is very charming to me now and I think is a full-blown Cannastra saint by now. I recommend Gould to you when you get back to NY. But Gregory's aright too, he ran into Kells and me in the Village and had a "novel" with him, short looking, written like Saroyan, and was humble and asked about you even.

Kells is a wonderful guy, made me mad as hell when he said he needed to go to a psychiatrist . . . the psychiatrist said "You need therapy immediately" so naturally Kells goes around borrowing huge sums, *a la* Burroughssian flair, and here I am raging at him to go down the public library and take out Buddha for god's sake. How silly. "At once" indeed, these conmen . . . as Bill would say, such impudence.

At your request, I pondered and remembered your 1948 Harlem visions, and they were the granddaddy of em all . . . accurate too . . . prophetic of Buddha. I would say you are a Sage, an elephant among Kings, a veritable Ananda among men, you have more naturals in you than Old Bull Balloon . . . Strange to say, tho, I see you very clearly now as more a Chinese type sage, a Taoist, a Chuangtse, than a Buddhist . . . I am now reading Tao over again carefully; Chuangtse especially, who is absolutely brilliant; I find Indian Buddhism almost impossible to practice; Tao is a more elastic, more humane philosophy whereas Buddhism is an ascetic way of life tacked on to a philosophy . . . ascetism and yogism are hard on a big boned fella like me, sensual wine lover,

[10] Stanley Gould worked for A. A. Wyn and was the model for "Portrait of a Hipster," by Anatole Broyard.

woman lover like me . . . bum like me . . . I think I'll become a wandering Taoist Bum . . . wanta come?

Allen, your visions of Harlem, your Leviathan, your reality opening itself a moment to reveal itself, your sudden recognition of ancient anguish and coyness on the faces of people on the sidewalk, your eerie discovery of the Idea behind objects instead of the apparent objects themselves, all smacks of clairvoyance

P.S. Don't forget to dig Frisco negro jazz with Neal in Nash—Loud!!

Allen Ginsberg [San Jose, California] to Jack Kerouac [n.p., New York, New York?]

ca. early August 1954

Dear Jack:

I keep thinking of writing you, since I sent last letter did you [receive] it? Sent to Richmond [Hill]. The duke doth not answer. Oh yet yes, I was to add a longer note in time later. The main problem, is, I want to send on a lot of poetry, to a sure destination, and it is not at all finished. Things go slowly. I put long poems aside for future endings. I read in basic prosody seeking for the yellow springs (of Chinese death) and conceive images, blasphemous and sensual "hidden in skin" and the airiest most abstract hymns to blue love, or green love or whatever, grasping stray vultures and hawks from the cages of heaven in this wooden house where I dwell in the prison of my life as thou dids't here too then untimely once or twice overing, or thrice was it?

There's too many poems to finish and not one really done, all these fragments small and large. And the possibility now after Indo China and Ike's admission that U.S. containment policy would be replaced by a weaker more limited policy of cold war—are we losing? Is the Fall of America already upon us? The Great Fall we once prophesied. I wrote my brother "and it will be horrible to see, broken machinery and cracked pavement I mean." My god all hell will break loose here when Asia begins fucking us, so the possibility of a prophetic poem, using ideas of politics and war and calling on love and reality for salvation, etc. Imagine throwing in Cayce ideas no—too complicated. What by the way do you think of rebirth? Is it also a Buddha Buddy Bhud Boo Oom sh-bam, idea? Have you heard "Life Could Be Dreamy" by that popular swinging group of spades, (and their imitators) I forgot. It has a ding a ling or ling a ling dining car harmony bob sonority. Also a canzon: "There's a riot going on (in Cell No. 9) / The scarface jones / come up and said / it's too late now / cause the fuse is lit / There's a riot going on (chorus)"

I am still not working, waiting to hear my fate at the railroad. I flunked the physical with that old evil mysterious (anti-Semitic?) Dr. STRANGE of the SP [Southern Pacific]; appealing speedily to Dr. Washburne head of SP Hospital Medicine he sustained me and accepted me. Now waiting in second week for verification of my victory or bureaucratic victimage. I tried for brakeman, no jobs, got OK'd by yardmaster for yard clerk. Waiting. Even if I make it business may be slow. But nonetheless trying to make it.

[. . .]

In Frisco I spent much time with Sublette and friend Vic, describe another time, big ex-army actor cat seaman a man and right hearted we drank wine in room for days. And walk a bit by the pool hall. Ed Roberts too, twice, another unidentified Gene, solomonesque, Neal once, other dark men. I also visited Kenneth Rexroth a poet who had read and dug *Junkie* on his own who conversed with me till 11 and drove me downtown for late train and is reader for New Directions—we must approach him with your work. Did Directions reject? What has happened there in the end, huh? We may be able to do something, maybe not. Anyway he'll read anything given him and is an old friend and worker of [James] Laughlin. Also a very easy guy ex hip about forty-five, speaks Greek, and Latin, Chink, Jap, etc. and is an anarchist and bleeding heart art martyr he says Kenneth Patchen he likes the most, and writes poem for all the dead great minor and major poets he's known that died too young or miserable lived or died. But very good, he likes to make believe he's tough and don't give shit and in a revolution against society and he does add to its small literature in a nice way. I mean he ain't Pound but one of the older disciples though he's independent etc. etc. all this crap. Big library, married, children, lives cheap as man of letters, knows everybody young and old subterranean or interested. Likes [Bill] Keck, respects his dignity that is. I told him something about you, Bill [Burroughs].

So as yet won't send poems. Maybe wait till you get here or till finished really. All I could send you is small and like my old style: but the longer more historic not done.

Bill writes still, he will be here at my invitation etc. September or later. Date not set, he'll visit family first. What are your plans? I really hope I'm working then because if so I hope to really have some kind of enjoyable life, not just an old mad city of fusty employed. Want to dig museums and movies and Yosemites, study, write, talk. And love? Well that comes from heaven I guess, or nowhere.

Love from paradise,
Allen

[. . .]

233

Also I have not said anything about the household, well here it is, Neal plays chess. I come 10,000 miles and he sits and plays chess with the neighbor and I baby-sit and goof, Carolyn out tonight for instance. Neal now back next doors where Dick Wood baby-sits for his wife, and, before, he stuck his nose in the chess book to read and could hardly be roused to a civil word. He wakes every few days or a week for surprise conjunctions—all too rarely with any pathos or feeling—of the bodies, but heaven refuses to fall and there is the usual discord between him and Carolyn, so bitter his behavior so long suffering, or abusive, or angry—never openly hurt. She's hurt. But she can be shrewish. Does she really love? I thought so. We were familiar awhile, and there is some coldness, now, though we patch up and are polite and sometimes involved in interesting conversation. Sometimes my mind drifts. Often I can't get across an idea, a new idea, an objective one, poetic. Political, religious, we nearly came to blows over what your nothing means nothing means. But Neal is a loss! what contradictions of character. What compulsive shuffling of cards sex cards. And the handkerchief. Tales of Watsonville, SF, uttered guiltily with eye out for wife secrecy. The mad chess. He won't talk to me. He hides in chess, he perfects his game. The time he's studying it now expertising WC Fields, "Tell Jack? Why . . . tell him I'll beat his lard ass in a chess game!" So the silence in the house I read and write. I bring out a poem and force it on him or her. He expresses like in the most general terms, won't hardly ever talk art or nothing . . . except Cayce that gets him in a good mood . . . a gleam in his eye . . . I express a doubt a heresy, he gets mad "at me! the poor fool (madman) He is not a man!" (Rimbaud) But the hopelessness of it, he won't be soft. His concerns are, if there, hidden except for flashes that you can't trust, they're so sudden and offhand, the really personal things. It's cold and bitter when we make it too. Well . . . I will I hope soon be working. Other here, perhaps I'll geta pad nearby. I have what to do, to keep me busy. But it's a sham. I feel strange. Today I have a cold, caught from Hinkle's kids.

". . . In a silence of facts to die?" Oh Jack, he's losing time, sweet earthly time. Is he waiting? Is he waiting—I mean for anything or life that was promised? He won't write because he wants to write sex and it's a Cayce sin. She agrees. But he won't write anything else right now. Says he's quit. He's quit. What? Why!? What future?? What will he do, what can he do? Trapped in R.R. etc. He doesn't want to leave here either really. This is the best deal. Why am I here? I hardly know.

But you come out too. We'll, we'll do something. Bill will be O.K. and write. I will make it.

Neal's basic grace is crowned
and uncorruptable but ask

such a life and waste
of sweetness.

    Love
        Allen

I'm afraid to say too much here—this is strictly for you not the public if any.

Jack Kerouac [Richmond Hill, New York] to
Allen Ginsberg [San Jose, California]

August 23 '54

Dear Allen,

Dedicating this joint to you as I start. Have a list of notes made from reading your letter and shall follow it as is writ. "Life Could Be a Dream," yes I dug that tune and the singers of it and it was a little Angel of Africa turned me on it, Bob Young by name, he's got close cropped (no) hair and black face and lisps and wanted me to go to his pad etc. but just bought me drinks on Bleecker Tavern and said really strange and mystical things about that tune, too, like you . . . I told him life IS a dream, he said no only if you lived with me . . . you might meet him someday if you want.

As for anti-Semitism on the SP, yes, the Okies on that railroad are anti-Semites, whatever that means in California.

Al Hink [Hinkle] you shouldn't encourage on his really simple-minded and ignorant commie kick, you shouldn't be such a fool Burroughsian liberal saying he really represents good old American dissent—"traditional American dissent" you called it, we don't call 18th Century Toryism, siding with the national military enemy, a "healthy dissent," it's really treason against the government and the army, what else? Let Al go to Russia if he can git there. Thomas Paine was not a Tory. [. . .]

I got Cowley talkin for me now—Arabelle Porter of *New World Writing* just bought Jazz Excerpts (of Neal and I digging Folsom St. Little Harlem, Jackson's Nook, and Anita O'Days nightclub on North Clark St. in Chi) (with things from *Vision of Neal* sneaked in, like "Lester is like the river, it starts in near Butte Montana at a place call'd Three Forks, comes balling down etc. etc.) (you know, one of the top passages of *Visions of Neal*, which at last can see light in print in *New World* within a year)—It was Cowley helped me, so I wrote and thank'd Cowley, and he wrote back and said "Maybe a publisher will take *On the Road* now" and he said "Show Arabelle Porter the chapter now about the Mexican girl in San Joaquin valley in the cotton tent"—So maybe you don't have to show me to Rexroth but I don't wanta get hungup on mail, is it because I'm lazy? or canny?) (and why should I be canny, I'm not a businessman)—I changed the title to *Beat Generation* of *On the Road*, hoping to sell it, and also I see "beatitude" in "beat" now than ever before, which might make it an international word understood in French, Spanish, most romance langues, just think of "be-at"—"be-at-itude"—and "beat" belongs to me as far I can see—(for use as title of book)—Little Shit Littlebrown Seymour Lawrence had all the half of 1954 and kept telling my agent it looked very good and finally it was rejected they say by one editor of LB altho accepted by twelve people elsewhere (on *Atlantic Monthly* board for some reason of merger) and to top it little shit Seymour writes me another, yet still another, severe note about "Craft" (the first one having come from rejection of Death of the Father George Martin, which everybody knows is a masterpiece and a classic chapter)—the nerve of that little queen. I tell you I get so mad-a-a-a-d! Am I good enuf though for good old soul goodman Malcolm Cowley to champion me?—Oh yes ps.s.s. I got $120 for the story, imagine. That's my first pay since 1950. No since 1953. Well Viking can still take it if they want it and make their $250 strait, and same with Wyn.

[. . .]

Maybe we should write no more letters but have absolute trust in each other till we meet. He who knows does not speak.

Incidentally I've lost my taste for booze, and don't hardly drink no more. You'll see. It's merely a matter of my *taste* changing again. Like no-smoke. Forc'd to it . . . I'm too old, I'm 33, to stay up all night drinking . . .

Love for you in Coast? Find a nice MG girl on Russian Hill, make it with the yacthing set, yatching set, Buddha boy . . . if you can, it's best for you . . . I can see you in hornrimmed glasses, bermuda shorts, and camera around shoulder at Yosemite. The queers of Remo [bar] as you know are in the Black Cat there, on Columbus at Montgomery.

[. . .]

I'm waiting till I see you again cause I'm not coming to California by a long shot, if anything I'm going nowhere . . . I have a little plan but my plans are always so poor . . . but I'll try it, tell you later . . . I hope to see Bill tho, he'll surely stop in New York. Maybe you and Bill should get yourselves a house in Mexico City, only cost $200 or $300 down and you have six or seven rooms and big teas at which Paul Bowles is not invited, and start your publishing house in an empty room upstairs. Both of you work and save for this, in Calif. Bill could work in a cannery maybe, hor hor hor.

What a magnificent letter I just got from him, one sentence says "He (Paul

Bowles Hobbes) invites the dreariest queens in Tangiers to tea, but has never invited me, which, seeing how small the town is, amounts to a deliberate affront"—

and

"I can't help but feeling that you are going too far with your absolute chastity. Besides, mast'ion [masturbation] is not chastity, it is just a way of sidestepping the issue without even approaching the solution. Remember, Jack, I studied and practiced Buddhism in my usual sloppy way to be sure. The conclusion I arrived at, and I make no claims to speak from a state of enlightenment, but merely to have attempted the journey, as always, with inadequate equipment and knowledge,—like one of my South American expeditions, falling into every possible accident and error, losing my gear and my way, shivering in the cosmic winds on a bare mountain slope above life line, chilled to the blood-making marrow with final despair of aloneness: What am I doing here a broken eccentric? a Bowery Evangelist, reading books on Theosophy in the public library, (An old tin trunk full of notes in my cold water, East Side flat) imagining myself a Secret World Controller in Telepathic Contact with Tibetan Adepts?—Could he ever *see* the merciless, cold, *facts* on some winter night sitting in the operation room white glare of a cafeteria—NO SMOKING PLEASE"—(You can't say nothin but trash, blues nigger new york song locally)—(me)—Bill:—"NO SMOKING PLEASE—*See the facts and himself*, an old man with the wasted years behind, and what ahead having seen The Facts? A trunk full of notes to dump in a Henry Street lot? . . . so my conclusion was that Buddhism is only for the West to *study* as *history*, that it is a subject for *under standing*, and Yoga, can profitably be practiced to that end. But it is not, for the West, An Answer, not A Solution. WE must learn by acting, experiencing, and living, that is, above all by Love and by Suffering. A man who uses Buddhism or any other instrument to remove love from his being in order to avoid suffering, has committed, in my mind, a sacrilege comparable to castration." (ya can't castrate tathagatas) (castrate the uncastratable? the invisible love?) (visible enuf when you open your eyes and look) (izzasso?) (I have my own doubts, you see, I make these little jokes) "You were given the power to love, in order to use it, no matter what pain it may cause you." (wow) "Buddhism, frequently amounts to a form of psychic junk . . . I may add that I have seen nothing from those California Vedantists but a lot of horse shit, and I denounce them without cavil, as a pack of frauds." "Convinced of their own line to be sure, thereby adding self deception to their other failings. In short a sorry bunch of psychic retreaters from the dubious human journey. Because if there is one thing I feel sure of it is this: that human life has *direction*."

But I dear Allen say, no direction in the void.

Also Bill says, for choice prose see this, "KiKi is slowly denuding me of my clothes. He enjoys them so much and I care so little." Talk about DeCharlus![11]

Okay, Allen, goodbye.

Jean-Louis

Extra p.s. Cowley says he mentions me twice in last chapter of his new book in October.

And incidentally p.s. I changed my writing name to Jean-Louis.

JAZZ EXCERPTS by JEAN-LOUIS Remember Incogniteau?

Allen Ginsberg [San Francisco, California] to Jack Kerouac [n.p., New York, New York?]

September 5, 1954

Sept. 5—Sunday 10:30 PM
554 Broadway, Room 3
Hotel Marconi, S.F. Cal.

Cher Jean-Louis Le Brie:

Thank you for your letters, all so kind, all so sweet to get, such a pleasure that tho it's a waste of time etc. I get more kicks from reading them than almost anything else,—but don't write if not so set up, natch. Hard to write with burn-blister on thumb (of pen hand) and no typewriter. Well: what has happened out here. [. . .] Carolyn caught me and Neal—screamed,—she is I think a charnel—yelled,—reversed her original hypocrisy—was it?—or I shouldn't maybe judge—but it was not comic, the intensity of insult and horror and even I think spite, indignation, etc. (She burst into my room one 4 AM at the house) (though you see I was hiding nothing—told her in fact—it was O.K.'d—but all the details are not for here can't write fast enough) but anyway a horrible scene—ordered me gone—Neal went blank, ran out to work—I sat and faced her. She talked and I thought her face waxed green with evil. "You've always been in my way ever since Denver—your letters have always been an insult—you're trying to come between us" and more, horrible—such force, Celinish, I went cold with horror—felt *steeped* in evil. They hate each other, charnels to each other she and Neal. But I can't picture it to you as I really see it, no Levinsky sacerdotal-ism involved. I was glad to get away. So took twenty dollars and went up to Frisco to the above address—(I had said nothing back to her—went blank with a kind of hopeless feeling she was mad—though tried to hold with some kind

[11] Marcel Proust's patron was Baron de Charlus.

of in-sad sight to it all—I didn't come to screw her up) and here moved into [Al] Sublette's hotel (he moved to the Marconi up a few blocks Broadway can see Vesuvios from his window) and pounded pavements madly. Got a job in market research, $55 a week, 9–5 next month—on Montgomery financial street— found a girl the first night—a *great* new girl who digs me, I dig—twenty-two, young, *hip* (ex-singer big buddy of [Dave] Brubeck, knows all the colored cats, ex-hipster girl) *pretty* in a real chic classy way, *straight*—she works in high teacup emporium store writing advertising—digs me—she has a wild mind, finer than *any* girl I met—really—a real treasure—and such a lovely face—so *fine* a pretty face—young life in her—and real sharp agenbite of inwit thoughts like Lucien—Thos. Hardy. So have been seeing her for a week we talk and neck and will make it sure—*but* she has a kid (married at eighteen, kid four years old) used to sing in San Jose roadhouses and knows Mrs. Green [marijuana], etc. What a doll. *And* she's not a flip thank god. Not a stupid square in any way but *not* a flip. Sheila Williams. She tried to get me a crazy job at store the first nite I knew her—instant digging each other—how wild and great. O well, to see how this proceeds—nothing ugly can happen anyway thank god, she's too fine—she dug Sublette, etc. But we wander around alone and sit and drink coffee at her apt. and talk—and she digs the *really* good lines of my poetry, not just generally digs, but digs the *specific* tricks—well enough.

So to continue otherwise: I live in the Marconi hotel—run by dykes—first night they say to me—"here's yr. key. You want to have anybody in your room go ahead and have a ball we're drunk all night ourselves"—and they are. Middle size room $6.00 carpet soft on floor privacy, Sublette upstairs and—horrors! Last Friday night Sheila takes me to big party of nowhere engineers on Telegraph Hill. I come home 4:30 AM meet Sublette, and Cosmo (a weird egotistic small poet smart aleck) go and get coffee, the cops look at us, search us, find white powder on Cosmo. To jail, all night, my first week here, as a vagrant (tho I have $18.00 and a job for Monday to come and a room and party suit on) in tank, me and Sublette horrified (I had a pipe in my room but they didn't look) but actually great kicks—set free the next day, Cosmo doesn't get out for 4 days—the powder was foot powder not junk all along—he kept telling them but didn't believe and had it analyzed and finally let him go. So Bill better be careful.

[...]

I at last enclose *Siesta In Xbalba*. It won't be finished (I won't quit trying to add) for a while but this is the best I can do with it after four months—five months. The handwritten part still doesn't get a vision of Europe like I hope for but just mentions it and signs off. Show this to Lucien maybe and Cowley maybe? if you dig it—maybe it's too revised and formal now.

Yes, Rexroth was only an idea just in case nothing else was happening, Cowley much better. By the way the Ansen type poet round here name of Robert Duncan, friend of Pound, runs a crappy tho sincere Pound type poetry circle here part of S.F. College came to my room and saw a typed copy of your "Essentials" of Prose (remember, you wrote it down on E. 7th St.) and *dug* it (strangely particularly the part of no revision and the general conception of spontaneity) and asked to borrow it to make a copy and wanted your address and wanted to know who you were etc. Well he's a funny guy, queer, his poetry is all crazy and surrealist and he's a friend of Lamantia and his poetry also is no good because too aesthetically hung up all about his sensibility faced with the precise tone of his piddle—Light, etc.—that's the subject matter—but it's all right he's nice a curious person, talks too much in front of his young Corso students.

Neal—he played chess with Dick Woods and was blind, etc. except in a weird way very nice to me, but he is *mad*—the thing is Jack he really is suffering some incipient insanity—the charnel Carolyn, the frantic sex—now it is terrible pathetic mad rushing around and can't even *make* it—getting caught masturbating by his conductor—fucking seventy year old spiritualist woman in S.J. [San Jose]—the crackpot Cayce which he holds on to like some doctrine in an asylum—half serious obsession—I see him driving now frantic with empty hatreds of other drivers on Bloody Bayshore—he hates Carolyn I think—but nowhere else to go—no way out of the three children R.R. After I left they both went and took (o comedy horror) the Rorschach Ink Blot Test (which is maybe more or less accurate in determining degree of clinical insanity if you believe in the word, which I don't for me and you, but sort of do now for Neal) and he told me, jumbled, four conclusions: 1). sexually sadistic 2). pre-psychotic 3). "delusive thought system" 4). intense anxiety prone. Well as to number 3 that means if anything he has some kind of mad "*Cayce*—sex—driving—T"— system which is operating independently sort of convulsively compulsively running him around a kind of rat race. He don't write no more "I was writing about sex and you dig it's sinful, I know etc." he says. And Carolyn agrees "What good is that sort of thing, you call that art? It's just dirt." I tell you that household is—and so much gold in trash now, the *chess*, maniacal. He won't talk to me, except in a sort of dissociated way. Comes to my room in Frisco gets in bed and plays with self. You know how I dig sex my way any kind but there's something wrong in the total sense of masturbatory insistence and franticness of that. He says generally "I have no feelings—never had." I mean we ball as ever still but read on. His stomach is bad—nausea at meals, maybe ulcers. His suffering is—well not suffering, his *pain* or dissociation from contact or good sweet kicks is more and more autonomous, more overloaded, heavy. He sees

240

it, no way out for him he says once in a while, drives faster. I do all I can to make it with him—as friend I mean,—I don't really care about the cock—it seems too dislocated for that. (I mean this judgment does not come from morbid lusting turning sour exactly.) Would be willing to take vows of leave him alone etc. if he only would be sweet and care-ful again and open to gentle kicks and images and poetry and digging things of all natures—and no time for kicks on jazz— he's too busy—Chess. Or if we did go it would be a ragged fury of being too high driving too fast, all too hot and horrible. Well he and I love each other, it's all *there* no doubt, but everything seems *impossible* as far as any real contact and natural enjoyment. He really gets no kicks from me as Allen or Levinsky or poet or old memory friend. I mean he does and I too from him but it's so fast it's unreal and most of the time driven into the background grim reality noth- ingnesses that happen. As for Carolyn, I know or imagine she has suffered as wife perhaps to justify any way she is now but I have strong impression she's a kind of death—she doesn't dig new things (statues or paintings when pointed out)—I mean she has no active curiosity or aesthetic or kicks interests and lives by this ruinous single track idea of running the family according to her ideas strictly, ideas which are mad copies of *House Beautiful* and are really nowhere in addition to being unreal on account of the horror of the house and the need for some real force of compassion or insight or love or Tao, or whatever. Maybe it's impossible. She's a hysteric type—that is, shifting layers of dishonesty which I first didn't dig but do so now. Will take it or leave it, it is only my reaction to the general scene. I felt relieved to get out to poverty—work worries free of the mad hassle of anxiety at the house, alone in Frisco. And if I feel relieved to get out of a situation with Neal there must be something screwy somewhere. I know what I was doing there with Neal sounds on the surface like a monstrous thing, as Carolyn with some justice suddenly exploded out with, but that isn't the cause of their woes, she forbade me by the way to ever see him again. I have horror of such insensitivity to the total situation *insisted* on as the *right*, self righteous *final* eternal etc. Oh well enuf of this it is too nasty and I can't give the picture as I saw it. But I mean I felt evil around me—her vehemence and the feeling of horror I had reminded me of moments in the N.J. hospital when my mother was seized by a fit of frenzied insistent accusation and yelled at me that I was a spy. If you remember the story I told you about the sense of finality and absolute tired despair and hopeless futility I felt when at age fourteen I took my mother on a mad horrible trip to Lakewood where I left her to fall apart in paranoiac fear with shoe in hand surrounded by cops in a drugstore. I felt the same tired inevitability and impossibility of fact and mad horror listen- ing to Carolyn, and afterward—tired exhausted feeling in the back, want to go off somewhere else from the impossible *end* of communication and sleep it off.

That's disappeared since I've been here running around, but it hasn't disappeared in San Jose, for Neal who lives in hell and for her who lives in hell, and I guess the children.

[...]

Well, Bill writes he leaves Sept. 7 from Gibraltar and he'll get here sooner or later. God knows what will happen. Jack boy now get on the ball. I will be trying to make it perhaps with Sheila, trying anyway. I will do everything I can for and to Bill, anything he wants, but the impossibilities of his demands are ultimately inescapable unless I let him carry me off forever to Asia or something to satisfy his conception of his despair and need. You must try and now straighten him out, you know. I'm not that [much] a bitch or unwilling to go to any lengths to help out. I do like him and would love to share a place with him here if it could be done which it will be, but he is going to be frantic and possessive you know. He was (against his own will) having tantrums of jealousy in N.Y.C., even over Dusty [Moreland] he was annoyed. The situation with Sheila will be a madhouse. I don't know how to manage it. Bill will enforce his idea so much he will *make* me reject it and take it as a hopeless horror. He has of course calmed down a lot since midsummer, but he still puts all his life in my hands. Even *I* never went that far. So you must make him understand to go easy. It's not a crisis of final communication, etc. Whatever it is—it is whatever he sees it as of course, except for the basic mutual bond which is so final and permanent which seems now unreal to him unless he possesses my very thoughts equal to his—it's a real bitch man. So you *must* try to give him some kind of strength or Tao and O.K. hipness to the situation so that he doesn't make a horror of it. I can't be his one sole and only contact forever, I can only be his nearest and best. Well you know, whatever so long as everybody's happy with the resources that are at hand. Christ what a situation. Surrounded by mad saints all clawing at each other and I the most weird? And tell Lucien to talk to Bill. He certainly knows about symbiosis and ought to have a helpful constructive word. As for me I am resolved to be patient and as un evil as I can manage.

No time to describe—too tired—North Beach—characters—one mad Peter du Peru (who has gestures and same tone as Peter Van Meter and *both* are from Chicago). But Du Peru (what a mad Subterranean name!) is also like [Carl] Solomon a Zen ex amnesia-shock patient who wears no socks and is always beat and *sensitive* and curious and interested and has the best mystic mind I've met here. Digs me too. We talk—have walked together him telling me about various Baroque and Regency and City Hall weirdness of architecture all over S.F.

And our friend Bob Young, why my dear I *believe* it is the very same little black angel I once *did already* make it with on E. 7th Street no less perhaps a year ago—ask him. Wears fine clothes? very sad sweet, yes it must be he, even the name I *seem* to remember. We met drunk at the White Horse. Actually a sad occasion, it made me shudder.

As for the American Revolution it *was* a revolution wasn't it? The "traditional dissenters"—well the Tories weren't dissenting it was our forefathers, the Paines. But Hinkle (nor I) don't favor revolution or conquest of U.S. by Red-East. Maybe Hinkle does, come to think of it. All I am saying is that the U.S. is in the hands of people like the publishers you hate and they are fucking us up in the rest of the world's Spenglerian schemes. We should be feeding Asia not fighting her at this point. And if we actually do (for some mad reason) fight, it'll be the *end.* The Reds are what Burroughs thinks they are—evil—probably—but enough bullshit on this. Yes, Al [Hinkle] is kind, and so Helen [Hinkle] too at time of crisis in Cassady household—they put me straight on the horror. I thought I might be going mad. They knew.

No more long letters, but short notes occasionally when there's news. Keep me informed on pleasant news of publishing. No space to talk about Shakespeare. I like your Tao, it's more humane. I also have read some Chinese cloud mountain—for as said in the *Green Auto* "Like Chinese magicians, confound the immortals with an intellectuality hidden in the mist." And my poem also by the way on Sakyamuni (who brought Buddhism to China) coming out of the mountain. I got most of my titles about it all from digging the *pictures* of the cloudy mountains and the sages that the *arhats*[12] painted—*dig dig dig* at the N.Y. Public Library Fine Arts room the great collections of Chinese paintings—visions of the physical Tao, if one can get a spiritual insight from the painter's material vision of the mountains receding into vast dream infinities series of mountains separated by infinities of mist. The paintings of the infinite worlds of mountains were my favorite, and next the great belly rubbing or beat or horrible looking W.C. Fields *arhats* in rags with long ears or giggling together over manuscripts of poems about clouds.

Also there is a book, *The White Pony*, ed. Robert Payne, which is translation of all kinds from thousands years Chinese Buddhist-Taoist poetry—easy to read, such a pleasure, so many—and Bill Keck has my marked copy of this book, unless he's given it to someone. Tell him "I ask him for Balloon's sake to recover it and give to you if it's not an impossible hassle"—if you see him.

When you send me essay on Buddha? I read it with pleasure.

[...]

Give Gregory my respects. Say I said "The accurate measure of a free verse line is at present impossible (so as to make free verse stanzas and base lines to

[12] An arhat is a Buddhist monk who has attained Nirvana.

vary your free song from, like musical variation), but it is I think a beautiful problem to attempt to solve. I am interested in hearing any results on this still." Give him my affectionate regards—tousle his head perhaps, poke his pap. He's alright maybe.

Remembrances to Kells. I'm a wandering Taoist Bum—as this Mex poem indicates—or would like to be *if* I could only escape this eternal fixation on the metaphysics of being one—tho I know that to be one you only have to forget it and let the thing and no thing whatever be. I am stuck on the paradox and can't get it out of my mind. It's a *hang up block*, my undoing. Madhouse.

Where where—is Carl Solomon?

Allen Ginsberg [San Francisco, California] to Jack Kerouac [n.p., New York, New York?]

before October 26, 1954

Dear Jack:

Confusion reigns! After an exchange of shocking letters Bill [Burroughs] seems to have come off the distraction-intensity. Now he's down in Fla. My letter to him was perhaps too strong but subsequent correspondence has straightened out some of the bad feeling and left the whole situation a lot relieved. If you are interested, I do hope he comes out here, have always wanted him to, but not with the kind of hang up he had. I should know. Anyway, so he's down in Florida. What happens next? His inheritance is disappearing on him— reduced to $100.00 per month or less he writes. Maybe can't get to Tangiers. Not sure what to do. Doesn't much want to come to California he says but also says he might like to under certain circumstances, etc. I wrote asking him to come out, offered fare back to Mex border if he wished to depart. And would pay rent in small apt. or room for him here.

[...]

I am living in a big crazy apt. on Nob Hill with Sheila [Williams] who incidentally tell Jerry Newman heard about him thru an ex-recording engineer friend of Brubeck who she knows. Al Sublette comes all the time and wines up or eats and talks and Sheila and he dig one another. She a sort of department store white collar Dusty [Moreland], but younger with a child and more a prey to girlish psychological semi-dramatizations (I'm an old man tired sort of, I can't make the flux of love-illusions)—and undoubtedly the seeds of dissolution of this affair have already set in, now that we are established. I wish it were just quiet domestic so I could write. But there is the strain of Burroughs on my

side and the strain of ex-lovers and department store cocktail friends and un-
certain childlikeness on hers. God knows what'll happen.

[...]

Because of Sheila and moving around and screwing and evenings full of
North Beach and department store types (who are a drag) I haven't written
anything since I left San Jose. Things have finally settled down and I am back
at work on book this week which is now ⅓ done about. Another month perhaps
and I will send you copy called perhaps *The Green Automobile*. I sent your letter to Neal asking to see what you wrote him and haven't got it to answer he
didn't reply—haven't seen him since the heat went on and off again, all's alright
now again no threat.

[...]

I will go write on your S.F. poems. They are nearer to center of poetry than
elsewhere can be found but since my effort in last two years has been to find a
formal look (as Cezanne said he wants to paint pictures that look like classics
in museums, and did) your poems are satisfactory at special moments in them
(Ted the F.B.I. for instance; parts of Neal in Court; other sketches from window). I'd rather not say anything till I go home. (It's Friday afternoon in Montgomery Street office I am writing from) and look again—when they seem
formal, too, as well as naked.

Sheila hates me because I am a stuffy old nay-saying abstractionist and not
a Dostoevskyan lover. I screw for the first time regular these days by the way,
what a relief to come home to. I hear Burford (and Baldwin?) put Bill and
me down. What's wrong? I don't see why Burford should come on that way
unless as Ed White said in Dusty's apartment he's just a continental snow-job
specialist.

[...]

I'll write subsequently,
Allen

Bill said you were angry at me because of my letter to him. You should not
be—I am doing all in my power for him. If I had not written so he would continue in state of tragic self-pity absorption perhaps. Even Bill knows at heart.

*Editors' Note: Ginsberg had been afraid that if Burroughs visited him in San
Francisco, Burroughs would want to take over his life. Allen loved him as a
friend, but did not want to be his lover, so he was angry when Kerouac wrote
Burroughs and told him Ginsberg wanted him to come to visit.*

Jack Kerouac [Richmond Hill, New York] to Allen Ginsberg [San Francisco, California]

Oct. 26, '54

Dear Allen:

Thank you for writing and implying that you forgive me and had gotten over that rage for a poor little kind white lie I told Bill—to make him feel good, almost droning like an old Grandmaw, I just said "He really secretly wants to be with you as before otherwise you see Bill he wouldn't write and discuss and re-hash so much"—My true feeling was that maybe *you* didn't want Bill anymore because he was become so strange and frightening and *secretive.*

1. He paid absolutely no attention to anything I said especially about Buddhism—like Lucien he "couldn't care less."

2. You should never have involved me in these judgments which relate to cupidities and concupiscences of homosexuals of which I am no expert.

3. Burroughs does not respect my intelligence but what really is, he does not respect my *power of deception.*

4. I am not going to deceive or conceal anything for anyone and I call now for all of us to return to Beat Generation 1947 confessions and honesties *a la* Lucien dawn drunks of truth.

The "white lie" was spoken to Bill *for* Bill—I was also well aware you wanted straightness with chick and also told Bill. I don't know what he wrote you, (about my opinions.) "Canuck unsaintly" prescribing liaisons for you not meet for me, how come, who is the queers around here, now really—how could I make sex with Bill and so what is un-meet about an old lover re-loving him? I mean, why did you get so mad? Are you sure it isn't Neal but *you's* crazy? I think you were distracted and your severe formal reject letter to Bill I know was written in distraction. I don't want to be unkind and I don't want to fight and I don't want to be misunderstood as "mean"—But I do think we'll need a serious mutual confession and admit the new backlog of secret hates we have for each other that if not uprooted will grow, [. . .]

[Bob] Burford did *not* put you down, on the very contrary is deeply respectful and wants to hear from you at once—care of American Consul or Burford, c/o L'Eau Vive, Soissy Sur Seine, France—he was knocked out by *Visions of Neal*, the A.A. Wyn part and wanted to take *Beat Generation Road* to Knopf but my agent is jealous of interference and I hope I didn't goof by sticking to agent's judgment—God he's, it's slow—that Cowley article shoulda done it don't you think? Book is at E.P. Dutton's—[James] Baldwin put Bill down, not you, saw Bill's manuscript somewhere.—Tell Al Sublette I met a great new pianist called Cecil Taylor, plays like [Oscar] Peterson gone Classical, fast runs but Brubeck-Stravinsky-Prokofieff chords, a Juilliard classicist—He, like Baldwin, colored, I think gay,—Baldwin is gay. I don't dig all this gayness. Burford put Bill down, says "If I believe in evil, he is evil." Burford says only other evil person he knows is Temko (!) (?)—I put [Eric] Protter down, was drunk there.—Bill has your poems—I think they are great, whattaya want Whitman to think of Melville.—

[. . .] I think Cowley should see *Naked Lunch*. I'm going to show *Sax* to [Alfred] Kazin, he was on air recently, TV, talkin about Melville stuttering breathlessly and great. My *San Fran Blues* poems did you know were all writ spontaneous fast? that's point. Not too good, really nowhere I'm sure, except some . . . images thin. Who cares? My poetry is prose lines.

I just took trip to Lowell, whole Duluoz Legend all thirty-five volumes of it flamed in my brain—should I bother with so much repetitious detail? haunting castle above my birthplace house I hadn't seen since I was three . . . so that's where Sax come from. In fact whole Lowell trip so vast I can't even begin to draw breath to tell . . . later. I tired. Glad you wrote and ain't mad and that I ain't mad and now let's rest in understanding. [. . .] Incidentally, if you have any questions and doubts about Luminous Truth, ask me. I am surer now than ever. As for Tao, it is just outer style, like in Mexico I be Tao hobo in beans and jeans, but etc. in other words, I have reached the Gnostic and apocalyptic certainty beyond all doubt and my mind is set to concentrate now to the end.

Jack

IMPORTANT! (writ after twelve hours sleep) I had $30 cash in my desk for a winter leather jacket and Bill took a cab to Richmond and looked crazy and wanted money (for Ritchie) and took it all—Instead of paying it back he went to Florida—Doesn't even write now—I don't have his address—It's getting winter and no coat for poor old Poe—send me his goddam address—I'm not the one with incomes around here. That's really my mother's money.—I want that money *back*.

Incidentally what happened to those power of attorney papers you have? My agent Sterling Lord is also planning to publish me in France in French and will handle everything. Unless he's a secret agent for Giroux, who recommended him.

So what else?—Looks like Neal has finally drowned in the plans of Karma-making Gea—we'll see him no more I'm afraid. (so all's fucked and lost).

J.

Allen Ginsberg [San Francisco, California] to Jack Kerouac [n.p., New York, New York?]

Nov. 9, '54

Dear Jack:

My rage was annoyance but I generally understood and took it as a minor thing. Certainly not enuf to make me think of not writing. Yes Bill has become too strange for me to live in such close quarters with—not absolutely frightening but I knew it would end in some kind of absolute sad idiocy, particularly with me off all the time with Sheila [Williams]. But even without chick, too much. Still I invited him finally to come here, I didn't want to put him down at soul. We are corresponding again. He's more distant. It's easier to read his letters. How hard it all is—I have to confess that as far as I'm concerned I dig Bill as ever and have no objection to anything and feel like an ego fool for the whole season but what could I do or should or whatever? I don't care really about straightness with chick or anything like that—I first knew he'd come here and I'd get him all involved and vice versa and there'd be a bust with the cops ultimately and I'd be coming late to work and have to sit and listen to him and routines mercilessly applauding and so on. I wasn't interested enough, I might be sometime when I want to return to saintly solitude and brotherliness to Bill. I lack solitude here and Bill is a power of solitude—got to give him *all* attention, I had my attentions turned in other (lesser) directions.

[. . .]

Sure I'm crazy. I begin at the local analytic clinic tomorrow—$1.00 an hour. Don't bust a gut.

I'm not a devil neither are you, stop saying things like that. I just thought you were on an angelic type jig so to speak, gleefully siccing Bill on—but really he's so far gone or was, you might just as well have humored him. In the long run the same thing that made you tell him white lies—the same madness—made me yell at him. I did everything I could not do for half a year.

[. . .]

Because of living in splendor with girl I do no reading no writing. Probably coming to the end of this, I'll move in a month or so and get secret nice pad on side street run-down height of Nob Hill I've elected, under a great concrete basement of the next top-of-hill block for $35 a month save money and read and write and pray to solitude. [. . .]

[Kenneth] Rexroth has Bill's book reading it. He advises at New Directions. He invited me to reading poetry at a series he's a manager of connected with a college here. [W. H.] Auden, [William Carlos] Williams, local poets including me. Sometime next month perhaps.

Damned [Jordan] Belson read Yage and put Bill down, refused to read *Queer* [...]. What madness inspires these semi-ignus? He gave me some peyote, I got hi with [Al] Sublette and Sheila and we dug S.F. midtown cable cars clanging skyline—looked out my living room vast window down into the bldgs.—especially the Sir Francis Drake hotel—which has a Golgotha-robot—eternal—smoking machine crowned visage made up of the two great glass-brick eyes on either side (the toilets men and women of the Starlight Room)—upstarting out of the paved mist ground—I wrote on it.[13]

[...]

Bill is at 202 Sanford, Palm Beach. He writes: "Oh God I owe Jack $30 and don't have it to send him. He will be hounding me like Friendly Finance. I feel so guilty I can't bring myself to write him." Write *him* a Friendly Finance letter maybe. He by the way you know (So doth the fixt foundation change) no longer has $200 per month—now only $100. How will he make it? I owe him $60, which I'll pay in a month.

[...]

What of yours has been published so far or accepted?

As to Neal: Since I been settled down here he comes by every week to borrow Miss Green or bring Miss Green [marijuana]. Last few times rushed in and out with Lucien, a high grotesque black man from Howard St., his pimp for Miss Green, unrolled her on the floor and proceeded to manicure and blow in midafternoon while I wandered around turning on and off lights and carried garbage downstairs and picked up child's toys. One thing I must say, I can see what a strain it has been for him to try and maintain a family household and at the same time run a mad pad. Sheila digs him, of course, but he's been very good about not coming on with her. [...]

Well Neal says I should write you for him. He is always rushing around. So he keeps telling me—"you know what to tell him, we're buddies, etc." He will be cut off the R.R. sometime early January. He wants to go to Mex City for kicks for a week or a few days, then go booming in Florida, and then go rush up to N.Y.C. for a day or two and then return to Frisco to job. Carolyn threatens to quit if he goes booming, wants him to get a filling station job in Los Gatos. He as yet seems undecided whether or not he can get away with it, but he's been talking about it since I first arrived. So he wants you to know his general plan. I don't think I'll go with him to D.F.—Scared of his driving, and

---

[13] This peyote vision was the original inspiration for Ginsberg's poem *Howl*.

I'll be working still, then, I suppose. Saving $ for Europe or the East. Anyway he wanted me to write you for him. Consider him. He's up for three investigations, everybody on the R.R. whispers about him blasting, "everybody knows I'm a cunt hound," Carolyn hasn't laid him in three months. I'll tell him I wrote. He seems lately a little cooler however than in the Hotel Marconi days—a few months ago. I even played him a game of chess. He's taught chess to Sublette and half of North Beach. Sublette beat him. He's still on Cayce, will bring it up out of nowhere on every visit. If I say something other than Cayce he says with a forbearing smile, "Well that's because you don't really understand Cayce." [...]

What is happening with yr. art? Send me, yet, the Buddha book to read.

[...]

Love,

Allen

Allen Ginsberg [San Francisco, California] to Jack Kerouac [n.p., New York, New York?]

November 26, 1954

Fri
Nov. 26

Dear Jack:

Last nite walked drunk [Al] Sublette over Chinatown at 3 AM to Hotel Marconi and packed him up for farewell to his fine window overlooking the corner Bway and Columbus and skyline ranging out above. Taxi to Pier 37 and aboard the Santa Lucia for him to South America, Acapulco and Chile. He staggered around lugging his sides [records] and record machine and I with two valises and then we wandered around the ship. I guess my next big move will be to ship again. Maybe sometime in spring and also as a yeoman or perhaps see if I can get a purser type shot and make money. Certainly to Europe in one and half years. Poor Bill's left by boat I guess, supposed to the 20th and I haven't heard since the 17th. What a sad mess. Amazing to think that (as I am sure) our relationship will suddenly have changed to some strange distant Bill distance in Bill—perhaps no longer the eager Bill of before (I mean a year ago, two years ago) with mutual ignu marks and stars. He feels maybe that I am a paranoid [Hal] Chase suddenly cutting off his finger, unforgivable, and will no longer be able to address me without self-consciousness. But I suppose if we were to meet again in some dark corner of a Kasbah we'd be all right understanding again with no thought of this woe. And how different will I feel toward him having "as it were" tweet tweet found a limit to what I would do for him and by implication for you or Lucien or Neal, and by implication vice-versa. Almost an F. Scott Fitzgerald disillusioning. And what would I do with a pilgrim soul if I did find a real one here in S.F.? I said to Sheila last night, in the middle of a hassle about why I don't love her really. I thought maybe because I loved men too much, but do I do that any more like I used to?

Neal came by the other nite and got me hi and I fed him, Sheila slept, we talked, he went out to wander in North Beach. Not much work on RR, off longer periods of time. But every time you talk to him as soon as it gets interesting he suddenly turns a switch in his head and the CAYCE Jones Locomotive blackens the horizon—he begins repeating the same ideas, more simplified and unrelated (whirling around fragments of former perceptions and mad thoughts) in answer to anything that he thinks about for more than 37 seconds. It all gets channeled. Except for chess, as he complains, cunt and chess and Cayce, beyond that he's a blank, can't listen to a paragraph of writing easily, nor read, hardly seems to notice the weird Chinese paintings I prop up for his delight on the table, says "uhhuh." Then looks up and sadly says, "Can't concentrate any more—except on chess." I can't concentrate enough to like write you a letter, he feels sorry, he wouldn't write me, no one, couldn't except a line a year, "well how's the old boy?" Said situation with Carolyn [Cassady] worse, now he no longer even shared room, but sleeps on the couch. This may be coming to some kind of break. She also has suspicious notions about me. He said he had "made the mistake of showing her this Miss Green" and she went into a rage accusing "Ginsberg of feeding it to him." The Hinkles were by and said she was continuing war against me in my absence, I mean real absence from the scene even in Frisco, I so seldom see him, alas. I really don't think she's all right Jack, maybe she's come to bugged end with him, but there's real nastiness coming out of her. Helen Hinkle, his old confidante up in arms against him—he comes around and plays chess with Al, all the time, bugs Helen tho why I don't know except jealousy, so she threatened to tell all his confidences to Carolyn unless he stopped coming and playing chess incessantly. Invited to come without chessboard. Nevertheless I do notice that when at my house he seems subdued and very warm, tho perhaps preoccupied, but very gentle and old friendly—the only franticism is the occasions he rushes in hardly without saying a word or inquiring whether squares are present with big black connecting Lucien spade and begins rolling huge mounds of Miss Green squatted beside green coffee table on white shag rug in my great living room. But after that's over (he often cursing, demanding paper, not sullen but bugged with his green, sometimes shortchanged and angry) he sits down over coffee like an old uncle, tho doesn't say much.

Well anyway, Jack, I'll be leaving here Tuesday nite December 14 and get to NYC noon Wednesday. I'll have to make it around with family since my brother [Eugene Brooks] sent me plane fare to make his wedding. But I won't spend much time, a fast visit to Paterson maybe Thursday afternoon, visit my brother Wednesday afternoon. Where will you be Wednesday night? I'd wish you to make the plane field but its a nonscheduled flight and I'm not yet positive when exactly it arrives where. If I find out I'll let you know. Anyway I stay around till Sunday evening and catch return plane then. Wedding is in Riverside cathedral?? NYC Saturday nite. So I'll be around Tues Nite, maybe Wed nite, Thurs Fri and Sat and Sun. Please leave time free to see me, we will make all the possible scenes, Montmarte and Village, Lucien, Kingsland, Dusty, ah Love. How I'd love to fuck Dusty again. I don't know where I'll stay, maybe Dusty or Luciens or my brothers or Kingsland or Greenwich hotel. I'm sure it will be a sad four day ball. *Write me before I leave here so I know you're in town and don't have to worry about seeing you.* I'll bring many poems, a note for you from Sublette, a note from Neal, the address of Sheila's girlfriend to look up, etc. I saw the Cowley chapters. Too objective and tentative, "this one and that one fits into such and such scheme of things," what horrors.

Love,
Allen

My appearance has changed a little—I have good tweed suit and close cropped head and gaunt perhaps rocky face. Amazing I get more beautiful as I grow older, thank god. A curious P.S. but I've been all hung up on the temporary miracle—Sheila thinks I'm beautiful—for two weeks. Her opinion's not worth too much but I feel that way anyway.

Editors' Note: Ginsberg flew to New York for his brother's wedding on December 18, and had a chance to see many of his friends, including Kerouac. Within a week he was back in San Francisco, where he had fallen head over heels in love with Peter Orlovsky, a handsome model for the painter Robert LaVigne. Orlovsky had recently been discharged from the Army with mental problems. Immediately, everything in Ginsberg's life changed and he moved out of Sheila Williams' apartment and in with Orlovsky and LaVigne, whose apartment and studio were on Gough Street.

Jack Kerouac [Richmond Hill, New York] to
Allen Ginsberg [San Francisco, California]

12/22/54

Dear Buddy boy,

I'm not mad. You didn't have to show off to the bearded bohemian hepcats in the crowd. I just saw a film of Alistair Sim in "Christmas Carol"—did you ever dig Alistair Sim? Did you ever know about Seymour [Wyse]'s appreciation of Alistair Sim? How great he is. Like some great English poet who became an actor instead. Greater than Dylan Thomas, like a real Herbert-Vaughan-Herrick-Wyatt greatness, in acting, in facial expression, in interpretation. I feel as sentimental as our dear rabbi.

The night is cold. Freezing. Snow. Ice. My legs are cold. This afternoon I had a long meditation and tried to dwell in Mind Essence. You can't dwell in it, can only glance and stare at it even, and think about it, but being hung with the three gunas of sattva, rajas and the other one [tamas] (intelligence of light, inertia of dark body, and energy that moves) one can't sit all the time, etc. But the greatness of Dickens is like the thing in [John Clellon] Holmes that does make him great . . . a vast O What The Hell Live It Up ness . . . like Holmes at old parties raising beerglass . . . with Lyndons and Durgins and what the hellers. . . . like Cannastra. May I someday be like Scrooge, a reformed dour Buddhist suddenly going mad dancing in the street? It doesn't matter, all's the same. Our Balzacs and Dickenses and Holy Dostoevskys knew that.

Goodbye,

Jack

P.S. Be sure to be sure to be sure to be sure.

But in truth, Scrooge was attached at first to his niggardly selfness; then he became liberated from that and became attached to people.

As for dwelling in Mind Essence, it's like Edie [Parker] who used to want to crawl up my ass hole she said and curl up. I can't crawl into mind essence and curl up because it is No Body, No Womb. But I can dwell *with* it. The secret of Buddhism is the practice of Dhyana in the morning, Dhyana in the afternoon, Dhyana in the night, every day. No other way. Finally when you've intuited so long it opens and opens to the illimitable void and vastness and etc. This is all clear. Don't show my stuff to [Robert] Duncan the Holmes. I'll see my agent soon about *Sax* mail. *BEAT* has been recommended now by editor in chief [Joe] Fox . . . the others are reading it. Happy New Year.

Jean

Allen Ginsberg [San Francisco, California] to Jack Kerouac [n.p., New York, New York?]

December 29, 1954

Dear Kind King Mind:

> I'm sick, kind Kerouac, your hallowed Allen
> Is sick in eternity! laboring lonesome
> and worse and worse by the day by the hour . . .
> but I need a little sweet conversation
> sad as the tears of that great prince Sebastian.
> (after Catullus)

Fraid you were mad then because of me unkind, the paper, was unkind. Never yet have seen Alistair Sim, I'm sick, home a day from work, deep cold, penicillin, I'm deaf almost, sick with love again also, moved to Gough Street artist bohemian pad, Sheila [Williams] comes surprise dressed up on her lunch hour to find me in clothes sweating in cell on pallet on floor, Neal is giggling and playing games with redhead [Natalie Jackson] in other room down the hall, I'm in love with twenty-two year old saint boy who loves me, lives there too, but terrible scene is here. I ran into painter Robert LaVigne, ignu-deep souled twenty-six year Polk-Sutter beard a month ago, we went up to see his paintings, walking up Sutter from Polk-Sutter Fosters Cafeteria where I went one night drunk to dig subterranean scene and look for Peter Carl—Sol DuPeru (who I met first nite in [Al] Sublette's room here in SF), so I went up to beard lonely to ask after DuPeru who he didn't know, we talked, he invited me to see paintings, went to house on Gough St. I walked in room—this was a month ago—and saw huge modern true painting of naked youth, and others of same, clothed and unclothed. Then in walked the boy his model, who painter, made it with too, gentle souled tall Russian red Kafka, respectful, silent, and so I came back that week, expected, and began season—great house, I told you, I brought Neal to dig the redhead girl, he made it with her last week and thereafter—long hall, big messy rooms, tea in kitchen, just like youth, we gather, talk, Neal rushes in 9AM WC Fields—Oliver Hardy pulling on or off his pants, makes it with girl, laughs again, puts on her clothes, she his vest, they blast,—and he and I agree on nostalgia of the front door, we've both gained so much tender youth kicks in last two weeks entering the apartment first floor of huge Victorian wood house, big smell of paintings and studio for LaVigne up front, Peter Orlovsky studying in a room in the middle (he's the boy) and Natalie the ex-Stanley

Gould girlfriend here for four months in the back—so sweet and promising 115th St. tender joys entering the house again, for me, Neal feels same like I say, so one night before I leave for NYC—LaVigne telling me he's leaving, mysterious, leaving town to go paint (after his show running now, wild colored nudes and pix of Fosters) near San Diego, end of his season with Peter as perhaps mine ended when I left Houston for Dakar Doldrums, so he says he's leaving, will I see please Peter much when he's gone, needs a friend, needs sweet companion, I shudder, I see the love, I'm doomed, my heart melts again—how I hate women, can't stand not to be in love, can't stand not to be melting with real tenderness, childlike need sweetnesses, that's what's wrong with me and Sheila, I don't love like sad love can be, my heart's chill there. So I tell LaVigne, OH, god not again, what lord are you asking me for? I can't kneel and cocksuck forever like of old—but he says Peter knows and digs me, mind, man, I'm changed in Calif., like a dream—I'm waited for. So I went to NYC with that in mind, except also a night I spend there and talk to Peter who tells me he dreamt that he had walked up to me, put arms round my waist, I was surprised in dream. Then in hall in life, embraced, real sweetness in my breast, too much, I'd almost cry, but it's such poor pitiful fleeting human life, what do I want anyway? Nature boy—to be loved in return. So followed a night of embraces, not sex. Then NYC, then I return, move out of Sheila's to here—meanwhile, she suddenly digs Al Hinkle in my absence (in fact had before I left one evening when I was out all night, Al came visiting, got some wine, they talked on the floor rapport)—so in absence she made it with Hinkle, sweet, I am pleased—so she waits for him one night, I'm in NYC, then she goes out, he cuts by, doesn't know where she is, nor know I'm in NY, he goes up to Polk and Sutter Fosters looking for me or her, she has just left there, he goes up to the Gough street house, looking for Ginsberg, redhead says I'm away, he asks to flop for few hours, sleeps, wakes up, goes to take a piss, turns hall corner, there's naked Neal bumping into him (he didn't know Neal ever was there—all in my absence) they laugh, the circles of Dostoevsky in this house. I return, everybody making it full blast, Peter having got hi first time with Neal and redhead Natalie and suddenly DUG also, in strange drooling Peter Lorre way—he's a Myshkin too—BUT alas, now the sad horrors begin, LaVigne also digs me, I make it with him in bed, for life's sake tho not really want to, then when I move here we set up bed, all three of us making it in same bed, but I only dig Peter really, Peter begins guilty only digging me, tho all love Robert LaVigne for sad genius ignu self and beard he wears—and one thing, I can't understand why he's bowing out, what genius of sad knowledge of loss he had (as I had with Neal in Texas)—meanwhile Peter and I have mad conversations about Thought, I read *Visions of Neal* aloud to Natalie and all, Neal expected hourly again, night of wild balling with Peter with Bob there too—and then Bob (LaVigne) goes mad, sees self losing, Peter changing, I seem smug and over bestial, he's angry, won't speak, locks self in room with Peter to plead, threaten? I never heard, we try to talk, Bob and I being more or less equal souls, fruits, can't say, hate and love each other, Peter scared and guilty and faithful to Robert, I suffer now, anger in the house, all wrought up for days, who will kill who? But I not want to deceive or offend Robert so drag pallet into my lone room, tension yet mounts, Bob feels I've betrayed him, I'm falling more in love, he's falling more in despair—love though he is leaving any week now, still can't give up hope for golden love boy, he thinks I'm evil mocking (Hal Chase thought) grabbing kid fast for kicks, Peter meanwhile promised to me, promise fades, we finally all three meet in kitchen and evil hate scenes, Peter loving both, old fidelities, new sensual mental kicks, Bob and I digging each other perhaps the most yet thru clouds of fear, the maya mists, irony between us, he accusing, I can't stand it as he thinks I'm being dirty toward Peter, but I love, meanwhile Peter more and more offended by scene we can't stop as it's in cards—Robert saying "You're both waiting for me to kick off so you can make it together." I saying, "We can't have a rose without your blessing = rose requires perfection which you added don't take it away now." Robert saying, "I won't again" irony, Peter saying finally ah comedies, "You're both a pain in the ass"—only Burroughs would appreciate. But finally we all melting in sadness, I can't hide that I want, Robert can't hide that he too wanted, Peter that he didn't need—his innocence going to see us old farts go woeful, he also wants girls, after all, as well as teacher kind king mind yet sweet prince would love us too, and me after all these hopeless years—that is to say, this be some self deception but actual promise of Peter nature more harmonious for kind of sweet comradeship than any other I had yet met, I having given up hoping long ago, so now hardly begun to thaw to the rue and sadness of love, just beginning tonight in my sick bed. Well we all made up in a kind, Peter to go alone, Bob to go alone, I alone, Sheila appearing at noon digging my kick sadly, she loves me, I dig her but can't make it, with final conversation neither of us really wanting to betray Robert between self and Peter, that we would wait and see—but already in sad old love heart I know it never came that way, that easy, unless this was prelude of torments to some bliss, will never manifest with such innocence again, I'm sad, lay in bed sweating with cold, too olden to really remember self pities of eighteen-twenty again, but unhappy till I began thinking of the unlikely possible accidental sweetnesses of life, maybe that's all they are, transient. And in his journal (where I peeked tho he would have killed me) Robert writing suffering lines about god shaping him with torment to bareness and true beauty, he really digs, though we can't talk.

So the situation stands now, Natalie making me tea to drink, meanwhile rent is due, Robert due to leave, house to break up, I have to find new pad or hotel—will move in or near area near Peter and Polk Gulch in some hotel for two weeks till paycheck comes enough to get small pad, meanwhile reading *Visions of Neal* and *San Francisco Blues*.

Yes, I know maybe you will wind up throwing up arms at life's mess and accept it Dickens way but I still say Jack that though I did not attain sanctity because I was too egotistically hung upon the idea of pure vision continuous in order to be saint, and had no stern bare guru who KNEW, just Van Dorens who made me doubt—there is the goal of the Nameless that is the most worthy for us if we've the faith or insight to persist. I wait for life like this to break me down to no attachments maybe because none so sublime as I can emotionally imagine exist

> not even the human
> imagination satisfies
> the endless emptiness
> of the soul

(This silly simpleminded after all our conversation and your last letter, maybe to a point where as before I'll sit in silence cooking vegetables again as I did in 49 in Harlem hopeless till my door was silent and silently swung open and let in heaven's light) to persist in seeking it whatever way is offered, directer the better. But what a madness gamble it is. I'll try to live it up first, then die again, when I'm sure there's nothing left in life for me to dig of beauty, but that's almost endless, at least sadness is, recurrent. So practice thy Dhyana and bring me holy news.

Will not show your prose to Duncan, will to Rexroth. Mail *Sax*. Now as to *S.F. Blues*, that excellent book: I've reread it (having read it thru over Kansas on plane back) slowly halfway thru taking notes on what I like. I'd say there were therein great original poems, so far I found namely: that is to say the absolutely most classic ones

> * in the reel of wake up
> middle of night
> flophouse nightmares
> *Then I'll go lay my crown
> *There was a sound of slapping
> *Rhetorical third street
> *Swing yr umbrella
> *Betwixt hill and house

 *Heart and heaven
 Your corners open out
 *I also have loud poems.

but it's obvious how many of them are great original poetry besides. By the way the plastic coverlets and several others are also very like imagistic poems and W.C. Williams. I haven't finished reading thru again tho. Where's Neal on Trial?

I had a copy of Joan Rawshanks typed up in case I need, otherwise you'll have that extra. Will publish Joan Anderson Neal letter.[14] Have written Bill the dope, and also long letter, he wrote me too. "Goddam there's nobody to talk to here," or "I wish there were somebody to talk to," he said.

Neal is going to NYC direct the 8th or 16th maybe of January he says at the moment. May bring Redhead, or Sheila, or anyone who knows. If he goes. If he does I'll write you when and where.

    Allen

(also received Xmas card via Paterson from Lizzie Lehrman in South Africa. She's married.)

Carl Solomon has not arrived, can you investigate?

---

[14] Cassady's epic, 13,000-word "Joan Anderson Letter" was written in December 1950. In it Neal described a brief affair he had, in a narrative style that profoundly altered both Kerouac's and Ginsberg's methods of writing. The letter was later lost, but segments were used as the basis for *The First Third*, Neal's autobiography and only book.

1955

Allen Ginsberg [San Francisco, California] to Jack Kerouac [n.p., New York, New York?]

Jan 12, 1955

Dear Jack:

I have your new letter—I can't answer, too much thought, tonight, must wait till tomorrow or Friday nite (today's Wednesday) but I did write you big letter, not mailed, was going to add to it, haven't yet, so I send it, it's all about world war-lings, forgive me for answering holy letter with inflammatory. Read other letters first.

Since then (I wrote it almost soon as got back) I've moved into room on corner Polk Sutter with sixteen windows on corner of building overlooking Polk Sutter Fosters cafeteria where everything happens red neon scene street-light, I look down from above, watch everybody's window, big secret plots, I'm still in love, boy loves me we don't sleep we talk, never flesh really yet (except a few times) we talk, great lover for me, young, digs my curiosity heart, I dig his saints, he has visions too, trees bowing in park on startled mornings for him on way to school—but Robert LaVigne hates me and him now, we all live across street from each other, I'm keeping an hour to hour journal of it, fifty pages since the first of the year, record for me, something great happens to me in Frisco after girl now for first time in life boy—I will at least be able to know what it is I am losing in losing life when I go by holy—if ever—

Will write you about this, but also I have not written more since I have been sick in bed New Years Eve, out of work four days too, every night home with fevers writing in journal, burning out self pity if can, new kind of boylove, making it not unsuccess, poems too.

> I'm happy, Kerouac, hallowed Allen's
> finally made it. I've found me a cocksman
> and my imagination of an eternal boy
> walks on the streets of San Francisco
> handsome, and meets me in cafeterias,
> and loves me. Ah don't think I'm sickening.
> It's hard to eat shit, without having visions,
> and when they're real, the world's like heaven.

I read carefully your new letter. I will write of doctrine in a day. I will send certain thoughts for your consideration, relating to stopping machinery of mind. I will be serious. I will read. One day more.

Letters from Bill in Tangiers. I enclose some of his writings. Return them to me immediately. Please. I want you should see. A short story about his finger, and a chapter CHAPTER I of his great new book now formulated begun Bill in Tangiers. Send them back. Reading *Visions of Neal*. That Duncan wrote his poem several years ago, his own ideas, not quite like yours. I steal from you, he doesn't. Bill mentioned you mentioned.[1] Another magazine connected with great Ford Foundation sponsored radio station, called *Folio* near here in Berkeley. Gerd Stern a publicity manager for station KPFA, called me asked for something of ours, may I give him a few sketches or a section from *Visions*? Say yes, I will use discretion.

Tentatively I will use a piece of *Visions of Neal* for Crazy Lights, as per your suggestion, unless I change mind, will inform you. I also enclose Power of Attorney form, I found it, see I'm honest, take it back, but don't destroy it, you never can tell, if you go desert and I'm left send it back, if you die, or something, will it to me, I'll guard your remains. I'll write. Thank you for asking I write, I always wanted to be asked, nothing gives me bigger thrill, like if Neal asked you (begged you) to write and wrote you big letters.

> Love
>> Allen

Is Carl Solomon free still? Not out here, not arrived.

Don't think I don't realize how great sketch by sketch and sentence by sentence *Visions of Neal* is. It's late for me to say it but I see how much better you are than I. Lonely eminence. Well maybe I'll create someday—but such suffering—I think of myself.

Neal now is not going to NYC but to Mexico fast and back. He's still working on S.P.

Allen Ginsberg [San Francisco, California] to Jack Kerouac [n.p., New York, New York?]

Friday Jan 14, 1955

Dear Jack:

Just returned from the library carrying Goddard's handbook (Golden Path), 1954 Philo Lib *Buddhist Texts*, thick book varied selections, and 2 vols (II and III) Rhys David's *Dialogues of Buddha*. I'll read in these for awhile, first.

---

[1] In his September 5, 1954, letter, Ginsberg told Kerouac that he had shown Robert Duncan a copy of *Essentials of Spontaneous Prose*. Kerouac was afraid Duncan might steal his ideas.

Reread your letter: keep writing. Since unfamiliar with the vocabulary difficult to follow actual thoughts. I'll familiarize myself with the titles and states soon, though, that may make communication easier for you, for me.

I have no, or few, doubts that you have conceived and touched (by means of mental, physical sensation) the basic single truth. This touch I distinguish from a general or even sharp idea, symbol in mind, or literary vision (emotional poetic passionate world ken) in that this touch is touch on another totally unknown sphere of let us say "inhuman" sensation, which I will call henceforth (the unknown or unknowable, outside conception of poetry or imagination and also outside possibility of representation by ideas). So I begin with a basic X which is "unspeakable," "unknowable" and "unthinkable." Believe this X can however be experienced. I image it can also be communicated, or hinted at, pointed to (with finger, image, X, poem, word, etc.) (letter too). Communications on the subject are limited.

One problem I have always found, that those who seemed to me to have experienced this "break in nature," or breakthrough of eternity into time, have different ways of describing it—I would think they all have the experience of the identical X—but when it comes to matching symbols and circumstances under which X was experienced, though the signs all point to an experience outside the limits of understanding (comprehension, imagination, even memory) (memory of the experience, as in Dante, "here fails me"), as I say though all signs point to some kind of break in nature, breakthrough of an X, the little descriptions of the X do vary, confusingly, and the circumstances under which X manifested itself or was experienced also seem to vary. Peter Orlovsky (who seems to me to have grasped something—actually) says it comes to him after torment struggle. With me only when I am totally empty. With others for no reason at all, etc. With you, with preparation. Now here you think in comparing our X's. I am presuming your Buddha experience and my Blake ones are on the same level. And I have no way of knowing.

My minutes after Blake were such that they satisfy above description of unspeakables etc. and such that at the time and to this day I vowed to believe in that One of which now I remember only the absolute absolute absolute absolute absolute absoluteness, infinite absoluteness, I mean, no possibility (no way for me to conceive) of there being any other One. But because I am unable to conceive other does not mean I did see the final X— perhaps there are further developments of X only imaginable after further experience, which you are offering me, with Buddhist doctrine and methods. For this I keep mind open and also for the reason that though at time I thought, hoped, had to, by its very nature, perfection, continue to undergo the experience, learning how, so to stay in bright room all the time, temporally, it was not under my control—sent perhaps when I was unaware as a sign, but no more.

Since its nature was to be unknowable by me, Allen mind, but only by not me, but it which I was while experiencing, I saw, after a year of every third thoughts, that thought on the subject (I had really reduced my mind to complete absorption, relatively complete, perhaps not absolutely complete though, no not absolute, was still on York Ave., etc.)—I saw, or thought, that having thought all things down to one thought, sooner or later the thought, still human, would embody itself in inhuman experience—the thought (an image of the thing, a shadow of the X) would terminate by becoming the X suddenly, and the thought disappear, (boat to cross river, image to concentrate on and discard) and I would be left in pure thought-less state of X.

The thought, thought toward X, I soon found (1950–1951), were themselves the wall, the door lock say, no key at all. I had replaced experience of X with thoughts of X. So I had to begin consciously to eliminate thought of X from my mind, thinking, paradoxically, that by sacrificing my continuous preoccupation with the goal I might attain it.

I also perhaps mistakenly (thru reading Taoism and Confucius and Yeats and Blake) followed the line thus: since all things are One, absorption in the idea of One is an absorption on the one thing that One isn't, so to speak. So that to enter the One I had to enter its manifestation, the world, picking up on concrete particulars (that's when I began writing free verse too)—and become so occupied with the world that I became thoughtless of the One, and therefore a part of the world, and therefore One with the One—sing as the Tao Bird sings. Also influenced by poem #1 in Lao-Tze (don't have it here, but it says, since the inner mystery, X, and the surface of the universe are One,—men give them different names are confusing the issue metaphysically—who names or touches surface touches the inner mystery.) Now, this line of sacrificing idea of the one (and ego aspiration toward sanctity and illumination, in itself a process of letting self like Christ descend from heaven nirvana in order to be crucified by the world—living in it, being mortal) I conceived of as the most sublime paradox, in itself probably the way toward sanctity. Twistings and turnings of thought. So you see in a way I have been—especially in this last lust affair—been steadily pursuing the path, however it may be only to find that it is the wrong path, despite my "faith" in the fashion I conceived to be indicated—by warnings from half-wise Van Doren, whom I took to be an angel advising me when he said forget about this metaphysics and read a book about modern Chinese sociology. Van Doren is famous for working by metaphysical paradox and I took it as serious pun *arhat* guidance toward austerity—no ego self-indulgence in sanctity to glorify Allen. I thought I was being punished for saying (several times) "I want to be a Saint." I meant it. Was prepared not to be, in order to be.

However through various experiences—trying to live in flatworld of work, particulars, empty love, etc., or rather unhappy love—I began in 53 to see (in "Green Auto"—and incidentally my poetry as I've said records stage by stage all the major moments of the cycle, Empty Mirror being the phase trying not to look for eternity) or think that after all, imagination painted pix of world as heart (I had a right to heart) wanted it, so I began developing my imagination again, in order to enjoy life, went to Mexico and to see Neal.

But now not even the "human imagination satisfied the endless emptiness of the soul," as poem on plane says. I am absorbed in the world. The world is real, as it wasn't to me when I had first visions of X.

And now it is perhaps time for training in the absolute illusion of absolute reality, that is, time for another approach to the unimaginable only this time not by thinking of X but by emptying the mind of all thought. I had no method then, though I knew early this was the way.

For this reason, above reason, I am hesitant to nowadays really seriously speak about Harlem Visions and treat them gingerly, as with Lucien, and also hesitant to involve my mind in doctrine of any kind. Now you come along with doctrine and method, backed up by all signs of successful method and right doctrine— that is, your descriptions, almost unmistakable (I have a shade of doubt) of your experience of X or its equivalent (now beyond my conception anyway).

For this reason be careful with me, with prose, in future letters. You see why? If you bullshit me you confuse issue in my mind. If you misuse the titles of states of enlightenment, or ascribe to an experience a description or a name which doesn't purely accurately truthfully (Chinese word for truth man standing next to his words) represent it, you'll be doing me harm, and also making it more difficult for me to follow. In enthusiasm of your prose, in its facility to imagine eternity, I detect your giving same importance to different levels of experience, over using lesser experiences so that I may not be able to tell the deeper from the less deep, and the deeper from the deepest.

I am not here doubting you, the deepest comes thru in the letters there's no mistake I believe.

It is that I am trying to distinguish accurately what you are saying, and the depth of significance of the different moments and expression and descriptions of the letters. You once accused me of confusing literary and actual visions.

Next: certain, I must begin Buddhist spiritual exercises. If you have clarity from—clearly observed stages and methods, an order of exercise, especially eyeball, earball bellyball kick etc. phenomena, exercises, specific bodily and mental inside signposts, hip me.

I not exhausted with human love—you for instance—and so will not yet give it up. This may cause confusion. But mean to conduct myself with less self-hood, self-pity, etc., meanwhile practicing some kind of study and austerity mentally, emotionally.

I haven't here discussed your letters really. Want first to give clearer picture of my past path, in light of possible seriousness you might interpret to it now since your seriousness began real serious. Want you to know what I've been through. This letter outlines clearly more or less what I've tried to get across on various occasions and maybe already said tiresomely in letter or in person.

The voice of this letter is that of a kind of *arhat* it strikes me, dry *arhat*, what? Unless I can't detect my ego except in this here break.

I'm keeping a world life journal more closely now as mentioned yesterday and will send it to you.

Forgive my not discussing matters in Buddhist technology yet but I don't know enough. I hate to send just gossip about interesting literary gossip things I find in it so maybe won't be able to discuss Dharma with you for awhile in Dharma terms till I have some experience with it in terms of my own sensations. Please continue writing. I'll answer speedily, and think of you if I have to delay.

Goddard is famous, I'll find out if he's alive.

Dig Suzuki's books.

Realize I am interrupting literary studies (Catullus, Latin, meter) to begin this project.

Allen

Jack Kerouac [Richmond Hill, New York] to Allen Ginsberg [San Francisco, California]

January 18–20, 1955

Jan. 18 '55

Dear Allen,

This letter is divided into three parts, the first joyous, the second regretful, the third serious and philosophical.

FIRST JOYOUS PART. I don't want to contaminate you with thoughts that relate to the existence of my self, your self, any selves, many selves divided into many living beings or many selves united into one Universal self; nor with ideas of or about phenomena, which I will eventually prove to you, with the aid of the Buddhas and their Sutras, is but figurative and only spoke-of. But later. In other words first the joyous human news about "me" and "such." No, I didn't sell my books. In fact Knopf sent back *Beat G.* after all that hassle about typing that had me up late night all December slaving and editor in chief Joe Fox's opinion is rather contemptuous saying it's not even a "good novel" which ain't true. (But Seymour Lawrence read *Subterraneans* and wrote a beautyful sad rejection about how beautiful my work is and "why don't K. get away from Beat G. themes." etc.)

Anyway, it concerns Eugene [Brooks] and me. We went to court together this morning and were sitting at the back looking anxiously through his brief-case for an affidavit of my sickness[2] Doctor Perrone (your Perrone) had written last night testifying saying, "I order this man to bed until his acute condition subsides." But I didn't get mad at Gene and he said don't worry. Enuf that he is kind enuf to get up early-in-morning and come help this helpless hunk soon returning to emptiness from which it came. But Joan Haverty was there, but hadn't been notified of my demand for a paternity test so did not have the girl daughter. But they told her right away about it, and how sick I was (from V.A. records). Sweetly she came and said may I sit with you? Sure. And guess what? She has been converted to Catholicism and talks of the Virgin Mary sadly and of Jesus etc. And how she has found peace. Hasn't changed in looks, thinner. Showed me pixes of the dotter who I think looks like me, especially frowning square-browed photo, so may be mine. But loves her so much doesn't want me ever to see her or ever have my Ma send involving presents etc. Said "I'm sorry I didn't know you were so sick." The V.A. must have given a report to the police about my condition that is worse than I realize. But joy floods by my being as I think I may die soon, or young, such emancipation, such universal sweetness. Joan was so sweet, paid attention to me, scoffed a little at my Buddha (I had big manila envelope ready for Tomb Incarceration, including *Buddhist Bible* of Goddard, my own typed-up PRAJNA selections from Public Library sources, and my new novel the long night of life and notebooks with Chinese inscriptions which I showed her but didn't look.) She said she didn't want money from me if I didn't have it; had reformed (as helpless woman) and decided to take bull by the horns and move to NY with dotter and work and eventually run day nursery etc. Love of children. Girl's name is Janet Michele Kerouac, born Feb. 1952. Blue eyes. Said my Buddhism, was my "little game" fitting in with my personality. "You play your little game and I'll play mine"—real hip coming on. Sweet glances. In fact Eugene said she was nice to me and seemed to like me. Gene interested. Gene cutting out to talk to lawyer, setting up case, calling my doctor, etc., at one point standing surveying entire hall of Negro beat mis-fathers and wives and kiddies with big glasses digging life. So at noon we all go

---

[2] Kerouac suffered from a debilitating form of phlebitis.

into judge chambers and judge so weary from case before ours, which is long, he just says "If this man is disabled, then we'll set the case aside." So now nothing will happen unless Joan gets mad or I get rich and famous, etc. and I smoothed waters by telling her if I am left alone I will not demand paternity test but give her money instead (for test). So case is suspended (Gene says for a year I guess) and Joan and my woman probation officer real buddy buddy shaking hands and woman saying "I told you, it's better to do things yourself" and big women philosophies but Gene leaning in listening to them digging women. So instead of going to jail I come home, memorize the heart of the Great Dharani of the Lord Buddha's Crown Samadhi, on knees recite it, drink wine and take benny and read your letter, and tape up legs. So now I see Gene Friday for shot of movies we took and maybe bring him a little money my mother says he deserves. My mother not home yet to hear great news. And Joan told me write and I will. Now I'm all set for desert, soon as I go down to south and clear the country lot my folks bought for house, cutting trees and burning stumps and cutting grass and sowing garden when able. Have nicotine habit, dammit, must break it again.

SECOND REGRETFUL PART. Your long letter about the sad love. If like me you renounce love and the world, you will suffer the sorrows of renunciation, which come in the form of ennui and "what to do, what to dream?" dig. But if you grasp at sadlove, ergo, you suffer from sadlove. I dug whole letter and loved the Dostoevsky and bare Neal bumping in[to] Hinkle in hall (like the time the three of us bumped in Watsonville and had big poker game with brakemen)— Peter O. sounds very great and I know that whatever happens, you will know how to reassure the sad heart therein. Be sure to do that, before too late, before disappears. Reassure Canuck painter too. Cut out. Or if not cut, out, for how can I know any more than Burroughs deal . . . at least never recriminate, never sadden others, always be kind and forgive and suffer. I suffer from loneliness, long afternoons after dhyana, or rather really before, what's there to do? The letter beautiful, I read it line by line in morning, savoring every bit of it, how I love letters from you my fine sweet Allen. And don't ever worry about me getting mad at you again—I swear off of that for the last last time, every time I get mad at you it later turns out imaginary reasons of dust. bah. Never again will you get a scowl, or a bad word, from me, and I dig you as a saint already and a real saint. I understand your concerns taking the form of big discussions of "X" as being solely due to long rational philosophical scholastic hip-poet grounding. Faith you need. What do I mean by faith? Supposing Buddha says that when you become enwrapped in highest *samadhis* all the innumerable invisible bodhisattvas come from all quarters of universe and lay their hand in a radiant wheel on your brow?—and my answerin in faith, is, WHY NOT? (since they're invisible, inscrutable, inconceivable.) So as to sadlove, sadlove equals sadlove and as to the Tao surface of reality, I see several mistakes in your phrasing concerning "reality." . . . your words: "ABSOLUTE ILLUSION OF ABSO-LUTE REALITY" and this is the crux of your misunderstanding due to lack of learning which now you begin to get. (Incidentally by abandoning Catullus and meter for study of the *basis* of poetry you certainly don't shirk scholastic-self-study requirements, there can be no poetry with any basis other than Buddhist that will have no holes. Later on I criticize Dylan Thomas for you on this ground, to show you childish innocence of his thought.) Phenomena is the il-lusion, reality is the reality. Phenomena is your Chinese surface, that you also mention saying "when visions are real it's like haven—heaven"—in other words, say, the body—the body isn't real, the vision is—*so the vision of nothingness is at least as real as the vision of body*—but the vision of nothingness is, right?, the vision of vision, mind essence. Now let me give you this: on the subway yesterday, as I read the Diamond Sutra, not that, the Surangama Sutra, I realize that everybody in the subway and all their thoughts and interests and the sub-way itself and their poor shoes and gloves etc. and the cellophane paper on the floor and the poor dust in the corners was all of one suchness and essence. I thought. "Mind essence is like a little child, it makes no discriminations at all." And I thought, "Mind essence loves everything, because it knows why every-thing is." And I saw that these people, and myself to lesser extent, all were buried in selfhood which we took to be real . . . but the only real is the One, the One Essence that all's made of, and so we also took our limited and perturbed and contaminated minds (hanking after appointments, worries, sorrows, love) to be our own True Mind, but I saw True Mind itself, Universal and One, en-tertains no arbitrary ideas about these different seeming self-divisions and suchness, is unlimited, unperturbed, uncontaminated by suffering self-hangs on form, mind is IT itself, the IT . . . The cellophane, when I looked at it, was like my little brother, I really loved it . . . so saw that if I sat with the True Mind and forgot myself and its limited mind and imagined and set-up sufferings (that as you know vanish at death) (like Melville's loomings on street 100 years ago in dark America with ice and snow on sidewalk that if he didn't have Body he'd a fallen through endless space) (no sidewalk even) (all empty, hallucination of forms) if I sit with True Mind and like Chinese sit with Tao and not with self but by no-self submission with arms hanging to let the karma work itself out, I will gain enlightenment by seeing the world as a poor dream.

This is not bullshit I really believe this and not only that I will prove it to you at some time or other. As to your going to desert, it ain't necessary (scorpions in your pockets), it is for me, if it turns out to be the way of really Sambogha-kaya staying-with-it all the time then I'll tell you and then it will be time to say you should do it. But nothing I can do to change your own vision of sad love which is after all Sebastian's [Sampas] and the other night I realize that when Sebastian died on Anzio he probably did so by rushing through bullets to aid wounded comrade (he was medic) and died a Tathagata in his sad Charles Boyer Algiers hospital. Who knows? Yet there is no other way but sitting. The trick is dhyana, twice a day. That's the trick. I'll hip you, as you ask, on "specific bodily and mental inside signposts."

THIRD SERIOUS PHILOSOPHICAL PART—As prelude, I showed your "X" letter to Eugene because he wanted to see your letters and dint show him Peter O. letter but made up for it with "X" and what his comment: "Don't show it to my father." Urp. The talk about "breaks" etc. I guess.

Right this minute, because of silly elation, wine and benny, I cannot sit down and practice true dhyana. But here's the trick:

Drink a small cup of tea, lock door first, then place pillow on bed, pillow against wall, fold feet, lean, erect posture, let all breath out of lungs and take in new lungful, close eyes gently and begin not only breathing gently like little child but listening to intrinsic sound of silence which as you know is the sea-sound shh under noises which are accidental. (It's the sound of the imaginariness of the scene—the mind-sound of mind-stuff everywhere). This is the Tathagatas singing to me. To you too. This is the only teaching. Babes hear it. It never began, never will end. Tathagata means "He who has thus come and thus gone." That is, the essence of Buddhahood. The first signpost is, that after five, ten minutes you feel a sudden bliss at gentle exhalation and your muscles have long relaxed and your stomach stopped and breathing is slow, this bliss of out-breathing means you are entering Samadhi. But don't grasp at it. The bliss is physical and mental. Now you're no longer interested in sounds, sights, eyes closed, ears receptive but non-discriminatory. Itches may rise to make you scratch; don't scratch them; they are imaginary, like the world; they are "the work of Mara the tempter" (in yourself) trying to delude you and make you break up your Samadhi. As the breathing is blissful, now listen to diamond sound of "eternity," now gaze at the Milky Way in your eyelids (which is neither bright nor dark, entertains neither arbitrary conception of sight). Body forgotten, restful, peaceful. I mention the tea, it was invented by Buddhists in 300 B.C. for this very purpose, for dyana. As bliss comes realize by INTUITION (this is where we leave the X) the various understandings you have concerning the day's activities and the long night of life in general, their unreality, eeriness, dream-ness, like Harlem Vision again. Then if you wish, use a lil tantrism to stop thought; to stop thought you may say "This Thinking is Stopped" at each out-breath or "It's all Imaginary" or "Mind Essence loves Everything" or "It's only a Dream" or "(Adoration to) the Tathagata of No-Contact" (meaning no contact with thoughts.) But cutting off contacts with thoughts, their clinging ceases; they come and go, certes, like dreams in sleep, but you no longer honor their forms, because you're honoring Essence. By a half hour of this a further bliss seeps in. But then there are leg-pains. Try often to stand the leg-pain as long as possible to dig that when it seems unbearable, at that instant, you can take it just one minute more, and suddenly during a few seconds of that minute, you forget cold about the pain, proving their imaginariness in Mind! But hung with body you have to come out. Try continuing with legs out, or better, rest, rub them, and start again . . . Practice ONE long *dhyana* a day, because it takes twenty minutes to quiet the machine motor of the mind. It's simply by *dhyana* that you'll come to what you seek to find because that in itself is, like in my vision of the subway, abiding "in self-less oneness with the suchness that is Tathagatahood." (emptiness, rest, eternal peace)

Now as to the word. What you need at once is the DIAMOND SUTRA. If you haven't got it in your Philo Collection (which I hanker to see) then tell me as swiftly I'll type it for you and mail it. It is the first and highest and final teaching. I think you're ready for the Diamond Sutra. All your "X's" are or is answered, therein. The "X" is simply essence underlying forms . . . as essence, it is the quintessence of emptiness, . . . it is Nirvana, Highest Perfect Wisdom. The crystal reality. Form is a dream, essence is reality. Creation is illusion with a real origin.

(Two days later) I know these letters have the sound of bullshit because of the same level of enthusiasm all the time for thoughts that are sometimes powerfully exploding and sometimes weakly imploding, but this is like *breathing* and enthusiasm is like the life the breathing makes possible.

I been thinking all day, there's just no point my trying to teach you via these letters. I'll just have to tell you in person; conduct sorta lectures off my Some of Dharma notebooks, because writing-of-it there's no beginning and no end to the work and the monotony. I don't make light of your X or of your Harlem Vision; it's only that you haven't described it sharp enuf to make it look any different from 1000 samadhi sensations I've had. Sending it to you, incidentally, so you'll be able to remember and judge.

Nothing "inhuman" about Buddhism, it's simply a religion for "sentient" beings meaning all beings possessed of sense and therefore liable and under punishment of suffering and death. Ah, I'm sick of talking. talking.

I think the best thing to do next out is just send you my personal dharma notes with no comments because these letters are getting too much. A million things in my notes, why re-word them for you?

Yes, publish Neal's Joan Anderson, it's a masterpiece and was the basis for my idea about prose, tho Neal himself doesn't care or understand; but that dense page where he breathlessly drew a diagram of the toilet window is the wildest prose I've ever seen and I like it better than Joyce or Proust or Melville or Wolfe or anybody.

Bill's Interzone Tangiers is great, haunting, it looks like he'll go very far on a hundred unpredictable tangents and be really a big writer especially because he is uncompromisingly amusing himself. His finger story is so accurate, the prose. Haunting concern with brevity. I should have written my ideas of that when I read his stories last week. I'm very mentally tired today; for two days I been wrestling like a mathematician with the problem of how the Seven Great Elements are sucked into action . . . a problem solved in the Surangama, but because of the poor translation or incomplete thought in Sanskrit, was not made manifestly clear; but this has wearied me so I rush this incomplete letter to you, begging for time to recoup. In my next letter I will simply chat awhile and then type up dharma notes. In them all the problems of karma, arbitrary conception, etc. Bah bah words words. Don't think for a minute I've lost my faith, no, I'm tired of words and writing letters like this; my progress is slow but sure. Carl Solomon must be in Denver seeing Rudolf Halley. How can I check on him? He musta left that place on Madison by now.

Bev Burford going to Frisco in March. One of the best parts in *Visions of Neal* is that part about Saturday Night Red Neons Making Me Think of Chocolate Candy Boxes in Drugstores, remember?—good for Crazy Lights—Excuse this tired letter. I very glad to be free of jail. Now I go to Frisco this spring or summer or fall and eat lotsa panfry chowmein and drink wine with Al—also will live in Chittenden Riverbottom and write more poems on tea—go to desert via the Zipper right outa 3rd and Townsend all the way to Yuma Desert—Here I am yelling about Dharma and I write nothing about it. Patience. Wait till my next. Meanwhile accept this, and enclosed stories by you and Bill, and write again if you have something. What are your virgin feelings concerning your first Buddhist studies?

Jack

Jack Kerouac [Richmond Hill, New York] to Allen Ginsberg [San Francisco, California]

Feb 10 55

Allen,

Just idly reading your last letter in the afternoon, with glass of hangover wines (after big weekend at Tom Livornese with Ed and Maria, drinks and piano-singings) and I see the sad letter about the "X"—your metaphysical concerns and doubts—I understand the seriousness of your past path and applaud it and there is no difference between your past path and the Buddhist one you enter . . . As I have in my notebook writ, *The life of an enlightened man is like a dream that is self-enlightening in which the dreamer knows that he's dreaming before he wakes up.*

And the reason why there is an Eightfold Path (of Purity) and why lust is unadvised is because a man led around by his dong will not have a mind free to realize that the dream of life is only an arbitrary conception (a conception arbitrated by false terrestrial judgment) (as a Judge arbitrating a court dispute between "two") and so he will go on perpetuating occasion for rebirth and seeking rebirth himself and thus the Ocean of Suffering rolls on and on thru Kalpa after Kalpa with no let-up, like traffic in a great superhiway and everybody driving to another birth and further graves and cribs and all longfaced and solemn in charnels of their own making, like butchers in bloody aprons at morn regarding the empty blue sky with self-believing huge ignorance . . . so.

Saw Lucien. He said he was actually an ancient ex-Buddha devoted now to the full enjoyment and investigation and digging of life, and suffering too, but I see that he's really only a dreamer absorbed in his dream, like my *Town and City* heroes Joe and Charley Martin *absorbed* fixing motors and so mystic Peter can't understand what their absorption is all about nor Francis' own silly absorption in denial. There is no way for a Buddha, an Awakened One, to reappear like a Lucien. But Lucien is beginning to know what I mean, his story is "I couldn't be less interested," which I see in his eyes; incidentally I've discovered that my little nephew in the south, Lil Paul [Blake], is Lucien really, and will grow up and be the same. How strange that I have to be hungup now with another seven year old Lucien and be his uncle and charged with the responsibility of watching over him and taking him [on] walks and giving him spiritual instruction . . . a little blond, green eyed desperate tortured introspection Lucien with unhappy life.

Anyway, to reap the realization that you're dreaming, and that nothing necessarily exists after all if you don't notice it, live in a childlike unconcerned contemplative way in the forest solitude. Or the city solitude, like a Seymour [Wyse] by the window, or a San Francisco Blues Poet sitting in skidrow rockingchairs. But the forest solitude, about which I know nothing yet, is traditionally handed down from the Buddhas and Buddies of old and *arhats* and cats and I am going to try it.

First I go to South, to help build the new family house, dig ditches and carry planks and saw boards. Then, July, I drive to NY with new auto license, in old panel truck of brother's, and pick up my mother and drive her back, with all our stuff. Then in August I go to New Orleans in bus and from NO to Del Rio

Texas on Southern Pacific freights and from Del Rio to Villa Acuna across river and from there to south and plateau and sweet Actopan and thence on up to West Coast via Mazatlan searching for best seasons and areas for bhikku life of future. And if you in Frisco around October I will go, otherwise no reason. Will go on 1st class Zipper freight from Yuma on thru, fast and free.

Rebirth. Perhaps you been wondering. Coming back to the dream in a rebirth is like myself when I've been to the Village and Stanley Gould has scolded me for some silly camp I put down, I want to go back and do it over and redress the silly camp, there's a residue called "cause for regret"—and this is now the phantom dreamer seeks his rebirth because of unmatured undeveloped unredressed Karma from the previous life dream. Though it's hard for me to realize there's no Stanley Gould, no scolding, no silly camp, no going back, and no coming-from, and no "I" in the matter, no individual in the matter, nothing but wholly imaginary burbujas possessing no more strength than imaginary blossoms seen in the empty sky, no more strength than forgotten images in forgotten dreams in forgotten centuries long ago, yet, Go! Svaha! Be Saved! Take up thy Staff! This is the Holy Life!—nevertheless it's the truth, there was no Stanley Gould, there was no scolding, the silly camp was a gesture in a dream, I cannot go back and straighten it out because there is no straightening of gray space and open rain, there is no Jack Kerouac in the matter, I don't necessarily exist except as an arbitrary conception stated by some fools.

Sunday I had the Dhyana of Complete Understanding—A happiness was in me, beyond the happiness of mortality, and neither a happiness nor not a happiness; and it was revealed and laid bare, not as a result wholly of my actions and efforts to realize the truth, but because it was already there, with no beginning, no ending—it was the bliss of knowing that our lives are but dreams and arbitrary conceptions, from which the big dreamer wakes—What could be more like a dream, with birth the falling-asleep, and death the awakening from sleep?—a dream, with beginning and ending and plot—a dream, with that which is not itself, bounding both it's sides—a dream, taking place in dark sleep of the Universal night—I had a clear *physical* realization that it's only a dream—

Practicing meditation and realizing that existence is a dream is an *athletic*, physical accomplishment—now I know why I was an athlete, to learn physical relaxation, smooth strength of strong muscles hanging ready for Nirvana, the great power that runs from the brow to the slope shoulders down the arms to the delicately joined hands in Dhyana—the hidden power of gentle breathing in the silence—it's *athletic*—somehow I realized why Bill and Lucien liked me—And the big dreamer wakes from dream-after-dream and wants to keep going back to rebirth in a new life-body to redevelop his evil deeds (cause for regret) his good deeds leave no karma, no need to redevelop, to redress—but his bad deeds, his lies, lusts, cruelties and thefts do haunt him and he has to go back and work it over better, to Good—but if he becomes enlightened in the midst of the dream he sees all things as arbitrary conceptions merely (form that is emptiness, emptiness that is form), he realizes he himself, the ego-personality assumed in the dream is inexistent, he realizes that things, if you don't notice them, don't necessarily exist (the wisdom of the Tathagata, Suchness-Arrived, the Unborn) . . . *that they are illusions that have no hold on reality* . . . an unconditional void realization comes to the big dreamer and he awakes in the dream—even before death—and there will be no more rebirth for the phantom dreamer—but as long as the big dreamer fails to see that even karma, rebirth and death, dream and non-dream and the whole Dharma of Buddhas and Tathagatas, all conditioned conceptual things, including himself, exist only as arbitrary conceptions and not in reality, then the big dreamer will go on dreaming, perhaps in heaven, where he is not exempt from pain. Form is Dust and Pain.

When a dreamer is enlightened inside the dream, it means his karma was thus intended to reach its end as enlightenment became revealed—so when he leaves his body and the Five Skhandhas and Suzuki's "pernicious corollaries of egoism" there is no gnawing need to pick up again and resume the dreaming again, because it is seen that "to come back" is only a dream, only an arbitrary conception, and there *is* no coming back and never was—these are the rough outlines of a complete understanding of the truth—I sat incidentally for mental inside hip signposts for you, with feet comfortably crossed under my legs, with the big toe of my right foot nestled in the hollow between calf and shinbone of the left leg—letting all my breath out slowly so as to relax the dangerous tense diaphragm—do that—I entered the Halls of Nirvana and understood—the hosts of Buddhas were there, the Bodhisattvas touched my brow, I felt a distinct touch on the brow (imaginary)—I distinctly heard a Chinese sentence sung—I realized that Sages and Saints are real men with astounding discoveries of the Mind, sitting plainly in assemblies waiting for supper, but with a smile—like Charley Parker I can see a Chinese Saint with Bird Parker's face, Bird's quiet virility and leadership and faint smile among the cats and *arhats*—Everybody is happy as they realize that Nirvana is the happiness that never ends! and that it was already there!

　　　　Write soon,
　　　　Jean-Louis

The "silly camp" referred to was when Stanley showed me a drawing of Pound by [Sheri] Martinelli and I said "I don't know anything about Art" and

Gould said "O don't give me that shit." Incidentally, that was an afternoon spent with Stanley and Dave Burnett in a girl's pad (Marylou Little) in Village and blasting and when I told David that Chris McLaine said he was the best poet in Frisco I heard D. say "He's just a crazy knot"—saying "nut" with inconceivably elegant L.A. languidity . . . dig . . . but I find generally that the subterraneans are quippers only and feel they should honor the nihilism inherent in quippery and that is their substance . . . the nihilism of Bill and Allen and Lucien and Neal was greater tho not much smarter (and Joan [Burroughs] and Hunkey). Anton [Rosenberg] is their best quipper because he can come up with cries like Bre-boac Karrak Kerouac (from *Finnegans Wake*) but I find David inherently the most interesting one and kinder and more humane.

I have been translating rare works written in French and translated from the Tibetaine, the Mahayana Samgraha of Asanga, a great saint scholar of first century, and have a whole lifetime of translating ahead of me, of works done by Great Rimbarvian Frenchmen in the abbeys of Tibet, here is an example I done out; "Sentient beings ask themselves: 'How can the inexistent be perceived?' To rid them of this hesitation, the Sutra compares dependent nature to magic (Maya) (magie)—" and etc., very easy and great career for me if I feel nothing to do. The Asanga was translated by Abbe Etienne Lamotte. Also I been looking up the secondary Buddhist works, such as Burmese etc. (Ledi Sayadaw) and the Tibetan book of the dead, etc., all about hallucinations, fantasies, etc. and I find generally that the scholars are merely secondary to the emotional geniuses of the sutra-writings. For instance, I believe the greatest writer in the history of the world, wrote the Surangama Sutra, without doubt, but we don't even have his name any more. But secondary scholarships, like this here that I translated, "If the object were really an object, the knowledge exempt from concept would not be born; without this knowledge, the state of Buddha could not be acquired." (Mahayanasamgraha) is hungup on words etc.

[. . .]

Allen Ginsberg [San Francisco, California] to Jack Kerouac [n.p., New York, New York?]

Feb 14 1955

Dear Jack:

Just got your second letter. I wrote Bill by the way and sent him $20 and will send him a little $$ now and then as I can afford. I owe him about 60 anyway. He sent me a story, which I'll forward to you presently, about man talking through his asshole. Also some notes on reports he's read about Englishmen making same mistake in William Tell as he.

Wish you would write him some encouragement re the method he's using toward prose, what he sends me is interesting like Kafka journals and fragments, he's worried apparently that the fragmentariness and "disorganization" of material depress him. I write back to let material take own form as it comes. You might advise him same from your knowledge to reassure that this *Naked Lunch* style from Tangiers is the correct procedure. Rexroth doesn't like Bill's work, Belson didn't nor does Gerd Stern. It will be difficult to promote to others or peddle.

Perhaps a shot of acceptance somewhere would do him good. If you can promote anything through *New World Writing* see if you can. I think the S.A. letters are the most presentable pack of his writing. He hasn't put together a complete set of writings since, that'll take some time. Also he says he has a *New Yorker* style letter from Tangiers. That would be good for *New World*, since it will be full of sharp scenes of decay. If you think you can do something to arrange for [Arabelle] Porter to really give it attention, I could send you the manuscript or send it directly to her. I'm not able to get anything for him yet out here except maybe a small magazine short shot.

Shot here is the local language, type-shot ("blood type shot drunk," says Sublette, returned from sea, out-luciening Lucien.)

Shit on shot.

Rexroth thinks your work is what it is, despite his lack of appreciation of Burroughs, and despite Rexroth being a bullshitter slightly, he's all right. However he does definitely admire Kerouac, whoever that is now, the most, realizes you're the wave of the future and would do what he can to promote publication. He advises Laughlin. He showed *Visions of Neal* to Laughlin and gossiped about all of us to him, and to Auden and writes Cowley discussing you, etc. and says by the way you're legendary already without having published. Now he advised three things. 1) Probably more action after *New World Writing* comes out. Wait till then and see manuscripts are shown that week. 2) Definitely contact Edmund Wilson. He's (according to Rexroth) the only one with any actual power to see that a book get published. Van D. [Doren], Cowley and Trilling, etc. have no practical power in that direction. Wilson is the power behind the throne in the literary world. He wrote Cowley suggesting Cowley get a manuscript to Wilson. You might ask Cowley about that, suggest or promote that, or have me do that if you're going away, or have your agent do that if he's able and understands. Rexroth suggested this course repeatedly and thought Wilson would pick up. 3) As to New Directions, that is a possibility. When I receive

Sax I'll give it to Rexroth and have him push it with Laughlin. He's already advised Laughlin to publish you, and I think needs only a regular complete publishable book to act more on it. That would serve with *Sax, Maggie, On the Road*, and maybe *Subterraneans* and later. The three named seem most likely for this purpose. I'm glad you mention sending me *Sax*. I prefer to start with that, as far as my tastes go. Do definitely have a copy sent me here. Maybe will work out.

I will send you *Visions* as soon as I have completely read it again, and the poems. No rush, is there?

[Gerd] Stern was "gassed" by Neal's Joan Anderson [letter].

Crazy Lights is as you prophesied stillborn, the editor is leaving town, has no money to make it. I know my projects seldom materialize but that's life, I keep trying. One will sooner or later. *Junk* did anyway.

Well enough of this matters.

Neal has your last big letter so I can't write you back from that. I tried reading Goddard's *Golden Path* and found it too diffuse. I returned the other books and ransacked the library till I came up with a revised (1952) edition of Goddard's *Bible*, same as you have, which I took home without checking out—didn't realize I had done so till I was on the street, I guess it's mine for awhile.

I read through the Diamond Sutra, which I found a perfect statement. I have marked passages and will note them presently and send them for your notation in relation to me. I was most stuck with use of word "arbitrary." All conceptions are arbitrary since they are other than suchness, they are conceptions.

The suchness of nothing is what I lack further experience of. Suchness, let us say.

To promote suchness I will endeavor to master Goddard book and practice physical meditation.

Peter O. [Orlovsky] by the way picks up on your letters and the Goddard book and is reading it through with great simple seriousness. I think he has some early stages (compassion) already but not familiar enough with the categories to point to them yet, in this respect. Beside myself, he is the only one I am in contact with who is on, consciously, around here. He also now sits and meditates and gets his weirds there from, seem on right track.

I'm near to exhausting my conception of even the dong. Seems like it can't be renounced, just used out till it becomes unreal. Even my own cock etc. grows yearly more unreal to me. The more satisfied it is, the nearer detachment. That's why I pursue.

Your letters are very useful, helpful, don't think empty effort, since I actually do pay attention to details and whatever signposts are legible, look for them. The more you write about Dhyana, physical meditation, crosslegs, etc. I think the more useful to me—that's what I need instruction in to develop suchness, that method I think. Also the novelist images of nothing are useful.

I will read Lankavatara next, then Surangama, then begin at beginning of the book.

Burnett's sweet alright, Anton [Rosenberg] the most cute silent quipper. I don't know Sherry well enough to use address but thanks, may someday. Get Chase's address I'll write him a letter with Neal. Maybe.

There are some Chan documents in French. You can get info on this type scholarship from Alan Watts of the Asia Institute in S.F. There's a Zen temple in NYC. Phonebook. I went there. Suzuki may be teaching NOW at Columbia. He's very great. His books are only collections of documents and intelligent in fact uncanny comments on them beside Goddard that I know.

You know by the way Irving Babbitt at Harvard at the turn of century wrote book on Buddha and influenced Eliot, etc. that way, so Eliot studied Sanskrit. And of course the Boston Brahmins, and Transcendentalists, Thoreau, were Buddhists. I think Thoreau or Emerson actually translated some Buddhist scriptures too. A New England tradition.

[. . .]

Do you by way remember similar poem of E. Harlem of mine: "Many seek and never see, anyone can tell them why. O they weep and O they cry and never take until they try unless they try it in their sleep and never some (summon) until they die. I ask many, they ask me. This is a great mystery."

I'll write you again soon. I got the idea from letter you were leaving NYC, would you send me your address if leaving now?

Perfect Forest for Bhikku solitude is near Palenque, skirts of unexplored interior Guatemala Peten Rain Forest. Where I stayed at the Shields finca, you can go clear mountain water and solitude and hammock and grasshut for nothing, maybe free food too. When the time comes let me know, I'll write the Signora, maybe probably in fact surely she'll set you up a grass hut alone at village outskirt in the midst of forest. Chiapas for Bhikku life best place in Mexico I know, unless you want to be desert Bhikku. Maybe also there are forests on relatively unexplored coast area no highway between Lake Chapala south to Acapulco way. Supposed to be wild country, lonely and not desert.

Love,

Allen

Jack Kerouac [Rocky Mount, North Carolina] to
Allen Ginsberg [San Francisco, California]

March 4, 1955

Dear Allen:

Enclosed is a letter for Bill I want you to mail because I actually cannot afford overseas stamp and anyway write to him. Here is my itinerary.

1. At present in South, babysitting and washing dishes for family, writing great new book already half-finished, about Buddha. *WAKE UP*

2. In May go to N.Y. and pick up 100 pounds of manuscripts and mother and bring down to here, in truck (brother's)

3. In July hitch and freight hop to Texas with pack and sleeping bag and sutras, for uninterrupted Samadhis—

4. Two months in desert

5. S.P. Zipper to Frisco in September—Now for Krissakes don't leave before I get there

6. November back to South via freights

7. Xmas work for Paris and Tangiers $ (for brother-in-law) (for boat and Arab bread)

8. Europe in '56 (Africa . . . India bus . . .)

I wrote to Cowley. If everything you say is true about Rexroth, etc., please write by letters to Sterling Lord (my agent) and tell him score, I will hip him about you. Has he mailed you *Sax* yet? I told him to. (All this Cowley talk and never any loot.)

After Buddhist handbook now, I shall write a huge *Visions of Bill* next, like *Visions of Neal* (don't tell him, please remember not to tell him, it will spoil great spontaneous studies of him.)

No typewriter so that ends my big dharma letters for awhile. *Some of the Dharma* is now over 200 pages and taking shape as a great valuable book in itself. I haven't even started writing. *Visions of Bill* will be very wild and greater than *Tristram Shandy*. I intend to be the greatest writer in the world and then in the name of Buddha I shall convert thousands, maybe millions: "Ye shall be Buddhas, rejoice!"

I've realized something utterly strange and yet common, I think I've experienced the deep turning about. At present I am completely happy and feel completely free, I love everybody and intend to go on doing so, I know that I am an imaginary blossom and so is my literary life and my literary accomplishments are so many useless imaginary blossoms. Reality isn't images. But I do things anyhow because I am free from self, free from delusion, free from anger, I love everyone equally, as equally empty and equally coming Buddhas. I have been having long wild samadhis in the ink black woods at midnight on a bit of grass. There is no need for you to go on in a state of ignorant worry and greed for worldly pops,

     Later

        Jack

See you in Sept.!

Allen Ginsberg [San Francisco, California] to Jack Kerouac [n.p., New York, New York?]

March 13, 1955

Dear Jack:

Enclosed find copy of letter I sent to [Sterling] Lord. Neal is here at 1010 Montgomery St. with Natalie [Jackson] for the weekend. He got beard, two weeks hobo like, sad face, vacation. So they went to L.A. for half a nite, returning with four speeding tickets (and him with his license already pulled) and Carolyn having warned him if he went not to go back (come back), and so they're here camping on my bed, Peter [Orlovsky] brooding alone in his room, gloomy Russian depressive, me trying to get lazy weekend work reading, so finishing Pound's newest translation book "The (Chinese) Classic Anthology (poems) defined by Confucius" (edited).

Still in Surangama Sutra, it is hard to read, I don't follow it though it goes somewhere, there, it works alright but I can't yet concentrate on the principles. I will keep looking at it till I do. Hard to follow understand. Huge structure, great terrifying structure of signposts. Most penetrating I ever saw.

I will join you to W. Europe in early '56. I had been thinking I would go that year early. I am in debt here and must keep working longer to raise money for trip. But I should be more or less ready by February or January a year from now.

My pad great, fireplace, long dark bohemia room, rugs all over Turkish, soft armchair to read in, Webcor Victrola three speed I just got from pawnshop, beds, desk and books, Neal and Hinkle all afternoon chess by sunny window on street.

Your ambition is justified.

I have had only a few moments of freedom walking up Monkey [Montgomery] Hill envisioning Telegraph Hill and the bank building as being neither a concept nor not a concept. Diamond Sutra has helped most clear the mind for a few minutes in the past month. I don't practice Dyhana.

Send me a Word on occasion.

Neal message? "Watch out for all the ripe red rock tomatoes that might show up." ???

      Love,

          Allen

Naturally I'll be here in September definitely.

Jack Kerouac [Rocky Mount, North Carolina] to Allen Ginsberg [San Francisco, California]

                                     April 20, 1955

April 20

Dear Allen,

What's the score on the manuscripts?

This is my new permanent address. Have you seen *New World Writing* and what do you think? Nonetheless *BGeneration* just been turned down again, by Dutton now.

What's the news from Frisco? Is that railroad rolling? How's Al Sublette, how's shipping?

Now I'm typing up whole new full-length *Buddha Tells Us*, which is materially (and mostly) a kind of American transcript, American explanation in plain clear words, of the grand and mysterious Surangama Sutra. I dug Suzuki in NY Public Library, and I guarantee you I can do everything he does and better, in intrinsic Dharma teaching by words. Nothin's happening in NY, was there three weeks ago.

Wrote new poems, Bowery Blues, *a la* SF Blues but unhigh (no good).

      Jack.

P.S. Got no reply from Tangiers in months.

Allen Ginsberg [San Francisco, California] to Jack Kerouac [Rocky Mount, North Carolina]

April 22, 1955

Dear Jack:

1. Rexroth read *Sax* and said "he wouldn't buy it"—"he'll leave it to some bourgeois publisher to put that out—now if I had 90,000$ to spend I'd publish

something like *Visions of Neal* which nobody would touch otherwise. I liked that better, it's original etc. but if you want me to use my position to put pressure on Laughlin its gotta be for something that nobody else would publish anyway and someone's sooner or later going to publish this (*Sax*). Sounds like it was written on Tea—like those askew spiderwebs on Benzedrine—the sentences are always diffuse, as if he were wandering not driving forward to the point of the book always. No I know it's great writing, I just have a feeling he's gone astray somehow, on the wrong track. Now you take Burroughs, he'll never amount to anything, like Kerouac, but he knows how to write,—though he can't write any-way—but he tells you straight off and you read thru in a rush and he's going to one direction, tells you what happened, catches attention and takes you fast."

That's not exactly verbatim but that was his answer. He obviously likes it and's read thru everything I give him (even asked to see Bill's Tangiers material) but can't get no action out of him. He keeps suggesting Edmund Wilson and Grove. I'll send the manuscripts back—where? *Visions* to you and *Sax* to [Sterling] Lord? I've reread both, they're both great, sorry Rexroth is so evasive, he's poor poet with big ego, but he dug them nonetheless. I've showed them to anyone around here I liked, Peter, Sheila, etc. and reactions have been very strong. "Joan Rawshanks" is by the way a local myth around N. Beach now. Rexroth without my knowing had read aloud long parts of *Visions* to several people including Duncan (who is now in Majorca) and keeps quoting Duncan's reaction—"As Katherine Mansfield said when she read *Ulysses*, this is obviously the wave of the future, I'm glad I'm dying of tuberculosis."

I'm not sure still that Rexroth is absolutely exhausted as a prospect. If you have an extra copy of *On the Road* or *Subterraneans*, have them or you send it to me, I'll try him with those. Maybe it's wasted effort maybe not. Meanwhile I'll return the *Visions* and *Sax* as soon as I hear from you where you want them sent. I have plenty of stamps around, and will send them insured, etc.

Edmund Wilson still a good idea.

[. . .]

If you have second or early version of *On Road* he's not circulating send it here yes? Might as well use every possible copy at once for every possibility.

I'll also return Buddha *SF Blues* which have been at my side for some time. I typed out passages of it and submitted it to a mag called *Voices* which had asked me for poetry (used to be edited by [Louis] Simpson) and they returned them and my poetry too. Well phooey. I enclosed the few sections I typed up, I just picked them at random. To show you I typed them up. They did take one short poem of mine, imitation of my sister's date-talk.

Herman Hesse has a novel called *Siddhartha* about a Buddha disciple, I read it last nite, nowhere particular. Still struggling thru Surangama. I can't finish it and keep turning aside to read things like [William Carlos] Williams' book of essays new published, Pound's *Translations from Chinese* odes, collected poems by Laura Riding, *History of Surrealist Painting*, [D. H.] Lawrence poems, [Aldous] Huxley's book on peyote (which has only one interesting thing—a description of a Cézanne he saw when hi)—(from memory)—"weird peasant goblin face leering from the wall of the page, leering out, a self portrait."

I have a great three speed piccolo I paid 40$ for second hand and one album of Bach *B Minor Mass* which I listen to every nite before sleep. I write hardly nothing, but I do write strangely.

> "there's nobody here
>   to talk to."
> San Francisco house
>   April 12, 1955.
> Slam of Neal's car door
>   outside my shade
> at twilight. Great
>   art learned
> in desolation.
>   An empty ashtray.
> Think another line
>   . . . .

Well that's just silly doodle. I am out of debt here and now just when I'm beginning to save money for Europe etc. I've been fired. As of May 1, I'm being replaced by an IBM mechanical brain, the whole office is closing. I may be asked to stay on another month or two or be invited to New York at same salary $350 per month, but maybe not. So now I have half year at $30 a week unemployment as my due. I don't know what to do. There's nobody here but Peter and Neal I like, SF is empty and I'm ready to take off and collect my 30 per in L.A. perhaps and dig LA. But I've got to work for Europe money perhaps, or should go to Shool? School? (*Shool* is synagogue)—Well send me some advice as to what to do. I won't know definitely till May 1 what gives with job here. Assuming I take off four or five months I will try to finish collection of poems which I haven't and can't without more love leisure whatever, in time—I mean I look to actually assemble it all in form when am free,—I am at the moment confused what I'll do. No able makeup mind.

Bill writes, he asked what your address was, no answer from you. I had told him to keep writing to NYC address, but will now send him 1131 Raleigh.

My brother wrote me that he received *New Writing*—which I have not been able yet to find in SF—and had been in Rocky Mount in Easter and had written you asking if you wanted a ride or your mother did, down there, but no reply except that you sent him *New Writing*. Thank you for being sweet to him. He seems responsive in a Gene [way].

He also wrote that Carl Solomon is in Building 22, Ward 3, Pilgrim State Hospital, L.I., New York, same as my mother. Carl's mother called Gene and said Carl asked me to write, I wrote yesterday. What'll happen to Carl in time?

Send me new *Bowery Blues* anyway.

Sublette working as waiter under Mew at Fisherman's Wharf—Sabellas restaurant, junking occasionally, drinking oft. I see him, he stops by semi-daily, but now except for Neal who's always welcome and Peter I can talk to no one and wish to be alone to read and write. Neal still with his girl Natalie, he has my key and brings redhead here to fuck, she beat, keeps hanging around to talk to me I can't stand it (tho she's a hip redhead frantic lost days), but I'm too weak to listen to lost talk, too tahred tahred.

Williams' prose in *Collected Essays* very like yours. When and if I finish what I am doing if he's still alive he'll amaze. Have been out of touch with him since NY.

Write me what you will do perhaps we can do something together.

New address instead of office 1010 Montgomery St., S.F.

Jack Kerouac [Rocky Mount, North Carolina] to Allen Ginsberg [San Francisco, California]

May 3, 1955

Dear Allen:

Please send all the manuscripts to me care/of this address soon as convenient.

Tell Neal I dig and everything is okay.

How come Bill doesn't answer my handwritten letter sent via you in February?—can you re-check on that.

Giroux has asked to see my B-works and so I want all my manuscripts now.

Sincerely,

Jean

The wild classic sentence in *New World* didn't come from *On Road* but from *Visions of N.*

Allen Ginsberg [San Francisco, California] to
Jack Kerouac [n.p., Rocky Mount, North Carolina?]

ca. May 10, 1955

Dear Jack:

I'm sending two packs of manuscript first class registered and insured to Raleigh Road, they're wrapped, I take them to P.O. tomorrow. Sorry I couldn't get anything done. Rexroth reviewed *New Writing* over the FM station here where he gives Saturday weekly book programs and spent most of his time talking about you as one of the greatest writers of the day, etc. I didn't hear the program but heard about it, he said you wrote like Céline and Genet. At any rate he reviewed the issue and gave "Jazz" most of his time. I gave Sublette the copy you sent me, it's not out here. Neal has his own, already worn and cumed-on, I wandered upstairs where he was with Natalie and he was naked and blasting and on floor by ashtray was thumbed-cover bent back copy, he'd been reading it, aloud.

He arrived here the other morning in Nash station wagon with his type-writer and clothes—he and Carolyn separated, now he has a room with phone for RR calls in North Beach, living with Natalie (the redhead I mentioned in earlier Polk Gulch letter). He's been out a few days, says he'll do nothing but fuck and play chess, left his typewriter with Peter, to type on, told me to wire you now here we *both* are in town rush right out. This is not the year of Great Ball however, though Neal is very demonstrative, still full of energy, I play my Bach partitas and he rolls stick, vainly, imitating unaccompanied violinist at same time, can't hardly get the green out of tube when the violin screeches, he throws arm up wildly scraping bow on string, he tries to lick paper, violin be-gins extended chaconne which leaves him thrashing on the floor (like Bill) scraping the bow wider and wider as the notes come out of phone longer and longer, balancing still his stick above head, playing with his feet finally to get the stick rolled, can't make it, Heifitz comes to a climax, he spills the T (but catches it with other hand) rising exhausted out of the floor to get the last high notes scraping the wall. Today he came in to tell me his address at 8 AM as I was leaving for first trip to unemployment office (and sat in nearby park wait-ing it open in piss park, dogs and old ladies and gents hurrying waving arms running down grass to busses to downtown, yellow morning I saw over Twin Peaks, now I'm at leisure, I wander lonely, through early morning in SF, wait-ing,) and Neal raised his chin and my hand to it, on neck, rubbing—"Am I full of sores there? my neck?" But no, just red from shaving, why did he ask? Just that, unexplainable intimacies.

He went to see Hugh Lynn (son of) Cayce at local conference, and talked to him four hours. Came out saying everything was fine, fine, everything's being solved just like I told you that guy Cayce, you just got to work on it, your Karma, now Cayce he's working off his Karma too just like the rest of us—he's quiet, I think he's queer too, it's his Karma we spent four hours talking, and I told him about T and masturbating and Carolyn and you (me) *et* you got to see him myself (and I did go one night, too late). Carolyn also went, but didn't get interviewed by Cayce self, but by one of the women, workers, and was given ten minutes and asked "Please, yes, That's it, don't say anything, I mean, just—shut—be—quiet, bear your Karma, I mean just don't SAY A THING," *a la* the man who married a dumb wife.

The Cayce interview seemed to set basis for the separation, which followed in a week, by mutual agreement, try out, says Neal.

What your plans? I have now extra big desk, reading Corbiere and Buddha and Pound, slowly rehabilitating my heart to write. [William Carlos] Williams coming out here next week. Corbiere by the way is a Lucienesque Breton who writes about Breton coast.

[. . .]

I have now a small panel truck, and can sleep (cramped) in back, go riding on Calif cliffs and to woods. Kingsland (John) is flying out here for a week's vacation visit—he arrives day after tomorrow—I'll put him up—he wrote and asked—and take him riding around. I like to look at the sea, nature, lately—no one to talk to otherwise.

> Love,
> Allen.

Jack Kerouac [Rocky Mount, North Carolina] to Allen Ginsberg [San Francisco, California]

May 11, 1955

Dear Allen:

Just an additional letter to go with the enclosed clipping and to let you know what I was thinking in the yard. I don't think you should be discouraged by the neglect you are receiving from publishers and poets and publics and fellow Jews. This is classic. The Jews have finally taken hold in America, like a well ripened plant, and the 20th century in America is a big thing in their general history; they have great national importance and international stature thru their Americana, their Amurica. It is only fitting that there should be a great Jewish Bard hidden among them, unknown, neglected, obscure, poor, sad,

classically Jewish (Ginsberg), classically learned, gentle, cultured, and classically pure as a writer of poems. It's most important for you to realize that it is
inherent, the Jews are bound to neglect their own best Ginsberg Jesus; the
prophet is without honor; it is classically a Jewish thing, due to fact, that Jew-
ism is a materialistic bigcity hard boiled hardminded ism and the high fine
cultured poet is like their finest silver, under the napkins under everything else
hidden in the mahogany commode, not to be tampered with, tempered, mixed.
It is also classic, plus your name, that you be Spy Rosenberg martyr-faced, your
clean collar, clean middleclass look, glasses, *shool* humility, when you wore
your black mustache you looked like the classic sad cultured Chaplin . . . (with
also romantic Fredric March *Trade Winds* Joseph Conrad aura of mystery). I
can just see it, the Jewish National Hero will be you, a hundred years from now
or earlier, Ginsberg will be the name, like Einstein in Science, that the Jews will
bring up when they claim pride in Poetry. They certainly can't say Shapiro or
Schwartz, these absurd piddlers with words. Everything you've done as you say,
in your later writings, to my mind, is valuable. Because original. Your earlier
works were imitations of tradition and had little value. I know this as I dig thru
my things and look at your letters and poems of 1943, 1944, etc. though some
of them were beautiful and will be well worth saving. But everything that has
come later, starting I'd say with the Sketching, or, the wildcity, the Harlem Vision, I just can't remember where, when it started, the poems that you began
to write I think around 1949 or was it 1951 or 1952 when you began to use the
first word that came to your head and sometimes words like "Amurica" (O
that's from Williams?)—I mean, I remember Lamantia remarking about a funny
unpoetic-like remark . . . the new poetry that you write, free, which now has
become a classic style in the beautiful Airplane Poems of last December. Whenever a true writer gets original, he can't do wrong any more. Like Bill. Also, the
classic thing about you, also, is your very great, superior learning, tremendous
sharpness, true ignuhood, ariya, elect, your unerring eye finding out not only
Burroughs and me but Neal and the greats, the Joanses, Hunkeys, Corsos, rejecting the Simpsonses, Hoffmanses, Holmeses, Harringtons, Temkos, who
will be nothings compared to even the lowest ravings of Neal or myself . . . I
know and realize that there are other writers in this country who think a lot of
themselves and exchange letters like this predicting their great future fame—
but I'm not whistling in no dark, I haven't seen anything yet, I'm not unmindful
of what Giroux said of me in 1950 and what Auden said of Bill nor am I fooled
by the great silence that always falls when your name is mentioned among
poets and writers. Besides why should we care, if we're whistling in the dark
and we're not "great" writers, then it will only mean that tastes and standards
will change into Apocalypse which is our message anyway. Bill with malicious

humour, you with voice eerie rock, Neal with babble stone story,—Your classic learning, your tremendous experience finding the ignus, your all-knowing range, your huge notoriety, your low (like rivers of valleys) hidden position, with a father who probably thinks you can't write poetry—Paste this in your hat, Ginsberg is the great poet of the Jews of the 20th Century in America and his position among Americans is commensurate with the extent of the importance of the position of the Jews themselves, naturally. When I heard your sad idealistic voice on an old wire recording of you, at Holmes' last year, I cried realizing this but hadn't figured it all out. I thought you were dead and we had lost our priceless high finery, which we'd taken for a turd while it was there, which is the classic situation. Like Lucien saying, "I can't think of anyone more disreputable than Kerouac." We're beggars.—Don't think I'll come to California, no money, no reason, write anyway and we'll thrash it out plans, etc. Davalos in Hollywood gives you good in there, maybe. Ginsberg in Hollywood.

Write—Mail my manuscripts.[3]

Jack

Jack Kerouac [Rocky Mount, North Carolina] to Allen Ginsberg [San Francisco, California]

May 20, 1955

Dear Allen:

Well today I wrapped up a 10,000 word short story called "cityCityCITY" and sent it to Cowley asking him to figure someplace to send it and recommend it too if he wants and suddenly in a P.S. I admitted I'd been a fool early 1953 refusing to publish *On the Road* with him . . . Allen do you realize if I had published then, by now I'd have been in the money all this time, would have traveled to Europe, Tangiers and maybe India or even China and Japan and would have probably published *Sax* and also written great new works obtaining from inspirations of travel. Now I suppose Cowley may laugh at me . . . I suppose he figures I'm big underground martyr hero ready to spend life unpublished like Grieg and Tashcaikowksy, crying in the dark . . . Suddenly the past two days I been watchin ants in the garden, their dry villages, their familiar dry travails in the grit, and it seems to me I have reached the point beyond Enlightenment now and can abandon Buddhism now because Buddhism is an arbitrary conception. I mean, in reality, there is no difference between Igno-

[3] On May 3rd Kerouac had sent a postcard saying, "Please send all the manuscripts to me care of this address soon as convenient . . . Giroux has asked to see my B-works and so I want all my manuscripts now."

rance and Enlightenment, they are both different forms of the same thing which is that unknowable unpredictable shining suchness as I say . . . a girl's ass is the same as nothing, life is the same as death, practicing discipline is the same as riot, what's the use of torturing your form? The mind-system *cannot* stop, the Lankavatara admits it, the habit, the seed-energy of mind cannot end, therefore there is no way to stop the mind-system as long as you "live" and therefore no way to rid yourself, or obliterate, the "external" world and therefore there is no reason for conceptions of enlightenment and paths and Tathagatas or conceptions of any kind. Your X essence is as it is, the Tathagata is the Attainer-of-X but it is a mental attainment and still the Tathagata dies of dysentery shitting imaginary shit . . . mindshit all of it is mindshit . . . I know that do and don't are the same thing, I know I can stay right here in this lonely cottonfield and do nothing the rest of my life, or suh around and do a million things, it be the same thing . . . As far as I'm concerned now the truth isn't worth a shit. So I think I'll just do anyway, take Krishna's advice . . . now that I know the truth and that it isn't worth a shit what's the difference whether I do or don't? right.

Sure I'd like to come out to the Coast, right now, eat chow mein, drink wine, blast with Neal etc. but have not the money. Think what I'll do is come out there and get a job running a typewriter in Frisco or perhaps baggage room of railroad (anything but railroad braking which I hate because I don't understand how do it).

If so, do I get to stay on your couch till I get paid and start fixin up my own room?

Also, I have an idea it would be good to show *Subterraneans* to Rexroth. It is the first of the "hip" novels and he might go for it, or else sneer at it like Alene [Lee] and Anton [Rosenberg].

That Sterling Lord who calls himself my agent hasn't even written to me, in three weeks or more, I have sent countless panicky requests for word, it started when he said Giroux wanted to see me and my Buddhy manuscript so I write big letter to Giroux and apparently both are bugged by something in it. I asked for a thirty day limit on the reading of the manuscript but does that sound like something to be bugged about? What does it mean when a business agent doesn't reply to you at all as if he was like dead? Can you assay guess? He wasn't pleased by you and *Sax* but what's the matter now? So I wrote and told him if he wasn't innerested in my books to forget about them and send them back EVEN THEN NO ANSWER. As Bill says, a deliberate affront. I am flipping like Bill, like Carl, I must run up to NY within a week and see what's wrong. Please please please the other night I dreamed I was suddenly taken with a convulsion in front of two men in the "synagogue library" and became screaming and flop-ping like maniac epileptic and they were not surprised nor frightened but merely interestedly awed by calm to see a real maniac and yet as I screamed inside of me there was that essential calm compassionating out to them, I remember, I was screaming and finally my face paralyzed in a contorted position and still I remember my calm eyes sad for them their fear . . . what does this dream mean? does it mean I am a maniac? If I don't get published soon I think I will go into a fit like this and be a lunatic—that's how orldgirl deshepishe ei feel, I feel real awful, these guys in NY are really killing me at last . . . please do something . . . pray for me, something . . . I want to kill myself . . . my family doesn't even want me to get drunk any more . . . I'm really a wretched paper pauepr paoeori like I said. I will write to Carl. Please let me know once and for all if you forwarded my letter to Bill last February. I sent him "cityCityCITY", no answer.

Got the manuscript packet in mail.

Jack Kerouac [Rocky Mount, North Carolina] to Allen Ginsberg [San Francisco, California]

May 27, 1955

Dear Allen:

Here are the prose samples you asked to show William Carlos Williams. I'll be proud as punch if he digs it.

Lissen I wrote a full length Buddhist Handbook called *Buddha Tells Us* and here these rats in New York like, Lord says, "Is it any good?" when I spend my last two dollars long-distancing him, and then Giroux, who'd earlier asked to see my Buddhist works (NOT the others, he was careful to emphasize to Lord) now lets it be known via Lord that he's changed his mind. Meanwhile the manuscript has been sitting neatly typed and ready and idle for a whole month. My sister who is taking over my business or the business managership of my scripts is disgusted and says we ought to pull the manuscripts off from Lord who hasn't done anything and has the nerve to say that we overestimate Cowley yet it was only Cowley who'd done anything so far. Lissen Allen, if you have any ideas just let me know, and I pass them through the sister—let me know what you think of Lord—and if we really should show *Subterraneans* to Rexroth—I would like to show *Subs* to you in fact, typed, and fixed, and also to Williams.

My Buddha book is a Lake of Light, really great, and guess what it is?—an embellished précis of the Surangama Sutra, just what the doctor ordered for you hey? a real simple explanation guaranteed to explain the inside secret of emptiness, how come, etc. Clear as day, look at the ground this morning and

291

the ants in it and the plants springing out of it like fantasies and think "Bring to naught, destroy, exterminate . . ."

Write soon as you can. Love to John. Am missing big times ain't I? Well, I'm broke and sick (phlebitis)—If you want to get a Jack-California fund together I'll hitch—would like to visit Santa Barbara monastery— **Be sure to dig the monastery at Santa Barbara for me on your way to L.A. or back—Be sure to reply about Bill where is he? What is he doing with the short story I sent him at cost of sixty six cents stamps? Neal and Carolyn and Cayce are all crazy. I guess it doesn't take much intelligence to tell you why—Karma like everything else is only a dream, appears to be happening, is not really there . . . it's all fantastic emanations from the Womb of Tathagata whatever that means and now my subject of thought—I mean, atom is made of nuclear protons and neutrons with outside electrons, and they themselves empty, empty, Karma Cayce is Ego-self-fool.

J

Be sure to tell W.C.W. I went to Horace Mann too.

Allen Ginsberg [San Francisco, California] to Jack Kerouac [n.p., Rocky Mount, North Carolina?]

May 27, 1955

Dear Jack:

[. . .]

Send *Subterraneans* here for Rexroth immediate, yes, this is a good idea, and in any case no harm can come of it and it may bring some results. I would do this. Definitely.

As to Lord your agent I guess the best thing is just to leave manuscript with him to work on and let him take his own time, apparently one thing I see, with these people, erratic behavior, or behavior which seems to them erratic, bugs them no end—Cowley (I hear from Rexroth) was bugged by your pseudonym shot in *New Writing*. But I think, seriously, the less talk about such the better with them, just let maybe them alone to work out fate. But who cares? Write all the big letters to Giroux you feel like, if he don't understand them maybe someone else will in 12¼ years. Leave your manuscript with Lord, I would say, for the time being, and work on other channels as you can, as with Rexroth, taking what opportunities rise. Send me the *Subterraneans*. Or to Rexroth if you wish, his address is 187—8th Ave., SF. But best send them to me, for my vanity reasons, I guess.

I guess best leave manuscript with Lord and forget about him till he writes you, but wherever you go send him notice of new addresses.

What is cityCityCITY?

I saw Williams here, he is old and sick, he asked me where I had been all this time, told me to send him new manuscripts, and I talked about you and Cowley (who is his friend) and Rexroth's appraisal, and he said he'd like to see some prose, he's really interested in it from your angle I think, see for instance the "Notes on the Short Story" and excerpts from his diaries published together in his *Selected Essays* last year, look them up maybe, he hasn't your power but he has the true spirit of originality and understands it. So select a few (two or three or five) pages of pure any prose and send them to me, I'll send them along with my own manuscript, or to him at 9 Ridge Road Rutherford, N.J. but here not for vanity reasons I suggest send them to me as his wife shields him from all strange correspondence, as his eyes are bad and she has to read to him I think. If he digs that prose he'll possibly connect for you with his editor at Random House, name of McDonald or something. In any case I should like to have him dig you before he dies, so he will understand the true historicity of my letter in *Paterson* mentioning you and Melville, he thought it was just a crazy subterranean mention.

Look up Kingsland in NYC for news of me—you said you were going there?

I guess you're going mad in a way, as the termination of the process of consciousness of vision or X or whatever should leave you beat before the absolute world not world as in Sakyamuni coming woeful out of the mount, nothing accomplished, but all finally understanded. I mean the absence of further inner effort, now, and what to do among all million things outside, but as Carl [Solomon] said "Everything that's going to happen has happened already." So DON'T FLIP, don't hurt your body, take care of yourself now, rest from fatigue and figure what next to do. This my poor advice. Love abounds. Since the mind system cannot stop, and since body and consciousness remain, we're limited to the absolute fact flat world around, and to the fact of our heart (human) loves and imagination, which latter cannot be destroyed, it pines too much. Can you come out here see me? I pray you do. I have an absolute extra couch here, have a big room, kitchen cheap food down the hall, and I have complete freedom and an income of $30 a week for next half year, which began only today, my first check. I have no money left except the checks, but that's enough to pay rent and food for both, for leisure. How much do you need to get here? Write me that fast, I'll see Neal and collect some cash from him for your visit, he'll come across, gladly probably, he's left his wife and is in town and freer than I've seen him yet. Yes absolutely come here. As for me I long to see you and this city is empty without you. Still, we can live quietly, I finish my book, and then we can maybe take off and once for all (I still dream of it) go down and conquer Hollywood. Yes that's a project, and believe it can be done. Davalos will be back here in a month if you don't see him in NYC. Over vodka we had a picture all lined up, he has a director, but we can connect maybe. Come, fantastic dream. There's so much money down there, and no one with any beauty around to spend it as we might. In any case to share grating poverty with you for a season again would be a pleasure. Ha! to Lucien if you see him, Kingsland says he's to be a father again soon. Or come out here and stay on my extra couch till you get your own pad. In any case what I have here's yours. Also come here and teach me Buddha doctrines and poetry. Unhappy that self esteem should be so battered by outer neglect but since this is the condition of the craft, must survive it—and poor Bill in Africy without even our literary illusions to sustain him. Hasn't he answered yet?

Write me immediate how much $$ needed to finance bus or whatever way trip out here and I'll go work on Neal for it.

We can make radio programs together here—Gerd Stern has been urging me to and I haven't yet.

     Love,

        Allen

I am really as hopeless as you but expect to live another fifty years if not forever.

Jack Kerouac [Rocky Mount, North Carolina] to Allen Ginsberg [San Francisco, California]

June 1, 1955
(drinking moonkind shocktails)

Dear Allen:

Okay, your letter convinces me I should come out, it was the best letter I ever got from anybody, your explanations about flat fact level world we have to face rather than try to mystic penetrate the X is rather good but I have another angle to explain to you, in person will be better, in any case for now let me say that "this world" *is* "X"—is a dream already a long time finished (as Carl says)— and salvation like everything else we can think about, is only an arbitrary idea. Being a Tathagata transformation oneself, you yield yourself up to all beings for the sake of their eventual emancipation—these beings and multiple million things are but manifestations, mere mental dreams, rayed forth from

294

the Tathagata's Womb (Christians will say, from God's Mercy) so that his (the Suchness-Master-of-Holy-Honey)'s Compassion may be understood as rays as seen as working here is where . . . I fail a little with words . . . you have no more desires inside, tho outwardly you desire to desire, no passions, tho you may take or leave, you make no more discriminations (really inside mind you don't care one way t'other, like New York Waterfront Tuff), and patiently you accept that you have no more ego (of course). "The life that you live thereafter is the Tathagata's Universalized life as manifested in its transformations."

[. . .]

In the solitude of the love life of reality—Truly you have nothing to do but rest and be kind and telepathize Samantabhadra's Unceasing Compassion. Samantabhadra's Unceasing Compassion is the transcendental sound of silence, hushsshhhhhh. The same Compassion is realizable in transcendental sight, the heaven rays of mothlight mentioned here. Transcendental thought is the Samadhi high thought, the Samapatti transformations and ray-ings . . . the other three transcendental senses, smelling, tasting, feeling, are on a more bestial level and on their level I do not know as yet how the Unceasing Compassion is manifested.

So for krissakes send me $25 and I'll hitch hike to Salt Lake City and from there ride Southern Pacific freights straight on in to the desert in Oakland . . . with a few free meals in Denver—en route—and we will all have ball—wine, women, and song—I'll bring my brakeman's lantern in case the railroad needs work for later for me—then from there, I'll go on down to Mexico—My big hope is that we can go to Tangiers together and see Junoesque Proportions Burroughs and maybe we make it anyway—my mother dreamed last night that I sold *Beat Generation* to Hollywood for 100,000 dollars.

I will, I have to go to NY to see Lord, Cowley, others, so I will look up [Dick] Davalos and say "Lookie here boy I want you to show *Beat Generation* to Perlberg and Seaton and tell em we'll make a great script of it for screen with Dick Davalos as Dean Moriarty (as Neal) and Montgomery Clift as Sal Paradise (Jack) and Marlon Brando as LuAnne and Allen Ginsberg as Carlo Marx and our second production will be *Burroughs On Earth.*"

Incidentally I have a concrete idea for Hollywood, it concerns a brand new writing form that combines novel with movie, the THE MOVIE NOVEL will explain—it will I think be the answer for you (and me) moneywise and Shakespeare-art wise—if anybody wants to do it—wait till I outline you the way—meanwhile, send that $25 and more if you can, if I had the bus fare I'd roll right on out now. As for my trip to New York, that's on my mother's poor $10 and I'll have to hitchhike both ways and stay on Stanley Gould's floor. Please write back at once, sending me John K [Kingsland]'s phone number and address, I called Kingsland last time and phone had changed. I will look up Kingsland, Davalos, and all. If you think the prose sample I sent you for Williams isn't good enuf let me know and I send some thing even better. I would write you greater letter today but my eyes hurt and I write you one grand doozy next week before I start packing for your couch. O boy I can hardly wait for the kicks and the good old buddyhood you me Neal.

I have phlebitis . . . but I think it will be gone in time for me to hitch hike to Denver . . . will stay there in Bev [Burford]'s basement, high . . . see [Justin] Brierly . . . then thumb on thru to Salt Lake Nealbirth City . . . Tell Neal, anything he might want done in Denver, like looking up his Dad, message, I will do, or anything else . . . Can you really get me that money? It means I can come out and be on the Coast with you and we go to chow mein together which is an old dream of mine and I want to dig Subterraneans Hep Frisco with you so much, Neal and I always goofed that end of Frisco with wild Folsom Street gogogogs . . . I really do believe now, that this world is just a mental dream rayed out from the Honey Womb of Heaven, even ugly lobsters know it . . . I say that, because, I have decided to go on wine and green again but not with goof, with conscious decision to remember center compassion I told you Holy Honey Nirvana and not get gone and hard on everybody (impenetrable lard-ass) because on green I always was ashamed of the natural kindness of my non-tea personality . . . natural, "forced," but official, religious, gay kindness, like with Jamie and Cathy [Carolyn and Neal Cassady's children] my wine-glasses and tapes and don't you know that God is Pooh Bear? Or that the Mountain is a Pipi?

Jack

Allen Ginsberg [San Francisco, California] to Jack Kerouac [n.p., New York, New York?]

June 5–6, 1955

June 5, 1955

Dear Jack:

My twenty-ninth birthday having passed June 2, I woke up the night after a wine drunk 2 AM in the silence of the void, birthday nite, with "I filled with woes the passing wind," concluding line of the mysterious Blake Crystal Cabinet: a poem I had never understood until that moment, as meaning he had dwelt in the crystal cabinet of his mind for years, but, though "another London there I saw"—I can barely complete a straight line of thought—when

"with ardor fierce and hands of flame
I strove to seize the inmost Form
But burst the crystal cabinet
and like a Weeping Babe became—
A weeping babe upon the wild

. . . . .

And in the outward air again
I filled with woes the passing wind."

This is another letter, I feel the most important of them since I am on the verge of true despair, and if only I could express . . . or better still accurately describe the mental state I am in, accompanied as it is with a sense of the void, headaches floating thru my brain like a thought for over two weeks now, at least since I return'd from Hollywood, and a daily wakening into the monstrous nightmare of my life, reminded continually by my own inevitable recurrent dreams that—but how can I express the desolation of the state, can't hardly define it, the repetitions of meaningless thoughts, the sense of living in a dream, which must now end or be broken by some bleak harsh realization of a great mistake of consciousness that I have daydreamed within for decades, now I am passing like all others out of youth, into the world where everybody else is the same, faced with financial problems that must be solved or will remain to nag all the rest of allotted span of 60–70 years, wherein Art, what little of it I can eke out, for I am blocked and burdened by this emptiness and so for the time can find no other subject, and this a deadly one, no one's interested and I haven't anything to say except complain, trouble deaf heaven with my bootless cries, though I had a vast fantasy of writing a modern *Crystal Cabinet*, in modern verse, with a big dream structure from which I wake to express in the end the sudden wareness

I had an angel for a friend
evening wearied him with me
midnight love came to an end
waking in the morning light
harsh and bleak he was a fiend.
    tho that's too simple, silly.

June 6, 1955
   Mostly my hangup with Peter, usual woes of lovelack, he won't sleep with me, finally last nite I made it with the girl downstairs who loves me, I feel better

today, because I worked myself in hole with Peter—you must consider him when you get here.

And also finally a letter from Bill today, I hope its true: "Just back from a fourteen day cure in clinic—lost thirty pounds—usual plus a substantial case of the horrors. Still sick and sensitized to the point of hallucination. Everything looks sharp and different like it was just washed. Sensations hit like tracer bullets. I feel a great intensity building up and at the same time a weakness like I can only keep myself *here*, back now in a doughy, dead flesh I have been away from since the habit started. I feel like I was back from years in a concentration camp. No sex. No hunger. Just not alive yet, but feel like I never felt before. Junk is death I don't ever want to see it or touch it or commerce in it. Way I feel now I'd rather sell lottery tickets than touch The Business."

He also mentions, "I have a long letter from Jack," and has by this time undoubtedly written you. It seems obvious from the above that it does make a difference what we do, that Bill has been in a hole as we all are, and that he at least for the moment, seems inspired with the apparent, obvious, need to do the necessary to get out of it. God knows what's the obvious for me or you but the cessation of junk death seems to be the thing for him, I only hope it lasts.

I sent your dreams to [William Carlos] Williams and also I sent with that manuscript a copy of twenty pages of *Visions of Neal*, "Joan Rawshanks in the Fog," which I had typed up a while ago. That ought to cover a lot, if he can only patiently read it, it may be that his wife has to read to him, in which case not much will get through since she may not be as receptive as he, it may not work out, thru accident. I hope he likes it though I don't know what he can do in his weak condition even if he does like it, it didn't help me any earlier. But it would be nice to get some appreciation for what is written down.

Neal seems not to be good for any money, or anything—he's there all right but not reacting, to me, you, at any rate not outwardly reacting tho he does assure me he's there and aware of me etc. but for instance I sit at his side all nite at The Place, a bar, and he plays chess, there seems to be nothing else interests him, and I feel helpless to invent any kick other to do with him.

I think it would help me a great deal if you could come out, how I know not, but wish you could. I am so disorganized. I am writing my brother asking him to send you some money and I don't know whether he can be counted on to do so or not, but I am not ashamed or afraid to ask. We'll see what happens. I hate to sound so ragged, dragged with life, but I have been hollow eyed for a week with worry over what has seemed to be a blind alley (of love and of writing, and living) (seemed more than the normal feeling of life for everybody as a blind alley to death) and not known what to do, just dragged myself.

A little note from the past: sketch:

"Back of the real R.R. yard, S. Jose in view dim of the white foothills beyond, in the foreground a factory with serried V roofs,—a flower on the hay on the asphalt—the dread hay flower perhaps, a brittle tough black stem like a vine, a halo of brown spikes like Jesus crown, several dozen, an inch long each, corolla of yellowish dirty spikes, and soiled and dry in the center cottony tufts sticking out like a dry dirty shaving brush that's been under the garage for a year— yellow, yellow flower, flower of industry, tough spiked ugly flower—but it has the form of the great yellow rose in its brain, it's a flower none the less—so brittle on the bench the wind keeps brushing it away from me where I sit near the shack in the sunlight writing—I have to get up and get it again. This is the flower of the world, ugly, worn, brittle, dry—yellow—miracle of gravel life springing to the bud.—Thistles."

There is also the possibility that Neal can get you a RR pass ticket to get out here, I have to check with him on that.

See Meyer Schapiro perhaps too?

Maybe visit Carl in Pilgrim State. Perhaps my brother will want to drive out to visit Naomi. But why these lacerating visits?

I can't make Miss Green often, I get too depressed and anxious. Every time I get on I come to a new deeper horrible realization of my life. Every thing seems too real, like it must be with Bill *off* junk.

I swear no real kicks here, they're all available, but I can't make the repetition of the scene unless you can buoy me up to enthusiasm, since Neal's so withdrawn still.

I liked "the saint grieves."

The trouble is that the money problems of reality are not ghostly at all, they're solid as rock, I keep hitting my head on. How the hell are we going to get up $$ to get to Europe, and when that $$'s gone what are we going to do? How can we live with no future a building? That's what's bothering me. Especially since no poetry I might possibly write will ever produce enough $$ to even think of that as solving any problems. Prose may be somewhat different, your situation seems to me remediable in the course of things.

Aw well on this lousy note I sign off. I've reread your outlines in last letter on Tathagata, but then I look out my window in the sunlight and realize that I will have to be eager and vigorous and full of plans for supporting myself in five months. I'm bewildered. And it's no joke.

      Yours,

          Allen, The Geek.

Jack Kerouac [Rocky Mount, North Carolina] to
Allen Ginsberg [San Francisco, California]

ca. June 10, 1955

Dear Allen:

Just a card, letter follows few days. Yes, the best idea of all is to get Neal's railroadpasses, tell him to get on the ball and put them together and repeat instructions, since now I know the routine lingo and jargon of railroading I can certainly pass as brakeman Cassady. (He knows). Tell him ole Sal Paradise wants to come out and re-visit the jazz scenes of Dean. As to your sad letter, yes, there's no hope, no money, feeding yourself is one "reality" essence doesn't have to bother with and since begging is illegal in the West, true absent-minded concentration on Essence is only just about possible in the nuthouse, since even in a hermit age such as I will have in Mex I'll have to come out every six months for turista and work problems even if only 8 $ month. But don't despair. You and I and Bill are in same hole and can help one another out when breaks come writing-wise. Now I'm going to NY to see Cowley with my Ray Smith "Road" A new one—and Giroux with Buddha book, etc.

     Yours,

        Jack

Jack Kerouac [New York, New York] to
Allen Ginsberg [San Francisco, California]

June 27–28, 1955

June 27 '55—Jim Hudson's Pad

Dear Allen:

Am all alone in this charming pad over Washington Square in window of which yesterday I wrote big poem "MacDougal Street Blues in Three Cantos."—Lots happenin, usually nothin.—First, I went and lost page three of your letter which Lucien said mentioned $25 and train tickets so in your answer repeat said information for I will be in Rocky Mount day after tomorrow ready to start thinkin of rollin west.

My news is beat, I guess—Davalos is in Provincetown.—An elegant gay publisher almost took *Beat Generation* but now Cowley wants it back—re-changed my writing name to Jack Kerouac, offered *New World* two new stories ("Joan Rawshank", and last chapter of *Subterraneans*)—Sold "CityCity" to David Burnett's *New American Reader* for $50, payable tomorrow.—Big drunks with Gregory [Corso] and everybody—sex everywhere but I have declined in general and on principle and *au naturel*.—Still I understand that Samsara is same as Nirvana, and Nirvana same as Samsara, but I came here I wanted my rightful [?] and money for Mexican loafs . . . tho I am wise I have to wait and endure like any other fool—Love to see you in Frisco, coming, soon, wait for me.

Will miss Peter [Orlovsky] by a week.—No money to hang around—will transmit message to Dusty [Moreland] today—*Doctor Sax* pronounced *Magnificent* by Giroux, in front of Corso, but company can't take—*Buddha* is being sent to Harvard U. Press—*Subterraneans* at a small publisher called Criterion—*Sax* now at Noonday Press, publisher Arthur Cohen, if sympathetic good possibility for all of us.—Stick to poetry and tears and never mind trying to impress Lucien with theories—Lucien loves you, don't be mad at sweet Lucien, he just naturally believes that Paul Bowles is a better writer than we are.—(He frowns over page one of *Sax*).—Gregory also to show his novel to Cowley.—Cowley got drunk with me in Village, said he will try to get me prize money, thought the novel-excerpt I showed him with idea of $25-a-month to finish it was too *Wolfean*—so is Norman Mailer *Wolfean*—(Cowley is old and insensitive sometimes to pain of young beat poets)—(he sleeps in letters)—but likes me—and I told him about your greatness. SO, here I am, still broke, bumming supper tonight off elegant Allen Klots of Dodd Mead, a sharp little Hohnstein hero. Must see Kingsland ere I leave.—Will find Stanley Gould and get high.—The music scene in Village is frantic.—I conducted jam session on sunup waterfront tell Neal, our tenorman has *same soul* as Neal (not good-looking) but *is Neal*—(George Jones).—Henri Cru is here, bouncer in our bar—the big meet bar (new one) Riviera—(bouncer in Remo, like).—Saw Alene [Lee], she made meet with me then didn't show up, I wonder if she thinks she's really hurting me—(hope so)—(for her sake).—I wouldn't have talked to her but Anton [Rosenberg] told me to.—Gregory has eighteen year old doll and many Harvard friends and is on the con. Please tell Neal to let Carolyn know I'll be by this summer, I have no time to write, I'm going out to get drunk in the Monday afternoon streets of Village.—I have just discovered Pound's *Cantos*, never realized poetry was free till now.

[. . .]

Love to Neal, Peter, Sheila, Rexroth, Mew, Sublette

Jack Kerouac [New York, New York] to
Allen Ginsberg [San Francisco, California]

June 29, 1955

June Prune

Dear Allen Old Bean:

[. . .] I got your dream about Joan,[4] and Lucien and I discussed it and got to talkin about Mexico your trip there. Lou still says he wants to go live there. Well you see, I came to New York with, to make a deal with fuck this typewriter it's a awful typewriter, I can't do nothing, I came to New York to make a deal with Cowley, said, "Here is twenty-seven pages of a novel in progress (the Ray Smith huge epic *Road*) get Viking to pay me $25 a month and I will go to Mexico and live in a hut and finish novel." Cowley laughed and Jennison[5] was with him and they said, "You certainly aren't holding us up, boy." So maybe I'll get it. Oh and also I talked about you at great length and told Cowley he must read *Naked Lunch* soon and he agreed and said he remembered Burroughs from descriptions of him in *Beat Generation*. Then he say, "You know a poet called Gregory Corso?" It seems Gregory has put out a book of poems and making big hit, *The Lady of Brattle Street* or something like that [*The Vestal Lady on Brattle*]. Lucien said Gregory was facile and would be a success but you were greater poet. But Lucien also said I and you are full of shit and can't write and live in literary illusion like idiots and said Paul Bowles was a great writer, I said for krissakes show me Paul Bowles' *Visions of Neal* and Paul Bowles' *Doctor Sax* and his *Some of the Dharma*, his etc. etc. etc. and then we'll judge. I got real literary then and jealous literary type and o we talked all night, I wish you weren't missing any of it. Further, I have "citycitycity" ready to go to science fiction mags with Malcolm's blessing. And calling Giroux today about *Buddha*. And *Beat Generation* is at Dodd Mead or something. And I'm here to try to get a few dollars and things going. I will be able to help you one day. Do you realize it was you got *Town and City* published, you gave it Stringham, Stringham gave it Diamond, etc. then Kazin. For god's sake, did Neal is Neal going to send railroad passes?

[. . .]

Write to me. We've got to get me out thar.

Jack

---

[4] "Dream Record: June 8, 1955."
[5] Keith Jennison was an editor at the Viking Press, who, with Malcolm Cowley's support, convinced the house to buy *On the Road*.

P.S. I wrote note to Carlos Williams, asking for recommendations to Random House.

Allen Ginsberg [San Francisco, California] to Jack Kerouac [n.p., New York, New York?]

July 5, 1955

Dear Jack:

Your June 27–29 letter received. Just returned from series of trips, Yosemite, Reno, Lucus Beebe's Virginia City, Lake Tahoe, hitchhiking accompanying Peter on first leg of NY trip.[6]

Neal says he can't get the RR ticket. He hasn't worked very hard on trying but perhaps he can't. He got one already for his girl Natalie [Jackson] which she didn't use and its expired and so he can't get another so soon. And Hinkle got one for Sheila [Williams] which she didn't use and that's expired already too. Hinkle's moved back into SF by the way, with family, and Neal still maintains love nest pad with Natalie redhead. Your letter and message to Carolyn he saw, he sees all your letters.

What does Cowley want with *Beat Gen*? to re try publish? Send instructions on what Burroughs I should send—all three books? I have not heard from Bill for several weeks and am worried.

Using your name Kerouac is the best thing.

What is "City City city"? you never described it.

The senora from Mexico is here and will be here the first of next month for several weeks again, she might be around when you're around in which case it might be able to occur that she invite you to loaf in Chiapas jungle, this is a real possibility, though it might take a few minimum bucks income for food since she's poor. But she has free housing and the cheapest food around in Mexico. Plus horses, etc., servants.

I am seeing Mark Schorer[7] to see if I can get teaching assistant job at Berkeley this fall when unemployment runs out and study Greek or prosody. If this doesn't work out I may join you in Mexico.

I don't understand Corso's celebrity. I saw a poem of his about [Charlie] Parker, beautiful blackbird in the horn longnose pelican, in *Cambridge Review*. But I still don't understand what or how he's doing that Cowley knew of him.

---

[6] Peter Orlovsky hitchhiked to New York in order to pick up his teenage brother Lafcadio. Their mother was on the verge of committing the mentally handicapped boy to a mental institution.

[7] Mark Schorer was a professor at UC Berkeley who later would testify in the trial of *Howl* in support of City Lights.

What did Lucien say about Joan [Burroughs] poem dream? I wasn't being mad at him I was saying your father in laws moustache via that paragraph I did hope he'd be impressed by theory. He's so frightened of science I keep using the word over and over, Merims like. Skip the last sentence. Anyway I'm not scared of his frown, not at this distance anyway.

I should send Cowley poems and will sooner or later when I have finished this season here. No word from [William Carlos] Williams. You?

My brother hasn't written me whether or not he sent you the gelt. I've re-written him, asking whether. If you've received let me know.

Neal gave me the enclosed Brotherhood of RR Trainmen dues receipts, to send you. He sez hitch to New Orleans, whence there are two trains leaving for L.A. daily, S.P. trains, and these plus a little talk should get you through. He says you know about this type shot. Ask the conductor first, and he'll mention it to the other conductors as they change sections or lines or what it is I dunno. If this requires further explanation write and I'll squeeze details out of him. I tried once and the above sentence was what came out. Is this any good? He says yes.

What is Alene's [Lee] address? I wanted to connect Peter.

I am poor but my rent's paid and plenty of food available by cheap shopping, steaks, etc. so the 30 per week is alright.

Yes, Gregory must be conning? for what who? What does he say of [John] Hollander in Harvard? My drear penmarks—I wonder if they helped or hin-dered Gregory's development.

I read your chess to Neal who just giggled.

Forgive me tonight dear skeleton.

I'll write again. This is just to send tix.

AG

Jack Kerouac [Rocky Mount, North Carolina] to Allen Ginsberg [San Francisco, California]

July 14, 1955

Dear Allen,

Just received a check for $25 from Eugene [Brooks]. Note says: "I have heard from Allen several times. He tells me you were in New York recently. He also asks me to send the enclosed. Look me up when you get into town. Sincerely"—Is he bugged because I didn't look him up in NY? Well, I'll write to him today and explain that I was on the mooch in my recent trip to NY and it's just as well I didn't get to him. I'll make it sound alright, that is, don't worry.

He's a big Dostoevskyan brother.

So now I have money to get to New Orleans where I will hop the Zipper flatcars with sleeping bag and roll 500 miles per night, unless sometimes (in rain) I may be able to wheegle caboose rides via Neal's brotherhood papers. Tell Neal I cannot wheegle rides on passenger trains because if he will recall, I was not a passenger brakeman and I don't know the lingo and the routine, but when you tell him this he'll just blow up but we don't all know what he knows. Anyway I'll get there.

Will leave within one week as I have to help my brother-in-law's business moving TV sets while his helper is sick, I get 75 cents an hour and it's making more loot for me to hit road with. So I should DEFINITELY AND WITHOUT DOUBT be in Frisco (for your DATE convenience I put big important capitals) no later than August 10 at the most outsidest and between Aug. 1 and 10th anyhow. That's the good (Aug. 1) season in California. We'll dig Frisco together for a few months and then I suggest we head south together to California Mexico border where we can rent dobe and you can save $20 a week out of your $30 California unemployment for return-to-NY-trip money or even, if we did it sooner, for Tangiers money. Actually, in a dobe hut, say, in Mexicali or Gadsden or Tijuana or any Calif.-Mex bordertown, we could live on $5 a week (on Mex side) and you could save 25 of your unemp.—that's 100 in a month. I think that's practical idea for in Frisco you're just letting it down the drain of big city rent. Then, when you ready to re-head East, I'm goin south to Mexico City via the west coast again (Mazatlan etc.) to rent me a hut. I have minimum travelers checks for that Mexican purpose after I leave you, and minimum cash for getting out to see you now—and then I'll get $25 from the blood bank as usual for wine and chow mein kicks—also, I may do part time jobs around Frisco, would love to get on railroad baggage room again (at $15 a nite).—

Meanwhile, I now answer your recent questions.

1. Cowley wants *Beat Generation* he says, he and Keith Jennison, "for another crack at it"—I told them, I apologized for goofing in 53 and Keith tapped me on back—Sterling Lord thinks they may publish it now—but I feel gloomy as usual—especially because I had come to NY with specific request for $25 a month for Mexico hut new-novel and Cowley goofed on that, overlooking my true need and bad foot, etc., vaguely said he'd get $250 prize for me from American Academy of Arts and Letters sometime, and sent a few of my stories to *Paris Review*.

2. "cityCityCITY" is my big science fiction fantasy preview of city of future which I sent Bill a copy of, very wild, I tell you about it when I see you, very hip, very tea-head writ, sinister, etc., not Burroughsian at all, tho—sort of thing I could do ad infinitum on weed—wrote it during Army McCarthy hearings and

so it has wildly hip political flavor. Dave Burnett took it and dug it and made only grammar changes but hasn't paid me $50 for it yet. Kafkaen horror etc.

3. I saw Dusty, told her Peter was coming, also told Gregory "Allen's new angel" was coming, etc. I owe Dusty a dollar—will mail Monday—incidentally she now lives at 38 Morton St. isn't that where Kammerer was?

4. To Cowley send ALL of *Naked Lunch*, titled *NAKED LUNCH*, I told him all about how we got to title—send it as ONE NOVEL, stop goofing with this three part business, it's ONE NOVEL, one big Vision . . . the *Junkie* part leads reader on to more complicated works of *Queer* and *Yage* ahead.

5. Corso's celebrity obtains from enclosed POEM book which I send you, hold it for me. Nice inscription. Also, he wrote a play which he was going to entitle *Beat Generation*, changed to *This Hungup Age* when he saw my *New World* shot—one act play, it was produced at Harvard, big hit, he got big write ups like in *World Telegram* a big write-up by one of the staff columnists with big headline saying "Gregory sends us poems we don't dig" etc. all about how the columnist found Gregory writing in an underground basement under the cave of the Village or something. Gregory makes big hit with Boston socialites. and Harvard boys. and girls. And now we got together and sent his poems to Burnett one poem entitled to Jack K. did I tell you?

6. Don't study Greek and Prosody at Berkeley, get away from this Pound kick, Pound is an Ignorant Poet—How many times do I have to tell you that it's a Buddhist, AN EASTERN FUTURE ahead—Greeks and poem styles are child's play, even Neal knows that (without college education). At Berkeley study Sanskrit and start translating big Sutras never before translated and write poetry with Buddhist base. The Greeks are a bunch of ignorant cocksuckers as any fool can plainly see,—better than that, even greater and deeper than Buddhism, is Primitive Africa where old men when it's time to die sit down and think themselves out to death, Pari Nirvana, they call it FACING THE WALL—

"If you need me call,
I'll be waitin at the final wall".

Get away from Pound . . . I dug him and he is deliberately Greek and fancy with his Oniothose Greek expressioni . . . balls. He and Hopkins suffer both from trying to show how fancy they are, and Yeats too . . . for Poets I like Dickinson and Blake . . . But even they are ignorant because they simply don't know that everything is empty in and out in ten thousand infinite directions of the undisturbed light. Please, Allen, wake up . . . if for one moment you doubt Buddhism because you're attached to I don't know how to say it, I just don't understand, I really thought you were intelligent and Bill too—like Neal is much more on the ball now with his Cayce who is after all close, Cayce is Purusha-believer but outside of that he is almost pure Buddhist. I'll explain Cayce to you. It's not that I'm so smart it's only that the light has been vouchsafed to me when I stopped thinking. I confess to a great deal of impatience seeing people receive the teaching and not absorbing it . . . habit-energy of ignorance has roots that get deeper and deeper as you get older, like tree.

6. No word from [William Carlos] Williams—at least write to him and ask him if he's read anything because if his wife read out loud all about the piss-bottles it didn't work (old harridans) what they're doing married to prose and poem geniuses I shall never know.

7. Alene's [Lee] address is still where it was, Paradise, I think it's 501 E. 11.

8. About Joan [Burroughs] poem dream Lucien didn't see it, I forgot it here, then later he saw it in your letter but by then you'd dubbed him "drunk and golden" instead of just golden and anyway I wasn't there when he read it so no comment—generally I would say that Lucien loves you and considers you a charitable saint . . . don't get so hungup on what he thinks, Old Priesthead Monacchio knows him better than you do and his judgment is: "You don't real-ize that Lucien is a relatively simple guy trying to enjoy life—much simpler than you or Ginsberg, for instance." Very very true. So I looked at Lucien and saw Tony was simply right. Like, Lucien spent a whole night describing to me how he beat a guy up in a fight even tho I told him I wasn't interested in who won—he's just a regular guy . . . Just, Tony says, an ordinary kid.

9. I hope I get to meet the Senora, I would like to try Chiapas in the winter in the summer I couldn't possibly stand it.

Turns out that all my final favorite writers (Dickinson, Blake, Thoreau) ended up their lives in little hermitages . . . Emily in her cottage, Blake in his, with wife; and Thoreau his hut. This I think will be my truly final move . . . tho I don't know where yet. It depends on how much money I can get. If I had all the money in the world, I would still prefer a humble hut. I guess in Mexico. Al Sublette once said what I wanted was a thatched hut in Lowell, a real wild thing to say. Anyways, I was headed strait for Mex City but now that Gene has sent the 25 I can afford Frisco and will come. I look forward to talks. Also chow mein and wine. Also walks. Neal. Maybe Miss Greenie [marijuana]. Also I want to spend one week in the river bottom at Chittenden pass. Also a week on the Santa Barbara channel coast. Also I want to visit the Buddhist Monastery at 60 Las Encinas Lane, Santa Barbara. Also I might try bhikkuing in early Salinas river bottom near Wunpost, very wild country. I just want a find some place, where, if I feel like being in a trance all day and don't wanta move for nothing, nobody there to stop me, nothin to stop me. I *know* that the secret lies in the old Yoga secrets of India, let alone Dhyana, and that any man who does not, as you, practice Dhyana, is simply wandering in the dark. The mind has its own intrinsic brightness but it's only revealable when you stop thinking and let the body melt away. The longer you can hold this position of cessation in light, the greater everything (which is Nothing) gets, the diamond sound of rich shh gets louder, almost frightening,—the transcendental sensation of being able to see through the world like glass, clearer; etc. All your senses become purified and your mind returns to its primal, unborn, original state of perfection. Don't you remember before you were born?

Read, as I'm doing, the Diamond Sutra every day, Sunday read the Dana Charity chapter; Monday, Sila kindness; Tuesday, Kshanti patience; Wednesday, Virya zeal; Thursday, Dhyana tranquility; Friday, Prajna wisdom; Saturday, conclusion.

By living with this greatest of sutras you become immersed in the Truth that it is all One Undifferentiated Purity, creation and the phenomena, and become free from such conceptions as self, other selves, many selves, One Self, which is absurd, "selfhood is regarded as a personal possession only by terrestrial beings"—no difference between that star and this stone.

Buddha Tells Us has been received codly [coldly] by Cowley, Giroux, Sterling L. [Lord]—a great book. It will convert many when it is published and read. If I can get it thru the money changers, the people who sincerely read it will dig. I mean, I've read it over three times and it definitely has magical powers of enlightenment, it is truly a Lake of Light. I wish I had extry copy for you. It is now (supposedly) at Philosophical Library in NY, people who publish Suzuki. I'm really curious to know the fate of that one. I'm really amused now, finally, but childish ignorance of said Cowleys, Giroux, peopleses everywhere, but I entertain no lasting notion that it's anything but a dream from which they'll awake a little later than I and maybe none the worse for it I guess, being chill un. My sister got mad at me and said I thought I was God, I say "What are ya jealous?"—O what a dreadful household this is, I'm in . . . leavin again . . . everybody resenting my cool Sihibhuto sittings in the morning, cool trances, they work hard to show me how busy they are, they putter around, restless, proud, indignant, call me this and that, O if I were not greased cool by the wisdom of the Indes (which is French for Nothingness) I would be madder yet and have more reason to be madder than even in 1952 when I was mad at everybody even you . . . but I see it's a dream, a disagreeable dream.

As for a woman, what kind of man sells his soul for a gash? A fucking veritable GASH—a great slit between the legs lookin more like murder than anything else.

Really, my dear, every time I look at a woman now I almost get sick thinking of it. As for codpieces they can bury em in the cottonfield and let em sprout moons for alls I care. Nevertheless one drap of vino and I'm all for anything. But I'm really getting sick and tired of the Western World and I wonder what will happen to me in Ceylon or Burma or Japan (yes Tokyo, that's the place). Did you see the *Compassionate Buddha*, a pocketbook? by E.A. Burtt, there is a great sutra in there by a mighty Chinaman called Hsi Yun, on page 194. "Because the understanding of the people of the world is veiled by their own sight, hearing, feeling, and knowledge, they do not perceive the spiritual brilliance of the original substance." I presume you know what this means, don't you?

It means, that there is One Essence, for instance every drop of rain contains infinite universes of existence the essence of which is undisturbed light. The essence of wood is the same as the essence of air. A hydrogen atom is arranged one way, another another way . . . both are empty in essence

> In and out in all 10,000 directions matter is ephemeral
> In and out in all 10,000 directions space is ephemeral
> And thought is ephemeral . . .
> Ants don't notice us, ant-ants don't notice ants, ant-ant-ants-don't
>   notice ant-ants
> Are you too "old" and too "cultured" to concentrate on this?
> Don't you remember your babyhood concerns any more?
> What, some Viennese Lecher told you something about "maturity"?
> Tell me about this Viennese Lecher, is there not an infinite direction of
>   infinite universes inward into the unnumberable atoms of his
>   body?
> Is there not an infinite direction of infinite universes outward into the
>   unnumberable atoms of space of the universes all 3,000
>   Chillocosms of em?
> Is this Mature Viennese too culturated to think about such matters? no
>   time for reality? Reality is Images? Appearances? Epiphanies?
>   Sprouts? Fantastic Emanations? Luvoid Madblake?
> Reality is Personality?
> Reality is Skeletons?
>
> In essence there is nothing
> but essence-
> And the essence is not disturbed.

Bellygoat boom
At ache of
Day bang.

P S P S: I also wanta dig the Buddhist church just south of Sun Hung Heung on Washington St. I helpt build one night drunk on wine with Al Sublette. We go in and sit and pray. I know a whole prayer to recite and chant in the church.

I ran into Jose Garcia Villa on street, he was with big loveboy of his, I converted both of them I think in White Horse bar, I mean both dug and were sad. Jose said he liked Hopkins best. He doesn't like Gregory. But nobody does, like Helen Parker put down G's book and said, "Well there's nothing to worry about there."

I was with Helen a few days. At pad. Etc. She holding out good.

Then I ran into old Wasp Bingle Frankel. and he said [Alan] Ansen is causing worry everywhere, has disappeared in Africa, North, or Italy or somewhere, no word from him since Xmas and Frankel thinks he's dead. He also said YOU would die young too. He was depressed and sat in bar with head down. Finally he didn't notice me any more.

I wailed at him a whole night with what I would have like tape recorded, explaining High Mystery Poetic aspects of Buddhism to him which he dug yelling Bravos in bar but next day he didn't notice me. The Riviera is such a scene. I am really lookin forward tho to Frisco, Allen don't get mad but every night, most every night, I want to lie down with Pat Henry in my ear, and I hope green, and wine, and dig newest music, after all I am America's new jazz critic expert ain't I?—I also look forward to usual Frisco wigs like seeing Leonard Hall the Buddhist and Chris MacClaine and the crazy twisted poets and Ed Roberts and Charles Mew and all the hep kicks and me 'n Al singin in the street jazz . . . and yes I would love to fuck Sheila [Williams] and everybody else too why not. All's I need is a drink . . . I drink eternally. Drink always and ye shall never die. Keep running after a dog, and he will never bite you; drink always before the thirst, and it will never come upon you. Argus had a hundred eyes for his sight, a butler should have (like Briareus) a hundred hands wherewith to fill us wine indefatigably. My apprenticeship is out, I am free man at this trade of wine bibbling. Come, my good buddy, fill me here some, and crown the wine, pray, like a cardinal. Would you say that a fly could drink in this? The stone called asbestos is not more unquenchable than the thirst of my paternity. Long clusters of drinking are to be voided without doors.

The river'll get none of it, I absorb it all.

Jacky Boy (Write)

Allen Ginsberg [n.p., San Francisco, California?] to Jack Kerouac [n.p., Rocky Mount, North Carolina?]

after July 14, 1955

July zoom, 55

Racketyjack:

I'll study any ole bloomin langwish I want, be it Greek or Greak and I might consider Sanskrit if anybody knows how to pronounce it since its sound I'm after, SOUND, Sanskrit being the right language for every other reason except who knows is it still spoke? Yes I suppose so but there's time for Greek, Chinese, Indian gelatin and pali Afrikaans, ten years apiece, I have fifty to go and can study Sanskrit in eternity as well maybe I will in fact maybe I was going to study Sanskrit (it passed thru my mind) I haven't decided what, yet, only wanted another non Latin sound in my brain to bop with: and in addition, now that I can ride horse and mule and drive green autos (120 miles and five hours behind my black buggy to my credit) I would if I can still use rusty mind and study musique herself, find out about harmonies and hemidemisemiquavers and write my own operas and particularly Zoroastrian masses,—particularly here the study of physical sound of time—maybe, as understood thru structures of Bach—you should hear, will hear, my fantastic Bach records, nothing but the purest most elevated in fact irrational moments, I even thought of studying numbers, mathematics, but that's silly to see the conscious structure he had, the brick shithouse I take it to be—all this because in recent poems I'm coming across rhythms I heard of but don't really know difference between and maybe digging them be greater kicks than market research, also I get teachers papers maybe, and review in detail the whole fucking history of the development of English prosody from Chaucer to Kerouac. Be all this as it may I took this programme along with the fifty pages fresh complete and new of my presently being worked on new book of poems 1952–55, it's half done now, another fifty to go I'll still be working as I am now—at last again ten hours adesk per diem—when you arrive, when you can instruct and chastise me for red pencils—for reading Corso's original good book I see what good verbal imagination he has and how beautiful it can be and how I have neglected that I realize (a thought of two days ago, that in attempting to capture prophetic rock of the voice of rock I rocked down my poems to the absolutely literal beginning with Williams' *Empty Mirror*, so that a literal voice could be heard saying something literal, world-real, if it be only: this tree before me rocks and the baby birds cry at the same time, and not saying the boidies [birdies] is frightened in the tree, so that I (me self) would have nothing to add, I just want to begin by

311

being an eye, in sound, later the eye will speak)—at any rate reducing the poetry to a monologue without images or music (title of long poem three years ago) and then when down to the bare bones of literal fact, adding music, which I'm working on now (or proposed to thru studying foreign sound and then music and prosody) and later add more enchanted hallucination rubber tires like the Denver, Dakar, and Holy Doldrums. Corso however has not only native genius for word slinging, marvelous delicacy, also an uncrystalized mystical thrill, if only he weren't such an egobugger, in his poetry. Still it's better than Hollander writes who is now a professor at Harvard I seen. Hollander's fault (I use this word as Faulkner says in [A] *Fable* in geological sense) was not that he's at Harvard but he isn't saintly enough to begin with—which reminds me of a Burroughsian phrase appeared to me in a dream, "We offer our goods to the market place and they are no not accepted by that cynical crew of confirmed fruits." Be that as it may I WENT to Berkeley and saw Blake student professor Berkeley's Trilling, Mark Schorer and concisely laid my manuscript down on his desk and said I wanted to study prosody for an MA and probably some music and Greek to go with it—and he said nobody here ever done that, I'm not sure, in fact no, you can't do it in the English department, you can only study English in the English department, no more than three points per term otherwise in unrelated (Music, Greek and Buddha) fields—maybe try comparative literature dept. But they probably won't allow it, either. Well maybe he'll change his mind after he reads my book-half, but I very seriously doubt that, so I will do as I please and take what I want without an MA, but I want that for distinguished loot-source as possible teacher in future if necessary whether it be in Winesburg or Cambridge, better trade than market research. There is another angle, which is that if I do go to a school and stick it out for five months to a year I think probably I'll wind up with fellowship, or easywork teaching assignment, to enable me to live at say $1,500 per year for years, maybe take me to Europe on Fulbrights, or near orient for Sanskrit, whatever, I may study Chinese, however this is all provisional fantasy since my poor unemployment will give out in October or November and I'll need loot then, only. The only thing I don't want to do ever again is work in an office like this year, complete waste of time, except that if I didn't—I'm sure I never done it before—I'd have to be in one of Neal's or Lucien's other lifetimes. Since you'll be here I'll send no samples of poems, except this piece of rhythm:

Leafy heads on long poles
revolve up and down
in the dangerous yellow breeze

and newborn robins cry in their nest
at the top of the whirling tree.

[. . .]

Besides I'm not having visions NOW. I wait for your arrival and will not resist then.

I saw Philip Lamantia, spent six hours allnite cafeteria talking with him at Kearney and Market after a party at Rexroth's and he told me how he made it with religious Indians in Mexico, met priest and had visions, illuminations, is now turned catholic, put down peyote, pot, lush and "am saving my seed" though married to a Gogo (name of girl) and is pushing Bibles at door fronts to the "laity." He thinks he's now accepted back into Christ's and Mary's fold on lower and humble level, been saved from madness and sin, and expects to have more direct contact with the source. Christ "crashed" through time. He talked (looking like James Mason serious, nervous trembling fingers, calm voice, like Huncke's charming smile when smiling) all night and left me bugged with what happened to MY visions? Anyway he's really sold, reading church fathers, erudite, learned on kicks of theology now like Pippin used and Durgin used to be, though he (Lamantia) having had visions (real ones of monsters on peyote and off, since he was fourteen) and now this final one which obliterated all before, while reading Mohammed, he floated above his body, bliss, an angel appeared and told him he had to go back, he wept and said no, bliss here too much, angel beckoned him down and said he'd been shown the true light once and for all and then he woke weeping and "rushed out into the street to look at the heavens and saw the earth too bathed in an illumination" from X which lasted fifteen minutes or so. The only really wild mind around here, I also thought him slightly mad, saving his seed and talking about Marian theology now, intellectualizing his visions. He knows some booda [Buddha]. You should talk with him also, except that he's a narrow-minded catholic too, but you being an old catholic might be interested in seeing about the most interesting mystical catholic I met personally, he makes it as interesting as Peyote, I mean a hip catholic, how the disciples "all flipped out when they saw Christ resurrected," not on nightclub level hiptalk application.

Peter's [Orlovsky] wandering around NYC now and from last letter can't find anyone home. He'll be here August late or September early.

[. . .]

Lovelovelove
Lovedog
Allen

Jack Kerouac [Mexico City, Mexico] to Allen Ginsberg [San Francisco, California]

Sunday Aug 7—'55
212 Orizaba St.
Mexico DF, Mexico

Dear Allen:

Am down here with Bill Garver—got routed off my Western course hitch hiking across horrible Texas and came down for kicks—but still en route Frisco, will be there September—mainly I want a full penicillin treatment for my leg here, minus American doctor bills—as I get older leg is more persistent—Bill Garver and I found old friends of Bill B's and Bill G. is straight—I have no eyes for anything but occasional drinking, got sick first day on shit. Feel aimless, ephemeral, inconceivably sad, don't know where I'm going, or why. Wish I was in Frisco now but such a long trip. Will make it to Nogales on SP railroad of Mexico for $10—accompanied as far as Culiacan by Bill—dig—in about a month. Meanwhile I been sleeping on Bill's floor. Tomorrow I get rooftop adobe. All I want as far as life-plans are concerned from here on out, is compassionate, contented solitude—Bhikkuhood is so hard to make in the West—it will have to be some American streamlined Bhikkuhood, because so far all I've done is attract attention. Maybe we go to NY together at Xmas—My mother may be there again—I am sick with dysentery, write me a letter. Bill sends you his warmest regards.

> Jack (Beat)

Message from Bill [Burroughs]: "I wrote you a letter a month ago and I thought you might answer it." P.S. "For Krissakes don't fool around with O or H in California, worst state in the Union." "Send him my regards."—

He is in bed reading Time—
Old Dave died, a year ago—the
Old Ike of Bill's book.—His wife
Is the most beautiful—wow—
What an Indian and what a
High priestess Billy Holiday—
Her name on the street: Saragossa—
Like Genet Hero name—
I fell in love with her
For an afternoon—

I've met Miss Green
Thru her and agree with
you, she is a drag.—

Don't get mad at me,
I'll be there in a month—
Write your plans—
Hello to Old Continuous Neal—

Conscious continual compassion and ordinary contentedness for whatever
way of making it,—I mean, simple kicks,—quiet—what more will we need? I
meditate, rest my belly, pray, eat, sleep, masturbate and pace, till my time of
now is up.

J.

Allen Ginsberg [San Francisco, California] to Jack Kerouac [Mexico City, Mexico]

before Aug. 15, 1955

Dear Jack:

Received your letter several days ago, then Peter Orlovsky blew into SF with
kid brother, fifteen years old hungup on toilet rituals, and getting everybody
settled.

Robert LaVigne the painter is somewhere near Mazatlan, if I get his address
I'll send it to you, on your way up you can sleep on his floor and eat.

If you still have dysentery, you know the Enteroviaforma brownpill cure, if
it persists I understand a heavy shot of antibiotics is good—Terramyacin, I
believe.

I enclose first draft scribble notes of a poem I was writing, nearer in your
style than anything. My book has fifty pages complete and another fifty to go
still I think. It won't be finished by summer end. I will unless you persuade me
that my sight saver lies elsewhere go to Berkeley, I found a cheap house ($35 per
month) one room, a Shakespearean Arden cottage with brown shingles and
flowers all about, big sweet garden, private, apricot tree, silence, a kitchen and
bathroom too, windows on sunlight, near Shattuck (Key System trolley) Avenue, six blocks from school, perfect place to retreat be quiet, which is my desire
since I am more absorbed in writing than before. I will have to go to work in
compassionate hospital possibly to support self, and start MA work, course on
Anglo Saxon they require and whatnot, not, and so will be alone there and so

you will be welcome to settle there for one year, two years, a month, however long, there'll be all foods around, I eat well, little money, but enough to get into SF, we'll make out alright. I will be here at 1010 Montgomery Street for three more weeks or perhaps more, and move across bay around Sept. 5. Neal has apt in town for you to stay in if you want to flop over in city anytime. My original invitation to come stay here etc. still same except now the cottage with garden makes it more Shakespearean Bhikku retired, better.

An art gallery here asked me to arrange poetry reading program this fall [this was to become the famous Six Gallery reading], maybe you and I and Neal one night give a program; also we can record and broadcast whatever we want on Berkeley radio station KPFA.

I have been seeing big Berkeley professors but I am anonymous nobody and can impress no one with nothing so I will have to work for a year, after I can have money from schools and make it thru PhD's Fulbrights to Asia Harvards wherever I hope. I guess I have to do this route for the moment, otherwise just work anywhere when money runs out and not be preparing for anything as far as money future. What you think?

Letter from Bill, he wants me to go to South America bisexual tribes, but how can I? no gold.

Come up here keep me company, there's no one to talk to. I am continuing Surangama Sutra. Also I am reading surrealist poetry and Lorca, translating Catullus from Latin.

I will see [Karena] Shields the Mexico woman and tell her you'll leave your address at the U.S. embassy for her, she'll probably pass thru Mexico City in a week or two.

I was thinking, would you be able to order Mescaline Sulfate from the Delta Drug Co. thru Mexican pharmacy and bring it up here? I'll send check for that, find out? Delta Chemical Works, 23 West 60th Street, NY 23, NY, it costs $7.00 a small bottle.

I'll write soon. Write, come for sure.

> Love
>
> Allen

PS: apropos messages from Bill Garver??? I didn't receive letter from him in last two months. I exchange regularly with Burroughs. I tried some "aich"[8] here but so expensive, a drag. Bring codeinettas up with you, a few tubes, yes? Regards to Garver.

Ed Woods, witness to Joan [Burroughs]'s death is here in town tending bar

---

[8] "Aich" meaning H, slang for heroin.

at The Place, main North Beach bar, and Sandy Jakobson, friend to Kells [Elvins], also in town on aforementioned radio station KPFA. [Chris] Mac-Claine is a cook-waiter at The Place also aforementioned.

I also want to get piano and study basic music, write blues poems.

Since Peter been away I've been writing a lot, solitude after all this year is good for me though I go blue depression mad in it too. I can't stand life.

Don't get mad at me, come when thou wilst, don't come only on account of Eugene's $25, but come anyway, soonest, make it in peaceful milk in Shake-spearean house.

I am trying to shepherd fifteen year old [Lafcadio] Orlovsky around thru life right now, like being married and having overgrown problem child, crazy kicks, pathos of real life. They'll take an apartment in town here, I'll move to Berkeley and get away from it all.

Guy Wernham the translator of Lautréamont is in furnished room across street, comes over and translates Genet for me, Genet poetry, drinks tea and shudders dignified and lost like Bill, looks like a sort of Bill without Bill's genius charm.

I'm alright, actually sort of happy.

Also we'll have a car to loll in.

> Love
>> Ginsberg

Jack Kerouac [Mexico City, Mexico] to Allen Ginsberg [San Francisco, California]

August
(not April)
19, 1955
c/o WM Garver
212 Orizaba St.
Mexico DF

Dear Allen:

Did you see Alan Harrington's review in *Time* magazine for Aug. 22-? Knopf has brought out his Saga, remember it? He seems to have compromised, by changing title from *An American Comedy*, to *Revelations of Dr. Modesto* . . . They make fun of it, *Time* and *Newsweek*, as they do of all current literature, as though the fact that it was current contemporary made it harmless.

Meanwhile, the geniuses of United Press keep turning it out pure. Lucien wrote: "I was going to sell your (seaman's) papers (that I left at his house) to an

African shipjumper but he said they were no good" and Hudson writes: "Are you going all over that ancient quiet land, Mexico?"

Myself I have just knocked off 150 bloody poetic masterpieces in *Mexico City Blues*, each one of uniform length and writing. It's an easy world, hard to die in—

Garver sends his best.

I don't want to see the Senora—I won't move from Bill's pad. I am hungup and very high on Mexican. Does Robert LaVigne know Miss Green and all the other maids of honor? (Be sure to tell me).

I'll be in Frisco Sept. 15 or Oct. 1st—you be in Berkeley I find you. Peter sounds like the idea I had for Peter Martin in sequel to *Town and City*, with all brothers gone mad. I'm sure he's a saint and would never make fun—of him or of fifteen year old brother.

Your *Howl For Carl Solomon* is very powerful, but I don't want it arbitrarily negated by secondary emendations made in time's reconsidering backstep. I want your lingual spontaneity or nothing, that goes for you and Gregory Corso, I won't read hackled handicapped poetry manuscripts.

Send Robert LaVigne's address (I want to swim a few days in Mazatlan) and some spontaneous pure poetry, original manuscript of *Howl*, I'll be headed out sometime Sept. 1 or 15th.

Fuck Carl Solomon. He's a voyeur in the madhouse. He's all right. Give my love to Al Sublette and Neal. Tell Neal that I still love him dearly and shall always, he's my brother all right.

Garver is great guy misunderstood by Burroughs who didn't listen because of Viennese preoccupations. Garver knew a Jewish promoter who conned his analyst out of $25,000 after the initial fee. Don't give me that shit about Innisfree.

Will read your poem again,—bring suggestion, which is, the first spout is the only spout, the rest is time's tired faucet—etc.

> Love to you too
> Jack

P.S. [. . .] And—I like, in *Howl*, "with a vision of ultimate cunt and come"—and—"waving genitals and manuscripts" (which is like your prose about Peter hitchhiking Texas with *Illuminations* under arm)—and especially I like "died in Denver again" (leave my Dying Denvers) and "self-delivered truth's final lobotomy".

Yes, I would agree with you that going to Univ. of Calif. for an M.A. or for anything is a good idea, it's your proper atmosphere, don't be afraid of becoming big college professor savant about literature and Buddhism and Oriental Art poet and critic like Cowley, *Allen Ginsberg.* Cowley and I walkin in the Village in June and Meyer Schapiro passes by, doesn't recognize me, or remember, but says, "Malcolm Cowley" and I say "Meyer Schapiro" on the street,— weird scene.

[...]

Allen Ginsberg [San Francisco, California] to Jack Kerouac [Mexico City, Mexico]

1010 Montgomery
August 25, 1955

Dear Jack:

[...]

The pages I sent you of *Howl* (right title)[9] are the first pages put down, as is. I recopied them and sent you the 100% original draft. There is no pre-existent version, I typed it up as I went along, that's why it's so messy. What I have here is all copies cleaned and extended. What you have is what you want.

I realize how right you are, that was the first time I sat down to blow, it came out in your method, sounding like you, an imitation practically. How far advanced you are on this. I don't know what I'm doing with poetry. I need years of isolation and constant everyday writing to attain your volume and freedom and knowledge of the form.

[...]

We wandered on peyote all downtown, P&I [Peter and I], met Betty Keck and saw Moloch Molochsmoking building in red glare downtown St. Francis Hotel, with robot upstairs eyes and skullface, in smoke, again. And I saw in me and he a void under the knowledged, of each other.

And then did [Meyer] Schapiro recognize you?

Ask Garver if possible to order the mescaline, leave him the Delta Co. address, and bring news, so I can order. One first arrest in California this last month on possession of peyote. Chap in San Mateo. Anonymous hipster, furnished room.

Remember cheap bus with wetbacks crossing desert from West Coast Pan-Am highway (inquire Guaymas, Culiacan or Hermosillo) to very Mexicali, thus cutting out all U.S. travel. Also beautiful busride crost Sierra Madres from Durango to Mazatlan, about sixteen hours each. Mexicali bus connects with main highway at Santa Ana I think.

---

[9] It was Kerouac who had suggested that *Howl* would be a good title for Ginsberg's poem. Allen had earlier called it *Strophes*.

I have no money but if in bad trouble $$ write immediately and I'll tap Neal or someone, and send instructions where to send it.

Bern Porter or City Lights bookstore here will publish a book of poems for me, possibly also for you, to be investigated. I had a little poem in small magazine in Southern California and my father sent me a copy republished from *NY Herald Tribune*, they do that every Sunday. Strange. Incomprehensible note about "The Shrouded Stranger," of all things.

One hundred fifty poems?! But I've labored all month putting together twenty little piffles! Fifty pages so far plus *Howl*.

Neal is off the extraboard on a regular job, so can schedule dates and nights.

As I say you have the original manuscript of *Howl*.

Blues samples lovely. I wrote Bill. He not dead. You know (snicker) I cut out truth's etc. lobotomy in new version. We'll talk.

> Love
> Allen

Allen Ginsberg [San Francisco, California] to Jack Kerouac [Mexico City, Mexico]

August 30, 1955

1010 Montgomery
August 30

Dear Almond Crackerjax:

[. . .]

City Lights bookstore here putting out pamphlets—fifty short pages—of local poets and one of W. C. Williams reprint and one of Cummings and will put out *Howl* (under that title) next year, one booklet for that poem, nothing else—it will fill a booklet.

I move in two days to Berkeley cottage with flowers and quiet. Send more MexCity Blues if you stay long. Regards to Garver. September heat in SF turning milk sour.

> "What Sphinx of cement and aluminum bashed in their skulls and ate
> their brains and imagination?
> Moloch Moloch Solitude Ugliness! Ashcans and unobtainable dollars!
> Children screaming under stairways! Old men weeping in parks!
> Moloch! Moloch! Skeleton treasuries! Ghostly banks! Eyeless capitols!
> Robot apartments! Granite phalluses and monstrous bombs!

Visions! Omens! Hallucinations! Gone down the American River!
Dreams! Miracles! Ecstasies! The whole boatload of sensitive bullshit!"
etc.

Love,
      Allen

Jack Kerouac [Mexico City, Mexico] to Allen Ginsberg [San Francisco, California]

September 1–6, 1955

Dear Allen:

(Thanks very much for the mad money—now I go mad)

Thou possessor of the tenderest heart and the highest wisdom. If I can ever crawl to your cottage of Blakean Horror in Berkeley (Yak!) and mack the bread-crumbs off your bone, Wak! Lak! The boy lak! Smak! Trak! Shak! Yok! pock—smock—there'll be a lotta typin to be done.

[. . .]

I have good news. Mr. Cowley got me Academy of Arts and Letters loot, to tune of 2 C's, which I get in monthly checks of 50 bucks, which I convert into traveler's checks and writ. Also sold "Mexican Girl" to *Paris Review* $50. Have big warm letter from Malcolm [Cowley]—and now he will write foreword for *Beat Generation* for Viking. I'm driving myself crazy Miss Greening. I don't know what I'm doing or where I am.

Need a typewriter, need friendship of you.

[. . .]

Friday Sept. 2. Threw green down the toilet, getting ready to visit you. No mescaline, man got arrested on the border with mescaline last week.—Want to get there.

My legs are very bad again, penicillin didn't work with Miss Green.

Holmes wrote me.—Also, publishers of Suzuki in N.Y. (Philos. Library) wanted me to guarantee 600 copies before publishing my "very well written" Buddha-book. I don't know no 600 people with $3.50. Will change title to *Wake Up.*

Saturday. Miss Green again, hard girl. Will leave one week from today, take train to Santa Ana, bus to Mexicali, bum to LA, Zipper to Frisco. Will come back for winter in Acapulco-district grass-hut, when we finish our talks in Berkeley and I have done some work and some roaming around Frisco. No typewriter, no imagination, I apologize for my poor quivering meat.

Afternoon—Now I'm drinking whisky like Lucien and flipping. I am *bored*. Garver talks but not to me. Wish Bill B. was here for old-time charm kicks at Mexico. He hasn't answered my letter of Aug. 30, written with Garver. If he got disemboweled by Berbers at Ouedzen I say he deserves it for snooping around and in Eternity for surreptitious mutilation of cats.[10] I can just see him being tipped over by non-committal disinterested Nomads and sliced nonchalantly as the afternoon drones on . . . Bill is saying "What? Wait? Where?" and he suddenly is face to face with his romance, a Arab hatchet.

If so, it means I will come face to face with *my* romance, sheeps in heaven.

See you between the 16th and 23rd of September, though by now you don't believe me any more.

Jockolio

Leaving Friday—can't wait to see you.

[. . .]

---

[10] For a while, Burroughs took pleasure in torturing cats, but in his later years he became a devoted cat lover.

1956

Editors' Note: In September 1955, Kerouac arrived at Ginsberg's Berkeley cottage door. At the very moment he was waiting for Allen to come home, Allen was meeting Gary Snyder for the first time and making arrangements for the Six Gallery poetry reading. Jack attended the reading, on October 7, but was too shy to read. Allen, Gary Snyder, Philip Lamantia, Philip Whalen, and Michael McClure read and Kenneth Rexroth acted as the master of ceremonies for the evening. In October, Gary and Jack went on a weekend camping trip that served as the basis for The Dharma Bums. *Then in November, Natalie Jackson committed suicide while Jack was supposed to be keeping an eye on her for Neal. Both men were shaken by her death and Neal returned to live with Carolyn in Los Gatos. After a short visit with the Cassadys at the end of November, Kerouac eagerly returned to his mother who was living in Rocky Mount with Jack's sister and brother-in-law. For the next few months, Jack remained in North Carolina working on several books, including* Visions of Gerard.

Allen Ginsberg [Berkeley, California] to Jack Kerouac [Rocky Mount, North Carolina]

1624 Milvia St.
Berkeley, Cal.
March 10, 1955 [*sic*: 1956]

Dear Jack:

Enclosed find letter from John Holmes. I'll write him too. Enclosed also find the letter from Jonathan Williams[1] I mentioned before. I have some notes I once showed you which I wrote in NYC which I will send him. I thought also to summarize Bill's *Naked Lunch* and send a sample of Bill's routines. Jonathan Williams' letter is what it is. *Black Mountain Review* is run by Charles Olson (poet whose poem about hairy table I showed you in bookstore in Berkeley). Robert Duncan is now in N.C. also, teaching at Black Mountain [College], which apparently has a crazy hip crowd. I wrote Williams telling him you were in N.C. too, suggesting Duncan look you up, since he read *Visions of Neal*.

W.C. Williams apparently either never received or read neither your prose which I sent him nor a subsequent letter from me enclosing *Howl* for him to read. He wrote City Lights he would write an introduction if I sent him the manuscript I haven't heard from him directly. I sent him another copy of *Howl*, and will inquire what happened to your prose later.

Cowley was in town, I spoke to him briefly, he didn't remember me, then we

[1] Jonathan Williams was the owner of Jargon Press.

got into an argument about Burroughs—"Keep away from him," he said "I understand he killed his wife." He mentioned *On the Road*, saying it would take time and was hung-up on the libel matter. Apparently they are all ballooned seriously on that issue. I didn't like Cowley this time.

Lucien wrote: "Jack stayed here coupla days. Seemed quite cheery. Thought his stuff about brother Gerard quite excellent also. Glad to see you both on a less obscurantist, obfuscating kick. Also enjoyed his story in *Paris Review*." . . . "I was made Night Bureau Manager recently which I guess means I'm white, if poverty stricken."

Orlovsky moved into big happy modern housing project, gave Lafcadio peyote and got him laid. LaVigne having big shows of spontaneous drawings at The Place and City Lights bookstore. I had a big dream last night that Neal moved into my old neighborhood in Paterson. I'm working lugging baggage at Greyhound Station in SF, $13 a day, and applied at MSTS and MCS for ship, hope to get one inside two months.

Snyder living with [Locke] McCorkle at Mill Valley, [Philip] Whalen comes over for supper a few times a week, I stay in town at Peter's a few nites a week when working. Revised Moloch which is now three pages long—"Moloch whose breast is a cannibal dynamo," etc.

See you in Time,
　　　Love
　　　　　Allen

Editors' Note: In April Kerouac returned to the Bay Area and moved in with Gary Snyder, who was living in a cabin in Mill Valley while preparing to leave for a Buddhist monastery in Japan. With Snyder and Whalen's help, Jack applied for work as a forest fire spotter on a remote mountain peak in Washington State that summer, while Allen found work in the merchant marines on a ship resupplying radar bases in the Arctic Circle.

Allen Ginsberg [USNS *Joseph F. Merrell,* San Francisco, California] to Jack Kerouac [Mill Valley, California]

ca. late May 1956

Allen Ginsberg, Yeoman
USNS Joseph F. Merrell
TAKV-4
c/o Fleet P.O. S.F., Cal.

Jack:

Enclosed $20.00 ten I owe you ten because I'm rich. If you need any more for north-ward trip let me know.

Received proofs on my book [*Howl and Other Poems*] and Ferlinghetti asked for extra poems to include so I sent him Holy! etc. and a new four page Greyhound poem you haven't seen yet. I leave 16th St. and 3rd shipyards pier 64 Triple A, on the 4th June to go to Oakland Supply Army Base, and sail on the 8th for Hawaii, then up to Seattle I think and then to Arctic. I maybe in Seattle till the end of June with weekends off so I'll hire a helicopter to visit Desolation Peak.

Several letters from Bill [Burroughs] in Berkeley I haven't seen yet. Eugene my brother had a baby boy named Alan Eugene Brooks. I didn't realize he loved me so.

I guess I'll see you before I leave, may in fact come out this weekend to Mill Valley. I gave Burroughs' Yage City to [Robert] Creeley.

Needle man won't print "Railroad Earth"—the young Italian Zoot Suit anarchists who support him think it's not political anarchism, and they pay him to publish latter. He says he's sorry. I saw him at Creeley reading.

I sent copies of *Howl* to T.S. Eliot, [Ezra] Pound, [William] Faulkner, [Mark] Van Doren, Meyer Schapiro, [Richard] Eberhart, [Lionel] Trilling, till they were exhausted (the copies). I wonder what T.S. Eliot will do. I wrote them each about you too. Funny letters to each. Imagine to T.S. Eliot.

I have a headache and am wandering around S.F. Friday afternoon with money and briefcase and poems and leather jacket and khaki shirt and pants and haircut with nothing to do. Stopped here in the Chinese Post Office by the Chinatown park.

What happened with Neal—you spent two–three days?

Love,

Allen

Allen Ginsberg [USNS *Sgt. Jack J. Pendleton*, Point Barrow, Alaska] to Jack Kerouac [n.p., Desolation Peak, Washington?]

August 12–18, 1956

August 12, 1956

Dear Jack:

[. . .]

So have been up and down north coast of Alaska for a month, now at northernmost Point Barrow. Sun is out all night or was in midsummer last week, dread ghastly pallor all nite thru clouds, and this week fantastic burning iron sun going down at edge of horizon every nite for a few hours, clear weather. The water always moving clouds always moving, birds same clouds and me same like a transparent shifting haze everywhere changing. I spend a lot of time at the prow at nite, often on my knees, praying, but don't know to who or what. I thought of you and wanted to write but didn't know what to say, what you would find acceptable, and still feel ill at ease. I thought of writing you huge envy-worry-love confession but the sun's in my eye and why bother you. And Gregory Corso is in S.F. heard so from Whalen and then got a short crazy letter from him—so sharp—.

". . America cry was embarrassing . . . but so was Novalis and Wackenroder. And Kleist had the Amazon eat her lover raw right on the stage the German poets are the end. Read *Howl* and thought why when Rimbaud put us all down by 19ing himself. You are old. I am old. Our cries sound more like cracked wheezes than GRRRRRRRRRRRRRRRRRRRRRS. And love. We are too old to say what love is. Easily enough we can call it Zen Polemic Boycock. If you didn't write and live a great poem before your 30th year give up. I told that to [Archibald] MacLeish, and he sent me away from Cambridge. Goodbye, Gregory Corso."

And he included a play, first art, crazy play called "Way Out" which is written all in style of his poem on Bird, in poetic hip talk, and is very beautiful too.

[. . .]

Letter also from Burroughs and Ansen in Venice where they're having a ball in "Mohammedan paradise with boys" and Auden is joining them maybe in the fall. Bill left London cursing London and Seymour Wyse too who he complains kept standing him up.

Finally came up against a sea full of ice floes and sailed around in that for two days, banged hull against one and cracked the fantail and flooded one of the rooms, that's all fixed, I watched divers all day the other day swimming in Mars suits underwater, and took a ride around Barrow waters under the huge hulls of ships in a small landing craft, delivering papers. Work's easy, lots of time off. Have not masturbated since leaving Seattle and so last week finally a flood of sexy daydreams and night dreams which came up like typhoon and I started writing a long poem of them, and finally it all stopped and left me more or less peaceful and undrowned. It's all in the mind. It went away.

Work here is finished (it's now the 18th August) and probably will leave here for S.F. today or tomorrow. I have weekend off to finish Bible if can.

Got a copy of *Howl* from City Lights, looks all right sort of sloppy and a few typographical errors and they left out Joan Dream poem I wanted in, and put in a few I didn't care about. Next time will take my time and not be so eager to finish a book.

Wrote Gregory to stay put in S.F. perhaps City Lights will do a book for him.

Have so far $850 in the bank in N.Y.C. from this trip plus my mother's money[2] (as of end of this month August). Will be in S.F. Hope to hear from you—when you get back?—earlier if possible—and make plans for soon return via knapsack thru New Mexico Grand Canyon and Chicago hitchhike, will buy sleeping bag, maybe stop off in Mexico? Anyway I should be in S.F. in two weeks if ship doesn't change plans. Mail service is irregular I don't know if this note will get to you before I leave here or be held on ship till S.F.

You must be lonely or strange in all that solitude on mountain if you don't get mail.

I've written journals and notes and a few psalms and the long sex poem, so far about Haldon [Chase] and Neal.

I wrote Hal also and sent him the clipping and your sympathies. Short note, said I might pass thru Denver and would look him up if he's there.

Saw [Bob] Merims also before leaving S.F. for half hour, he on way to Japan, gave him Gary's [Snyder] address. Heard from Whalen, Marthe Rexroth back in S.F. Whalen *is* a pillar of strength like you said.

Picture of Walt Whitman—I just finished last month also a huge biography. Notice ever that guarded look in his eye? Nothing like the poetry. I finally understood it when I quit masturbating for the trip—he's hiding his queerness and tenderness, fear and shame. So the blank guarded lidded look, he put himself down. His journal note, poor Whitman, "his emotions are complete in himself (indifferent) of whether his love, friendship etc. are returned or not." That's why Whitman never made great lovely saintly photos of himself entreating the world of boys. Remarkable thing is the complete openness of the writing.

[. . .]

But after all the reading of Bible and thinking I am more confused as usual about the holy life to come. Sooner or later I guess I'll have to start out totally poor and give up altogether. I guess when I finish taking care of Bill if I do so and return from Europe, it'll be hard to live and get job and I'll be too old for fucking with boys so I'll be thrown into the outside and go friendless and not know what I'm doing anymore at all. We'll see. Let me know where you are and will be September.

Love as ever.

Allen

Editors' Note: *After he returned from his fire-spotting job, Kerouac stayed only a few days in San Francisco before moving on to Mexico. Later in the year, Ginsberg, Corso, and the two Orlovsky brothers met him there.*

[2] Ginsberg's mother, Naomi, had unexpectedly left him $1,000 in her will.

Jack Kerouac [Mexico City, Mexico] to
Allen Ginsberg [San Francisco, California]

Sept. 26 1956
(Love to Peter)

Dear Allen:

Well here I am—Just (in my rooftop cell) wrote (by candlelight) first sad serious chapter of "The Angels In The World" which is about our most recent season in San Fran and which I'll hold on to for three, four years while I publish other things, for it will be intensely wild and personal—All about you, me, Peter, Gregory, Lafcadio, Neal, etc., angels, etc. with invisible wings that don't help—(and my vision of the silver crosses I saw).

Neal saw me off with that muddy hashish of his and near scared me to death with his railroad anxieties ("Keep out of sight!" he whispers from passenger coach as freight engine turns corner and puts big light on me)—Otherwise I woulda hopped freight with a song. As it is, you see, I made it, and what does it matter anyway?

Allen I want you to know I'm sorry I mistrusted you a while, now I trust and love you completely, even *like* you, so don't worry—You are martyred type of pure goodness wearing mask of evil, for martyr-reasons. Go around tell these bums you have a good heart—I know you're lechering but aren't we all—(that is evil-seeming ulterior motives of sex-seekers but I do same to girls)—Just laid a fifteen year old gorgeous girl for 48 cents, tell Peter—Name is Rosa, I'll bring Peter right to her—If you come. *Are* you coming? What precisely is the plan for our going to Europe?

I think I'll go cause I don't like Mexico anymore, shoulda stayed in Frisco for *Life* magazine,[3] these Indians of Mu ain't got no vibrations— Esperanza flipped on goofballs and tried to beat me and Bill up—Bill himself flipped and pissed in my bed poor dog (I was mad)—Awful first days.

What shall we do? I am lost in the world night. I'd like to go to Europe, yes, but let's be careful of Tangiers, the Arabs will want to kill whites very soon. I may not go with you to rat hell hole. I'd like to eat bread and cheese in Paris garrets, visit museums and cathedrals, drink in sidewalk cafes.

I haven't heard a word from my mother and I'm worried. It's like being born into a new hateful world today, tonight, this week. I don't understand anything. I told Neal to love Gregory but he don't. I wrote Creeley and apologized for telling Duncan to stick the rose up his ass.

---

[3] *Life* magazine planned to do an article on the San Francisco Renaissance.

Let me know definite plans. Neal wants to drive you down, that would be best way and Neal needs a vacation I think (from Oral Roberts). I'll look up boat fares to France outa Vera Cruz. I'm sorry I'm not God—I wish I was God. I'd make everybody's wings appear and bring heaven on—why wait? What *is* this shit?

> Your brother,
> Jack

Allen Ginsberg [San Francisco, California] to Jack Kerouac [Mexico City, Mexico]

October 1, 1956

5 Turner Terrace
SF Cal

Dear Jack:

Send poems or prose to Gregory for *I.E.* [*The Cambridge Review*]:—will publish Whalen, Snyder, me, you, etc.

Work ends here the 1st November I will hang around (I don't think I'll be shipped out again) till the 23rd or so for poetry reading with Gregory. Then leave for Mexico. All provided I don't firewheel get shipped dynamite out.

Beginning to get long admiring letters from starry-eyed Parkinson[4] and NY types about *Howl*. Did you see the *NY Times* September 2 article—I don't remember? Yes, you must have I guess. You left about two weeks ago. Agh! I'm sick of the whole thing, that's all I think about, famous authorhood, like a happy empty dream. W.C. Williams wrote he dug it and read it to "young artists" in NY and they were excited and "up their alley" and ordered five copies extra to pass around to the young. How beautiful, tho. I guess I really feel good about it. It's assuming proportions of an "it" in my life. I will be glad to regain organic contact with Burroughs.

Here enclosed a letter from Sweet Prince Creeley. He writes me, sending incomprehensible short clipped poems—I don't understand them, anyway usually.

I'll maybe drive down with Gui De Angulo,[5] Gregory and Peter—they'll come too—and Lamantia? Regards to Garver. Tell him I send a book to him, autographed.

Peter and I unable to sneak into *The Lark* (Joan of Arc) with Julie Harris left her a crazy note about not being able to pass the angels at the door and would

---

[4] Thomas Parkinson was a professor at UC Berkeley and the editor of *A Casebook On The Beat*, one of the early Beat anthologies.
[5] Gui was Jaime de Angulo's daughter.

she arrange for me and Peter to sneak in? So she sent back a letter via the manager giving us free tickets, and a $1.00 free program and invite to meet her after—we did—Peter will describe.

With Gui (she is sensitive she has shrunken freak red area sunken strange breasts—horrible—that's why so dignified and private, suffering, set off apart) will drive to Big Sur this weekend stay maybe at her family house and visit Henry Miller at the baths Sunday morning and dig eternity in the landscape.

See you in maybe a month. Gregory writing long crazy jailhouse howl.

Allen

Allen Ginsberg [Berkeley, California] to Jack Kerouac [n.p., Mexico City, Mexico?]

1624 Milvia
Oct 10, 1956

Dear Jackie:

Sorry not answer sooner—been running around, hanging around SF allee time, waiting for Neal to decide, what and when. Just returned to Berkeley for settle down a few weeks before heading for Mexico.

Me, Peter, Gregory and possibly bearded Hubert [Hube the Cube], possibly Gui de Angulo, will all go to Mexico City November 1. Peter and I will bring Gregory. I'm buying his records (for my brother) for 100 dollars, so he'll have money to go anyway.

So much happened—first Neal—he went for his eye test, color blind, and he flunked, Dr. Strange rejected him—the same Dr. Strange that bugged me. He's still working, but may be fired from S.P. as brakeman this week. Still up in air, he has to go to S.P. Hospital for retest—they can't believe it. He doesn't know what will happen. I'll write further on this the end of the week. Era ending, Neal probably finished with SP unless he gets job in baggage room or otherwise. Also he says he wants to write again, maybe, on his post Cayce ideas. He has a new girl who loves him, a Bette from Chicago "No. 1 girl" in the rackets, book-ies, gangsters, Mission Street, round eyes, mascara, slacks, cute little body, cool as cucumber, junkie, head, balls with spade chicks, blows Cowboy (trumpet) in alleys, thrice married, twenty-eight years, cars and babies and husbands back in Chicago, digs his body, doesn't want him to make her hustle for his racetrack money. "Baby I don't dig the horses but if you do I guess I got to now." Gui gave her a pair of earrings. Peter, Greg and I made further friends with Gui, so we spend days and nites at her pad, Gregory yapping at her. She in hospital for operation, removed her female insides, no can have babies—nor has she breasts,

Gregory one day saw by accident. Strange girl. Thinks about death and extinction, out of hospital, can't stay home when no one is there, we keep rushing down to North Beach where she's walking weak and twisted around a lamppost exhausted, bring her home. She was to drive us all to Mexico City—but she's too ill, from operation, to make strenuous trip, nor can her car probably, so she will follow if at all by train, or see us in NY Xmas.

Neal says he won't go, on account of job, and promises to Carolyn. But there is still some hope. You write him asking again maybe. He has to settle new job—nothing's happened yet, maybe nothing will—waiting on SP action, maybe they won't even take any.

Gregory wrote his great poem, a great great final poem called "Power." Extremely funny—and it all means something, hangs together about eight pages so far long, still in making—read aloud (with tape) for first time two nites ago at Gui's house, Hubert, me, Pete, Lamantia, Gui there, all knocked out—good great poem, like *Howl*. And in town that week, Randall Jarrell, poet and in residence at Library of Congress, so I meet Jarrell and offend him at Witt-Diamant's house,[6] offend his wife mostly, by drunk arguing silly, then party several nites later at Parkinson's in Berkeley for Jarrell, which Whalen, Gregory, Hubert, Peter, and I crash, Temko is also there, we corner Jarrell, make him sit down on floor with us in the middle of the crowd of silent professors, Gregory begins yakketing, "are you really a fascist like Rexroth told me??" . . . Shelley . . . little Gregory . . . Jarrell gets all hung up with us, party half forgotten—after awhile he gets up to say goodnight to professors and Gregory sits down on couch with Jarrell's wife holding her hand, charming, I recite a poem of Gregory's to her as she goes to ladies room upstairs . . . goodnight . . . then Witt Diamant calls Gregory two days later, the Jarrells want to see him, take him out to dinner . . . he goes, with "Power" under his arm he declares himself a vegetarian, so he has to eat eggs and lettuce while they're swilling wine and crabs and lobster soon he's holding hands with them and skipping down the street from Fisherman's Wharf . . . they want to adopt him . . . Jarrell had read his book at Diamant's house, thought it was great . . . if he needs any money just write to them . . . Jarrell will review his book, better, write an introduction to the next one . . . he must visit them and stay with them in Washington . . . he is a great poet . . . if he wants to go to Europe, Jarrell will help him get a grant from Guggenheim . . . come to Washington and record for Library of Congress. The whole works. Insane. So now Gregory has finished this great "Power" poem, has publisher in Ferlinghetti, backing from Jarrell, promise of money, fame etc.

[6] Ruth Witt-Diamant was a patroness of the arts and the founder of the San Francisco Poetry Center.

Imagine, just like that, in days days. He hipped Jarrell to your work also, he'll look it up. He doesn't like *Howl* too much, alas, I guess I really bugged him, but that's alright, I got W.C.W. [William Carlos Williams] and I want to go back to anonymous anyway. But just think for little Gregory, what windfall of fortunate love. Too much. Even [Michael] McClure, sidled up to me at Duncan's reading (literary mystical I couldn't understand it) and asked where he could get in touch with Gregory. Ah, gold, honey, I haven't lost my way.

Well I am out here with Whalen for the rest of the month, retired. I go to S.F. October 21 to give a reading on same platform with Gregory, both of us together, the final reading in SF, Gregory with great "Power" to unveil that nite, the audience will go mad. I'll read big queer poem, maybe. Then I'll leave maybe the 23rd for L.A. to see my relatives. Maybe with Gregory. Peter will work thru the 1st November and join us there. Then we'll all go to you in D.F. This is the tentative plan. So: You can expect us definitely by October 7—at 212 Orizaba. Look around see if there's someplace we can all live for a few weeks—hurray, in Mexico together at last! What have you found out about boat fares from Vera Cruz? Wait, this is my plan after Mexico—I have to go back East for a month to see my parents anyway, visit my brother, see Lucien, Village, etc. I want to and must. So I will take ship from NYC, since I know for sure you can get a boat for 160 or less from there. But there is also the strong possibility of legal workaways, on foreign ships, which will save the carfare for me and Peter, maybe you if you want to, tho carfare saving is not so important, just a minor detail. If you want not to have to hang around, but would like to leave directly from Mexico, then find out about Vera Cruz or elsewhere and I'll get $$ and you go on ahead of us and see Bill, or get him to Paris, or do what you like. We can settle this when we get there—to D.F.

Ark is out, they'll send you ten copies probably, the dazzling obscure parade and etc. . . . is Shakespeare like you say.

Heard from your mother yet?

Yes we will be careful of Tangier. I hear from Bill, he's still off junk, still waiting, expects us by January at least and can wait he says, expects us all and sounds pleased.

No more waiting we all go to heaven by boat this Xmas or sooner.

So . . . glad, happy, you will come to Europe . . . will also portion out money in advance so there be no money hassles and dependencies, everybody to be free to goof on their own, no strings just ball around . . . if I dole it out in small amounts we'll all goof each other unhappily, I know me, by now. So don't worry nothing about Europe. Also Gregory will get us all fellowships and grants and awards.

Peter wants to make your Rosa. We've also balled Ruth Weiss together, finally, I screw dog, her, and she kneeling blows Peter, then we change around. She shy at first but after awhile we all began goofing happily with our cocks and cunts and everybody woke up pleased.

So you have my precise plans . . . answer soon, are you there I mean still there? I sorry not wrote earlier directly but I been hanging around in SF without day to day plan, expecting to return to cottage to write and finally did.

[. . .]

Love

Allen

Jack Kerouac [Mexico City, Mexico] to Allen Ginsberg [San Francisco, California]

Oct 10 '56

Dear Allen:

The literary news is that Grove will want *Subterraneans* for their first issue or *Evergreen Review* (a quarterly) this winter, at 1¢ a word, and it's about 50,000 words so $500—money for Paris—but Sterling Lord is disappointed because Don Allen won't do hardcover of it first—and I'm disappointed because Don Allen wants to meld *Doc Sax* with *Gerard* "to make a good book" as tho *Sax* wasn't by itself a *chef d'ouevres*. Further, I'm completing the second and final part of *Tristessa* now, it will be, together with last year's rather light touch, now, a big sad novel. I no longer blast to write, benny is better. My prose now is very choppy and terse and funny to the point and painful—no flowery—so first flowery part of *Tristessa* take care of flowers.

I lost a whole new book of beautiful poems to Fellaheen thieves, they were better than *Mexico City Blues* too. Maybe you and Peter and Gregory and Creeley can help me recover them? We can bring baseball bats and knives and rocks in our pockets. It's disappointing, I don't feel like writing any more poems—Agh.

How'd *Mademoiselle* pictures come out?[7]

Get a picture of mine at Walter Lehrman's or somebody and show to *Life* photographer so I can be in *Life* too.

I should have stayed at Peter's instead of coming here because Garver is awful and I feel terrible here. Only good thing is, I started to paint—I use house

---

[7] *Mademoiselle* was featuring the Beat Generation in an illustrated article and Kerouac posed for his picture with a crucifix around his neck, which caused some controversy.

paint mixed with glue, I use brush and fingertip both, in a few years I can be topflight painter if I want—maybe then I can sell paintings and buy a piano and compose music too—for life is a bore.

Jack

Editors' Note: *As planned, the group reconvened in Mexico City following a reading in Los Angeles by Ginsberg and Corso. After a brief stay in the city, Allen, Jack, Peter, and Lafcadio headed back to the United States via car, while Corso awaited an airplane ticket to Washington, D.C., where he intended to live with Randall Jarrell for a while.*

Jack Kerouac [Orlando, Florida] to Allen Ginsberg [New York, New York]

December 26, 1956

Dec 26
1219 Yates Ave.
Orlando, Fla.

Dear Al:

Far from sending you the $6 I owe you, I've already asked [Sterling] Lord to lend me and send me $40 for my return trip with the manuscript because of Merry Xmas I had down here buying turkeys and whiskey for everybody and presents. Also, I don't know where those passport photos went, so I'll have to apply for my passport around Jan. 8 and so, three weeks from then will be Jan. 29 which oughta be just a hairline under our sailing date so I guess we'll make it.

In Washington Gregory said he would sail with us on the same ship . . . But he thought Paris was a port so when I told him we were sailing to Le Havre or Marseilles or Gibraltar he got mad and said he'd take a ship to Paris by himself because he doesn't want to ride beat trains overland to Sura . . .

We had a ball in Washington, I wrote the Washington blues in Randall's living room while he and Greg went out to yak at some psychiatrist . . . Jarrell is a big kind Merims types and very sweet man indeed . . . The first night I arrived me and Gregory started to paint an oil on canvas together then G. went mad and said, "Stop, let me do this myself, I'VE GOT IT," and he proceeds to bash and smash at the canvas with big popping tubes of every color . . . the next day we have a surrealistic city . . . next night I take big tubes and paint a huge frightful Dr. Jekyll face, and also a surrealistic cat . . . which I gave Jarrell as a gift, he wanted it . . . then I drew his beautiful daughter (stepdaughter) Alleyne

Garton . . . who sorta loves me and G both. We raced around in a Mercedes Benz, bought $10 Xmas trees, visited zoo, antique shops, etc. G. got bugged at me because I was bored with his goddam antique shoppes . . . but he felt better when I left. I drank up all the family whiskey and left high, rushing off with big Washington hipsters into alleys and almost missing my bus and losing my rucksack with all manuscript and paintings and gear . . . but God is good and got it back for me. Randall gave me as a swap for the huge long coat, a huge long leather coat with fur collar, a red sharp sweater and a sharp hep cap for Paris . . . but even this new coat is much too heavy for the world . . . don't know what to do.

In my *Berkeley Blues* I found this haiku: "Flowers / aim crookedly / at the straight death", which I think is better than "heavy rain driving into the sea" . . . and the reason you never mentioned it was because you secretly hoarded it up for your crooked flower poem without remembering where you saw it. But you know what I think, while I gave you "America," which you finally dug from *Visions of Neal* type America, you actually gave me *Visions of Neal* type prose, it was not only from Neal's letter but from your wild racing crazy jumping don't care letters that all that sketching came out, it broke me off from American formalism *a la* Wolfe. So we all learn from one another and wail along but my God too much is being written by too many people even good writers, mountains of useless literature are rising all over the modern world and whole unnumberable hordes of not-yet-born writers in the womb of time'll come and raise the mountain higher yet, a pile of pure shit, to reach the masquey stars of Neal, till Céline piss, Rabelais laugh . . . ough. And everybody in NY so involved in IMPOSSIBILE multiplicity reads fast like Howard and really doesn't care and doesn't look or listen, it's just one vast excited over-excited ulcer all this. 'S why I don't know, I think my *Some of the Dharma* exceeds my other books because it is mindful of this problem of stupid multiplicity and blind raging wordage.

Anyway I wrote to John Holmes and arranged for our later visit in January so you'll be hearing from him. Gregory wants to go to [William Carlos] Williams' with us, so wait for me too, make it after Jan. 8th so I can meet Williams. I can now use Jarrell's name for fellowships so find out about fellowships, Guggenheim is too hard, find out about others, if you have time in all that nervous madness there.

I've made the arrangements for my mother to move after I leave, and for further little monies for Europe, minus the fare . . . that is, do you still intend to pay my fare? Otherwise I won't be able to go, because that's her moving bill. By Autumn I'll have money to repay you, make it a loan, I already owe you $40 from last spring, lend me the fare now, and next Xmas I'll give you $200 in all, when by that time my mother'll be ensconced in Long Island and I'll have her monthly S.S. checks. Okay? But if not okay let me know. Besides I haven't signed those contracts yet and something might go wrong. Moneywise it will all come back to you from me, don't worry about that aspect, Jarrell said I'd be rich. More anon, another letter, longer, but shoot me one meanwhile.

      Jack

1957

Editors' Note: In mid-February, Kerouac sailed for Morocco to visit Burroughs and help him put together the manuscript of Naked Lunch. Ginsberg and Orlovsky followed in late March, meeting up with Jack in Tangier. Corso decided to head directly for Paris, where he hoped to renew his relationship with his old girlfriend Hope Savage, whom he called Sura, but she was eager to see India and left soon after Gregory's arrival in the city. Kerouac, tired of life in Morocco, set out from there for Paris, only to find that he wasn't welcome to stay with Gregory or any of the other acquaintances he had there, and after a brief stop in London he headed home. No sooner was he back in the U.S. than he and his mother, Gabrielle, decided that they'd move to Berkeley.

Jack Kerouac [New York, New York] to Allen Ginsberg and William S. Burroughs [n.p., Tangier, Morocco?]

ca. late April–early May 1957

c/o Whalen

Dear Allen and Bill:

Yes the manuscript safe in the hands of Frechtman in Paris. When I left he hadn't yet read it. Writing you this from Joyce [Glassman]'s pad in NY preparing to move out [to California] with my mother, only waiting to see if Neal agrees, if not, bus. The 4th class packet is nowhere, never take it, take it 3rd class, I had to scrounge around for my food like a stowaway, woulda starved without my camp pots, slept on burlap mattress, among soldiers and Arabs, no blanket even, and had to have my camp pots filled by surly cooks in the kitchen. Tried to hitch hike from Aix en Provence to north, no rides, no good hitching in Europe. However dug the Cezanne country and also Arles, tell you more later. Paris bugged me because no rooms and no fine American friends could let me sleep on their floor, Mason Hoffenberg could've but didn't want, Gregory was nix because of his landlady, spent five furious days digging everything on foot then went to London and pickt up advance, bought boat ticket, dug all London too, including performance of *St. Matthew Passion* in St. Paul's Cathedral, and saw Seymour [Wyse] who is at 33 Kingsmill . . . Last I heard of Gregory he was at Hotel des Ecoles, Rue Sorbonne, Paris. He got me drunk and made me spend most of my money the first night, 's why I had to leave Paris so soon. Paris better than I dreamed, great, unbelievable, Allen you will love it . . . but do NOT live in St. Germain Montparnasse, go instead to old Montmartre where it's cheaper, children's carousels in the street, artists, beater artists, working class district . . . (not fashionable now, the idiot Americans all sit in Montparnasse cafes as if they didn't get enuf of that in the Remo and The Place ugh).

So live in Montmartre when you get there. Don't miss the Louvre, I saw it all there . . . voluminous notes on the pictures I saw, in my diary. In Paris even Frechtman wouldn't let me sleep on (apartment) floor . . . as a result, all I got were one-night hotel rooms, kicked out in morning, spent most of time sight-seeing Paris with full pack on back, sometimes in hail rain and snow. But really loved it and this whole trip, now I'm back in NY, I see as having been worth it, worth the money spent and the hassles. Now I'm in touch with Whalen and ready to go out there. Latest news: in this week's *Publishers Weekly* [April 29, 1957] a long paragraph about *Howl* banned, and invitation to editors and writers to contribute to the fight against the ban, the court trial coming up.[1] Nothing wrong will come of it, and anyway American edition will then sell like hotcakes. I hear Viking is excited about *On the Road*, expect it to be a bestseller (old story, hey?).

Bad news is that Joan [Haverty] is after me with the cops again already, they think I'm in Europe still (I hope they didn't check boat lists) and are about to clamp on my source of income at Sterling Lord's and attach it, etc. just as I'm struggling to move Ma to coast. What I'll do is order a blood test in a few months and settle it once for all. That bitch, and I was feeling so good because no lushing and happy thoughts of concentrating all attention on Duluoz legend, damn her, she's like a snake snapping at my heels. She got some doctor to prove that she couldn't work and support her child, because of TB. She made sneaky calls to Sterling who dug her right away without my telling him and kept mum. So what I'll do Allen, when I get their roundabout letters, is answer them, mail the letter to you to mail from Casablanca, as tho I was there.

And how is the deal in Casa, any jobs? Is Bill with you? Peter? Is Peter's cure working? Saw Elyse [Elise Cowen] who misses you so much, almost cried, told her what I could. Even Seymour dint put me up in London because of some cunt in there who hated me, I'm gettin to be like Burroughs. Seymour still slim and boyish but strangely unemotional, tho as we were strolling through Regent Park one evening and I told him he didn't have to be fooled every second (by false mind) he let out a shout of recognition. He's alright but England not good for him, nothing but drear there. Anyway good contact for you in London. Go to the Mapleton Hotel in London and get a "cubicle" room, cheapest possible (Mapleton and Coventry Street). In Paris, Montmartre. Be sure to dig the Ce-

---

[1] Ginsberg's book *Howl and Other Poems* was seized by the San Francisco Customs Inspector when it arrived from the British printer. Later in May, the case against the publisher, Lawrence Ferlinghetti, was dropped after Ferlinghetti decided to order a second printing of the book made in the U.S. to circumvent the jurisdiction of the customs agents. This strategy worked until June, when the San Francisco Police Department arrested Ferlinghetti for publishing and selling obscene material.

zanne country which looks (anyway in spring) exactly like paintings, and Arles, too, the restless afternoon cypress, yellow tulips in window boxes, amazing.

Whalen and Rexroth and Ferlinghetti and Spicer making tape recordings for Evergreen, will dub yours and Gary [Snyder]'s in. I got letter from New Haven poet man [John Wieners], having *Book of Blues* sent to him. "cityCity-CITY" has ended up (unfortunately) free of charge with Mike Grieg in Frisco (New Editions).

Esquire to write piece about you, I hear, and they want a chapter from *On the Road*.

Joyce is going to get $200 option for her novel from Random and is coming out to Frisco to live awhile, Elise also maybe coming to Frisco with her.

I will see Lucien before I leave. Dumb Don Allen still wants to "improve" *Subterranean*, this is a secret (says Sterling) we will probably remove it from them and give to MacGregor[2] (keep this secret he says) . . . But they did take "October Railroad Earth" UNTOUCHED (!) to go with your poems in *Evergreen* #2 which is good and will make a sensational issue.

I feel gloomy and bugged and Gregory didn't help in Paris accusing me of gloom and bugginess, we did have one gay day drinking cognac in Luxembourg gardens with big gang of French girls and Irish queers on bikes . . . and that night met all the Paris American hepcats and painters, Baird, and others. I saw Jimmy Baldwin who also wouldn't let me sleep on his floor. I simply had, was forced to leave Paris, in England the immigrations wouldn't let me in because they thought I was a bum (with seven shillings left) and suspected my big oriental stamps from Tangiers as me being a spy . . . awful . . . till I show'd them Rexroth's article in *Nation* and the inspector beamed because Henry Miller had been to his hometown and written about it (Newhaven, England). So now I'm back, came on the *Niew Amsterdamn,* don't ever take a "luxury liner" it's one big drag, in my jeans among fops, waiters staring at me in the dining room, old freighters are better, food not so sensational after all and who wants to eat at sea . . . cost $190.

Was planning to write you huge happy letter full of news about my trip but this Joan shot has brought me way down to utter gloom again, there's a subpoena out for me and everythin . . . just like before. How can I ever make it as a Bhikku? Even if I prove it ain't my baby, the expense, the hassle, having to see her horrible haughty face again, the judge might still make me support the kid because no one else will, then what do I do? Give up writing and bhikkuhood and get a steady job? I'd rather jump off Golden Gate Bridge. And if I run away

[2] Robert MacGregor was the managing editor at New Directions.

my mother can hardly make it on $78 a month and they'd come sneaking around for her little pennies even. In which case I end up murdering somebody, guess who. I have a machete too. I'll take the Prophet's advice. By their fruits ye shall know them. O God all my crimes have been big gentle crimes of omission and at worst "subterranean sabotage" as Billy says. What would everybody say if I suddenly exploded with a sword of intelligence? Nothing . . . because nothing ever happened. Listen here Bill Burroughs whenever you say that what I say "means nothing" that's what I mean!

Allen, when you leave Africa, be sure to take lots of cigarettes with you, cigs in France and England cost equivalent of 60 cents a pack and are nowhere. Moment I hit New York I bought tobacco like a madman happily. In Paris, get a stove pad, because food on the street stalls dirt cheap and sensationally delicious . . . pates, cheeses, head cheeses, unbelievable. What beautiful churches I saw, Sacre Coeur on Montmartre butte, Notre Dame, etc. etc. Only thing I didn't see, go dig, was Eiffel Tower, which I'll save for you and me, within next five years. Montmartre will call me back . . . and that was where Van Gogh, Cezanne, Rousseau, Lautrec, Seurat and Gauguin were, all together, wheeling their paintings upstreet in wheelbarrows.

And listen here Bill Burroughs whenever I say "I know everything" it is because I know nothing, which amounts to the same thing.

Take it from there.

Write me, Allen, care of Whalen, where I'll be in ten days or so, . . . love to Peter . . . I waved at you finally from the packet but you and Pete can't see that far and there you were on the windswept sea wall peering blindly to sea. Love to good old Bill who is a gentle soul I say and fuck all his talk. Meet you all in Heaven.

> Jack

Jack Kerouac [Berkeley, California] to Allen Ginsberg [Tangier, Morocco]

May 17, 1957

1943 Berkeley Way
Berkeley, Calif.

Dear Allen:

Please mail enclosed letter for me to Joan Haverty (Kerouac) in N.Y. who will then send me something to sign in Tangiers for her Porto Rican divorce (she says). A subpoena out for me but everybody thinks I'm in Tangiers still. When you get divorce paper, mail to me in Berkeley—(at my new above address permanent home with my Ma) (a $50-a-month great furnished pad) and I'll send back to you to mail and that will do it. She says she wants remarry a guy who will adopt kid, says she wants no money just divorce.

Will get my typewriter soon and write you long letter. Neal's wife mad at *me* now for being bad influence on him, says at least you had "a motive"—flippy world. Whalen is well. Your name in local gossip columns (Herb Caen), Phil sending you clipping. Bill's book looks greater and greater. Ansen, I'm so sad I didn't see you but I had time-problems—We'll meet again.

Have you heard from Frechtmann?

Don Allen very pleased with "Sather Gate"—and tapes too. W.C. Williams is sore about a big con letter *Gregory* wrote from Paris asking for personal loan, I saw letter, *you* didn't say anything wrong. Any chance my getting Mad Checks like Peter?[3] I saw Ronny Lowenson [Loewinsohn] on Beach, he reminds of Lamantia. Al Sublette arrested for shoplifting, [Bob] Donlin a bartender in Monterey. [Gene] Pippin asked for you. Hal Chase left Berkeley. Neal still the same, borrowed money from me and yakked of Cayce.

Please rush Joan's letter on.

Love

Jack

Allen Ginsberg [Tangier, Morocco] to Jack Kerouac [Berkeley, California]

May 31, 1957

c/o US Embassy, Tangiers
May 31, 1957

Dear Jack:

Received your two nice letters, one from NY and your note from Berkeley and got homesick for cottage and Frisco and Mill Valley, seeing you were back there already snugly with your mother and permanent home apartment under the green Ginny trees. Later—first—enclosed find letter from Joan Haverty answering yours with paper to sign. Far as we (Bill, me, Peter) can see she actually wants divorce. Best then forget embarrassment of being discovered on W. Coast USA and sign papers—they have to be notarized there so no use pretending longer you're here—and send them on to her lawyer. Needn't send return address if you're afraid she'll nonetheless track you down. Her return

---

[3] Orlovsky was receiving monthly veteran disability checks due to his medical discharge from the Army.

address on letter was 200 W. 68 St. Apt 4-c, NYC. (We can't have them notarized here since can only be done at Embassy, with passports etc.) Presumably
this will free you finally from the whole deal.

Ansen is here and wanted to add a note, only he left this morn for a five day
tour of Southern Spain, Grenada and Cordoba. While he was here we got a lot
done on Bill's manuscript. We typed up the whole word hoard (including part
you'd already typed—with some changes, punctuation, separation into paragraphs), and then moved backward on other related *Interzone* materials, whole
chapters, routines all packed together and integrated from the letters—till at
this point have about two hundred pages of material finished or ready to be
finished—even had Eric hired out typing. *Interzone* appears now as a mosaic
of all the routines, scenes in the Socco Chico, dreams, scientific theories and
thought-control fantasies Bill made up the last three years, and it ends with the
revelation (radio broadcast by maybe a mad prophet) of *Word Hoard*. All this
will be through, and typed duplicate, by June 8, when we all leave here for
Spain. The only thing left will be to go back thru earlier letter-autobiographical
material to fit in another hundred pages of personal narrative between *Yage*
and *Interzone*—work on that's started already. I don't know where we'll do it.
(Ansen was great, came and started typing immediately, read through all the
notebooks and in fine hand made a huge index of all the material in the letters,
sentences, announcements, routines, all to be integrated chronologically.)
(Worked on it like a great professional pedantic scholar with an unruly library
full of dignified ancient manuscripts of the Venerable Bill.)

We worked every day, then Peter and I went shopping—Ansen and Bill sharing expenses—and cooked huge meals nightly, Paul Lund still there. Bill and
Peter not making it greatly; and I offended at Bill often till one night when he
mocking me high on majoun I leapt up and ripped open his khaki shirt with
hunting knife and felt bad later.

Ansen comes back in few days to resume work; then he leaves for Venice,
and we leave for Madrid. After that dunno. I ran out of money and sent frantic
letters to Neal and WCW and home. Williams (I guess you saw thru Whalen
letter) came up with $200 thru National Institute Arts and Sciences. But what
did Gregory do? He really almost fucked me I guess. Anyway that's my present
capital. As soon as you have enough surplus to send me any, please do so. Bill
said you were loath to since you thought I was only wasting it. Be that as it may,
later on this year I will be getting on toward broke here, so don't withhold any
money you can send me then for that reason—I'll be too broke to waste any. I
can go from Spain to Venice, and stay with Ansen—But Bill don't want to go
there. Though it might be cheap, Ansen has a pad and great to dig Italia. Also
invite from Bill Ullman to spend summer cheap in Italian villa he rented near

Florence—eighteen rooms at eighteen dollars a month. Strange, he suddenly wrote us here out of the blue and offered refuge. Or else we can leave Spain and make it to Paris. I'd rather do that and Bill would go. Merims is there too. So anyway tentatively it looks like we leave here (me and Peter) with knapsacks and make our way to Madrid and meet Bill there—he wants to go direct and fast, we'll go by 3rd class buses. Maybe stay in Madrid awhile and then in July head for Paris. Meanwhile mail'l be forwarded from here, whenever we leave.

Bill sitting on bed now reading new *Time* about Formosa riots. Paul Bowles arrived three weeks ago and came calling, with [Ahmed] Yacoubi, who is a young handsome good humored Arab about twenty-five, sits in Paris Cafe relaxing in sports shirt bought in India and whistles at girls. Bowles laid on us some Tanganyika T and said Kenya was armed starving concentration camp for natives. Peter and I been over visiting his place and all very friendly, he took me out to escargot and talked about Gertrude Stein and we went over his house and Ansen fell asleep on couch at 3 AM and he played Indian music on tape and rolled huge bombers and talked medicine with Bill. Jane B. [Bowles] also on scene, she thought Peter was a saint. Also a great English painter Francis Bacon, who looks like overgrown seventeen year old English schoolboy, born in Dublin, started painting late at thirty and now he's forty-seven and wears sneakers and tight dungarees and black silk shirts and always looks like going tennis, like to be whipped and paints mad gorillas in grey hotel rooms drest in evening dress with deathly black umbrellas—said he would paint big pornographic picture of me and Peter. He's like Burroughs a little—painting a sideline, gambles at Monte Carlo and wins and loses all his paint money, says he can always be cook or trade if he fucks painting—most interesting person here. Bowles wears nylon suits and is very intelligent and sounds like Bill Keck, tho he's small and has nervous stomach and Bill is going to teach him opium and he has blond close hair. Yacoubi paints childish camels like Klee and is great hipster and loves T, Neal would dig him. Sometimes he cuts around whistling at girls in radiant white robes—says he's descended in holy family from Mohammed, and has big parchments from Sultan to prove it. . . . But otherwise Tangiers is still a drag. I can't wait to leave, except we've done so much on manuscript I don't regret tarrying.

Peter upstairs reading *Bartleby*, started drawing pictures of the Bay last week. I'm reading Israel Potter and read lot Koran and also *Typee* and many Melville. Written nothing, except dreams and some journal. Ansen goes to Catalana and brings home, "has a boy every day after lunch." He sent his regards and said sorry no see you. How are you doing and what you doing? Bill quieter lately, had liver trouble so not eat Majoun nor drink so much, easier to live with. We don't know where we're going for sure. Peter unhappy here, wants

347

to get on with girls and Europe—soon, soon. But he read a lot. Send me news. What's with your books and what's happened to my own in court? Write.

> Love, as ever
>> Allen

Editors' Note: *The following note was written by Ginsberg the same day on a letter to Kerouac from Peter Orlovsky.*

Interruption, Allen Speaking—no, not heard from Frechtman yet. What was Gregory's letter to WCW like? and your visit to him? Where's Sublette in jail alas now? See Chase before he left, or did anybody see him? We sent Juan [Joan Haverty] her letter you sent us, and this her reply enclosed as I say in my letter formal. By all means pick up that great LaVigne picture of Peter, keep it for us, or lay it on Whalen. What New Haven poet man??? Was this John Wieners of Boston? Tell Whalen to send, definitely, manuscript of poesy to Wieners—he has address—for *MEASURE*. Am sending Wieners some Burroughs too. This a long range little mag deal, like *Black Mountain*, with same personnel practically and Olson and WCW blessing. He wrote me today asking for material and wanted to know where Lamantia was, and also Whalen and Snyder, said he received something he liked from [Sterling] Lord, of yours, and would publish it. (received "ten pages of the Book") (I assume it's *Book of Blues*). Tell also, for Whalen to give the "Green Auto", which I sent him, to Grieg for *New Editions*, if he can't or hasn't given it to *Berkeley Review*. Elise writes that the girls are all three headed for Frisco soon. What happen with Lucien when you saw him? (his name is now out of my book). Fuck Baldwin, Corso, Frechtmen, Wyse for their inhospitality, I hope they all do better by me.

> OK signing off again,
>> Love,
>>> Allen

Jack Kerouac [Berkeley, California] to Allen Ginsberg, Peter Orlovsky, William S. Burroughs, and Alan Ansen [Madrid, Spain]

June 7, 1957

Dear Allen and Peter and Bill and Monsieur Ansen:

Well, first, Allen, I got the divorce papers you nicely sent, had them notarized, signed, mailed registered mail, with all kindsa receipts to prove, and so I hope now I'll be left alone in peace so's I can build me that hut for solitude . . .

And I revealed my presence on West Coast but said I was en route to Florida or Mexico or someplace (in case of big tricks to trap me) . . . mwee hee hee ha ha . . . I did not ever think I shouldn't pay you that $225 because you'd waste it, tell Bill to stop presupposing his own thoughts in my mirror, I only just don't have it but wait till October when big things will be popping in NY with publication of *On the Road* and maybe pocketbook offer and movie options and excerpts etc. so you ought definitely get it ere Xmas, don't worry. As for Neal: yes, Peter, he fine but he borrowed ten dollars off me saying his children were hungry and then I had to go to Frisco one month later and trap him at his train but he only shoveled up two bucks and kept talking all the time. He's just as mad as ever, cunthappy, but I got a big letter from his wife saying I was a bad influence on him because he was making progress in trying to change to the better things, she says (she defines Dharma as the right way, tho it really means "the meaning"). So Neal persuades me to spend the night in No. Beach and line up some babes, I spent overnight with one gal, but she was a dyke I'm afraid. I met the magnificent Hubert Leslie who is just like DuPeru (who I saw also, he still the same) and Hubert in fact is even coming to visit me at my house in Berkeley (imagine Hube the Cube and my mother in the same room!) Hube is a great painter, he used butter on his last work, he really is not so dumb, he knows PLASTICITY of painting even if he uses shit for his browns, that's as it should be). Also Leonard Hull and Doris are two very great people, Doris is Hube's "mother" etc. and they have big mad friends who come around and tiazurpen with big neezzeedles . . . However, first, let me report on *Howl*. The whole (case) thing was put down and laughed at in Washington by big hep customs inspector lawyers or whatever, so the local dumb Irish cops rushed up on their own initiative and bought *Howl* in the store and arrested the nice Jap cat who was instantly bailed out by Civil Liberties Union but I went there and there were no more *Howls* on the shelf. Ferling was out of town and will show up soon to go thru formality of arrest and bail out. It's disgusting—what's worse is even some intellectuals are saying it's too dirty, I have a hunch the intelligentsia of America is really so gutless they might knuckle under the dumb fat Irish cops in time and it'll be like Germany, a police state. I'm really worried and Bill [Burroughs] was always right. However Rexroth is burning and there are some who won't be gutless so Allen do not worry. Write a big poem called "Wail" beginning "Wail for the cripples of Morocco crawling on their bellies in the Socco Chico, Wail for the homeless Arab boys sleeping on tables by the sea with their heads in their hands, WAIL for etc. etc." a big super World Fellaheen *Howl* instead of just dumb Amurica hepsters. Wail for the boyos with their Catch Mohammed pants!—Wail for the outraged American Queers throwing dirty pictures to the wind!—Wail for the seven foot pederasts leading small boys up the hall!—Allen, I just wrote a mad poem and sent it to John Wieners, yes Whalen and I sent him a big mad letter with Corso, him and me poems, and Gary [Snyder] too, all's set, we're all accepted and to be published in the next three issues: My poem went: "Pulling off the human drawers of girls! / Leaving whole pussywillows unblown! / Because I'm a breathless tree!" which I read to Ronny Lowensohn [Loewinsohn] the other night in Place. Mike Grieg of New Editions is publishing my "Neal And The Three Stooges" in this issue, shall I mail him your "Green Auto" now? It's at Phil [Whalen]'s round the corner. It was turned down by prissy jealous Berkeley high school boys. Tell Ansen I'll be seeing him within a year anyhow as, if I make loot this fall, I'll meet you all in Paris and go to Venice. I can't get over Paris and it was greater than you'll ever dream in advance!—so I'll meet you there within a year or two . . . Allen G., that is so mad, so mad, Allen, that line "Ansen worked on the manuscript (of Bill's) like a great professional pedantic scholar with an unruly library full of dignified ancient manuscripts of the Venerable Bill" (!)—Gregory wrote a big letter to Williams last March or April asking for money saying you and I were loaded but he was poor but somehow it came out sounding like a con organized by us. Yes, you should pick up on Ullman's offer and Florence is a gas. As to my recent work: poems and some prose, trying to write a huge novel call'd *Avalokitesvara* but at the last benny sitting it bogged down in metaphysical discussions . . . however I painted The Vision of the Goatherds, which is red shepherds looking at a creamy cross in the heavens, with swirling blue clouds around, and also painted (on peotl at ?'s cottage) more mad flowers exploding out of a (black) pot, and one painting of the yard that I dragged thru the grass like a mad bohemian modern (which I'm not) and painted Smerdyakov[4] in the Garden (nowhere) and painted another flower and painted a girl in bed and finally a chalk of Mary and Joseph but I ain't even started yet. O yes, a perfect drawing of Whalen sitting crosslegs with his pipe, called Buddha Red Ears, or did I tell you all this?

Allen, meanwhile there are big rumors around town here that you were seen several times on the street and in The Place, as tho you were Hitler and nobody wants to believe that you're really "dead". Also you were "seen" in New York even and everywhere I go I'm introduced as "that guy that *Howl* is dedicated to!" (you rat!) [?] So anyway *Howl* was cleared in Immigrations Customs Court or whatever (let Whalen explain details) but now local police step in. Write to Frechtman for God's sake, show to someone else if he don't like it, like Cocteau or Genet himself. Al S. [Sublette] is in jail for shoplifting, he will be freed in

---

[4] Pavel Smerdyakov is one of the characters in Fyodor Dostoyevsky's novel *The Brothers Karamazov*.

thirty days for good. My visit to Gregory was a big story in itself. Yes I will pick up the LaVigne painting of Peter, wanta study it. "New Haven Poet man" was John Wieners (he has already bugged Sterling Lord with his "illiterate" letters). Gary sent Phil Whalen big Buddha robes—also, Gary's sister is in Mill Valley and I am going to latch on. Send Wieners your and Bill's material and Pete's too and he wants snapshots too, he's open to everything. I think he would be better for "Green Auto" because I think *New Editions* is square. When I saw Lucien he wasn't drinking any more, quiet, had to quit, I drank, got drunk, he was very friendly and nice and I told him whole story of everybody and he laughed. In Paris latch on to American girls at Bonaparte Cafe near the Deux Magots Cafe near the church St. Germain de Pres, better than men like [James] Baldwin etc. they have loot and wanta be loved, that's how Gregory makes it, but try to live in Montmartre only half hour hike. London nowhere, don't ever even go there, except unless you want to strangle bobbies in the fog. Try to go thru Aix and Arles too, and don't miss Louvre, don't miss anything . . . (you won't) . . . wish I was with you. Now that my mother all settled and happy I feel like becoming happy too—but the three girls are arriving soon (Joyce, Elise, Carol) and Neal all blowing hot and big season to begin. New poet on scene, little incunabular Burroughs with glasses called Dave Whitaker . . . (seventeen). Send me instructions about "Green Auto", whether for Grieg or for Wieners. I hear there's a picture of you and Gregory and Laff in new issue of *Esquire* (for July) and that dumb Rexroth article is in *New World Writing* no. 11 where I'm "in his small way" peer of Céline and Beckett. *Esquire* has turned down what we offered them after a big hasselous lunch where they wanted to stare at me the pricks . . . I should have shoved my prick in their mouth, that's what they really want . . . I will write big separate letter to Pete now but also for everybody to read.

        Ti Jean

Editors' Note: Kerouac's mother wasn't happy living in California, so they moved to Orlando in order to be near Jack's sister, Nin Blake.

Jack Kerouac [Orlando, Florida] to Allen Ginsberg, Peter Orlovsky, and Alan Ansen [Venice, Italy]

July 21, 1957

Dear Allen and Peter and Alan:

    Finally re-settled my mother for good in nice pad here in Orlando, which has my own room—cost me hundreds of dollars and's left me destitute but all is set, she says she never wants to leave here and cheap rent of $45 she can make it herself, on her social security monthly checks—so tomorrow I leave this heat wave horror for cool plateau of Mexico City where I will arrive with $33 and must write despairing letters to Malcolm Cowley and agent for money. If Garver is dead, and my rooftop room is taken, I'll go to 7 peso-per-day Hotel Solin where Esperanza liveth and buy candles and holy weed and alcohol burner and potatoes and write second half of *Desolation Angels*. Allen, crafty Cowley wants me to write more childhood scenes for *Doctor Sax* and deliver them by Oct. 1st and I suspect he will yank fantasy out of it without my permission, as he yanked much out of *On the Road* (review copies of which are out) (*On the Road* undecimateable, unlike *Sax*) without my permission or even sight of galley proofs! Oh shame! shame on American Business! So I may get *Sax* publish't as is by Mike Grieg for the record (free) and let Viking fuck *Sax*? You are very famous now, Allen, incidentally I will be getting money this fall undoubtedly and will send you cashier's check for $225 before Xmas I hope. Reprint people ought to take *Road* any week, it's only 305 pages as published hard cover. Wild book, by the way—(first Dostoevskyan pure novel in America). *Evergreen Review* No. 2 is also great, "Howl", "Railroad Earth", good Gary, McClure, everybody blowing, nice cover. Elise [Cowen] came to Frisco mysteriously, Joyce [Glassman] in N.Y. wondering where I am, has $500 to travel. Rather be poor than bugged. Received your Angel postcards of Spain. If all goes as it should, I ought to meet you all in Paris in May. Have to explain *Beat* for *Harper's* or *Saturday Review*, big article, by Aug. 15th. LuAnne [Henderson] and Neal and Al Hinkle floated into my Berkeley door *just* as I was unpacking boxful of *On The Roads* from Viking, all got high reading, LuAnne wanted to fuck me that next night, Ow, had to leave (bus tickets). Saw Stanley Gould and Al Sublette in one mad night that exhausted and scared Elise. Tell Gregory I wrote him letter but where mail it? Lafcadio brooding in N.Y. *Desolation Angels* all scattered. Is Bill alright? Will you see him in Paris? does he know I love him? (I mean, in my letters, I never mention him affectionately). Shall I have Viking mail you copy of *Road*?—don't be bugged by what Cowley wanted put in, on page six or so, about "intellectualism" of you and Bill and Joan [Burroughs] as against Neal's hard-on hungry purity. Cowley thinks I'm Simple Simon, I'm a fool alright. Who will really justify us shits?

Peter, I didn't get that LaVigne painting, no time. Peter, write a mad story, Mike Grieg wants to publish my "hidden geniuses"—you, Jack Fitzgerald, Hunkey, Laff, etc. in his *New Editions*. How about a nice essay on Portuguese Baroque by Sr. Alan Ansen? Don Allen came to Frisco with Jonathan Williams, Whalen doesn't like him much (he's contemptuous of so many things including my way of writing, say "*On the Road ought* to be a good book, the Viking editors spent three years revising it")—and Rexroth saying at big get-together, "We who have power with publishers" like, they're all getting hungup on the power poetry gives, not poetry itself. Rexroth says *Road* is great and sent me message saying so. Even Mark Schorer tried to reach me. Anyway, spending all my money *before* I get rich so now I can make me fine pad in Mex City and come home winters, all's finally settled. Now for Panama Street.[5] Write to me care of here till I send you Mex address. I'll write long letter soon to all of you. Are you going to file for Guggenheim now, deadline Oct. 1st? I will. Gary coming to Calif. within months, it seems, on freighter. Well, end of sheet.

DIAMONDSHATTERING BULLSHIT

Jack

Jack Kerouac [Brownsville, Texas] to Allen Ginsberg [Venice, Italy]

August 9, 1957

Dear Allen:

This is by way of being a letter to Bill also, to tell him that Bill Garver is dead, buried somewhere in Mexico City with Joan [Burroughs], died last month or so. That was the first catastrophe, then I went to Esperanza's hotel, she's disappeared, then that night the earthquake which made me tremble and hide under the bed in this hotel room with a twenty foot ceiling (woke up from deep sleep to what I wordlessly thought was the natural end of the world, then I said "It's a giant earthquake!" and waited as the bed heaved up and down, the ceiling creaked deeply, the loose dresser doors moansqueaked back and forth, the deep rumble and SILENCE of it in my Eternity Room). One horror after another as usual in Doom Mexico. Now, a few days later, I walk and see the building that used to say "Burroughs" on it is divided in two, all the windows broken and only "Burrou" left of the name in front. Anyway I wrote the article they want, EXPLAINING THE BEAT GENERATION, all about our visions, yours, mine, Bill's, Philip Lamantia's, Gregory. Visions of "devils and celestial heralds," Joan's, Hunkey's, Gary's, Phil's— even Alene's and the Times Square kid of the Second Coming. I hope they publish the article, in it I show that "beat" is the Second Religiousness of Western Civilization as prophesied by Spengler. I also mention Neal's religiousness and Lucien's attempt to gain asylum in a church, which is really the most Gothic mad event of all. Also, I'm writing new scenes for *Doctor Sax* but I've decided to showdown with Cowley by inserting a clause in the contract against removal of (Gothic)

---

[5] Panama Street was a well-known area of prostitutes and brothels in Mexico City.

fantasy and in fact against extensive editorial fucking-up. I have $17 left, however, and am waiting to be saved. Will start back September 15 and go to New York in October. Joyce [Glassman] wanted join me here.

I keep thinking of Bill Garver . . . and of November when we were all together here. Have no typewriter and thinking of looking up old painter Alfonso for one, or Donald Demarest of the *Mexico City News* who mentioned you and Denise Levertov last Sunday in a review about a painter's autobiography (the painter, Lester Epstein, is an "aficionado" of you and Henry Miller, it says). I asked Viking to send you copy of *On the Road*. O what a loney room I have, twenty foot ceiling, whorehouse mirrors, no windows, right downtown. Except for writing-work, I haven't got a single reason in the world to be here, especially since Catastrophe No. 3 was my visit to Panama Street. The whores have been driven off the streets *completely* apparently by spreading cancer of Americanism. And I'm without my holy weed too! Write to me in Florida, am leaving.

Jack

Latest latest news—I got Asiatic flu and going home.

Allen Ginsberg [Venice, Italy] to Jack Kerouac [n.p., Orlando, Florida?]

August 13–September 5, 1957

August 13, 1957
American Express
Venice, Italy

Dear Jack:

Got your letter today, of Garver's death, and the other letters before, and answering with big long letter now, I've been putting off, it's such a big terrible letter, telling all about Europe, I'm sorry I waited so long, but thought every day and couldn't sit at typewriter for fear of not writing something beautiful. But Bill is only in Copenhagen, after London, after Spain, waiting what to do, we (me and Peter) in Venice with Alan Ansen, Gregory (we hear from oftener) in Paris still (with big apartment someone loaned him and broke and hungry we sent him five dollars but he ate with Genet and met Brandos), and now we are all ready to take off it costs only twenty and go to Greece and further Istanbul, before even seeing Paris—but all our plans are not fixed, so when you are ready in October after NY where else is there to go, come join us in Istanbul or Paris or live free at Ansen's (pay for your own food rent free and lots free liquor) in Venice—we been here month and half now.

354

Peter and I left Alan and Bill in Tangiers and took off on our own with knapsacks into Spain [. . .]⁶

Sept. 5. Never finished this—Leaving for Paris day after tomorrow and cleaning up desk—will pick up from there and tell you everything else we've done so you don't miss nothing of Europe. I got fare to Venice a few days after writing you last—write us c/o American Express—are you in N.Y.C.?

Love

Allen

Ferlinghetti sent me check for $100 royalties (unexpected) for *Howl*, all sold out printing a 4th printing. Probably more loot coming in a few months—helps solve money problems which is a lot better now. Will file for Guggenheim soon—if you get chance ask Cowley if he'll write for one for me. Should he? Have Viking send me a *Road* in Paris if they haven't already.

Allen Ginsberg [Amsterdam, The Netherlands] to Jack Kerouac [New York, New York]

Sept 28, 1957

Dear Jack:

Passed thru Vienna, Munich, week in Paris, then up here to Amsterdam, sleeping on Gregory's floor here. Mad scenes in Holland—it is a great town—everybody speaks English, they have hip poet's bars, bop bars, surrealist magazines that publish Gregory's poetry and will review *Howl* and *Road*, and Burroughs get pieces published here. Canals, quiet streets with weeping willows and psychiatrists offices, no housing shortage, cheap food, 12 cent big rare roast beef sandwiches, beer and cheese, magnificent museums with Rembrandt and Vermeer—and a museum with fifty-five Van Gogh paintings—another one twenty miles away with ninety-five Van Goghs—and the whore streets—huge red lite district neat and clean and quiet—girls sit like mannequins in windows, like Dutch dolls in dollhouses, on ground floor, windows bright and clean, they sit in chair and cross legs and knit quietly waiting for customers on quiet streets—whole blocks and blocks of girls in bright ground floor windows—like a heaven—and they don't yell at you or grab your arm—just go on with knitting. Neal would go mad. And lovely canals on side

⁶ Ginsberg continued this letter for several pages, giving Kerouac a complete rundown of his trip through Spain and France. He wrote extensively about European and Indian trips, but because Jack never responded to the specifics of these letters, the editors have not included them in this volume. This particular letter can be found reproduced in toto in *The Letters of Allen Ginsberg* (DaCapo, 2008), pp. 158–168.

streets. Peter's shaved his beard and moustache. I spent all nite awake wandering round Les Halles (market) butcher district till 7 AM writing huge poem about carts full of lungs and horns still sticking out of naked goat's head—in Paris—we went up Eiffel Tower, beautiful dream machine in sky—greater than I imagined—and hitch hiked to Belgium—saw Rotterdam and went to museums there. Tobacco cheap here too—friends here and girls nice—sweet town—we almost go on to Sweden.

Bill is in Tangier writing, he's OK will perhaps join me in Paris when Peter leaves for NY.

We saw *Times* September 5 review,[7] I almost cried, so fine and true—well now you don't have to worry about existing only in my dedication and I will have to weep in your great shadow. What is happening in NY? Are you being pursued? Is there a great mad wave of fame crashing over our ears? What does Lucien say about *Road* review? I thought his father-in-law must have arranged that extra space and picture.

I am writing a short intro. to Gregory's book *Gasoline*, why don't you also write a page of intro—send it to Ferl to use with mine—we unite and give him send off—for he is sure to be generally put down unless people are made to dig him—everybody in S.F. according to Ferlinghetti puts him down as a "showman" and for that reason Ferlinghetti won't even publish "Power". Tell Don Allen about "Power" too.

Will return to Paris room with gas stove Oct. 15 and settle there. Write soon, what's news. Love to Lucien—you seeing him?

Allen

Jack Kerouac [New York, New York] to Allen Ginsberg [Amsterdam, The Netherlands]

October 1, 1957

New York Oct. 1

Dear Allen:

Of course now in a position to send you your $225 sometime this Fall. Did you see Gregory in Amsterdam? I writing to him separately. First, you must tell Peter that I wrote him a long beautiful letter about the Russian Soul but mailed it c/o Orlovsky instead of c/o Ansen, Venice, so it's probably still there and he must send for that letter for sure . . . it was to you too . . . important you should

---

[7] Gilbert Millstein's glowing review of *On the Road* in the *New York Times* made it a best seller and launched Kerouac's career.

read it. Everything's been happening here, including this last satori week-end with Lucien and Cessa and kids and Joyce [Glassman] at his upstate coun-try haunted New England house with birds peeking in the holy windows, a big blurred Dostoevskyan party with socialites where I was The Idiot, etc. so mad in fact I could write a novel about just this last weekend, Lucien and I went mad in moonlight haunted house yelling coyote cries and gibbering and seriously insane sitting in our shorts in the old parlor as girls tried to sleep. Then when all sleep I played four hours massive musical suck-out of everything in pump-organ incredibly long sonatas, thundering oratories, shoulda heard. A guy called Leon Garen (who you better meet, twenty, hepcat) will produce a play about Neal if I write it, offers me a weekend in Taft Hotel in room over-looking Broadway with free sandwiches and typewriter if I knock it off, which I might (big play about Neal, horses, the night of the Bishop, etc., with you and Peter in it). But another guy called Joe Lustig backed by money also wants a play about Neal. Meanwhile Hollywood somewhat active on *Road*, Marlon Brando's manager (his Dad) I heard was interested. Italian publishers bought *Road*. Grove Press bought *Subterraneans* on new hard cover big-time basis. *Esquire* bought casual baseball story for $400 (all spent now). *Pageant* bought article on Beat for $300. I wrote intro to a book of photos by Robert Frank, to be translated in French for the English edition (Delpire publishers). Ferlinghetti getting my *Blues* by mail. Letter from Robert Olson saying I am a poet, he says, from reading Ontario stuff and "Three Stooges" (by the way, I sent you a copy of the "Three Stooges" New Edition to Venice, did you get it?) Bob Donlin was in NY (with evil Hittleman) got photographed by *Playboy* with me kissing me on street, after photo I feed him hand to mouth in Cedar bar Creeley artists madbar. Donlin and I fell on sidewalk in Bowery, I also fell on Bowery with Stanley Gould. Unbelievable number of events almost impossible to remember, including earlier big Viking Press hotel room with thousands of screaming interviewers and *Road* roll original hundred mile manuscript rolled out on carpet, bottles of Old Granddad, big articles in *Saturday Review*, in *World Telly*, everyfuckingwhere, everybody mad, Brooklyn collidge wanted me to lecture to eager students and big geek questions to answer. Of course I was on television, big interview bit, John Wingate show, mad night, I answered angelic to evil questions, big letters poured in saying I was beloved, finally a phonecall from Little Jack Melody. I had nervous breakdowns, two, now I got piles and I lay up read *The Idiot* and rest mind. I had final evil flips of evil spirits and most insane dreams of all time where I end up in leading big parades of screaming laughing children (wearing my white headband) down Victory Street Lowell and finally into Asia (parade is intended to cover me up from cops, when they look kids surround me hide me singing, finally cops join parade happy and it ends big blur of robes in Asia). I been preaching Peterism, on TV too, about love, preaching Nealism, everything, I have just made big final preachment in America that would flip you if you knew details . . . big roaring parties finally where I see old enemies in a blur shouting round me—(Bill Fox, etc.) . . . new that Norman Mailer pleased with me, telegram from Nelson Algren praising me, etc. etc. in short we don't need press agents any more (I told Sterling to leave minor details of our poetry and Burroughs to us, he is busy with contracts and $$$ and bewildered by your innocent demands, you being poet do not realize the madness of NY). You will when you get back. Now listen Viking wants to publish *Howl* and your others and also Grove they racing to reach you first take your choice I think *Howl* needs distribution it has not even begun to be read.

But I don't understand politics, if this would fuck up Ferlinghetti don't do it. I'm just telling you the news . . . they sense you will make money with *Howl*. *Howl* nowhere Whalen says in Grove recording because cut while [James] Broughton drones on and on, Whalen very mad. A million more things happened, I only wished you and Peter and Greg be here, not to mention Burroughs and Ansen, it was too too much, especially TV which killed me, big camera coming close, "Do you ever smoke dope?" "What you think of suicide?" final big question "What you seeking?" "I am waiting for God to show his face." (which I meant, having thought of it just a week previous lying on sickbed in sad south). I flipt and had to cancel further publicity with Tex and Jix, Barry Gray, etc. on and on, Look, and finally tho I did manage two radio shows etc. etc. getting all involved with sexfiend radio man who finally made big drunken tape of me and him and Leo Garen explaining young cunts of Organo Street and that sexfiend reformed drunk rushes to Lucien to bring him into AA which is Lou's I don't want to hear it about dept. in fact a perfect raving scream of furiously funny events rivaling anything in Dostoevsky. Joyce and I in fact leave phone off hook all day till four because it was ringing every mad five minutes. Ed Stringham keep rushing up with mad "hipsters like Neal" who insist on driving me 110 miles an hour down Fifth Avenue, one of them Howard Schulman, poet, who took me to Lafcadio and we knocked on a evil door and somebody inside yelled at us to go away, two men, not Laff . . . don't know where Laff is, except rumor he was in Fifth St. bookshop making speech (I think about us). Schulman like Ronnie Cherney if he don't watch out but might be good. Incidentally I got roar drunk with John Wingate the TV interviewer after the show, we had to be dragt away from each other . . . so there . . . I mean, he wasn't so evil, but an evil business TV. His girl interviewer wanted to know if I thought sex was "messy," I said "Who said that?" she said "James Gould Cozzens" I said "No it's gateway to Paradise." "O I don't think so" "Close the door and let's do it!" I say softly, she turns color, "DID YOU FEEL IT?" I yell . . . big Zen. Saw Anton [Rosenberg] who had book covered with plain white paper, on one side, writ in ink, "ZEN" on other side "HOO". He tried to drag me away from Don Allen to go get hi with him and Burnett. Anton being very friendly, calls me Playboy of "our" generation he said, and tried to sell me a car worth $20,000 as if I had that . . . "You haven't got it yet" he shouted, in shop. Even Thurston Wallace I saw, pounced on me in a bar, gad I felt like Burroughs . . . didn't even go to Columbia, of course, where West End Bar full of young kids reading *Road* . . . piles of fan letters, some from sixteen year old girls who saw me TV love me . . . what an opportunity for a Great Lover, which I'm not . . . I being quiet Sam Lunatic, actually quiet dreamy Hinayana coward . . . or, Hinayana of Avalokitesvsrs. Ralph Gleason of Frisco had better review of me than Rexroth! Best review of all was written inside Michigan State prison where all convicts dug Neal of course. Best review of all from Mississippi where a reviewer signed "O I wish I was young again". Everybody talking about you . . . you must go to town now in Paris and get things done . . . money coming your way. Tomorrow I'm sposed to get *Life* spread of my own, but am getting so bugged I may finally get bugged and flip and tell *Life* fuck. Already had one hundred fifty color shots taken of me squatting on Sheridan Sq., talking, screaming to bums drunk in Bleecker St., etc. . . . also pictures in *Harpers Bazaar* followed by interview with intelligent middleclass lady who got drunk in my arms practically. I been getting fan mail from middleclass ladies and like, Cessa's mother mad about book. My big satori was when Cessa screamed at me "Shut your big mouth" when I was being idiot at party upstate, a doctor wanted to give flu shots to her babies and I yelled, "Don't torture your children" and doctor everybody shocked finally everybody drunk on the floor. Lucien and I were insane, I drove car myself thru the woods crashing thru little trees and over dumps . . . never loved Lucien mo . . . and he kept singing "Getting to know you". And I thought (thru all this) of Burroughs all the while. I delivered manuscript to [Donald] Allen, separated *Word* from rest of manuscript for him to start on. I made big friends with Mr. Von Hartz.[8] Lemme know about Paris as soon as shock wears off and you quiet somewhere, for sure if movies buy I go see you this winter rather spring, May, then you could wait confidently there for my temp. support. Write. Many more things happed but I save it for next time.

Jean-Louis

---

[8] Ernest von Hartz was Lucien Carr's father-in-law.

Allen Ginsberg [Amsterdam, The Netherlands] to Jack Kerouac [n.p., Orlando, Florida?]

Amsterdam Amer Express
Oct 9, 1957

Dear Jack:

Received your October 1 wave of beauty crashing over you in America—reading left Gregory exhausted, universe turned sweet for Peter. I thought what inevitable mad dream of life we've turned up. SAVE YOUR MONEY!!!!!! God knows what oblivion we'll wind up in like unpopular Melvilles when Russia gets to Moon and world is bugged with US! (last nite in great calm queer club, men dancing, I thought, Gregory in fact thought, he heard Bill Haley R&R singing "Little Rock, Little Rock, Little Rock, Little Rock, Have Yourself a Ball"). Yes we are sleeping in Greg's bed in nice room in Amsterdam, we cook steaks and eat mad Dutch bread and Swedish bread and Gregory writes mad poems "O People O My people / something weirdly architectural / like a rackety cannibal / came to Haarlem last night / and ate up a canal" and "Four windmills, acquaintanceships / were spied one morning / eating tulips" and we go around Amsterdam in mists by vast museums full of Vermeer bugging the Dutch with insane demands that they join us in eating canals. Stayed up all nite last nite in Paris in Les Halles meat and truck butchery writing big meat poem about trucks full of lungs, ending "Fellow Conspirators, Eat." And here last night we got drunk and wrote huge chain poem manifesto of our demands for the coming moon—very beautiful lines, dozens of small notebook pages, Peter blowing: "I can't wait till when I get to the moon till I see thereon the round plain the naked human gazelle crying with long hair and high bony cheeks running 50 mph like a jeep over nowhere land after trout,"—and Gregory, "Nor can I wait to see the sad angel of streets in his own personal alley, hands to face, wings covering all, weeping his heavenly woe and lack of Ebbets Field scream."

I sent Bill tonite a clipping from *London Daily Telegraph*, describing New Guinea Disease, "Kuru" or "Laughing disease." Rare tropical disease perhaps Bill not heard of yet, closely related to Latah and Amok according to the paper, "Twenty natives are now virtually laughing themselves to death in Okana hospital . . ." Some villages are said to be full of "laughing men and women." "This uncontrollable laughter is followed by exhaustion paralysis and death." Gregory just now wrote the poem. I sending it to Bill, he should dig Gregory now. As epigraph to title page of *Gasoline* book, Gregory quotes Bill's lines about "Gaming tables where games are played for incredible stakes." I sent my intro to Don Allen to give you to read. As I said in card, write a note or page if want on Gregory and send it to Ferl to use also as preface or book jacket. His book is mad and perfect. God knows what will happen to poetry when that explodes and if Ferlinghetti takes your book. Give this poem "Zizi's Lament" to [Donald] Allen.

Back to Business: on Bill's manuscript I know full well how idiotic my letters to [Sterling] Lord sound but on such small details Lord builds his Paradise. He has two letters full of instructions. Well you take over there and I'll work here. Philip Rahv of *Partisan Review* has a section ("The Market", I think). Please call him up and find out what he'll do. We read him some in Venice and he said he dug it, so Alan Ansen sent him that piece.

Wieners took and will publish one page. He might publish more if he sees more.

Mike Grieg should be able to publish a section.

Don Allen Grove etc. you know all about.

Combustion might spread a page but I not in touch. If you have time send them something.

The *Needle*, too, if still running?

It's just a question of running around talking to people. Probably *New World Writing*, if you can phone Arabell Porter. Use your imagination I guess. You must be busy to madness. Well, let me know what you think. I mention these small places so that at least tastes and sections can reach select audience and create subterranean fame and response for Bill.

Ferlinghetti once thought about publishing South American letters *Yage* section, as a small pocket book of prose. Well, he writes he would sympathetically read the manuscript to see if maybe a mad sixty page section, like "Market", can be issued. I will put as much golden pressure as I can on him to do so. When NY people are thru, send him book. New Directions, this year's annual no good, all foreign translations material.

Meanwhile in Paris, will find Beckett and see if he'll help. Frechtman has it, but he'll be only a bug on this. (He offers to try find you translator—maybe good idea, since he would care about literary stylistic matters, which might be neglected in ordinary commercial negotiations. In any case, no harm if you can send him a copy, either thru me or his address: 27 Rue de la Michodiere, Paris, France. He translated Genet and Guignol's Band—so he might actually be helpful artistically—not a question of publicity, but getting inspired translation.)

I not received copy of "Three Stooges", nor *Road*—send me also extra *Road* to put in hepcat American Jerry Newman bookstore Mistral window. If you got them. If can send any interesting mag or news clips—I see nothing—like oblivion.

No news on trial, tho I guess it's over. Is Lucien carrying the story at all? I wish he would, his name's out. [Henry] Miller attended trial—and later developments may wind up freeing Miller's books—and maybe Bill's—not inconceivable—maybe Ferl [Ferlinghetti] try other test cases in SF. Show Lucien this. Hello Lucien. Make Jack save loot.

All your mad news so fine. Write more details, O heroic! TV answers great—what'd you say on smoke dope?

Re *Howl*, Ferl sent me 100 dollars, has 4th printing, sold 5000 already, will sell more,—it's circulating a lot. Could Viking or Grove actually do better? I wonder. However I don't know. But City Lights took it, way back, and fought trial, and Ferl went into red once for it, so I have already told him I won't go whoring around NY. Tell Lord, if he can reprint *Howl* itself (or any other poem) anywhere, and get me some loot—in *Life* (maybe Rosalind Constable would even back that you know) or *Look* (who knows?) or *New World Writing* (more likely) to do try do so and be agent if he cares and will. That won't fuck up Grove, since their issue is over, and will only help City Lights sales. Anyway, tell Lord, and ask him to inquire around and think it over if he will.

I sent you big letter from Venice, about Europe, you get it?

I sent in Guggenheim—used references: Van Doren, Williams, Bogan, Rexroth, Eberhart, Josephine Miles, Witt Diamant, and you.

Would have used Cowley but didn't know what he thought.

If can sell Hollywood god—good, but maybe hold out for real great fantastic original creative treatment—use Neal and me and you as actors—but anything so movie is pure, even if big commercial flop. Of what other use, and what other power, has Zen poverty—except to demand everything? Make mad bold history, O world smasher!

What and where the big final preachment?? You mention.

I know about Grove record nowhere. City Lights and Fantasy want me to record whole book in Paris and will issue great record when I do. Will do soon.

Beautiful line about being quiet dreamy Hinayana coward. What you hear from Neal? Write me in Paris, tell all, it's so great. I'll write soon. I wrote Bill your news. Goodnight.

     Love,

       Allen.

Allen Ginsberg [Paris, France] to
Jack Kerouac [n.p., Orlando, Florida?]

Paris,
American Express, Ginsberg
October 16, 1957

Dear Jack:

Got back to Paris last nite, have nice warm room, large, with two burner gas stove, five floors up, 9 Rue Git Le Coeur, one block away from Place St. Michel, out window I can see Seine.

Peter's letter tells details. It seems that Lafcadio is holed up in the Orlovsky chicken-shack, is flipping. Mrs. Orlovsky is also flipping. Who is worse flip we can't tell since Laf doesn't write. At any rate situation sounds very bad—i.e. we're afraid from sound of letters that she'll call cops and put Lafcadio in bughouse. (He's probably flipping because she's bugging him, won't take care of him, trying to make him go see his father Oleg and threaten his own father for money, and wants him to leave.) (She on other hand is bugged with him, he's flip, and she's broke and in debt and probably frightened). Anyway big mess.

We figure we ought to do something because situation sounds like its getting out of hand and he might wind up being committed by her. Similar situations in past with other brothers, whom she committed.

Peter thinking of immediate return to states—if nothing else can be done, and if situation is as bad as above.

Therefore, if you can, will you investigate for us and see what you can do? Thing to do is go out there, see if she hasn't already committed him, bring him to city (if he'll go), get him a room and leave him enough money to eat. You can use the money you owe me to do that on.

I don't know if you yet have enough money to do that—this is all hypothetical—we're trying to figure a way so that Peter doesn't have to return immediately.

Peter plans coming back in two months, before Xmas, in any case. If you can straighten out matters at least temporarily and solve this present crises, it might all blow over and be alright for Peter to stay here till then. If you can't and the situation is still bad, he'll leave for States immediately—get Embassy to send him back because of family emergency.

Sending this letter air special etc. I know the responsibility might bug you, it would bug me, the whole proposition.

I don't know what's up this week with you and what the pressure of other wild events is, and if you are in a position to do anything anyway.

If you can try, please go out there with one of the aspiring hot rodders immediately, and write us what's up.

If you can't do anything, please write back, immediately, and let us know, so that we can make arrangements for Peter to return. What I mean is we got to hear from you in a matter of a couple of days—can't afford to wait.

Normally I'd assume such matters settle themselves Buddhist-wise and no point doing anything (The sun rises and sets without my help)—but something real evil might happen to Laf, Beloved Laf, we're worried.

But so, I mean, man, Jack, write us immediately if you can go out there, or not, so we can take big hysterical actions.

Peter worried, sad.

Everything else fine, we rescued Corso from Amsterdam, had a three week ball there. Saw [Barney] Rosset today, he's in NY by time you get this letter. Saw Frechtman, he hadn't even read Burroughs manuscript. I took it back and have Beckett's address and will take it to him tomorrow. KiKi[9] was stabbed to death in Spain by jealous orchestra leader, says Bill. Jane Bowles flipped and is in English Hospital. Bill writing more. I wrote you the other day. Gregory's book will be great. My family saw you on TV and said you talked about *Howl* too, great. Case is won I hear, headlined in *Chronicle*. I'm writing big poem to rest of Universe, now that we are out of Earth—biggest news event (tell Lou) since invention of Fire. Do you realize we'll soon (ten years) be on moon, and in our lifetime get high with brother Martians? There'll be others out there, and we'll reach them, I'm certain—and our poems too—I go rewrite Whitman for the entire universe—have big poem started. Other night in Amsterdam I looked at moon with new eyes.

So, so, so dear Jack, please write us back, rescue Lafcadio temporarily (even if it's a big mess) and if you can't rescue him, don't worry, don't be bugged at us, but write us back what situation is, you can't go out there, so we find other practical way. Hard to deal with events from so far away.

Can call Eugene and ask his car and help, if want—he'll probably come on alright and sympathetic, tho he may be bugged being dragged—but probably not, he'll think it an adventure and be glad to shine in your company.

Gregory alright, staying with us, writing. Paris great. Would there were no worm to mar my happiness. I'm free and don't suffer anymore, in fact never did, but everyone else seems in trouble. Regards to Lucien and Merims (who wrote the other day about big party at his pad)—saw Dexter Allen and Baird

[9] KiKi was a young boyfriend of William Burroughs in Tangier.

and Mason, today, ah, I'm willing to cook beans in my room and not go out except to see pictures and meet 18–24 year old unspoiled angels—old angels are too down. Haven't started making it with female angels yet, just got here, but soon have nice scenes I bet.

Write what's new.

Love,

Allen

What does Holmes say? (John Clellon)

Jack Kerouac [Orlando, Florida] to Allen Ginsberg [Paris, France]

October 18, 1957

Dear Allen and Gang:

I've just sent in my 2 cents to Ferling on the subject of Gregory's poesy: as follows: "I think that Gregory Corso and Allen Ginsberg are the two best poets in America and that they can't be compared to each other. Gregory was a tough young kid from the Lower East Side who rose like an angel over the rooftops and sang Italian songs as sweet as Caruso and Sinatra, but in *words*. 'Sweet Milanese hills' brook in his Renaissance soul, evening coming on the hills. Amazing and beautiful Gregory Corso, the one and only Gregory the Herald. Read Slowly and see."

(Okay?) As you know, (or do you?) Ferling asked for my *Blues* from Sterling and we mailed them to him. I told Ferling if he follows up to call my book *Blues* . . . nice sequence, *Howl, Gasoline, Blues*!!! Meanwhile I typed up "Zizi's Lament" and sent it to Don Allen, who crossed me in the mail with your preface to *Gasoline* which is alright, in fact rather good . . . especially "hip piss." So all's swinging . . . but here (I think, I hope) is the truly great news: I wrote a play, a three-act play for Broadway or off-Broadway, *one*, definitely Leo Garen will produce it in his 2nd Avenue Yiddish theater but we also have Lillian Hellman and big producers on the line, big press agent Joe Lustig who is also going to organize such immense poetry readings in the Spring that it will be worth all your whiles to come home early Spring and do it . . . he wants to do it with jazz and I'm going to tell him definitely to play a number, let a poet read a poem, play a number, let a poet read a number, but NOT mix up jazz and poetry together like SQUARE OF SAN FRAN. Joe will take all our advice, he is nice Yiddish saint, in fact Allen you must ally yourself with him and advise him, to have people like Chas. Olson and Gary [Snyder] read instead of Richard

Howard and Popa Ididoud. (tho he sounds like he might be interesting.) The play will be called *Beat Generation*[10] and is only the beginning . . . meanwhile too Leo Garen is eager to see Gregory's plays . . . you can reach this mad little (director) cat thru Joyce Glassman, 65 West 68, get on ball. Plays! Productions! Leaping from the author's box to the stage to make flower speeches! Homburgs! Operas! Red linings to black cloaks! Millions! Money! Cunts!—Drunk on the Bowery like Jack Dempsey! Falling on our head with Stanley Gould in the Ritz! Early morning whiskey sours in the White Horse! Throwing garbage pails at Caitlin Thomas! Kissing the feet of Nuns!—Do you rats realize that the Fathers of St. Francis of Assisi church 34th Street New York are actually saying a Mass for my spiritual and temporal welfare, at the request of two secret Dostoevskian nuns in a Connecticut monastery, because of what I said on TV? I wrote my play in 24 hours, no less, couldn't sleep till it was done, there.—all argues in favor of spontaneous. Here's the big news I wanted to say: ALLEN! you will play Allen Ginsberg in the play! rush to NY and become big actor, scream Rimbaud on the stage, sprawl between the Bishop's mother and Aunt in Neal's imaginary living room! it's all about the Bishop Night, preceded by a day at the races and a first-act scene in Al Sublette's kitchen with big Al Hinkle and little Charley Mew! A Comedy! the dialog pours like waterfall across the pages!—big part for Peter as Peter, Peter singing "can't recall the hours, flowers" (Peter please send me title and words of that tearful rock and roll number so I can insert it in playscript in time for big producers to understand with cigars in mouths *— big part for Peter finally Peter Allen and Jack start screaming holy holy holy in front of Bishop . . . I have ah hunch I've re-done the American Theater with this one . . . it's not even typed! I just finished it! Leo Garen is driving to Florida to see it! Airplanes are flying overhead!—When I get back N.Y. around New Year I'll take up business on Burroughs manuscript, meanwhile Don Allen has it, I had Joyce Glassman call Philip Rahv, answer forthcoming . . . Peter's gazelle on Moon beautiful . . . all beautiful, Gregory, Allen, all . . . My latest poem is: "Flesh the payer/spirit bills." (I call them little ones "Emilies")—Very latest poem: "I wooed her with the soft young glue."— ooo—(meaning America, me young once). I wrote a poem "Too ashamed to show my asshole to Jesus Christ" and next day I had piles.

        Jean-Louis

P.S. You won the trial in SF. My money not in yet—soon!

P.S. Germany just bought *On the Road*, Rowohlt Verlag Publishers.

Allen—my money so far has been one short story loot—but more coming

---

[10] *Beat Generation* was published in 2005.

366

and in January $8,000 royalty check! When and how and where you want your loot? (Rumor in N.Y. that I don't want to pay you!)

Allen Ginsberg [Paris, France] to
Jack Kerouac [n.p., Orlando, Florida?]

November 13–15, 1957

Nov 13, 57 Paris

Dear Jack:

Gregory brought his letter over, I'll add a page and save stamps and reassure you, we are all still here, not bounded over Atlantic—reason I'm so still is I'm confronted with great backlog of unanswered letters, have just been sick in bed with Asia flu for two weeks, ago to now and been reading book on Apollinaire and learning more French. Suddenly I can read French a little better—not enough to read books, but enough to read poems I see quoted in books—I am all hung up on French poetry, I went into a big bookstore, saw French translations of whole plays by Mayakovsky, pamphlets of fine funny poems by Essenin, then the big bookshelves of XX century French bohemians, Max Jacob, Robert Desnos (a French girl said I looked like Desnos profile), Reverdy, Henri Pichette—all their huge books, Fargue, Cendrars etc., names, I never read them, but read a few by each, all personal and alive, Prevert, and all the funny surrealists, so I want to improve French and dig them, none translated, and all fine fellows, I can see from the pages of loose sprawled longlined scribblings they've published for fifty years here now—what sad treasuries for Grove or City Lights if anybody ever were able to have time and intelligence enough to organize and edit and transliterate them all, would be marvelous to read in U.S.—most of it almost unknown really. Anyway my French I happy to say, getting better so one day I'll be like R. [Richard] Howard with French books in my house in Paterson and be able maybe to enjoy them.

Gregory as you can see, he improved in Frisco, and he improved since, and now is even riper, and is like an Apollinaire, prolific and golden glories period for him, in his poverty too marvelously, how he gets along here hand to mouth, daily, begging and conning and wooing, but he writes daily marvelous poems like the enclosed—enough already for another huge book since last month's City Lights manuscript. Gregory is in his golden inspired period, like in Mexico, but even more, and soberer solemner, calm genius every morning he wakes and types last nites two or three pages of poems, bordering on strangeness, now he's even going further, will enter a classical phase seen and possibly construct structural poems and explore big forms, his genius showered with strangeness.

We are getting lots of great junk too, better than anything I ever had with Bill or Garver, so pure horse we sniff it, simply sniff, no ugly vaginal needles, and get as good almost a bang as a main line, but longer lasting and stronger in long run. Very cheap here too, and this around for Louvre visits.

Not yet explored Paris, just inches, still to make solemn visits to cemeteries Per Lachaise and visit Apollinaire's menhir. (MENHIR) and Montparnasse to Baudelaire.

Granite surrounded by ivy.

I sat weeping in Cafe Select, once haunted by Gide and Picasso and well dresst Jacob, last week writing first lines of great formal elegy for my mother—

> "Farewell
> with long black shoe
> Farewell
> smoking corsets and ribs of steel
> farewell
> communist party and broken stocking
> O mother
> Farewell
> with six vaginas and eyes full of teeth and a long black beard around the
>   vagina
> O mother
> farewell
> grand piano ineptitude echoing three songs you know
> with ancient lovers Clement Wood Max Bodenheim my father
> farewell
> with six black hairs on the wen of your breast
> with your sagging belly
> with your fear of grandma crawling on the horizon
> with your eyes of excuses
> with your fingers of rotten mandolins
> with your arms of fat Paterson porches
> with your thighs of ineluctable politics
> with your belly of strikes and smokestacks
> with your chin of Trotsky
> with your voice singing for the decayed overbroken workers
> with your nose full of bad lay with your nose full of the smell of pickles
>   of Newark
> with your eyes
> with your eyes of tears of Russian and America

with your eyes of tanks flamethrowers atom bombs and warplanes
with your eyes of false china
with your eyes of Czechoslovakia attacked by robots
with your eyes of America taking a Fall
O mother O mother
with your eyes of Ma Rainey dying in an ambulance
with your eyes of Aunt Elanor
with your eyes of Uncle Max
with your eyes of your mother in the movies
with your eyes of your failure at the piano
with your eyes being led away by policemen to ambulance in the Bronx
with your eyes of madness going to painting class in night school
with your eyes pissing in the park
with your eyes screaming in the bathroom
with your eyes being strapped down on the operating table
with your eyes with the pancreas removed
with your eyes of abortion
with your eyes of appendix operation
with your eyes of ovaries removed
with your eyes of womens operations
with your eyes of shock
with your eyes of lobotomy
with your eyes of stroke
with your eyes of divorce
with your eyes alone
with your eyes
with your eyes
with your death full of flowers
with your death of the golden window of sunlight . . ."

    I write best when I weep, I wrote a lot of that weeping anyway, and get idea for huge expandable form of such a poem, will finish later and make big elegy, perhaps less repetition in parts, but I gotta get a rhythm up to cry.

    Re Lafcadio: Good news, suddenly the long-lost father Orlovsky appeared on scene, visited, promised $10 a week support family, talked gravely and digni-fied with Laf, the crises in household still go on, but now not critical, no mad deeds will be done, so it can wait Peter's return—we wrote you unrealizing you were already out of NYC—meanwhile Joyce Glassman wrote us and pro-posed she investigate with Donald Cook, so the situation's there in hand and we got sensible fine letter from Laf, he has beard he says and will be great artist of space and time and draws constantly and sent us a burning red face in crayon of Laf-spaceman-mystic with eyeshields of red glasses.

Let me know when plays are ready. I think play down the Beat Generation talk and let others do that, it's just an idea, don't let them maneuver you into getting too hung up on slogans however good, let Holmes write up all that, just as "S.F. Renaissance" is true, but nothing to make an issue of (for us). I mean I've avoided generally talking in terms of SF as if it were an entiry. You only get hung on publicity-NY-politics if you let them or be encouraged to beat BEAT drum—you have too much else to offer to be tied down to that and have to talk about that every time someone asks your opinion of weather—it'll only embarrass you (probably already has)—Let Holmes handle that department. Next time someone asks you say it was just a phrase you tossed off one fine day and it means something but not everything. Tell them you got six vaginas.

[...]

Bill's manuscript [*Naked Lunch*] was read by Mason Hoffenberg who pronounced it the greatest greatest book he read of all time, Mason brought it to Olympia [Press] and assures me it'll be taken (Mason wrote a porno book for them and knows them and is also an advisor) he is astounded by WSB and his reaction I gave great sigh of relief, I think everything'll be alright with the book, it'll be published here in toto intact. Meanwhile Bill sent me another thirty pages and says he has another hundred coming up with new final character like Grand Inquisitor who will wrap the whole book up in one unified theme and stream and interspace—time plot and fill in all lacunae and unify everything into perfect structure and delight, so.

I guess it will be published here then in the Spring. I wait to hear word this week and then will notify Bill. If. I think it'll work out they'll buy it tho terms are lousy, they only pay $600 per printing (i.e. if reprinted he gets another 600) but I'll try get a formal contract reserving all mag. rights for *Evergreen* to Bill etc. I have to contact [Sterling] Lord and get name of his Paris office and have them arrange legal details as I personally don't want to be responsible for another fuckup like Wyn. However with fugitive shady Olympia, the terms of publication seem bound to be disadvantageous and nothing much can be done, except the great main thing get book into print once for all. Perhaps I'm proceeding too nervously and in too much haste merely to get book in print irregardless of business hallucination dignities Bill deserves and might demand—what you think? I don't know, I be relieved to see it actually accepted. But I'll try to have Lord's Paris office protect Bill.

[...]

I get lots of letters, also from many unknown young businessmen who tearfully congratulate me on being free and say they've lost their souls. I have to answer them all and have several dozen letters to write—which is why I seldom go near the typewriter, which is why I haven't written you. And then I owe LaVigne six letters, and Whalen, and McClure started writing me again (he was seized with madness when he saw your *Blues* book, evidently Ferl is showing it around) and called it the great poem since Milton—also said he wept reading *Road*, in urinal scene with Neal, where you quarrel. And I always owe letters to Bill—and my unfinished project to finish another fifty pages letter to you recording continuing our Europe tour—still have all Italy and Vienna and Munich and Amsterdam to tell you about—which will do soon—and typing up poetry which I rarely do—there isn't enough time for all the great flowery tasks. You must be snowed under, more than me, I wish I knew all details. (Oh, I found Lord's address, never mind).

Still no sign Genet. What novel you writing? "Zizi's Lament" is incidentally about a new disease we sent Bill a clipping about, KURU, a relative to Asian Amok and Latah, a laughing disease, "whole villages laughing themselves to exhaustion and death."

I thought record was rotten (I played it in front of painter hipsters here and cringed) but Ferl says I should make a new full length LP he'll put out with Fantasy records (it's all signed up and arranged) so as soon as I get voice back after flu will record whole book and new poems too. My record with Grove is censored and I'm mad and I got embarrassed, by my own tone because where I really rescued tearful seriousness in that particular reading was in parts two and three (which continued upward in beauty and non-goofing intensity tears)—and I asked Grove to print those parts on record—which advice ignored—so far as I think it's all a goof that record—they missed the big meat, those vultures. However it don't really matter. Besides I put out good record in time, or not, but will. So disgusted I sold my copy of record here for 800 francs to eat with (less than $2 to someone who was going to England). Bookstore friend of Ferlinghetti here has big window display of fifty copies of my book[11] and sells a few a week so I get small income from that.

What number best seller are you nowadays? How dreamy that all is. Thank god. Neal wants $5000 or has he not written? We were talking about your money, our own fantasies and demands, but nothing we grub for will match Neal's final Great Demand for fifty or ten thous for the hosses. Whatcha gonna do? I should write him a letter. I wonder what he's thinking. When *Howl* trial was over there was a front page banner headline all across page of *SF Chronicle* announcing results—wonder what he thought—and did he see you on TV?

[...]

---

[11] The Mistral Bookshop was owned by George Whitman, an old friend of Lawrence Ferlinghetti.

I haven't ever received a copy of *Road*, if you ever get time to take necessary steps. Tell Viking there's not one copy on sale in Paris and they could make a fortune here too. In English—several hundred copies anyway. Shortage I guess.

It was I suggested to Ferl several months ago for the 10th time that he reread your blues for City Lights, may I add. I also told him to read Bill's book for a short printable selected Burroughs—perhaps *Word*. However, whether it was my suggestion that prompted him or no, when he contacts you about your book (presumably I guess he'll do something) remind him to read Bill's and get it to him after Grove is done, I think he might do it. That way some Burroughs in U.S. I looking at your recent letters for unfinished business. (Never got Peter's Venice letter).

My father and brother write you seemed confused and nowhere on TV, were you high? I supposed they missed the mad drama, dream.

I got mad long Rimbaud letter from boy in Bordentown Reformatory.[12] I wrote mad Rimbaud letter to [Rosalind] Constable at time saying Luce should send me (and you) (and Peter and Greg) on secret trip Russia. She said she passed letter along, who knows? And wished us well, was sad, in our greatness. I wrote Gary. Whalen in N.W.

> Love,
> Tears and Kisses
> Allen

Nov. 15: Olympia rejected Bill's book but will still try change their mind and might. *Partisan* sent me $12 for a poem and I sent them three Corsos. We could get free ads and advertise to get $ to publish Bill ourselves or by subscription if worst comes.

Jack Kerouac [Orlando, Florida] to Allen Ginsberg [Paris, France]

November 30, 1957

Dear Allen:

Your poem very beautiful, especially "eyes of Ma Rainey dying in an ambulance." (why don't you spell it "aumbulance" which would mean aum-vehicle . . .) . . . well, and Greg's "sweetlys in sun-arch" indeed amazing . . . I'm very drunk as I write this, forgive, I too have a thousand new poems but I'm

---

[12] This is a reference to the poet Ray Bremser, who was in this New Jersey jail at the time.

tired and too tired to send you some . . . later. I'm going to NY in three weeks to appear twice a night at Village Vanguard nightclub to read my prose, starting with *Road* and later I'll stick in *Visions* and *Pomes* . . . at plenty money a week I'll do it and if this doesn't make me a drunk, nothing ever will . . . actually I look skeptically towards this adventure but the money is necessary. Holly[wood] ain't buying my book probably at all, Brando is a shit, doesn't answer letter from greatest writer in America and he's only a piddling king's clown of the stage, I bugged, so your $225 I'll send as soon as I can probably December or January when I get royalties, don't worry, and it'll be your return fare security anyway. Like you paid my way over to the other shore, I'll pay your way back. Without movie sales I really only have not much more than *T & C* [*The Town and the City*] loot, which is a shame. You guys were all het up about nothing. I be bhikku till day I die. But I hope to meet producers et al as nightclub performer and I will come on like a cool SOUND MUSICIAN like Miles Davis and not drink too much I hope. I'll be living at Henri Cru's pad which is 307 West 113th St. in three weeks. [Paul] Carroll at *Chicago Review* askt me send him stuff, I sent "Lucien Midnight" poems (new ones you didn't see, wrote em last night in fact) and other poems. Jay Laughlin is going to do a selected edition of *Visions of Neal*, maybe one hundred pages, of best prose, in fancy $7.50 thin volume private edition, he says to begin with, is very nice and polite in letters and sent me little brochure of his really most excellent poems. He's very good poet. I am afraid of this coming New York trip but I was getting fat and bored down here. I'll probably end up in the Bowery this trip but as Esperanza used to say I DUNT CARE. No, Gregory, I won't go cry on Lucien's floor, Lucien makes me laugh happily. Lucien is my brother. I'll this time find Laff and take him under my tutelage when he hits town. With loot from Vanguard I'll buy oils and paint more holy pictures of Virgin Mary my mother. and your mother, mother. I am vast endless nakedheaded giant cloud making no sense even to members of the nut ward, what a fate for a simple footballplayer! I got a nutward letter from a certain B. Zemble and am sending him back a spontaneous poem so crazy Gregory would flip over it, in which I say "science statement is million years over owned by pens as treacherous as Aga Arnold of Good Day Biddy Father Uptown—see? I'm a fool! I love reverse! I got hidden Moo-Flutes in my horn cow. I did it dad because I dood it money—I am Governor President!"—etc. and it ends with "My conscience is all snow. In fact my conscience is coldspot."

In other words I have discovered Gregory's secret because I'm so smart and crazy. But I don't care. I'm rather good novelist now, my in-progress work is *The Dharma Bums* about Gary [Snyder] and 1955 and 56 in Berkeley and Mill Valley and is really bettern *On the Road*, if I can only stay sober enuf to finish it now that I know I'm going to make big fool of myself with evil Gilbert Millsteins in New Yoik. If I can swing the sale of *Road* to movies, on this jaunt, Brando may come dig me in nightclub, I'll make a trust fund and disappear on Zen Lunacy Road and you can all join me. That's my purpose in this blear deed. "All of Medieval Europe in a Shakespeare inch," I wrote last night, where says: "Poor perdu! thin helm!" Wow. Also I'm reading *Don Quixote* which is probably most sublime work of any man ever lived, thank God for Spain! All living creatures are *Don Quixote* of course, since living is illusion. Ho ho ho ho ho ho ho ho ho ho ho ho ha ha aha ah woeieield.!"k3738#%#"($& So I'll send your money soon, All, don't worry, *Alle, ubers ober* and did you get the letter I sent you to mail to Burroughs a month ago? Well, I'll write later. I am bugged and sad and mad and writing a great novel, *The Dharma Bums*, wow, wait'll they read that one! How great Gary is in it, and Whalen . . . you'll see. Meanwhile all I gotta say is: We're all going to die. Neal don't write. Neal great. Neal says "Ha! I shall now succumb to victory" as he plays chess with me, satirizing where I'd said to him I let him win chess games because I a bodhisattva . . . I wrote great play about Neal, too, which was mentioned in *Herald Trib* and now four producers reading it, but it's woefully short, but that's all right you sweet daddies please pray that I can join you in Paris in April because I want to embrace you, poor perdus. Well, this is John the Roi saying, Don't step on the candy gal.

  Joh Perdu

Allen Ginsberg [Paris, France] to Jack Kerouac [New York, New York]

December 5, 1957

Dear Jack:

  Got high on junk last night and thought of you, said to myself we must— now we are famous—not get drawn apart by varying fames or worlds but get closer in unfamous solitudes brothers, I am just adding this as extra to Petey's letter so do not expand but will write big letter I thought about your writings, again. Yes Brando must be a shit it's too long he's not got in touch ever with us anyway and makes bad movies now a pitiful karma. Ferlinghetti sent me $100 yesterday so we eat I paid Gregory's 20 dollar back rent and he's moved in with us temporarily and we bought Genet and Apollinaire dirty book and a paper of junk and a matchbox of bad kief and a huge quart expensive bottle of perpetual maggi seasoning-soy sauce. Ah, that Village Vanguard sounds maybe blear, they won't listen to you, I wish we were there to raise spirits of audience and stir them up as you did for us in SF, but maybe it will be alright—you should do it like a saint to talk to them even if humiliating, maybe it will be but a ball though—good luck and don't drink too much and be not unhappy with NYC. It would be a beauty to see, you sound lonely facing NY, I wish we were there comrades in that madness. No rush about $224 now, Grove Press will publish seventeen page Mexican "Xbalba" poem and pay me this month probably, and I still got $35 from Feldman-Citadel Beat Generation anthology (I guess you know all about) (for reprint *Howl*) and also more money coming in from City Lights—you realize by miracle I've got (in addition to two hundred free copies) so far 200 dollars from them? You'll make a little loot like that for *Blues* if they print. So send the money when you have it I have not been at all bugged or anything (you mention it often I thought you thought I was impatient) and had not expected it till after New Years. News of *Visions of Neal* is great, that is the great prose marvel, what will they select and why only one hundred pages? Perhaps later hope for Burroughs in same way. Olympia rejected manuscript. City Lites eager to see Burroughs also. Don Allen taking too long. Bill writes he's expanding into huge formal structure accidentally—the present manu-script will have to be fitted into the cracks of the new leviathan conception— hundreds of pages of that done already he says—and will be in Paris after New Year. *Partisan Review* took two poems by Gregory now after big mad letter from us—should get them to pre-publish passages from *Visions of Neal* before ND [New Directions] comes out with it. They also took two poems of Lever-tov—the plague is on (as we wrote them). Letter from Holmes he comes here Xmas. And Parkinson unseen yet in town yestidy. Yestiddy. Peter and Gregory paint a lot, Peter strange red angels in red trees, Gregory make this week spar-kly abstracts on our wall on canvas-paper. I shy, so don't dare touch brush—so also same reason write so little, but I'm getting over it I think, I hope, I feel ashamed write so poor and little now. Doleful. I feel ashamed as a pear. Is G. Millstein evil except that he's full of NY? His review brought tears. Van Doren you remember always hung on *Don Q.*, and I hung on last pages when he "wakes" up. I mailed your letter to Burroughs, he not written you? I don't think I come home yet awhile but stay on here six months in Paris and then perhaps with you and Bill in spring journey eastward—first I want Moscow if can, after circumnavigate globe. I want to have a big vision before I return in U.S. Come Paris soon if you can honey. I thought last nite you only write well (aside from the prose) about those you love imaginarily—Bill, Lucien, Neal, Huncke, your father—I mean those who are your fathers, who hit you in the nose and not about us who kiss your feet (me and Peter for now)—what you do with Phil and Gary—with big sad depth 3-D details about them and not rush thru incidents too fast as in *Desolation*. Perhaps you not paint me Peter in detail then for fear of offending us (with what you see)—but I rather be writ in tragical detail than kist in passing as giddy kid. But it's exhausting to write. Beautiful young backstreet Rue Huchette bar here with runaway high school existential boys seventeen and their fifteen year old girlfriends nobody got 40 francs for a glass of wine, we took Ansen there, to look at boys with shoulder long hair and D'Artagnan beards. Peter be in NYC in a month or so we hope and will see you in Vanguard with Laff maybe. Love, stay with us, I repeating in answer I felt your letters said that too.

       Allen

Jack Kerouac [Orlando, Florida] to Allen Ginsberg, Peter Orlovsky, and Gregory Corso [Paris, France]

December 10, 1957

Dear Allen and Peter and Gregory:

Just got your wonderful letters today and haven't even had time to re-read and digest them but I want to leap up and answer right away with blah blah blahs . . . Wanta tell you, I just finished writing my shining new novel *The Dharma Bums* all about Gary [Snyder], the real woodsy vision of Gary, not surrealistic romantic vision, my own puremind trueself Ti Jean Lowell woods vision of Gary, not what you guys will like particularly, actually, tho there's a lot of Zen Lunacy throughout and what's best: all the tremendous details and poems and outcries of *The Dharma Bums* at last gathered together in a rushing narrative on a one hundred foot scroll. So I wrote Cowley and told him, and if Cowley don't want publish it, someone else will, as it's like *On the Road*, real muscular prose. But when *Subterraneans* comes out February I'll be so proud that a real sweet poem of mine is finally out, and the next drive is for: *Doctor Sax*. On *Subterraneans* manuscript I labored days undoing the wreckage of Don Allen's commas and dumb changes . . . so it's now as original, shiny, rhythmic, bespeaking future literatures by great young kids. May I say, Peter's poems about red footprint in snow is real great poetry, I now pronounce Peter Orlovsky a great American Surrealistic Poet of the First Magnitude. Peter, I hope you do come back to New York within a month and as I say I'll be at Henri Cru's but be SURE NOT TO COME THERE! Henri has laid down a strict law with me that I can stay there PROVIDING none of my friends call, so just telephone me there, and we'll make our meets wherever we want, Fugazzy's, Helen Elliott's, Joyce's, anywhere, in fact Peter why don't you take up with Joyce Glassman at her new address 338 E. 13, where she has full huge pad with big kitchen and all where you can stay because I want to make it with Helen W[eaver]. I just wrote big letter to Laff telling him I'll see him. Yes, Al, I know reading will be fiasco-ish but I think I'll make them vibrate just so's I can be held over an extra two weeks and send you your money and also set some aside for my own triumphal visit to Paris (bleak, meet on the street) in March where I'll rush up and find Burroughs, Ginsberg, Corso, Orlovsky, Ansen and Cocteau all in one bed of rocks I was going to say Roses, I mean all in one stew, I mean all at one time, besides Gallimard has just bought *On the Road* and advanced me francs and it will be published in French in Paris 1958 so now Genet and I have same publisher. Frankly, last two months, I haven't been interested in anything but peace. You know what Christ said when he entered a house "I bring you my peace," or, leaving, "I leave you my peace." That is the greatest kick of all. Just sit all day doing nothing, enjoying cats and flowers and birds. My swift finger in writing poetry is swiftfinger but Gregory you're right, beauty is slow, but you see, if you don't speak now your own blurt way you may forever hold your tongue, this was Shakespeare's law, how do you think he wrote so fast and so much and so sublime? The hawthorn sleet of Lear fool and the dancing fool and Edgar in the moor, was all fast wild thoughts. O, I've pissed more water as a sailor of the several seas than sallow's aphorism will allow, and had I written slowly and deliberately, might you call me Sallow then. Aphoristic Lionel Trilling deliberating like Henry James over his imaginary sentence structures. Poetry is Ode to the West Wind! ? Wake Up Poetry is Shakespeare and nobody but Shakespeare and don't Pound me no Tolstoy me broach me no rejoinder! Shakespeare is a vast continent, Shelley is a village. Why do you insist, Gregory, on being DIFFERENT and choosing unlikely Shelley for your hero, why do you be afraid of being like everybody else and admitting the Supreme Greatness of Bard Will Shakespeare? How, ask Burroughs about Shakespeare, he spent years with the Immortal Bard on his lap . . . Burroughs in fact bespeaks himself like Shakespeare. Listen to Burroughs talk. Don't be fooled by Mighty Burroughs. Gregory, you are about to come in contact with the greatest writer alive in the world today, William Seward Burroughs, who also says that Shakespeare is the end. Apollinaire is a veritable cow's turd in a meadow in the continent of Shakespeare. The greatest French poet is Rabelais. The greatest Russian poet is Dostoevsky. The greatest Italian poet is Corso. The greatest German poet is probably Spengler for all I goddam know. The greatest Spanish poet is of course Cervantes. The greatest American poet is Kerouac. The greatest Israeli poet is Ginsberg. The greatest Eskimo poet is Lord Bleaky Igloogloo. The greatest Burroughsian poet is World. Well, boys, I'll be seeing you in March in Paris and don't flog your dummies, and save some girls for me, and some harry, and don't upset the tables, and don't worry, I don't give a shit what I saw, when I sawyeouek what I sawk woue and that's that. I'm drunk. You can see I'm writing this letter drunk. Okay. Tell Alan Ansen to go to that queer bar on the same street as Cafe Napoleon about five blocks down where they all sit around listening to classical jukebox sipping coffee and vermouth, I went there with Irish motorcyclist from Dublin. Or is Ansen yearning for long haired youths from nature boy caves? Poor Ansen? Bless his eyes, kiss his eyes for me! Hello Ansen! Hello Burroughs! Hello out there you mothers! How are you? Hello Allen! Eyes of Ma Rainey dying in an ambulance! There are sweetlies in sun-arc! the little purple women monsters are straddling the sun! The black cowboy! The cottage without bacon! Hello Peter Brother, how are you son, kiss the ground you walk on! Hello all you Franciscans! Hello out there! have another cognac! Hello you miserables . . . end of magnificent message, end of blah hoard, see you all in Paradise Paris in March when we'll light the torch of saint.

Allen, you know why I said I was greatest American poet and you greatest Israeli poet? Because you didn't pick up on Americana till you read *Visions of Neal*, before that you were big Burroughsian putter-downer of Americana. Remember Hal Chase and the Wolfeans and the Dark Priests? You suddenly saw Americana of Neal and all, and picked up on it, and made a killing on it, but your heart's in the mountains, O Tribe of the Mountains, the Mountains of Judea! Am I not right? You KNOW I'M RIGHT. Burroughs' own Americana is effortless, it's Brad coming on the red leather seat, so he is intrinsically Americana, like me (with teenage poems to Americana) but you only got in the act later. This is pure vision of Ginsberg's poetry history. Because you are not an American, you are a Magian man, and belong to the yearning new culture of the 21st century, which will be Magian, Orthodoxy, Cavern-feeling . . . s'why old tired Western Franciscan monks of Italy can't convince you, because you are really an Arab and above all an Aramean Russian Motherlander. Jews and Arabs are Semites, and Jews and Arabs and Russians are all Orthodox in the deepest sense. If you want further information, mail 25¢ for booklet.

[. . .]

Well this was a strange letter but it's all true. . . . When I come to Paris in March and get drunk and pass out you may all stomp me to death in the gutters of St. Danis and I will rise going Hm he h eee hee hee he ha ha and be Quasimodo and run down the bloody flowery streets of sacred heart and tear little girls apart from limb to limb, my dear, and then you'll have to trap me on top of old Smoky with Lucien and we'll dump molten buckets of Wilson Rye Whiskey on your beholden heads and crown you with garland gain . . . see?

Jack Kerouac [New York, New York] to
Allen Ginsberg [Paris, France]

December 28, 1957

Dear Allen . . . Dear Alleyboo:

I'm in Joyce's kitchen and brooding at the table suddenly sad (as she's cooking hamburg supper) "I wish Allen was here" and she said "That's right, we have
enuf meat for another hamburger."

Mad pad in Porto Rico 13th Street near Avenue A . . . where I'm hiding out,
this afternoon I finally told everybody I was thru with publicity for rest of my
life. I see where Rexroth says I am an "insignificant Tom Wolfe" (can he really
say that bout *Sax*?) Everybody attacking us like mad, Herbert Gold, etc. etc.
you and me now equally being attacked. My mother says every knock is a boost.
I saw your sweet sweet cousin Joel [Gaidemak] the other night, he gave me
bottle vitamin pills, your father wrote, wants me come out Paterson "talk." O
talk talk, I've talked to 1,500 people in past week. I read fine. Lucien said Yes, I
read fine. Lucien sad, admires my sticking it out, dear Lucien slept on my bathroom floor on two day binge. Wish you were here. Broke up with Joyce because I wanted to try big sexy brunettes then suddenly saw evil of world and
realized Joyce was my angel sister and came back to her. Xmas Eve read my
prayer to drunken nightclub, everybody listen. Lamantia was here and had mad
days with him walking five miles down Broadway yelling about God and ecstasy, he rushed into confession and rushed out, he flew off to Frisco, back
soon, he got in big publicity interviews with me and was full of sacred elo-
quence. Great new poet: Howard Hart, a sheer Peter, a Catholic, Lamantia's
buddy. I will write big novel about past week so you can dig the whole scene
entire and to warn you about something. You'll see. . . . Excuse my last letter,
paranoia lapse I guess, I am funny kind of hungry fool. I hunger for final ultimate friendship with no hassles, like with Neal early days, not for part time
sneer friendships like with Gregory. You have never sneered at me but I have
sneered at you. Now why? I tell you this is the beginning of something great,
let's do it, put it down, put down publicity, go underground for final great
maybe caves of gold. with Gary and Pete. and Laff. and Bill. And if Greg wants.
I say, I say, fuck the monster. No more poetry for poetry sake, either, like word
slinging, but actual me-to-you and you-to-me hey-listen hey-say saying like
Neal Joan Anderson [letter] (re that, I see from Robert Stock article that Gerd
Stern is now regarded as an SF poet so I figure, yes, he did steal Joan Anderson, let's get it back for sure now.) Well, actually, I won't do anything, probably

never see you again, don't know what I'll do, I just dig peace. You come see me in my cave. Wish I was talking to you on transatlantic cable. You're right, you're right, you're forever forever right forever forever you're right. Goodbye. Go d be w ye. Las ombras vengadora DO WHAT YOU WANT DON'T LISTEN TO ME

     Jack

1958

Allen Ginsberg [Paris, France] to
Jack Kerouac [Orlando, Florida]

9 Rue Git Le Coeur Paris 6
Jan 4, 57 [*sic*: 1958]

Dear Jack:

Don't yell at me so drunk and wicked as in first aerogram from Fla., it is actually very upsetting, I don't know how to answer—teach gentler. My writing is all fucked up it's true, I write too little and am continually rusty at the black piano instead of blowing and ecstatic. Lately only time I can write well in fact is on junk (a shuddery dream)—tho I have great ideas. Latest is ten pages of political poetry (like Blake's French Revolution) (Then Necker got up his robes full of the shrieking of golden babes and his voice shook the dank walls of the cavernous Louvre crying "Guillotine!" sample Blake type). Blake fits Whitman like a glove to apply to present day epic of Fall of America. [. . .]

We saw Sterling Lord, he took us all three to supper with his friends and kindly sat talking to us most of time, we read him Gregory's new mad poem about SF—which he wrote per request of *Esquire*. "I looked at Alcatraz clutching my Pan's foot with vivid hoard of Dannemora O stocky Alcatraz weeping on Neptune's table and saw Death seated like a huge black stove." He's putting on his clothes now Sun nite, going with borrowed 10 mil franc note with foggy upstairs hipster by train to be a salesman in Germany—been sleeping in sleep bags on our floor last months—try to sell drawings of ghouls or Encyclopedia Britannica to soldiers in Frankfurt just decided to leave today try his fortune and see Germany. Told me to send you enclosed girl name Joy who's waiting for you he's been balling her but tired she lives in Paris and is Indonesian simple art model mostly homey type girl he say you can have her, make up for [Alene] Lee and Paris goil.

Anyway *Esquire* wired us both promising $35 on delivery for SF poems, he wrote one and I sent "Green Auto" fixed up but still dirty and "Over Kansas", they won't take them, but they sent me money, the $35—maybe they'll print a poem too who knows.

[. . .]

Yes, no more poesy for poesy sake—though I have not yet as you and Greg gone thru a purely maniac unrevised phase of writing and still have to loosen me up—as you can see the above tho imageful is rather harsh and unmellow and too directed—tho I'd like to write a monstrous and golden political or historical poem about the fall of America, even talking about [John Foster]

Dulles[1]—if poetry can be made of ashcans why not newspaper headlines and politics? Talk about Dulles the way Blake talks about the kings of France shuddering icy chill runs down their arms to their sweating scepters. But I write so little painfully and revise and I can't get settled down to free expression and have nightmares about ever holding my piece. It's not that I don't really agree with you about method of writing—I don't have your football energy for scrawling endlessly on pages. I am nervous and fretful and have to force myself to sit down—at least lately—other seasons it's been more natural. I guess all this publicity is bad. Well like I say I prophecy a natural obscurity will befall me anyway and take that problem out of my hands. Fuck this bullshit. And Bill is blowing in Tangiers has several hundred more pages, I sent some to *Chi Review*. Get on Don Allen's ass and find out what's up—he's been silent on it for months. Say Hello Lucien and best for New Years to everybody's families. I'm triste it's raining out today in Paris and there's an empty room down the hall. Maybe I'll go to London this month, I had sad exultant dream, parapets of England and couldn't get in, I had no pounds or something to change—same dream as when I dreamt two years ago of going to Europe. Next year I guess will be sad dreams of exultant entry to India on backs of elephants. Do write me news and analysis of NY monster scenery—particularly what Lu says of it all. I wrote him awhile back. All I think it's strangely up to us to save U.S.—who else—or what else to do next? Quixote wakes in the end last five pages.

    Love,

        Allen

Write me back about money so I'll know.

Jack Kerouac [Orlando, Florida] to Allen Ginsberg [Paris, France]

January 8, 1958

Dear Allen:

My royalty check comes in February, I send you money then in one lump. Sterling tells me you and Gregory wonder about my riches . . . didn't he tell you I'm only going to get about $4500 from all that *ROAD* noise? No movie sale, of course, and little dribbles from everywhere. With that loot I gonna make down payment on a cottage for me and my mother, my later old age Emily cottage of haikus, way out on Long Island, furthern Lafcadio Northport. Just sent Bur-

[1] John Foster Dulles was the U.S. secretary of state under President Dwight D. Eisenhower.

roughs manuscript (the one he sent me about queer fuzz who calls counterman by first name and another about Joseliot) to Ferlinghetti, who askt, giving Ferling Don Allen's home address so's to get all of *Naked Lunch.*—Ferling doesn't believe *Mexico City Blues* is poetry because I say so in it . . . In *Chicago Review* I will be lead poem (quivering meat conception) and lead note on what is SF poetry, so there. I told Ferling off about this. Ferling thinks like Gregory that I wrote prose (as I state myself) LINES DONT MAKE A POET, . . . Poetry is poetry, the longer the line the better when it comes finally to two page Cassady sentences hooray. Big attack against me in *Nation* saying I a fool boy poet and Richard Wilbur a heroic man poet. Do guys like [Richard] Wilbur and [Herb] Gold stay up nights hoping we'll hurl critical attacks at them? Geez. Everybody down on me for reading my heart out in Village Vanguard careless of my appearance, my "poise," etc., read like Zen lunatic saint, like you said to do, would have anyway but you gave me confidence ahead of time. Steve Allen will make album with me, just wrote me. Your cousin Joel was there, sweet, your father wrote me from Paterson. I had wildest time of all time. Met great new cat Zev Putterman, from Israel, play director. Saw Leo Garen again (your brother, he's like) . . . Got heeazi on your Paris kick but straight with Allen Eager. Had three girls in my bed one night. Me and Philip L. [Lamantia] orgied one together. Philip really wailing these days, got in the papers with me, *NY Post*, made big Marian nervous speeches to Mike Wallace tape. Tryna think of all thousands of details you'd like. I should write novel about it all. I read last part of *Howl* in the club, it's mentioned in newspaper. I also read "Arnold" the few lines I could remember and got big yoks, of course I repeated that it was Corso's, twice . . . I even read one of Steve Allen's sensitive lil poems . . . I even read Dave Tercerero's confession . . . (Esperanza's old husband) . . . The Negro dishwasher said "Nothin I like bettern go to bed with two quarts of whiskey and hear you read to me" and Lee Konitz said I blew music, he could hear music. At Brata Gallery I read your latest Mother elegy poem [*Kaddish*] and Gregory's "Concourse Didils" and use use use use to big audience of pale faced sober shits, at Philip's and Howard Hart's request, but later, after I left, a wino stumbled in from the Bowery Street and got everybody drunk and the reading was big success I hear (at same moment I was reading in club to big opening night audience and being photoed as I read and sneered at and thunderous applause and big swigs and long talks with hepcats in back). One young hepcat from Denver said everybody was going to start imitating Neal. In fact you shoulda been there, for all the handsome teenage boys came up to talk to me (hundreds). Trying to sleep days, my floor was covered with sleepers: musicians, editors of small mags, girls, junkies, it was a spectacle. Robert Frank is going to be our boy: Robert Frank is greatest photographer on scene, has already shot an experimental movie on Cape Cod, with free nutty actors who only want wine, and is going to make a movie with me in May in New York wherein I will get my experience for later in the year when you come back we will begin work on our first great movie. He says it only costs about $200 to make a movie but we'll have sound too; he will get money from big Meyer Schapiro foundations. I already have an idea for a great movie about Lafcadio and Peter as brothers, Frank's wife their sister, and you the father, or and you the father with your evil brother Uncle Willie Burroughs (incest). This Frank is no bullshit a future Rossellini but refuses to write own movies, wants me to. I told him of our old dreams and plans. With Bill back in New York we could really in 1958 do Burroughs on Earth. Gregory knows Alfred Leslie, don't he, and Miles Forst, they were in movie, Leslie technician, wildhaired subterraneans running off their holy movies against pockmarked walls of Bowery lofts is the scene. Then all rush down to Fivespot . . . poor, crazy, future moguls of Hollywood like D.W. Griffiths actually. I have discovered cat to play Neal in *On the Road*, Kelly Reynolds, Irish nervous Neal with blue eyes and imperious Neal look in profile and nervous Neal of 1948 . . . (he's an actor, MCA) . . . Got big letter from Gary Snyder shuffling around the world on a ship, India to Italy, etc.* (*and *back* to India). Got big letter from [Elbert] Lenrow who told me [Archibald] MacLeish at Harvard praising my book. Rexroth however is down on me, called me an "insignificant Tom Wolfe" on KPFA, because, why? I'll write and explain to him I disassociated myself from his sphere of influence because I DON'T WANT NOTHIN TO DO WITH POLITICS especially leftist west coast future blood in the street malevolence (there will be a revolution in California, it is seething with incredible hatred, led by bloodthirsty poets like "Jean McLean" and Rexroth keeps yapping about the international brigade etc.). I don't like it, I believe in Buddha kindness and nothing else, I believe in Heaven, in Angels, I eschew all Marxism and allied horseshit and psychoanalysis, an offshoot therefrom . . . beware of California.

Dear Buddy Gregory . . . Thank you for beautiful Buddha postcard, dig the monks, the one young monk so cool and free that he can stand in the street and do nothing but gaze at his reflection in streetpuddle . . . I dig you sending me that. I announced you in NY, I hope somebody heard, well *Gasoline* is coming out so you're in . . . I see now, tho, that fame makes you stop writing, why should a man stop and sketch a railyard when he has to make a publicity appointment? So I am quitting all publicity appointments from now on, including *Life* and all that shit. If they want my picture they have to chase me down the street. Big new years eve party. Jay Landesman (this for Allen too) will pay big money for poetry readings at the Crystal Palace in St. Louis. You and Allen can actually make a big living now just touring the country and reading. Good for both of you, but I read no more. I get too drunk. I even burst into the New School, as asked, a read to bunch of seminar squares. Saw Alene [Lee], who is very mean now. She lives at 5 Jones. Saw [Stanley] Gould who is great guy. See Anton [Rosenberg] all the time. I wore crucifix around my neck, stuck in shirt, while reading in club. Beware of fame, poems will become *non sequitur*. I am worried about myself now, I feel that poems aren't as important as writing a letter to my publishers, that's bad. Allen, when is Peter coming back? It was humanly impossible for me to go see Laff. Is Bill now with you in Paris? give me news of Bill, and Ansen. Has Holmes come to see you. What an enormous number . . . and to think that this is going on in all directions of the universe, this multiplicity of Angels which was all once ONE ANGEL.

   Write, here, Florida. Love
   Yes, love
     Jack

P.S. Big article about Zen in new *Mademoiselle* quotes from *Howl*.

Allen Ginsberg [Paris, France] to Jack Kerouac [n.p., Orlando, Florida?]

Jan 11, 1957 [*sic*: 1958]
9 Rue Git Le Coeur
Paris 6, France

Dear Jack:

 Wrote you to NYC about five days ago and received your aerogram today, I guess you've not yet received my letter, 'twas long, full of instructions about nonexistent money and gloomy manuscripts. Well February's fine by me for money, I'm going to spread out use of it for months anyway, it's the last assets I got for the moment (barring happy fortune of *Esquire* publishing "Green Auto" which is Tank Dieu doubtful anyway). However I'm broke now and don't have enough money to get through this month, the grocer ask't me today when I pay my four day old small milk and eggs bill. I need at least 20 or $25 to see me through the end of the month—please send that airmail fast if it's at all possible—I really be starving otherwise. I've used all other dribbles of ready cash, hawked my book and *Evergreens* in various bookstores, spent my Xmas $15 family money sent me and am down to stamp money for this and one last lugubrious letter to Bill saying when's he arriving and send me some Tangerian Francs if he has any. So send me now please enough to get thru till February— don't need much, just food money—I had thought you were sending loot January and getting royalties January as of letter some months back and so your new arrangements catch me short. Don't be mad by this dunning letter.

Bill no write, I don't know what he'll do, he's supposed to show up this month, I reserved a rare cheap hard-to-get room for him in this great hotel—only $25 a month—and wrote him last week that everything was clear, but silence from Tangiers. Maybe he's incestuously miffed, Peter still being here waiting for government to ship him home. He'll probably show up February.

Government called Peter last nite to say they would ship him home this coming week—probably the 17th he leaves and be in NY before end of the month. Too bad you didn't have his two poems to read in Village they would have been the final naive bug of all dark-suited Manhattan. He'll send them soon. We got letter from Laf, everything's mad at cottage but everybody still hanging on waiting for him to swoop down angelic on wings across oceans and save everybody there. His long lost father even showed up home and had great manly talk with Lafcadio who liked him.

Oh, Ferlinghetti! I don't know what to do, I'll write him another letter. He resists other people's advice tho, would never take my word on Gary [Snyder] and Phil [Whalen] and I suspect is suspicious about Burroughs too. Well, we'll keep trying. He hasn't written me about your book tho McClure has, thought it was greatest long poem since *Paradise Lost*—he read it thru. Sooner or later.

As related in last letter: What's with Don Allen's reaction to *Interzone*? Have him send me *Queer* and *Yage* to try publish first thru Olympia which won't publish *Interzone* but wants to see *Queer* and *Yage*, that's a beginning anyway. And fine he should send *Interzone* complete to Ferlinghetti.

I saw the Gold piece, not the later Wilbur, and many others, got all worked up one day on T and almost wrote huge manifesto of nonsense but it's all transient and illusory aftereffects of writing and not writing itself, so decided to shut up. Maybe someday later if I write something by divine accident which applies—but these people are filled with the worst bullshit and nonsense, it's almost unbelievable how unhip and what bad artists they are. It's all off the point. No pay care what people saying; important thing about it all (the publicity) that we'd have chance to sow our dreams in market and lots of souls will read and see without doubt—those who have doubts have doubts what can you do? Undoubt them and the whole civilization in one year?—how many literary sputniks necessary—we just keep sending up one a year. . . . Read all your lovely gossip of Lamantia (he writing too?) and Gary and various unknown Garens[2] and [Lloyd] Reynolds and [Howard] Harts I guess I'll have ball when I get back.

I'm trying to go to England February, stay free with [Thomas] Parkinson and

[2] Garens was Ginsberg's nickname for Snyder.

meet some English hipsters there, see fogs and make BBC paid reading (says Parkinson but I won't censor no more so doubt it)—I had dreams of London last week. Gregory still in Frankfort, flipped he writes in front of Army red tape on selling encyclopedias and is only visiting museums and conning poetic Germans, maybe be back soon. I know [Al] Leslie and [Miles] Forst. [Chris] Mac-Claine and SF bullshit will die a natural death and Rexroth's cornier remarks also, so no need replying there any more than Gold, etc. Let works speak, they speak. I had long dry period chasing editors in NY and slowly coming out. No Holmes yet. Send loot.

     Love All

      Allen

You can transmit loot easiest by personal check. If no one around has checks, send cash, my father does, it arrives.

Jack Kerouac [Orlando, Florida] to Allen Ginsberg [Paris, France]

January 16, 1958

Dear Allen:

Alas, you'd a got this money three days earlier but for an ankle that prevented me from walking to the bank, some kind of swollen rheumatism, and no one to drive me. I hope now you'll have a great time, next three months. Please don't blow your substance on fools and parasites, but try to enjoy Paris nice now. Take long walks with Bill. I just got paid by Vanguard nightclub thus this loot. Germany advance just came in, this is what I'm sending. I will be in Paris this summer unless Hollywood calls me to go work on the script if they take the book which looks extremely likely now, I just got big letter from producer Jerry Wald at 20th Century, he wants to make big melodramatic changes in format but his ideas aren't too bad and besides I want to get rich so I can make my own movies with Robert Frank later. *BMR* [*Black Mountain Review*] is out with Bill's *Yage* in it, looks great. Your "America", what is this kind of addition to America you pasted on? . . . Anyway I only told Hollywood one rule: no brutality in my movie. I really told them sumptin. "The secret of the beat generation, you wouldn't kill anybody even if you were ordered to (by a commander or sumptin.)" I know I wouldn't. Jerry Wald seems to see *On the Road* like a kind of Wild Ones brutal bit. But it ain't as bad as I make it sound. I want to dig Hollywood (as scenarist, and sitting next to directors on set) so I can write big final Hollywood novel of all time. Otherwise, if things go slow, I will be in Paris this summer. Is Bill with you yet? Is Peter really coming NY? Did Grego run away to Frankfurt because of those bad checks? I'm going to order *Gasoline* from Ferling and read it. This is big year of Zen on Madison Avenue, Alan Watts the big hero (the wisdom of insecurity, his new book, big hit among executives of security) . . . so we also come in now . . . but in my *Dharma Bums* new novel I do make the distinction between "Zen" and original Mahayana Buddhism. Well, many things to say and do, write me when you can, please notify me if you got money okay, and I write back big letters answering all your questions (ask some, I probably answer em all)

Jean Louis

Jack Kerouac [Orlando, Florida] to Allen Ginsberg [Paris, France]

January 21, 1958

Dear Allen:

Your writing is not fucked up, never was, I mean technically, technically you're probably the best writer in the world . . . it's only your depressing ideas, when I feel happy and pure from weeks of studying sutras and praying suddenly I open one of your letters (sometimes) and feel a nameless depression, as tho black scum over my lucid bowl. Well you know you ARE a black blob so sorrow . . . but no, don't forget I love you, but I'm afraid of you now, and for you, such depression. Why, for instance, well it's none of my business, but why don't you ignore war, ignore politics, ignore samsara injust fuckups, they're endless . . . why is Chiang Kai Shek worse than Mao? and why shouldn't a saint walk thru the white house someday? Why are you so depressed, angel? so what, rhinestone autos from Detroit, there are rhinestone buyers and blueberry spies. Chaplin was just as bugged with "America" as U.S. with him, a double hatred . . . and when the universe disappears no movie can stick in God's throat because God is nothing (thank God, go ahead, thank God for that!) Money is money, why shriek at money (especially now that I'm going to be rich.) Allen, cool it. Rid thee of thy wrath, go lamby, isn't it a better thing to do in eternity to leave everybody alone good and evil alike and just pile along glad? Aha, our old 1946 argument.

Just got this note from Ferlinghetti: "Thanx for sending Burroughs sample. Would like to read more and will write Don Allen for it tho I doubt there will be much left for me by the time Grove and ND are thru wid it . . . Where is Allen? no word."

Marlon Brando doesn't want me or Sterling to sell *Road* without giving him a chance to bid, that's the news on movie.

In two weeks I going to NY put down payment on a house and be near city for all this sixnix. Way out in L.I. [Long Island], like fifty miles or more. Lucien go with me drive around . . . looks like I'll be able to go to Paris see you and Bill this summer, if movie is sold and I have my trust fund established, we can all travel on that money, free money (interest). I'd like to repay Bill a little for his many kindnesses in the past including that last importuning steak in Tangiers the night I should av ordered spaghetti. Trust fund will be in my mother's name and she mail me loot. This is wiser than you think (considering Donlins and Neals).

If Peter is still there, give him my warmest love and I mean it. Your description of Gregory going to Germany is amazing! I know what, Allen, you must write prose masterpiece now and make a million: write a big VISIONS OF GREGORY, call it something else, Joyce Glassman is going to write a big VISIONS OF ELISE just for me (then publish it later as is, tho she doesn't believe it) . . . Give my love to Joy [Ungerer], tell her I want to kiss her everywhere soon's I see her, tell her I'm free. In NY somehow somewhere somebody stole my copy of Gregory's use use use use poem, tho I may find it later* (*Could Lamantia do that? for secret kicks?—or did I just misplace it? Tell Greg—) . . . But if you write prose you can make living, like me, and don't tell me you can't, your prose letters are the best I've ever seen, so come on. We'll, I'll definitely get a tape recorder, and you tell me long stories of everything that happened. I'll find some way to get you loot. But don't get hungup on bitter thoughts, and don't ever get mad at me permanent. Carl Solomon was out with someone in a bar in NY three weeks ago, I hear . . . all I know. Secret fellow in shadows of vanguard who dug me was, yes, Lucien . . . but also others, like a young kid wrote big poems about it, and many others. I can't understand *SRL* [*Saturday Review of Literature*] saying I "lost friends" during that reading . . . I really can't understand all this bitterness and malice sweeping around lately. I myself, like Whalen, feel "indefinitely happy" (he says) . . . What am I doing today? typing up *Dharma Bums*, all day, every day, while people ball in bars (it's Saturday night) I toil and toil on my typewriter and get bored and so revert to letters like these . . . what a scribbler I am now. I have to complete a story about desolation peak for *Holiday* mag., etc., have to figure out a movie for Robert Frank, have to write big 5000 word letters to Hollywood producer giving ideas, etc., it's getting out of hand . . . have to complete typing of *Dharma Bums* and at same time they're starting to tear down house around me and I'm racing against time. Ah, how I'll relax and do nothin when I get to Paris (I hope sometime soon). You shouldn't have got that $25 room for nothing, supposing Bill arrives in March? That's what I meant by don't spend your money I sent you, foolishly . . . that wasn't practical . . . but if Bill does arrive soon then its okay. Holmes is in England, not yet in Paris, he wrote big article about the beat in *Esquire*, about me mostly, at behest of that fine young editor there who wants you too, Rust Hills Jr., nice kid . . . don't despair, everybody wants you. Don't start screaming at robot America with its secret hidden Lafcadios in the night etc. its millions of Lafcadios, all Americans with birth certificates, etc. America is not going to take a Fall . . . there's your France with its "ideal" setup and shit, France is dull. America's flaws go with her immense virtues, don't you see that . . . France has no flaws, really, and therefore no virtues. Glad you're reading *Caesar Birotteau*, great novel, you know the greatest of all Balzac's novels is *Cousin Bette*. All the Orlovskys sleep a lot, and so do I, so did Joe Louis world heavyweight champ . . . it's the custom of the champs . . . sleep a lot alla time . . . then you store up vibrations . . . turn them on in shining life. Of monster scenery in NY Lou said, anyway, said, "I admire you for putting up with it, K." or something like that, meaning, my nightly appearances among sneers. But I had a big ball alla time reading and yakking with new friends, I don't understand what *Village Voice* is putting down, recent most terrible attack I haven't seen yet is said to gloat at our downfall (you and me) at last! this I gotta see, with *Subterraneans* coming out in two weeks, and movie of *On the Road* almost sure bet and with big company too (20th Century) and the completion of a new novel just as good (salable, readable) as *Road*, and a thousand other things, not to mention, via your side, your new poems. Yes, Spengler says Russia next, but he said it would be long time yet, America ain't reached its Faustian ripe moment yet and won't for long time, will blow, in fact may not fade at all actually since history being bypassed now by nature-laws (of science). I'd say, Africa will then absorb Russia that follows. But meanwhile Asia will have joined with West, so finally big worldwide daisychain . . . just as you wished . . . because everything, Allen, you ever ever wished for, will come true in TIME, don't you know what that means?

           Jean-Louis

Allen Ginsberg [Paris, France] to Jack Kerouac [n.p.]

ca. February 26, 1958

9 Rue Git Le Coeur Paris 6, France

Dear Jack:

    Got letter from Peter, your notes—I wrote you awhile back to Fla [Florida]—so thought I had been waiting to hear from you since. Wrote Peter five pages the other day including two page Lion poem ["The Lion For Real"], and been writing letters, to Phil, LaVigne, Gary today, *Climax, Yugen*, etc. etc. have to write Lucien still. Well, just sitting here in Paris, in my room. Bill today and Gregory talking about sword swallowers and juvenile gangs in NY. I been moping and gloomy, write desultory, my bowl unlucid. Tho six hours staring at ceiling and reading a pack of Whalen manuscript wound up happy again. [. . .] You got your house yet, what's it like and where's it be—maybe near my brother's out in Plainview—Huntsville? That's near Whitman birthplace cottage too. Also near Peter's family. And *Dharma Bums* sold? You know we still haven't got a copy of *On the Road* here I haven't seen it tho received *Subterraneans*—can't you get Cowley or Lord to (airmail?) us a copy? It's not on sale here that I've seen. Herb Gold was here, as I wrote Peter, I was very paranoid about him. Bill thought too much so, but finally settled down he came by often, dug Bill, I read him County Clerk, explained what I could about your actual method of writing, perhaps he be more sympathetic. First nite I screamed at him but then cooled it. He's just another race or something. Depressing. How you taking NYC? I'm afraid to come back and face all them aroused evil forces for fear I'll close up and try making sense and then really sound horrible. About reading, I have record to make for Fantasy records, and have been to studio here twice and tried but I can't do it when I know it's for real, money, contract that I can't re-record it for five years, etc. I just daze over and can't read with any feeling and don't know what I do want to sound like and get self-conscious. But when I was in England I went to BBC studio got drunk a little with Parkinson and blew into Blake's secret soul weeping, tremendous recording—they played about seven minutes of it and it got great rave staid review in the *Listener*, demanded the rest. But I can't record or read under formal auspices, only accidentally. Like I find I can't write when I'm expected to write, something to cap *Howl*. It's bothered me all along. It's fortunate in a way, keeps me from getting to be a sort of pro—it also leaves me wild and free when I do uncork and blow—but couldn't read steadily by schedule, too shy or ambitious to really do well—so when I get back I'll give mad readings but accidental ones and won't be able to make any real loot on it—I think. I don't know. Anyway shouldn't come back for that. I'd like to give one classical drunk blowout in NY and disappear. I'll stay here four months more and be alone, more or less till I straighten out more, meanwhile want to dig Berlin, Warsaw and maybe short Moscow trip if can get invited, that's the only way I could go anyway. Money is ok Bill has some and City Lights owes royalties this month maybe 200 so I'm fine. Gregory is back from Venice, he wrote some great long poems there and sent them to Don Allen especially "Army Army Army" a great weird war cry about Nebuchadnezzar. Card from Gary, I wrote him today. What's up in NY? Is Lafcadio weirder like Peter says? How's Peter seem? Bill sends love. Saw few reviews yet of *Subter-*

raneans tho Peter writes it's already sold 12,000. How's *On Road*? You're right tho should get *Sax* out before they try to type you with Beat scene—it was in Pogo I saw, I guess you're permanently in History—Wow! I'll write Lucien in a day or so too, so will Bill.

       Love

           Allen

Jack Kerouac [New York, New York] to Allen Ginsberg [Paris, France]

April 8, 1958

Dear Allen:

    My mother didn't forward your letter from Fla in keeping with her feeling you're bad influence on me but please don't get bug'd but as of yore we will be friends in our own milieu. I've quieted down completely now after the other night stumbling helplessly drunk set upon by faggot ex-boxer and his two fairies who held me outside San Remo knocked me out twice and cut me with ring finger, Stanley Gould ran away also new poet Steve Tropp ran away more or less, in the Dorothy Kilgallen column it said I was "knifed" . . . went to hospital, taken by kind Lamantia and Joyce [Glassman] and Leroy MacLucas friend of LeRoi Jones, got fixt finally by good doc, gave me pills stop drinking, feel fine, a little bored but that's because in two days now I go driving south with photographer Robert Frank in his station wagon go get my mother, cats, typewriter etc. and bring back to new house in Northport L.I. where I am going to live very quiet secluded monastic life actually, announce to eager Northport author-lovers I am there to work and won't have no social life except when I come into NY to see Joyce, Lucien, Sterling, Peter, you, et al. House is old Victorian type with banister to slide down from bedrooms, and cellar, attic, etc., big yard with grape arbor and rock garden and PINES to meditate under in dark of night, everything will be fine I think after this nightmare beating-up . . . cause of fight I cannot tell, don't know, think Stanley Gould said something loud about "faggots" and they took for me. Your new G.J. hepcat sounds like repetition of same old horseshit, let's change, besides who could ever blow like Neal did at his peak, tell this G.J. he don't begin to realize how much Neal really did swing. Herbert Gold is a nowhere nothing as a writer, why don't he leave you and me alone, we have suffered in the Hell of Poetry, been busted, fucked up, lost, starved, ask him how much he's suffered for his dinky little craft. I have policy now of completely ignoring all Golds and suchlike they really dying for a rebuttal, like the other night a big discussion by Young Socialist's League called "The Kerouac Craze," one of my spies reports that the chairman tried to put me down but a big funny sixty-five year old Russian leaped up and with Russian accent said my whore house scene in Mexico (in *Road*) spoke for itself and he kept yelling about revolution and everybody cheered, revolution of novel, etc. Trilling's friends also writing about me, *Subterraneans* has finally (because of obvious intellectual content) flushed out intellectuals of *Partisan* and *Kenyon* etc. *Dharma Bums* is sold, getting advance . . . coming out October, will be big number of Fall for Viking, you in it as Alvah Goldbook . . . they made me change your *Howl* (by Goldbook) to *Wail*. Yes the scene in NY aroused with evil forces but you can howl them down easy, don't worry. You can make much money if you want now, reading, and touring country, like [Jay] Landesman St. Louis,[3] etc. New Orleans, etc. Lamantia ran away to Mexico today, he also was mugged and robbed of a buck and says the great purgation is coming in NY . . . all you gotta do is stay sober. I will never get drunk again now. Pills for five weeks then will power like Lucien. Lucien not drinking and feeling fine and being sweet beyond words . . . Can't you offer your BBC reading tape as an album for Fantasy? I made an album with Steve Allen, drunk, and three with Norman Granz, drunk, and they great, in fact so way out I wonder if they'll release them, sooner you come home the better, Rexroth opening in Five Spot[4] next week at good pay, I don't go see him, he insult me in *Subterranean* review saying I don't know nothin about jazz and negroes, how silly, and him don't let negroes into his house even ever. Lafcadio is same, he said to me "You're gettin old, Jack" and told Peter "Don't be a poet". Peter I never see but twice so far, he a great angel nurse far as I can see and handling everything well . . . he's shy of me I think. *Road* also still selling, two hundred a week, sometimes four hundred. What did it say in *Pogo*, I didn't see that? I got lead review in *New Yorker* for *Subs*, very snotty, by Donald Malcolm my dear, who doubts my virility . . . I will move into new house (*Life* mag assignment on trip down) furnish it, tape recorder and all, furniture, etc. and settle down quiet and write big tearbook about Lowell boyhood which will fit around *Sax* like halo. Only trip I really contemplate is this Fall to Gary [Snyder] for Dharma Bumming hike to Sierras and up Oregon way etc. and maybe not even that, I inward . . . France some day. I did TV show too, to question what is a Mainliner I sang "Skyliner" melody with words "Mainliner," very Zen, even Giroux dug. Fuck it all, tho, this fame, these punches, I be lamb and people call me a vicious lion [. . .]

Jackiboo X

---

[3] Jay Landesman owned a nightclub in St. Louis, which offered poetry readings as well as more traditional entertainment.
[4] The Five Spot was a jazz club on the Bowery.

Is Bill coming back with you this summer?

I can't send *On the Road* without enormous hassle, you read it anyway once—tho I wish Bill and Gregory could see. People keep stealing my own copies. I'm sick of poetry and going back to "no-time-for-poetry" prose of old. But you and Greg and Lamantia are [?]

Allen Ginsberg [Paris, France] to Jack Kerouac [n.p., Northport, New York?]

9 Rue Git Le Coeur Paris 6, France
June 26, 1958

Dear Jack:

Wrote you last month, no answer, are you mad at me? Write honey, I'm full of snow right now, strange interesting rich acquaintances here, one a young Rothschild junior Burroughs, he and Bill will go to India someday together, I'll—somebody, another blonde young millionaire just brought up some old suits, Bill now smoking Green all drest in distinguished Averill Harriman black worsted flannel, thin, graying temples: he brought me my first suit in years, fine English grey wool, last a thousand winters—but later—Alas Alas Jack I got final word from LaVigne today, long letter, Neal is in jail, LaVigne not seen him, talked to Carolyn on phone to find out for me and wrote me—he's in San Bruno County jail, waiting trial, "Two facts are 1) that he was arrested selling to Narco agents, has been tied (mistakenly) into series of other arrests as source of supply (since he comes up in trains from south), there is a long list of charges against him (tho Carolyn didn't enumerate them), 2) that he is discovered as Dean M. of *On the Road* by the fuzz." That's what LaVigne says Carolyn says, though I doubt the latter means anything, maybe just her paranoia. Tho I hear scene in SF is very bad, saw a girl from there who showed me evil Herb Caen column innuendos about marijuana smoke stronger than garlic these days on North Beach, anyone can pick up Columbus and Bway, fuzz is all over on account of all the publicity, city officials cracking down, The Place raided, and its balcony use forbidden and only thirty-five people at time allowed in LaVigne was having a show there and they ordered him off balcony—some guy name Paul Hansen fall off a building last Sunday, and finally skull struck again, Connie Sublette[5] was strangled last "Tuesday AM by a spade seaman who confessed that PM."—I met someone here two months ago that knew her said she had a codeine habit and was slightly crazy, calling cops to arrest people, I don't know

5 Connie was Al Sublette's wife.

what—long saga of drunken week following her around feuding with some evil tea heads or something, I don't know. Haven't heard anything of [Al] Sublette, I guess he's ok—in jail I had heard for a burglary. . . . everything I hear from there sounds evil . . . except letters from Gary [Snyder] who's in hospital for ball operation, and [John] Wieners who's living at the [Hotel] Wentley with LaVigne, they're friends now, I guess I think even making it . . . but what to do about Neal—I wanted to write Carolyn, don't any longer have address on Bancroft, got letter back—LaVigne forgot to send it—you have it? I'll try write him in jail. Carolyn added that she thought he'd get two to five years maybe—god knows what he's thinking. I had a shuddery premonition, thought he was committing suicide, yesterday when hi, suddenly thought of him maybe in jail, then got this letter today. But little doomed Connie is sad.

I'm coming back to New York in a few weeks, hope to leave here, have to get up the fare but that'll come, or else family said they'd send it if no other way. Gregory and I interviewed by Buchwald, Art, silly interview, he tried to be sympathetic but we were drunk and kookie, but next night I sent him big serious prophetic godly letter, said maybe he'd publish that, and Gregory will send him another Luciferian sweet one—but at end of article he said we were trying to raise fare, I was, for return, maybe someone send it. [. . .]

But is there anything we can do about Neal? Character witnesses—he'll be all alone only haggard Carolyn probably angry at him, Gary's in hospital can't find out anything, he's wise enough to know if anything to do, no one to write to there who could help—thought maybe Ruth Witt Diamant or Rexroth, just some letters that he's a writer or something, say—he being crucified, evil laws on T, trapped by decoy cops, all nothing for him to suffer for—and probably big mistaken spider web paranoias by cops—though I guess maybe he's having some peace and have plenty time to meditate and stay way from horses and RR and T and Carolyn and house and his life, forced vacation, maybe blessing in disguise and he grim and peaceful in jail, or writing prayers to Saturn, maybe he write again, die, I'll stay in NY-Paterson-Long Island Eugene's, wherever, a year, maybe Peter get Veterans apartment in Bronx—have endless notes, poems, to type, finish "Fall of America" poem, maybe, Bible Jeremiah book, China have billion people by 2000, we'll see it, be industrialized as much as England in fourteen years I read, must call for Holy America make it on beat angel soul promote Walt [Whitman] comrade to Budh ambassador—otherwise maybe paranoia machine sink down on us from new Asia—we may be visionary island America after all—still interested in *Democratic Vistas*, he says if we don't produce bards and spiritual America and if materialism greed takes over we be "the fabled damned among nations"—can see it happening from year and half in Europe, from Europe,—yes I see the vast virtues but family Sunday house with eternal TV like *T&C* [*The Town and the City*] solidity strength—even that and spume in history waves—white race too small—smooth metallic faced chinamen in space suits maybe go to Mars. Burroughs horrified by all tales of communist dullness, we hear here in Paris from travelers, shot all hop smokers in China etc. etc.—now T is banned (legally and slightly enforced) in Tangiers (Arabs have to hide their pipes under table in cafes now)—so America got to be peaceful wiseman among nations, and survive—maybe take vow of poverty and give away Empire State Building possessions to India. I dunno, just a gleam. [. . .] (Door just knocked, I got it locked so I can keep private 3 AM feed of coke and write you letter.) You ever get a coke letter before? Dear Jack, you love me still, I love you, don't be mad I make long remark last time and about mother—that why you no answer? [. . .]

Well, yesterday Art Buchwald, we were looped, I see not much gets across in interview that way, tho he was simpatico, I wrote him serious prose poem letter last nite for his column. I see what you had to go through, wish I'd been there, I feel now too tired tongue stricken to blow, afresh, when I get home, my virgin kicks and energy and sense of mission like I had with Gary in Northwest, or earlier in SF, seems gone—nothing new to say, repeat poetry novelties—wonder how I'll do in NY and if I'll have to do anything wild—don't even feel like reading, *Howl*, can't even make ecstatic tape in soundproof French Vogue studio room, tho I've been paid $50 advance on it, can't make it right now, maybe in Newman's studio in NY can get drunk—make last weep record. Help me. What you do—I heard your record (records?) out—Steve Allen? Tho not heard anything about it. Enclosed find letter from Terry Southern, friend of Mason [Hoffenberg], wrote pointless tho hip N. West book published by your Deutsch in England—perhaps you can answer him—I'll write him that queer sections, some libel characters, and whole scroll long syntax of *On Road* was tampered with by Viking—they take out any tea? I seem to remember they broke up prose a lot to shorter sentences often and disturbed the benny flow. He (Southern) seems well meaning and interested in prose and took trouble to write and investigate and so I feel like answering informationally. You seen review of *Road* from England *Times* and *Observer*? One (John Wain) quoted both of us at length attacking etc.

Buchwald said he'd introduce us (and Bill especially) to John Huston who's here, making picture. Bill has idea for Tangiers panorama film (episodes seen thru eyes of bill-junky looking for drugstore sick on Ramadan holiday, street boy looking for a score from fag, effeminate tourist with mother), town seen thru different Burroughs eyes, juxtaposed. Or maybe Greg [Corso] and I make travel loot in bit-parts—or maybe just watch Huston Burroughs talk.

x

398

Lentil soup and Bayonne hambone on stove, blue dawn rainy cloudy sky all week, coke descending, been grinding my teeth all night, cat's on bed washing his breast, grey calm cat Bill no longer torments at all, why don't you write me love letter, you ashamed of me I don't write enough or not sufficiently entered void ready for death? Ah Jack, are you tired—you have been writing long solitudenous halo for *Sax*? I'll be home in NY see you within a month, let's meet like angels and be innocent, what are you brooding about in Long Island, hold my hand, I want to see Lucien again and shade of Rubenstein and London Towers and 43, 1943, our walk by 119th St. to Theological Seminary when I told you about saying farewell to Lucien's and my door on 7th floor and adieu prayer to stairway there, is not Sebastian [Sampas] faithful to the end? Saw [Seymour] Wyse in London a month ago grinning over counter of his Chelsea record shop, indifferent, serious, no change in his face looks same as once, not even fat now. Write me a note, I'm coming home, write Neal, what's new, how's hicks, snow's melted, now I'll sleep.

      Goodnight,

        Allen

Editors' Note: Kerouac had difficulty dealing with the pressure that fame imposed on him. He began to withdraw even more from the world of the Beat Generation, a world which Ginsberg would continue to enthusiastically embrace in the years to come. The following letter illustrates the growing distance between the two writers.

Jack Kerouac [Northport, New York] to Allen Ginsberg [Paris, France]

                                   July 2, 1958

Dear Allen:

By now you must have gotten my mother's letter to you, which she wrote and mailed before telling me and thus only put a 6 cent stamp on it? did you get it? anyway, whether or not, it's nothing new from 1945 Ozone Park hangups only now I more agree with her not because what she says, but I have withdrawn (as you saw me begin to withdraw in Tangiers and Peter objected, recall) and want to live my own kind of simple Ti Jean (whatever you may think of it) life, like in overalls all day, no going out, no weeping mobs of Asia under my midnight Buddha pine, no "horde of silver helmets" (that alright for great historian and poet Corso who is a Romantic like Shelley)—I am just a Buddhist-

Catholic and want no more shit nonsense and roses. What does this mean? O by the way I wasn't angry by your earlier letter, I've just been pondering what to say to you, it has nothing to do with that or with anything you've done since you never change, it's ME that's changing. Outside of a few calm visits with you in NY or preferably Paterson at your father's house I don't want no more frantic nights, association with hepcats and queers and Village types, far less mad trips to unholy Frisco, I just wanta stay home and write and figure things out by myself, in my own Child mind. This means of course I wouldn't dream of interfering with Julius [Orlovsky] shitmouth or Neal's fall, how many times have I in fact you told him to cool it, it was no longer feasible in California or anywhere in USA and on top of that he goes and pushes for the sake probably of saving a dollar for extry breakfast, poor N always did save a penny to spend dollars. He may write *The First Third* now, by the way, I think—what else do? as long as it ain't a Dostoevsky-Siberian term in hard labor snow. Carolyn may be wrong about the fuzz knowing Dean but in any case what's the real connection? in fiction, as it says on jacket, and Dean never pushed. I read all about the Frisco horror suicides and murders and Lucien came over and had me bat out a UPI interview to disassociate me from such shit. I agree with my mother on the point of your not using my name in any activities of yours (other than pure poetry and prose) such as politics, sex, etc. "action" etc. etc. I'm retired from the world now and going into my mountain shack later and eventually just disappear in woods as far as it can be done these days. That's why I've made no effort to see poor Peter or even Joyce [Glassman] anymore, Lamantia bugged the shit out of me in the spring using me to publicize his poetry readings rushing into Joyce's with screaming Howard Hart (was fun for awhile) then vanishing as tho nothing happened anyway, he really a con man. Very beautiful about Bill's great new Proustian sick-in-bed aesthetic millionaire genius, hope they do something together like India, because where can Bill go now? He said Portuguese East Africa last time. Does Gregory know that he was mentioned in Dantono Walker's column (*NY Daily News*) saying "While Beat Generation writers are raking it in in night club readings, Gregory Corso, who originated the idea years ago, starves quietly in Paris." Also Robert Frank the great photographer thinks he's the greatest poet. Also there's a girl I know (twenty, rich) who's in love with him already. Yes, I'm beyond the idea of falls and orients and masses, the world is big enough to right itself, *Sax* said the universe disposes of its own evil, and so does history. You underestimate the compassion of Uncle Sam, look at the record. I know it will all come raining down in our paranoiac minds but maybe not in nature. As for a peaceful wiseman America I think you got that now. I just believe it, I have no facts to back it up, like Einstein don't have no facts to back up what Buddha knew in full (electromagnetic-gravitational ecstasy). Well Burroughs, okay, Great Teacher, the universe is exactly two billion years old—as for the 2,999 other Great Chilicosms guess. Don't get mad, Allen. I'm not screaming at you. I'm just like Lucien now, a quiet family man, of *T&C* solidities again, and not rolling in dough at all. No money from movies yet, and royalty monies gone in house . . . but I wanta figure it out by myself from now on in . . . I tired of outside influences. I'm getting at something in solitude halo. Besides I'm only interested in Heaven, which is evidently our reward for all this screaming and suffering going on. When you come back we'll discuss in detail all the publishing items for you and Bill and Greg . . . Be careful of NY this time, you know I got beat up almost killed when drunk by Henri Cru's enemies and people write on walls of Village shithouses "Kerouac Go Home" . . . that don't leave me much stomach for the same old shit of past years, man. Me for midnight silence, and morning freshness, and afternoon clouds, and my own kind of Lowell boy life. As for the Freudian implications, or Marxian, or Reichian, or Spenglerian, I'll buy Beethoven.

O why don't I shut up, always showing off? Your letter very great and I'm sorry and yet glad that now we'll have new quiet Van Doren type relationship. Lucien by the way approves of you altogether, says I'm nuts, and says all women afraid of manly queers who put shoulders to wheel but ain't afraid of swishies. My own reason is: Peace. And the Dove. In my ceiling crack, the dove. George Martin dying in the kitchen. Baseball games. *Memory Babe* my new book big RR Earth run on Lowell memories. I'll see you around September, won't leave house till then, according to June vow, for work reasons.

Alas, Allen Goodnight

Jack Kerouac [Northport, New York] to Allen Ginsberg [Paterson, New Jersey]

August 11, 1958

34 Gilbert St
Northport NY

Dear Allen:

As you can see, I sent you $5 check a while back but the address Peter gave me I mustav imperfectly remembered. Anyway here it is. I notice you haven't written to me so you must be alas goodnighting too but that's alright because for now and next months I be going to town on *Memory Babe* which is big Xmas weekend in Lowell climaxed by huge vision of Bethlehem star and Child.

A great new poet has arisen out of Chicago, Stan Persky, who sent me his long poem "How The Night Came To Me" and I wrote back and (rightly) praised him as greatest new cat since Gregory (you'll agree, this time) (I was lukewarm, after all, about [Jack] Micheline-Silver) and I wrote back and he wrote back saying: "Dear Mr Kerouac, And cried a hundred house in insane halls to read your message and the fruit upon the tree of Snaketown life is in season. I pray for you when I pray to God at night. And have just been inducted into the Navy and that day I got your card I stood around all day with naked multitudes and we gazed in embarrassment at each other with our mutual cocks and I thank you and thank you crazily in my young joytears and my name is Jewish and I come from hundreds of thousands and uncounted generations of brown shepherds in the wisdom of Kabala night." Then in a Gregory-like burst, after saying how he reads your poetry to his hobo father "Overland Jackie" he says: "At what point in sad history will I be privileged to sit at your feet and watch you with my unabashed idolatry?" Ends, with, "Will meet you soon in neon mirages and night and desolate rivers." How's he sound? I told him to send poems to Don Allen. You should write to this kid because he's the new great one, Stan Persky, 17, 27 N. Menard Ave., Chicago 44, Illinois.

I gave him your imperfect address so write to him, maybe, after all this is your meat. Poet meat.—Bill Burroughs wrote to my mother saying "I will not forward any more of your insane letters to Allen. Please stop bothering me."—In the Fall I will come out of my writing fog and come see everybody in town when the winds blow. Meanwhile I'm having trouble with Hollywood who refuse to pay for any of my material. I don't know why. They all seem to want it free. I have just enuf money to furnish this house, pay it, and then no more money, so I better make Hollywood do some paying somehow. Gary [Snyder] gone to mountains Holmes wrote me, would like to see you at Saybrook Old. Don't be afraid to write me if you want, like we planned. Have you seen Lucien? I'd like to go to his country house with you in Fall, since by then he'll be drinking again and we can howl under Adirondack stars and crash his car through woods and go to big cocktail parties with Gov. Harrimans. Until then I write. Soon I buy oil paints and (for first time oils) start painting in my attic room. That's why I'm not worried about Laff, I be greater painter maybe someday. Laff no talk to me on train. Quiet letter from Gregory in Stockholm, says he going to Lapland.

Well, okay, and give Peter some of this money I guess. See you in Ha He Her Had Hea Hero

Hok

Allen Ginsberg [New York, New York] to
Jack Kerouac [Northport, New York]

Tuesday Aug. 20, 1958
170 E 2 St Apt 16 NYC 9

Dear Jack:

Fast note, I have no comfortable table to type on yet. I'm living at 170 East
2nd Street, apartment 16, New York—that's between Ave A and B—great Lower
East Side neighborhood, I take long walks around Orchard Street—walked into
Hebrew Funeral Home and saw a big display tombstone GINSBERG. We (Peter
and me) got four rooms—front, overlooking all night rye bread bakery with
noisy trucks, but that's nice all night, the lights and tinkle of glass—we got no
furniture yet, but an extra pallet in one room and some Indian rugs—have
heat, great huge new stove, icebox, shower, hot water, etc etc. big solid family
type apartment—$60 a month between us tho Peter's paid it all so far. Com-
fortable boxlike square apartment square rooms, not too big, but big thick
doors so lots of privacy from room to room—spent this week washing walls
and cleaning up. You can stay here all you want if need NY refuge—new policy that nobody visits, it's silent castle for sleeping, balling, cooking and writing. I see Peter off to work at 11 every night, then take tour of bars, visit Five
Spot, nobody knows me except the waiter who lets me in free and gives me
an occasional beer and gossip, I hear hours of anonymous Thelonius Monk.
Then maybe I see Lucien at after midnite and watch the late show with him,
we don't drink, so we don't yet have talked much, deeply. He goes to three
week upstate vacation today. Saw Monacchio and Merims there yesterday,
and Luce and Hudson there last week. So far Lou and I talk politics. Then I hit
San Remo or Cedar Bar, see [Michael] Rumaker once, and Edward Marshall, great religious poet, often, he's the best of the young poets—you saw his
long mad poem in *BMR*?? [*Black Mountain Review*] I thought he'd be cranky
strange pimpled schizo, but he's stocky blond manly queer who reads Episcopal
bibles theology and works fulltime Columbia Library, and writes long primitive original confessional poems. Also saw [Frank] O'Hara one night, just
talked, and the girls (Joyce [Glassman] and Elise [Cowen] and Helen Eliot)
one night, and Dusty [Moreland] another, and Walter Adams, I visit them all,
sneak up like a ghost and spend all evening talking about what happened to
them. Then I go home, I brought my books from Paterson, read the *Iliad* or
whatever, lay and think, cook. Saw Don Allen also again—this week all week
will be in Easthampton, Peter has five day vacation, we'll go screw on rocks in

sun, stay at Richard Howards and meet all the rich painters. So be back next Thursday.

Got your letter in Paterson, late, and thanked for check, happy you wrote, I wasn't sure you wanted me to write so waited for a sign. Also got letter from Gregory, he visited Lapland is back in Paris, no word from Bill yet, Whalen says (he wrote) he'll be visiting here in the fall or winter,—also Sheila Boucher [Williams]—my old girl—showed up, run away from husband, I took her on walk thru Bowery over the Manhattan Bridge for eternity wink of Manhattan. She was four days in jail in Minnehaha, midland, US, I forget, for vagrancy, met your sweet painter cat and traveling with him now. She says Gary [Snyder] came to her door, walked past her outraged husband, said, "Sheila are you ready?", helped her pack, and drove her to SF. Gary wants to marry her she says—make her have babies in Japan. So Gary, she says, will be here later in Fall too. Also LaVigne coming. September. New York will be great this winter. Maybe we all give one mad poetry reading together, free to multitudes, no bullshit. I met Howard Hart, I didn't dig his poetry, he recited me some, and all he talked about was bread and loot and wanted me to give expensive reading with him as partner, tried to hustle me I thought. I think you're right, Lamantia and he are conmen of poetry readings and only give it a bad name. He fought with Lamantia in Frisco, on top of everything. Fuck that shit.

[. . .]

Lucien says you say you have Buerger's disease—have you got a really good doctor out there? If not you should come in and see [Dr.] Perrone and get that straightened out. It sounds like it's getting beyond the point where standing on head is effective treatment. Please take care of yourself you shouldn't give up and go die now. I always needed you.

Sneak in and come see us in a week or later if you stay there till September. I don't want no wild scenes and drinking, nor want to see you drunk, nor will partake of big suicidal drunks no more. I'd rather just walk or sit and talk or go to the Metropolitan Museum of Art and read Brueghel picture there.

[. . .]

Well later on—I'll write again, send me a postcard to 170 E. 2nd Street so that I'll know you did receive this letter safely and it didn't fall into the sad hands of fate.

Oh yes, I saw [William Carlos] Williams in Rutherford, had supper with him, his wife and he said they thought you were very charming and sweet, said to give you their regards. [Ezra] Pound came stayed overnight there after he got out of hospital—they thought he was wacky. He brought five people with him, wife and he also has a little girlfriend. WCW showed me a picture of them—W sad, sitting, Pound behind him thin and wiry and bare-chested both looking

404

into home camera. Tell you about that later. Talked about measure and wailing with him.

okokokokokok

Kokomo

Jack Kerouac [Northport, New York] to Allen Ginsberg [New York, New York]

August 28, 1958

Dear Irwin:

Gone from the earth to a better land I know, I hear their angel voices calling Old Black Joe . . . I'm coming, I'm coming . . . for my head is bending low.

That's a nice song, now playing on my FM talkless Sunday music program. "Why do I sigh, that my friends come not again . . ." and that was the song I played on the zither on a stage before huge audience at age eleven. My favorite song, I see now.

Yes, Edw. Marshall is a fine poet. But haven't you discovered Stan Persky yet? I'll bring in his work next time.

Carolyn put me down in Berkeley last year so I'll just stay quiet. Neal has money enuf I know. He never writes, if he does write to me that'll be different because I'll never forget the time I brought him candy and magazines in the hospital and he told me I had "descended on him." Bleakjawed Neal was mad at me and one day I jumped off the engine at Bayshore and suddenly saw him, and he drove away guiltily.

You're probably right about rights for *On the Road* getting more valuable, but I want to see what happens with this mess now, they want Joyce Jamison to play LuAnne and that would make the picture a hit and I get five percent and Mort Sahl said he wanted the picture to hew very closely to the book, that's better than MGM. Meanwhile MGM making a movie called *Beat Generation* with Jerry Lee Lewis, haven't even consulted me about my copyright of that title in 1955 (remember, Jean-Louis, *New World Writing* #7, from a novel-in-progress *BEAT GEN.* copyright 1955 Jean-Louise etc.). So Sterling will sue for copyright payoff. I also have Holmes article attributing coining of phrase to me, and other stuff. They are really crooking me in H'wood, *The Subterraneans* for peanuts, etc. Imagine Sloane Wilson getting a half million dollars for *A Summer Place*. I don't want all that but certainly fifteen grand is nothing in H'wood, or the 25 offered then reneged for *Road*. This sounds silly to you in your poverty but if I ever get an income (trust fund) started I'll have money for you once in a while, gratis. Not for everybody, not for voracious Gregorys and Neals, but

405

for kindly poet saints cooking lung stew in East Side quiet palaces. No I don't have Buerger's disease, I have a good doc called Rosenberg, I had boils and I guess they came from poison ivy getting right into my system from my constant retrieving of basketball from poison ivy patches. No, no phlebitis, nothing. My real problem is drinking. I drink alone and sometimes too much even alone. I take dexamyls to write and they not healthy (prescription). Do you remember that wonderful Benzedrine used to make us shit and sweat and piss and lose weight and get holy high, this dexymal constipates, fucks up, screws, agh, ugly depressions worse than benny. Our prurient medicos, wouldn't give me benny. They got goddam codeine in those dexamyls, bet you any money, causes constipation. So I'm still fat.

Glad you have long quiet talks with Lucien. I wonder how he can stand all those shouting visitors including me,? poor dog has no life of his own. He is really and truly a gracious aristocratic man. He said my "Lucien Midnight" was pejorative about him, shoulda been majorative. Can't even find words in dictionary! I just wrote long letter to Joyce [Glassman] describing my current work, ask her to read it to you, if you want idea. I'm bugged and bored by it, but I was bugged and bored by *Dharma Bums* too. No more fun in writing for me. Blah. Bought a Webcor three speed and played my own record albums, my Norman Granz three albums are greatest poetry records since Dylan Thomas and I do think Granz is not going to issue them at all from prurience. I really read like a bitch. Nice low voice, too. Steve Allen album said to be coming out with Hanover Records, it is quite a little gem too. If you have a box I'll bring them in. My own box weighs ton. Yes, and did Hart fight Lamantia physically or what? If you have big free poetry reading with Gary [Snyder] et al please don't urge me to join in, I'll just listen like in Frisco. I have offers to read for money all over country and reject em all. Too bashful, goddamit I don't like to be on a stage. If Gary does come, and Phil [Whalen], it will be strange won't it. If you want to get to Bob Lax, he's phone TWining 9-1323, and lives at 3737 Warren St. Jackson Heights. He just sent me a letter, an empty envelope (!) (?) Great day in the morning, I go die now, I feel awful (dexies). See you soon. Snipsnip snip.

They wanted me write commentary to Norman Mailer's Hip and God talk, he says God is dying etc. kinda nonsense tho he is nice serious kid. But I don't wanta get involved with him and his gang. They also wanted me to talk on stage with Max Lerner for $100 honorarium at Brandeis Univ., don't think I'd like that, big gray faced liberal sneers . . . goodbye poor $100. When you and me and Bill have ALL our work published they'll be no more talk about Nabokovs and Silones. What a long time it will take, and when it comes, it never matters anymore, and then we go into eternity and don't care anyway. And so it's already eternity and here we inward tomb bliss our sleep.

Meanwhile Jonathan Williams sent me his awful list of dissident pisspoor intellectual wrecks, that whole BM [Black Mountain] gang is full of shit if you ask me . . . big abstract conceited tracts about nothing.

> Following each other,
>   my cats stop
> When it thunders

And as for Alan Watts, I call him Arthur Whane in *Dharma Bums*, which is Old English for horsefly, for the way he bit us in *Chicago Review*. Ah, Heaven will respect us. In fact I'd better start respecting poor Mr. Watts. This fame shot makes you gripe more than blow, doesn't it?

> Adios
>   Jack

Rosenthal at *Chicago Review* wants you to send him *prose*. Will write you c/o Paterson soon. Send him letter excerpt.

P.S. I decided to accept that Lerner invitation and buy full set of oils and canvases. Royalty check just came in, half of what I expected.

Allen Ginsberg [Paterson, New Jersey] to Jack Kerouac [n.p., Northport, New York?]

ca. August 31, 1958

Dear Ghost:

Well you're the smart one. Why didn't you tell me life was a dream? I got on some Nitrous Oxide, twice in a row for experiment, in dentist's chair today—went thru all the kalps, kalpas, "in all directions" inside and out, like you say—never had such a time. Much to talk about, wrote some apt lines, dammit it's all a big cheat—great universal razz like ridiculous woody woodpecker disappearing laughing into the receding eyehole of cosmic cartoon, all the universes disappearing all at once. I'm sorry I was so deaf, I was hung on Harlem God—I still don't understand how both absolute impressions can exist without contradiction in the same universe. But I'll let anything go in one ear and out the other.

I want to reread your poems and Buddha books, now. Bring them in, the manuscript, please please—no joke serious. When you come in.

All sorts of things falling into place, and plenty of time to let them, so don't worry I'm not flipping. I just didn't understand what you were talking about before, or Gary or Phil for that matter.

I'm in Paterson, I'll write from NY—got your letter.
What a funny thing.

> Irwin

P.S. Gregory's letter was great—like Neal's old one. I read "Bomb" drunk in Five-Spot at 3 AM to three people.

Jack Kerouac [Northport, New York] to Allen Ginsberg [New York, New York]

September 8, 1958

Dear Allen:

Got your letter about the dentists gas satori . . . or maybe supreme enlightenment I guess . . . yes, and if you want to follow up on the words on the subject, you know where to go . . . Surangama Sutra, Lankavatara Scripture, Diamond Sutra, the MAHAYANA WRITINGS (not Hinayana earlier crude moral stratagems) (tho Mahayana even more moral) . . . so, just get Dwight Goddard's *Buddhist Bible* in library unless they haven't replaced the copy I stole) . . . we'll talk about it anyway. I don't want to leave my unpublished *Some of Dharmas* etc. out of house and Don Allen (if you want see) has *Mexico City Blues* sutra at his pad now. Anyway, don't worry. I just wrote big letter to Gregory praising him to heavens for making me cry at last, after all these years since Neal's great letter. How sweet it is that a word-slinger can sling in prose or verse, hey? What mighty prose it is, what sounds emanate from his gregorytongue! Just as good as Neal. Both better than me, except I guess in *Sax* there I gets supernatural assistance and prose-tricks . . . but prose-tricks don't add up to sighing tears prose. Poor great Gregory and Jesus how he suffered! Well, we'll discuss that too. There's a girl here, Jill Lippman, rich, sexy, thin fucky, who went with me to visit Lafcadio last Saturday nite and we saw him wandering in the moon and went in and talked in drear kitchen with Marie [Orlovsky] and looked at his paintings, his "simple" ones, that is, I know that he's going thru a strange little rococo phase of his own . . . so we gave Marie Jill's number so when you and Peter come you can call her and she comes in big car and gets us all for big moonlight swims but actually now it's almost too late, she going to Yale school now . . . anyway. Did you see new *Horizon* magazine where you and me raked over coals again by another Columbia Trilling fink? But every knock is a boost and we sure gets boosted knocked raked and everything in this. Once more accused of fomenting teenage murder atrocities. That, my friend, you can lay back to Mr. Holmes who said in *Esquire* that it was extremely "significant" that a little nigger cretin pulled the knife out of Michael Farmer's chest and said "Thanx, man, I wanted to see what it was like." How a man can make irresponsible statements like that from his cloistered position I shall never know but anyway it appears these Trillingers seem to think WE said such a silly thing and that's two critics now lay murder at our feet, . . . and you and me who don't even hunt or even fish. They have our pictures, our poems, etc., they print the first page of *Subterraneans* saying and showing nothing because the book got rolling two, three pages later. Is it really true that Phil and Gary are coming? let me know. Sterling is dying to nab Gary for his future novels, . . . and Phil. (O yes, the murder hints from Columbia from Trilling I just realized today pretty soon they'll be digging out Lou. If they do that they might have another murder on their hands.) Kingsland wrote me letter from Philly said he would drive to Northport and drop in, I told him it was my mother's house, I guess he'll be bugged, imagine huge swishy Kingsland walking into my mother's innocent rosy kitchen. Paranoiac rosy kitchen but she did rise at 6 A.M. for a decade while I was allowed (believed in utterly) to stay home write my saxes and sexes so don't forget that. [. . .] Don't worry, I won't maddrunk begscenes in your quiet stately pad when I comes in, if I comes in . . . ur ur ur . . . be in soon few weeks. *A ton coeur.*

Jean

Allen Ginsberg [New York, New York] to Jack Kerouac [Northport, New York]

ca. September 16–17, 1958

170 E 2 St NYC
Sept 17 [*sic*: 16?], 1958

Dear Jack:

Quiet stately path pad alas alas hell, the girls are all here, plus a few tomcats and FBI agents wandering around the Village inquiring of me if I'm from SF (a spade agent I heard about from paranoiac girlfriend of Peter—who's temporarily moved in with us to satisfy his cunt Karma)—came up to me in Jim Atkins—as prophesied he always does to Village cats from SF—and said "don't I know you from SF"—but I didn't want to bug him so I said, no, which was true, and also, "I come from New Jersey really" which was also true, so he retired a little baffled—anyway Sheila [Williams] my old girlfriend is in one room here (been here two weeks and says she's returning to SF as soon as someone bugged at her on the coast sends her the plane ticket, probably before this weekend)—she has nice painter boyfriend in side room with her they sleep all day and vanish gloomily onto the street for the night and come home and argue about his manhood.

She says she and Gary were having a kind of affair, and Gary came got her with little car at her husband's to rescue her drove her to Frisco and said he'd meet her in NY. But now she's changed her mind and's going back.

Well, also, another girl named Sheila [Plant] from SF who'd made it with Peter and Laf there, and subsequently various hospitals, also today settled in, preparatory to her return to SF also ("I don't believe I'm in NY. Is this NY?") Peter's having a nice time, so am I, it leaves me free to lie in bed stare at ceiling and read. What I'll do is move into a private isolated side-room in the apartment and it'll be like I had a lonely furnished room. So actually that's all ok, and maybe even the present wave of dependents will unwave.

So come in and get drunk as you want to, or not. I'll be here, would like to talk to you.

Better later, tho, Lucien invited us both out to upstate this weekend, but I have things to do here this weekend anyway and Lucien it turned out couldn't get a car. He says later on in the fall.

I went to New Directions to pick up copy of [William Carlos] Williams' new *Paterson* which has a letter of mine, and met [James] Laughlin, talked to him. Explained to him about Gary and Phil's unpublished books, he said he wanted to read them and maybe would publish them. I explained him how poetry appearances were getting fucked up by absence of their high-class work and Ferlinghetti's blindness etc. I had just seen Don Allen for two minutes to pick up your *Blues* (which I had with me) and Laughlin said he wanted to see that also, maybe he could publish it complete I suggested. He said he was still interested and working on *Visions of Neal* he thought was great prose, but having trouble with fearful printers—but would sooner or later be able to find one and would definitely do it. Also he asked for Gregory's address and would write him a card.

Yes, I saw the *Horizon*, and broke my rule about not answering, several weeks ago, and wrote them objecting to their chopping out endless balls and cock from line eleven and leaving out two lines and patching in again, saying it "broke my rhythm" and they had to announce next issue that I disapprove and was not consulted and felt it was insult to the structure (which it actually is in a way since two lines they left out were the rhythmic come of the eleven preceding lines). I'm curious how they'll handle that. They first wrote back saying they meant no harm and consulted Grove, so I wrote back detailed one page explaining rhythm and offering to read it to them over telephone if they couldn't hear it themselves and requesting prompt reply. But they never replied. Besides

I said, I had copyright anyway not Grove. I dunno just a funny piece of spleen like arguing with a bus driver.

However considering all that bullshit about no form it be funny if they had to print an announcement they'd fucked my form.

Also I went off my head last week and rapped out twelve page single-space heap of complaints to [John] Hollander in a girl's school in Connecticut.

Meanwhile I'm reading the Goddard book which three years ago I stole from I think San Jose library and have been carrying around since. Phil wrote that Gary was now up there with him, that he, Phil, would stay in Oregon till after the elections (he has to help his Judge friend be re-elected) and then maybe come here (he'd said earlier) around Xmas. He hadn't met Gary yet when he wrote (he was expecting him next day.) Gary'll write in a few days I think. But he'll not come I don't think.

I reread all of the *Bles Blues* and'll return that to Don Allen. I would like to read *Some of Dharma* etc. later. I've never lost your manuscript and had lots of them around. *Blues* are great, I understand them more perfectly now and they're like a monumental Shakespeare sonnet sequence.—all to be published entire—it's a good thing Ferlinghetti didn't publish a selection, actually. Maybe Laughlin could do it. They're a marvelous explanation and reaction to *Dharma* and it's as good as any late novel, better in fact, all poetry.

I read *The Dharma Bums* in one sitting, about five or four hours, the nite Peter brought it back. The whole thing's a great piece of religion testament book, strange thing to be published, I'm glad it is now tho before I'd worried should it be published out of chronological order—but the definite believable presentation of Buddha material is inspiring like a mad movie about St. Francis. The last pages of haikus are good prose. Sentences seem shorter and not so energetic continually as before, and not so mad. You settling down in simpler prose or just tired as you said? [John] Montgomery is great in there, and Gary is fine too, I don't dig myself (too inconsistent mentally) (in the arguments). It is a big teaching book which is rare and spooky. It is spooky, I wonder how XX Century NYC newspapers will react to that? This time it should be funny. You'll get attacked for being enlightened. I made marks on which pages and sentences I thought were groovy, but can show you that in the book when you're here. Rats in attic sentences at end was sublime, so were all the haikus and rainbows at the end. Meditation in the woods I read aloud, or Sheila [Williams] read aloud, great funny sustained serious final testament prose. Amazing after all these years there would be incarnation of some pre-prophesied romantical sense of The End.

Did I tell you, Gregory's, "Hay like universe, golden heap on a wall of fire, sprinting toward the gauzy eradication of Swindleresque Ink"—I decided finally it must be prophecy of disappearance of cosmic illusion. I'd never really understood that in Paterson. Did you see that?

[...]

My poetry is getting to be like your Blues. God knows how I'll get out of that and what literary hassles that will lead to but now does it make difference? I'm also writing like Whalen also.

[...]

Gave my book to Thelonius Monk—he was silent a week—then saw him outside Five Spot and asked him if he'd read it—"Yeah, I'm almost through." "Well?" "It makes sense," what a funny answer.

Owe Gregory a letter. Bill should be back in Paris now—was in Tangiers—the heat's on fairies—"India roll out your carpets" he writes.

When and where is the platform with Lerner? I'd like to go along and hear it all. I never saw you in public.

As ever,

Allen

Jack Kerouac [Northport, New York] to Allen Ginsberg [New York, New York]

October 5, 1958

Allen:

Came home full of exhilaration which became mental exhaustion. I don't think I can do the Hunter College thing now. Like America I'm getting a nervous breakdown. I am going into exile. Wrote Whalen big description of day. All these well dressed people looking at me with slitted eyes, why don't I just retire from the universe. Ah fuck it, I'm going back to Li Po. I hate my beating heart. Something's wrong with the world. I'll be alright in the morning. Grandfather Night in this old house scares me with its black coffin.

See?

Jacky

Jack Kerouac [Northport, New York] to Allen Ginsberg [New York, New York]

October 28, 1958

Dear Allen:

Here's what I'm telling Sterling to do, and it's what I want: to get that new publisher to buy *Sax* for $7500 advance but without a single change; thereby

Sax gets published, what does it matter who? or hard or soft cover? it's still publisht and read and can be reprinted in five years hard. I need the $7500 now to complete the buying of this house so I can put it up for sale, if I don't buy the house now I'll lose the $7000 already in it, by big defaulting suits. A hard and evil world. But *Sax* will be angelly published. If they make changes, no go, I give it back to Don Allen. Meanwhile, I'm insisting that Viking take and publish glorious *Visions Of Gerard* next. No changes except where I'm going to take out the Buddhist imagery and transfer Catholic since the story is about a little Catholic saint. There will be no theological difference . . . The Holy Ghost is Dharmakaya (the body of truth.) See? Etc. Dharmakaya literally means the Holy Spirit, or the Holy Truth, so what's the big tzimis? So I told them, okay I'll go to Paris but I won't write the book about Paris till a year later when I've had time to digest the events. Meanwhile, even, in fact, I think now, I know now, when I get to peaceful Florida this Xmas I'm going to write *The Beat Traveler* anyway about my trip to Burroughs in Tangiers then on up France and London and back, and all the mad sea-writing around that, when I got caught in that great tempest and we had to flee south and almost foundered and I saw the whole jacobs ladder into the sea and saw Stella Maris too and thought NOTHING HAPPENS EXCEPT GOD which was the only thing I could think about because I thought we were all going to drown now . . . O poor seamen.

Okay. I think this is right. Meanwhile I'm sending "Lucien Midnight" to [Irving] Rosenthal[6] and if he rejects it he's crazy but he may reject it because also I told him to give me whatever payment he can, or wants to pay.

My hand is shaking so today, Henri Cru came suddenly as I was balling with my baby and the house then became full of local drinkers and if it hadn't been for the girl cleaning an cooking it would look like hell now. She's coming back Thursday to take care of things while I try to answer a thousand letters. So today I tried, alone, in house, to sit and write you big glorious poem about golden eternity and couldn't because I've so been importuned by this world lately I can't even push a pencil any more so now I know if I want to take Lucien's advice and write more I must leave NY, and will (not so much "importuned" but pleasantly partied, actually, but my god every day, every night, no rest, no solitude, no reflection, no staring at the ceiling or clouds possible any more.) Big mad telegram, for instance, from Lucien, a British lord wants to rush out and interview me and I just GOT interviewed yesterday by *Herald Tribune* here in house, "millions of cool beautiful Marlon Brandos" I told him to say is what Beat Gen is . . . And *Look* mag is sposed to be coming out to interview me too, and meanwhile I try to feed and mind my poor frightened cats, the yard

---

[6] Irving Rosenthal was an editor for the *Chicago Review.*

full of cars. When do I find time to type up Neons from Neal. Allen, can't you go to New Directions office and type up whatever you want (and Laughlin allows). If you need note of intro and permission I'll send. Short of that, okay, I'll type up Neons, let me know. As for poems, I just don't know which ones are forever eternal, goddamit, they the forever eternals I gave Don Allen on that roll but after all I got many more. Why don't I just send some and you judge, I don't know. Besides what's your deadline with City Lights? Let me know deadline, that'll help prod me in ass.—Bruno never came back the next day, he probably went away saying "Ah he's just another fag," you don't know how those characters are, unless you're right about river-of-shit I-don't-care-everything-okay. In any case, whenever I come on with fuck I don't mean it, it's just a Zen joke. In fact it's the one thing I've never done, recall.

The situation about Tuttle etc. and Grove[7] I just don't understand but let me know when time is ripe tho for krissakes yes I don't care but it's a good idea for Phil and Gary to get busy and blow out some poems.

Dody [Muller] is a painter, a big Alene-Esperanza combination in looks (laughs exactly like Alene) but not frigid like Alene, not junky like Espy, built better too, great woman, part Comanche Indian and French, a good painter (huge Al Leslie canvases of pink and blue women bathing) (also little tiny ones so big) and is regular barefoot Provincetown and Mexico City Helen Parker sophisticate also and fantastic cook and clean when does dishes, makes kitchen all beautiful with flowers and displays of vegetables and in the candlelight her face is holy and has black eyes and high cheekbones like I like and everybody likes her and is a young widow. And loves me. And I love her. Don't know what will happen. Used to draw pornographic pictures in her notebook which her mother threw into the sea weeping. In other words big Neal-favorite good doll and so fucking sensual I can't believe my good luck. She knows everybody, which is too bad. Altho good because I know everybody too. What a complicated scene is on now, wow, too much. Henri [Cru] lost his apartment by being evicted, bums he left there lost his cat, he came back no apartment, furniture impounded by marshal, is wandering around looking for cheap pad in Lower East Side, let me know if you know one. Henri great man. Likes you now, he told me. Mustv read your book or something.—I sent off a piece of *Book Of Dreams* to Robert Lowry[8] and also part of a letter from Gregory I'd just got, about his theory of poetry. You'll see it.—What to do? Have another beer.

And to add to all the confusion of my book coming out and all this new spate of publicity and nervousness my sister had to go and throw HER complications

[7] These are references to several anthology projects Ginsberg had proposed to Kerouac.
[8] Robert Lowry was an editor and novelist who wrote reviews for *The Saturday Review*.

in making my mother babysit for a month and here I am no time to shit and the house getting dirtier every day. If you do come, you could in fact come and browse among my manuscripts and type up what you want for anthology, come with in mind not to dirty house and Peter too, like I'm really harried. I wish you would come, like right now this weekend, fuck Norman Mailer he's trying to get in the act. Why wasn't he a hipster when it counted? Why didn't he talk about God when everybody else was talking about Freud? On Friday night Nov 6 I'll be at Hunter Playhouse 68th and Park and will drive back with Dody. I still don't know what I'll say. I'll talk a little, give them their money's worth of Kerouac Beat Generation, then start reading "Bomb" I guess, unless you think of something else and new. (Because I don't really agree with "Bomb" world-apocalypse is good, I believe in people saying it won't happen at all because we've evolved now and become smart human race. I hope). (microphone in heaven). I'd rather read "Marriage", can you bring that for me? And do I shoot you question in audience? Will I be in the enemy camp on that mad night? Do I wear Mighty Goodwills? Am I Sirdanah the Mighty Goodwiller? Do I have to be smart? Do I even have to think? Can I drink beer on the stage or shall I show up quiet wordless sober? Will I address Dean Kauffman directly? Oh yes, don't miss my interview on the editorial page of *Herald Tribune*, by Ray Price, in which I said the old hipster saw, printed for first time now, "Wouldn't it be wonderful if Ike and Dulles and Macmillan and DeGaulle and Khrushchev and Mao and Nehru should all sit around a table and smoke tea? what humor and openmindedness would result, what tender perception." He said he would make that his lead. When the fuxx fuzz comes to my house there won't be a joint or pill in the house so never bring any you and Pete. All I have is dexhamyls by prescription from local doctor. [. . .] Mike Goldberg was telling me how terrible you and Pete were in the Hamptons, says Joyce [Glassman], I don't even remember, I was answering eagerly yes to everything he said (blind drunk) and Joyce said I sold you and Peter down the river and that I was a balloon and that I was always worried what the neighbors would think and etc. embarrassing her in public she added and really, now, when we went to Hecht show you remember we tried to sneak out the back way. Is she demented? I hope she doesn't shoot me before I see *Sax* in print, and *Gerard* next fall. As for new chick (new, NEW, I had no old chick) Henri says because she Indian and French she knife me if I ever kid around other girl. O boy, here goes Léon Robinson into the ends of the night.⁹ What with being pulled apart on earth by you and my mother, in heaven by Buddha and Christ, none of whom can get together I don't know why except over my suffering carcass, wow, this will be the end of

---

⁹ Léon Robinson was a character in L. F. Céline's first novel, *Journey to the End of Night*.

me, I always thought I was too strong to be Stephen Craned like Louis Simpson but it's almost happening and NOBODY IS RESPONSIBLE? You see Nobody is Responsible. Not even me. Not even my mother. I forgive myself first and then all of you for the origigan original ignorance of wanting to be born in the first place but we're doing alright, especially you sweetie.

Jack

Allen Ginsberg [New York, New York] to Jack Kerouac [n.p., Northport, New York?]

170 E 2 St
NYC 9
Oct 29, '58

Dear Jack:

Called Don Allen. He says Grove will really put out books for Gary and Phil, and he wants to publish *Mexico City Blues*. Says Grove wouldn't want all that poetry given to Tuttle they'll print it. I wrote Gary and Phil saying, then, ask Grove to shit or get off the pot (oops excuse) and find out Grove's plans, and then do what they want, choose their publisher—or let Phil henceforth deal with Tuttle—either arrange and edit or let them know no—so they don't get confusing letters from anyone. I also wrote Tuttle that Phil would get in touch with them, that Gary and Phil might have other commitments I dunno, that their letter was sweet and that even if they didn't get the Zen book of our poems, there were still several manuscripts of yours—poetry, *Some of the Dharma*, and biography of Buddha and gave them Lord's address if they wanted to investigate more that. So now I cut out and leave it to Phil and Lord can get in touch with them, tell him, if you want to try *Some of the Dharma*—which might be great to have them publish.

Don Allen was also upset—hadn't received *Dr. Sax* and wanted to know if anything was wrong. I told him I dunno, but you were finished or near finished with work on it. My opinion—don't let Madison Avenue try water you down and make you palatable to reviewers mentality by waiting on wildbooks and putting out commissioned travelogues (however good). *Sax* is logical next book and you're in a position to do what you want now. Aesthetically *Sax* and *Visions of Neal* and *Poems*. After *Sax* they'd have to see prose beauty of Neal and also the hero's real beauty—they been shitting on that poor boy and comparing him unfavorably with nice Japhy [the *Dharma Bums* character based on Gary Snyder]. Perhaps [Sterling] Lord is impressed with that mentality.

Sent [Irving] Rosenthal all Burroughs' manuscript *Interzone* to use as much as he can next issue.

Please send me excerpts from *Visions*, and your best poems forever for the City Lights anthology. There was a long shortline poem adieu / goodby / bonsoir etc. for man in Lowell who dies, GJ's father? you showed me in Berkeley. Also in Helen Weaver's pad two years ago a poem in "long lines" about wine trickling down alley in moonlite. Would like those and choose your blues. Yes? Or not—should I get poem from manuscript at Don Allen?

Navaretta from the party wrote "At his most drunken, or rather ecstatic point, Jack continued to prove that he could take all of it and sing back. This, after all the fancy words, proclaims the poet and artist. It is a question of enduring, and Jack endures—Please tell him he writes like a brother and that I love him like a brother. And thank him for coming to our party as we also thank you, Allen Ginsberg." And he wants to have me write a 3¢ a word an article on extreme abstraction in poetry. I dunno anything about that. Do you? Gregory's a little abstract, that's all I know. Maybe midnight might be considered abstract type prose. I'll say I don't know what it's all about to him.

Your public? Goof! how many times have you (forgotten, drunk) challenged me (and Peter and who?) in public anyway, "C'mon I'll fuck you." Screw public relations let's be kind and truthful. Who else dare?

> Love,
> Allen

Allen Ginsberg [New York, New York] to Jack Kerouac [n.p., Northport, New York?]

170 E 2 St
Mon Nov 17, 1958

Dear Jack:

Just brought in some furniture from Paterson so have set myself up a nice workroom and desk in the apartment. Enclosed find article from *Village Voice* I wrote. Also enclosed a letter from Robert Cummings, editor of *Isis*, the Oxford undergraduate magazine. I gave him some poems of yours while I was in Europe, so he'll publish them with some of mine and Gregory's.

Rosenthal of *Chicago Review* wired me asking me to phone him Saturday Nite. I did, and he said that the University of Chicago had forbidden him to publish Winter issue, which would have consisted of thirty-five pages select cleanish Burroughs, "Sebastian Midnite" complete, and thirty pages [Edward]

Dahlberg. Also said that in future they'd forbid him to publish any of Bill, or you, maybe Dahlberg too even (he wrote a book about Priapus.) Also the University may forbid my poetry reading December 5 under *Review* auspices. So Rosenthal doesn't know what to do. I asked Don Allen and McGregor of New Directions to ask Laughlin, but they don't offer any ideas. I told Rosenthal to write Ferlinghetti and have him print it up as the banned issue *Chicago Review*, City Lights probably would. Meanwhile Rosenthal and staff not made up their mind whether to go ahead and screw the university and end the review—but they probably can't anyway as it's printed at the University of Chicago Press. He'll probably write you. Meanwhile I'm supposed to go there anyway in two weeks (December 5) and read, somewhere, except won't get no pay for it, was supposed to get $150. Want to come to Chicago and be communist hassle martyr with me? (Seems the Hearst press there is trying to bug the university, had last year got book by Maud Hutchins, ex-wife of prexy, banned; and new stink comes from Herb Caen type gossip columnists circulating news stories that filthy magazines are being sponsored by the university. So the school gave in.)

[. . .]

Went to Paterson and brought old letters and documents etc. including some other writings by Huncke buried in attic five years now. Have to look it over yet.

Last Friday lunch with Rosalind Constable and gave her outline of all your books chronologically, she asked for.

House looks great now, special private rooms for writing, huge Brueghel picture of children's games hung by rope from wall, used rope to frame a cardboard picture.

Guess I'll settle in to type last couple years scribbled poetry, ignus etc.

Gregory writes he's feeling fine back in Paris wants to come home, going to be on radio-TV in Berlin to read "Bomb", they invited him. Nothing from Bill. [John] Montgomery's started to bombard me with letters.

Don Allen says [Barney] Rosset turned down separate volumes for Gary and Phil but would do a book of Gary, Phil and myself and you. However Rosset still reading *Blues* and Allen thinks he'll put that out complete.

Don Allen also said he wants to print *Dr. Sax*. Also wants to read *Visions of Neal* again and study it and see if it can be legally printed complete here. Said *Gerard*, "more sentimental" would be good later on for an Xmas book.

Sterling Lord doesn't seem to realize how good *Sax* is literarily nor how good it might be commercially, nor how good it would be for your reputation.

He (Lord) is thinking a good deal in reputation terms. He thinks *Dharma Bums* was good for your intellectual and commercial reputation. He thinks a book on Paris would be, like, new material for the *Spokesman* to deal with. All this is on Viking-Madison Avenue mental level.

I tried explain to him that nite with Deutsch that I agree it's a good thing to consider reputation, I'm in favor of it, *Sax* would be the book to do it with. He asked me did I really think so literarily? I said yes and he seemed surprised. So I gather that the reason he's shopping around with *Sax*, promoting the Viking–Paris book as the next Good Thing, is that he doesn't dig how good *Sax* is.

We talked about that. He says, Jack's next book should

1. deal with different material

2. have more of regular structure-form

I explained that *Sax* does deal with small-town myth-gothic new material, and that it does have, more than any other book, what could be called a regular recognizable classical structure. He didn't seem to understand that either of these points were relevant to his reputation plans, and that *Sax* had them.

So I say, perhaps both Viking and Lord are neglecting your good books and trying to get you to write "potboilers" according to their ideas of what your writing career should develop like.

So I say that since Grove wants to print *Sax*, as your next book, this spring, you ought to let them do it. If Viking objects and wants to print a book first (tho they had the last one)—see if they'll do *Sax* or *Gerard* or *Neal* or a book you *want* printed.

Also, says Don Allen, the *Subs* did well financially, they spent lots money advertising ($6000 he says), made money for you anyway on resale—he also said they'd probably match anybody else's financial offer. Ask Lord to try. Also says Don Allen, they've asked for and wanted the book a long time, and have already signed a contract for it (signed and handed it to Lord, he hasn't signed yet) so they wonder what he's doing. I told Don Allen to have lunch with Sterling, and talk business. So I don't know.

All I'd say, it doesn't matter who prints *Sax* really, except it should be done next, by someone. I dunno. Anyway I get the impression from Lord the basic reason for all this hang-up with Viking, *Sax*, Paris, etc. is that they don't realize how good *Sax* is, otherwise they'd just publish that next and then go on chronologically.

I told Allen you were sick of publishing hassles and wanted quiet and so were leaving all arrangements etc. to Lord, and Tao.

What's new?

As ever,

Allen

Jack Kerouac [Northport, New York] to
Allen Ginsberg [New York, New York]

November 19, 1958

Dear Allen:

I told Sterling that Don Allen said he would match anybody's offer for *Sax*
and I'm seeing Sterling Friday night—I'll be at Dody's [Muller] loft Thursday
evening at 81 Second Avenue above the bakery, will go see you unless you call
first. I told Sterling I want *Sax* published this spring (for $7500 advance, why
not?) and then *Gerard* by Viking in the Fall and then for 1960 my Paris book
which will be alright, in fact it will be called *European Blues* and be all about
Spain and Italy and Hamburg too—(me and Dody digging fishermen's
wives)—or *God Over Europe*, or something—in fact I'll get the title high. I just
wrote my first column for *Escapade* magazine all about Bill and Gregory and
you and me and current state of American Lit being shitty because not yet
published on accounts editors and writers themselves who discard their best
manuscripts. Your *Village Voice* review best I ever got, of course, but *Road* was
not written on benny, on coffee, and in 1951, (May), and wasn't onionskin tele-
type roll but Bill Cannastra's drawing paper etc. we should have consulted
somehow. I thought page 34 to page 25 a real silly maneuver—(by wiseguy
editors who don't believe you anyway).[10] But you told them off. Next time you
start an article say, "Now to put an end to all this cowflop." Okay with me about
Cummings in Oxford—Now that Ferling may do the rejected *Chicago Review*
I guess our anthology is off for a while, anyway I had figured it out, your notes
amount to thirty pages of material and then I was going to throw in the "Three
Stooges" (already printed in Mike Grieg's *New Editions*, without any errors
except dashes) and "Old Bull Balloon" for fairly complete picture. We can do
that on a deadline, anyhow, I'm good on deadlines. Tell me this weekend. No,
don't go to Chicago, what's the use, t'would be better to go nowhere and just go
have long talks with LeRoi Jones or somebody or even arrange yourself a week
of poetry reading at Village Vanguard or something, could be done, would be
great, make a little loot ($400 a week). Or read at Half Note, or don't read, just
type up your poems. Take this advice from a man who has created a masterpiece, what's the sense of traveling around to the midlands of America unless
you have a car or something, I don't know. Just type up your poems. Put together a brand new book of your own stuff for Don or Ferling. If you do go to

---

[10] Ginsberg was annoyed that the first portion of his review of *The Dharma Bums* appeared in the November 12, 1958, issue of the *Village Voice* farther back in the newspaper than the second portion.

Chicago then you should go all the way to the west coast before Gary leaves. I am home alone now with my mother and still can't sleep too good and very nervous and twitchy, I going to get advance from Viking and fetch passport and go to Europe then. I hope Gregory comes back ere that. I will bring Dody so I can have companion of love and also get to know ladies as well as gentlemen of Europe, move around more and be spectacular scott fitzgerald type investigators instead of just me like a thief. Nobody trusted me when I was in Paris because they knew I was an English thief—with Dody I can go to big cocktail parties in Paris and meet fashionables and pass out and be cute, not bummy— either that or I don't go at all. I mean, maybe I won't even go. What I care about Europe? How's Peter? Has he written new notes? Tell him Lafcadio came over with his paints and a bare canvas and painted my portrait in the kitchen making me look small childlike Jake Spencer and took it home to show to his Ma, wants me to buy it but I'm going to save my money now, spent $150 last week on food and liquor for everyone, too much—I'm not William Faulkner movie writer yet. But painting is fine and he said he would not show it to you or Peter at all, so don't mention it. Dody says he is a nice boy, just shy, not crazy at all. Don't press him too much, he told me he was bugged by you and Peter pressing him to "come out." He don't want come out. Everybody wants him come out— even strangers like Henri Cru—let him dream. My mother and I going to stay in Northport now so all's well and I see you often. Hearst-political hassles in Chicago not worthy of your time. Whow Who's Hearst in Eternity? When you see Lucien tell him I see him this weekend. Actually I don't know what's going on and don't really care, maybe I will leave everything in Lord's hands and just go on, I feel like taking sketches of Europe now, as well as Manhattan when I'm there alone in cafeteria. See you soon. (Friday or Thursday or Saturday.)

Jean
Jack

Jack Kerouac [Northport, New York] to Allen Ginsberg [New York, New York]

December 16, 1958

Dear Allen (Dec. 16):

Just got "Midnight" from [Irving] Rosenthal, he doesn't like Jean-Louis so I decided once for all on "Old Angel Midnight." I'd stayed up all night trying to find names in Bible and Dictionary, gave myself a headache, listed down such names as Lauschen M., Listen M., Lumen M., Luscious M., Labium M. TiJean M., Jean-Louis M., Jeshua M., Hezion M., Vision M., Grecian M., Goshen

M., Nimshi M., Ziphion M., Nineveh M., Neriah M., Misham M., Mishma Midnight, Misham Midnight, Leshem, Shelah, Shelumiel, Shelomi, Sheshan, Elishua, Enosh, Ephean, Eliatha, Shimeon, Marcion, Halcyon, Elysean, Lover Midnight, Illusion Midnight, Notion M and finally couldn't sleep and watched Charley Van Doren on morning TV show where he suddenly begins telling Ling Giggling Ling tale by Mark Twain about an "old angel" in heaven and it was like the magic of his father and I took it. So I'm sending it tonight with these changes, using Lucifer Woidner at one point since he's an old angel of light they say. Rosie says he has the $600 for the publication so it's all set.

I'm sending you enclosed in this letter your story we writ at Lucien's farm, which has bit poems here and there for you, of yours, and I'm going to quote you a letter I just got from Henry Miller:

"Big Sur 12/9-58 Dear Jack Kerouac—I don't know where Ginsberg gets his mail, so you write him a postcard, will you, and thank him for his letter. Tell him that the review he wrote of your *D.B.* [*Dharma Bums*] in the *Village Voice* (N.Y.) struck me as quite, quite wonderful. . . . I felt, when I read *D.B.* that you must have written millions of words before—and I see, via A.G., that you have. Salute! P.S. Do you read French? I know, or hear, that you are French Canadian, but—? Anyway, if you do, I'd like to send you "Salut Pour Melville" by Jean Giono." etc.

I'm putting down most everything, I've decided, except you and Dody and Peter in NY with a few exceptions, I really don't care if I ever see six million of those madcaps ever again. I'm really all up to here now. Have mad new great novel in mind I think I'll write after Christmas, beginning right after *Desolation Angels* in Arizona desert, to down to Mexico with Bill, you and Greg and Laff and Pete in Mex., pyramids, etc. floating gardens, etc. up to NY in that mad packed car, the Helens, WCWilliams, Yugo freighter, Tangier, Paris, Greg, (Bill), London, ship back, Florida, mad bus trip with my Ma to Berkeley, Whalen, back again to (after little North Beach anecdotes) Fla., back alone on bus to Mexico in time for earthquake, back to Fla., illness, then up to big "what you call October wave of beauty crashing over my head" publication of *Road* on up to nightclubs, readings, albums, interview, the whole mad scene in its entire nutty entirety (including Lucien weekends, Pat McManus,[11] etc etc.) showing how it starts I'm a rucksack bum in the desert trudging along not knowing fortune is a crock in America. Think of a nice title for me. Fame in America? Trial on Earth. Through the Wringer. Love on Earth. (The weight of the world is love indeed). (O yes including the mad nun scene I made, etc.) A big epic book telling all the critics and reviewers how full of shit they are, right

[11] Patricia McManus was the publicity director at Viking Press.

in their faces. Well, I'll write a book soon anyway, maybe get mad and just do *Memory Babe* childhood *Town City* reminiscences in real life non-fiction setting.

Meanwhile it looks like Viking okay for *Gerard*, and Allen (Don) wants *Sax*, and Jerry Wald interested in *Road* again he says. I'm being quiet and healthy and happy taking long walks in sub zero I mean freezing yard in cold moonlight and have color and clear eyes, don't drink at home, do my exercises and feel great. Eat big meals in kitchen and sneer at TV and say to people on TV "Oh ain't we smart!" which is my old original self okay. I mean, all this consanguine diamond sutra vow to be kind to every tom dick and harry and waste my energy and health. Kind to sportswriters and priests, kind to memo book salesmen and reel engineers. O yes, have a tape, just recording jazz now, later languij.

See you this weekend 19th and 20th and 21st.

Jean-Louis

1959

Editors' Note: In January 1959, Kerouac and Ginsberg performed in Robert Frank and Al Leslie's movie, **Pull My Daisy.** When Jack was in the city he tended to drink to excess and retreated more frequently to his mother's house for solitude. Ginsberg became more occupied with readings, interviews, and public appearances around the country. On March 26, Allen was scheduled to read at Harvard and had hoped that Jack would go with him, but Kerouac sent his regrets. In order to keep his sanity, Jack was trying to keep out of the limelight.

Jack Kerouac [Northport, New York] to Allen Ginsberg, Gregory Corso, and Peter Orlovsky [New York, New York]

March 24, 1959

Dear Allen, Gregory, Peter:

It looks like I can't go to Harvard anyway because *Holiday* magazine wants those two articles by March 30th and it will take me several days to type them and also make bigger sentences out of our material. In other words I'm staying home to make your money for India and Crete. Besides, I'm tired. Hearing your Chicago records (tapes) made me feel depressed all over again about poetry readings. Too much repetition of same material for new audiences, etc. Too much the eagerness to be accepted. O well, you know how I feel and felt about that in Frisco.

Here's your check for 15 bucks I owe you. If I suddenly go mad and decide to go to Harvard with you anyway I will be at your pad at 3 or 4 on Thursday.

But then that would only be if I finisht and mailed off those two articles to *Holiday* by then. Almost impossible.

How you like my new typewriter type?

American College Dictionary sent me their big square definition of "beat generation" and wanted to know if I would revise, emend or make a new one. Theirs was awful, "certain members of the generation that came of age after World War II who affect detachment from moral and social forms and responsibilities, supposedly due to disillusionment. Coined by John Kerouac."

So I sent in this: *"beat generation,* members of the generation that came of age after World War II-Korean War who join in a relaxation of social and sexual tensions and espouse anti-regimentation, mystic-disaffiliation and material-simplicity values, supposedly as a result of Cold War disillusionment. Coined by JK"

If I don't come to Harvard, read them this definition and tell them that I "plead work as my excuse for not attending the reading at Harvard, for every Massachusetts boy dreams of Harvard."

My mother (not wanting me to go get plastered so often in NY, and me too I get sick and dirty and don't work) invites all three of you come out here any time you want, so after Harvard let's do our tapes etc. Also you can see my paintings etc. Also, Allen, I have copy of *Jabberwock* sent to you care of me, by big Scotland types, who want our work published there in fall, and other items.

Anyway, I'm not a liar. As to my recent belligerent drunkenness I just noticed today it all began last April right after that bum pounded my brain head with his big fingered fist ring . . . maybe I got brain damage, maybe once I was kind drunk, but now am brain-clogged drunk with the kindess valve clogged by injury.

More anon. Addio.

Jack

Editors' Note: In April, Ginsberg took his first jet flight, traveling to San Francisco, where in addition to various public events, he visited Neal Cassady who was in San Quentin prison serving time on drug charges. The relationship between Kerouac and Ginsberg was becoming strained, in part due to Jack's drunken and abusive phone calls to Allen, and in part due to Allen's continuing promotion of the Beat Generation.

Allen Ginsberg [San Francisco, California] to Jack Kerouac [n.p., Northport, New York?]

City Lights
261 Columbus
S.F. Cal
May 12, 1952 [*sic*: 1959]

Dear Jack:

Fine, your check came a day after I delivered typewriter to Neal—cost exactly $50—a secondhand rebuilt portable—noiseless for tact's cell sake. No not paranoiac about kitchen yakkings tho if I shut up (as before) and didn't yell back I would wind up paranoiac. Just thought it was time to scream back and you were receptive. I wrote big two page letter to *NY Times* about *Dr. Sax* yesterday, said it was a "grand luminous poem" and maybe they'll publish it. I saw so far *NY Post*, *SRL* and *Times*. Any others? I mentioned Melville in letter. Sneaky queer article on me in *Partisan* by Diana Trilling. She thinks "Lion" is a faggy poem to Lionel. Ugh, Icky. Don Allen was here preparing a new SF issue [of *Evergreen Review*], and he mentioned he hoped to get more Brakeman on

RR ["October in the Railroad Earth"] from you for it so it's a happy holy coincidence you sent it in when you did.

Yah, Yah, and Sterling Lord sent us big fat check for $450 last week. O how delightful, thank you very much, how noble that we all have that easy money thru your typings and friendlies. I also got some money from City Lights so I have $600 and will take slow trip home in drive-car-east for someone if can find car needs driving and see Death Valley and Grand Canyon, be home June mid-most. And Bill says he's coming to NYC late June or July—and Don Allen says he'll try arrange an advance for Bill thru Grove to cover round-trip boat-fare. Burroughs now in Paris fled from Tangiers—police after him there on suspicions, but nothing real so he's alright.

I'll try bring Phil Whalen up, east, with me, he's broke anyway now and has nothing to do here but get job which he doesn't want to.

Gregory wrote me nutty postcard after I sent him $40 saying Nicholson[1] had given him 675$ is that true?

When you leave for Fla?? Bill probably come down there to see Willie [Burroughs's son] so you'll see him.

Giving reading here with all the poets, Wieners, McClure, Whalen, Duncan, etc etc. to raise loot for *Measure* mag. and also giving free reading at the Mission, and then I'm done with all reading for good for years.

Do you want the *Kaddish* for your Avon Book?[2] *Big Table* and *Yugen* have parts, and [Stephen] Spender asked me for it all for *Encounter* but probably can't since mags already have it. Let me know if you want it for Avon. How you coming? It must be a lot of heroic beer. Let me know whatever you want from me. Maybe the politics poem?

Don Allen has a lot of material he assembled from SF too. Duncan has a beard and looks like Whitman and rough and bearded and lives isolate on the coast and comes to town once a week to dentist and is much more vigorous than before, less pansy aesthetic, loudervoiced, grey hairs in beard—much better appearance. Just as stupid tho. And met [Brother] Antoninus who was always looking like ready to cry, and talks squeezing his hands in crotch in black suit bending head down low to the floor and whines. Strange pipple. Weather here just like Tangiers. Bright sky and bay. I saw Neal thrice in S.Q. [San Quentin], he's hung a little on his martyrdom doom of five-to-life for three sticks. and not people to organize pro-marijuana societies.

Love,

Allen

[1] Johnny Nicholson was a wealthy restaurateur and friend of Kerouac's.
[2] Kerouac had been asked by Avon to edit a book of contemporary poetry. Although he worked on it and mentioned it in the next few letters, it was never published.

Gavin Arthur, teacher of Neal's S. Q. religion Saturday morning class is doing my horoscope. I read "Caw Caw" there and all the cons go around in cells now saying "Man then really wails—Caw Caw." Next week I go down to Stanford to take LSD 25.[3]

Jack Kerouac [Northport, New York] to Allen Ginsberg [San Francisco, California]

May 19 '59

Dear Allen:

Please forward this to Neal, I don't know his "number" and also, when answering me, please, send me Neal's entire address. Read letter then seal. It's just a little note.—So much mail in my room I can't sit. Will you ask Ferlinghetti if 5,000 additional words of "Old Angel" enough? They are written and ready to mail, also the cover (ink and pastel, weird). But that goddam [Irving] Rosenthal has not gotten our release for Old Angel yet! And never paid me $50 token as promised! What IS Irving's ax address?

Glad about typewriter. Now Neal can work. And he will. I never saw *NY Post* review of *Sax*, musta been awful, but *Time* waxed good. *Time* likes to be put down, Dennis Murphy threw them off porch and they gave him swell review. Had we ever mailed that madletter to Lipscombe? Didn't see Diana Trilling's, heard much sick reaction everywhere even Wesleyan college where on whim went to accompany Gregory and had big fantastic time almost endless to describe. I danced with teenage girls in shorts, like a kid I was (they had shorts) . . . Wesleyan is run, I mean led, the boys are led, by two strange Russian jews with phony names (Charley Smith and the guy who wrote the introduction at the reading). I told them we would convert Moscow or something. I was a bit silly. Mason H. [Hoffenberg] drove us back in hotrod to Persia New Haven. I autographed twenty *Saxes* and *Roads* and *Subs*, etc. with all weird poems in them and drawings by Gwegowy. I banged piano. I wrestled wrestlers in the grass. Gregory went to a picnic with three hundred girls while I slept. We had to flee. The reading: G's "Bomb" reading made me weep (quietly), I read "Doc Benway" to roars of laughter, read just like Bill does. Also read last two pages of *Bums*. Got nice letter from Gary Snyderee. All's well. I leave for Fla. I don't know, six weeks or so, I guess, will see Bill in NY I guess. With Whalen also in town we

---

[3] Ginsberg volunteered to take part in experiments to study the effects of LSD on the human brain. It was to be his first exposure to the drug.

better cool it, Gregory almost started race riot in Seven Arts when Negro slapped him, mad Italian rage, Lucien and Cessa were there. Our movie ([Robert] Frank) is best movie I seen. Germans buying it. Also TransLux chain I guess. But it's all too much and I'm afraid now, we gotta get out of NY. Arch Washington Square on Sundays crowded with thousands of beatniks. Thru which Gregory and I and Persian and Stanley Gould walk highdown billkick. Why don't you write a new poem about jet plane adventure for Avon anthology. Please tell McClure and McLaine that I rec'd manuscripts and that anthology people at Avon are slow. Write new poem for me, or anything you want. Antonius [Brother Antoninus] sounds great. Reading at SQ [San Quentin] a triumph of your prophetic soul, boy. You were prophetic right about *Sax* too, *Sax* instead of Mad Avenue Winking Wiking Pwess. Caw Caw. You're the hippest kid. If Irving Layton or whatever his name is, I mean Lawrence Lipton knew how hip it is to be hip like you . . . ah shit, that book is awful, all about his own barefooted bearded non-working art friends who don't write but just talk and show off and the things about us who started it all are pejorative. *Holy Barbarians* is the first full-scale attempt by the communist party to infiltrate the Beat Generation, and please tell everybody I said so, if you want. I don't want to have anything to do with no communists: tell them to leave my name out of it. And they even can get poor innocent pure jazz musicians in hot water: their awful hot water of hatred. You and I and Burroughs and Gregory and Peter believe in God and TELL THEM THAT, YELL IT! (Burroughs said so in *Word*.) (But why was it deleted from original manuscript of *Word*, which I have here)?—God is what everything is. Everything is a vision of God's mind which is No-Mind. When people are shitty it's because they don't know. don't know this. And God in his mercy gave me alcoholism instead of leprosy. Got big mad letter from Lamantia in Mehico. Also an enormous huge spread in Copenhagen Denmark paper with big pictures of me and [James] Dean and [Norman] Mailer and all about you inside and all in Danish. Saw John Holmes, okay, we went to opening of awful *Nervous Set* musical by Jay Landesman, music was good, story itself is middle-class play about lumpenproletariat beatniks. Condescension dripping from stage. The beatnik himself a silly fool. Jay was sad. But he will get his money back anyway, it'll run about six weeks. Why don't somebody produce my angelic play I wrote? Why don't Hollywood buy my angelic *Road* if they want beat movies? What's going on, Allen? It's not money I'm worried about any more, but the perversion of our teaching which began under the Brooklyn Bridge long ago? Gregory and I also crashed in on Jay Laughlin, and on Richard Wilbur, and I got Samuel Greenberg poems for anthology (from Mr. Laughlin). I haven't even had time to write my new column. I'm not going into NY any more, except when

Bill gets here. I have a broken leg. All day yesterday I was wearing a hat that wasn't on my head (tell that to Creeley).

Goombye.

Don't steal that hat. I want it. Grook. Yak. Kitchen yakkings. Not important. Come on. Besides soon we'll part, later grow old, die, you won't even be at my funeral . . . we'll remember with tears. I'm sorry I hurt you. Our lives are no longer ours. So we'll go home. Far away. Goldclime. Don't waste your energy on the frenzies of mediocrities. Genius is Calm. Whalen is a Genius. Caterpillar genius. Peter is a Saint. So sleep. Write hymn for me.

Jack

Jack Kerouac [Northport, New York] to Allen Ginsberg [San Francisco, California]

June 18 1959

Hello Mike!

Dear Allen:

Received all your poems and everybody's poems, Whalen's etc. (including your recent batch with Burroughs letter enclosed) so all is set except the kind of mad man who is the editor at Avon who keeps taking me out on binges that always end the same way with him flipping beating his girl who cries on my shoulder etc. I keep getting the feeling the anthology will never out, he'll kill himself or something (insane Tom Payne) . . . I told him and told him to rush on this job because I'm leaving but he does nothing, so it looks like I'll have to write my running commentary on the (now) two anthologies (have that much material!) in Florida or even Mexico since I'm leaving Northport here within a month . . . actually might get it all done at last minute. Will leave present pile at Sterling's. If this guy flips (and W. R. Hearst just bought Avon Books!) and everything falls thru I will be accused by all the poets of stealing their manuscripts! But I'll have to mail them all back at my own expense. The trouble with these (like you sad) (said) guys in "business" (Payne is the guy who wrote that letter about the disastrousness of publishing *Sax* at this time) is that they don't have the quiet serene sense of work-accomplished that we "beatnik" poets have, they flip and let everything go to pot!! I could have all this anthology, both of em, ready in two days if he'd simply send me his batch, which I would collate with my new batches, tack on commentaries, and send to printer!—Anyway, we'll see.

Allen, Hanover records who made my Steve Allen record now want to advance you $500 to make an album with them, in NY here, also they want Gregory. So there's your money you need! THAT could be your last reading.

Sterling is going to be your agent in this deal anyway so write to Sterling and get all the details. He SHOULD be your agent or you'll get screwed on subsidiary rights later on, so stick to him, he's been fair and honest with me, and he is willing to arrange for Gregory too. The guy looking for you is Bob Thiele.

Everything is too much, I'm trying to run away back to my quiet soul now but so many things hanging, so I turned down another album offer (was to cut it tomorrow) and turned down even articles with *Playboy* etc., I am mentally exhausted and spiritually discouraged by this shit of being of having to do what everybody wants me to do instead of just my old private life of poesies and novelies as of yore.

I met Eugene your brother on the train and said I would like him to be my attorney in the closing sale of house but when I got back to N'Port it turned out the broker had arranged for local lawyer and I want to tell Eugene but lost his card and don't have his address or anything, so tell him? He did send me a penny postcard with a completely illegible illegible return address.

Even Lucien came to get me last night for wild weekend in woods, can't do it, have to concentrate on packing and escaping all this. Lucien said I had become strangely philosophical. I saw a snapshot of myself taken recently in which I could see with my own eyes what all this lionized manure has done to me: it's killing me rapidly. I have to escape or die, don't you see? I can't get all hungup at this time on anything ANYTHING. So what I can do, as last thing, is ask Laughlin to write to Neal and offer him a job, okay. I haven't even got the spiritual energy to write a preface to *Visions of Cody* like Laughlin wants.

As for Jacques Stern, if he can write prose like *Subterraneans* and has imagination to conceive a *Dr. Sax* and the energy to write an *On the Road* and the spiritual fervor to write a *Visions of Gerard*, I'll believe what Bill says about him. Sounds like he's hypnotized Bill, to me, what with all the drugs too. There will be a great writer who will rise above us but I'm sure he will be a young American kid in about ten or twenty years, like after Melville and Whitman there came Twain. Don't be discouraged by talk like that from Bill, he sounds jealous now. I'm so sick of being insulted by every critic and everybody and now even by Bill whom I lauded so much and put over so well at Wesleyan! Fuck him. Besides no Stern Jackes can write a "Bomb" like Gregory, I can promise you that. Have you seen Dr. W.C. Williams' weird statement about Peter Orlov?—that we have a lot to learn from Petey?—in that new magazine put out by Willard Maas' son? Somebody stole my copy of it. Wagner College magazine.

Meanwhile, I hope I see you, when you get back just come with Peter to visit his mother and drop over, my mother won't mind and we'll say goodbye here. If you're too late, I'll see you in India or in Heaven . . .

Hasn't it been awful? We were so swingy? And now young poets are sneering at us? And saying that we're merely mellow classics now? without even reading *Sax* and *Kaddish*? in fact they're all screaming at the same time, how can they read?—Ho Ho!—I know what part of the blue sky. I go to . . . Ho Ho I'm happy. I'm happy to be free again . . . Ho Ho.

    Cruseke. fool him all

                Jean XXX

Allen Ginsberg [San Francisco, California] to Jack Kerouac [Northport, New York]

July 1, 1959 c/o City Lights

Dear Jack:

    Living in dank hotel on North Beach last few days preparing to leave. Still working on Neal—endless complications, newspapermen with wisecracks and political connections, lawyers, etc. once I set whatever impulse I can going in the machinery, I'll leave—just a few days. Laughlin wrote a beautiful letter, rapidly.

    Sorry I will miss you before July 4—the Fantasy record was slow making and then this Cassady dilemma. Maybe see you in Florida with Burroughs. Thanks for arranging deal with Hanover, but I'd already signed good contract with Fantasy and was working on the tape. They also sent Gregory $150 to Venice, he wrote he was in jail. You're right to disappear to Florida and take it easy. All the poets here Duncan (who is a good poet) and the lousy ones are tearing me apart psychically with their joyless ambitions. John Wieners by the way—I heard him read his *Hotel Wentley* poems—it made me cry, they are classic like Hart Crane's "Behind my fathers cannery works"—You have that book? He is a real poet, sad and damned and tender. I mean better than anything else here except Chances.

    Oh Bill must be a little nuts with dope now, that's all, and Stern has him hypnotized by flattery and junk and yachts. Also Stern's intelligent—they must be on some strange kick. Bill probably write disillusioned Mediterranean letters soon. Yes he forgets the art-devotion pact, and mellowness under ten year bridges. But he never dug that as much as mysterious sorceries with chemicals and psychic strange victories. So he's doing fine up his alley. I saw the Wagner magazine, it was funny and full of attention, but it depressed me, nobody gets the joke. Williams on Peter is golden hearted though. I dunno why old English Anarchist [Sir Herbert] Read thinks we're Nihilists, but he's more sympathetic than most big shots.

    After a year's stupidity I finally got the point—Peter's typing his poem up *with* spelling mistakes. They're part of the beauty of his soul I see. I was always trying to clean them up to be neat. So far, find what we got enclosed. There are some more but he types so slow and I only goof when I do them for him, tho I did type some.

Anyway, we'll leave here very soon, and in a car, with a few hundred $ from Fantasy, and swing into the West and wander hand in hand in small towns by deserts and forget the world awhile anyway, I want to see Grand Canyon still. We'll drive over Yosemite Sierras and down the east side of the mountains and maybe thru Death Valley.

From my LSD poem—take *out* that little section of lines "Gods dance on their own bodies . . . This is the end of man"—and put it separate as a little poem. It doesn't belong *in* the LSD notes, I added it later.

Keep Peter's spelling the way it is, if it looks alright to you—change what you think necessary if any.

I'm dragged and depressed by literary politics—my own fault for even getting involved at all—OK be free under blue sky soon. Flowers,

Allen

Jack Kerouac [Northport, New York] to Allen Ginsberg [New York, New York]

October 6, 1959

Allen:

Truman Capote notwithstanding,[4] I'm still catching up with the stuff I wrote by hand, am only now (like you) typing up *Orlando Blues* written in 1957, also busy. Running the anthology isn't as hard as you think, I can answer [Marc] Schleifer[5] myself, in fact am doing so this minute, okay I can do whole thing by myself if you want. I thought you might need the money and ALSO have a better knack than me for picking up true gems and historical diamonds . . . more opportunity, that is, hanging around Village etc. Let me know what you secretly really feel you want to do about working with me or not on Avon anthology. The second number is already well set with Ed Dorn's great new poems, his "Buck" story, with [Bob] Donlin's great story, with [Herbert] Huncke's new gems you mentioned (Huncke, all he has to do is keep writing those gempy vignettes and then we'll have a whole BOOK and take it to Sterling)—(Peter too)—(you too). Tell your story, you lazy bastards, people pay

---

[4] Capote had dismissed Kerouac's work, saying, "That's not writing, it's typing."
[5] Marc Schleifer was the editor for *Kulchur* magazine.

money for stories not just easy pomes rattled off couches. Yes we can have Avon send back what we don't want with big diplomatic notes by Preston or Payne, easy enuf. In fact Schleifer already recovered his manuscript and wants to bring it back again! You don't have to visit Payne and bother him, do all by mail. As I say, I can do it alone—I am going to start writing longer smarter running commentaries for this material too—first time is short drunk notes—Time to get Tough, like *Time* magazine—SO MAKE UP YOUR MIND ABOUT CO-EDITORSHIP.

What radio station will you be on with *Mexcity Blues*, when, date? I am going to H'wood Nov. 12th in train for 2 G shot with Steve Allen, want to read railroad prose or something—or from *Visions of Neal* about west—golden west—so won't leave NY till then, go to Mexico after. Got a note and a poem from Creeley, will ask him for stuff for second anthology.

The only way to detach yourself from all this frantic non-literary activity is go away, to Greece join Gregory write golden poems under fig trees of Crete. If you work like your father keeps yapping in Paterson you could fritter away in office desk—travel! That $100 you spent last week was half fare to Greece. When my *On the Road* deal is set, if ever, I'll give or lend you the money for any trip you want. We'll try to make a trip with Lucien to mountains this October, okay?

Big Table sold 7000 copies of that mag., made enough money to pay me my measly $50 for "Old Angel", haven't done it, in fact have the nerve to write nasty notes to Sterling who's only doing his job, and then on top of all that hold back my Ferlinghetti deal, just a bunch of greedy sneaky shits and you can shove them up your ass, and on top of that they use MY title. Start a magazine of your own—why fiddle around with Paul Carroll⁶—who is dying to put not only me down, but poor McClure and Whalen and Lamantia, like a virago—who cares about him anyway? What has he done to command your attention?—and what's so great about the magazine? LeRoi [Jones] is starting *Kulchur* and you have *Yugen* and *Beatitude*, all those lil things will grow into big *Dials* in time.

Okay for mescal, be in soon, but waiting for you and Pete come out here like you said to pick up clothes and dig basement . . . altho, wait, then, I'll come out myself soon and bring the clothes a neat package. Everything mixed up, in fact—movie men coming this afternoon, silly telegram just came, I can't even write letters, bulletins everywhere.

[. . .] Virus gone now, except big cough like I had remember in January 1957 at the Helens' when we all had coughs from Mexico trip in car. Yes I remember Spencer . . . I don't have the Dutchman's address—why don't I do that in your

---

⁶ Paul Carroll was one of the founders of *Big Table* magazine in Chicago.

kitchen, on white sheet. That's nice the nice things you write about me. In next anthology I will try to match that.

Just wrote the finger sutra, in my yard, t'other night, pod. silly, I guess. am kinda bored. Enclosed is a seminar where they lump beatniks with delinquents and drag what's left of the segment of America that's artistic into the criminal muck. Thought you might want to throw a bomb at them. This is the good work of Alfred Zugsmith emerging, like last night a parody on me on TV "Jack Crackerjack" I leap up (hair pasted on brow) and start screaming "I saw the best minds of my generation destroyed by naked hysteria . . . Kill for the sake of killing!" (Louis Nye the actor) ugh.

Jack

Allen Ginsberg [New York, New York] to Jack Kerouac [n.p., Northport, New York?]

October 16, 1959

Oct. 1959

Dear Jack:

Got your letter, and had sent one yesterday answering some questions, yes, I'm working, and been to see the material at Avon as said and did not bother Payne—in any case he'd asked me to come up independent of that material and suggest some other books to him (collected Melville poems, Dickinson, Lindsay, etc.).

I sent that piece back to Schleifer as I said. The magazine *Kulchur* will be edited by him—he wants some kind of satire magazine which will be mostly *Village Voice* sociology like his Mickey Mouse routine, that's his deal, it's not really a literary magazine unless people send him poems, which I will.

Yes I'm happy about working on the Avon, finish up a few pet projects. All we'll have to do is spend a day assembling everything.

I don't want to tell my story, easy poems is enough, I don't like work, life is too short. I worked too much in Bickfords,[7] I refuse to write prose till it comes out without work like a dream like poetry.

Good thing to get tougher on Avon book, yes let's be serious.

Have a nice trip thru west on train—try and stop and see Grand Canyon. I'll watch you on TV. I go make a tape with Casper Citron [at] WBAI next Monday morn, I don't know when it'll be broadcast.

---

[7] Bickford's was a cafeteria on Times Square where Ginsberg washed dishes and many of his friends hung out.

Lucien'll get in touch with you about mountains.

The printing bills on *BT* [*Big Table*] I & II are just about being done paid off by now, I unnerstand, but there's no money to give printer for next issue, which is where they have financial problems. They did not have enough money to finance SF poets trip, they weren't putting down the poets. In fact Podell the business manager arranged for *Playboy* to finance the trip for a TV shot, so *BT* will sponsor a reading, to split dividends and help raise money for next issue. Paul Carroll has lost his job at Loyola because of scandal of involve with *BT* and is himself broke and paying for mag out of his own pocket, but now has no job. They are not holding back Ferlinghetti deal, he is not I mean, Ferl himself wants to wait till post office OK's "Midnight"; the matter of selling out *Big Table* I is a consideration but not a primary one. *Big Table* would not offer objections to Ferl going ahead I don't think. If you want Ferlinghetti to publish it now, write him and tell him you want him to despite the fact that he doesn't have clearance from P.O. Is not that big a problem and if you would really like the book out right now soon I'm sure he would be agreeable.

I mean I refuse to get mad and het up about Carroll who's a horses ass as far as that goes and a mild virago but is working within his limitations as best he can and is not a total loss. In any case I refuse to get mad at anything now because beauty is the great murderer. I would like to see *BT* continue if it can because I already put time and effort into it, it first published Burroughs and Carroll is still fighting that in courts, it did first print "Old Angel Midnight" which the Harvard people refused to do, and it's a lot of trouble to start a new one, besides we have a new one in Avon already, but not a Little Magazine which can have criticism if any and book reviews of *Gasolines* and *Mexcity Blues*, and *Kaddishes*, and *Kulchur* is not going to swing with Poesy, and *Yugen* is only Poesy, and *Beatitude* is run by the SF Bread and Wine Mission now but is half for the purpose of publishing local teenage poesy around North Beach, which it should be. Not that *BT* is *that* necessary. But *Evergreen*'s already gone to French pot. So while it's alive I don't want to discourage it worse than Carroll's done already and maybe help him get himself straight. Meanwhile for next issue he has Peter poems, "Laugh Gas", a Selby prose, an article by Creeley on Olson's prosody, etc. so maybe it not be totally dead.

In fact I sent Carroll that essay on your prose, get it out faster than Al Leslie. No need to get excited about him—but I must say Carroll does manage to bug more people faster than I dreamed possible—even Irving [Rosenthal] won't write him at the moment, insulted. What a—I mean it's a big Buster Keaton comedy not serious as Oatmeal. It's all a bunch of shit, nothing to get excited over. Carroll has temporarily (maybe permanently) lost his mind, because he's always had money, and nice jobs, now he's in debt and involved with life and is hysterical. Maybe recover.

I went out to Paterson last weekend and sat with Uncle Abe.

I'll send a note to the seminar.

OK—As ever

Allen

When you be in? Don't answer with big letters unless you're bugged with everything else. I'll see you in town soon. Everything fine here, new postcard from Gregory with Greek Charioteers. I'll be in India next year there's time enuf then for solitudes.

The general public image of beatniks built up from movies, *Time*, TV, *Daily News*, *Post* etc. is among the hep a fake and among the mass evil and among the liberal intellectuals a mess—but that is weirdly good I dig, that we are still so purely obscure to philistines that it's inevitable that it be misunderstood— since how can a whole nation perceive the illusion of life in one year? and since we wind up upholders of comradeship and satori, how can that be expected to be massly understood in warworlds? Mockery is inevitable compliment. Look what happened to poor Christ, he got crucified.

[. . .]

Love,

Allen

Jack Kerouac [Northport, New York] to Allen Ginsberg [New York, New York]

November 2, 1959

Allen:

Here is Herbert [Huncke]'s check. He asked for $25 on the phone but this is a huge sum, I'm not Frank Sinatra. I would appreciate if he would pay it back when *Playboy* takes his story. Send "Hermaphrodite," they won't take "A Sea Voyage" because of queer scenes. Huncke's "Sea Voyage" shows that he is a perfect writer. (Also send "Cuba" to *Playboy*).

The amphetamine was the cause of Lois' [Sorrells] flip and my own when I got home, exhausted and to the point of madness. So I'm glad I didn't bring it. Don't anybody use it.

When I got home there were thirty letters and telegrams each one insanely demanding something. I see now clearly that I have to quit the whole scene for good. I don't want to see anyone or talk to anyone, I want to go back into my own mind. It's murder pure and simple.

One was a telegram from William Morris demanding I read at the monster poetry rally. The list would kill you. Demands for free prose and poetry, for me to phone at once, for me to attend receptions and Halloween parties, for me to write the publicity for MGM's *Subterranean* movie, for me to answer obscure literary points in England, for me to appear in public, for me to write columns I never planned, for me to send books to all parts of the world, for me me me in my one trembling body . . . so I'm cutting out. After [Steve] Allen show in H'wood I'm going to Mexico and won't be back till my birthday March 12. Give my love to Huncke, Petey, Lucien. This is awful. I'm going OUT. There's nothing personal. I feel I need Gary's Way now. For a while, a long while. This is serious. I'm mad. There's no hope. Eugene Burdick was right when he said "bemused spectators crowding around have suffocated the beat vision." I know you have fun spending mornings answering letters but my prose work takes more energy. I have last part of Tristessa all set to do the Lucien story and if he changes his mind I'll hide it okay. There is a dream of cold mountain ranges on a gray day with clouds that open silent window. Cities and poets are repetitious. It's time for the world to change. Nobody believes in enlightenment, i.e., kind tranquility, kind silence. I know you and Petey are trying hard without phone etc. but get thee to that finca. Anyway, love as always and see you.

> Jack

I'm not a Messiah, I'm an artist.

Allen Ginsberg [New York, New York] to Jack Kerouac [n.p., Northport, New York?]

November 5, 1959

Yes, glad you forgot the amphetamine—can only be used one day rarely, by me, for writing—then I leave off for half a year. Can't be used consecutively.

Decision to cut out is a good idea. You are "outnumbered" and too many things to do, drive reality from the mind. Lay what you think need be done on me, or on Sterling—make him handle *all* requests, I'll not send any to you henceforth—all literary requests—but give him orders to not be too worried about money, I'd say. If you want to quit anthology hassles which also could be done lay it on me and I'll arrange with Payne, compile the second and arrange to add some Burroughs and more Huncke to the first. then you be done with that responsibility. Keep your name on as editor of second book if that be advisable from any point. Perhaps also stop writing sidepieces, let Lord select from the multitude of manuscript he has already, no need dribble your time doing that secretarial and primarily agent-type work. He has typists there. Well anyway have a weird good time, I'll miss you.

I went to Lucien's last night, he talked with me at length after he phoned you—mad at me for hovering over and clapping hands and enjoying his telling you to write about him if necessary. He doesn't really want you to, is serious, and I am to blame for urging you on all this time. He scared me. Encountered something in him I had not felt before, or realized, apparently he been ill since that drunken night, not eating much, having nightmares—keyed off by this situation. Communicated some of the chill dread to me. It's more than I can bear, I'm sorry I intruded at all, Lucien feels I have tried to harm him, makes me feel it is so. Said he spoke to you on the phone and you were not going to write it, that's good. Because it really pains him that much, and seems a life and death matter to him. He has lost weight suddenly and seems changed and naked, or I am mad, or both, it scares me. He loves us, reassure him better than I can. (And I accede to his wishes and feelings here).

I guess I won't see you for while til March. I'll be here til then, and if go to Chile will stop over in Mexcity see you if you let me know where you are. Write if you can, postcard, if not don't worry I be OK. Silence for me later if at all, in India—McClure and Whalen arriving here this weekend, I'll take care of them, in fact am undisturbed—not as much pressure on me, and *Kaddish* getting finished and be ready soon. Tho disturbed by Lucien last night, upset.

Let me know what to do with Avon, or maybe best lay off it entirely whatever you want it's your cherub.

Peter typing poems and Huncke in bed with hemorrhoids, say hello to silence.

> Love, As ever
> Allen

Jack Kerouac [Northport, New York] to Allen Ginsberg [New York, New York]

December 24, 1959

Cher Alain:

Just concluded an amiable wrangle over *Tristessa* and am going to have it published just as it is (no additions) just like Lucien and Cessa said it should.

Seduction after all, doesn't make a book sexy, or dithyrambs.

It is such a short book that I myself gaze with amazement at the few words she spoke (you never read the whole thing tied up with the second year of composing so you don't know what I means).

Am playing *St. Matthew's Passion* as I write this, marveling at your taste when I came to your cottage in the western night in October 1955 from Mexico and nobody home I played your St. Matthew and waited for you hi on benny, remember?

Well, and I got big letter from Grove Press girl asking what I planned to do in Chile, I never GOT no invitation to go to Chile, did you intercept it for Peter's use? If so your schemes mell with my rhyme because I don't want to go away . . . am happy in my attic with the bat. The only explanation I can think of is that you bit your lip, tweaked your beard, and took my invitation and gave it to Peter, which is okay with me. Who wants to go south of north? But write to me from there and also find out why I didn't get an invitation: am I too crude? Too crude to be a Mahatma? I, the ponsell dinker?

Drama ain't nowhere without poetry (see Broadway), and poetry ain't nowhere without drama . . . s'why I write what you call PROSE, novels, see? My model is Shakespeare. In the interests of which I advise you, really, to plan now a big Miltonesque dramatic poem for your next pook. Boog, I mean. Imagine you getting hungup on big modern Shakespearean city tragedies using long line, short line, prosody, ellipses, etc. see. I decided this when looking over my poetry and my "novels" which have better line in em.

Karl Paetel[8] is giving Sterling [Lord] a bad time. What is he, a German con man? a sinister Burroughsian debt collector? a slinker? Sterling only claims that in every new anthology I should get "premium" payment because they can't make it without my name . . . that's all. I got with Sterling because I've had a long talk with Albert Saijo who reminded me that "money is poetic" (*viz.* Balzac, Shakespeare, etc.) and should not be put down per se by per se William. In fact, I intend to make a million and when I'm sixty I'll give it away and walk away with rucksack, gray-haired, across the roads of America, everybody will be amazed. Imagine, like, if Hemingway did it tomorrow. No cops would arrest him. Everybody would listen. S'why Buddha was born a KING, a Maharajah. Only trouble is, I ain't got no message.

Well sweetie, anyway, I'll see you New Years Eve at Lucien's or around Lucien's orbit, me and Lucien never miss a New Years Eve.

I hope Peter out of doldrums. Saw Laff in the road, at night, stalking, looks happy. Anybody'd be happy with all that good star of solitude.

I'll get you a copy of my new album when come to NY, you and me go to-

---

[8] Karl Paetel was the editor of *Beat, Eine Anthologie.*

gether maybe to Hanover Records 57th St. and pick up four or five and hand them around. free. Money for *Tristessa* will be 7500 dollars and's going right in bank. Won't start spending till I have 50,000—like I mean on crazy things. Am still Canuck and smart. Never draw money out of the bank unless I put MORE in. That way I can always write a check with confidence. Nothing to do with American ideas. Got Xmas card from Neal.

Only writing this to wish you big happy welcome holiday

Anyway writing it

Write me note

Ton Jean, Jean Louis

Allen Ginsberg [New York, New York] to Jack Kerouac [n.p., Northport, New York?]

December 29, 1959

New Years

Dear Jack:

Lafcadio o'th'moonlight arrived here last nite with Peter, strange. Him and Peter now watching Chaplin and Harold Lloyd at Museum. I been sick, spent four days Xmas in Paterson on couch wrapped in blankets listening to the *Messiah* late at night in dark when house was asleep, drifting out of my body into the music, a new kind of Jewish Yoga. I'm reading about medieval Hebrew Mystics and Isaac the Blind, who said that the Nameless was "that which is not conceivable by thinking" as if he'd read the Diamond in Toledo. There is also an old Kabalistic formula explaining in 1300 that "God in Himself, as an absolute Being, and therefore by his very nature incapable of becoming the subject of a revelation to others, is not and cannot be meant in the documents of Revelation, in the canonical writings of the Bible, and in the rabbinical tradition. He is not the subject of these writings and therefore also has no documented name, since every word of the sacred writing refers after all to some aspect of His manifestation on the side of Creation," rather than his perfect state as Nothing. In fact all the Rabbis always are talking about their meditations as trying to "make Something into Nothing," and are always making big doctrines about "the Nothing" and praying to it.

Anyway I'm reading up about the Kabala and Zohar and Gnostics, I always been curious and never did find the right book about them till lately. Same as Zen, when it all boils down.

No, I never got a ticket for Peter even. For that matter I haven't yet actually received my own ticket just an invitation. I'd thought you were invited because Ferlinghetti told me so. Maybe you weren't. The reason I am is that a Chilean Professor at Berkeley stole *Howl* and translated it in a black market edition in Chile and now he wants to make up for not telling me and paying me by getting me invited.

Yes, poetry ain't nowhere without drama, go back to writing big dramaturgies and I will too. *Kaddish* is actually a forty page story, narrative. Except that I never know what I write and haven't the novelistic strength to sit down and continue on one track for more than thirty hours at one stretch—can't pick up. Or never have tried. Maybe with benny might be able to. It takes strength of body to continue, unbroken, the same line in several sessions. I just never had that trick, like I never went to graduate school.

Paetel no stinker, I presume, I never found him to be so, in fact he's scholarly bibliographist, the only one with patience to make a scholarly bibliography. I don't know anything about his business relations and don't care. Leave that to agents. Yes money in your case is poetic. WHY NOT? In fact think of Shaw, the mad socialistic mentalist capitalist.

When I get up out of apartment (I'm taking antibiotics) I'll phone Lucien and find New Years eve, I phoned him from Paterson to say Merry Xmas on Xmas eve and told him to call you and relay same. Peter is happy with Lafcadio here. That's what he's been waiting for.

50,000 is not much money, make it 100,000—invest that in something stable, and live off the income.

I got $500 check from Ferlinghetti and paid all my debts for years—$60 [Bob] Merims, $50 Al Leslie, $203.11 to Columbia, $17 dentist, $5 doctor, and $100 State Department to get Peter's passport back. Wiped us out but now I don't owe anyone anything. Feels strange. Fucking Columbia people began suing my brother for the money—somebody anonymous had put up $100 to reduce the debt—and Barzun wrote me he couldn't get the finance committee to erase the debt in return for the big reading I gave there. They really are evil. I wrote them mad three page insane I ACCUSE letter demanding they stop teaching my poetry at Columbia—then tore it up, paid the $200 left, said farewell to them and now it's forgot forever and I don't have to hassle over it.

[Ray] Bremser still in jail and looks like he'll be sent back for a year. Seems that the chaplain at Bordentown heard him spouting on radio against prisons and pot laws, reported him, and now the bureaucracy got him in maw. He's charged with "associating with undesirable characters" among other things. That means me. The institutions and academies are really heartless. Anybody wants to have a revolution I don't want to be in the middle of it but I couldn't care less.

Neal's Xmas card to me said "Kneel!" nothing else for signature.

Finished typing Laughgas notes—now the whole poem's eleven funny pages and done.

[...]

Allen

See you tonite.

1960

Jack Kerouac [Northport, New York] to
Allen Ginsberg [New York, New York]

January 4, 1960

Dear Allen:

Got your long letter which I put away in my new INTERESTING LETTERS folder. I have a FAN LETTERS folder, and CREAM FILE, and BEAT ANTHOLOGY folders and that is a good way to dispatch.

Not that your letter wasn't cream file but it was your new poem which is very good and will be published.

Enclosed find $40 to cover taxi fare, other taxis, bottles and part of Chinese restaurant bills.

I got long letter from Lew Welch, a funny card from John Montgomery who is actually a pest because he wants me to send him albums, books, and puts down *Mexico City Blues* ("low material").

I am home safe now for a thousand years.

I want to write. I don't want to write letters (I got big huge letter from some Brierly type saying Neal isn't as great as Jerry who stole from private homes and got elected president of high school class and why don't I write about HIM instead of Neal) (isn't that awful?) (Neal who read the *Lives of the Saints* and never stole anything PERSONAL from poor people).

So I'll stay home 1000 years now and write *Beat Traveler* fast (soon as Don Allen comes through with my needs) (which aren't drastic demand) and one slow book about something probably Harpo Marx vision . . . Me and Harpo and W.C. Fields and Bela Lugosi hitch hiking to China together.

Note, send me note before Chile.

Or not . . . or from Chile . . .

[. . .]

Jack

Editors' Note: *In January 1960, Ginsberg and Ferlinghetti went to Chile for a writers' conference. Allen decided to stay in South America, and remained there for six months, searching in remote regions for yage, the hallucinogenic vine that Burroughs had described ten years earlier.*

Jack Kerouac [Northport, New York] to
Allen Ginsberg [Paterson, New Jersey]

June 20, 1960

Dear Allen:

Peter sent me your aether notes, I numbered the pages before they get screwed up and even tied a paperclip on but if you want me to type them up for you also, I will, I probably will anyway as I would like to read it en toto fast. Great new long poem of yours. I haven't really studied it yet, answering letter first—But it surprised me that when you were really hi on ether and heard the bells ("The sound of the bell leaving the bell," said Basho in a haiku) you thought of me, as I thought of you at the highest hi on mescaline last Fall. When on mescaline I was so bloody high I saw that all our ideas about a "beatific" new gang of world people, and about instantaneous truth being the last truth, etc. etc. I saw them as all perfectly correct and prophesied, as never on drinking or sober I saw it. Like an angel looking aback on life sees that every moment fell right into place and each had flowery meaning. Your "universe is a new flower" is a perfect statement like that, as tho thought on real hiness [high-ness]. But I'm making no effort any more (like you) to get real high and write visions, it seems I have to wait right now, I'm a little exhausted actually from all those Angel Midnights of past few years when I went all out. But what I really must do is get off by myself for first time since *On the Road* 1957 so I'll take a secret trip this summer and live alone in a room and walk and light candles, in Mexcity probably, where nobody'll know me or see me. Have to have a holiday to rediscover my heart, like—These innumerable friendships of mine are too much. Do you realize what happened just this last week for instance and as example: Jack Micheline writes big nutty letter all dabbed with tears from Chicago finally asking for ten dollars—Gregory writes "Come to Venice at once! Money is my friend!" (when I'd told him I might be sent there by *Holiday* on assignment)—Charley Mills and Grahame Cournoyer call me insistently from the Village for money and I have phone number changed—My sister wants to borrow a thousand for her house—(ahead of even the house)—Lew Welch hints he needs a hundred for his jeep. You invite me to fly to Peru, Gary [Snyder] to Japan, [Alan] Ansen to Greece, [John] Montgomery to Mill Valley to go live with him mind you, old Horace Mann school chums to reunion, art galleries to their art shows to buy stuff, etc. etc. I didn't put you in there because you belong in the battalion of money-askers (look, if I complied with all these recent wishes, including the other ones, I'd have no more money! always wondered why "rich" people were "tight" like Jay Laughlin or old 1945 Bill now I realize it's because, it's NOT because they're tight but they're outnumbered by money demands (and saddened too). Anyway how can I get into contact with the Nameless One by leaving myself open to all this? I must go and be quiet and alone, like God, awhile, again. To come back with something to write. Not that I haven't written enuf and god I'm sick of poetry and literature. Maybe everybody else is and that's why they're starting a war. Well I still haven't shown you my mescaline notes of last Fall. I will when you get back—Much like ether. When we had ether with Jordan Belson in 1955 we were not alone to lie down and think and listen to bells and scribble, instead we talked and went to Chaplin movie. I only saw Peter once or twice since you left, and Laff, and Huncke, usual Chinese dinner. Laff told Lois [Sorrells] he was a nice young boy blown out of a volcano with a gun—(quote)—I told her to write down notes of all he said, he talks to her a lot as they walk arm in arm to Chinatown behind me and Petey and Hunk. Mainly I sit under the stars and realize the same old blooey samsara is nevertheless empty. Feel like going to Heaven, now, in fact. But I could really write a wild doosy book to knock out everybody—including myself. Don Allen's anthology was fine. Our own anthology I think Tom Payne is being fired for, he will go to Bantam books and work there with it and my future novels—*Tristessa* out this week—not a word changed. Good review by that penthouse Dan Talbot of West End Avenue we saw, remember, in 1957, the two Israeli girls night, with Sterling—Where he says that people who claim the "immense sincerity" of the beat generation is a literary racket, is wrong. Anyway I'm bored with all this again, the whole present history of the world bruits on the horizon but I'm watching the freedom of eternity in the starry sky and wondering why the dream of life and history seems so real except to remember old dreams (sleeping dreams) when a tree was thought real, an attacker was thought real, in fact, oh yes, Ferling is putting out *Book of Dreams* with all my great NEW dreams at the end including the Flying Horses I saw and a final great dream about shit—That'll be: for this year: *Golden Eternity* by LeRoi [Jones] put out: *Tristessa*, by Avon put out; *Lonesome Traveler*, by McGraw-Hill put out (I put together 250 pages of pieces from mags including our beatnik nightlife new york and Gregory bums hobos and bullfight and statue of Christ all new stuff about Henri Cru, Mexico, railroad (all of railroad earth and new chapters) and things about mountains, Tangiers etc. not a bad book and to be on non-fiction list)—I now have 18 grand in the bank and not touching it—4 grand in checking for expenses—taxes took 16 grand last year—(this year paid)—not much compared to Senator Herbert Lehman and his half a million dollar donation last week to the Zoo.

But my mother is guarding over my money, my health, Lois comes to fuck and suck, Tom Payne (newly married) comes with new millionaire wife to get smashed. Has a cabin in Vermont I may live in soon. Think I'll just quietly sneak to Mexico (don't tell anybody especially Lamantia!) and get my visions in.

If perchance you will be in Mexico in late July or August on your itinerary let me know, I'll have nice pad with flowers in window, you can stay a week or so or two. That is, if I go. See, that's my life now, I never go anywhere or do anything. My last run to New York was so awful, a month ago, I haven't been back—I had nightmares, I saw ghosts—Bill Heine scared me, Charley Mills scared me, a big nutty trappist priest kept making me kiss a relic encrusted in rubies (but he did play me Bach for two hours). Everybody was smiling at me even Ornette Coleman, I was in torn blue jeans Lucien had torn, also had torn off all my underwear in front of Cessa in the house and I didn't even remember the next day. There is a great deal of talk about Voodoo, too, in the Village now, which scares me. People are sticking dolls. The police just closed down Gaslight [Cafe] and few other places for no good reason 'fire hazard'. Henri Cru is presently rushing back from Genoa to see me and tell me all about Fernanda Pivano the date I arranged for him with her and that will take up a thousand hours of energy could go on solitude visions, see? And remember, remember my introspective laziness not at all like your great social energy. Oh yes, John Holmes they said in the *Times* that I was a disciple of his and [Anatole] Broyard and [Chandler] Brossard in 1952 (forgetting 1950 *Town and City* hipster chapters) so Holmes get drunk and writes big sentimental letters about my boyish smile and "little Allen"—Is he crazy? I think Holmes is going crazy—Micheline is out of his mind. I enclose the letter he forwarded you about one of his nutty woodcut visions (you know, remember those woodcuts we saw with Gilmore in 1945 showing "the young poet in New York"?) the sentimental view of the "youth" in the white shirt among dark towers—this is Micheline, his vision—I mean, dearie, strictly from Marc Brandel.

Don't hear from Burroughs but was pleased he mentioned I named *Naked Lunch* (remember, it was you, reading the manuscript, mis-read "naked lust" and I only noticed it) (interesting little bit of litry history tho). James Wechsler has come out with his book *Reflections of an Angry Middle-aged Editor* where he excoriates me (maybe you too) for political irresponsibility and complicating up America with poetry. [Al] Aronowitz will come out soon I guess, I got mad at him for million mistakes, I straightened out a lot of them (mostly about me but some about others).

Well what am I living for? all I'm good for now is to graipe gripe gripe like this?—if I could only have a month alone, and smile and talk to myself quietly in French in a flowery sad Mexican midnight study, with a big garden wall with lizards maybe . . . by god I'll do it! don't tell anybody! Of course, in the Fall, new energy will come to all of us. I'm really afraid to go to India because we may be caught here in a big Red Chinese invasion and wind up emaciated torturees in prison camps because we won't admit to insects in the snow. Now, no, I'll buy a five hundred acre mountain and build a cabin on the southern slope of it. Tom Payne wants to go on a big gay Paris trip with Scott Fitzgerald women in the Fall, I dunno. I've been making wonderful tape recordings off the radio jazz, FM, and have hours of jazz. Just wrote a column on jazz for *Escapade* all about Seymour Wyse. Previous column about Zen, mentions you and Peter. But mainly, I'd like candlelight novel now. But, you know, it seems I'm getting to be like the old Kerouac of 1944, when Lucien and you talked and I just sat brooding, remember, because I was bored and confused. Maybe that's better for rest of my life that silly Zen Lunatic yakking on Brandeis stages I don't really mean anyway—yes—but I love you, Allen, don't bug me when you come back to New York about all your enthusiastic plans to go here, go there (like the fiasco of taking me to the Living Theater when I wanted to go hear jazz and I got in trouble with Butch [Frank] O'Hara)—just a gag—but forgive me and love me, if I seem not to share your particular enthusiasms, and those of poor dear Gregory, I just don't care the same way any more, I am going to become now a hairy loss old man with not-thoughts and no-talk almost. I'm trying to stop drinking—my soul is deeper than ever maybe because emptying—all you write in "Aether" is true and forever true. Pray for everybody, I guess. And Old Neal is out—wow—but I don't want to see him because, in the past he scorned me for being a drunken yakker, now he'll also laugh at me for making money at it (tho I know he has serious Jesuit undergarments where he knows I'm just a funny humble priest). But here's to our Birthday! Much love.

  Come back soon
  Ti Jean XXX

Editors' Note: *While Ginsberg was away, Kerouac continued to struggle with alcoholism. In July he went to Ferlinghetti's cabin in Big Sur to try to dry out once and for all. He was unsuccessful, but while in California he saw Neal and Carolyn Cassady for the last time.* Big Sur *is based on this period.*

Allen Ginsberg [New York, New York] to
Jack Kerouac [n.p, Northport, New York?]

Sept 19, 1960
170 E 2 St NYC

Dear Jacky:

You home? You home? You home? Leave home again! Fly to the Congo! Rush to Tibet! Be with Cuba! Jump underneath Algeria! Flop on Taiwan! Screech to a stop on the Isle of Weight! Warble!

Well all's the same here, except Huncke moved up to Hotel Belmore Lex and 25th St., but down on cocanyl intake to one bot a day and sold a story (Cuba) to Seymour Krim at *Swank*. Carl Immemorial Miel Solomon comes out weekends and so's stayed at my apartment drinking tranquillizers and talking all night, mostly complaints about his identity. I laid on him the fact that he is the one who is making up all these here identities but it don't seem to penetrate much. Anyway he's less violent than he was.

Thank you for the love of God which arrived by telegram from Frisco followed next day by a green pill from [Bob] Kaufman who lies upstairs but doesn't bother me, a pill he said they give to people the night before they go into gas chamber in Alcatraz, I sat down at desk 3 p.m. last Wednesday and did not rise except to pee till 9 p.m. Thursday nite, having typed up complete *Kaddish* manuscript adding in various Shelleyan hymns written in sob-racked exhausted trances, and took it to 33rd St. post office to mail to Ferlinghetti special delivery Saturday nite at 4AM, that's done.

Gregory in Berlin asks me should he come home? Bill writes he is sifting and panning thru cut-ups of his prose for the gold and joining them together with virus glue. I think he hasn't been laid so long he's going fruity . . . however latest letters are very sweet and kind, he even cut up and typed out some of my poems to show me how he's working. So Peter and I cut up some of our magic psalms to shuffle rearrange and send him. Just having a little fun mother.

"I went in—smelt funny the halls again—up elevator—to a glass door on a Woman's Ward—to Naomi—two nurses Buxom white—they led her out—Naomi stared—I gaspt—

too thin, shrunk on her bones—age come to Naomi—now broken in white hair—loose dress on her skeleton—face sunk, old!—cheek of crone—

Heaviness of early 40s and menopause reduced by one heart stroke—one hand stiff—a scar on the head, the lobotomy, her ruin—the hand dipping downwards to death—

O Russian faced, woman on the grass, your long black hair is crowned with daisies, the mandolin is on your knees

Communist beauty, all this summer promises to share its flowers everywhere you have your hand

Holy mother now you smile on one you love, your world is born anew, your children run naked in the field spotted with dandelions—

eat in the plum tree grove at the end of the meadow and play their games near the cabin of a white-haired Negro who shows them the mystery of his rain barrel—

sister of exile the new age is yours, your happiness is the Revolution and your hope is the only war no one will lose

Blessed daughter come to America I long to hear your voice again, remembering your mother's music, in the song of the Natural Front

O glorious Muse that bore me from the womb, and taught me talk and music—whose pained head gave me Visions—O mad hallucinations of the damned

that drive me out of my own skull to seek Eternity till I find peace for Thee—O Poetry!—and for all humankind call on the Origin—O beautiful Garbo of my Karma, your face of old movie stars—white flowers in your hair—

now wear your nakedness forever, no Revolution might destroy this maidenhood—with all the teachers from Newark—nor Elanor be gone, nor Max wait for his specter, no Louis retire from his High school.

Back! you! Naomi! skull on you! gaunt immortality and revolution come— wrinkle cheeked, lip sure—and ashen eyes of hospital indoors, ward greyness on skin—small broken woman—

This come to you now?—what I'll be when I'm mad as your hair in future 90s, when I scream on the rooftops of Synagogues, bearded toward Heaven?"

So I sent all that to City Lights. I still have to assemble type all other poems—this is already forty pages, maybe I'll put two books out at once. Sent him "Laughgas" for *Beatitude* and crazy Orlovsky-Corso-me chain poem on the moon writ in Amsterdam. Peter's going out to take Laf to NY State Unemployment office to inquire about special part time jobs for him and Laughcadio is going along all dressed in brilliant black, agreeable, they're leaving door right in a minute.

I'm writing intro to [Ray] Bremser's book.

Took a lot more ayahuasca and realized I AM the emptiness that's movie-projecting Kali monster on my mindscreen, projecting mindscreen, even. So not scared anymore. But I still can't stop the appearance of the fucking mindscreen, I mean I can't quiet my organism to total silence. I'll have to study yoga or something, finally.

If Castro pays, I will go for two weeks to Cuba late October to dig that revolution. My laughing gas uncle dentist who's a liberal but not a radical spends his vacations down there last twenty years just come back and says everybody is all happy and amazed and enthusiastic and big money revolution is going on, social progress, schools, works, etc. and U.S. newspapers are mainly full of shit. LeRoi [Jones] says same. Both agree big Marxist nasty enthusiastic mind-control is also going on, but isn't so mean yet as former dictatorship nor so savage when weighed against U.S. hysterical mind control. My book'll be done so I'll go on short weird Cuba trip and come back and write big revolutionary poem attacking Red China and U.S. and then go to India and shut up.

So that's me, bubbles. I read long sections of *Visions of Cody* to Stanley Gould who had a nervous breakdown in my kitchen due to excess goof balls and he said it was the finest thing he heard ever, even he stopped being mean to Neal. How's Neal? What happened? You saw him I heard from Whalen I think. I still haven't written him, tho I wrote long poem to/about him three years ago that I finally typed up this week. Is Neal just the same or soberererer?

Peter has been sad all week. Oh also he's making it with nice nineteen year old Janine [Pommy], sometimes I jump in bed with both.

Taking Lafcadio to see Marcel Marceau tomorrow night, pantomime at City Center. Going with Robert and Mary Frank. He's done with Babel picture almost, next wants to make full length. I said why don't you do *On the Road*? He said good idea but Jack wants to sell it to Hollywood. I said who knows. I saw *Subterraneans* it was no good. Why don't you give it to Frank free (on profit-sharing % basis) on condition he make a naked epic? Otherwise he wants maybe to do *Journey to End of Night*. Or write a script for a movie, new, for him.

[. . .]

Well, let's see. I have money. How're you doing, need a loan $2 bucks? Tell your mother you're the man in the moon. God I'm having trouble with Poppa over *Kaddish* he wants me to excise interesting parts about his own private life, about an affair he had with grocery man's wife twenty years ago. Doesn't even want to appear human. Well I'll excise. He's retiring this January and plans to trip to Paris in September. Also wants try mescaline. Wrote his doctor asking advice and a prescription for mescaline.

[. . .]

Lucien, he moved, same phone, Peter and Laf and I went over for huge days of painting his walls white. Then I went home and painted my apartment dazzling white too. All new and clean where I live with Chinese scrolls hanging on wall. Threw out TV set and a lot of other unworkable junk.

John Wieners much better lives with Irving [Rosenthal], wrote a book called *Jewels*. So we went to a party he all dressed up, over 8th St. Bookstore, he's so hard up, drunk there, loning like an elegant alcoholic, not the cockroach of last year, so he starts feeling me up, I drag him in the bathroom blow him, he's under the sink and can't even come. I say, "alright skeleton art thou not yet disillusioned with they orgasmal corpse?" He says "Long ago" and pulls out his false teeth and shows me his death's head. We sit laughing on the bathroom floor over our decaying bodies, me pointing to my balding skull. What a gas all this is! what a weird eternity we live in!

Peter moans, John isn't satisfied, May's the same, Irving longs, Bill cuts up, Gregory wrestles Berlin, Laf gets dressed, Janine she lays, Huncke hides, are you not tender today? Some more strange young spectral kids appeared on scene hang around 2nd Ave. and 8th St. broke near Jazz Gallery wait for Monk to walk up street to buy a paper and gape gently on'm. Peter met them while I was in South America, one's named Turk, one is Mickey, they read *Alice in Wonderland* and take ashmador powder you buy it in drugstore for asthma if you eat it you go blind, hallucinate cigarettes and doors, think you're walking on the street when in bed, they watch the weird, for twenty-four hours, then are OK again.

I have a 1½ foot long knee drum someone brought from Africa, and play it well after two months practice at odd moments every day. Has a nice sound, best drum I ever had near.

OK I'll shut up.

> Love
>> Allen

Jack Kerouac [Northport, New York] to Allen Ginsberg [New York, New York]

Dear Allen: (Sept 22 60)

Yes, just got back, big TWA Ambassador flight tax deductible with wine and champagne and filet mignon and Chinese Tapei ambassador's wife in front of me etc. New York seems cowed and nasty after anarchistic crazy freewheeling Frisco. Saw everybody. Neal greater than ever, sweeter by far, looking good, healthy. Walks to work in Los Gatos now as tire recapper—would be willing to play Dean in *On the Road* movie, anything better than tire recapping. SP railroad won't take him back but want ME back (Al Hinkle reports) (because all read "Railroad Earth", forgetting what a lousy brakeman I was). Much to tell you about Neal and everybody. Gave Neal money in crisis, he very glad now, crisis was solved and he got fine new rubywine Jeepster with good motor—gave him 100—(for rent) (he was fired). He got new job he walks to. Had love affair (I did) and almost got married with his mistress Jacky [Gibson] but I was drunk. Prior to drunkenness I was alone three weeks in woods in fine quiet fog with animals only and learned a lot. Have changed, in fact—Am quieter, don't drink as much, or so often at least, and have started new quiet home reading habits. For instance had 11th edition of *Encyclopedia Britannica* mailed to me (35 bucks whole price) 29 volumes containing 30,000 pages and exactly 65,000,000 words of scholarly Oxford and Cambridge prose (65 million that is) and last night stayed up till 5 A.M. amazed in that sea of prose—looked up Logia where Jesus is reported to have said (on old Egyptian papyri dating to 2nd century) that one must not cease seeking for the kingdom and WILL WAKE UP 'ASTONISHED' in the kingdom! (just like my bliss-astonishment of golden eternity faint). Apocrypha, Shmapocrypha!—Thought I'd also look up bats as there was a bat in Big Sur kept circling my sleeping bag every night til dawn, was referred to *Chiroptera* (*chirop* is Greek for "hand," *tera* "wing")—found what amounts to a small volume of complete technical explanation with pictures and diagrams. This is the prize of prizes! I've been waiting for this 29 volume edition since I first saw it age sixteen in Lowell High Library. It's possible to make complete studies in Theology of ALL religions, for instance, or study of all Tribes in the World, or all Zoology, all History to 1909, all Campaigns till then in detail, all Biography till then, all Mysticism, all Kabbalas and Shmabbalas, all rare scholarly treatises on Old and New Testaments, all about Buddha, Hindus, rare exotic Malayan religions, visions, all Ornithology, Optometry, Pasometry, Futurometry and in other woids ALL. I simply can't believe such an Ocean as the Pacific any more'n this encyclopedia—so my new reading habits: also bought fifty bucks worth of books from Ferling and have those (Pound, etc.)—and soberly studying now, writing new book (started anyway)—doing exercise (headstands, snake pushups, bent bow and knee bend and breathing)—feeling fine—lost ten or fifteen pounds—only got drunk once since home two weeks. Wanted to get new novel in or underway before calling you but made a false start. Had to keep Henri Cru away who went and got himself job as electrician in Northport (!) and wanted to inundate my life as usual with all the ridiculous trivialities of his fancy—so he mad. But I can't worry about every tom dick and harry who used to leave me alone to write *Visions of Neal* at my lonely happy rolltop desk in the early fifties.

Meanwhile, at Big Sur, I sat by sea every day, sometimes in dismal foggy roaring dark of cliffs and huge waves, and wrote Sea, first part, SEA: the Pacific Ocean at Big Sur California. All sound of waves, like James Joyce was going to do. Wrote mostly with eyes closed, as if blind Homer. Read it to gang by oil lamp. McClure, etc. Neal etc. all listened but it's just like Old Angel only more wave-plop kerplosh sounds, the sea don't talk in sentences but comes in pieces, as like this:

> No human words bespeak
> the token sorrow older
> than old this wave
> becrashing smarts the
> sand with plosh
> of twirléd sandy
> thought—Ah change
> the world? Ah set
> the fee? Are rope the
> angels in all the sea?
> Ah ropey otter
> barnacle d be—

(barnacle d be), rather, with the "d" all alone. Anyway this, and what Logia Jesus said about astonishment of paradise, seems to me much more on the right tracks of world peace and joy than all the recent communist (and general political) hysteria rioting and false screaming. Cuba Shmuba—I will come New York, open your lock with key you gave me, wait if you not there, am buying rucksack etc., will see Lucien etc. so see you and Petey soon. Okay.

Will come around the 28th—meanwhile please drop another line and enclose *Mescaline Notes* and *Gregory Letters* for the Cream File.

Jean

Allen Ginsberg [New York, New York] to Jack Kerouac [n.p., Northport, New York?]

ca. October 13, 1960

Dear Jack:

Just finished hamburger sandwich. Pete and Laf on 14th St. helping LeRoi Jones paint new huge apartment. I didn't mean to sadden you leaving you in taxi alone speeding away uptown. Here's a poem. You OK? Your book [*Lone-*

some Traveler] is very good, I sat down and read it yesterday at one reading and laughed aloud tickled by sentences lots times, aloud. I don't know what Lucien was screaming about except he thought you shouldn't have been so nice to McGraw Hill filling out their form. However saw Cessa last nite to watch Nixon Kennedy debate, and later found, what upset her and Lucien, you drunk started telling her kid brother Lucien saga 1943 she said and were talking to Lucien about writing book on him. I heard that part in passing but hadn't known it was the center of the evening for him. You ought to go there non-drunk some time and just have a nice quiet evening chatting with him and makem happy. The biography of him is just an open nerve if you throw it at him, particularly when drunk.

I also read Leadbelly's poems (songs) this afternoon. He's great poet. Also reread *Happy Birthday of Death*, Gregory is even better than I thought. I hadn't read anything of his or thought about him for a month and read this and it made so much ethical sense, especially his poem about Clown.

Anyway two days ago I finished my book [*Kaddish and Other Poems*] and sent it off airmail special complete to Ferlinghetti. I have one more big raving politics poem to add in if I finish it ever.

Saw the debate. Nixon is saying we should war against China for Matsu and Quemoy [Islands]. Kennedy is saying, no, which is a mistake to say tactically. But Nixon is taking advantage of this and talking hypocritically about U.S. not "giving an inch" to the communists. He is very evil, like that. I registered I'll vote for Kennedy. Both are phony and both are outright warmongers, the communists are right on that. Both want to START physical war on Cuba—have said so. But at least Kennedy's hypocrisies on this seem to mask some desire to withdraw from the whole U.S. aggression shot, and Nixon seems like he really wants war, like the *Daily News*. The *Daily News* really is asking for war, I read it. Or at least Nixon seems the more loudmouth super-patriot demagogue of the two. I don't see why you've switched your judgment back to favoring him. Obviously Kennedy is more liberal and for more foreign wheat aid type and less tied up with phony military patriotic grandeur and less an FBI type, in intention. Not that it makes much difference America is sunk either way because it's just plain selfish. The more extremely nasty we get the worse the communists get and anybody who doesn't want to give a shit gets caught in the middle.

Like it occurred to me today we already have a planned economy but all the planning of most of our government huge budgets is military. So we're already socialist so what's all the shouting about why don't we be hip planned socialists and make food and power instead of gas bombs, to defend ourselves against socialism. You don't think anybody's starving in the world. Nobody in America thinks so. This country is evil and Whitman and I now spit on it and tell it to be nice or die, because that's what's coming. I HATE AMERICA! Ugh, and Nixon and Kennedy combine all that's most obnoxious. But Nixon does take the cake.

I suppose all this hate is unpatriotic to eternity but fuckit I'm going to die anyway.

The subliminal suggestions I receive reading the papers are horrid. I don't see why you like Nixon already, yet. AGHHHHHhhh! I gotta go uptown see my father for supper he goes to a play tonight I have supper. Forgive my rant.

Love,

Allen

Jack Kerouac [Northport, New York] to Allen Ginsberg [New York, New York]

October 18, 1960

No, I was kidding about 1943 biog.—also about Nixon—making old argumentative scenes on couch, see—tell them. I not goin vote but would for Kennedy— everybody should simply make a vow of kindness and let it go at that, try to stay sober too—start new party Vow of Kindness party. Yes, starvation in world, because too many new babies everywhere, so no need for vow of poverty. Make vow of kindness. All hate unpatriotic to eternity after all—people forgetting that lately, even you, me, s'why world blooing. I gotta stay outa NY now, no more go there now—if Greg come you come him Petey you we talk in Mrs. O's big pad. Me no drink no more—me crazy now—me see hoodoo voodoo—is your chimu turtle voodoed? I can't answer you questions bout politics because it is all bloody impossible discrimination of riots and yelling horror on account don't blame em for fear of bombs, I pray for world and pray it works, I feel awful today, can't write later.

J

1961

Jack Kerouac [Northport, New York] to
Allen Ginsberg [Paris, France]

April 14, 1961

Dear Allen:

Just read narrative section of *Kaddish*, which has impact of Dostoevskyan novel. The whole package, with later visionary poems, makes one explosive book. No reviews yet, as tho they just wanted to wish you out of existence, the big Wilburs and Hollanders weeping in their pillows—no reviews either of course of *Book of Dreams*. Time for us to quit the literary scene and talk to none of them any more, I say. Things okay here, Gene doing good, we move soon, me free soon—me prayed also to cut lush, prayers answered so far. When have time give me rundown on latest Gregory soul-mind. Your early prevision of police-cabaret-beatnik troubles coming true—big political out-in-the-open battle now with John Mitchell coming on like Mayor. I studying Kant, Schopenhauer, Spinoza etc. all great minds agreed with Buddha—Lucien and Harry Smith called me high on phone. Why Bill "fled"?—Infinite Swarming Light—Bill's Hassan Sabbah says there is no Time and no Thing in Space—Well? he no agree in 1957. Oh Hum, vanity is a bore. Brand new world a-coming—Hello.

Jean-Louis

1963

Jack Kerouac [Northport, New York] to Allen Ginsberg [Kyoto, Japan]

Dear Allen: (June 29, 1963)

Was hesitant to write to you care of damned India where letter might be lost but hope you gets this anyway—Just now had a flash of understanding what a gone friendship we've had really, not only all the wild letters we exchanged (I have all your letters neatly filed here in my new steel office file and you can browse anytime and use them etc.) and all the wild adventures together on Brooklyn Bridge, Columbia, Frisco, Mexico, etc. and elsewhere later, but all that bombed-out literature we started (bombed-out-of-mind) and all the swirls and levels, like just now I was sitting daydreaming of Burroughs and Huncke finally meeting again in your 7th Street kitchen tomorrow and you and I are wringing our hands with delight and winking at each other as Huncke says, "Well, well," and Burroughs replies etc. Which is just another way of saying how much I respect you and value you, Poit. When you come to my new house in N'Port it will be perfect if you don't have that beard and long hair, who cares about that shit anyway? Let me see your cherubic haircut. Just saw Eugene [Brooks] who just came to my house and I really wanted to chat with him (have been conversing with Eugene a lot since you left and find him highly intelligent, as much as you in a way) but he brings a crazy Rabbi who wants me to rush around like Norman Mailer renting out Carnegie Hall and going to Stork Club and getting in Winchell because "great works of art" should be publicized etc., his name is Richard something-or-other, actually nice guy but I don't want to abandon my solitude and reading and quietude for just a lot of horseshit showing-off in public. Besides *On the Road* is finally contracted for a movie, I'll get five percent of the budget when shooting starts, five percent of the budget when picture released, and then five percent of the net profits of the company which will be headed by the guy who will turn *Road* into a scenario and also direct: name of Bob Ginnet . . . so I don't need to make money scenes, just enough for me anyway, since as you know I always collect my change when I leave a woman, and besides I hate the bitches now they're all such a bunch of whores and liars like Joan [Haverty] doubly ly lieing yet—Lies about me that hold *me* up to the world as

469

a liar![1]—But to hell with that, I'm thinking of something else, it's just started raining: my new pad here is at 7 Judyann Court, off Dogwood Road, keep that address a secret and put it in your notebook under the name of The Wizard of Ozone Park, under "W", and when you come to N'Port, there's the house, 7 Judyann Court, off Dogwood Road, instructions, etc.—Best house I ever had with big backyard with thrity-two trees all around and six foot tall wood fence of Alaskan cedar, basketweave style, nobody see me as I read in sun or goop among tomato plants and my mother feedeth the birds and they thrash in the birdbath and in my room is groovy new Telefunken FM (West German) set with big Bachs and Mozarts or jazz anytime, and full finished basement with den and FM music and records and later maybe a pooltable— Nothing fancy, just right—Only problem is too much local visitings from bores—No Lucien come yet, no Allen, just pain-in-the-ass visitors, as usual— One new friend rather nice, Adolf Rothman, schoolteacher and clamdigger, learned and quiet—Jewish Lenin face—But tonight, ugh, unavoidable visit from 2 teenagers who want me to go meet girls in dance bars, will not go but just play them music awhile—Please tell Gary [Snyder] when you see him, or write him, to excuse me for the enraged letter I wrote him drunk on a quart of Canadian Club whisky in which I excoriated women forever, tho I meant it, I didn't mean to be mean to Gary, who however didn't seem to mind and wrote back he was sending me a present. (Some dopey Jap cunt "psychoana-lyzed" *Subterraneans* in school like a real square Vassar shot.) A "living woman" indeed, what do they want me to do, screw cadavers? All mixed up letter, this, I really ain't got my heart in it, had so much to say when I got on typewriter just now, well anyway this'll let you know I'm with you all the way, but I want you to know, no like writing letters any more, getting like Neal now, I dunno why, sure would like to see you instead. Having Giroux look at Whalen's new book of poems (very good), returned McClure's novel without comment (hated it, cheapskate beatniks with guns in their briefcases kicking girls and sitting around being dull on pot), am recording great library of clas-sical and jazz tapes, saving letters, filing them, wrote letter defending *Subs* to Italian Judge in Milano where *Subs* being on trial for banning with bishops of Milano behind it with Montini was the bishop of Milano, my painting of Montini might be color photoed in *Time* or *Satevpost* [*Saturday Evening Post*], just sold a chapter from new novel to *Holiday* mag about "On the Road with Memere" (me and my mother in Juarez reroute Frisco 1957), and gener-

---

[1] An article by Joan Haverty, describing Kerouac as a deadbeat dad, had just appeared in *Confidential* magazine.

ally I being clam and readable tho had to quit local bars because a big blond fag wants to shoot me with gun because I called her a fag I guess, don't remember, cops watching me, local clamdiggers fucked up, my cousin Mooncloud came to see me here to tell me his story was just a lot of shit (I still don't know), we went Lucien NY and girls and scenes, all a mad mixed up mess whenever I leave the house so I stay home and this summer I think be nice go to Quebec and write that for *Holiday* and then in the Fall, when *Visions of Gerard* is out, take off for Cologne Germany, London, Paris, Cornwall and Brittany although I don't know, don't care much, all's in my heart HERE IN MY HEART, Ami.

In any case we take big trip together somewhere, or do something, sometime, again, copain.

I recently had horrible visions of the too-muchness of the world which requires really too much of our attention, our mind essence is completely blasted by music, people, books, papers, movies, games, sex, talk, business, taxes, cars, asses, gasses yak ack etc. and I almost died chocking over this (choking)—Like, now I'm outs with Gregory almost, we had a big jubilant reunion in April or so and hallelujahed to write a big article for *Playboy* about Beat and so he'd have money for his wedding with Sally November who hates me I think and it all deteriorated with Gregory rewriting the whole thing behind my back and cursing me and Luce and everybody as creeps, and him a "pure lyric poet" which is what Lucien told him the day before and it went to his head—Mainly, I had the sensation that Gregory is insane, because he kept me up and down all the time with him, suddenly realizing he's crazy and doesn't want to be friends with anyone at all, maybe wants to be punished for this? The article we wrote together, dictating to girlfriends of mine etc., was ridiculous, not even an article but a drunken whisky chain poem meaning nothing whatever—I think H [heroin] is going to G[regory]'s head really—That Sally of his is sullen, I think—But maybe they'll have a baby and coo quietly together and it might turn out good for poor tortured Gregory Corso—But on these visits to NY, worse than ever, I come back with visions of horror as bad as the Ayahuasca vision on the Neanderthal million years in caves, the gruesomeness of life!—Yet all my future be bright, with *On the Road* gonna be a movie, a new novel in the Fall, two new novels not yet published (*Desolation Angels* and its sequel about you and me and Pete and Laf and Gwegowy in Mexico *Passing Through*) and I see nothing ahead for me but ease and joy and yet my mind is so dark, and so lonesome sometimes I could cry on your shoulder or Bill's or Neal's any minute. And what of poor Neal? Carolyn marrying another man, couldn't I be a millionaire and make Neal my chauffeur? Do I need a crazy teahead chauffeur with broads hiding in the trunk? And Bill, how come I don't ever get to see him anymore and if I journeyed to Paris via Air France or Lufthansa jet would he be kind to me when I rushed up to him? or laugh at me for being fat? or WHAT? Where's Peter, why did you leave Peter? Why did you and Peter leave Laf to such a fate? How could you carry Laf around the world on your shoulders anyway? It's hopeless. How's Gary? I guess he's alright. Whalen is very sad and neutral with big sad neutral blue eyes. Scares me sometimes. Lew Welch is spending his time in an isolated shack, naked, at Forks of Salmon Calif. and says he's going crazy like Han Shan. Did you see *Big Sur* novel which I had sent to you? and what you think of the ridiculous denouement in THAT? all too true. Ow. Meanwhile all these subsidiary bores keep hammering at ya, Aquinas monks denying my theology in long silly letters writtenlikethiswithJoycean arrangements, or bores around Los Gatos assuring me I WAS of some importance while America needed me and thanks,—nevertheless, Allen dear friend, I feel a strange ecstasy, right now, always in fact, always. Holmes has been bombarding me with huge questions for his non-fiction book which will be about everything: I spent three nights answering his questions in detail, on typewriter, he oughta be glad right now. Book will be about you, me, Mailer, Baldwin, etc., whole scene . . . But it's raining, great straight drops of sheet rain falling through glen dark tree glades . . . very pretty day. A day for getting drunk on whiskey, in fact, but dammit I did that yesterday. A lost day. Wonder what Joan Adams is thinking . . . Where's Huncke? How's Laf? What is Paul Bowles thinking, and where? And Ansen? And Walter Adams? How sad the garbage can! Anyway, when you get back here, I'll show you all the piled up papers relating to everything since you left, letters, poems of Gregory, etc. and let us hope that the great calm hearts of Melville, Whitman and Thoreau do sustain us in the coming hectic years of overcommunicating Americas and Telstars and other Galaxies . . . What have we accomplished? Good new poetry, that oughta be enough. "Charming bedraggled little princes" everywhere on accounta you . . . and sudden waves of intelligent teenage football players somehow. Somehow my ass. Incidentally I liked your "honking Eliot" dream and just now in fact was studying an old dream of yours in a letter from Chiapas, no San Jose, about Chiapas, a dream you had there of Burroughs being photographed in a Rome trolley, and a dream of me leading tourist millions wandering in endless Brooklyns . . . I just had drink dream that I was shitting all the time whether I was in the toilet or not, shit all over the floor, over my hands, shoes, over my face really, just shit all over, like balloons . . . Lucien Ah . . . He had a little fling with Lois [Sorrells Beckwith] but Cessa straightened that out . . . not a fling really, but lying around all day on the floor with her at Jacques' [Beckwith], as Jacques fumed—I just can't keep up with Jacques and all that, I wanta go back to my simple Lucien and Allen and Bill. Anyway my present job is to write *Vanity of Duluoz* novel about 1939 to 1946, won't be easy, football, war, Edie, etc. Bronx Jail, you, Columbia, etc. ouch.

> Come home soon
>
> Jack

Allen Ginsberg [San Francisco, California] to Jack Kerouac [Northport, New York]

City Lights 261 Columbus
SF Calif USA
Oct 6, 1963

Dear Jack:

Kept thinking I should write you back fast huge love lovely belly flowers letter, received yours in Japan, I just got TOO MUCH to tell you TOO TOO TOO much whoops where could I begin Japan or somewhere? India, Ganges I'm bathing all the time and praying for transcendentalist Blakes and visiting holymen and all they got to say is "Take Blake for your Guru," or "Your own Heart is Your Guru," or "O how wounded you and Peter are, Oh how wounded, Oh how wounded," till finally I left when time was up and flew to Viet Nam and everybody killing everybody else hardhearted America paranoia and weeks in Cambodia ruins Ankor Wat and pot and Bangkok Chinese boys and finally peaceful Kyoto, sat in monastery with Gary [Snyder] and did belly breathing and that calmed my mind and then the sweetness of all those Gurus sinking in to me and then Joanne [Kyger] and Gary both so nice to me both took me to bed even Gary made love to me and all of a sudden I dug Joanne since it was alright for me to feel what anyway I felt, I want a woman wife lady, I want I want, want life not death, wound up crying on train from Kyoto to Tokyo and wrote final poem: On My Train Seat I Renounce My Power: So That I Do Live I Will Die therefore accepting Christ see also, and no more mental universe arguments: I am that I am and what exactly am I? Why I'm me, and me is my feelings by gum and those feelings are located to be exact in my belly trembling when eyes say Yes and in my breast all along that's my me NOT my head not Christ ideas not Buddha—Christ and Buddha are in my body not no where else. And everything else is arbitrary conceptions. So from now on I won't take nothing but love and give same, in feelings, except—well I came back weeping to Vancouver and there was Olson Duncan Creeley Levertov all to teach together and I said, I can't eliminate them from my universe or anyone even Norman Podhoretz they are all selfs too like me alas we been arguing and seeing each other like beatniks and poets and everything but crying self so I just cried and didn't teach just went around feeling everybody up till we were all there together having a happy earth picnic with no ideas in head about put up poetry or put down poets NO MORE WARS all are immortal laugh and lie down no superior poets no inferior poets furthermore no more need ayahuascas or peyotes because already flowing from belly and breast is infinity when feeling's open and that feels good not scary—all I saw in Blake 1948 finally came true, lasted weeks and weeks, lovely Jerusalem blisses, I even realized (finally) my mother died having seen and told me her last day the key is in the sunlight, but I didn't realize what she meant and felt till I felt myself back home in my own body on earth and knew she had been there and knew it. So all's well, I go get married and have little hairy losses someday—and I am not a hairy loss, I'm me, and me's nameless, but certainly not a bad feeling OOK like hairy loss, you put me under a spell for years, and Burroughs about killed me off with his cut ups—his cut ups fine since it cuts up the head but he wants to cut up his body feelings too, and that don't feel good at all—your hairy loss served to get me down off my high head too, but you coulda saved me faster by calling me tender heart, honey—everything's fine we're all going to be what? be what we is! ain't that great. I'm too mental and hungup to explain right, but anyway Jack I'm telling you like you tell me, yup, everything is alright, in fact I can't explain it anymore I just FEEL it and that's better than explaining so next time we meet I'll make you feel good. I'll kiss you and pet you and read you little poemlets about ispy diddle and I'll also kiss your mama and ask her forgiveness and ask her to love me and I done already prayed for your poppa and I go see my poppa and thank him for borning me and make him feel it's all alright and I go back to human universe just as in prophecy of *Dr. Sax* (which last chapters of which I read to class in Vancouver) THE SNAKE'S ALL TOOK CARE OF. And your letter full of tenderness so I won't sermonize you anymore either, despite I do detect doubts in your mind whether it's alright for you to have been born, well you go right over to your mother and REASSURE her that she did right giving life to you. And why right? Because god is feeling and it makes her feel bad you complaining alla time you didn't want to be born. Wouldn't you feel bad if your son told you he was mad at your for borning him. And wouldn't you feel good if son came home and said, dad, we made it, I'm glad I'm alive you did right. Wouldn't you feel better? and what else have we got but feelings, have we got some big ideas, or something else to be? besides our hearts? All the gurus in India say Abhya mudra abhya mudra and so says Buddha and so I say to little English Kerouac, except we NOW are in the tents of god so let's like lambs rejoice: and no more specters.

So now I'm here in SF going around asking everybody if I can kiss them.

Pathetic isn't it, asking everybody to love me? Which seeing I'm such a fucked up longhair goof naturally they melt and do, except it gets to be hard work. Nonetheless you look in those faces everywhere and what's to be seen but same self all over been wounded and pissed on—and Lucien was here and we blessed each other anew—and Neal now. Well I'm in a big apartment with some quiet young Kansas poets I got backroom and Neal and his girl have another room (same Ann [Murphy] you saw in Northport) and he understands why it was too difficult there (in Northport)—and beginning I hope Monday we sit down and Neal actually write his blop again, anyway he quit job and Carolyn divorced him (I spent days with her) and I singing hours of calm hindoo mantras to him soften the air till he get back in his body from racetrack specters and unfeeling frenzy and we all be back together again o la tierra est la nostra. I come see you Xmas without hair if you so desire me or with hair if you so accept me, if you want calm weeks come here reunion NO LUSHING it destroy feeling in fact get off that lush. I no take drugs no more nothing but belly flowers. I sleep with girls I reborn I happy I sing harikrishna lords prayer ipsky diddle I weep Sebastian [Sampas] knew all we know nothing unless we do love. Now we go out save America from lovelessness. I reverse *Howl*, I write white *Howl*, no more death O Walt Hello Jack!

I make movie of *Kaddish* with Robert Frank later you help me with dialogue?

I'll write you soon again. Will you love me ever? Peter heading his footprints across Pakistan toward Persia and New York by Xmas.

We are all babies! Feels good. The word at last!!!

INDEX

Note: AG refer to Allen Ginsberg. JK refers to Jack Kerouac.

Academy of Political Science, 38
Acavalna (Mexico): AG visit to, 214–18, 222, 230
Ace Books
  and AG works, 169
  and Burroughs works, 169, 189–92
  and JK finances, 158, 161
  and JK publications, 160, 171, 173, 176, 195–96
  Solomon at, 133–34, 133*n*
  See also Wyn, A. A.
Ackerman, Mary, 223, 224, 225–26
Adams, Joan Vollmer
  AG comment about Celine to, 25
  AG comments about, 9, 184
  AG inquiries about, 106
  and AG in jail, 67
  and AG in mental hospital, 98
  and Burroughs trust fund, 109
  and Columbia get-together, 22
  and JK concerns about morality, 21
  JK relationship with, 14, 53
  JK sees, 3, 22
  JK thoughts about, 472
  pseudonyms of, 3*n*
Adams, Walter, 51, 91, 91*n*, 100, 108, 109, 114, 195, 223, 403, 472
Adler, Alfred, 5, 5*n*
Admiral Restaurant (New York City), 17, 18, 20, 25
"Aether" (AG), 453
"After Gogol" (AG), 145
aging: AG views about, 457
Airplane poems, AG, 288
Alaska: AG in, 327–29
Alfred A. Knopf Publishers, 246, 267, 317
Algren, Nelson, 358
Allen, Donald
  AG comments about, 384
  AG discussions/meetings with, 403, 410, 416, 428–29
  and AG preface to *Gasoline*, 365
  and AG request for copies of JK poems, 417
  AG sends introduction to, 361
  and AG works, 361, 420
  and anthology, 451
  and banning of AG and JK works, 418
  and *Beat Traveler*, 449
  and *Book of Blues*, 410, 411, 418
  and Burroughs, 366, 375, 388, 390, 429
  and Corso works, 356, 385, 393
  and *Doctor Sax*, 335, 413, 416, 418, 420, 423
  and Ferlinghetti, 385
  and JK Buddhist writings, 408
  and JK contracts/finances, 419
  JK gives poems to, 414
  and JK-Rosenberg meeting, 359
  and JK views about publishing, 419

  JK visit with, 359
  and Lamantia works, 416, 418
  Lord lunch with, 419
  and *Mexico City Blues*, 408, 416
  and Persky works, 402
  and publication of JK works, 416
  in San Francisco, 352, 428–29
  and "Sather Gate," 345
  and Snyder works, 416, 418
  and *Subterraneans*, 335, 343, 376, 419
  and *Visions of Gerard*, 335, 418
  and *Visions of Neal*, 418
  and "Zizi's Lament," 365
Allen, Steve, 385, 395, 398, 406, 432, 436, 440
"America" (AG), 337, 389
Americana: JK views about, 378
American Academy of Arts and Letters, 305, 321
American Mercury magazine, 161, 172
American Revolution, 232, 243
Amsterdam, The Netherlands: AG in, 355–59, 360–62
Anderson, Joan, 270, 271–72, 278, 379
"The Angels in the World" (JK), 330
Ansen, Alan
  AG invitation from, 195
  AG letters to/from, 328
  and AG as literary agent, 173
  and AG in Mexico, 230
  AG reading works of, 138
  and AG in San Jose, 229
  AG visits with, 141–42
  and AG writing abilities, 230
  as Auden secretary, 133*n*
  and Burroughs, 229, 346, 350, 361
  on Cape Cod, 105
  disappearance of, 310
  and drugs, 347
  Duncan abilities similar to, 240
  in Europe, 328, 345, 346, 347, 348–53, 354, 355, 376, 450
  and Gaddis, 224–25
  influence on AG of, 162
  invitation to JK from, 450
  JK comments about, 224–25, 345, 378
  JK inquiries about, 387, 472
  JK letters to/from, 348–51
  JK missing of, 358
  and JK-Orlovsky letters, 356
  and JK plans to visit Europe, 350, 377
  and JK in San Francisco, 352
  JK sends regards to, 148
  JK suggestion for writings by, 352
  JK visits with, 222
  nihilism of, 276
  publication of works by, 133, 142, 150, 172

Ansen, Alan (*cont'd*)
    and Whalen, 352
    writings of, 141–42
anti-Semitism, 235
Antoninus, Brother, 429, 431
Apollinaire, 4*n*, 367, 368, 374, 377
Aronowitz, Al, 452
art
    AG views about, 10, 26, 52, 297
    JK views about, 5, 24–25, 26, 27, 63
Arts and Sciences grants, 154, 158
Associated Press: AG job with, 63
Atlantic Monthly, 227, 236
Auden, W. H., 133*n*, 140, 142, 155, 223*n*, 249, 277, 288, 328
Avalokitesvara (JK), 350
Avon Publications
    JK-AG editing anthology for, 429, 429*n*, 431, 432, 435–36, 437, 438, 440–41, 451
    Tristessa published by, 451

Babbitt, Irving, 279
Bach, Johann Sebastian, 284, 311, 452
Bacon, Francis (English painter), 347
Baker, Jinny, 45–46
Baldwin, James, 245, 246, 247, 343, 348, 351, 472
Balzac, Honoré de, 140, 186, 253, 392, 393, 442
Bantam Books, 451
Barnes, Djuna, 103, 103*n*
Barzun, Jacques, 444
Baudelaire, Charles, 4*n*, 368
BBC, 393, 395
Beat Generation
    AG advice to JK about writing about, 370
    AG promotion of, 399, 427, 428
    and brutality, 389
    and Burroughs *Junkey*, 189
    communist infiltration of, 431
    confessions and honesties of 1947 of, 246
    definition of, 427
    Feldman-Citadel anthology about, 375
    Holmes article about, 392
    Holmes as co-expert on, 190
    image of, 439
    JK articles about, 353, 357
    JK-Corso article about, 471
    JK interviews about, 413
    JK views about, 190, 389, 427, 432
    and JK withdrawal, 399
    key figures of, 190
    as literary racquet, 451
    Mademoiselle feature about, 335, 335*n*
    as "San Francisco Renaissance," 370
Beat Generation (Corso), 306
Beat Generation (JK)
    and Cowley, 300–301, 303, 305, 321
    dreams about Hollywood buying, 295
    Giroux requests copy of, 289*n*
    Harper article about, 352
    publication of, 253, 267, 282, 285, 300, 302, 303, 305
    as title for *On the Road*, 227, 236
Beat Generation (JK play), 366, 366*n*
Beat Generation (movie), 405
Beat Generation Road (JK), 246
The Beat Traveler (JK), 413, 449
Beatitude magazine, 436, 438, 455
Beckett, Samuel, 351, 361, 364
Beebe, Lucius, 97, 303

Beethoven, Ludwig van, 5, 185, 401
Belson, Jordan, 249, 277, 451
Berkeley Blues (JK), 337
Berkeley, California
    AG in, 318, 320, 321, 325–26, 332–35
    AG plans to move to, 315–16, 317
    JK in, 325, 344–51, 352
    JK move to, 341, 342
    JK writings about, 373
Berkeley Review, 348
Bickford's cafeteria (New York City): AG job at, 437, 437*n*
big meat poems, AG, 360
Big Sur: JK at, 453, 459–60
Big Sur (JK), 453, 472
Big Table magazine, 429, 436, 436*n*, 438
"Birthday Ode" (AG), 89, 89*n*
Black Mountain Review, 325, 348, 389, 403, 407
Blake, Nin (JK sister), 73, 178, 291, 308, 325, 351, 414–15, 450
Blake, Paul, 59, 75, 175, 273, 306, 307, 383, 384, 474
Blake, William, 38, 49, 89, 90, 263, 264, 296–97, 383, 393, 473
Bles Blues (JK), 411
Bloom (mental patient), 104–5
Bobbs-Merrill, 184
Book of Blues (JK), 343, 348, 357, 365, 371, 372, 375, 410, 411, 412, 418
Book of Dreams (JK), 224, 414, 451, 465
The Book of Martyrdom and Artifice (AG), 27*n*, 89*n*
Bowery Blues (JK), 282, 285
Bowles, Jane, 347, 364
Bowles, Paul, 197, 236, 301, 302, 347, 472
Brandel, Marc, 452
Brando, Marlon, 295, 354, 357, 373, 374, 390, 413
Brata Gallery: JK poetry reading at, 385
Bremser, Ray, 372, 372*n*, 444, 455
Brierly, Justin, 31, 73, 73*n*, 74, 75, 81, 97, 98, 105, 108, 296
Brody, Iris, 223
Bronx County Jail: Kerouac in, 3–4
Brooks, Eugene "Gene" (AG brother)
    AG buying Corso records for, 332
    AG dream of killing, 207
    and AG financial affairs, 193, 203
    and AG in jail, 67, 67*n*
    as AG lawyer, 154
    AG letters to/from, 284–85
    and AG in mental hospital, 105
    and AG in Mexico, 203, 207
    AG relationship with, 327
    and AG return to New York City, 252
    and AG trip to New York City, 397
    and AG views about U.S., 232
    AG visit with, 334
    and AG X letter, 270
    and bed for AG, 75
    children of, 327
    and closing on JK house, 433
    Columbia lawsuit against, 444
    Garen resemblance to, 385
    and JK book contracts, 133, 142, 148
    and JK child support payments, 157, 160, 267–68
    and JK finances, 304, 307, 317
    JK house near, 393
    JK letter to, 304
    and JK-Orlovsky (Laff) investigation, 364
    and JK plans to visit California, 298, 304
    and JK television appearance, 372

and JK trip to New York City, 299
JK views about, 157, 304–5, 469
JK visit with, 469
and keeping in touch with AG, 70, 105
and Naomi in mental hospital, 69, 299
in North Carolina, 285
and Solomon in mental hospital, 285
wedding of, 252
Broyard, Anatole, 231*n*, 452
Brubeck, Dave, 239, 244
Buchwald, Art, 397, 398
Buddha Tells Us (JK), 282, 291–92, 301, 302, 308,
  321
Buddhism
  AG comments about, 221, 473, 474
  AG interest in, 222, 228, 243, 244, 250, 262, 265,
    271, 273, 278, 279, 281, 283–84, 287, 294, 316,
    407, 408, 411
  AG writings about, 243
  Burroughs interest in, 237, 246
  and Carr, 246, 273
  and Elvins, 231
  JK belief in, 218–20, 221, 223–26, 228, 231–32,
    253, 263, 266–72, 273, 281, 294–95, 306–8,
    309–10, 386, 399–400, 465
  and JK-Orlovsky (Laff) investigation, 364
  JK thoughts of abandoning, 289–90
  JK translations of works about, 276
  JK writings about, 280, 282, 290, 291–92, 300,
    301, 302, 308, 309–10, 390, 413, 416
  and Lamantia, 313
  and Orlovsky (Peter), 278
Burford, Bev, 272, 296
Burford, Bob, 147, 147*n*, 162, 169, 172, 184, 245,
  246, 247
Burnett, Dave, 276, 279, 301, 306, 359
Burroughs, Joan (common-law wife), 126, 131, 168,
  170, 268, 276, 302, 304, 307, 316, 352, 353
Burroughs, William "Bill" "Denison"
  Adams as common-law wife of, 3*n*
  and Allen, 366
  and Americana, 378
  and Avon anthology, 440
  Bacon as similar to, 347
  Baldwin comments about, 245, 246
  banning of works of, 418
  and *Big Table* magazine, 438
  and Buchwald interview, 398
  and Buddhism, 237, 246
  Burford comments about, 245, 247
  and Carr, 242, 394
  and changes in world, 211–12
  children of, 138
  code names for, 71
  and Columbia get-together, 22
  and communism, 243, 398
  and Corso, 360–61
  and Cowley, 247, 302, 306, 326
  as crazy, 99
  criticisms of, 13, 245, 246, 247, 288–89
  curiosity of, 25
  "Doc Benway" by, 430
  drawling act of, 64
  and drugs, 239, 286, 298, 299, 334, 347, 368, 396,
    434
  in Ecuador, 156, 157
  in Europe and North Africa, 203, 204, 207, 211–12,
    222, 229, 262, 277, 294, 328, 334, 341–44, 346–
    47, 348–51, 354, 355, 356, 393, 412, 429, 454

and extinction of human race, 80
as Factualist, 63
and Ferlinghetti, 361, 372, 385, 388, 390
finances of, 244, 247, 249, 393, 429, 451
finger story of, 272
Florida trip of, 244, 247, 249, 434
and Frechtman, 364
and Garver, 138*n*, 318
help for compiling and typing works of, 346, 350
as homosexual, 201
and Huncke, 69
and Huston meeting, 398
as Ignu, 86
illness of, 229, 298, 347
imitations of, 165
inquisitiveness of, 26
intelligentsia views of, 349
Interzone by, 272, 346, 388, 417
Junkey by, 150, 152, 155, 156, 168, 173, 189–92,
  227, 233, 278, 306
and KiKi, 238, 364, 364*n*
lack of information about, 21, 404, 418
and laughing disease, 371
and LaVigue-Orlovsky-AG relationship, 256
Lee as pseudonym of, 189, 190, 191
as "leprous," 21
as lost, 222
Marker relationship with, 201
in mental hospital, 100
and Merchant Marine, 21
in Mexico, 124, 131, 138, 144, 147, 152, 156–57,
  162, 167–68, 169, 173, 176, 178
Mexico knowledge of, 206, 211
mind views of, 98
money views of, 82
and morality, 20
movie idea of, 398
Naked Lunch by, 247, 277, 302, 306, 325, 341,
  370, 385, 452
and New Guinea Disease, 360
and new literary movement, 158
New York City trip of, 196–97, 429, 430, 432
nihilism of, 276
in Peru, 193
as picking up women, 15
police search for, 429
publication of works by, 133, 143, 159, 161, 169,
  172, 277, 355, 370, 372, 375, 384, 388, 389, 401,
  406, 417, 438
and publicity for *Junkey*, 189–92
Queer by, 156, 159, 168, 172, 173, 176, 249, 306,
  388
and religion, 431
return to U.S. of, 242
and Rexroth, 233, 248, 277, 283
Rothschild friend of, 396, 400
San Francisco visit of, 233, 245, 246
"saving" of, 44
"Sebastian Midnite" by, 417
and sex, 156
Shakespeare knowledge of, 377
at Sheepshead Bay, 15, 16, 17, 19, 21
and Solomon, 150
and South America trip, 316
Spenglerian and anthropological ideas of, 27
Stern praised by, 433
in Texas, 86
trial of, 131, 144
trust fund of, 109

Burroughs, William "Bill" "Denison" (cont'd)
  and Vidal, 175
  Wernham compared with, 317
  and White death, 138–39
  and Wieners, 348, 351
  and *Word Hoard*, 346, 359, 372, 431
  writing method of, 277
  writings of, 138, 162, 247, 384
  Yage Letters of, 193, 196, 249, 306, 327, 346, 361, 388, 389
  and yage vine, 449
  Yiddishe Kopfe of, 12
Burroughs, William "Bill" "Denison," and AG
  advice to AG from, 9, 13
  AG in agreement with, 90
  AG comments and concerns about, 13, 76, 201, 222, 228–29, 234, 242, 245, 294, 303, 434, 454, 457
  AG desire to make movie about, 204
  AG dreams about, 115–16, 207, 209, 472
  and AG fears, 127, 173
  and AG finances, 170
  and AG as genius, 94
  AG inquiries about, 86, 106, 229
  and AG and JK helping each other, 300
  and AG-JK letters, 374
  and AG legal problems, 67, 69–70, 71, 87
  AG letters to/from, 27, 171, 196, 203, 211–12, 213, 220, 228–29, 233, 244, 245, 258, 262, 272, 276–77, 284, 298, 316, 320, 327, 328, 334, 360, 362, 371, 387, 388, 454
  AG as literary agent for, 143, 160, 172, 173, 189–92, 325, 361
  and AG-Lord letters, 361
  and AG madness, 50
  and AG in mental hospital, 92, 93–94, 98, 100, 103, 104, 106, 108–9
  and AG in Mexico, 173, 203, 204, 206, 207, 209, 210, 211, 213, 230
  AG ode to son of, 89, 89n
  AG plans to visit, 334
  AG references to, 195
  AG relationship with, 242, 244, 245, 246, 248, 250–51, 329, 331, 346, 358, 399, 474
  AG reliance on, 59
  and AG self-image, 11
  AG sends money to, 276–77
  and AG views about death, 48
  AG views about writings of, 143, 155
  and AG and women, 126
  and AG writing abilities, 230
  analysis of AG by, 99
  and Burroughs as complication in AG-JK friendship, 246
  and *Howl* trial, 362
Burroughs, William "Bill" "Denison," and JK
  advice to JK from, 344
  in *Beat Generation*, 302
  and Burroughs as laughing at JK, 59
  and "cityCityCITY," 291, 305
  comments about JK of, 246
  as complication in AG-JK friendship, 246
  And the Hippos Were Boiled in Their Tanks (with JK) by, 144
  and JK and AG helping each other, 300
  and JK-AG letters, 374
  and JK article explaining Beat Generation, 353
  JK borrows money from, 178
  JK cancels appointment with, 23

JK comments and concerns about, 82, 156, 168, 212, 238, 246, 268, 272, 288–89, 290, 307, 322, 345, 349, 377, 378, 389, 391–92, 400, 401, 465, 472
JK daydreams about, 469
JK desire to visit, 160
and JK divorce, 345
JK fear of, 26
and JK finances, 160
JK hope to see, 236
and JK idea for movie, 386
JK imitating style of, 34
JK inquiries about, 193, 292, 342, 352, 387, 390, 396
JK letters to/from, 53, 108–9, 133, 137, 156–57, 196–97, 222, 236–37, 245, 246, 280, 285, 291, 298, 314–15, 322, 341–44, 348–51, 352, 353, 375, 432, 452
JK loans money to, 247, 249
JK love for, 54, 197
JK missing of, 358, 359
JK plans to visit, 391
and JK plans to visit Europe, 109, 295, 377
JK promotion of works of, 277
and JK psychic balance, 24
JK relationship with Burroughs, 9, 15, 168, 246, 274, 344, 352, 358, 375, 379, 391, 433, 473
and JK self-image, 274
and JK as success, 359
JK thoughts of murdering, 53
and JK views of half-of-life-is death, 63
and JK views of people as godlike, 53, 59
JK visits with, 124, 341
and JK writing of *Doctor Sax*, 185
and JK writing method, 393
JK writings about, 144, 173, 230, 280, 413, 420, 422
letter to JK mother from, 402
and *On the Road*, 156, 173, 396
and *T&C*, 118, 156
Burroughs, Willie, 89, 89n, 168, 429
Butorac, Pete, 223, 226

Caen, Herb, 345, 396, 418
California
  JK decides not to go to, 289
  JK plans/desires to visit, 22, 290, 292
Cambridge Review, 303, 331
Cannastra, Bill, 105, 114, 127, 142, 151, 162, 170, 209, 231, 253, 420
Cape Cod: AG's desire to go to, 105
Capote, Truman, 81, 186, 435, 435n
car crash: of AG, 67–68
Carman, Dean, 87, 87n
Carr, Cessa von Hartz, 42, 138, 158, 161, 176, 224, 231, 357, 359, 431, 441, 452, 460, 472
Carr, Lucien "Claude"
  and Beat Generation confessions and honesties, 246
  in Brazil, 217
  and Buddhism, 246, 273
  and Burroughs, 242, 394
  Celine relationship with, 22
  code names for, 71
  and Corso, 224, 302, 431, 471
  drinking by, 35, 37, 42–46, 161, 219, 224, 230, 322, 351, 358, 359, 395, 402
  egocentrism of, 26
  as family man, 401

Garcia Villa meeting with, 223
and girl on skates, 43–44
and Hardy poetry, 70
heroes in writings of, 174
illness of, 441
imitations of, 165
in jail, 140
and Joan poem dream, 304, 307
jobs for, 326
and Kammerer murder, 3, 12, 12n, 44n
and liberation of Paris, 4
Livornese relationship with, 46
and love, 101
and "Lucienism" efforts, 16
marriage of, 134, 135, 138
and Mexico, 169, 170, 176, 302
and new literary movement, 158
and new vision, 24
New Year's Eve parties at, 57, 442, 444
and New York monster scenery, 384
nihilism of, 276
at parties, 123
in prison, 4n, 44, 44n
publication of work by, 144
and reality, 99
religion of, 353
resentment of, 21–22
Robinson as friend of, 61
in San Francisco, 475
"saving" of, 44
self-image of, 5, 124
self-understanding of, 42
and shrouded stranger phrase, 158
spirituality of, 222
views about New York City of, 392
at Village Vanguard, 391
wedding of, 152, 156
women/lovers of, 86, 472
Carr, Lucien "Claude," and AG
    AG comments about, 124, 196, 222, 229, 239,
        277
    AG desire to see, 399
    AG dreams about, 106
    AG inquiries about, 222, 229, 348
    and AG-JK letters, 230
    and AG legal problems, 71, 77, 85–86
    AG letters to/from, 394
    AG as living with, 190
    and AG in mental hospital, 93, 100, 106
    and AG in Mexico, 204, 213, 217, 220, 230
    and AG new faith, 50
    and AG New York City visit, 252, 334
    AG painting house for, 456
    and AG poems, 152, 159, 364
    AG poems dedicated to, 145
    AG regard to, 294, 364, 384
    AG relationship with, 51, 251, 301, 307, 441, 475
    AG reliance on, 59
    and AG self-understanding, 49
    AG sends love to, 356
    AG similarity to, 64
    AG talks with, 406, 444
    AG views about, 10, 26, 162
    and AG views about death, 48
    and AG views about hate, 59, 60
    and AG views about systems, 117
    and AG visions, 265
    AG visits with, 403
    AG at wedding of, 152, 156

and AG and women, 126
and AG writing abilities, 159, 230
and Burroughs-AG relationship, 242
comments/views about AG of, 44–45, 302, 401,
    406, 409
and Howl trial, 362
influence on AG of, 88
invitation to AG from, 410
and Siesta in Xbalba, 239
understanding of AG poems by, 151
Carr, Lucien "Claude," and JK
    advice to JK of, 413
    and Baker-JK relationship, 45, 46
    as character in JK writings, 162
    comments about JK of, 24, 44–45, 289, 302, 326,
        406, 409
    comments about T&C of, 123
    and Doctor Sax, 177, 301
    and JK-AG letters, 230
    JK car rides with, 230, 231, 359
    JK comments about, 135–36, 180, 219, 224, 231,
        273, 307, 312, 373, 401, 406
    and JK as "disreputable writer," 43, 47
    and JK drinking, 42–46, 460
    and JK finances, 158, 300
    and JK illness, 404
    JK as imitating, 156
    JK inquiries about, 41, 402
    and JK interview about San Francisco murders,
        400
    JK letters to/from, 393
    JK love for, 54, 440
    and JK madness at AG, 185
    and JK memories of, 453
    and JK move to California, 343
    JK need to impress, 42
    JK New Jersey trip with, 231
    and JK in New York City, 302, 357, 358, 359, 391,
        452
    and JK Paris trip, 94, 378
    JK relationship with, 138, 274, 375, 433, 441, 473
    and JK in San Francisco, 326
    and JK self-image, 274
    JK settling of arguments with, 62
    JK similarity to, 64
    and JK views of half-of-life-is death, 64
    JK visits/talks with, 351, 357, 421, 436, 459, 465,
        470, 471
    and JK wedding, 158
    and JK withdrawal, 394
    JK writing compared with that of, 181
    JK writings about, 422, 440, 441, 460
    and On the Road, 356
    and selling of JK seaman's papers, 317–18
    support for JK by, 379
    and T&C advertising, 123
    and Tristessa revisions, 441
Carroll, Paul, 373, 436, 438–39
Cassady, Carolyn
    Ackerman similarity to, 223
    AG comments about, 234, 240, 241, 251
    and AG in Mexico, 201–11, 213–18
    and AG in San Jose, 234
    and AG-JK letters, 145
    AG letters to, 201–11, 213–18, 219, 238
    and AG-Neal relationship, 238–39, 241
    AG relationship with, 229, 234, 251
    AG visits with, 475
    in Arizona, 163

Cassady, Carolyn (*cont'd*)
  and Cayce, 287
  divorce of, 475
  Horney influence on, 212
  as JK advisor about women, 155
  and JK and Buddhism, 218
  and JK-Cassady visit with Lamantia, 166
  JK comments about, 292, 400
  JK contemplates living with Neal and, 193
  and JK influence on Neal, 345, 349
  JK relationship with, 186, 405
  and JK San Francisco visit, 301, 303, 325
  and JK trip to Mexico, 163
  JK views about, 148, 166
  JK visits with, 453
  and JK writings, 223
  and Neal cross-country car trip, 56, 57
  and Neal in jail, 396, 397, 400
  and Neal jobs, 166
  Neal relationship with, 218, 234, 238–39, 240,
    249, 250, 281, 286, 287, 293, 325, 333
  pregnancy of, 57*n*
  in San Jose, 201–11
  second marriage of, 471
  Tennessee trip of, 146
Cassady, Diana Hansen, 114, 121, 123*n*, 126–27,
  182, 223
Cassady, Neal "Pommy"
  and Ansen, 141
  in Arizona, 163
  birthday of, 137
  Brierly offer to help, 82
  car trips of, 55–57, 281
  Carolyn relationship with, 234, 238–39, 240, 249,
    250, 251, 281, 286, 287, 293, 325, 333
  and Cayce, 234, 240, 250, 251, 287, 307, 332, 345
  and Chase letters, 279
  childhood and youth of, 104
  children of, 126–27, 219, 223, 240, 242, 296, 349
  code names for, 71
  in Colorado, 90
  and Corso, 330
  Diana relationship with, 126–27
  divorce of, 475
  and Dostoevsky story, 92
  dreams of, 175
  and drugs, 212, 249, 251–52, 255, 286, 330, 394,
    396, 400
  finances of, 154, 166, 345, 349, 371, 405, 458
  The First Third by, 155, 258*n*, 400
  Garen play about, 357
  and Gould, 456
  and Greek and poem styles, 306
  and Hinkle, 251, 255, 268
  as Ignu, 86
  illness of, 332
  imitations of, 385
  injuries of, 146, 146*n*, 193
  and Jackson, 281, 286, 303, 325
  in jail, 34, 104, 396, 397, 400
  "Joan Anderson letter" of, 258, 258*n*, 271–72,
    278, 379
  jobs of, 34, 56, 145–46, 166, 249, 262, 320, 332,
    333, 433, 457–58, 475
  and Lamantia, 140, 165–66
  Lustig play about, 357
  and Mann lecture, 76
  marriage of, 114*n*, 126
  and Mexico, 127, 249–50, 262, 331, 332, 333

  and new literary movement, 150, 158
  and New Year's Eve party (1948), 57
  New York City trip plans of, 258
  nihilism of, 276
  picture of, 144
  in prison, 359, 428, 429, 430
  publication of works by, 140, 149, 174, 416
  relationship with people of, 68
  as religious, 212–13, 212*n*, 213, 220–21, 353
  in San Francisco, 56, 74, 86–87, 113, 131–35,
    137–45, 149–50, 165–66, 212, 232, 240, 281,
    286–87, 316
  in San Jose, 178–80, 201–11, 213 18, 219
  and Six Gallery readings, 316
  and Solomon, 124, 158
  soul of, 152, 222
  as stealing book from Giroux, 180
  stealing of car by, 55–56, 57
  and Sublette, 227, 233, 250
  Tennessee trip of, 146
  and Williams (Sheila), 249
  and women in The Netherlands, 355
  women/lovers of, 109, 254, 258, 258*n*, 285, 332,
    349, 475
  writing abilities of, 230
  writings of, 123, 132, 134, 140, 234, 240, 332,
    430, 475 Cassady, Neal "Pommy," and AG
  AG comments and concerns about, 124, 149,
    152, 155, 169, 213, 221, 222, 228, 229, 230,
    234 35, 240–42, 249–50, 251–52, 299, 396, 397
  and AG decision not to go to San Francisco, 152
  AG dedication of poems to, 145
  AG dreams about, 36, 326
  and AG in Europe, 346
  AG feelings about, 54, 59–60, 121, 140, 143
  and AG finances, 346
  AG first meets, 31
  and AG illness, 114
  AG inquiries about, 70, 75, 100, 362, 456
  AG jealousy of, 120
  AG job recommendation for, 87
  and AG in San Francisco, 251, 254, 255
  and AG in San Jose, 220–21, 222, 228, 233, 234
  and AG-JK letters, 172, 303, 304
  and AG legal problems, 71
  AG letters to/from, 131–35, 137–43, 145, 155,
    184, 201–11, 213–18, 397, 445
  and AG as literary agent, 173
  and AG in mental hospital, 100, 104, 108
  and AG in Mexico, 201–11, 213–18, 220
  and AG plans to leave San Francisco, 284
  AG poems about, 84, 91, 329
  AG relationship with, 119, 121, 134, 238–39, 240,
    241, 251, 255, 265, 285, 286, 475
  AG requests letter/poems from, 135, 153
  AG sends writings to, 38
  AG visit with, 428, 429
  AG working with, 434
  comments about AG poems of, 143
  feelings about AG of, 145–46
  and *Howl* trial, 371
  influence on AG of, 258*n*
Cassady, Neal "Pommy," and JK
  as actor in JK plays/movies, 362, 366, 457
  borrows money from JK, 56–57
  as characters in JK writings, 295, 371
  and Cowley changes to *On the Road*, 352
  and *Doctor Sax*, 177
  as hating JK, 54

influence on JK of, 134, 258*n*
and JK-AG letters, 172, 303, 304
and JK and Buddhism, 218
JK comments about, 212–13, 219, 247, 248, 288, 289, 292, 301, 307, 312, 335, 349, 374, 394, 400, 449
JK desire to see, 31
and JK finances, 391, 405–6
JK first meets, 31
JK imitation of, 181
and JK in Berkeley, 351, 352
and JK in Denver, 108
JK influence on, 345, 349
and JK in Mexico, 318
and JK in San Francisco, 330
JK job recommendation for, 34
JK letters to/from, 108, 245, 249, 252, 262, 278, 282, 333, 374, 399, 405, 408, 430, 443
JK living with, 178, 186
and JK move to California, 341
and JK on television, 371
and JK plans/desires to visit San Francisco, 302, 303, 305, 307
and JK plans to visit Paris, 94
and JK plans to visit San Francisco, 290, 293, 294, 296, 300
JK play about, 374
JK reading poetry to, 459
JK relationship with, 147, 148, 185–86, 262, 285, 318, 375, 379, 405, 453
JK thoughts about, 81, 471
and JK trip to Mexico, 163, 166
JK trip to San Francisco with, 67
JK views about, 158, 166, 179, 186, 271–72, 408
and JK views of half-of-life-is death, 63, 64
and JK visit to Denver, 296
and JK visit to San Francisco, 296, 298, 299, 301, 303, 304, 320
JK visits with, 325, 327, 453, 457, 459
and JK withdrawal, 470
and JK works in *New World Writing*, 286
JK writing compared with that of, 181
JK writings about, 137, 157, 175, 235, 245, 258, 295, 330, 449
and jobs for JK, 146
and *On the Road*, 137, 173, 174, 177, 178, 179, 183, 352, 362, 371, 386, 396
See also *Visions of Neal*
cat joke, Hoffman's, 139–40
Catholicism, 413
cave: and AG in Mexico, 216–18, 229
"Caw Caw" (AG), 429
Cayce, Edgar
and AG in San Jose, 220–21
AG views about, 240, 287
and AG views about U.S., 232
and Cassady (Carolyn), 287
Cassady (Diana) letters from, 223
Cassady interest in, 212–13, 212*n*, 234, 240, 250, 251, 287, 307, 332, 345
and JK and Buddhism, 218
JK comments about, 213, 292, 307
Céline, Louis-Ferdinand, 104, 121, 121*n*, 286, 337, 351, 415*n*, 456
Cervantes, Miguel de, 71, 374, 375, 377
Cézanne, Paul, 42, 47, 50, 100, 104, 151, 245, 284
chain poem manifesto, AG, 360
Chaplin, Charlie, 288, 390, 443
Chase, Hal

AG comments about, 256
AG compared with, 250
AG inquiries about, 134, 279, 348
and AG introspection, 77
AG letters to/from, 329
AG reliance on, 59
AG sex poem about, 329
AG thoughts about, 79
and AG views about hate, 60
and Americana, 378
and Cassady, 87
death of, 98, 108
in Denver, 9
JK views about, 179–80
and JK views about people as godlike, 53
lack of information about, 138
leaves Berkeley, 345
and love, 101
lovers of, 22, 126
profoundness of, 32
reputation of, 207
and seminarists, 53
T&C comments by, 31–32
vision of, 58
Chicago, Illinois
AG trip to, 418, 420–21
JK in, 235
Chicago Review, 373, 384, 385, 407, 417–18, 420
children
AG's views about, 54
and JK's child support payments, 157, 160
JK's views about, 54, 97
Chile
AG trip to, 449
JK invitation to visit, 442, 443–44, 449
Citron, Casper, 437
City Lights Bookstore (San Francisco, California), 303*n*, 320, 325, 326, 328, 362, 367, 372, 375, 393, 414, 417, 418, 429, 455
"cityCityCITY" (JK), 289, 291, 301, 302, 303, 305–6, 343
Civil Liberties Union, 349
civil war novel, JK, 174
clairvoyance, 186, 224, 232
"Classic Unity" (AG), 61–62
Climax magazine, 393
Cloud of Unknowing (anon.), 209
Cocteau, Jean, 210, 350, 377
Cold War, 232, 427
colleges/universities: AG views about, 444
Colorado
JK in, 73–109
See also Denver, Colorado
Columbia Presbyterian Hospital, 92
Columbia University
AG debt to, 444
Ginsberg as student at, 9
See also specific person
Combustion magazine, 361
Commentary magazine, 159, 161
communism, 235, 243, 386, 398, 431, 455, 460
"The Complaint of the Skelton to Time" (AG), 78–79
Confidence Man (AG), 196
Constable, Rosalind, 362, 372, 418
contemplatives: AG views about, 209
Corso, Gregory
abstract poetry of, 417
as actor, 398

Corso, Gregory (*cont'd*)
  and Allen, 393
  "Army Army Army" by, 393
  "Arnold" by, 385
  Beat Generation views of, 400
  "Bomb" by, 408, 415, 418, 430, 433
  Buchwald interview of, 397
  and Buddhism, 224
  and Burroughs, 360–61
  and Carr, 224, 302, 431, 471
  and Cassady, 330
  as celebrity, 303, 306
  and City Lights, 328
  "Clown" by, 460
  "Concourse Didils" by, 385
  and Cowley, 301, 302, 303
  and de Angulo (Gui), 332, 333
  drinking by, 301, 343, 397
  and drugs, 471
  Esquire picture of, 351
  European trip of, 333, 336, 341, 343, 345, 355,
    356, 360, 364, 365, 368, 376–78, 389, 391, 393,
    402, 421, 434, 436, 439, 450, 454
  and Ferlinghetti, 333, 356, 365
  finances of, 333, 334, 346, 350, 367, 429, 434,
    471
  Garcia Villa views about, 310
  Gasoline by, 356, 360–61, 365, 386, 390, 438
  as greatest Italian poet, 377
  and Hanover records, 432, 433
  Happy Birthday of Death by, 460
  and Huston meeting, 398
  in jail, 434
  and Jarrell, 333–34, 336–37
  Laughlin inquiry about, 410
  as leading poet of Beat Generation, 134*n*
  leaves New York for West Coast, 134
  and Lee copy of *The Subterraneans*, 231
  and Lord, 383, 409, 433
  in Los Angeles, 336
  Mexico trip of, 329, 331, 332, 335, 336
  moon chain poem by, 455
  and Moreland, 134
  Negro incident of, 431
  and Orlovsky visit to New York City, 306
  paintings/drawings by, 336, 375, 383
  in Paris, 354, 374, 400, 404, 418
  Persky compared with, 402
  plays of, 366
  poems by, 303, 306, 375, 383, 393, 411–12
  poetry readings of, 331, 334, 336
  "Power" by, 333, 334, 356
  publication of works by, 333, 355, 372, 375, 401,
    409, 417
  and religion, 431
  as romantic, 399
  style of, 373
  This Hungup Age by, 306
  "use use use" poem by, 385, 391
  The Vestal Lady on Brattle by, 302
  in Washington, 336–37
  wedding of, 471
  at Wesleyan College, 430
  and Wieners, 350
  and Williams, 337, 345, 348, 350
  women/lovers of, 301, 341, 351, 383
  writing by, 332, 360, 367
Corso, Gregory, and AG
  AG borrowing money from, 374
  AG comments about, 304, 312, 332, 348, 367,
    408, 417, 457, 460
  and AG in Alaska, 328
  AG letters to/from, 328, 404, 408, 412, 418, 429,
    439, 454
  and AG poetry, 331
  AG reading of works of, 311
  AG relationship with, 224
  AG sends respects to, 243–44
  AG views about works of, 364, 411–12
  and *Howl*, 328
Corso, Gregory, and JK
  and Giroux views about *Doctor Sax*, 301
  and JK article explaining Beat Generation, 353
  JK comments about, 288, 373, 377, 391, 421, 461
  JK copies of poems of, 472
  and JK-Corso article about Beat Generation,
    471
  and JK finances, 384, 405–6
  and JK idea for movie, 386
  JK inquiries about, 356, 390, 465
  and JK in Washington Park, 224
  JK letters to/from, 352, 356, 367, 376–78, 386,
    402, 408, 414, 427–28, 450
  and JK lifestyle change, 453
  and JK losing copy of Corso poem, 391
  JK missing of, 358
  and JK plans to visit Paris, 377
  JK poem about, 373
  JK praise for, 365
  JK proposes AG write book about, 391
  JK reading of works of, 385
  JK relationship with, 379, 471
  and JK stolen poems, 335
  JK views about, 179, 224, 318, 377, 399, 402, 471
  and JK views about poetry, 377
  and JK visit to New York City, 301, 306
  JK visit with, 351
  JK writings about, 330, 361, 420, 422, 451
  On the Road copy for, 396
  poem about JK by, 306
Cowen, Elise, 342, 343, 348, 351, 352, 391, 403
Cowley, Malcolm
  and AG copy of *Subterraneans*, 393
  and AG Guggenheim application, 355, 362
  AG meeting with, 325–26
  AG views about, 229, 326
  and AG writings, 239, 302, 304
  and *Beat Generation*, 300–301, 303, 305, 321
  and *Buddha Tells Us*, 308
  and Burroughs works, 247, 302, 306, 326
  and "cityCityCITY," 289
  and Corso writings, 301, 302, 303
  and *The Dharma Bums*, 376
  and *Doctor Sax*, 352, 353
  JK compares AG with, 318–19
  JK drinking with, 301
  and JK finances, 352
  and JK grant, 321
  JK letters to/from, 196, 280, 321, 352, 376
  JK mentioned in book by, 238, 246, 252
  and JK offer to go to Mexico, 302
  JK relationship with, 292
  as JK supporter, 194, 196, 235–36, 240, 246, 266,
    277, 302
  JK views about, 291, 301, 308
  and JK visit to New York City, 295, 300, 302
  and *On the Road*, 194, 194*n*, 235–36, 289, 300,
    302, 302*n*, 326, 352

and publication of JK works, 194, 196, 240, 277, 302, 305
and Rexroth support for JK, 277
San Francisco trip of, 325–26
and Solomon knowledge about publication of JK's works, 196
as Viking Press consultant, 194*n*
Williams-AG discussion about, 293
Crane, Hart, 14, 97, 154, 434
Crazy Lights (AG), 262, 272, 278
"A Crazy Spiritual" (AG), 143
credo, AG's, 221
Creeley, Robert, 327, 330, 331, 335, 357, 432, 436, 438, 473
crime: JK's views about, 82
Criterion Publishing, 301
critics: JK views about, 422–23
Cru, Henri, 139, 139*n*, 222, 226, 301, 373, 376, 401, 413, 414, 415, 421, 451, 452, 458
crucifix, JK's, 335*n*, 386
Cuba
  AG story about, 454
  AG trip to, 202, 456
  U.S. war with, 460
culture: JK's views about, 82
cummings, e. e., 140, 320
Cummings, Robert, 417, 420

Dahlberg, Edward, 417–18
Dakar Doldrums (AG), 31*n*, 38, 141, 312
Dancingmaster. *See* Brierly, Justin
Dante Alighieri, 36, 263
Davalos, Dick, 170–71, 170*n*, 172, 176, 289, 294, 295, 296, 300
Davis, Miles, 163, 373
De Angulo, Gui, 331, 331*n*, 332–33
de Angulo, Jaime, 149–50, 149*n*, 165, 204, 228
death
  AG views about, 48, 49, 50, 75, 90, 115–16, 151, 221, 475
  and JK self-image, 53
  JK views about, 53, 63–64, 180, 275, 290, 406
  lack of imagination as, 221
  madness as, 50
  as subject of poetry, 180
  Williams views about, 151
  of world, 115–16
"The Death of George Martin" (JK), 51–52, 51*n*, 227
Delpire Publishing, 357
Delta Chemical Works, 316, 319
Dempsey, David, 189, 190
Denver, Colorado
  AG plans to visit, 329
  JK trip to, 31, 73–79, 80–109, 296
The Denver Doldrums (AG), 31*n*, 37, 108, 312
Desolation Angels (JK), 352, 375, 422, 471
Desolation Peak, Washington, 327–29, 391
Deutsch Publications, 398, 419
The Dharma Bums (JK), 325, 373–74, 376, 390–91, 393, 395, 406–7, 411, 416, 418, 420*n*, 422, 430
Diamond, David, 53, 53*n*, 302
Dickens, Charles, 4, 33, 54, 253, 257
Dickinson, Emily, 49, 97, 175, 306, 307, 437
Doctor Sax (JK)
  and AG as agent for JK, 192–93, 194–95, 196, 257, 278–79, 280
  AG letter to *NY Times* about, 428
  AG reading in Vancouver of, 474

AG views about, 177, 180–83, 184, 185, 186, 228, 418–19, 431
and Allen, 335, 416, 418, 423
and Carr comments about JK, 302
characters in, 183
contract for, 353–54
and Cowley, 352, 353
and criticisms of JK, 434
Giroux views about, 301
JK autographs copies of, 430
and JK finances, 412–13, 420
JK poems in, 182
and JK reputation, 419
JK views about, 408
and JK views about U.S., 400
JK writing new scenes for, 353
and Lord, 290
as myth, 177, 181–82, 183
origins of, 247
prophecy in, 474
publication of, 173, 184, 193, 194–95, 247, 253, 280, 289, 301, 352, 376, 394, 412–13, 415, 418, 419, 420, 432
reviews of, 430
revisions for, 352
Rexroth views about, 282–83, 379
sex in, 184
Van Doren views about, 226, 228
writing of, 94, 174, 178, 185, 399
Dodd Mead Publisher, 301, 302
Donlin, Bob, 345, 357, 391, 435
Don't Knowbody Laff Behind My America Hunchback (AG), 143
Dostoevsky, Fyodor, 20, 22, 33, 41, 50, 91–92, 96, 135, 161, 179, 245, 253, 255, 268, 305, 350, 350*n*, 352, 357, 358, 377
drama
  JK views about, 442
  and poetry, 442, 444
dreams
  JK views about, 274–75
  See also visions; *specific person*
drums: AG playing, 457
Dulles, John Foster, 383–84, 415
Duncan, Robert, 240, 253, 257, 262, 262*n*, 283, 325, 330, 334, 429, 434
du Peru, Peter, 242, 254, 349
Durgin, Russell, 37, 50, 153, 209, 313
Dutton Publishing, 227, 246, 282

Eager, Alan, 201–2, 201*n*, 227, 385
earthquakes, Mexican, 213–17, 353, 422
Eberhart, Richard, 327, 362
Ecuador, 156, 157
education: JK views about, 82
Einstein, Albert, 114, 288
Eisenhower, Dwight D., 232, 415
"Elegy for Mother" (AG), 368–69, 372
Eliot, T. S., 89, 96–97, 107, 108, 120, 228, 279, 327, 472
Elvins, Kells, 86, 86*n*, 137, 138, 156, 163, 169, 171, 193, 223, 231, 244, 317
Empty Mirror (AG), 184, 265, 311
Encounter magazine, 429
Encyclopedia Britannica: JK reading of, 458
Enrique (Mexican hipster), 163–64, 165, 166, 167–68
Escapade magazine, 420, 453
Esoteric Records: JK reading for, 209*n*

Esquire magazine, 343, 351, 357, 383, 387, 392, 408
Essentials of Spontaneous Prose (JK), 240, 262*n*
Europe
    AG in, 341–59, 360–62
    AG plans/desire to visit, 204, 209–10, 250, 281, 284, 295, 299, 305, 329, 334, 393
    AG poems about, 239
    AG reluctance to go to, 155
    JK in, 341, 399
    JK plans/desires to visit, 108, 146, 158, 280, 289, 330, 331, 334, 336, 350, 395, 421, 471
    See also Paris, France; *specific person*
European Blues (JK), 420
Evergreen Review, 335, 343, 352, 370, 387, 428, 438
evil
    AG views about, 117
    Burford views about, 247

Factualists, 63
"Fall of America" (AG), 397
fame: JK views about, 387
"The Fantasy of the Fair" (AG), 36
Fantasy Records, 362, 371, 393, 395, 434, 435
Farrar Straus, 176
fathers: JK views about, 33, 375
Faulkner, William, 135, 140, 142, 154, 207, 229, 312, 327, 421
Federal Bureau of Investigation (FBI), 409
Feldman-Citadel: Beat Generation anthology of, 375
Ferlinghetti, Lawrence
    AG comments about, 388
    and AG finances, 374, 444
    and AG recordings, 371
    and Allen (Donald), 385
    arrest of, 342*n*
    and banning of AG and JK works, 418, 420
    Big Sur cabin of, 453
    and *Big Table* magazine deal, 436, 438
    and *Book of Dreams,* 451
    and Burroughs works, 361, 372, 385, 388, 390
    Chile trip of, 449
    and Corso works, 333, 356, 365, 385, 390
    Evergreen recordings of, 343
    and *Howl,* 327, 342*n*, 355, 358, 362
    and JK *Blues,* 357, 365, 371, 372, 411
    JK buys books from, 458
    and JK finances, 430
    and JK invitation to Chile, 444
    JK letters to/from, 390
    and JK writing about Corso, 361
    and *Kaddish,* 454, 460
    and Lamantia works, 410
    and *Mexico City Blues,* 385
    and "Old Angel" poem, 430
    and rejections from *Chicago Review,* 420
    and Snyder works, 388, 410
    and Whalen, 388
Field, Joyce, 21, 22
Fields, W. C., 151, 234, 243, 254, 449
Fitzgerald, Jack, 124, 124*n*, 174, 352
Five Spot bar (New York City), 308, 386, 395*n*, 403, 412
Florida
    AG in, 201–2
    Burroughs in, 244, 247, 249
    JK in, 336–38, 351–53, 354–55, 360–74, 376–78, 383–92
    JK plans to visit, 413, 429, 430, 432

JK trip with Frank to, 394
JK writings about, 422
Foley, Martha, 193, 193*n*
Folio magazine, 262
Ford Foundation, 262
Forst, Miles, 386, 389
Fox, Bill, 225, 358
Fox, Joe, 253, 267
"Fragments of the Monument" (AG), 145
Frank, Robert, 357, 385–86, 389, 391, 394, 400, 427, 431, 456, 475
Frechtman, Bernard, 341, 342, 345, 348, 350, 361, 364
friendship, 116, 196
    See also relationship, AG-JK
Fromm (mental patient), 101–2

Gallimard Publishing, 377
Garcia Villa, Jose, 158, 223, 310
Garen, Leon, 357, 358, 365, 366, 385
Garver, Bill
    and AG, 204, 205, 316, 320, 331
    Burroughs views about, 318
    death of, 352, 353, 354
    and drugs, 138*n*, 319, 320, 368
    and JK, 212, 318, 322, 330, 335, 354
    in Mexico, 204, 205, 212, 314, 318, 320, 322, 330, 331, 335
    and White death, 138
Gellhorn, Martha, 154, 154*n*
Genet, Jean, 104, 133, 140–41, 147, 151, 155, 161, 162, 169, 171, 175, 286, 317, 350, 354, 361, 371, 374, 377
genius, 52, 63, 94, 184, 197, 352
gentleman's agreement, 47, 48
Geological Institute of Mexico, 216
Gide, André, 14–15, 21, 368
Giggling Ling, 80–81, 88, 89, 145, 422
Gilmore, Bill, 17, 18, 21, 26, 27, 36, 452
Ginsberg, Allen
    accomplishments of, 472
    appearance of, 252, 288, 469
    birthday of, 137, 296
    depression of, 297, 298, 299, 317, 390, 435
    double nature of, 25–26
    dreams of, 115–16, 207, 209, 297, 302, 326, 328, 384, 472
    drinking of, 229, 233, 250, 296, 360, 393, 397, 398
    and drugs, 221, 239, 249, 251, 255, 299, 316, 319, 346, 368, 374, 383, 397, 398, 399, 407, 440, 450, 454, 475
    education of, 4, 4*n*
    ego of, 25–26, 40, 58
    fears of, 127, 170
    finances of, 126, 133, 170, 172, 193, 203, 204, 205, 207, 217, 218, 281, 284, 293, 299, 304, 312, 316, 320, 327, 329, 329*n*, 334, 336, 337–38, 346, 355, 362, 372, 375, 377, 383, 384, 387–88, 389, 390, 391–92, 393, 401, 404, 429, 432–33, 435, 436, 444, 456
    Gold story about, 161
    grants and awards for, 346
    homosexuality of, 121, 124
    illness of, 19, 20, 114–15, 254, 261, 367, 443
    imitations of, 165
    insecurity of, 70–71
    introspection of, 46–47, 48–50, 75, 76–77, 88–90, 98, 138, 263–66
    in jail, 67–68

jobs for, 116, 193, 229, 233, 239, 284, 326
journal of, 68, 153, 261, 266, 329, 347
legal problems of, 67–70, 76–77, 85–86, 87
lovers/women of, 14, 124, 125–26, 134–35, 170*n*,
    239, 242–43, 244–45, 248, 251, 252, 255–57,
    297–98, 335, 351, 365, 456, 457, 473, 475
madness of, 41, 49, 50, 59, 69–70, 77, 80, 248
in mental hospital, 68, 92–93
metaphysical concerns of, 263–66, 268–71,
    272–73
and need for independence, 160
New York apartment of, 184, 456–57
Partisan article about, 428
"regular guy" mask of, 13–14
reputation of, 333–34
schooling of, 51
self-concept of, 184
self-image of, 10–11, 41–42, 60, 123–24
soul of, 93, 113, 143
true nature of, 41–42
visions and hallucinations of, 38–40, 41–42, 87,
    144, 153, 228, 231, 232, 265, 270, 288, 313
Ginsberg, Allen—poems/writings of
    AG comments about, 38, 61, 88–90, 151–52,
        230, 265, 331, 365, 383, 412
    and AG desire to write, 71
    and AG difficulties writing, 393
    and AG dreams, 83–84
    and AG in jail, 67–68
    and AG legal problems, 77
    and AG in mental hospital, 99, 105
    and AG method, 79, 132–33, 258*n*, 319
    and AG plans to leave San Francisco, 284
    AG working on, 311
    banning of, 418
    dedication of, 145, 146
    as greatest Israeli poet, 377, 378
    images in, 79, 83–84
    in Japan, 473
    JK encouragement of, 391
    JK influence on, 145, 146, 147–48, 315, 337
    JK sketches as similar to, 172
    JK views about, 80, 81, 135–36, 143, 144, 146–47,
        151, 152, 154, 179, 247, 287–89, 311–12, 377,
        378, 390, 449, 450
    at Maritime Training Station, 14
    method/style of, 288, 412
    modern, 152
    nonmetrical, 121
    publication/rejection of, 36, 84, 107, 120, 122,
        123, 132, 145, 150, 159, 172, 178, 283, 287–88,
        320, 331
    queer, 334
    references to JK in, 24
    revision of, 84–85
    sent to JK, 27, 27*n*, 229, 232
    titles for, 36, 143, 145
    topics of, 84, 91, 135, 257, 356
    typing of, 150
    untitled, 79, 90–91, 99, 105, 133, 170, 254, 257,
        261, 284, 297, 312–13, 320–21
    See also specific poem, person, or topic
Ginsberg, Louis (father), 38, 50, 68, 69, 70, 71, 72,
    94, 113, 114, 116, 132, 157, 160, 170, 184, 289,
    320, 334, 372, 379, 385, 389, 436, 456, 461, 474
Ginsberg, Naomi (mother), 69, 80, 105, 157, 170,
    241, 285, 299, 329, 329*n*, 368–69, 454–55, 474
Ginsberg, Sheila (sister), 115, 283
girl on skates: story about, 43–44

Giroux, Robert
    AG advice to JK about, 292
    and AG cave discovery in Mexico, 218
    and AG-JK letters, 109
    AG views about, 118
    and AG views about *T&C*, 117
    and AG works, 107, 120
    and Burroughs writings, 168
    Cassady stealing book from, 180
    in Denver, 98, 108
    and *Denver Doldrums*, 108
    and *Doctor Sax*, 301
    as editor for woman in Mexico, 206, 211
    and JK Buddha works, 289*n*, 290, 291, 300, 302,
        308
    JK comments about, 180
    and JK compared with Goldsmith and Johnson,
        113
    and JK "Go, Go, Go," 157
    JK letters to/from, 292
    and JK New York City visit, 302
    JK relationship with, 108, 288
    and JK on television, 395
    JK views about, 308
    Lord recommended as agent for JK by, 247
    and *On the Road*, 108
    and publication of JK works, 285
    and *T&C* advertising, 123
    and Van Doren (Charles) work, 226
    and Whalen works, 470
Glassman, Joyce
    and AG in Hamptons, 415
    AG visit with, 403
    Berkeley visit with JK of, 351
    as contact for JK, 366
    and JK-AG relationship, 379, 415
    and JK-Carr visit, 357
    JK letters to, 406
    and JK move to California, 341
    and JK move to New York City, 354
    and JK popularity, 358
    JK relationship with, 341, 379
    and JK withdrawal, 394, 400
    and knife attack on JK, 394
    and Laff situation, 369
    move to California of, 343, 352
    and Orlovsky, 376–77
    and Orlovsky-JK meeting, 376
    and "Visions of Elise," 391
    writings by, 343
"Go, Go, Go" (JK), 157
God
    AG views about, 40, 47, 48, 58, 88, 101
    Beat Generation leaders belief in, 431
    JK views about, 43, 52, 53, 55, 58, 59, 63, 113,
        331, 431
    Mailer views about, 406
Goddard, Dwight, 262, 266, 267, 278, 279, 408, 411
Gold, Herb, 161, 379, 385, 388, 389, 393, 394
Gould, Stanley
    and AG, 127, 456
    appearance of, 127
    and Cassady, 456
    and drugs, 301, 456
    girlfriends of, 254–55
    JK comments about, 274
    JK drinking with, 394
    JK relationship with, 227
    and JK visit to New York City, 295, 301, 357

Gould, Stanley (cont'd)
  JK visits with, 352, 366, 387, 431
  and JK in Washington Park, 224
  and knife attack on JK, 394
  and Pound drawing, 275–76
  as Subterranean, 142
  and Subterraneans, 231
  as Wyn employee, 231, 231n
goyeshe kopfe (goy's head), 12, 16
Granz, Norman, 395, 406
Great White Myth, 100, 101
The Green Automobile (AG), 243, 245, 265, 348,
  350, 351, 383, 387
Green, Julian, 21, 24
Greenwich Village
  JK views about, 452
  and JK visit to New York City, 301
  parties in, 33
  police/FBI in, 409, 452
Greyhound poem (AG), 327
Grieg, Mike, 343, 348, 350, 351, 352, 361, 420
Grove Publishing, 283, 335, 357, 358, 361, 362, 367,
  371, 372, 375, 390, 414, 416, 419, 429, 442
Guggenheim Foundation, 333, 337, 353, 355, 362

Hale, Barbara, 35, 40, 42, 45, 46, 52, 53, 54, 57, 60, 123
Hall, Leonard, 227, 310
Hamptons, New York: AG in, 403–4, 415
Hanover Records, 406, 432–33, 434, 443
Hansen, Diana. See Cassady, Diana Hansen
happiness: AG views about, 52
Harcourt Brace Publishers, 107, 123
Hardy, Thomas, 70, 140, 239
Harlem
  AG in, 37–40, 41–42, 50, 60, 144, 152–53, 247,
    265, 288
  AG poem about, 279
Harper's Bazaar magazine, 352, 359
Harrington, Alan, 54, 107, 107n, 126, 150, 158, 161,
  162, 172, 173, 288, 317
Harris, Julie, 331-32
Hart, Howard, 379, 385, 388, 400, 404, 406
Harvard Law School, 186
Harvard University, 306, 312, 427, 438
Harvard University Press, 301
hate
  AG's views about, 54, 59–60, 99
  JK's views about, 54
Haverty, Joan, 131, 148, 157, 160, 162, 163, 267–68,
  342, 343–46, 348–49, 469–70, 470n
Hearst publications, 20, 418, 421, 432
Hemingway, Ernest, 126, 154n, 155, 442
Henderson, LuAnne, 108, 108n, 146n, 352
Herrick, Robert, 81, 90
Hesse, Herman, 140, 283
Hindus, Milton, 121, 121n
Hinkle, Al, 56, 134, 142, 235, 243, 251, 255, 268,
  272, 281, 303, 352, 366, 458
Hinkle, Helen, 243, 251
And the Hippos Were Boiled in Their Tanks (JK and
  Burroughs), 144
history: JK's views about, 82
Hodos Chameliontos, 88–89, 96, 177, 182
Hoffenberg, Mason, 341, 365, 370, 398, 430
Hoffman, John, 139–40, 139n, 165, 288
Holiday, Billie, 150, 197
Holiday magazine, 391, 427, 450, 470, 471
Hollander, John, 88, 88n, 145, 151, 152, 304, 312,
  411

Hollywood
  AG trip to, 297
  AG views about, 294
  and JK dreams about Beat Generation, 295
  and JK ideas for movies, 386, 391
  and JK plans to visit California, 294
  and JK plans to visit Paris, 389
  JK trip to, 436
  JK views about, 295
  movie novel for, 295
  as refusing to pay JK, 402
  See also specific work
Holmes, John Clellon
  AG inquiries about, 222, 365
  and AG as literary agent, 173, 184
  AG as reading works by, 140
  and AG in San Jose, 229
  and AG-JK friendship, 59
  AG lack of contact with, 133
  AG letters to/from, 325, 375, 389
  and AG recording, 289
  AG regards to, 229
  and AG soul, 93
  AG talks with, 70
  AG views about, 141, 155, 161
  Beat Generation article by, 392
  as Beat Generation co-expert, 190
  and Beat Generation writings, 370
  on Cape Cod, 93, 105
  and Cassady marriage, 126
  Dickens compared with, 253
  and Doctor Sax, 184, 186
  drinking of, 225–26, 452
  in England, 392
  finances of, 226
  Go by, 141, 154, 155, 157, 178, 186, 189, 190, 191,
    226
  Harrington as friend of, 107n
  as jealous of JK, 178–79
  JK comments about, 225–26, 288, 408–9
  and JK copyright for Beat Generation, 405
  JK as disciple of, 452
  JK inquiries about, 176, 387
  and JK letter to Temko, 53
  JK letters to/from, 321, 337, 402, 472
  JK views about, 54, 179, 186, 452
  JK visits with, 222, 431
  Marian relationship with, 141, 155, 226
  and new literary movement, 158
  and New Year's Eve party, 57
  Newman house near, 227
  and On the Road, 159, 176
  publication of works of, 150, 172, 178
  and publicity for Burroughs Junkey, 189, 190, 191
  and Schapiro arrangements, 119
  and Solomon work, 123
  title for book by, 154
  writings about JK and AG of, 472
Holmes, Marian, 54, 57, 141, 155, 179, 226
Holmes, Shirley, 225, 226
homosexuality
  AG views about, 251
  Cru views about, 226
  JK views about, 196–97, 236, 246, 247
  as power in American Literature, 196–97
  See also specific person
honesty, 55, 60
Horace Mann School, 139n, 179, 292, 450
Horizon magazine, 408, 410–11

Horney, Karen, 212, 212*n*
Household, Geoffrey, 67
Howard, Richard, 365–66, 367, 404
Howl and Other Poems (AG)
  admiration for, 331
  and AG finances, 355, 362
  and AG invitation to Chile, 444
  AG reading of, 398
  AG sends other authors copies of, 327
  AG views about, 393, 475
  banning of, 342, 342*n*
  City Lights publication of, 320, 328
  Corso "Power" similar to, 333
  Corso views about, 328
  dedication of, 350, 356
  and Ferlinghetti, 327, 342*n*, 358
  Jarrell views about, 334
  JK copy of, 318, 319, 320
  JK influence on, 319
  JK reading of, 385
  JK suggests title for, 319
  and JK on television, 364
  JK views about, 318, 352
  Joan Dream poem in, 328
  Mademoiselle quotes from, 387
  peyote vision as inspiration for, 249, 249*n*
  reprints of, 375
  reviews of, 355
  revisions to, 395
  and Solomon, 103*n*
  trial concerning, 303*n*, 342, 342*n*, 349–50, 362, 366, 371
  and Whalen, 358
  and Williams, 325
Hudson, Jim, 230, 231, 300, 318, 403
Hudson Reviews, 104, 172
Huncke, Herbert
  AG comments about, 76, 457
  AG copies of work by, 418
  and AG introspection, 77
  and AG legal problems, 68–69, 71, 77, 87
  and AG as literary agent, 173
  AG meeting with, 184
  and AG in mental hospital, 104
  AG poem about, 84
  as AG roommate in Harlem, 50
  AG views about, 313
  and Avon anthology, 435, 440
  and Burroughs, 69
  code names for, 71
  dehumanization of, 68
  finances of, 439
  illness of, 441
  indictment and jailing of, 67, 87
  and JK article explaining Beat Generation, 353
  JK comments about, 80, 212, 288
  JK daydreams about, 469
  JK inquiries about, 32, 472
  JK relationship with, 375
  JK visits with, 451
  maudlin phrases of, 119
  in Mexico, 166, 167
  and new literary movement, 150, 158
  in New York City, 454
  nihilism of, 276
  publication of works by, 150, 172, 352
  relationship with other people of, 68–69
  revival of work of, 150
  saying of, 76

and shrouded stranger phrase, 158
and stolen property case, 67, 68–69, 87
Hunter College: JK appearance at, 412, 415
Huston, John, 398

Ignu, 86
imagination: AG comments about, 293
immortality: JK views about, 63
India
  AG thoughts of visiting, 384, 439, 441
  AG trip to, 456, 469, 473
  Burroughs plans to visit, 396, 400
  JK views about trip to, 453
intellectuals
  and Cowley changes to *On the Road,* 352
  and image of Beat Generation, 438
  JK views about, 349, 395
"Introduction to the Prose of Jack Kerouac" (AG), 195
Isis magazine, 417

Jackson, Natalie, 254–55, 256–57, 281, 285, 286, 303, 325
Jackson, Phyllis, 193, 194
James, Henry, 175, 377
Japan: AG in, 469–73
Jargon Press, 325*n*
Jarrell, Randall, 333–34, 336–37, 338
jazz: JK writings about, 235, 238, 286, 452
Jennison, Keith, 302*n*, 305
Jews: JK views about, 287–89
Joan Dream poem (AG), 328
"Joan Rawshanks" (JK), 258, 283, 298, 301
Johnson, Samuel, 41, 113, 114
Jones, LeRoi, 394, 420, 436, 451, 456, 459
Joyce, James, 5, 153, 173, 178, 181, 272, 276, 283, 459
Judgment Day, 82, 156, 159

Kaddish and Other Poems (AG), 385, 429, 434, 438, 441, 444, 454, 456, 460, 465, 475
Kafka, Franz, 39, 100, 140, 277
Kallman, Chester, 155, 223, 223*n*, 226
Kammerer, David, 3, 12, 12*n*, 44*n*, 306
Karney, Varda, 117, 119, 226
Kazin, Alfred, 57, 247, 302
Keck, Bill, 142, 209, 212, 233, 243, 347
Kennedy, John F., 460, 461
Kenyon magazine, 36–37, 104, 395
Kerouac, Edie Parker (wife), 3, 3*n*, 4, 22, 94, 97, 100, 108, 109, 113, 179, 253
Kerouac, Gabrielle (mother)
  advice to JK about work from, 62–63
  AG gets manuscript from, 162, 193, 194
  AG inquiries about, 90, 100, 334
  and AG-JK relationship, 394, 398, 399, 400, 402, 433, 474
  as babysitter, 415
  in Berkeley, 422
  and Brooks in North Carolina, 285
  Burroughs letter to, 402
  California move of, 341, 342, 345, 351
  and criticisms of JK, 379
  in Denver, 73, 90
  dreams about JK writings of, 295
  financial affairs of, 344
  and Hube the Cube, 349
  invites AG to Northport, 428
  JK concerns about, 330

Kerouac, Gabrielle (mother) (cont'd)
  and JK finances, 158, 160, 247, 268, 391, 452
  JK living alone with, 421
  and JK loan to Cassady, 56–57
  JK love for, 54
  JK "official" residence with, 190
  and JK paternity suit, 267
  and JK return to North Carolina, 325
  and JK thoughts of Mexico, 219
  and JK travel plans, 273, 280
  and JK visits to New York City, 295, 314
  JK writings about, 422, 470
  and Kingsland visit, 409
  Long Island move of, 337–38
  and meeting JK women, 35
  moves back to New York City, 94
  Northport home for, 384, 394, 421
  Orlando move of, 351–52
  and police search for JK, 157
Kerouac, Jack
  accomplishments of, 472
  birthday of, 440
  in Bronx County Jail, 3–4
  childhood and youth of, 24
  child support payments of, 157, 160, 267–68,
    342, 343–46, 349
  depression of, 230
  diary/journals of, 18–19
  divorce of, 344–46, 348–49
  dreams of, 290–91, 312, 357–58
  drinking by, 223, 224, 225–26, 230, 236, 270, 272,
    291, 301, 309, 310, 314, 322, 337, 343, 351, 358,
    359, 372, 373–74, 378, 385, 387, 394, 395, 404,
    406, 409, 410, 423, 427, 428, 453, 458, 460, 461,
    470, 472
  and drugs, 164, 165, 166–67, 169, 197, 212, 223,
    270, 296, 301, 307, 310, 316, 318, 321, 330, 359,
    406, 415, 420, 439, 442, 450
  fame of, 399, 440, 472
  favorite song of, 405
  favorite writers of, 307
  finances of, 94, 108, 133, 133n, 142, 146, 158,
    160, 172, 178, 184, 236, 289, 290, 292, 294, 295,
    296, 298, 300, 301, 302, 304, 305, 307, 321, 334,
    335, 336, 337–38, 341, 343–44, 349, 351–52,
    353, 354, 356, 360, 363, 366–67, 373, 377,
    387–88, 389, 391–92, 404, 405–6, 407, 412–13,
    400, 401, 402, 419, 420, 421, 427, 429, 430, 431,
    436, 443, 444, 449, 450–51, 452, 453, 469
  happiness of, 280–81, 391
  Haverty relationship with, 267–68, 342, 343–46,
    348–49, 469–70
  illness/injuries of, 267, 292, 296, 314, 315, 354,
    404, 406, 432
  imitations of, 165
  jobs for, 11–12, 11n, 16, 80, 146, 178, 189, 305,
    326, 329, 458
  knife attack on, 394, 401, 428
  lifestyle change of, 453, 458
  as mad, 53, 55
  marriage of, 4, 131
  marriage thoughts of, 53
  Mass for spiritual welfare of, 366
  in mental hospital, 75, 76, 107–8, 107n
  nicknames for, 119n
  "official" residence of, 190
  "personal-ness" problem of, 34
  and police, 3–4, 19
  popularity of, 357–59

pseudonyms for, 421–22
psychic balance of, 18, 19–20, 23–24
reputation of, 333–34
self-image of, 124, 377
self-understanding of, 49–50
suicide thoughts of, 291
transgressions and regrets of, 23–24
visions of, 42, 58, 230
wedding of, 158
withdrawal of, 399–401, 427, 433, 439–40, 450,
  469
women/lovers of, 22, 23, 35, 45–46, 53, 108, 109,
  143n, 147, 148, 158, 169, 179, 223, 225, 226,
  310, 330, 342, 349, 352, 377, 394, 414, 415, 421,
  452, 458, 469
Kerouac, Jack—poems/writings of
  AG as agent for, 189, 192–93, 194–96, 229,
    257–58, 262, 277–78, 283
  AG influence on, 147–48, 337
  AG inquiries about old, 182
  AG reading of, 407
  and AG requests for poem/excerpts from JK,
    153, 417
  AG views about, 71–72, 85, 88, 100, 153, 155,
    230, 245, 257, 263, 265, 411, 420, 420n, 422
  anthology of, 414, 414n, 415, 417, 420
  banning of, 418
  contracts for, 195, 353–54, 419
  and crazy poems, 80–81
  criticisms of, 379, 385, 392, 408, 452
  images in, 80–81, 83–84
  and JK desire to be greatest writer in world, 280
  and JK desire to write, 449
  and JK in Florida, 366
  and JK as greatest American poet, 377, 378
  JK interviews about, 413–14, 415
  and JK lack of interest in writing, 335
  JK problems with, 413
  and JK reputation, 418–19
  and JK request for AG to send copies of all his
    works, 289, 289n
  and JK style, 411
  JK views about, 81, 247, 337, 373, 414
  method in, 181, 258n, 393
  publication/rejection of, 51–52, 172, 229, 277–
    78, 331
  reviews of, 411, 417
  Shakespeare as model for, 442
  sketches in, 172, 174–76, 245, 337
  stolen, 335
  symbolism in, 71–72
  untitled, 80–81, 106–7, 223–24, 257–58, 314–15,
    459
  See also specific poem, person, or topic
Kerouac, Janet Michele "Jan" (daughter), 131, 267
Kerouac, Leo (father), 375, 474
Kilgallen, Dorothy, 394
Kingsland, John, 9, 14, 21–22, 151, 155, 209, 222,
  223, 228, 252, 287, 293–96, 301, 409
Knopf Publishers. See Alfred A. Knopf Publishers
knowing: AG views about, 48
KPFA radio station, 262, 316, 317, 386
Kulchur magazine, 435n, 436, 437, 438

Lamantia, Philip
  AG comments about, 140, 240, 388, 404
  and AG interest in Buddhism, 407
  AG letters to/from, 416
  and AG peyote request, 133

and AG in San Francisco, 227
and Allen, 416, 418
and *Big Table* magazine deal, 436
and Buddhism, 313
and Burroughs writings, 345
Cassady meeting with, 140
and Corso poetry reading, 333
drinking of, 385
Hart fight with, 406
and JK article explaining Beat Generation, 353
and JK-Cassady argument, 166
JK comments about, 226, 288, 400
and JK copy of Corso poem, 391
JK letters to, 393, 431
and JK Mexico plans, 452
JK orgy with, 385
JK publicizing poetry of, 400
JK relationship with, 375
JK visit with, 165, 313
and Keck, 142
and knife attack on JK, 394
Loewinsohn as similar to, 345
Mexican hipsters views of, 165
in Mexico, 331, 395, 431
in New York City, 379, 409
in Oregon, 411
poetry of, 140
publication of works by, 410, 416, 418
and religion, 313
in San Francisco, 165
Six Gallery reading of, 132*n*, 325
and Snyder, 411
visions of, 313
and Williams, 348
and Williams-AG correspondence, 132
Landesman, Jay, 122–23, 122*n*, 127, 386, 395, 395*n*,
     431
"Laughgass" (AG), 445, 455
Laughlin, James, 138, 138*n*, 233, 410, 411, 414,
     418
Laughlin, Jay, 108, 143, 152, 277, 278, 283, 373, 431,
     433, 434, 451
LaVigne, Robert, 252, 254, 255–57, 261, 315, 318,
     326, 348, 351, 352, 371, 393, 396, 397, 404
Lawrence, Seymour, 51, 51*n*, 227, 236, 267
Leadbelly, 461
Lee, Alene, 142, 222, 225, 231, 290, 301, 304, 307,
     353, 383, 387, 414
Lee, William. *See* Burroughs, William
Lenrow, Elbert, 70, 71, 86, 86*n*, 88, 120, 386
Lerner, Max, 406, 407, 412
Leslie, Alfred, 386, 389, 427, 438, 444
Leslie, Hubert "Hube the Cube," 333, 349
Levertov, Denise, 354, 375
Library of Congress, 333, 333*n*
life
     Burroughs views about, 237
     as dream, 225
     JK views about, 63–64, 82, 225, 336
Life magazine, 122, 330, 330*n*, 335, 359, 362, 386,
     395
limerick, of AG, 139
"Lines Writ in Rockefeller Center" (AG), 80
"The Lion for Real" (JK), 392, 428
Listener magazine, 393
literature
     AG comments about, 221
     homosexuals as powerful in American, 196–97
     JK views about, 185, 197, 317–18, 420, 451

Little Brown & Co., 227, 236
Livornese, Tom, 42, 43, 44, 45, 46, 272
Loewinsohn, Ronny, 345, 350
London, England
     AG visit to, 384, 388–89, 393
     JK in, 341, 342, 343
     JK views about, 351
Lonesome Traveler (JK), 451, 459–60
"Long Live the Spiderweb" (AG), 132, 135, 144,
     151–52, 158
"Long Poem" (AG), 145
Look magazine, 362, 413
Lord, Sterling
     AG advice to JK about, 292, 293
     as AG agent, 433
     and AG copy of *Subterraneans*, 393
     AG dinner with, 383
     and AG finances, 429
     AG letters/requests to, 281, 358, 361, 371
     AG returns material to, 283
     AG views about, 292, 419
     and AG works, 362
     Allen lunch with, 419
     and Avon anthology, 432, 435, 441
     and *Beat Generation*, 305
     and *Big Table* publication of JK poems, 436
     and *Blues*, 365
     and *Buddha Tells Us*, 308
     and Burroughs works, 361, 370
     and Cassady works, 416
     and Corso works, 383, 409, 433
     and *Doctor Sax*, 290, 412–13, 418, 420
     and French publishing of JK works, 247
     Giroux recommends, 247
     and JK Buddha works, 290, 291
     JK complaints about, 290, 291
     and JK contracts, 419
     and JK copyright for Beat Generation, 405
     and JK finances, 352, 384, 429
     and JK-Haverty relationship, 342
     JK meetings with, 420
     and JK New York City visits, 295
     and JK reputation, 418–19
     and JK request to AG to inform Lord about his
          activities, 280
     JK views about, 308
     and JK withdrawal, 394, 440
     and Lamantia works, 416
     and *On the Road* movie, 390
     and Paetel, 442
     in Paris, 383
     and powers of attorney for AG, 247
     sends JK works to Williams, 348
     and *Subterraneans* publication, 335, 343
     and Talbot meeting, 451
     Wieners letters to, 351
Los Angeles, California
     AG trip to, 334, 336
     JK desire to go to, 12
love
     AG comments about, 221, 293, 475
     AG desire to write about, 36
     and AG-JK friendship, 197, 219
     AG views about, 10, 26–27, 47, 48, 49, 60, 88, 98,
          99, 101, 161, 221, 255, 265, 266
     Burroughs views about, 237
     JK comments about, 358
     JK stories about, 12
     JK views about, 43, 44, 54, 63, 268–69, 270

Lowell, Massachusetts, 247, 307, 357, 395, 401
Lowell, Robert, 107, 140, 151
Lowry, Robert, 414, 414*n*
LSD, 430, 430*n*, 435
"Lucien Midnight" (JK), 373, 406, 413
"Lucien's Face" (AG), 36
Lustig, Joe, 357, 365–66
Lyons, Martin Spencer, 32

McCarthy hearings, 305
MacClaine, Chris, 227, 310, 317, 389, 431
McClure, Michael, 325, 334, 352, 371, 388, 429,
    431, 436, 441, 459, 470
"MacDougal Street Blues in Three Cantos" (JK), 300
McGraw-Hill Publishing, 451, 460
MacGregor, Robert, 343, 343*n*
MacLeish, Archibald, 328, 386
McManus, Patricia, 422, 422*n*
Macmillan Publishing, 415
Mademoiselle magazine, 335, 335*n*, 387
madness: AG views about, 39
Maggie Cassidy (JK), 192–93, 194–95, 196, 278
Mailer, Norman, 57*n*, 301, 358, 406, 415, 431, 469,
    472
Mann, Thomas, 5, 10, 22, 25, 76, 82
Marconi Hotel (San Francisco, California), 238,
    239, 250
Maritime Service Training Station (Sheepshead
    Bay, Brooklyn): AG at, 9–14, 16–17
Marker, Lewis, 138, 144, 156, 169, 201
marriage: JK views about, 63
"Marriage" (JK), 415
Marshall, Edward, 403, 405
Martinelli, Sheri, 275, 279
May, Joe, 60, 158
MCA, 184, 185, 191, 192, 194, 195, 196
Measure magazine, 348, 429
meat poems, of AG, 360
Melody, "Little Jack," 42*n*, 67, 69, 87, 357
Melville, Herman, 95, 124, 134, 141, 174, 185, 213,
    247, 272, 293, 347, 428, 433, 437, 472
Memory Babe (JK), 401, 423
men: JK views about, 53, 307
mental hospital
    AG in, 92–106, 113, 124
    AG mother in, 241, 285
    AG released from, 120
    AG tales about, 101–5, 107
    AG to go to, 68, 76–77, 85
    Burroughs in, 100
    doctors in, 103
    JK in, 75, 76, 107–8, 107*n*
    Orlovsky (Laff) threatened with, 363–64, 369–70
    Pound in, 107
    Solomon in, 103, 104, 285, 299
Merchant Marine: and AG, 9–11, 326
Merims, Bob, 201, 201*n*, 209, 304, 329, 336, 347,
    364, 403, 444
Merton, Thomas, 107, 123
"Metaphysics" (AG), 131, 132, 135
Mew, Charles, 310, 366
Mexican author. *See* Shields, Karena
"Mexican Girl" (JK), 321
Mexico
    AG in, 170, 201–18, 220, 265, 279, 302, 329, 334,
    471
    AG plans to visit, 176, 303, 329, 331, 332, 333, 441
    AG reluctance to go to, 169–70, 173
    and drugs, 316, 319

    earthquakes in, 213–17, 353, 422
    JK in, 124, 125–27, 162–72, 173–78, 314–22,
    329, 330–36, 471
    and JK offer to Cowley, 302
    JK plans to visit, 146, 147, 274, 295, 300, 303,
    305, 307, 352, 353, 432, 436, 440, 450, 452
    JK views about, 330
    JK writings about, 422
    See also specific person
Mexico City Blues (JK), 318, 320, 335, 385, 408, 416,
    436, 438, 449
MGM, 405, 440
Micheline-Silver, Jack, 402, 450, 452
Michigan, JK in, 4, 9
Michigan State prison, 359
"Midnight" (JK), 421–22, 438
Mill Valley, California: JK in, 326–27
Miller, Henry, 82, 140, 332, 343, 354, 362, 422
Mills, Charley, 450, 452
Millstein, Gilbert, 356*n*, 373–74, 375
Milton, John, 371, 388
mind
    AG views about, 135, 293
    JK views about, 97–98, 135, 253, 269, 290, 308,
    471
Mistral Bookshop, 371, 371*n*
Mitchell, John, 465
"Moloch" (AG), 326
Monacchio, Tony, 35, 180, 307, 403
money
    AG comments about, 221, 444
    JK views about, 82, 442, 443
    See also specific person
Monk, Thelonious, 197, 403, 412, 457
"The Monster of Dakar" (AG), 160
Montgomery, John, 411, 418, 449, 450
Montini, JK painting of, 470
moon chain poem, AG, 455
Moore, Marianne, 151, 155
Morales, Adele, 57, 57*n*
morality, 20–21, 33
Moreland, Dusty
    AG dreams about, 139, 209
    AG inquiries about, 222
    and AG New York City visit, 252
    and AG poems, 135, 151, 152
    AG relationship with, 154–55, 184, 231, 242, 252
    AG visit with, 403
    apartment of, 134, 138, 139
    and Burroughs-AG relationship, 242
    Corso watching, 134
    and Davalos, 176
    JK meeting with, 231
    and JK New York City visit, 301, 306
    JK relationship with, 148, 174
    and Orlovsky New York City visit, 306
    Williams (Sheila) as similar to, 244
movie novels, 295
movies
    and image of Beat Generation, 438
    See also Hollywood; *specific movie or work*
Muller, Dody, 414, 415, 420, 421, 422
Mulligan, Jerry, 197, 212
Museum of Modern Art (New York City), 86, 86*n*,
    203
Museum of Natural History (New York City), 204
music
    AG interest in, 317
    genius in, 197

See also jazz; *specific person*
myth
   Doctor Sax as, 177, 181–82, 183
   JK views about, 63
   See also Great White Myth
Myth of the Rainy Night: AG views about, 89

Nation, 343, 385
National Institute of Arts and Sciences, 346
National Maritime Union, 135, 142
Navaretta, Emmanuel A., 417
"Neal and the Three Stooges" (JK), 350, 357, 361, 420
Needle magazine, 327, 361
Negros
   and AG as "regular guy," 14
   Corso incident with, 431
Nervous Set (musical), 431
Neurotica magazine, 122, 122*n*
New American Reader, 301
New Directions Books, 132, 138*n*, 143, 145, 177, 184, 229, 233, 248, 277, 343*n*, 361, 375, 390, 410, 414, 418
New Editions, 343, 348, 350, 351, 352, 357, 420
new literary movement, 150, 158
New School, 40, 212, 387
New Story, 160, 172, 175, 176
new vision, 4, 4*n*, 5, 24–25
New World Writing
   AG wants copy of, 284–85
   and AG works, 362
   and Burroughs writings, 277, 361
   Cowley-JK letters about, 196
   and JK copyright for Beat Generation, 405
   and publication of JK works, 193, 194–95, 227, 235–36, 277, 282, 285, 286, 292, 301, 306
   Rexroth article in, 351
   Rexroth review of, 286
New York City
   AG apartment in, 184, 456–57
   AG car trip to, 435, 437
   AG in, 3–5, 11–27, 33–42, 46–50, 92–109, 117–20, 137–45, 149–55, 159–62, 176–78, 180–85, 189–97, 262–66, 436–38, 403–23, 427–28, 435–45, 449, 454–61
   AG plans to return to, 252, 334, 397, 399, 429
   AG views about, 393
   AG visit to, 252, 255, 336–38
   Carr views about, 392
   drugs in, 457
   JK in, 3–5, 9–27, 31–52, 58–64, 67–73, 113–24, 190, 194–97, 218–58, 261–79, 296–303, 341–44, 355–59, 374–76, 379–80, 394–96, 427
   JK plans to move back to, 94, 108
   JK plans to visit, 173, 295–96, 300, 314, 354, 373
   JK views about, 33, 395, 431-32, 461
   JK visits to, 300–301, 302–3, 341–44, 391, 452, 459, 471
New York Daily News, 20, 400, 439, 460
New Yorker magazine, 123, 395
New York *Herald Tribune,* 320, 374, 413, 415
New York Post, 385, 428, 430, 439
New York Public Library, 243
New York State Psychiatric Institute: AG at, 92–106, 113, 120, 124
New York Times, 190, 331, 356*n*, 428
Newman, Jerry, 138, 172, 209, 209*n*, 226–27, 244, 361, 398, 449
Newsweek magazine, 317

Nicholson, John, 429, 429*n*
Nihilism, 434
Nixon, Richard, 460, 461
Noonday Press, 301
North Carolina
   Brooks in, 285
   Cassady car trip to, 55–57
   JK in, 52–57, 178, 280–96, 300, 304–13, 325–26
   JK plans to go to, 40–41
Northport, New York
   AG visit to, 415
   JK house in, 394, 433, 470
   JK in, 396–402, 403–23, 427–45, 449–61, 465, 469–75
nothingness: JK views about, 269
"Now Mind Is Clear" (AG), 145

"October Railroad Earth" (JK), 343, 429
O'Hara, Frank, 403, 453
"Old Angel Midnight" (JK), 421–22, 430, 436, 450
"Old Bull Balloon" (JK), 420
Olson, Charles, 325, 348, 365
Olympia Press, 370, 372, 375, 388
On the Road (JK)
   advance for, 133*n*
   and AG as agent for JK, 195, 196, 283
   AG copy of, 352, 354, 355, 361, 372, 393, 396
   AG influence on, 146
   AG inquiry about, 394
   AG review of, 420
   AG sends copy to JK, 171
   AG views about, 134, 159–60, 176–78, 179, 180–81, 183
   Beat Generation as title for, 227, 236
   as best seller, 356, 356*n*, 371
   and Cassady, 177
   characters in, 46*n*, 137, 139*n*, 156, 174, 396
   classic sentence in, 285
   closing lines of, 136
   contract for, 133, 133*n*, 148, 176
   Cowley revisions of, 352
   Cowley's support for, 194, 194*n*, 235–36, 289, 300, 302, 302*n*, 326
   Dharma Bums similar to, 376
   Esquire piece about, 343
   European rights for, 357, 366, 377
   as Factualist art, 63
   and Giroux-JK relationship, 108
   and JK-AG "stealing from each other," 146
   JK autographs copies of, 430
   JK comments about, 136–37, 156, 172, 173, 174–76, 178, 179, 185
   and JK finances, 384, 436
   JK views about, 174–75, 373
   and JK visit to New York City, 300
   JK wants news about, 169
   and "Kerouac Craze," 395
   McClure reaction to, 371
   movie version of, 349, 357, 362, 373, 374, 384, 386, 389, 390, 392, 405, 423, 431, 456, 457, 469, 471
   paperback edition of, 144
   picture for cover of, 143–44
   poems in, 95
   publication of, 133, 142, 143–44, 148, 149, 157, 159–60, 171, 173, 176–77, 178, 194, 194*n*, 195, 227, 235–36, 278, 289, 302*n*, 342, 349, 422
   reprints of, 352
   reviews of, 355, 356*n*, 359, 398

On the Road (JK) (*cont'd*)
  revisions of, 398
  Rexroth views about, 353
  "The Rose of the Rainy Night" section in, 94–96
  sales of, 395
  scroll version of, 131, 420
  title for, 176, 227, 236
  Village Vanguard reading of, 373
  Whalen views about, 352–53
  writing and typing of, 96, 134, 142, 146, 148, 174,
    175–76
"On the Road with Memere" (JK), 470
Orlando Blues (JK), 435
Orlovsky, Lafcadio "Laff"
  AG comments about, 457
  AG inquiries about, 393
  AG letters to/from, 388
  AG relationship with, 317
  AG visit with, 376, 443, 444
  and drugs, 326
  Esquire picture of, 351
  as homosexual, 421
  JK comments about, 318, 392, 442
  and JK idea for movie, 386
  JK inquiries about, 387, 472
  JK investigation of situation with, 363–64,
    369–70
  JK letters to/from, 377
  and JK New York City visit, 373
  JK relationship with, 379, 395
  JK visits with, 358, 408
  JK writings about, 330, 422, 471
  jobs for, 455
  at Marceau show, 456
  as mentally handicapped, 303*n*
  in Mexico, 329, 336, 471
  in New York City, 352
  and painting Carr house, 456
  painting Jones apartment, 459
  paintings by, 402, 408, 421
  and Peter, 303*n*, 326, 363–64, 369, 421, 443, 444,
    455, 472
  publication of works of, 352
  in San Francisco, 315
  and sex, 326
  and Sorrells, 451
  threatened with mental hospital, 363–64,
    369–70
  women/lovers of, 410
Orlovsky, Marie (sister), 408
Orlovsky, Oleg (father), 363, 369, 388
Orlovsky, Peter
  as actor in JK play, 366
  AG comments about, 454, 457
  AG first meets, 254
  AG inquiries about, 393
  AG letters to/from, 393, 394
  AG moves in with, 252, 254
  and AG plans to leave San Francisco, 284
  AG relationship with, 252, 255–57, 261, 285,
    297–98, 317, 319, 327, 472
  AG writings about, 261, 318
  and AG X concept, 263, 270
  appearance of, 356
  Asian travels of, 475
  and Avon anthology, 435
  and Bowles (Jane), 347
  and Buddhism, 278
  and Cassady, 349

and characters in JK writings, 318
and Corso poetry reading, 333
and de Angulo (Gui), 332
depression of, 281, 442, 456
and *The Dharma Bums,* 411
and drugs, 255
and European trip, 334, 341, 342, 346, 347–53,
  354, 355, 356, 360, 363–64, 369, 376–78, 388
finances of, 345, 345*n*, 402, 403
in Hamptons, 403–4, 415
and Harris play, 331-32
and Jarrell San Francisco visit, 333
and JK-AG letters, 278
JK challenges to, 417
JK comments about, 268, 301, 344, 392, 442, 461
and JK divorce, 345
JK feelings about, 330, 358, 391, 440
and JK idea for movie, 386
JK inquiries about, 342, 387, 390, 421, 436, 472
and JK invitation to visit Chile, 442, 443–44
JK letters to/from, 348–51, 356, 360, 363, 372,
  374, 376–78, 392, 427–28, 450
and JK New York City visit, 306
JK Northport house near family of, 393
and JK Paris visit, 377
JK relationship with, 375, 379, 395, 422
and JK in San Francisco, 298, 301, 335
and JK stolen poems, 335
JK views about writings of, 376
JK visits with, 415, 451
and JK withdrawal, 394, 399, 400
JK writings about, 330, 422, 453, 471
and Laff, 303*n*, 326, 363–64, 369, 421, 443, 444,
  455, 472
LaVigue picture of, 348, 351, 352
LaVigue relationship with, 252, 254, 255–57, 261
and Mexico trip, 329, 331, 332, 334, 335, 336, 471
Monk meeting with, 457
in New York City, 303, 303*n*, 304, 306, 313, 376,
  388, 397, 403, 408, 410
and painting Carr house, 456
painting Jones apartment, 459
paintings by, 375
passport for, 444
pornographic picture of, 347
publication of works by, 438
reactions to JK writings by, 283
and religion, 431
and Russian Soul, 356
and sales of *Subterraneans,* 394
in San Francisco, 315, 319
visions of, 261
and Wieners, 351
Williams comments about, 433, 434
women/lovers of, 330, 335, 376–77, 409, 410, 456
writings of, 352, 376, 388, 434–35, 438, 441, 455
other-ness, 39
"Over Kansas" (AG), 383

Paetel, Karl, 442, 442*n*, 444
paintings/drawings
  by AG, 106
  by Corso, 375, 383
  by JK, 335–37, 350, 373, 375–76, 402, 428, 470
  of JK, 421
  by Leslie, 349
  by Orlovsky (Laff), 402, 408, 421
  by Orlovsky (Peter), 375
  pornographic, 347

Paris, France
AG in, 356, 360, 361, 363–80, 383–401, 465
AG plans/desire to visit, 154, 160, 210, 334, 355
AG poem about, 155
AG reluctance to go to, 155
friends of AG and JK in, 147, 147n, 172
JK in, 341–42, 421
JK invitation to AG to go to, 157
JK plans/desire to visit, 4, 94, 108, 147, 330, 350, 351, 359, 374, 377, 378, 389, 390, 391, 413
JK views about, 341–43, 344, 351, 378
JK writings about, 413, 419, 420
women in, 351
Paris Review, 305, 321, 326
Parker, Charley "Bird," 197, 275, 303, 328
Parker, Edie. *See* Kerouac, Edie Parker
Parker, Helen, 125–27, 222, 224, 225, 229, 310, 414
Parkinson, Thomas, 331, 331n, 333, 375, 388–89, 393
Partisan Review, 104, 120, 361, 372, 375, 395, 428
Passing Through (JK), 471
Paterson, New Jersey
AG description of, 85
AG dreams about, 326
AG in, 9–11, 42–46, 51–64, 68–92, 113, 114–17, 120–27, 131–37, 143–48, 151, 153, 162–76, 178–80, 185–86, 401–2, 407–8, 450–53
AG-JK meeting in, 400
AG plans to go to, 38, 189
AG views about, 160
AG visits to, 252, 418, 439, 443, 444
politics in, 116
Williams book about, 85, 131, 135, 177, 293, 410
Payne, Thomas, 432, 436, 437, 440, 451, 452, 453
Persky, Stan, 402, 405
personality: AG views about, 48
Perspectives publishing, 195
peyote, 133, 140, 142, 163, 176, 227, 249, 249n, 284, 313, 319, 350
Philosophical Library (New York City), 308, 321
Pippin, R. Gene, 143, 143n, 151, 313, 345
The Place (North Beach bar), 317, 326, 350, 396
Playboy magazine, 357, 433, 438, 439, 471
plays, JK, 365, 370, 374, 431
Podhoretz, Norman, 473
"Poem Decided Upon in Ohio" (JK), 74–75
Poems (JK), 373, 416
Poesy magazine, 438
"The Poet: I and II" (AG), 27, 27n
Poetry magazine, 120, 152
poetry/poets
abstraction in, 417
AG interest in French, 367
AG views about, 11, 47, 434, 444
and drama, 442, 444
JK views about, 180, 269, 377, 379, 385, 387, 396, 442, 451
poetry readings
BBC, 389
Big Table as sponsor of, 438
at Brata Gallery, 385
at Columbia University, 444
Corso views about, 400
in Germany, 418
at Half Note, 420
at Harvard University, 427
at Hunter College, 415
and jazz, 365–66
JK views about, 386–87, 406

Lustig, 365–66
for *Measure* magazine, 429
in New York City, 373, 374–75, 385, 404, 406
requests for JK at, 440
in St. Louis, 386, 395, 395n
in San Francisco, 334, 429
at San Quentin, 430, 431
Six Gallery, 132n, 316, 325
as source of money, 395
at Village Vanguard, 373, 374–75, 385, 388, 389, 391, 392, 420
at Wesleyan College, 430
police, 67, 157, 239, 342, 350, 429, 471
politics
AG views about, 383–84, 460–61
AG writings about, 383–84, 460
JK comments about, 386, 416, 459, 461, 465
Pommy, Janine, 456, 457
Porter, Arabelle, 235–36, 277, 361
Pound, Ezra
AG interest in, 281, 284, 287, 306
AG sends *Howl* to, 327
Buddhist works of, 281
Cantos by, 301
and de Angulo's book, 150
Duncan as friend of, 240
JK interest in, 301, 306
JK reading of, 458
JK as similar to, 146
and JK views about poetry, 377
Martinelli drawing of, 275–76
in mental hospital, 107
Rexroth compared with, 233
Translations from Chinese by, 284
Williams-AG discussion about, 151, 404–5
Yeats description of, 71
prayer: AG views about, 88
Price, Ray, 415
Protter, Eric, 175, 247
Proust, Marcel, 12, 149, 210, 238n, 272
Provincetown, Rhode Island, 125, 300
psychoanalysis: AG views about, 39, 47
Publishers Weekly, 342
publishing/publishers
AG views about, 120, 149, 159, 161–62, 229, 243
JK views about, 31, 40, 419, 420
power of, 353
Rexroth comment about, 353
See also specific publisher, author, or work
"Pull My Daisy" (AG), 84, 122
Pull My Daisy (movie), 427

Rabelais, François, 71, 377
radio programs, 294, 316
Rahv, Philip, 361, 366
"Railroad Earth" (AG), 327, 352, 458
Random House, 145, 146, 158, 159, 293, 303, 343
Rauch, Jerry, 99, 99n
reality
AG views about, 47–48, 99, 101
JK views about, 106, 135, 269, 275
reason: AG views about, 101
rebirth: JK views about, 274–75
recordings
of AG, 427, 432–33
of JK, 398, 442–43
by JK, 209n
See also specific recording company

Reich, Wilhelm, 94, 100
relationship, AG-JK
    and AG as agent for JK, 194
    and AG decision not to go to San Francisco, 152
    and AG and JK as brothers, 60
    and AG as missing JK, 140, 143
    AG views about, 27, 52, 473–75
    and AG views about hate, 60
    break in, 180
    Burroughs as complication in, 246
    change in, 9–11
    and clairvoyance compatibility, 186, 224
    distance in, 399–401
    freedom in, 58
    Glassman comment about, 415
    and helping each other, 300
    honesty in, 60
    hypocrisy in, 55, 60, 64
    and imitation of each other, 60
    jealousy between, 178–79
    and JK as genius, 27
    and JK fondness for AG, 113
    and JK invitation to AG to go to Paris, 157
    and JK missing AG, 379
    and JK mother, 394, 398, 399, 400, 402, 433
    and JK need for AG, 321
    JK views about, 24, 25, 54, 330, 379, 469–73
    and JK views about AG, 80, 179
    as loving relationship, 54, 135, 156, 197, 219, 390, 398, 453
    and madness between AG and JK, 59, 185, 268, 391
    and "our poem," 72–73, 83–84
    philosophical excitement in, 64
    and pleasing each other, 63, 64
    police take custody of letters between AG and JK, 67
    as stealing from each other, 146, 154
    strains in, 428
    suffering as basis of, 60
    trust in, 236, 330
    and truth, 54
    as Van Doren–type relationship, 401
religion
    AG views about, 47, 221, 329, 411, 443
    and "beat" as Second Religiousness of Western Civilization, 353
    and The Dharma Bums, 411
    JK study of, 458
    JK writings about, 413
    and Lamantia, 313
    See also Buddhism
Revelations of Golgotha (AG paintings), 106
Rexroth, Kenneth
    AG comments/views about, 233, 283, 389
    and AG Guggenheim application, 362
    and AG as literary agent for JK, 257, 279
    and AG at poetry reading, 248–49
    and AG in San Francisco, 227, 233
    AG views about, 278
    and Burroughs works, 233, 248, 277, 278, 283
    and Cassady arrest, 397
    and Cowley, 278, 292
    criticisms of JK by, 282–83, 379, 386
    Doctor Sax comments of, 279, 282–83, 379
    Evergreen recordings of, 343
    at Five Spot, 395
    and Howl trial, 349
    and Jarrell, 333
    JK comments about, 301

    and JK New Writing works, 292
    Nation article about JK by, 343
    as New Directions advisor, 248
    New World Writing publication of article by, 351
    and On the Road, 353, 359
    party at, 313
    poetry readings of, 248–49, 325
    and power of publishers, 353
    and publication of JK works, 236, 240, 277, 278–79, 282–83
    radio program of, 286
    reviews of JK works by, 359
    in San Francisco, 329
    as San Francisco poet and writer, 227n
    and Subterraneans, 290, 291, 292, 395
    support for JK of, 280, 286
    and Visions of Neal, 278
    Visions of Neal reading by, 283
    Williams-AG discussion about, 293
"Richmond Hill" (JK), 136, 144, 153
Rilke, Rainer Maria, 20, 145
Rimbaud, Arthur, 26, 27, 52, 88, 103, 140, 210, 234, 328, 366, 372
"River Street Blues" (AG), 154
Riviera Bar (New York City), 301, 310
Roberts, Ed, 135, 227, 233, 310
Robinson, E. A., 87, 97
Robinson, Jethro, 61, 64, 84, 226
Rochambeau bar (New York City), 42–43
rodeo: JK in, 81
romantic: AG as, 77
romanticism, 16–17, 18
rooming house poems, AG, 135, 152
"The Rose of the Rainy Night" (JK), 94–96
Rosenberg, Anton, 142, 209, 276, 279, 290, 301, 359, 387, 406
Rosenthal, Irving, 407, 413, 417–18, 421–22, 430, 438, 457
Rosset, Barney, 364, 418
Rotha, Paul, 203, 203n
Rowohlt Verlag Publishers, 366
Rubens, Peter Paul, 74, 80, 97
Russell, Vicki, 42n, 67, 68–69, 71, 87

Sampas, Sebastian, 114, 114n, 270, 399, 475
San Francisco Blues (JK), 224, 247, 257, 282, 283
San Francisco, California
    AG decision not to go to, 152
    AG in, 227, 233, 238–58, 261-313, 314–22, 327, 330–32, 335–36, 428–35, 473–75
    AG jet plane trip to, 428
    AG plans to go to, 207, 211, 218, 329, 334
    AG plans to leave, 284
    AG views about, 396
    and Beat Generation as "San Francisco Renaissance," 370
    Corso poem about, 383
    FBI investigation of people from, 409
    JK-Cassady trip to, 67
    JK in, 113, 131–62, 165–66, 180–86, 189–92, 310, 326, 329, 330, 335, 349, 352, 457–58
    JK plans/desires to visit, 272, 274, 280, 290, 293–94, 295, 296, 298, 300, 301, 302, 305, 307, 310, 314, 316, 317, 318, 321, 322
    JK views about, 400
    JK writings about, 330
    poetry readings in, 429
    and SF poetry, 385
    See also specific person

San Jose, California
  AG in, 218–38, 299
  Cassady in, 178–80, 201–11, 213–18
  JK in, 178–80, 201–18
San Luis Obispo, California: JK in, 192–94
San Remo bar (New York City), 394, 403
sandwich of pure meat (AG poem), 159
Saroyan, William, 34, 120, 120n, 160, 231
Saturday Evening Post magazine, 470
Saturday Review, 352, 357, 391, 414n, 428
Schapiro, Meyer, 69, 69n, 103, 119, 120, 299, 319, 327, 386
Schleifer, Marc, 435, 435n, 436, 437
Schnall, Norman, 108, 108n
Schorer, Mark, 303, 303n, 312, 353
Schweitzer, Albert, 98, 98n
Scribner's, 33, 34, 37, 171, 176
self
  AG views about, 98
  JK views about, 266, 308
sex
  and AG at Maritime Training Station, 14
  AG poem about, 329
  AG views about, 77, 90, 139, 154–55, 229, 278
  Burroughs views about, 156
  Cassady writings about, 234, 240
  in *Doctor Sax*, 184
  JK views about, 223, 301, 358
  and JK visit to New York City, 301
  JK writings about, 181
The Shadow of Dr. Sax (JK), 173
Shakespeare, William, 36, 37, 59, 61, 70, 97, 135, 157, 175, 243, 334, 374, 377, 411, 442
Shelley, Percy Bysshe, 20, 377, 399
Shields, Karena (Mexican author), 206, 211, 303, 307, 316, 318
"The Shroudy Stranger" (AG), 84, 120, 145, 147, 154, 157–58, 184, 320
Siesta in Xbalba (AG), 239, 375
Sim, Alistair, 253, 254
Simpson, Louis, 171, 184, 283, 288, 416
Simpson publishing, 176
sin: AG views about, 47
Six Gallery reading, 132n, 316, 325
sketches, 172, 174–76, 245, 299, 337
Slochower, Harry, 63, 63n
Snyder, Gary
  AG comments about, 326, 388
  AG first meets, 325
  and AG interest in Buddhism, 407
  AG letters to/from, 372, 393, 411, 416
  AG possible visit with, 421
  AG relationship with, 398
  and Allen, 416, 418
  and Buddhism, 326
  California trip of, 353
  and *The Dharma Bums*, 325, 373, 374, 376, 411, 416
  Evergreen recordings of, 343
  and Ferlinghetti, 388, 410
  illness of, 397
  invitation to JK from, 450
  in Japan, 450, 473
  and JK Beat Generation article, 353
  JK camping trip with, 325
  JK comments about, 352, 414
  JK inquiries about, 472
  JK letters to/from, 386, 393, 430, 470
  JK lives with, 326
  JK plans to visit, 395
  JK relationship with, 375, 379, 470
  and Lamantia, 411
  lovers of, 410, 473
  and Lustig poetry readings, 365
  and Merims, 329
  in Mill Valley, 326
  in mountains/Oregon, 402, 411
  New York City visit by, 404, 409
  nickname for, 388
  and poetry readings, 325, 406
  publication of works by, 331, 410, 416, 418
  in San Francisco, 397
  and Whalen, 351
  and Wieners, 350
  and Williams (Sheila), 404, 410
  and Williams (William), 348
  world travels of, 386
society
  AG views about, 87–88, 98, 121–22
  JK view about, 82, 88
  Van Doren views about, 82, 87, 88
Solomon, Carl
  at Ace Books, 133–34, 133n
  AG comments about, 103, 161, 293
  AG first meets, 103
  AG inquiries about, 222, 244, 258, 262
  and AG-JK meetings, 117
  AG letters to/from, 285
  and AG as literary agent, 173, 196
  AG recommendation to Landesman of, 122–23
  AG visits with, 454
  and Ansen works, 150
  and Burroughs writings, 133, 150, 159, 161, 189, 190, 191
  and Cassady-AG relationship, 124
  Cassady-Lamantia meeting at home of, 140
  and Cassady writings, 140, 149, 150, 158, 174
  and de Angulo works, 149–50
  in Denver, 272
  du Peru's similarity to, 242
  and *Empty Mirror*, 184
  and Genet, 162, 171, 175
  and Harrington books, 150
  and Hoffman joke, 139
  and Holmes works, 150
  homosexuality of, 103
  and *Howl*, 103n
  and Huncke works, 150
  identity of, 454
  as jealous of JK, 178–79
  JK comments about, 158, 179, 272, 290, 294, 318
  and JK finances, 160
  JK letters to/from, 291
  and JK writings, 155, 179, 184, 196
  in mental hospital, 103–4, 285, 299
  in New York City, 391
  and *On the Road*, 133, 134, 142, 143–44, 148, 149, 157, 159, 160, 171, 173, 176
  in Paris, 103
  personal background of, 103
  problems of, 149–50
  and publication of AG works, 150, 157
  publication of works of, 122–23, 122n, 172
  suicide attempt by, 103
  trips of, 119, 149
Some of the Dharma (JK), 230, 280, 302, 337, 408, 416
"Song: Fie My Fum" (AG with Landesman), 122, 122n

497

Sorrells, Lois, 439, 451, 452, 472
South America: AG trip to, 449
Southern Pacific Railroad, 34, 233, 235, 262, 274, 295, 304, 314, 332, 333
Spender, Stephen, 108, 429
Spengler, Oswald, 27, 40, 136, 243, 353, 377, 392
Spokesman, 419
Sputnik: AG views about, 360
Stanford University: AG participation in LSD experiments at, 430, 430*n*
Stendhal, 53*n*, 140
Stern, Gerd, 262, 277, 278, 294, 379, 434
Story magazine, 193*n*
Stringham, Ed, 57, 105, 302, 358
Sublette, Al
  as actor in JK play, 366
  AG comments about, 229, 277
  and AG in San Francisco, 227, 229, 233, 239, 244, 249–50, 285
  arrest and imprisonment of, 345, 348, 350–51, 397
  and Cassady, 250
  drinking of, 229, 233, 250, 285
  and drugs, 212, 239, 249, 285
  JK description of, 212
  JK friendship with, 212
  JK inquiries about, 282
  JK letters to/from, 252
  and JK in San Francisco, 310
  and JK-Taylor meeting, 246–47
  JK views about, 158, 227, 301, 318
  JK visit with, 352
  and JK works in *New World Writing,* 286
  jobs for, 285
  at Marconi Hotel, 239
  New York City trip of, 158
  South America trip of, 250
  views about JK of, 307
  and Williams (Sheila), 239, 244
Sublette, Connie, 396–97
The Subterraneans (JK)
  and AG as agent for JK, 283
  AG copy of, 393
  and Allen, 343
  characters in, 53*n*
  criticisms of, 392, 409
  Italian trial concerning, 470
  JK autographs copies of, 430
  and JK finances, 419
  and JK at Lee house, 225
  JK requests copy of, 292
  JK views about, 376
  Lee copy of, 231
  movie version of, 405, 440, 456
  "psychoanalysis" of, 470
  publication of, 267, 278, 301, 335, 357, 376, 392
  reviews of, 393–94, 395
  revisions to, 343, 376
  and Rexroth, 290, 291, 292, 395
  Trilling comments about, 395
  and Williams, 291
suffering
  AG views about, 39–40, 60, 88, 262
  as basis of AG-JK friendship, 60
  Burroughs views about, 237
  JK views about, 273
summer camp: JK work at, 11–12, 11*n*, 16
Surrealism, 140, 140*n*, 177, 316, 367

"Surrealist Ode" (AG), 89, 89*n*
Suzuki, D. T., 266, 279, 282, 308, 321

Tejeira, Victor, 46, 46*n*
television
  and image of Beat Generation, 438
  JK interviews on, 358–59, 362, 364, 366, 371, 372, 395
  JK views about, 423
  parody of JK on, 437
Temko, Allan, 37–38, 53, 108, 147, 147*n*, 247, 288, 333
Tennessee: Cassady trip to, 146
Tercerero, Dave, 168, 168*n*, 169, 385
Texas: JK in, 353–54
Texas, Li'l Darling (musical), 122, 122*n*
Thomas, Dylan, 123, 253, 269, 406
Thoreau, Henry David, 82, 279, 307, 472
time
  AG views about, 78–79, 89, 91, 137–38, 153, 234, 263
  AG writings about, 58, 59, 78–79, 91
  Bloom talk about, 104–5
  Van Doren views about, 87
Time magazine, 317, 347, 430, 436, 439, 470
Times Magazine, 189
"Tip My Cup" (AG), 91
Tolstoy, Leo, 20, 174, 377
Tombs (Riker's Island), 138, 138*n*
Town and City "T&C" (JK)
  advertising for, 123
  AG comments about, 115, 117–19, 183, 184, 220
  AG gives Parker copy of, 127
  and AG views about U.S., 398
  Carr (Cessa) copy of, 158
  Carr views about, 123
  characters in, 156
  and Edie-JK relationship, 94
  JK comments about, 273
  and JK as disciple of others, 452
  and JK finances, 73, 94, 373
  and JK "personal-ness" problems, 34
  JK views about, 62, 423
  and JK views about immortality, 63
  lines from, 33
  paperback edition of, 184
  publication of, 31, 34, 37, 40, 41, 51–52, 51*n*, 193, 302
  and publicity for Burroughs *Junkey,* 189, 190
  reviews of, 123
  sequel to, 318
  West End bartender requests copy of, 225
  writing of, 142, 186
"Trembling of Veil" (AG), 152–53
Trilling, Diana, 87, 428, 430
Trilling, Lionel, 9, 17, 18, 20, 21, 25, 27, 69, 76, 87, 277, 327, 377, 395, 409
Tristano, Lennie, 42, 42*n*
Tristessa (JK), 335, 440, 441–42, 443, 451
truth
  AG views about, 98
  JK views about, 275, 290, 308, 450
Tuttle Publications, 414, 416
Twain, Mark, 32, 37, 422, 433
20th Century Fox, 389, 392

Ulanov, Barry, 176, 176*n*
Ullman, Bill, 346–47, 350
United Nations, 186

United Press, 41, 317
United States
  AG views about, 121–22, 232, 243, 383–84, 392,
    397–98, 460–61, 475
  JK views about, 392, 400, 461
University of California at Berkeley, 303, 306, 312,
  316, 318
University of Chicago, 417–18
unknown/unknowable: AG views about, 263–65
USNS *Joseph F. Merrell*, AG on, 326–27
USNS *Sgt. Jack J. Pendleton*, AG on, 327–29

Van Doren, Charles, 226, 422
Van Doren, Mark
  and AG book, 105
  AG comments about, 228
  and AG Guggenheim application, 362
  and AG-JK friendship, 401
  and AG legal problems, 77, 87
  AG lunch with, 159
  and AG madness, 69
  and AG in mental hospital, 94
  AG reliance on, 59
  AG sends *Howl* to, 327
  and Cervantes, 375
  and Giroux, 108
  humility of, 32–33
  influence on AG of, 257, 264
  JK views about, 32–33
  JK visit with, 226
  and JK writings, 31, 32, 33, 185, 226, 228, 277
  and Melville notes, 134
  as moral man, 33
  and people at Columbia views of AG, 70
  and publication of AG poems, 120
  Shakespeare comments of, 135
  society views of, 82, 87, 88
  and *T&C*, 31, 32, 33
  time views of, 87
  writings of, 87
Van Meter, Peter, 142, 242
Vanguard Publishing, 373, 376
Vanity of Duluoz (JK), 473
Vidal, Gore, 168, 175, 196–97
Vietnam War, 473
View magazine, 140
Viking Press
  AG views about, 419
  and *Beat Generation*, 321
  Cowley as consultant to, 194*n*
  and *The Dharma Bums*, 395
  and *Doctor Sax*, 419
  and *Howl*, 358, 362
  and JK finances, 302, 421
  and JK Paris book, 419
  and *On the Road*, 194*n*, 236, 302, 302*n*, 342,
    352–53, 354, 355, 357, 372, 398
  publicity for JK at, 422*n*
  and *Visions of Gerard*, 413, 420, 423
Village Vanguard (New York City), 373, 374–75,
  385, 388, 389, 391, 392, 420
Village Voice, 392, 417, 420, 420*n*, 422, 437
The Vision of the Goatherds (JK painting), 350
visions
  of AG, 38–40, 41–42, 87, 144, 153, 228, 231, 232,
    265, 270, 288, 313
  AG views about, 221
  JK views about, 269
  JK writings about, 96

Visions of Bill (JK), 230, 280
Visions of Cody (JK), 173*n*, 209*n*, 433, 456
Visions of Gerard (JK), 325, 326, 335, 413, 415, 418,
  419, 420, 423, 433, 471
Visions of Neal (JK)
  and AG as agent for JK, 196
  AG comments about, 183, 262
  AG influence on, 337
  AG reading of, 255, 257, 262, 277, 378
  AG requests excerpts from, 417
  and Allen, 410, 418
  Americana in, 378
  Burford views about, 246
  and Carr comments about JK, 302
  Cassady reading of, 222
  changing title of *On the Road* to, 176
  classic sentence in, 285
  Duncan reading of, 325
  in "Jazz Excerpts," 235
  JK happiness while writing, 458
  JK readings from, 436
  JK views about, 272
  Laughlin reading of, 373
  publication of, 246, 277, 375, 410, 416, 418, 419
  reviews of, 375
  Rexroth views about, 283
  Village Vanguard reading of, 373
  and Williams, 298
  writing and typing of, 414, 459
Voices magazine, 283
Von Hartz, Ernest, 138, 217, 359, 359*n*
VVV magazine, 140, 140*n*

"Wail" (JK), 349–50
Wake magazine, 51*n*, 227
Wake Up (JK). See *Buddha Tells Us*
Wald, Jerry, 389, 423
Wallace, Mike, 385
Warren, Henry Clarke, 228, 228*n*
Washington Blues (JK), 336
Washington, DC: JK in, 336–37
Watts, Alan, 279, 390, 407
WBAI radio station, 437
Weaver, Helen, 377, 417
Weitzner, Richard, 59, 59*n*, 61, 62, 105
Welch, Lew, 449, 450, 472
Wesleyan College: JK at, 430
West End Bar (New York City), 25, 214, 225, 359
Whalen, Philip
  and AG in Alaska, 328
  AG comments about, 326, 372
  AG letters to/from, 329, 371, 404, 456
  AG reading work by, 393
  AG visit with, 334
  and AG writing style, 412
  and Ansen, 352
  and Avon anthology, 432
  and *Big Table* magazine, 436
  and *The Dharma Bums*, 374
  Evergreen recordings of, 343
  and Ferlinghetti, 388
  finances of, 429
  and Giroux, 470
  happiness of, 391
  and *Howl*, 350, 358
  and Jarrell visit to San Francisco, 333
  and JK-AG letters, 341, 344
  JK comments about, 345, 414, 472
  JK drawing of, 350

Whalen, Philip (*cont'd*)
JK letters to/from, 412
and JK move to California, 342
and JK in San Francisco, 326
JK views about, 432, 470
and Levigue picture of Orlovsky, 348
New York City trip of, 404, 409, 429, 430, 441
and *On the Road*, 352–53
and poetry readings, 325, 406, 429
publication of works by, 331
and Snyder, 351
and Wieners, 350
and Williams, 348
"What the Young French Writers Should Be Writing" (JK), 175
White, Ed, 37, 37*n*, 105, 147*n*, 162, 172, 174, 176, 225, 245
White Horse Bar (New York City), 310, 366
White, Phil, 64, 138–39
Whitman, George, 371, 371*n*
Whitman, Walt, 134, 136, 155, 174, 247, 329, 364, 383, 393, 397, 429, 433, 461, 472
whys and whats: G-K exchange about, 17–18, 32
Wieners, John, 343, 348, 350, 351, 361, 397, 434, 457
Wilbur, Richard, 385, 388, 431
Williams, Jonathan, 325, 325*n*, 352, 407
Williams, Sheila Boucher
and AG appearance, 252
AG first meets, 239, 256
and AG interest in Buddhism, 411
AG meeting with, 404
and AG-Orlovsky relationship, 252
AG relationship with, 239, 242, 244–45, 248, 251, 252, 254, 255, 409–10
and Burroughs-AG relationship, 242
and Cassady, 249, 258
and Cassady-AG relationship, 248
and drugs, 249
in jail, 404
JK comments about, 301
JK desire for, 310
Moreland as similar to, 244
in New York City, 409–10
railroad ticket for, 303
reactions to JK writings by, 283
returns to San Francisco, 409–10
and Snyder, 404, 410
and Sublette, 239, 244
Williams, William Carlos
and AG in Europe, 346
and AG finances, 346
and AG Guggenheim application, 362
AG and JK visit, 337
AG letters to/from, 131–32, 325, 348, 410
and AG in NMU, 135
AG reading works of, 140, 284, 285
AG relationship with, 334
AG views about, 132, 134, 258, 293
AG visit with, 293, 404–5
and AG writings, 131–32, 145, 147, 150–51, 152, 159, 304, 325, 331
Arts and Sciences grant for, 154
City Lights publication of work by, 320
Collected Essays of, 285
and Corso, 337, 345, 348, 350
death views of, 151
at Horace Mann School, 292

and JK-AG letters, 136, 151, 160
JK comments about, 307
JK letters to/from, 303
JK meeting with, 156
and JK writings, 137, 162, 291, 293, 296, 298, 325, 348
JK writings about, 422
and Lamantia, 348
Lowell letter to, 151
and *Measure* magazine, 348
mind views of, 135
"Notes on the Short Story" by, 293
Orlovsky comment by, 433, 434
Paterson by, 85, 131, 135, 177, 293, 410
Patterson trip with AG of, 151
and Pound, 404–5
and Rexroth poetry readings, 249
San Francisco trip of, 287, 293
Selected Essays by, 293
and Snyder, 348
and Whalen, 348
Wilson, Edmund, 277, 283
Wingate, John, 357, 358
Witt-Diamant, Ruth, 333, 333*n*, 362, 397
Wolfe, Thomas, 4, 10, 13, 16, 17, 33, 38, 42, 121, 122, 272, 301, 337, 379, 386
women
AG views about, 54, 77, 255
Carr views about, 401
at Ginsberg (Sheila) party, 115
JK views about, 53, 54, 81, 82, 97, 308–9, 469–70, 471–72
and JK views of half-of-life-is death, 63
in The Netherlands, 355
picking up, 15
See also specific person
Woods, Dick, 234, 240
world: as death, 115–16
writing
AG views about, 160, 388
"bad," 43
JK views about, 18–19, 337, 406
theory of, 35, 36
Wyn, A. A., 133, 133*n*, 134, 142, 149–50, 152, 192, 193, 194, 195, 231*n*, 236, 246
See also Ace Books
Wyse, Seymour, 162, 169, 172, 210, 226, 253, 273, 328, 341, 342, 348, 399, 453

X concept, of AG, 263–66, 268–71, 272–73, 290, 293, 294

The Yage Letters (AG and Burroughs), 193, 196, 249, 306, 346, 361, 388, 389
Yeats, W. B., 58, 61, 71, 88, 90, 101, 106, 174, 177, 264, 306
yiddishe kopfe (shrewd Yiddish foresight), 12, 14–15, 16, 31
Yokley, Sara, 143–44, 143*n*
Young, Bob, 235, 242–43
Young, Celine, 3, 3*n*, 4, 9, 14, 18, 22, 25, 35
Young, Lester, 37, 197
Young Socialists League, 394–95
Yugen magazine, 393, 429, 436, 438

Zen: JK writings about, 453
"Zizi's Lament" (AG), 361, 365, 371